LIBERIA

Political Map
(Before 1964)

The Official Papers of
William V. S. Tubman
President of the
Republic of Liberia

His Excellency William V. S. Tubman, G.C.O.P., K.G.B., G.C.B., G.C.M.G.,
Grand Croix Légion d'Honneur, President of the Republic of Liberia

The Official Papers of William V. S. Tubman President of the Republic of Liberia

Covering Addresses, Messages, Speeches and Statements 1960–1967

Edited by E. Reginald Townsend
Secretary of Information and Cultural Affairs

Assisted by Abeodu Bowen Jones, B.A., M.A., Ph.D.
Department of State, Monrovia, Liberia

Published for
The Department of Information and Cultural Affairs
Monrovia, Liberia
by Longmans Green & Co Ltd

LONGMANS GREEN & CO LTD
48 Grosvenor St, London W.1

PO Box 1176 Freetown

PO Box 2051 Accra

Longmans of Nigeria Ltd
PMB 1036 Ikeja

Associated branches companies and representatives
throughout Africa and the world

Department of Information and Cultural Affairs
Monrovia, Liberia

First published 1968

Printed in Great Britain by
Western Printing Services Ltd, Bristol

Contents

Acknowledgments   xv

Preface   xvi

Introduction to the Second Volume   xvii

Introduction to the First Volume   xix

INTERNAL AND POLITICAL AFFAIRS

Fourth Inaugural Address, Monrovia, 4 January 1960   3

Independence Day Message, Monrovia, 26 July 1960   16

First Annual Message delivered before the Second
Session of the Forty-fifth Legislature, Monrovia,
22 November 1960   22

Independence Day Message, Monrovia, 26 July 1961   43

Second Annual Message delivered before the Third
Session of the Forty-fifth Legislature, Monrovia,
9 January 1961   49

Independence Day Message, At Sea, 26 July 1962   62

Third Annual Message delivered before the Second
Session of the Forty-fifth Legislature, Monrovia,
23 November 1962   65

Independence Day Message, Monrovia, 26 July 1963   83

Fourth Annual Message delivered before the First
Session of the Forty-fifth Legislature, Monrovia,
23 December 1963   89

Fifth Inaugural Address, Monrovia, 6 January 1964   102

Independence Day Message, Monrovia, 26 July 1964   114

First Annual Message delivered before the Second
Session of the Forty-fifth Legislature, Monrovia,
24 November 1964   123

Independence Day Message, Monrovia, 26 July 1965   135

Annual Message delivered before the Third Session of
the Forty-fifth Legislature, Monrovia, 16 November
1965   141

Independence Day Message, Monrovia, 26 July 1966   153

Third Annual Message delivered before the Fourth
Session of the Forty-fifth Legislature, Monrovia,
15 December 1966   163

Speech delivered at the Executive Pavilion in reply to
Speeches of Welcome by Leaders of the Three Branches
of Government, Monrovia, 6 November 1960   175

At the Dedication of the Unification Monument,
Kolahun, Loffa County, 5 January 1961   180

To the Men who returned from Services in Congo
Kinshasa, Monrovia, 23 January 1961   183

Responding to the True Whig Party during a
Demonstration in his Honour for the Convening of a
Conference of African Leaders, Monrovia, 30 May 1961   185

A Panegyric to the Memory of the Late President of
Liberia, Charles Dunbar Burgess King, Monrovia,
8 September 1961   191

Broadcast on the Eve of his Departure on State Visits to
the United States of America, and to the Kingdom of
Ethiopia, Monrovia, 4 October 1961   198

To the National True Whig Party expressing Gratitude
for its Loyalty and Devotion against Subversion,
Monrovia, 16 November 1961   204

A Broadcast on the Eve of his Departure on a State
Visit to Israel, Monrovia, 1 June 1962   208

Response to the County Branch of the True
Whig Party of Grand Cape Mount County after holding
a Mass Demonstration in which the Citizens of that
County pledged their Support to President Tubman,
Monrovia, 31 October 1962   212

A Response to the National Convention of the True
Whig Party endorsing him as Candidate for the
Presidency of Liberia for a Fifth Term, Monrovia,
7 February 1963   215

At the Opening of the Third Biennial Unification
Council, Kolahun, Loffa County, 14 February 1963   220

At the Closing of the Third Biennial Unification Council,
Kolahun, Loffa County, 19 February 1963   228

Broadcast on the Eve of the 1963 General Elections,
Monrovia, 6 May 1963   231

Reply to the True Whig Party following his Re-election
for a Fifth Term of Office as President of Liberia,
Monrovia, 13 May 1963   237

On the Occasion of the Formal Announcement by the
Legislature of Liberia of his Re-election to a Fifth Term
of Office, Monrovia, 14 August 1963   241

On the Occasion of Accepting the First Executive
Mansion built by the Government of Liberia, Monrovia,
3 January 1964   249

On the Occasion of the Laying of the Cornerstone of the
Edward T. Roye Memorial Headquarters of the True
Whig Party, Monrovia, 8 January 1964   255

On the Occasion of the Dedication of the Temple of
Justice, Monrovia, 7 January 1965   259

A Broadcast to the Nation on the 153rd Birthday
Anniversary of Joseph Jenkins Roberts, Liberia's First
President, Monrovia, 15 March 1965   263

To the Nation on his return from a State Visit to the
Kingdom of Morocco, Monrovia, 12 April 1965   269

To the Civic League of Crozerville, Liberia, Crozerville,
10 May 1965   274

Speech made during the Presentation of Resolutions to
President Tubman by the Women's Political Movement
of Liberia, Monrovia, 5 August 1965   281

Speech of President Tubman to the Liberian National
Guard, Monrovia, 5 February 1965   285

To the Nation on the 154th Anniversary of the Birthday
of Joseph Jenkins Roberts, Monrovia, 15 March 1966   287

To the Nation on his return from State Visits to the
Republics of Togo and Dahomey, Monrovia, 7 May 1966   291

Speech on his return from Zürich, Switzerland,
Monrovia, 1 October 1966   297

Speech at a Dinner held in Honour of the Forty-fifth
Legislature, Monrovia, 10 October 1966   303

Speech made at Barclay Training Center, Monrovia,
30 October 1966   309

At the Fourth Biennial Unification Council and
Unification Fair, Lower Buchanan, Grand Bassa County,
8 December 1966   311

Acceptance Speech for a Sixth Term of Office as
President of Liberia, Monrovia, 21 February 1967   319

To the True Whig Party upon his Election to a Sixth
Term of Office, Monrovia, 5 May 1967   324

ECONOMIC AFFAIRS

To a Business Club, New York City, U.S.A.,
13 October 1961   329

Address at Dinner in his Honour tendered by the
American Business Leaders, New York City, U.S.A.,
18 October 1961   332

Remarks at Luncheon in his Honour before the
Washington Press Club, Washington, D.C., U.S.A.,
20 October 1961   337

A Radio Broadcast to the Nation on Austerity Measures,
Monrovia, 15 April 1963   340

At the Dedication of the Lamco Joint-venture, Nimba
County, Liberia, 15 November 1963   344

At the Ground-breaking Ceremony for the Walter F.
Walker and Thomas R. Faulkner Hydro-Electric Power
Plant, Mount Coffee, Liberia, 29 January 1964   346

To the International Labour Conference, Geneva,
Switzerland, 26 June 1964   349

At the Opening of the Conference of State and
Governments of Guinea, the Ivory Coast, Liberia and
Sierra Leone on the Free Trade Area, Monrovia,
20 August 1964   351

A Broadcast to the Nation upon the Establishment of a
National Development Bank, Monrovia, 19 October 1964   355

At the Opening of the National Industrial Relations
Conference, Monrovia, 27 January 1965   358

To the Board of Trustees and Officers of the National
Iron Ore Company, Monrovia, 13 May 1965   362

Speech at Dinner in Honour of A. G. Lund, President of
Firestone Plantations Company, Monrovia, 28 June 1965   365

At the Formal Opening of the Bong Mining Company,
Bong Mines, Liberia, 12 November 1965   368

Tribute on the Passing Away of Lansdell Christie,
Friend of Liberia, Monrovia, 24 November 1965   371

A Nation-wide Broadcast on the Firestone Strike,
Monrovia, 12 February 1966   375

At the Salzgitter Corporation, West Germany,
8 September 1966   379

To the Liberian Businessmen's Conference, Monrovia,
11 January 1967   381

Speech to the Rubber Planters' Association of Liberia,
Monrovia, 14 March 1967   387

EDUCATION

At the University of Liberia, Monrovia, 13 March 1961   395

Address to the College of West Africa, Monrovia,
9 July 1961   398

Statement on the Goals of Liberian Education,
Monrovia, 24 August 1962   401

Speech delivered at Haile Selassie I University in Addis
Ababa during the Conferal on President Tubman of an
Honorary Doctor of Laws Degree, Addis Ababa,
Ethiopia, 16 May 1963   409

Speech delivered at Cuttington College during the
Ceremony for Laying of the Cornerstone of the Bishop
Harris Building, Suacoco, Liberia, 1 December 1963   411

Speech delivered at the University of Liberia, Monrovia,
8 March 1965   414

Statement on Liberian Education, Monrovia,
3 July 1965   420

Statement to the National Teachers' Association,
Gbarnga, Bong County, 26 March 1966   422

An Appeal to the Nation for a Fund Drive for the
University of Liberia, Monrovia, 23 June 1966   424

Statement to the National Teachers' Association,
Monrovia, July 1966   426

HEALTH

Speech delivered to the Annual Convention of the
Liberian Midwives' Council, Monrovia, December 1963   429

An Address to the 1964 Graduating Class of the Tubman
National Institute of Medical Arts, Monrovia,
6 February 1964   432

World Health Organization Day Message, Monrovia,
7 April 1964   437

Speech delivered at the Dedication of Phoebe Hospital,
Suacoco, Liberia, 16 May 1965   439

At the Laying of the Cornerstone of the John F. Kennedy
Memorial Hospital, Sinkor, Monrovia, 2 August 1966   442

Address delivered by President Tubman during the
Dedication of the St. Joseph Hospital and Medical
College, Monrovia, 19 March 1967   445

RELIGIOUS AFFAIRS

On the Thirty-fifth Anniversary of the Establishment of
the Liberian Mission of the Seventh Day Adventists,
Monrovia, 27 January 1963   451

Announcing the Retirement of the Rt. Reverend Bravid
W. Harris of the Protestant Episcopal Missionary District
of Liberia, Monrovia, 12 January 1964   454

On the Retirement of Bishop Bravid W. Harris,
Monrovia, 18 January 1964   456

On the Tenth Anniversary of the Establishment of
Radio Station ELWA, Monrovia, 18 January   459

To the Methodist Annual Conference, Monrovia,
23 January 1964   461

To the Annual Methodist Conference, Monrovia,
26 January 1964   465

To the 133rd Session of the Liberian Methodist Annual
Conference, Careysburg, 4 February 1965   469

On the Closing of the 133rd Session of the Liberian
Methodist Annual Conference, Careysburg, Liberia,
7 February 1965   473

At a Dinner honouring the Vice-President of Liberia,
the Honourable William R. Tolbert, Jun., as President of
the Baptist World Alliance, Monrovia, 14 July 1965   476

In Memory of the Rt. Reverend Bravid Washington
Harris, Monrovia, 14 November 1965   479

On the Special Week of Prayer and Fasting, Monrovia,
21 February 1966   483

A Closing Statement on the Observance of the National
Week of Prayer and Fasting, Monrovia, 28 February 1966   485

SOCIAL AFFAIRS

At the Acceptance of the Tubman Center of African
Culture, Robertsport, Grand Cape Mount County,
Liberia, 29 November 1964   489

Remarks made at the Celebrations of his Seventy-first
Birthday Anniversary, Sanniquellie, Nimba County,
29 November 1966   493

AFRICAN AFFAIRS

At the First Independence Celebration of the Republic
of Guinea, Monrovia, 2 October 1959   499

Broadcast to the Nation on Africa Freedom Day,
Monrovia, 13 April 1961   502

Welcome Address to the Heads of State and Governments
and Delegates to the Conference of African Heads of
State, Monrovia, 8 May 1961   504

On the Occasion of the First Anniversary of the
Independence of the Federation of Nigeria, Monrovia,
12 September 1961   510

Speech delivered upon his return to Monrovia from the
Lagos Conference and State Visits to the Federation of
the Cameroun and the Republic of Gabon, Monrovia,
16 February 1962   512

Broadcast to the Nation on the Eve of his Departure to
the Addis Ababa Conference of the Organization of
African Unity, Monrovia, 11 May 1963 — 517

Speech at a State Banquet given in his and Mrs.
Tubman's Honour by Emperor Haile Selassie I of
Ethiopia, Addis Ababa, Ethiopia, 15 May 1963 — 521

Speech at a State Dinner in Honour of Emperor Haile
Selassie I during President and Mrs. Tubman's State
Visit to Ethiopia, Ghion Hotel, Addis Ababa, Ethiopia,
18 May 1963 — 524

To the Addis Ababa Conference of African Heads of
State and Governments, Addis Ababa, Ethiopia,
25 May 1963 — 526

To the Nation on his return from the State Visits to
Ethiopia, Yugoslavia and Austria, Monrovia,
13 July 1963 — 529

Speech delivered during an Official Dinner held in his
Honour, Tunis, Tunisia, 1 October 1963 — 539

On his return from a State Visit to the Republic of
Tunisia, Monrovia, 14 October 1963 — 542

Broadcast to the Nation on the Eve of his East African
Visits, Monrovia, April 1964 — 553

To the National Assembly of the Malagasy Republic
during his State Visit, Tananarive, Malagasy Republic,
31 May 1964 — 557

At a Dinner held in his Honour by the President of
Tanzania and Mrs. Julius Nyerere, Dar-es-Salaam,
Tanzania, 2 June 1964 — 561

To the Second Summit Meeting of the Organization of
African Unity, Cairo, United Arab Republic,
10 July, 1964 — 564

To the Nation on his return from State Visits to the
Republic of Malagasy and Tanzania, Monrovia,
13 July 1964 — 569

On the Occasion of a Dinner in Honour of President
and Mrs. Nicholas Grunitsky during their Visit to
Liberia, Monrovia, 25 July 1964 — 575

To the Nation on his return from the Cairo Non-aligned
Conference, Monrovia, 30 October 1964 — 577

Speech at Dinner in Honour of the Secretary-General of
the Organization of African Unity, Monrovia,
8 February 1965   583

Speech delivered to the People of Togo on a State Visit,
Lomé, Togo, October 1965

To the Accra Organization of African Unity Summit
Meeting, Accra, Ghana, October 1965   588

Statement on the Rhodesian Situation, Monrovia,
18 December 1965   592

Speech at Banquet in his Honour by the President of
Dahomey, His Excellency Christopher Soglo, Cotonou,
Dahomey, 29 April 1966   594

FOREIGN AFFAIRS

Speech at Dinner in Honour of the Diplomatic Corps,
Monrovia, 2 March 1960   599

To the Sixteenth Session of the United Nations General
Assembly, New York, U.S.A., 23 October 1961   603

To the Nation on his return from a State Visit to the
United States of America, Monrovia, 13 November 1961   610

Speech at a Luncheon in Honour of Her Majesty,
Queen Elizabeth II of the United Kingdom, Monrovia,
23 November 1961   614

An Address to the Diplomatic Corps and Officials of
Government, Monrovia, 23 April 1962   617

Speech on the Occasion of a Dinner in Honour of
President and Mrs. Tubman by the Israeli
President and Mrs. Ishak Ben Zvi, Tel-Aviv,
Israel, 15 July 1962   621

To the Nation on his return from State Visits to the
Republic of Israel and the United Kingdom,
Monrovia, 31 July 1962   624

Speech at a Dinner tendered in Honour of a British
Parliamentary Delegation, Executive Mansion,
Monrovia, 15 March 1963   629

To the Inaugural Session of the Seminar of the
International Alliance of Women, Monrovia,
29 July 1963   631

A Panegyric to the Memory of President John F.
Kennedy of the United States, Monrovia,
25 November 1963   634

Speech in Honour of Dr. Eric Williams, Prime Minister
and External Affairs Minister of Trinidad and Tobago,
Monrovia, 23 February 1964   639

To the United Nations Conference on Social Defence,
Monrovia, 18 August 1964   642

Speech delivered to the Second Conference of Non-
aligned States, Cairo, United Arab Republic,
7 October 1964   645

Welcome Remarks during the Visit of Lord
Mountbatten to Liberia, Monrovia, 8 October 1964   650

Speech at Dinner during Dedication and Opening of
the Embassy of the Federal Republic of Germany,
Monrovia, 1 March 1965   652

On the Occasion of the Sudden Death of Ambassador
Adlai Stevenson, United States Permanent Representative
to the United Nations, Monrovia, 15 July 1965   654

To the Nation on his return from Zürich, Switzerland,
Monrovia, 2 October 1965   655

Speech at Dinner honouring the Israeli Prime Minister,
Levi Eshkol, Monrovia, 2 June 1966   660

Speech at Dinner in Honour of the Prime Minister of
Israel, Monrovia, 3 June 1966   662

APPENDIX A. *AFRICAN AFFAIRS*

To the Parliament of Sierra Leone, Freetown,
20 June 1959   667

Opening Speech at the First West African Summit
Conference, Sanniquellie, Nimba County, 16 July 1959   671

APPENDIX B. *ON EDUCATION*

Address at the University College of Fourah Bay, Fourah
Bay, Freetown, Sierra Leone, 16 June 1959   675

Address to the Graduates of Cape Palmas High School,
Harper, Cape Palmas, 14 December 1964   678

APPENDIX C. *POLITICAL AFFAIRS*

To all Units – Armed Forces of Liberia, Monrovia,
8 February 1967 683

APPENDIX D. *SOCIAL AFFAIRS*

Eulogium on the life and character of Mary Euphemia
Barclay, B.A., widow of the former President of Liberia,
Edwin J. Barclay, Monrovia, 18 January 1967 685

Acknowlededgments

The Editors wish to accord in this public manner their thanks to those who assisted in the preparation of this book for publication. Dr. Augustus F. Caine, Secretary of Education of Liberia, has caused me to participate actively in this assignment upon his recommendation to the President. The result was the development of an excellent working relationship with Secretary Townsend. Joseph Gbayue of the Department of Information and Cultural Affairs collected the papers.

H. Deyio Wilson, Press Secretary to the President, gave valuable suggestions, and his helpfulness in many ways including arrangements for several interviews with the President made this task a pleasurable one. Augustus F. Caine, nephew of the Secretary of Education, Thomas K. Browne and Stanton B. Peabody provided assistance during the preparation of this work. E. Boima Fahnbulleh, George Sherman, Soni Sherman, E. Rame Bowen, Fred David and others gave full-time assistance in typing the manuscript. My husband, Dr. A. E. Nyema Jones, Chief of Geological Survey, Bureau of Natural Resources and Surveys gave me constant supervision.

ABJ

Preface

In 1959, *President William V. S. Tubman of Liberia Speaks* was published. That book contained the official papers of President Tubman during the period 1944–1959. Since then the need has been felt for the publication of a second volume of the President's papers.

The Official Papers of William V. S. Tubman is therefore companion to the first volume mentioned above. In order to preserve a sense of continuity in these papers we have included the preface from the first volume.

These then are the first serious attempts to gather the collective writings of our President and to make them available for purposes of research. The publication of these papers has been further motivated by the need to preserve a valuable portion of our national heritage and traditions and to present a portrait of Liberian Democracy in action.

Finally, it is our hope that these papers will make a contribution to Liberian scholarship and serve especially as a repertoire of events during the Tubman years in our history.

The planning and publication of this book has been under the direction of the Department of Information and Cultural Affairs.

E. REGINALD TOWNSEND

Introduction to the Second Volume

The spirit of the Liberian is a free spirit, one imbued with the kind of freedom which man in his primeval state enjoyed and was bequeathed to him as a free gift of his creator, unchained and uncaged. Not even the Industrial Revolution introduced into Liberia by President Tubman has succeeded in its attempts to discipline that freedom and to curb its excesses.

In these papers we have what amounts to a working plan or formula to guide our freedom so that it may become productive and meaningful. Indeed, in a real sense, that has been the burden of every President of our nation. These utterances of President Tubman have meaning only when seen and understood in the light of that burden and with a constant and active awareness of the policies at work which have wrought profound changes in our way of life especially since the end of the last war. These policies, chief among which are the Open Door and National Unification, have been operative features of our daily living and the life of every Liberian has been affected by them.

These papers therefore portray a constant review of these policies so that their meaning and effect be not lost. Indeed, it is this element of constant review in terms of what has been accomplished and what lies ahead that is central to any appreciation of them.

The papers have been grouped along the following themes:

1. INTERNAL AND POLITICAL AFFAIRS — The complimentary papers in this group are the Inaugural Addresses, Independence Day Messages, the Annual Messages and to a lesser degree those delivered upon his arrival home from trips abroad. The Inaugural Address was generally a policy statement, the Independence Day Message a mid-year review of all policies, and the Annual Message an annual review and recommendations for further implementation and new programmes. National unification is an ever recurring theme.

2. ECONOMIC AND INDUSTRIAL AFFAIRS — The self-help approach to our economic development within the framework of the free enterprise system is defined and must be understood as a serious attempt to plan and implement economic policies while in effect remaining unaligned to any international economic block. Despite a few set-backs our economic boom was not affected. The Open Door Policy with its physical transformation of our society is seen in its proper perspective. Our stable government remained a major attraction for foreign investors.

3. EDUCATION — The Government's programme to provide mass education was further expanded during these years.

4. HEALTH — Our health programme was given more attention than ever before and along with our education programme both can be considered as initial steps toward the implementation of a national social welfare programme.

5. RELIGIOUS AFFAIRS – The Liberian temperament is basically a religious one and has portrayed this conditioned attitude since the founding of this nation as a modern state in 1822. The Missionary and Government have been harbingers of westernization in Liberia and partners working for progress and development in our land. The Government subsidized all religious programmes and encouraged a movement for an independent Liberian Church.

6. AFRICAN AFFAIRS – The Continent of Africa gave birth to more than thirty-six new states. The decade starting with the year 1960 saw the independence movement at its peak and the impact of this movement on the international scene was not to be taken lightly. Africa, however, stood in need of a guiding hand to channel her new freedom along lines of national and continental unity, meaningful programmes for the welfare of all of its peoples, commitment to the total liberation of Africa from European domination, and her own rôle in international affairs in the fight for world peace. As one of Africa's oldest statesmen, President Tubman took an active interest in all of these matters. Moderation, tolerance, patience, love and peace were recurring themes in nearly all of his addresses on this subject.

7. FOREIGN AFFAIRS – President Tubman's prestige in international affairs rose to new proportions and he became more widely respected abroad. Indeed the foreign world came to appreciate him in much the same manner as Liberians had grown accustomed to doing. A man of peace, he felt that regional conflicts frequently arose between peoples who have much in common to unite them and some compromise along with free discussions around the conference table is a *sine qua non* for the restoration of peace.

It was further found useful to include a short introductory note to each of the topics contained in this second volume of the President's papers so that an extended statement is out of the purview of this introduction. This collection begins with his fourth Inaugural Address and ends with his acceptance speech after the elections of 2 May 1967, to succeed himself for a sixth term in office as President.

ABEODU BOWEN JONES

Robertsport
Grand Cape Mount County
Republic of Liberia
21 May 1967

Introduction to the First Volume

In his years of Presidency, William V. S. Tubman has made hundreds of speeches to the Liberian Nation. Through them he has not only succeeded in establishing an intimate relationship between himself and the people, but he has won national support for his bold development programmes, which have pushed Liberia half a century ahead.

No President in our history has spoken so frequently, travelled so extensively among his people and listened so patiently to their grievances. And no President has addressed as many foreign audiences. Mr. Tubman has truly set an unprecedented record. He has addressed every type of audience: religious, social, political, educational.

His speeches now form a unique part of our cherished heritage. He made it understood in the beginning of his administration that he was wedded to a cause. That cause rings out clear and loud: 'To rouse a nation long forlorn to nobler destiny.' This he has succeeded in doing both by precept and example.

Mr. Tubman assigned to himself the arduous task of awakening national consciousness to the menace and tyranny of disease, illiteracy and poverty. And he has done so by the use of his soft, inspiring voice. Only time and the searchlight of history will tell how effective his speeches have been, and how commanding his stature. But it is evident that he has moved the Liberian people to action and has gained international confidence and renown.

A witty, jovial, open-hearted and free-handed youth, he early captured the hearts and won the confidence of his comrades. His childhood friends often tell how his parents on many occasions scolded him for sneaking out with his 'Sunday best' tucked away under his arm, to help one of his less-fortunate playmates.

But little did they realize that their kind-hearted son from among the towering palms of Harper City, Maryland County, on the easternmost tip of Liberia's coastline, would rise to place the capstone on the first century of our national existence and plant the foundation stone of the second. Or, that he would so ably merit the epithet of 'the greatest leader in our history'.

Never tired of meeting people, the President has always been surrounded by a host of admirers from all walks of life. With his pungent good humour and genial personality, he early developed the enviable characteristic of showing a convincing understanding of other people's problems and helping to solve them. He is possessed of the rare ability of remembering names and faces of people he has met and recalling many years later even their conversation.

By this peculiar trait he has developed an astounding power of quickly attracting men, women and children from all classes and races to him, thus winning their esteem and affections. He is hardly ever too preoccupied, no matter in what group or company, to give a warm, friendly greeting and a pleasing smile to the humblest person. It is a fact that no one who meets him can ever easily forget him.

Equipped with such potentialities, he came to the Presidency thoroughly aware of the problems of the Nation and the idiosyncrasies of the people. The tide of progress was at a low ebb. Everywhere the teeth of depression were biting hard and bitter. The Nation was choked almost to despair by the unrelenting hand of a financial burden. Relief seemed centuries away and the threat of stagnation was everywhere apparent.

It was at such a time that William (Bubber Shad) Tubman emerged on the national horizon. A buoyant, confident voice was heard sounding the clarion call for a New Day: 'I bring a new approach and a new outlook . . .' Some were happy. Some were hopeful. Others looked askance. But from that point onward hearts began to be lifted, hopes revived and the future seemed bright. A New Day was dawning. A New Nation was being born.

The President felt it was the people's right to know the policies and programmes of the Government. And he busied himself travelling and telling them. In launching his now celebrated Executive Councils, he trekked through dense forests over century-old trails that took him to the heart of the far-away interior. He risked his life in frail dugouts and surf boats. He slept in mud huts with thatched roofs and even held councils in make-shift assembly halls. But despite it all, he carried his message and his new programme to the people in every section of the country.

In some instances as will be seen in this collection he had to tongue-lash a few who, because of shortsightedness, parochialism or sheer clannishness, tried to weaken and defeat him even to the extent of attempting to assassinate him and so bring the nation into disrepute. But even in such cases his speeches have been seasoned by the depth of his transcending vision. To all these, the people have listened. They have been convinced, impressed and inspired by his leadership and they have willingly followed.

Thrice they have called him to the Presidency, and thrice he has accepted. But the call has continued to come and to be more mandatory. Even in the second month of his Third Term, they began to urge him to accept a Fourth.

For two years he baffled, hesitated and delayed a reply. But the pressure continued to grow and the call became louder and clearer. He accepted a Fourth Term and the people were happier. It cannot be doubted, therefore, that he now enjoys the implicit confidence of the entire nation, and the people are solidly united behind his enlightened leadership.

Mr. Tubman is no part of a dictator; not even a benevolent one as some of his detractors have attempted to label him. He is by nature a lover of men — all men — regardless of race, creed, nationality or status. He stands among the greatest democrats of his generation, and in him the Free World has an unequivocal advocate in Africa. Not even in one instance has he flirted with 'seducing ideologies'.

When travel by hammock was the customary means by which important Government Officials reached the interior of the country, the President would step down from his hammock and walk the entire day's journey because 'it is iniquitous to ride on the heads of one's fellow men'. It was he who introduced the 'buffet service' to the tribesmen; and when he discovered that minor employees hardly got anything to eat because they had to be last in line, he would, without warning, reverse the order and come to the table last in line 'to show that we should be considerate for those who come after us'. Thus has the President succeeded in leading Liberia, not by force but by love.

Try as I have, it has not been possible to include herein every speech he has made. Many of them were composed while on his feet. Some were made from notes written on the backs of an envelope or a scrap of paper. But they were none the less as forceful as the ones found in this collection.

It would be impertinent to say these are the best. He, himself, would be hard put to make a selection on that basis. But these have been chosen because I believe they express most accurately and clearly the political, social and economic philosophy of Liberia's eighteenth and best loved President.

As for me, I still think his First Inaugural Address is his best. It revived the hopes and aspiration of his fellow citizens who were anxious for a change, hungry for a real democratic leadership and concerned about their future. It was the magic word that broke the spell of darkness, doom and despair – the three D's which had long overshadowed the Liberian people.

I must confess that in this introduction it is not possible for me to focus attention on the many sterling qualities of a person so unusual, yet so dynamic as Mr. Tubman. He is one of those truly rare leaders who appear in the life of a nation and on the international scene only once in a century.

If, therefore, this collection of his speeches can give to this generation only a partial insight into the inner workings of his prodigious mind; if it can show some of the reasons why Liberians laud him as their man of steel with a heart of gold and continue to call upon him to lead them, then my humble endeavours will not have been in vain.

E. REGINALD TOWNSEND

Schieffelin
Marshall Territory
28 June 1959

To the People of Liberia

INTERNAL AND POLITICAL AFFAIRS

Fourth Inaugural Address

Monrovia, 4 January 1960

*We consider as one of the most burning issues of the world today,
the achievement of self-determination and independence for all of
the peoples of Africa and of the world, and that this right should be
conceded and inspire all world leaders and nations as a* sine qua non
for peace.

*The Unification Policy has worked marvellously and the whole
nation is now united as one people.*

*The Open Door Policy has brought a virtual transformation of our
nation in many respects, and all parties concerned — concessionaires,
Government and the people — have been the recipients of the benefits
that have accrued from this bold policy.*

Introductory Note

The inauguration of William V. S. Tubman into a fourth term of office as
President of Liberia was a period of unusual significance. By that year he
had broken all previous records of tenure in that office, having been President of Liberia for sixteen unbroken years. The period also ushered in the
famous decade of the nineteen sixties which historically became known as
the African Decade. During this period the number of independent states
in Africa rose from ten to thirty-six. President Tubman's inaugural
address viewed this phenomenal development with pride and satisfaction.

His inaugural addresses were further policy statements. In this his fourth
inaugural address, he defined the objectives of his new government, a
blue-print of what he would accomplish in a period of four years. National
Unification and the Open Door Policies had long ceased to be mere
slogans and were now operative features of the daily lives of all Liberians.
The President renewed the commitment of his new government to these
policies, and launched an appeal for the greater industrial growth of
Liberia. Out of this address have come the National Education Fund
Drive, a Special Commission on Government Operations, the Liberian
Development Bank, improved communications networks, a National Ship-
ping Line, and the Rural Teachers Training Institute. The nation was
forging ahead with great strides.

Monrovia, 4 January 1960

IT IS my distinguished, rare, and unprecedented privilege and honour to
respond to your free, voluntary and spontaneous call to serve you for a fourth
term in the high and responsible position of President after three successive
tenures of eight, four and four years, respectively, in all sixteen years. This
expression of your abiding confidence, faith, trust, satisfaction, and affection,

exercised by you under the provisions of the organic and statutory laws of the country, is beyond my ability to comprehend, especially so when there are so many others of my fellow countrymen, equally and perhaps more qualified to be presidential timbre than I am, available, ready, anxious and willing to serve. I make no attempt, however, at trying to ascertain the reasons and causes that have actuated your action, but leave it to you who are the custodians of your own liberties and who, under the Constitution, have a right to decide and make your own choice.

It is, therefore, incumbent upon me at this time, without reservations or evasions of any kind, to declare the complete surrender and devotion of myself to the cause of your welfare, well-being and progress, and to defend and protect your liberties and that of the Government under the provisions of the Constitution to the best of my ability, thereby fulfilling the solemn obligation implicit in the Constitutional Oath of Office to which I have just subscribed in your presence.

This great distinction and honour bestowed upon me by you greatly humbles me and in great humility, with a deep and abiding consciousness of my unworthiness, I acknowledge, with gratitude and thankfulness, this sublime gift from you freely and spontaneously given and I give myself, body, mind, strength, and spirit to the service of our common country and you its people.

In 1944 when we first appeared before you to be inaugurated for the same office we enunciated in detail the policies that we designed and intended to pursue and demonstrate. How far we have succeeded in pursuance of those policies, you are the best judges. It is now our determination to continue in pursuance and demonstration of the general principles of those identical policies in the new administration, with the necessary alterations and changes that internal and external conditions may require. Some of the changes in the execution of these policies will be revolutionary in character, but we intend to pursue them as far as possible by evolutionary processes, and to the extent that the people will approve and follow should they deem them in the interest of the state and themselves; for we believe in the fundamental principles of democracy and the administration of the affairs of state in such a manner that the will of the people prevails.

Our earthly reliance is upon the united hearts of you, the people, whose high resolve animates and actuates us to higher endeavours. Looking back through the past sixteen years and recognizing the tender mercies which God has extended unto us, with implicit faith in Him for the future, I should renew my belief in these words of the Holy Writ: 'Paul may sow, Apollos may water, but the increase comes from God.' Therefore as it has been my practice on each previous occasion that I have appeared for induction into office (and more necessarily now than ever), it is my obligation and inescapable duty to utter a fervent prayer of thanksgiving and intercession for the many great gifts and blessings received and for the miracle wrought in our behalf; for continued gifts and blessings of peace, prosperity and solidarity at home; for friendship abroad and for guidance, direction, wisdom, understanding and the abiding presence of the Holy Spirit. Consequently, I ask those of you who have no scruples against it to join with me in exercising our religious freedom in prayer, and those of you who may entertain scruples to exercise your freedom by abstaining as you may choose.

God, the All Terrible, Thou Who ordainest, look down upon us, the children of Thy creation; show forth Thy pity on High where Thou reignest, give unto us peace, O Lord. God, the All Merciful, earth hath forsaken Thy ways of Holiness, slighted Thy Word; let not Thy wrath in its terror awaken. Give us peace in our time, O Lord.

We confess our sins; we acknowledge our iniquities but through the mercies of Thy Son Jesus Christ, we have intercession to Thy Throne of Grace; forgive us our sins we humbly beseech Thee and we prostrate ourselves in the dust of humility before Thee as nothing, unworthy of the life that we live, of the breath that we breathe, of the good things of nature and of the world which Thou hast freely and bountifully created and permitted us to enjoy. We thank Thee that Thou didst found this nation one hundred and twelve years ago and wast with our forefathers in the days gone by, when the odds preponderated, when great uncertainties attended their efforts at making this nation and maintaining it; for Thy mercies and blessings unto us since our incumbency; for guidance, protection and deliverance.

As in the past, O Lord, we earnestly and fervently pray the continuation of Thy loving kindness, tender mercies, blessings, protection, guidance and guarding of the nation and of each and all of us. We pray Thy blessing upon all nations and peoples of the earth: those here assembled and those who are absent. Give us clean and upright hearts; help us to love each other as we ought to love, as individuals and as nations. Remove all bitterness and hatred, suspicion and guilt from the hearts of men and of nations and assist us in establishing a reign of peace on earth with goodwill toward all mankind. Amen!

EXTERNAL AFFAIRS

Current trends in world affairs lead us to the hopeful conclusion that the prospects for peace are better now than at any period since World War II. The behaviour and attitudes of nations, in the United Nations where the course of peace is charted, seem to be undergoing reasonable transformation, and from the standpoint of Liberia's relationship with Member States of the United Nations, we advocate better understanding, unity in essentials for human welfare, peace and harmony between all men and all nations by the application in word and deed of freedom, justice and independence for all men of all lands as an inherent right. We believe in the doctrine of the golden rule, 'Do unto others as you would that they should do unto you.'

We are deeply concerned for a just and lasting peace in the world and shall always endeavour to contribute to the fullest extent of our ability towards this end. We shall commit no acts nor engage in any activities or contrivances that will make world conditions worse and more complicated and thereby endanger peace; nor shall we exploit rifts and misunderstanding between nations for personal, material or individual gain.

We consider as one of the most important and burning issues of the world today, the achievement of self-determination and independence for all of the peoples of Africa and of the world, and this should be conceded and stimulated by all world leaders and nations as a *sine qua non* for peace. We implore those that are strong to utilize their strength to relieve all men of the unjust and heavy burdens of oppression and repression which they bear and assist in restoring and placing them on the high plane of free men enjoying

the benefits and privileges of human dignity, self-determination and independence. This is the legitimate aim of all men.

At Ghana, Sanniquellie, Monrovia and Guinea the three African states
proposed a Community of Independent African States in an attempt to
avoid the pitfalls of the old nationalism; to avoid the fatal luxury of racial
bigotry, class hatred and disregard for the natural rights of others; to apply
their resources to the good of all with ill-will, malice or prejudice toward
none.

As a *means* of cultivating stronger ties of friendship between Africans, we
envisage an accelerated programme of cultural and economic exchange
between African states as a basis of lasting and fruitful co-operation. We
now advance the proposals of regional economic and trade councils with a
view to:

1. Negotiating and concluding treaties and instruments of friendship,
   commerce and navigation.
2. Opening doors for multinational investment in enterprises which require greater funds, greater markets, greater resources than would be
   available in any one state.
3. Investigating and presenting proposals for regional marketing programmes of products of regional importance on the assumption that
   even the largest and strongest unit would benefit from additional size
   and strength through association with its neighbours.
4. Studying, adapting, rejecting or adopting experience in regional economic co-operation amassed elsewhere.
5. Training a sufficient number of persons and even more to man government, businesses, schools and hospitals as well as other enterprises in
   Africa, as there is no need in Africa at the present time as great, pressing
   and important as the need for trained people. With a need so great
   African nations could use the greatest imagination, show the greatest
   flexibility in finding ways to fill this void.

We propose a detailed survey of the resources for education, training and
research which exist in African states and we suggest the pooling of those
resources so that each nation might have access to existing institutions of
education and training and contribute to their support, enlargement and
improvement in proportion to its size and ability to use such an institution.
For example, Nigeria has the Medical School at Ibadan; Ghana, the new
business administration course at its university; Liberia, the new Forestry
School and Guinea, the Mali Federation, and other African states with such
specialized institutions as they may have. Without committing any unit to
refrain from establishing such schools for themselves later (the need will
increase with time for more and more schools, so this seems inevitable), the
purpose would be to enlarge and make widely available the facilities which
now exist.

If acceptable, we could launch an appeal to friends and all interested in
Africa to support such a co-operative programme by:

1. Asking the United Nations and its Specialized Agencies to concentrate
   their efforts on those fields which the African states select for emphasis.
2. Asking those interested or becoming interested in Africa to centre their
   assistance on such projects as:

(*a*) Helping to obtain professors, teachers, etc. for this expanded educational programme.

(*b* Providing scholarships for African students to study in Africa as as well as overseas.

(*c*) Helping to obtain the equipment, buildings, libraries and study materials involved in such a programme.

3. Suggesting to the foreign businesses operating in Africa that they work with the regional organization to plan their participation in this effort by:

(*a*) Establishing or endowing chairs for teaching and research in fields of regional importance.

(*b*) Establishing scholarship programmes in Africa and abroad in some cases and,

(*c*) Helping with equipment, books, etc.

As Africans, we face grim imperatives. Africa is not a world unto itself but an integral part of our one world. We have to make a new Africa in which all races of men may live and work together in the great task of reconstruction.

INTERNAL AFFAIRS

In the prosecution of the internal policies begun in 1944, we still place great emphasis on the Open Door and Unification policies and we again register our solemn pledge of regarding commitments whether they be concession agreements, treaties or even oral pledges and assurances as sacred and inviolable.

The Unification Policy has worked marvellously and the whole nation is now united as one people.

The Open Door Policy has brought a virtual transformation of the country in many respects and all parties concerned – concessionaires, Government and the people – have been the recipients of the benefits that have accrued from this bold policy.

A Plan for Economic and Social Development

The security, safety and preservation of the state is the first duty of any government. Consistent with this, the highest purpose of any economic or fiscal policy is the securing and providing of equal opportunity for all alike; and the promotion of the happiness and prosperity of the citizens of the country in an atmosphere of peace and tranquility.

But economic security, prosperity and happiness can never be only the result of casual reaction or sensitivity to the developmental measures of Government. In a country such as ours which has had to devote all of its energies to the supreme struggle for survival against encroachments, intrigues and other basic assaults on the sovereignty of the nation from its inception for almost a hundred years, progress is a most pressing demand if we are to catch up with the advanced nations of the world. Consequently, the action of Government in initiating, sponsoring, and promoting economic and social developments must not only depend upon spontaneous actions of individuals, but also upon clear leadership spearheaded by a deliberate development process.

In the historical view, the presence of natural resources has been considered the fundamental prerequisite to any development activity. Our forefathers and our fathers have spoken about the natural richness of this land.
However, not until recently, by careful, expensive, scientific investigations
have we been able to ascertain the actual extent to which this country is
naturally endowed by the presence of mineral, timber, and water resources
and of soil most suited to the production of certain types of plant life. In this
regard it is perhaps one of the great acts of Providence that many of the rich
deposits of iron ore which we are now in the process of exploiting were not
discovered before now or else they might not have been within the present
territory of Liberia.

To exploit this natural resource we embarked, nine years ago, upon a programme, first, to map and survey what we had; next, to plan a road and
harbour construction, telecommunication and electrical power development
programme.

In the tenure of office commenced today, this administration will
endeavour to carry out a development plan by which it will:

1. Seek additional revenue by enforcing the collection of all taxes due
   Government. It will see that taxes are not evaded or avoided. They
   must be fully paid and on time.
2. Expand and improve the arterial road system by establishing a network
   of secondary roads that will connect all important points in the country
   with the central arteries which at present run from north to south and
   east to west.

To facilitate this development it is proposed to create a Rural Road
Administration to be responsible for the implementation of this project. This
is not to be just another permanent body. It should be a Commission consisting of a representative of the Public Works, Interior, Agriculture and
Commerce Departments and the National Production Council. It should
have a life of four years and a set objective for each year; that is, to see that
either a fixed number of miles of road are actually built each year, or that
the responsibility for the lack of accomplishment is directly placed, and those
responsible disciplined.

The Government will provide a pool of heavy equipment and be responsible for the construction of large bridges or carry out large excavations as
necessary. The Government will also give the necessary small tools. But the
rural towns working through their tribal authorities should bear primary
responsibility for construction. Within the next four years every important
town in the country should be connected to the National Highway System.

3. To further expedite transportation and travel, the schedule of our
   National Airline should be extended to provide for stops at most major
   towns where it is profitable or safe to do so. Further, within the next
   year, an expansion programme must be inaugurated to include international flights for passengers and freight to other parts of Africa,
   Europe and possibly America. This international programme should be
   undertaken in co-operation with any other airline or on a basis which
   would invite private, foreign or domestic capital.
4. Negotiations have been commenced to facilitate the creation of a
   National Shipping Company. This venture will be executed in co-

operation with foreign capital and the extent of the lines to be undertaken and the number of ships to be put into service will depend upon
the size of contracts for conveyance of iron ore and rubber.

The shipping line would not only provide the means of connecting our
harbours and seaports at road terminals, but would insure Liberia's exports
and imports against discriminatory freight rates. It would further provide
training and employment for many of our citizens long recognized as
naturally adept in the arts of seamanship.

Although the power capacity of the country has more than doubled in the
last few years and will further increase as soon as the new electrical units in
process of construction in the counties are completed, it is now evident that
unless our water resources are exploited we will experience serious retardation in the economic growth of our country. If it is possible we should not
permit this to happen. The Government will undertake to see how this
needed cheap hydro-electrical power can be introduced within the next four
years.

For many years there have been many attempts to get Government
involved directly in the pricing and sale of certain commodities such as
coffee, palm oil, palm kernels and piassava. We have resisted this in the
interest of free trade. There is to be no basic change in this policy.

However, to facilitate uniform processing and pricing as well as the
assuring of a year-round market to our farmers, the Government, in co-
operation with the Chamber of Commerce, will seek long term contracts for
the sale of our domestic commodities. And through the National Production
Council in the next four years, coffee and palm oil processing mills must be
located at strategic points in the country; and an organized market for the
pricing, sale and support of these commodities created so that farmers, no
matter where they are, can know the real prices being offered and can be sure
of getting a sale of their produce the year round.

Although the presence of natural resources in an appreciable quantity has
for over three centuries been considered the *sine qua non* of economic
development, since the beginning of this century it has been recognized that
capital is also a requirement, sometimes of even greater importance.

In the absence of sufficient domestic savings, it has been necessary for
Government to induce foreign capital to come in to assist in our development
programme as a result of measures which assure it freedom of action and
through the provision of tax incentives and other encouragement.

Direct Government loans have also been made to build roads and other
public utilities and guarantees have been made to foreign-owned financial
institutions to facilitate the lending of capital to citizens of the country to
enable them to purchase machinery, equipment and other things necessary to
promote private agricultural, industrial, commercial, and trade activities. In
addition to this an Agricultural Credit Corporation with a modest capitalization has been organized as a Government agency to assist Liberian agriculture and industry. But these are not enough.

If our development activity is to move forward at a more rapid pace more
capital must be made available. New sources must be tapped. All available
savings should be marshalled for the titanic effort which must be made to
raise ourselves.

The Government will therefore in the foreseeable future request help from

the World Bank or other sources to assist in the creation, systematic
organization and detailed operation of a Development Bank. We believe that
such an institution should guarantee various types of agricultural, industrial,
commercial and other loans made to Liberians by foreign or domestic banks.
It should discount the notes of the Agricultural Credit Corporation and in
general underwrite sound financial institutions of this type. Under certain
special circumstances it should also be able itself to invest in the exploitation
of some of our natural resources.

The capital of the bank, facilities and earnings should be free from taxes
for a number of years.

5. Consistent with their primary and God-given duty of producing and
caring for children in a family, the female population of the country
should be encouraged to do such farm, domestic or industrial work as
is not considered injurious to their health. This is the case elsewhere in
the world and especially in the rubber producing areas of the Far East.
Our women should not be kept back from earning a living and contributing to the welfare of their country where they can.

The Labour Laws should be revised to give them the necessary protection
against exploitation, including equal pay for equal work, adequate maternity
leaves, insurance against harsh and injurious treatment; and they should be
admitted into all labour unions on an equal footing with men.

Whereas exploitable natural resources and adequate capital are necessary
for any development programme there is another factor which is now considered of equal importance if the people of any country are to participate
fully in their own development and receive the maximum benefit therefrom.
There must be available a sufficient number of trained technicians, scientists,
engineers, doctors and skilled workers to evolve, execute and carry on the
development activity. These in turn must come from a well trained, literate
and educated public.

This factor in development is often the most difficult because it is
certainly the most time-consuming and cannot be easily telescoped. One cannot train a scientist in a year; neither can one educate engineers and doctors
in a matter of months. Furthermore, they must be a part of a total educational system which prepares them for advanced training.

We shall seek to overcome this handicap to our rapid development by
engaging upon a three-fold educational and health programme.

To ensure adequate capital for the bank's operations a fixed percentage of
Government's royalties from, or participation in, iron ore concessions should be
invested in the capital stock of the bank each year for a period of twenty years.

The co-operation of foreign capital in the exploitation of our natural
resources has proved mutually beneficial and has enabled us to avoid the
pitfalls of extremist nationalist policies. Under the Open Door Policy many
concessions for various purposes have been granted. Most of these have
operated very successfully. But it is now evident that if maximum benefits are
to be derived from them all, the labour supply of the country must be
increased.

Of course, the various health programmes which will include maternity
and child care should in the long run increase the total population. In the
meantime certain steps must be taken immediately to alleviate this situation.
Among these:

1. Work hours of Government as well as private industries and businesses must be increased.

2. To decrease absenteeism due to illness, all foreign or domestic agricultural or industrial employers employing more than fifty labourers should by law be required to install a small clinic, if none is available in that area, for the use of their labour.

3. In cases where there are twenty or more children of employees under the age of fifteen living in the camps, they must provide elementary school instruction for them, provided a public school is not within a radius of three miles.

4. New vagrancy statutes must be enacted and enforced vigorously by the police constabulary and the Interior Department. This country can no longer afford the luxury of able-bodied men loafing from one centre to another and living off their brothers who are gainfully employed. We shall strictly enforce the proposition that he who is able to work and can find work but will not work, should not eat.

5. We shall create in the University of Liberia an Institute of Technical Studies which shall be responsible for training our physicists, chemists, geo-physicists and other advanced technologists.

6. We shall undertake a nation-wide vocational education training programme adapted to training in the agricultural, mechanical and other industrial arts.

   A survey team of specialists has been requested to develop a master plan for the Booker Washington Institute which should become the National Centre of Vocational Education in the country.

7. Higher education whether it be vocational, classical or technical rests squarely and ultimately upon a base of elementary education. Therefore we shall embark upon a national programme of mass public elementary education, literacy and health. *Our aim is to wipe away forever the blight of ignorance and illiteracy from the children of this land.*

Within a bold framework, the following steps shall be taken to implement this programme:

(a) Through multi-lateral or bi-lateral arrangements a corps of teacher-training specialists will be invited to Liberia to organize at once at least three additional rural teacher-training centres.

(b) A low-cost but durable elementary school building will be designed and constructed in co-operation with local labour in every major town or village in the country.

   Until the teacher-training schools have graduated sufficient rural teachers contract employees will be brought in to man some of these schools after construction is completed.

(c) The Department of Public Instruction will be required to develop suitable curricula, consonant with modern world-wide trends yet related to the historical tradition of the people and need of our country.

(d) As an inducement to qualified persons to pursue the educational profession as a career the salary scale and retirement scheme of teachers will be revised and improved.

FINANCING THE SCHEME

Despite the fact that the local towns and communities to benefit from these programmes will be requested to provide material and manual help to assist in the construction end of the programme, its total magnitude is such that a tremendous outlay will be required beyond the practical limits of the Government to finance from its normal current revenues.

It is consequently proposed that an Educational and Health Fund be created.

The fund would be subscribed to on a voluntary basis by civil servants but supported as a matter of public and party policy by all persons holding political appointments or elected by popular vote.

In an under-developed country permissive or casual action in the field of development often proves ineffective in inducing growth; in some cases more compulsory steps are necessary through active leadership.

Persons subscribing to this fund would receive bonds every quarter which would mature ten years from the date of their issue and the income and earnings from these bonds would be exempted from income and other taxes.

A fixed proportion of the fund would be invested in the capital of the Development Bank so as to facilitate the easy retirement of the bonds as they become due.

Parallel and in conjunction with the education programme a broad health programme must be undertaken to assure maximum health of the public. This should be financed from the Education and Health fund an should include a rural health training programme, the location of clinics in the new school buildings in major towns and the organization of a nation-wide itinerant maternity and nursing service.

From experience it has been discovered that given the necessary exploitable natural resources, adequate capital, trained technicians and an educated and healthy population, there is still a fourth and final prerequisite to dynamic economic development.

This fourth factor is *the will* of the people to progress, their determination to raise themselves up through hard work, sacrifice and co-operative self-help. It is inconspicuous and invisible but powerful and has no substitute.

A man or a woman wants a thing in an instant but to will it requires the insight and understanding to plan for it, the stamina to work for it, the courage to fight for it and the endurance to see it through to materialization. It commands our own efforts and solicits the assistance of our friends who in the past have co-operated with us under the Open Door Policy in so many fields. Foreign merchants and businessmen resident in Liberia will we hope, be willing to steam out of the harbour of over-the-counter sales and into the channels of unexploited opportunities which beckon from every stage of our economic development.

The will to move forward must be the cement which binds us together in mutuality.

In the final analysis, fellow citizens, if we are to build a great country, we must believe in it in our hearts and in our minds. We must be unshakeably determined to work out the scheme of our salvation. Our determination to progress must be commensurate with the blessings which God has so bountifully bestowed upon us.

PUBLIC ADMINISTRATION

It is obvious that with the meteoric growth of our economy and of the Government's activities which have expanded rapidly, some waste and inefficiency would inevitably occur, and these should be corrected. Therefore the following means should be applied as correctives:

1. Discover where waste and inefficiency actually exist.
2. Suggest specific programmes to eliminate these.
3. This to be done without disrupting the Government, dampening the enthusiam of the people or embarking on utopian or quixotic projects but with a programme which shall be practicable, realizable and genuinely effective in view of the funds and trained personnel available.
4. Such improvements to be accomplished in the light of new demands which will result from expansion of our economy due when Mano, Nimba and other industrial enterprises come into production.

PROCEDURE

1. We shall seek to establish a Special Commission on the Government's Operations:
    (a) To consist of seven men with experience both in and out of Government.
    (b) The chairman will be a man of recognized ability, experienced and intelligent, who is known to have a somewhat critical attitude and who will be willing to work hard and risk being unpopular.
2. It is but natural that heads of branches of Government and Departments as well as their immediate staffs will defend the status quo; the Commission must therefore be stocked with critical minds without too great a risk of undue radical action.
3. The Commission and Chairman will speak and act only in the name of the President who will have final authority to approve all actions proposed and submit them to the Legislature.
    Other members will reflect a variety of views; some critical, some not; and of backgrounds, some technical and some legal.
4. The Commission will be charged with:
    (a) Investigating the programmes, practice and procedures of every Department and Agency of Government.
    (b) Investigating the use of funds, personnel and equipment. It would have access to all records; be empowered to discuss with all persons, public or private, involved in the various branches of Government. It should review all past proposals and policies to ascertain what current regulations are being enforced and whether useful ideas have been discarded or ignored.
        We shall establish specific programmes for dealing with any shortcomings and failures revealed by the investigation. In this and in other investigations the Commission will have available to it all specialized and technical personnel necessary from Government and we will seek assistance from ICA and U.N. Agencies.
5. We shall establish procedures for regular, systematic policing of the implementation of its recommendations. A watch-dog committee will be set up for each department or agency and should survey, at least

three times per year, the manner in which suggestions are enforced
when they are successful, and change them if not successful.

6. We shall direct the Commission to begin its work with the Executive
Mansion.

The foregoing programmes are far-reaching, bold and ambitious and will
require strong, able, selfless, honest, devoted, honourable and patriotic men to
execute and translate them into realities.

They will require men whose burning desire it is to have their country
grow, develop and prosper; they will require men consumed by zeal for their
country to take an outstanding place in the comity of nations, not men who
will devote their principal time and energies toward developing their own
resources.

OUR ACCREDITED HONOURED GUESTS

It is exhilarating to look at the faces of the honourable representatives of so
many friendly governments accredited to these ceremonies by their respective Sovereigns and Chiefs of States. Each of their presences here in Africa
to do honour and pay respect to this Government, its Representative Citizens
and the Vice-President of the oldest Republic in Africa who have now been
inducted into office, betokens what a wonderful transformation is taking
place in our time.

Here are met together representatives of nations from all of the continents
of the earth and some of the isles of the sea. Their presence unquestionably
establishes the fact that there is a strong desire to develop good relations and
fraternity among all nations and we associate ourselves unreservedly with
them. In us it inspires new hope that as we thus meet and are associating
together, exchanging courtesies, a new day has dawned in international relations which we think could make the nucleus for better understanding between ourselves and ensure the universally just and lasting reign of peace on
earth for which we have all been striving and seeking.

The warmth of the welcome we extend to you emanates from hearts overflowing with love and goodwill and carries with it a yearning for peace,
independence, goodwill and brotherhood among all nations and people of
the earth which we feel can only be attained by developing in each of us a
new spirit of tolerance in things non-essential and unity in things essential.

I note with joy the presence of the President of the Republic of Guinea
who has come to associate himself with the Liberian Government and people
in these festivities. He is a great nationalist and his presence is an indication
of the closest ties of friendship, fraternity and oneness subsisting between our
two States.

It is also invigorating to observe attending these ceremonies representatives
of so many African states, a situation hitherto unknown. As we view this
grand array of African personalities, and expect other African territories to
come into nationhood within the foreseeable future, we are overwhelmed and
over-awed by the sight, and by the implications which it connotes for the
future. May each and all of us resolve here and now that we shall lend our
best efforts to see that men everywhere become free and be permitted, without molestation or hindrance, to organize themselves into political communities and nations under such forms and frames of government as they

may choose; this we know to be a fundamental right to which all men are entitled.

As we view the changes that are rapidly taking place on our planet we are lifted to a higher plane in ecstasy and praise, and express the magnitude of this feeling by reciting the lines of Julia Ward Howe:

'Mine eyes have seen the glory of the coming of the Lord;
He is trampling out the vintage where the grapes of wrath are stored;
He hath loosed the fateful lightning of His terrible swift sword;
His truth is marching on.

'In the beauty of the lilies, Christ was born across the sea,
With a glory in His bosom that transfigures you and me;
As He died to make men holy, let us die to make men free,
While God is marching on.'

We ask you to be kind enough to convey to your respective Sovereigns and Chiefs of States the felicitations and gratitude of the Government, the people of Liberia and myself for this high recognition and distinction extended to us, our Government and people; we assure them of the encouragement which it gives us for greater efforts on our part to work and strive with might and main for the development and strengthening of our own country, meanwhile wishing for their respective nations, governments and peoples internal peace, happiness, prosperity and solidarity.

We have the pleasant privilege of noting the presence of numerous of our invited guests from abroad — men and women who have been particularly and genuinely helpful to the country in its struggle for development. Many of them are men who have vested interests here in concessions and other business — men who, in the early years of the present administration, seeing our struggles to get started, rendered us assistance and advance, and even extended us endowments, gifts and grants in different fields of endeavour. We welcome them and hope their stay will be most pleasant and enjoyable.

Nearer home, we have the good fortune of being blessed with the extremely rare privilege of having one of our former Presidents, an octogenarian, one of those who weathered the storms that attended the nation in the perilous years when there was no United Nations.

We give thanks to God for sparing his life and sustaining him with a reasonable portion of health and strength to be with us in these days of re-construction to give counsel, advice and encouragement.

May his years continue to accumulate and as his years shall be so may be his strength.

Now to you, my fellow countrymen, let us with united hearts, minds and strength press vigorously and persistently forward to raise our nation to a higher and yet higher stratum of nationhood.

MAY GOD KEEP, PROSPER AND SAVE THE STATE.

Independence Day Message
Monrovia, 26 July 1960

Liberia is the happy home of a unified people.

Introductory Note

The winds of change were blowing over the continent of Africa with breathtaking velocity. There was to be a new world order. President Tubman here gave probably his greatest philosophical message since he took office and we get a real understanding of the Liberian way of life.

Monrovia, 26 July 1960

I REMEMBER reading somewhere that prominently displayed in one of the galleries of Florence, Italy, is a group of half-finished statuary known as *The Prisoner*. Art experts say that Michaelangelo merely attempted to give a glimpse of human figures emerging from marble struggling to emancipate themselves, and that the work needed the finishing touches of future artists to bring out the true artistic splendour and greater symbolism. This illustration recalls to my mind that task of building this nation from a mere nebulous concept of liberty sketched with foresight and wisdom into the Declaration of Independence 113 years ago by the early hardy, brave and patriotic pioneers. Like Michaelangelo they must have left the full flowering of this concept to future generations of leaders, governments and people.

From that time on, we, their progenitors, have been working to put on the desirable finishing touches to the national statue carved by them. Future historians of this nation I know will record that their successors did not fail in this, that they proved themselves worthy representatives and worked constructively and persistently toward the goal of completing the national picture to a point of great beauty, honour and significance. We of this generation should pledge ourselves to carry on to the end that we too may hand to future generations, greatly enhanced, the noble task begun over 113 years ago.

As we have gathered here today to celebrate the 113th anniversary of our nation's independence, I am at a loss to find words in the English language that would adequately or even approximately express the contrasts between those early years of then and the present years of now.

Then, the pioneer fathers came from the United States determined to return to the land from which their ancestors had been ruthlessly taken away, and to identify themselves with their kinsmen and kinswomen. While the integrating process which has taken place was long, bitter and punctuated with war and bloodshed, nevertheless with determination, education, the orderly process of government, the co-operation of the lords of the soil, and the people whom they met here, the Republic of Liberia was ultimately founded and made into a stable and orderly government where the greatest hopes of those who had returned and those who had remained could be realized in the contest of mutual understanding, oneness, peace, prosperity, and solidarity.

Now, Liberia is the happy home of a unified people who resolved that on these shores they would find an asylum from the most grinding oppression, the home of countless others who love and cherish the blessings of liberty and who have thrown in their lot with the people of this nation in the march toward the things which make for an enlightened, stable and progressive government.

Then the political recognition of the infant colony entailed personal visits by President Roberts to European capitals where the force of his personality, the earnest and compelling logic of his appeal won the hearts of influential men and moved them to action on behalf of the new state, conceived merely as an experiment of a philanthropic ideal.

Now, political recognition has lost much of its former trappings and exchanges of notes and diplomatic representation from one country to another have raised diplomacy to a higher plane of international understanding and procedure, and membership in the United Nations has become an accepted norm.

Then because her natural and human resources were hardly discovered or touched and faced with internal dissensions, external indictments of illiteracy, poverty and disease, it was felt this nation was doomed to failure, and thus the suggestion that it should be reduced to a sphere of influence by a vicious international enquiry.

Now, the story of progress over the years has staggered the imagination of even her bitterest detractors; with the discovery of great natural potentials, and the backing of world magnates, with considerable progress in education, health and sanitation, roads and communication, the presence of Technical Assistance Programmes, United Nations Specialized Agencies, an awakened people conscious of and determined to play a magnificent rôle in the second century of their country's national existence, a revived economic system and programmes in every field of national endeavour designed to accelerate the country's progress and bring to fruition the ideal of the founding fathers, the idea of liberty, justice and equal opportunity for all this nation has gained international prestige and status.

BITTER FRUITS

The history of our own country has taught us the evils which emanated from the bitter fruit of indoctrination sown by our enemies between the indigenous population and the colonists. On the one hand the former were told that the colonists were the agents of the 'white man', that therefore they had come only to enslave and dispossess them of their land, that they had not come to throw in their lot with their own, to lead them from darkness to light, but that they were dangerous enemies of whom they had to beware.

On the other hand the indigenous peoples were represented to the colonists as cannibals, barbarous peoples who were incapable of civilization and that they had sworn eternal hatred and to do warfare with them at all times. Thus the psychological warfare raged, nourished constantly by the agents of evil and disharmony: those were dark and dismal days, critical and stormy, even public sentiments frowned down on us from all sides. But endowed with an irresistible will and in divine economy of things the guiding hand of

Providence pointed out the way and national leaders arose and international friends appeared strong, valiant and selfless to champion and plead a nation's cause and plan a nation's strategy.

Now we look with gratitude to the 1862 treaty of friendship with the United States, the gesture of friendship with Queen Victoria, the token of the British Admiralty, Lord Ashley's generosity, and all those whose investment in this nation are helping to pave the way to a better economic future for the Liberian people and others whose support and friendship constituted strong bulwarks to the young nation.

TRANSFORMATIONS

As in the tides of the world great transformations have followed wherever the winds of change have blown, science and technology have completely changed the complexion of what were once the unknown continents. The new and the old have merged at many useful and desirable points and out of this synthesis there has evolved a new system of values. Progress in the educational, social, cultural and health spheres has been phenomenal; vast water power schemes to supply hydro-electric power for irrigation, large agricultural experiments, gold and diamond mines, rubber and iron ore concessions, cocoa and aluminium plants and a textile factory in the Belgian Congo – South Africa, Sierra Leone, Liberia, Nigeria, Guinea, Ghana – all Africa is bursting and bristling with useful activities, for the peoples of the continent are awake and on the march.

But need I remind you of the responsibilities which true freedom imposes? The breath-taking process seen all over Africa is truly remarkable. But we cannot be complacent. We must not be content to rest. World conditions compel us to persevere within the bounds of nationality never permitting our egos, personal ambitions or ethnocentrism to overstep our discretion and good judgment, for good judgment is always the better part of valour.

This sense of our responsibility in this new era calls upon all African leaders, governments and peoples to combine their resources in the formulation of (a) correct internal and external policies for the public welfare; (b) a burning desire to work selflessly in the interest of the democratic ideology; (c) a programme designed to seek and achieve co-operation with the nations of Africa and the rest of the world.

Great human potentials have been unleashed and millions of Africans and peoples the world over have become conscious of the supreme rôle which man under the impulse of freedom can now play. It was with such thoughts in my mind that I said in a major policy address that I believed that those African nations which have been independent for many years and those which have recently achieved freedom or will be independent in the years to come should remain fully committed to a policy of friendship and love for all, regardless of racial differences, in order to demonstrate to the world that we recognize our responsibilities and have the capacity to administer equal justice and opportunity for all in an atmosphere of malice towards none.

THE CONGO CRISIS

The prevailing conditions in the Congo Republic naturally cause us grave concern but there should be no need for a attitude of panic or despair, for the Congo Republic must survive. Arising from this realization we need to apply to this and all other similar situations, a calm and sober attitude, since it is only within such an atmosphere that the desired results can be achieved. As the United Nations forces therefore take over to restore law and order, it is my hope that other peace media will be utilized, so that the arms theory will not be the only determinant and that the desirability of peace *per se* as an instrument by and through which goodwill and the blessings which come from a united front of all the political parties of the nation be ensured. This appeal to the reason, to the nationalism which has been the motivating factor to unity of purpose for the welfare of the Congo Republic should accompany the task of restoring peace and order in a nation now torn asunder by misunderstanding, intrigues, strife and mutiny.

There is one vital lesson which we in Liberia should learn from this unfortunate and regrettable situation: it is that the millennium foretold and believed by Christians where law would reign and armies, police forces and courts would no longer be required has not yet dawned.

UNITED NATIONS

I am convinced that the United Nations is the greatest bastion and the greatest international citadel of peace, human liberty and fundamental freedom. This great organization has brought together nations, if not in total peace and harmony, into a framework where appeal to reason has been encouraged rather than resort to passion; where the cause of nations great and small has been heard and decided and armed conflicts avoided. I know that the hope of the people of the world depends upon the decisions in the halls of this great symbol of peace, in the resolution of the differing ideologies and the achievement of man's ultimate hope of a world devoid of war, human suffering and misery. I am happy that the Great Powers have set the pace in not wantonly and flagrantly disregarding, ignoring and violating the fundamental principles of the United Nations.

While it is true that some of the great powers have threatened to contravene the principles of the United Nations Charter against the balanced and preponderant judgment of member states, not one has yet, when the United Nations was handling a situation, proceeded to act unilaterally in a crisis. In this example alone the pace has been set for small nations in the grip of the tide of political nationalism. At a time when the world is in a great upsurge of nationalism, nations should hold as their ultimate objective the constructing of a pathway for peace.

It is my hope that all nations will come to believe and support the work of the United Nations and work in close collaboration to achieve the ideals of permanent peace and brotherhood, and thus make the world safe for democratic ideology. I salute the work of this great organization.

LESSONS AND TRIALS

In this second century of our nation's history, and with a full realization of the lessons and trials of our past political struggles and experience, we look forward to an era of great economic prosperity for all our people as a realistic foundation to our political independence.

We look forward to the effective exploitation of our natural resources and abundant opportunities of work for all peoples everywhere.

We look forward to education as the nation's highest form of investment for the moulding of its future leaders in Church and State and the acceptance of an educational philosophy based upon the needs and aspirations of the country.

We look forward to all the various areas of government which have contributed and continue to contribute to the security, maintenance and perpetuity of our nation.

We look forward to men and women, boys and girls in all strata of our citizenry using their vital resources toward the building of a stronger and truly united nation.

This nation looks forward with hope to a promising future for mankind everywhere in an era of continued peace and happiness.

On this historic occasion we do well to ask ourselves: What has been the secret of the progress of our country over the years of our national existence? Has there been a continuity and consistency of policy through the years as outlined for the nation in 1847? Toward what goal may we look in the future? How much of this will depend upon the elected and appointed leaders, how much upon the citizenry, how much upon those who continue to befriend and champion the cause of nations great and small in the battle of human freedom?

From my point of view, the true and faithful answers to these questions will depend upon the affirmative, sound, well regulated, sacrificial, and patriotic actions of all in order to ensure forward and progressive strides in the second century of our national existence. On our part we regard agreements, contracts, treaties, concessions and all other obligations, together with oral or verbal promises and commitments to be religiously sacred and binding.

We are happy and indeed extremely proud to extend on this occasion heart-felt greetings to the doyen and members of the Diplomatic Corps accredited to this Government as representatives of their several governments and peoples. Amidst uneasy international world conditions, it is my proud privilege to mention that no significant incident has occurred between our countries capable of marring the good and happy relations which exist between us. That an atmosphere of friendship and harmony has prevailed, I attribute to the high degree of statesmanship and devotion to duty of those filling these positions of great responsibility in our capital. May we ever continue to strive to maintain such harmonious relationships between our countries to the mutual benefit of ourselves and the world in general.

I note with deep appreciation and satisfaction the presence of the Minister of State of the Ivory Coast and his Deputy at this 113th anniversary of our nation, for the people of the Ivory Coast and Liberia have, even during the period of colonial administration, maintained warm and friendly contacts. This relationship grew out of the fact that Liberians from the south-east section of the country went freely to the Ivory Coast and vice versa. We appreciate greatly their presence and welcome them to this independence celebration, and because visits between African states have greatly engendered better understanding, it is my hope that our two countries will continue to maintain the closest of ties.

I extend congratulations to the Prime Minister for the strides towards independence which will take place at zero hour on the seventh of August (1960) and to which I have already accredited a special delegation.

It is my special delight and a very great pleasure to welcome the President of the Community of County Councils and the County of Grand Canary, Las Palmas and Mrs. Matias Vega Auerra. It was my privilege to meet these distinguished officials in 1952 when on a state visit to Spain in response to an invitation extended by Generalissimo Franco. We were given the most lavish welcome and every time since then when either Mrs. Tubman or I broke our journey at Las Palmas, we have been accorded every official and friendly courtesy just as though each visit were the first. We have invited them to witness this 113th Anniversary celebration and wish them and all our visitors a very warm welcome and a very pleasurable stay.

Fellow citizens, each recurring national birthday should bring vividly to remembrance the highest gift of patriotism — SERVICE. It is recorded that the soldiers of Napoleon received from their 'Little Corporal' after a famous battle, a simple medal inscribed with the name of the battle and the words, 'I was there'.

The tangible manifestations of this day's celebration will soon be over, the voices of those who this day have spoken across the nation in patriotic orations and speeches and those who proposed toasts will be stilled and perhaps soon forgotten. We shall return to our homes and our daily pre-occupations. As we do so, may we in our hearts pledge ourselves anew to the true ideal of service to our nation, and thus have the privilege not only of saying, 'I was there', but 'I SERVED': Served with fervency and zeal the best interest of my God, my country, and my fellow-men.

First Annual Message delivered before the Second Session of the Forty-fifth Legislature

Monrovia, 22 November 1960

The tremendous changes that are taking place in Africa today create great thrills of joy, not only because the people of our continent are emerging into nationhood and gaining the national and individual dignity to which all mankind is entitled, but because these changes are evidence of the recognition of the errors and sins that have been committed in the subjugation, oppression and repression of the people of Africa and elsewhere in the world; and this I believe indicates further repentance.

Introductory Note

In 1960 Africa made headlines and the world witnessed the political awakening of an entire continent. European domination became a thing of the past and now Africa began to speak with her own voice in international affairs. In Liberia this was a year of great jubilation and the birth of each new state was hailed with special significance and honour. Recommendations in this message included a change of name of the Liberian Frontier Force to the Liberian National Guard, the creation of a Produce Marketing Board and revision of the Charter of the University of Liberia. The President further reported that contracts had been made for the setting up of a Medical College in Liberia.

Monrovia, 22 November 1960

SINCE THE adjournment of your last session, events of both national and international significance have occurred and many important decisions have been made which we feel are bound to affect the peace and safety of the world.

To an increasing degree it has become obvious that our age calls for men of stalwart stature, stern determination and unflinching patriotism and loyalty who will help to deepen the national consciousness, broaden and enrich the basis of world understanding, and thereby bring faith and dedication to the supreme task of nation building. These qualifications have already been exemplified by you in your service to the nation. I trust, therefore, that you will at this session enter upon your duties with the same earnestness, patriotic enthusiasm, and loyalty as you have done in the past.

Because of the numerous duties attendant upon the inauguration, the formation of a new Government, the reception of foreign dignitaries, and my two State Visits to the Republic of Guinea and the Federation of Nigeria, it was not practicable for me to take advantage at an earlier date of

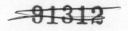

the health and rest trip which you so generously and spontaneously granted me, until August of this year. It is on this account that I was not at the seat of Government during the opening of your present session.

I now appear before you at this time with the full assurance of your continued co-operation and loyalty toward the achievement of those goals which we have always believed are fundamental in the building up of a sound socio-economic and educational system for our people.

My basic belief in the democratic process is well known to you. You are fully aware of my thesis for the full development of the human and natural resources of our nation. I continue to look forward to the development of the ultimate value of the human being. In these ways, I have come to believe that together we can achieve for ourselves and our posterity the blessings of the sacred heritage which our Founding Fathers have bequeathed unto us.

I pray that God will guide and direct you throughout your deliberations so that wise legislations and beneficial statutes may emanate from your present session. With dependence upon your loyalty, faith in your sense of responsibility and your dedication to service, let us all forge ahead to another year of peace, progress and prosperity. I challenge you to utilize the magnificent opportunities which these ideals hold for us and for all mankind.

It is now my pleasing duty to report to you on the condition of the State and what has transpired in the administration since your last session.

FOREIGN AFFAIRS

Our relations with member states of the United Nations, including those governments which have diplomatic representations near this capital, continue to be characterized by increased understanding and goodwill.

We are pursuing a policy of peace and friendship with all nations of the earth; a policy of deep interest in and profound concern for all under-privileged, oppressed and subjugated peoples of dependent and independent territories. In our relations with other nations, we have been and are still, persistently exerting every effort within the bounds of reason to contribute fully to the relief and liberation of subjugated peoples everywhere.

The tremendous changes that are taking place in Africa today create great thrills of joy, not only because the people of our continent are emerging into nationhood and gaining the national and individual dignity to which all mankind is entitled, but because these changes evidence the recognition of the errors and sins that have been committed in the subjugation, oppression and repression of the peoples of Africa and elsewhere in the world, and I believe, indicate repentance.

While there are still some instances of persistent indulgence in the degrading and vicious policies of discrimination and apartheid, these practices are almost universally condemned and find little or no public support in international circles.

During the course of this year fifteen African States emerged from colonial administration into full sovereignty and independence with relatively no acts of violence or shedding of blood. The attainment of nationhood of these African States has been marked with great jubilation throughout Africa.

To all the independence celebrations of these States, the Liberian Government accredited special representatives, and at home, the day on which a particular State celebrated its independence was proclaimed a national holiday; its flag flown at Fort Norris alongside our own flag and a national salute of twenty-one guns fired.

The majority of these new independent nations have emerged from the French colonial administration in Africa. Therefore credit is due the French, in our opinion, for this great step forward, and we trust that they will bring the same sense of justice to the Algerian question. Meanwhile we pay tribute to the British for the rôle they have played in this changing Africa, their last act being to grant independence to Nigeria, the largest African territory.

While our hearts are uplifted by the birth of so many States and while we watch with pride the steady progress of most of them, the situation in the Congo has baffled, if not frustrated, all attempts at finding a formula for solution of the problems of that country.

The situation in the Congo became so acutely dangerous that the United Nations decided, upon the request of the Congolese Government, to send a United Nations Force to restore and preserve order and peace in that country. In response to a United Nations appeal, the Liberian Government despatched a contingent of a rifle company of two hundred and forty-five men; this contingent is still serving in that country.

Regrettably, allegations have been made against the Liberian contingent in the Congo to the effect that they caused or permitted the suffocation of a number of people who were being removed to safety. These allegations are now being investigated and the Government has sent Counsellor Turner W. Stewart and Major William O. Kun to Leopoldville to hold a watching brief of the investigation.

The mission of the United Nations in the Congo has been made difficult in our opinion because, in the first place, there appear to be many conflicting, opposing and rival groups who are striving to seize political control of the nation, regardless of whether or not their ambitions injure the interest of the country. Besides, there are upstart foreign groups from other areas, including Africa, who are exploiting the situation.

Notwithstanding these obstacles, the Congo crisis *shall* and *must* be solved and the country remain the unified Republic of the Congo, politically and territorially, as when power was transferred from the Belgians to the Congolese. This can only be accomplished by patience and tolerance on the part of the Congolese as well as by disinterested and altruistic assistance and urgent contributions through the United Nations, on the part of foreign governments, including the governments of African States.

It was my great pleasure to make my first State Visit during May of this year to an independent African State when I visited the Republic of Guinea upon the invitation of His Excellency the President, at N'Zerekore, just across the Liberian border, and we travelled by rail and motor cars from N'Zerekore to Conakry, the capital of Guinea. It took five days to accomplish the journey and throughout our travels there were continuous chantings of praise, unabating and spontaneous outbursts of tumultuous welcome, a demonstration of friendship and fraternity. Our reception in Guinea was the greatest display of friendliness and welcome that I have ever witnessed or that has ever been bestowed upon me. The activities in connection with our visit to Guinea were crowned by the opening and naming of one of the streets in Conakry after the President of Liberia.

At the close of the visit, President Touré and I issued a Joint Communiqué embodying our views on some of the problems of Africa and the world. We specifically agreed upon a solution for the boundary dispute that had existed between France and Liberia up to the time when France transferred that territory to the Republic of Guinea. The Joint Communiqué will be transmitted to you.

In June of this year, upon the invitation of Her Majesty Queen Elizabeth II, we visited Nigeria as guests of the Governor-General of Nigeria. At the time Nigeria was a British Colony and was in a state of expectancy, as October 1, 1960, had been set for its dependence. During this visit great courtesies were extended us by the officials and people of that country wherever we went. We visited the three Regions of the Federation and found great progress and striking evidence of social and political maturity.

Since our visit, Nigeria has become a sovereign and independent state, and during the ceremonies marking her independence, the Honourable William R. Tolbert, Jun., Vice-President of Liberia, and the Honourable Charles D. Sherman, Secretary of the Treasury, were accredited as my personal representatives. I am pleased to state that these gentlemen fulfilled their mission with dignity and credit.

The Swiss Government granted permission for us to visit Zürich, Switzerland, for a medical check-up and vacation and during our stay in Switzerland, that Government generously provided us with security measures and extended to us the usual courtesies and considerations accorded a Chief of State travelling *incognito*.

Accompanying Mrs. Tubman and myself were the Honourable H. Mac White, Father J. D. K. Baker, Counsellors Samuel W. Payne and D. C. Caranda, the Honourable C. O. L. Bonner and Honourable Marshall Roberts, besides military, secretarial and security personnel.

While we were in Zürich the local authorities took special interest in our happiness and welfare and were helpful in making our visit enjoyable and restful.

During our stay there we received an invitation from Her Majesty Queen Juliana and His Royal Highness Prince Bernhard of the Netherlands to pay them a private visit. We accepted the invitation and spent three days with them. This visit was very pleasant and afforded us the opportunity of meeting again Her Majesty and the Prince whose guests we were four years ago.

We returned to Liberia on November 6th and were received, greeted and welcomed by Government, citizens and foreign residents with extraordinary fervour and enthusiasm.

The report of the Secretary of State that will be transmitted to you deals in detail with this matter and others in connection with our foreign relations, and he will be available to answer questions or give explanations on any matter referred to in his report.

RECOMMENDATIONS

The following are recommendations of the Secretary of State, for which I request your favourable consideration:

1. That plans be made for the creation of a Central National Archive;
2. That a new building be provided for the Bureau of Printing;

3. That fifty thousand dollars be provided in the 1961 Budget for the procurement of modern printing equipment;
4. That the new Foreign Service Manual be approved;
5. That an Act be passed penalizing Registrars of Deeds who fail to send the record books to the Department of State; that assignments be made for the indexing of registered deeds; and
6. That ordinary passport fees be increased from five dollars to six dollars.

In the report of the Secretary of the Treasury it is noted that for the first time in many years Government revenues exceeded Government expenditures at the close of 1959; hence it was not necessary to use any Government revolving credits to balance the Budget.

The Government has, in the reporting period under review, received an increase of $6,145,866.15 over the similar preceding period 1958 to 1959. Furthermore, for the period January 1 to September 30, 1960, $22,182,874.80 has been collected against estimated revenues of $22,500,000.00 for the whole year. This means that as of September 30, 1960, total revenue collections had exceeded estimates for the year. If this is compared with the eighteen and a half million dollars collected in 1958, it represents a very substantial rate of increase.

On the basis of past yields for the last three months of the year, it is reasonable to predict that revenue collections and receipts for the present fiscal year ending December 31, 1960, will aggregate in the neighbourhood of $20,000,000.00.

On the subject of Uniform Accounting and Reporting, the Secretary of the Treasury has commented that it has become quite evident that there is a very limited use which can be made of statistical reports where there is a continuing shift of the reporting periods. And, of course, there is concurrent risk in using such information for any worth-while economic analysis.

It is therefore recommended that a uniform reporting period for the Government fiscal agencies as well as all statistical reporting departments be adopted so that a basis for comparison and analysis would be permanently established, and that all future reports should conform to this period irrespective of the time when the Legislature meets.

The Secretary of the Treasury recommends, and I request your favourable consideration, that the Government create a wholly owned Development Corporation for the purpose of financing its participation in business development enterprises. The direction of such a corporation would be restricted to the Treasury, the Department of Justice, the Bureau of Economic Research and the President of the prospective Development Bank.

Considering the extreme importance of an Emergency Reserve Fund, it is hereby recommended that such a fund be established and the Secretary of the Treasury authorized to set aside 1 per cent of the annual budget in the years 1961–62, and that said rate be increased in each succeeding year as may be reasonably safe.

If illiteracy is to be banished, as it must, the high economic potential of our citizenry fully realized and our health programme expanded, expenditures for education and health will have to be increased at an extraordinary rate. It is therefore recommended that implementation of the proposed Education and Health Fund suggested in the 1960 Inaugural Address be undertaken during the year 1961. Such a fund was recommended to be subscribed to on a voluntary basis by civil servants but supported as a matter of public policy by all persons holding political appointments.

It is pointed out in the report of the Secretary of the Treasury that as a result of a careful study, we have come to the conclusion that existing pre-financing practices should be given a re-examination. In the past such financing served the useful purpose of introducing Government securities to the world market in so far as the Government did not have any credit rating in most foreign banks and the capital required for development activities was extremely scarce. It was then necessary for large contracting firms to make their own contacts and arrangements for financing construction projects. Some of these firms contracted with the Government for interest rates of 5 per cent but had to accept credit from 10 per cent to 12 per cent, plus insurance charges from 3 per cent to 5 per cent, and in some instances discounts on Government notes.

The net result of this is that construction costs of various projects are very high because they carry a hidden financing cost. Worse than that, however, is the depression this can cause to the level of prices of Government bonds, and thus reflect an undeserved lack of confidence in their value.

The bank credit situation seems now to have improved and there have been specific requests by certain banking interests to undertake part of Government bond financing.

It is therefore recommended that future proposals for pre-financing be carefully examined against the possibility of securing banking credit or normal investment finances so as to have such projects executed on a cash basis. This would save the Government multiple interest rates, reduce construction costs and at the same time save the contractor from having to go out of his way and become a banker or be taken in by bankers.

In the meantime our economy continues to function in a period when prices are constantly rising. Especially is this true in the case of building materials. In an attempt to curtail these mounting material prices and thus boost the construction industry, over a decade ago Government lifted the duty on all materials imported for construction purposes.

The prices of building materials continue to rise, however, despite the waiving of duty, because it has been argued by importers that wage rates and material prices in the countries of origin, coupled with transportation charges, are contributing factors to the high prices. The ultimate outcome is that unit prices charged by contractors for private as well as Government construction are still inflated by these factors.

To review the whole area of construction cost, excluding financing charges, the Treasury has secured, through the co-operation of the United States Operations Mission in Liberia an expert in construction engineering, Mr. Karl Smith, who, in association with Mr. P. Ernest Parker, Director of General Accounting, is conducting a study and collecting appropriate data to ascertain what prices a contractor should charge to do business in Liberia and at the same time be able to realize a reasonable return on his investment. An interim report of this team indicates that their review is progressing satisfactorily.

It is recommended that the Bureau of Audits should take primary responsibility for a systematic periodical auditing of agencies of Government which are handling funds. In these auditing operations, except where it is directly involved, the Treasury should be represented.

It is further recommended that an addendum to the codification contract be entered into to provide for the compilation, in loose leaf binders, of all Concession Agreements entered into by Government since 1900 where these are still in force.

Since the delivery of my last Annual Message, the Government has established an independent Power Authority and all income from this utility has been separately deposited under the control of that Authority. However, collections were not made up to date by the contracting collecting agency, the Liberia Company. As a result, the Government had to honour its existing commitments with the Port Management Company for the supply and purchase of power by advancing to the Power Authority the sum of $150,000 to meet its current obligations.

The Secretary of the Treasury reports that there is a submission of additional invoices totalling $263,000.00 which has been certified as the Government's indebtedness to the Port Management Company. In view of the termination of the contract of the Liberia Company, this is an obligation which has to be honoured and arrangements will be made for payments.

In view of the fact that under existing agreements pre-financed projects are increasing at a very rapid rate, it has been necessary to establish reserve funds at the Bank of Monrovia to meet these obligations. It is therefore recommended that the Treasury be given authority to place parts of these reserves on fixed deposit from time to time in order that the Government might earn interest on them to offset interest payments on short-term obligations.

The Intra-Bank of Switzerland is completing the organization of a new Commercial Bank of Liberia and 40 per cent of the shares of this bank are to be offered to the Liberian public as soon as plans are completed.

The Port Management Company has made a proposal to Government for a general 20 per cent increase in existing tariff rates and approval of this proposal is being recommended.

On January 1, 1960, half a million dollars worth of Liberian coins which had been struck by the United States Mint, were put into circulation. These coins are in denominations of 50 cents, 25 cents, 10 cents, 5 cents and 1 cent.

Other recommendations of the Secretary of the Treasury will be submitted to you through his annual report to Your Honourable Body.

The detailed financial accounts of revenues collected and expended as well as all other matters of a financial nature are contained in the reports of the Bureau of Audits, Accounts and Revenues which will be transmitted to you in the usual way.

The Attorney-General reports that during the course of the year under review, Volumes III through VI of the Liberian Law Reports were published and are now in use by the various courts in the Republic as well as by members of the Bar and the public in general; also that copies of Volume VII are now available for distribution and Volume VIII will shortly be sent to the press.

The Attorney-General's recommendation for procedures having to do with easing the congestion in the dockets of the Civil Law Court of the Sixth Judicial Circuit and of the Circuit Court for the First Judicial Circuit will be forwarded to Your Honourable Body at a later date for approval.

The following are the Attorney-General's recommendations for which I respectfully request your favourable consideration:

1. That responsibilities of the Tax Division be increased to include direction and supervision of prosecution, in all courts of the Republic except the Supreme Court, of all cases to which Government is a party;
2. That the Research Division be merged functionally with the Codification Division because the functions of the latter absorb those of the former.
3. That two new divisions be created so that one of them may be in charge of co-ordinating technical services and the other charged with co-ordinating non-technical services of the Department of Justice.
4. That every concession area be declared a stipendiary magistracy with the appointment thereto of the usual law enforcement officers.

The following are recommendations submitted by the Postmaster-General for which I respectfully request your favourable consideration:

1. That a programme aimed at giving specific specialized postal training for persons in the postal service be inaugurated under the directorship of the Deputy Postmaster-General;
2. That the rates of airmail postage be increased;
3. That the Liberian Official Postal Guide be revised;
4. That a biennial convention of all postmasters within the Republic be authorized; and
5. That scholarships be granted ten persons to study abroad in the following fields: Postal Accounting; Parcel Post handling, including registration and insurance; Money Order and Postal Saving System; Postal Administration, including the setting up and operation of branches and Rural Post Offices and systematized handling and distribution of mails.

A telecommunication project which was negotiated some time ago has made some progress and it is hoped that work will soon begin on establishing the system.

Other matters covered by the Postmaster-General will be made available to Your Honourable Body in his report to be submitted to you.

Our military, defence, police and security forces must be re-organized and the laws and regulations appertaining to them reviewed and revised so as to insure greater internal security and safety. A programme to effectuate this has been commenced.

It is recommended that the strength of the Liberian Frontier Force be authorized to be increased to a Brigade and that action be taken to provide for compulsory training of two militia Brigades to be equipped with up-to-date and modern military accoutrement. To carry out this programme it is respectfully requested that construction of a training camp in Montserrado County for training officers and men of the First Brigade and one in Sinoe County for training of officers and men of the Second Brigade be authorized. This is of utmost importance and I pray your favourable consideration during your present session.

The assignment of Liberian Frontier Force Officers and men to do Customs, Internal Revenue and Police duties throughout the country is having an adverse effect on the Frontier Force and authorization is therefore requested for the organization of an Interior Police Force to perform these services.

There appears to be no legislation giving the size of the Liberian Flag, or the exact description of the shade of red and blue of the flag, nor prescribing the number of points the star should have; nor has any law been found describing the President's standard. It is therefore recommended that legislation be enacted to supply these requirements.

We also recommend that a law be enacted to legalize the Liberian National Anthem.

The following are recommendations of the Secretary of National Defence which I respectfully submit for your favourable consideration:

1. That the name of the Liberian Frontier Force be changed to the National Guard of Liberia;
2. That appropriation be provided for a suitable mooring pier to be constructed for the coast-guard crafts;
3. That authorization for a 327 foot and 311 foot cutter as well as a 295 foot patrol boat and two 40-foot cutters be made available to serve and to enable regular patrol of our coastal borders.

The administration by the Department of the Interior of that portion of the territory of the Republic beyond the 40-mile limit established in 1847, has been the subject of controversy and considerable contention between the Legislature, the Judiciary and the Executive for some time.

It was not until the year 1919 in a matter of *Habeas Corpus* brought by Ballah Karmo and WorhnBeh, Appellants, against John L. Morris, Secretary of the Interior and Major John H. Anderson, Officer Commanding the Liberian Frontier Force, Appellees, that a clear pronouncement was made on the question of the administration of the hinterland by the Interior Department and its relation to the Republic under the provisions of the Constitution and the Act of the Legislature of 1914 relating thereto.

In that case it was alleged that the appellees illegally imprisoned the appellants under the authority of the said act and therefore the appellants issued a writ of *Habeas Corpus* to procure their release.

In contesting the imprisonment, the constitutionality of the Act of Legislature approved October 13, 1914, which places the administration of the hinterland (that portion of the Republic beyond the 40-mile limit), under the authority of the Interior Department, was questioned by Counsel for Appellants, L. A. Grimes, then Counsellor-at-Law, while Edwin Barclay, then Attorney-General, in support of the Act of Legislature above referred to, and its constitutionality, raised the following contention that:

1. 'The jurisdiction conferred upon the Secretary of the Interior in relation to matters of administration and justice in causes arising in the hinterland districts is not unconstitutional.
   (a) 'Because the rules of the Liberian Constitution apply only to territory defined in the municipal law of the Republic of Liberia and to such other territories appurtenant to Liberia over which the laws and Constitution of Liberia have been extended.
   (b) 'The territories acquired by the Republic outside the forty-mile zone fixed in the statutes as the boundaries of the Republic are governed only by such regulations as the Legislature may prescribe, which regulations furnish the character of their rights and government.
2. 'That as the native territories outside the forty-mile zone do not belong to constitutional Government, no action of the Secretary of the Interior in relation to matters arising in the hinterland can be tested by constitutional rules, etc.'

The Supreme Court, in an opinion handed down on the 2nd day of May, A.D. 1919, by Mr. Chief Justice Dossen, referred to the constitutional issue raised by the Attorney-General in support of the Act, the division of the country into county and hinterland jurisdictions and the position of the Executive Government, as grave and momentous.

Said Mr. Chief Justice Dossen:

'We propose to consider, firstly, the grave, momentous questions raised by the Attorney-General, which attack the sovereignty of the Republic beyond the limits of forty miles from the Liberian littoral, and the limitation of the Constitution and the judicial power created thereunder to the territories embraced within the said zone of forty miles.'

After reviewing *in extenso* the Constitution, the Act of 1914, the several treaties of the Republic, the deeds of cession, and the methods of acquisition of territory in Africa by the Colonizing Powers from the time that the Pope claimed the authority to grant individuals of European descent the right to acquire, hold and govern African territory down to the Berlin Conference on Africa, he laid down the following provisions for the appropriation of land on the coast of Africa:

'The theory upon which a civilized state may extend its sovereignty and laws over uncivilized tribes who may not have previously come under the political and governmental control of some other civilized country, was developed and carried further at the Conference on Africa in Berlin. When that conference was laying down conditions for the appropriation by the signatory powers of territory on the coast of the African continent, the plenipotentiary of the United States declared that: "His Government would gladly adhere to a more extended rule, to be based on a principle which should aim at the voluntary consent of the natives whose country is taken possession of in all cases where they have not provoked the aggression." Protocol of 31 January 1885. But the conference took no action on this invitation of the United States' Plenipotentiary – it was merely recorded that in the unanimous opinion of the conference its Act did not limit the right which the powers possessed of causing the recognition of the occupations which might be notified to them to be preceded by such an examination as they might consider necessary. . . .'

It would be most interesting to repeat the entire opinion here but time will not permit.

The decision of the Supreme Court in the case just cited settled the question once and for all, nullified and abrogated that portion of the Act of Legislature of 1914 limiting the county jurisdiction to 40 miles inland and placed an interpretation upon the Constitution of 1847 with reference to the forty-mile limit. But because of the lack of communication and transportation, and the availability of facilities for ready contact with the hinterland, the Executive Government had not been in position to give force and effect to the implementation and execution of the decision.

Besides, the tribes were more or less hostile to each other and very often to the Government. This condition was mostly created by lack of contact of the tribal peoples with the Central Government or even the local county governments. A feeling of antagonism and hatred, influenced more or less by outside intrigues, developed over the years and internecine wars persisted.

However, with the change of the Government's policy and the amendment of the Constitution and laws of the country, particularly the enunciation of the Unification and Integration Policy, which provided for representation of the people of the hinterland in the legislature and the extension of suffrage to all alike regardless of tribe or sex, these dangerous conditions have substantially improved and the people of the hinterland have shown themselves loyal, patriotic and devoted citizens – equal to each other and to all other citizens of the Republic, sharing the mutual weal and woe, and bearing the burdens of taxation and other responsibilities implicit in citizenship. Furthermore, since the creation of the United Nations Organization other outside intrigues have been diminished.

Now that road transportation and communication by air, radio, telephone and other media with the interior have improved, all parts of the interior are accessible and education, religion and civilization have penetrated and are being carried throughout the hinterland, and it is constitutionally obligatory that the Legislature and the Executive at this time take action to implement and execute the mandate, judgment and decision of the Supreme Court referred to above.

We contemplate a rearrangement of the political sub-divisions of the country and in this connection strongly recommend for your favourable consideration and action that a Special Commission be appointed and authorized to examine, study and survey the present political sub-divisions of the country.

This Commission would be responsible to make recommendations for the necessary readjustments and changes to meet the requirements of the decision of the Supreme Court, and their recommendations would be submitted to Your Honourable Body at your next regular session.

It is my feeling that that portion of the Act limiting the county jurisdiction to forty miles inland should be repealed and that the county jurisdiction be extended to the limit of the territory of the Republic.

As a first step towards the rearrangement of the political sub-division of the country, perhaps the present forty-mile county limit could be extended to include more territory inland, thereby reducing the present territories of the three provinces. After annexing portions of the provinces to the counties, the remaining territories of the three provinces should be raised to county level. The Commission however need not be limited to the views expressed herein.

Another reason which makes the rearrangement eminently essential is that the present hinterland administration was patterned upon the colonial system and must be abolished.

Last but not least, it is to be noted that these suggested changes are not courtesies to be extended nor privileges sought to be bestowed but natural, inalienable and inherent rights to which each and every citizen of the nation is entitled under the provision of the Constitution that 'all men are born equally free and independent'. I attach great importance to the immediate necessity for this change.

The following recommendations of the Secretary of the Interior are submitted and your favourable reaction solicited:

1. That appropriation be provided for the construction of Provincial Headquarters for the Western Central Province and

2. That Paramount and Clan Chiefs be placed on annual salaries and the
   hut tax be increased to ten dollars per hut per annum.

In our last Message we emphasized the eminent importance of the over-all
reorganization of our school system with a view to strengthening and raising
the standard of education at all levels, particularly in the elementary schools.
The need of well-trained and amply prepared teachers to carry out this programme is of the utmost urgency.

We recommended the enactment of several projects of law during your last
session to meet some of the education demands, and recommendations
received your favourable consideration. Now we are pleased to report that
programmes for the implementation of these legislations are being undertaken and progress is being made.

The universal urge and anxiety of all our citizens, girls and boys, women
and men, to improve themselves, present a great challenge to the Government, and this challenge must be met by providing well-trained teachers and
better school buildings adequately staffed and equipped. This calls for increased appropriation and therefore we request that Your Honourable Body
give consideration to increased appropriation for education in next year's
budget.

It is necessary that the Foreign Scholarship Programme be revised and
that the needs of the country in technological, professional and other fields be
ascertained and evaluated; that scholarships be granted only for a specialized training in these fields determined by Government and that all such
awards be made only to students who have successfully passed competitive
examinations and aptitude tests before a Board of Examiners appointed for
that purpose.

The Fundamental and Adult Educational Programme must be expanded
and intensified and to accomplish this, the appropriation for this programme
should be increased. This we respectfully recommend for your favourable
consideration when preparing the Appropriation Bill for 1961.

Considering the importance of scientific, technical and vocational education
to any national development and educational programme in this scientific and
technological age, we recommend the expansion and intensification of vocational education at Booker Washington Institute, the establishment of
vocational schools in each of the counties and provinces and the stressing of
the sciences in all institutions of higher education with special emphasis on
the applied sciences.

As the country's highest institution of learning, the standard of the University of Liberia must be improved and strengthened and qualification for
full professorship in the University should be a doctorate degree. To give full
vigour to the new programme envisaged for the University of Liberia, it is
recommended that the Charter of the University be revised and that lawyers,
politicians and statesmen do not comprise the majority of members of the
Board of Trustees of the University.

Scholarships shall therefore be granted to present professors with Master's
and Bachelor's degrees to enable them to obtain their doctorate degrees
should they so desire it. Similar scholarships will be awarded other students
under the scheme herein mentioned after competitive examinations. A more
precise and definite plan for the new charter and programme for the University will be submitted to you for action.

The Government has consummated plans for the construction of another elementary school in the City of Monrovia. It is therefore requested that appropriate legislation be enacted for the appropriation by Government of lots numbers 30, 31, 32 and 48 on Broad and Carey Streets with the following description for the construction of that school.

Commencing at the South-west intersection of Broad and Lynch Streets and running thence on Magnetic bearings North 54 degrees West 247·5 feet parallel with Broad Street; thence running South 36 degrees East 132 feet; thence running South 54 degrees East 165 feet; thence running South 36 degrees West 132 feet; thence running South 54 degrees East 82·5 feet parallel with Carey Street; then running North 36 degrees East 264 feet parallel with Lynch Street to point of commencement, and containing one (1) acre of land and no more.

The following recommendations proposed by the Secretary of Public Instruction are hereby submitted for appropriate action:

1. That a National Public Library be erected in the City of Monrovia.
2. That legislation be made for the school year to begin in September and end in June instead of beginning in February and ending in November, and that an emergency school year be created in 1961 to carry three semesters so as to facilitate the change-over and thus provide for utilization for an extra semester which will be created during the change-over period.
3. That the Education Act of 1912, amended in 1937 and 1944, be further amended to include the present organizational chart of the Department of Public Instruction and redefinition of the functions of its staff.
4. That in order to encourage missions and private schools in improving the quality of the academic standard required by the Department of Public Instruction the Education Act be amended to provide subsidy only to private institutions which have attained the standard set by the Department.

Most of the burden of the development programme rests upon the Department of Public Works and Utilities, and the importance of the efficient maintenance and administration of this department cannot be over-rated.

Recently, the Secretary of Public Works and Utilities, the Honourable Thomas E. Buchanan, after protracted and recurring illness, upon the advice of his physician, tendered his resignation. It was with reluctance and regret that I accepted Mr. Buchanan's resignation for he was a hard, persistent and devoted administrator. There was no task in the line and course of his duties that he did not tackle with bull-dog tenacity and astute acumen. The word failure was not in his vocabulary and whatever his hands found to do he did with all his might.

I cannot forget the early days of the administration when our Development Programme was just being formulated. Our effort to forge ahead in this key programme of the administration was rendered difficult because World War II had just ended and building materials were virtually unobtainable. Supplies for the construction and remodelling of old buildings, particularly for the construction of the original Centennial Pavilion and remodelling of the Executive Mansion, were also unobtainable. Mr. Buchanan undertook the construction and renovation of these buildings and, by what I consider almost a miracle, completed them in time for the observance of the Centennial celebrations in 1947.

Since those early days when there were but few engineers, and no construction companies, he has been in the forefront of our development programme and is credited with the most outstanding contributions to the success of various projects under the Department of Public Works and Utilities.

It cannot be overlooked that two successive Secretaries and one Under Secretary of Public Works and Utilities have suffered heart attacks in recent years and these officials developed these conditions, I believe, because of the heavy responsibilities, duties and obligations imposed by the onerous burdens of the office of Secretary of Public Works and Utilities.

To lessen the burdens and to meet the growing demands of that Department, it is respectfully recommended that two additional Assistant Secretaries of Public Works and Utilities be appointed.

To cope with the many involved and intricate issues arising ever and anon concerning lands, surveys and titles, we propose the organization of a Bureau of Lands, Surveys and Titles under the Department of Public Works and Utilities and that one of the additional Assistant Secretaries of Public Works and Utilities recommended, if approved, be appointed head of this Bureau.

While the Honourable Mr. Buchanan has been certified as being unable to continue carrying on the duties of Secretary of Public Works and Utilities that Department should not lose the benefit of his vast experiences and specialized knowledge. I therefore recommend that the position of Consultant to the Secretary of Public Works and Utilities be created.

The Senior Under Secretary of Public Works, the Honourable Stanley L. Borland, because of health reasons and upon the advice of his physician, tendered his resignation as Under Secretary of Public Works, which has been accepted.

The Honourable Joseph W. Boayue, Junior Under Secretary for Utilities, has by operation of law, assumed the functions and responsibilities of Acting Secretary of Public Works and Utilities. The following are recommendations submitted by him for which I solicit your favourable consideration:

1. That the Division of Municipal Engineering should be absorbed by the Division of Highways and maintenance of Monrovia streets should be contracted;

2. That an amendment requiring practising electricians and plumbers to qualify for licenses by passing basic examinations in their respective fields, be made to the Act of Legislature passed during your 1959–60 session to provide for penalties for violators.

3. That the Pre-engineering Programme at the University of Liberia be extended to three years.

4. That funds be appropriated to recruit graduate engineers to be assigned in the counties as county engineers.

5. That the Mesurado River Bridge be widened, along with that section of United Nations Drive between Water Street and the proposed Freeway from Bushrod Island to Mt. Barclay and Johnsonville.

6. That a Commission be appointed and charged with the task of readjusting property boundaries and providing an adequate system of streets and alleys. This Commission should operate under the proposed Bureau of Lands, Surveys and Titles.

Liberia is essentially an agricultural country and the creation of the Department of Agriculture and Commerce was intended to strengthen the extension service with emphasis placed on increasing rice and a great variety of other agricultural products.

The increase in the rice-eating population and the demand for increased labourers for concessions and local farming are affecting the production of rice by farmers in the interior, and this has made it necessary to import large quantities of white polished rice, which contains little or no nutrition value. This condition is affecting the people's health as evidenced by the increased incidence of beri-beri.

As rice is the staple food of the country, its production cannot be neglected. A programme, therefore, is being formulated to ensure the increase of rice production and permits for the importation of polished rice will either be discontinued or reduced to the lowest minimum.

The Secretary of Agriculture and Commerce reports that a committee has been set up to examine and recommend means by which the use of labour in the development of commerce and industry can be effected.

On the 14th June 1960, the Secretary of Agriculture and Commerce recommended the establishment of a Produce Marketing Corporation for the purpose of finding a remedy for the malpractices which now plague our produce trade.

It will be the responsibility of the Produce Marketing Corporation to develop to the fullest extent the export trade of our produce by the following activities:

1. Purchase produce regularly throughout the country at prices previously fixed at each point and made widely known;
2. Ensure that there are buyers at each point at which the price is fixed. This can be done by making the fullest use of the already existing merchant organization in the country;
3. Establish very high standards so that we can obtain the best possible price in the world market;
4. Provide machinery and equipment for the processing of products such as palm oil, palm kernels and coffee; and
5. Explore world markets so that we can increase the sale of these products.

With reference to the Act creating the Bureau of Labour, the Secretary of Agriculture and Commerce has submitted the following recommendations and I request consideration of them:

1. That immediate action be taken by Government to have section 1416 of the Revised Statutes of Liberia repealed, as this section is now obsolete;
2. That the Interior Regulations be amended, particularly that section dealing with porterage; and
3. That Liberia lend financial assistance to the proposed Institute for Labour Studies by the ILO.

The Director-General of the National Public Health Service, Dr. Murray Barclay, being out of the country at Harvard University for specialized training in Public Health Administration, the duties of this office devolved on the Assistant Director-General, Dr. C. F. Scarbrough, as Acting Director-General.

Plans for the construction of the Monrovia General Hospital are well advanced. The drafting and planning for this hospital are being undertaken by the firm of Litchfield, Whiting and Browne upon contract with the Department of Public Works and Utilities.

While in Europe on vacation, the Rector of the University of Zürich and a group of medical professors offered to supply professors for the proposed Medical College of the University of Liberia. To follow up the offer, the President of the University of Liberia, upon my request, went to Zürich and met with me and these medical professors and the Rector of the University of Zürich. After several conferences a tentative agreement was reached and a memorandum drafted and signed by the Rector of the University of Zürich and the President of the University of Liberia. The memorandum embodies the kind and nature of assistance that the Rector and the professors contemplate making in connection with the proposed Medical College. It will be transmitted to you.

It is intended that the proposed Medical College of the University of Liberia be integrated with the Monrovia General Hospital, or at least constructed near the hospital as a part of the hospital plan.

The Nurses Training School in Monrovia should also be integrated into the hospital and form a part of the Medical College.

I think it should be mentioned that Dr. Paul P. Meyer, my personal physician, who accompanied me to Zürich, played a very important part in initiating and promoting the arrangements that led to the offer of the Rector of the University of Zürich and the medical professors to supply professors for the proposed Medical College. They request that he be the liaison between them and the Government.

The registration of births and deaths is too important to be handled as carelessly as it is at present. A project of law will therefore be submitted to Your Honourable Body to effectuate the general reforms contemplated in this connection.

The Acting Director-General of the National Public Health Service has submitted the following recommendations for which I solicit your favourable consideration:

1. That the salaries of nurses and midwives be increased;
2. That all buildings being used by the National Public Health Service be maintained by the Service;
3. That the first contract salary for foreign medical professionals be $6,500 per annum, the second contract $7,000 per annum and the third $8,000 per annum and that retirement benefits be provided for such foreign medical professionals who serve for a period to be designated;
4. That appropriation for five additional garbage collection units for Monrovia be authorized;
5. The scholarships be authorized for four students for first clerical training;
6. That authorization be given for the engagement of the services of two qualified persons from abroad in gathering and compiling vital health statistics; and
7. That two scholarships be authorized for a course in vital statistics.

The following are recommendations submitted by the Director of the Bureau of Natural Resources and Surveys for which I solicit your favourable consideration:

1. Authorization of a mapping project on a contractual basis, utilizing the aerial photographs to produce a topographic map, a geological map and a forest service map in combination with ground survey teams.
2. Appropriation for a twin-engine aeroplane of the Apache type to be used for new photography and to assist in the survey project recommended above.
3. That funds be provided for implementing the Hydrographic Service which was recommended in last year's report and made law by the National Legislature;
4. That additional funds be allocated for expanding the staff to include geophysicists and provide for additional equipment.
5. That the National Public Health Service be requested to provide mobile medical units to be stationed in the vicinity of diamond mining centres in the interest of the workers.

The Director of the Liberian Information Service postulates that 'constructive publicity is one of the surest methods of advancing the frontiers of national prestige and creating international understanding. It is the dissemination of information by means of letters, interviews, lectures, travels, books, pamphlets, posters, displays, films, filmstrips, photographs, and radio broadcasts, designed to promote the interests of a person, place, cause, etc., so as to secure favourable public attention. And this is the task to which the Liberian Information Service is firmly dedicated and the principle upon which it has operated during the fiscal year just ended.'

The following are recommendations submitted by the Director of the Service for which I recommend favourable consideration:

1. That the Public Relations Programmes now being conducted through Liberian Embassies abroad be discontinued as of December 31, 1960, and replaced by the employment of two reputable and experienced public relations firms, one in New York and the other in London, to conduct international public relations and publicity for Liberia under the direction of the Liberian Information Service;
2. That to encourage the Organization of Liberian Orchestras to popularize Liberian music for broadcasting and making phonographic records, the duty and luxury tax on the importation of bands and musical instruments be waived for a period of five years;
3. That appropriation be provided for the opening of three Regional Information Centres in 1961 to be situated in Zorzor, Sanniquellie and Tchien, respectively, to support the national development programme in preparation and dissemination of information and educational material by films, radio broadcasts, etc., to the populations and
4. That authorization be given and appropriation provided for the Liberian Tourist Organization to become a member of the Union of Official Travel Organizations and a fellowship be granted for a qualified Liberian to go abroad for six months to study and observe techniques in the development of tourist agencies.

Mr. Allen, a representative of Hill and Knowlton, a public relations firm, undertook an extensive survey of our public relations and publicity programme and has pointed out that in most countries and certainly in all business organizations the person charged with the responsibilities of administering an effective Public Relations or Information Programme is a member of the Policy Planning Board. He therefore suggested that the status of the Liberian Information Service be raised so as to enable the Director to be a member or at least an *ex officio* member of the President's Cabinet.

The Bureau of Economic Research was established recently by authority of an Act passed during your last session. Since the organization of this Bureau, it has been operating with zest and both the Director, Mr. J. Milton Weeks, and the Deputy Director, Mr. Henry Yaidoo, are exercising great diligence in the discharge of their duties.

The following are recommendations of the Bureau of Economic Research which deserve your favourable consideration:

1. That caution be exercised in further extension of rubber planting because at least 6,000 acres of mature rubber are not tapped at present due to shortage of labour, particularly tappers; and an additional 70,000 acres of rubber will mature within the next seven years;

2. That a compulsory general registration system be instituted to cover all business establishments including tree crop farms, all eligible taxpayers and all employed persons, so as to facilitate development of better tax administration;

3. That compulsory registration of real estate be conducted in order to promote development of better administration of Real Estate Tax;

4. That promotion by an objective publicity programme to educate the taxable population and business entities on taxes which affect them be planned and undertaken so as to change the present attitude on the part of many persons of avoiding taxes due to a lack of knowledge. While tax evasions may be curbed by a system of universal registration, tax avoidance may also be reduced by objective education or publicity on fiscal legislation;

5. That appropriate legislation on economic research and statistics be enacted to change the name of the Bureau of Economic Research in order to reflect operational requirements for research and statistics, because statistical investigations are the basis for research and it is natural that this fundamental aspect of the Bureau's activity be so reflected even in its name;

6. That the Secretary of the Interior be authorized to permit the Bureau to guide and develop the potentialities of Section (k), Chapter 14 of the Interior Administrative Regulations for purposes of inaugurating a national statistics reporting system;

7. That the Immigration Law authorizing the Bureau of Immigration and Naturalization to seek statistical information on all persons leaving and entering the country be amended since the present law does not apply to citizens and the Bureau of Immigration and Naturalization is doubtful whether it has authority to collect, for research work, statistical data on citizens.

8. That a larger budgetary appropriation be made for economic research and statistics to provide for the expansion of varied field work and the installation of better equipment.

9. That five scholarships be granted to suitable candidates for training in statistics.

Legislation is requested for these recommendations.

GENERAL MENTION

The proposals advanced in the last Inaugural Address and approved by you suggesting the cultivation of stronger ties of friendship and co-operation between African States by an accelerated·programme of cultural and economic exchange between these States as a basis of lasting and fruitful co-operation, have been submitted to the various African States and several have acknowledged receipt and have indicated interest. Because there were several states awaiting independence, we decided to await the consummation of their independence before proceeding further with these proposals.

The Economic and Social Development Plan proposed in the same Inaugural Address, which was approved by Your Honourable Body, is being activated in the following respects:

1. Item one of the Economic and Social Development Plan which provides for seeking additional revenue by enforcing the collection of all taxes due Government is being implemented.
2. Item two is being activated by the expansion and improvement of interior roads and letting contracts for new roads, but this programme is in its initial stage.
3. The Joint United States–Liberian Commission for Economic Development has proposed plans for teacher education expansion, staff organization, description of the Department of Public Instruction and other improvements in the educational field. These plans together with estimates of costs of the expansion and improvement suggested in my last Inaugural Address will be submitted to Your Honourable Body, and where legislation is required we ask your favourable consideration.
4. It is hoped that Item Three which deals with the expansion of our national airline to include plans for international flights will be activated soon.
5. Negotiations to facilitate the creation of a National Shipping Company which were initiated last year, are being pursued further and most of the concessionaires have agreed to apportion a certain percentage of their iron ore and other Liberian products, when required by the Government, for shipment in Liberian bottoms by the National Shipping Company. The only question raised is that of competitive prices.
6. In my Inaugural Address a proposal was made for the organization and operation of a Development Bank and you approved this proposal. Negotiations for such a bank have been initiated.
7. The Public Administration reform proposal postulated in the same address has not yet been activated; however, we expect to do so before the adjournment of your present session.
8. The Labour Code prepared by the Liberian Codification Project at Cornell University, upon the Government's request, has been completed, submitted and circulated among individual members of the Legislature. It is hoped that this Code will be approved by you at your present session.

I am of the opinion that we can no longer fail to utilize where possible all avenues available to us in promoting our economic development programme. In this connection I have directed the Treasury to reopen talks with the International Monetary Fund and World Bank for the purpose of securing

Liberia's admission to these world bodies. I trust that this will not only promote the interests of Liberia but will at the same time enable us to make a further contribution to world economic co-operation.

Heretofore, the Government has pursued a policy of awarding grants-in-aid and subsidies to Liberian students studying abroad on scholarships granted by foreign governments and individuals but it has been insisted upon by the donors of such scholarships that they evaluate the cost of the courses before offering the scholarships just as they do in the case of all other foreign students. These donors also contend that the funds provided the scholarship students should be adequate to meet the needs of the Liberian students because similar grants prove adequate for other foreign students who do not receive grants-in-aid or subsidies from their governments or any other source.

Speaking with some of our Foreign Service Officials and other foreign friends during my last visit to Europe, it was confirmed that funds allowed Liberian students from foreign governments and friends are adequate to meet their needs but that some of the Liberian students complain of the inadequacy of the funds and request additional funds because they desire some luxury.

As a matter of policy the Government cannot countenance the providing of funds to meet the luxury expenses of students who enjoy the facilities of scholarship awards from foreign governments and individuals. Therefore, no additional grants-in-aid or subsidies will be given by the Government to Liberian students who have accepted foreign Government scholarships. All subsidies and grants-in-aid extended such students will be discontinued on 31st of December, 1960.

In our relations with foreign concessionaires, businesses, religious and educational groups and other foreign enterprises, the Government has sought and will continue to seek and develop conditions and a climate favourable to close co-operation and understanding between us and these foreign establishments; and the Government expects reciprocity. There must be mutuality between parties if they are to work together.

In this anonymous manner I wish to express my recognition of a great act of national kindness extended to the Government and people of Liberia in a matter which involved the vital interest of both the Government and people. This act came from the representative of the oldest foreign concession in Liberia but propriety and his special request prevent me from being more specific.

THE SUPREME COURT

The Honourable Supreme Court had its regular semi-annual sessions and disposed of matters that were pending in that Court with dispatch and notable juridical action. The Court continues to hold the confidence and respect of the public.

OBITUARY

All men are born to the inheritance of death from which there is no escape, exemption, evasion or defence. Thus during the year the arms of conquering death have invaded the Legislature, the Executive and other services of Government and borne away the following persons:

The Honourable H. B. Duncan, former Secretary of Public Works and Utilities, statesman, architect and industrialist, whose remains lay in state in the United States while we were delivering our last Annual Message.

The Honourable J. Lemuel Gibson, President Pro-Tempore of the Senate, statesman, parliamentarian, politician and cleric.

The stroke that brought Senator Gibson his inheritance of death while serving as President Pro-Tempore of the Senate has also, within less than a year, handed to his predecessor in the Senate, the Honourable Edwin A. Morgan, *his* inheritance; and so within a year the Gentlemen of the Senate have been deprived of the association of two Senators and two Presidents Pro-Tempore.

I know that these two colleagues and intimate friends, Senator Morgan and Senator Gibson, have met somewhere in heaven's auroral bliss to talk of things on earth, in the Senate Chamber and elsewhere, which they never can forget.

Also brought to their inheritance of death during this period were:

His Honour Emmanuel W. Williams, jurist, scholar and advocate,

The Honourable William Burth Geegby, parliamentarian and statesman,

The Honourable George A. Dunbar, genius and builder,

Drs. J. B. West, E. H. Allen, T. R. Lalana, medical specialists who made valuable contributions to our Public Health Service.

Mr. Werner Schultz, architect and engineer,

Mr. Clifford Brown, architect and engineer whose name shall be known while the many public and private buildings, the result of his handiwork, endure,

Mrs. Victoria Payne, Mrs. Sophronia Gant, Mrs. Malvania Brewer, Mrs. Fannie Dunbar, mothers; and octogenarians.

May their souls rest in peace.

And now once again we commend our nation to the safe keeping of our Creator who has guided her destiny from its birth to this day.

Independence Day Message

Monrovia, 26 July 1961

Changes of great political significance have occurred on our continent during the past few years precipitating peaceful as well as bloody revolutions.

Introductory Note

This year the Independence Movement in Africa reached its period of greatest momentum and the tide of Independence could not be turned. Now instead of only a few independent states on our continent more than thirty-five new states were to be born before the decade was over. The President was pleased to participate in the emergence of these new states. He recounted our efforts and trials in having successfully escaped the yoke of colonialism through the mercies of a benevolent God. He was further concerned about Africa's future and her new rôle and status in international affairs.

Monrovia, 26 July 1961

ON THIS 114th anniversary of our national existence, we recall the dramatic incident of June, 1822, when the Pioneers becoming discouraged by seemingly imponderable drawbacks in the establishment of a new nation, and surrounded by nations which had taken part in the partitioning of the African continent, were confronted with continued and bitter resistance and bloody attacks by their tribal brethren.

We have often referred to the immortal words uttered when the captain of a foreign frigate, hearing gunfire, came into harbour and offered the Pioneers help provided he would be permitted to plant his nation's flagstaff on Liberian soil. 'No, we want no flagstaff put up here that will cost us more to get down than to whip the natives,' replied the brave and fearless Elijah Johnson. In Liberian history these words will also constitute a classic example of the determination, the heroism and indeed the patriotism of those who fought fearlessly in the cause of our freedom and independence.

Or consider the pitiful plight of those indomitable souls who had set out with high optimism and radiant hopes to found the nucleus of a nation which would reflect the dreams of a new social-political order, where economic opportunities and religious liberty in a novel orientation would be vouchsafed them and their children. But with their numbers now sadly decimated, exposed to divers sicknesses, harassed by the rigours of the tropical climate and faced with continued opposition from the hostile tribesmen who did not then understand what it was all about, it seemed to many that the realization of their hopes was a mere fantasy.

Removed as we are by the comfortable and secure distance of time which intervenes between those years and the present, it is difficult to visualize

43

accurately the terrible conditions, the excruciating hardships and the heart-
rending experiences which the Founding Fathers underwent – poverty, disease,
unpleasant climatic conditions, inexperience in statescraft, and even death.
They suffered great agony of body and spirit, many of them reaching the
point of despair and abandonment. But, to their eternal glory, they were not
deterred by these external and internal circumstances, and although aware of
new and hidden dangers, they yielded neither to threats nor intimidations,
disease, battle nor death. They reposed their faith in God and in their own
indomitable will, and in those moments of darkest despair one of their leaders
uttered the memorable expression, 'Two long years I sought a home; here I
have found one, here I remain,' words which will always be remembered in
the history of mankind as symbolic of the guiding spirit and fierce determination of those who seek the blessings of liberty and freedom at great peril to
themselves.

Then try to contemplate the incident of the ultimatum given to the
Liberian Government during President Payne's administration by the captain
of a naval vessel when he threatened to bombard the capital unless the
Government complied with the conditions of the ultimatum. He received the
reply, 'bombard and be damned'.

Today, we do well to pay high tribute to the vision which inspires men in
all ages, the hardihood which enables them to face fearful odds, the faith
which nourishes and steels their souls in times of storm and stress, and the
patriotic fervour which provides strong motivation for fervent nationalism.
We think today of the vision, faith, courage and determination of our forefathers which enabled them to forge ahead once they had embarked upon the
quest for the blessings of liberty and freedom. Because of their supreme
sacrifices they bequeathed to us a noble heritage for whose safety, maintenance and perpetuity we of this generation are personally responsible to the
end that it may be guarded zealously and transmitted to posterity unimpaired.

Re-reading the cultural history of Liberia, or looking at it in ethnic
retrospect, the people of Liberia who came from the United States in 1822 to
establish a home on this coast of Africa together with the chiefs and tribal
people, their kith and kin, were and still are an integral part of the people
from all over Africa. It is a history which extends beyond the Empires of
Sokoto, Gando and Kano to an area beyond Songhai through the various
dynasties of Egypt, and the Africans' passage to America was but an extension of the Divine Plan designed to prepare a whole people for the future
service of their kith and kin. Thus it was that the records show that among
those who returned to Maryland County the first man to leave the boat when
the Pioneers arrived there was one Anthony Wood whom the Greboe chiefs
recognized as one of their own sons who had been taken away some years
before.

I verily believe that nothing happens by chance and that behind all
phenomena in the universe is the unseen hand of God. I believe, therefore,
that the accident of African slavery, while iniquitous, criminal, devastating
and degrading, was a part of the Divine Plan, and that Liberia's rôle in that
great drama makes her an indivisible component of all things African.

My fellow citizens, only those who lived here, fought here, and died here
in the struggles for freedom could fully appreciate all the implications of the
blessings of liberty. It is for their heroic deeds that we have persevered to

maintain the government of this Republic for which they laid down their lives; it is for our own ideals that we strive continually to keep faith with those who fought to preserve this noble heritage; it is for succeeding generations that we continue to forge ahead to share the momentum of history.

But more than these considerations, the political and social revolutions which have taken place in Africa and in the world have aroused in us a newer and greater sense of nationalism and we must dedicate ourselves again and again to the ideal 'The Love Of Liberty Brought Us Here'. Let those who find creative joy in unfair and useless criticisms of us continue to do so; but let those who also share our ideals and ideas and sympathize with our struggles for freedom extend to us a helping hand so that the future years of the nation will be one of peace, progress and prosperity, and let us, citizens all, work hand in hand towards the achievement of the greater day which awaits us.

Let those who continually aver that Liberia has done very little or nothing of significance during a hundred years of sovereignty look at the past in true historical perspective and judge us in the light of that history. We know that however slow our progress may have been there has been no standing still and a forward and progressive movement has been clearly perceptible all the time, and thus there was laid here a solid and unshakable foundation for democracy in Africa.

Our struggle as a nation at a time when the forces of colonialism and imperialism were taking a heavy toll of the peoples of Africa, when to stand alone was considered an affront to international diplomacy and a stand devoid of political wisdom, the mere fact that we took that stand and survived is a lasting reflection on our political history, a miracle in international achievement and a most outstanding evidence of the ability of the African for self-government. But we do not boast of our strength alone. We express continued gratitude to the God of Human Affairs Who guided us and the unconquerable spirit of the Founding Fathers who led the nation during those critical years.

The events of history continue to move urgently and progressively on and most of the strides which today characterize the twentieth century were woefully absent from the national and international settings of a hundred years ago. There were no such projects as Technical Assistance Programmes, UNESCO, WHO, ILO, FAO and other specialized agencies to underdeveloped countries. The United Nations, that world organization which has ushered in a new day of great promise and help to nations great and small, old and new, was not in existence a hundred years ago. The rattling of the sabre, gunboat diplomacy, the 'might-makes-right' policy and the law of the jungle were the order of the day in those first one hundred years. The nation stood alone in the great onslaught of ruthless territorial expansionism while the rest of Africa was partitioned and brought under colonial domination. Amidst all this, Liberia maintained her sovereignty and kept the Lone Star at full staff.

And yet during the course of our hundred years foreign attitudes towards this nation were inimical to her retention of sovereignty and consequently there were attempts to obliterate her from the political map. Then internal and external wars, foreign criticisms, ridicule, unjust accusations, indignities, and humiliations became her lot. But, ever mindful of their commitment to found on these shores an asylum for the enjoyment of the blessings of liberty, our forefathers did not swerve from their path of duty. How binding is the obligation upon us, their successors, to protect, preserve and defend this sacred heritage!

The twentieth century is an era of great and unprecedented material progress and unparalleled intellectual achievements. Stupendous advances in science and technology have transformed the world and given mankind the secrets of the unknown forces of nature. But despite his mastery the conquest of man himself remains to be achieved, to which his new and great powers will be directed. Great scientific researches, breath-taking discoveries, an insatiable desire for more knowledge have enabled him to probe the wonders of outer space and his attempts to send man to the moon, establish communications with the planets Mars and Venus, and send satellites around the earth at speeds exceeding the wildest imaginings of man, have been given great impetus. But man, in the midst of all these accomplishments, must acknowledge the source of his intelligence and power – God. Natural forces such as earthquakes, tidal waves, hurricanes, and cyclones, and diseases like cancer and insanity are still unleashed upon mankind and science must muster its forces for the ultimate conquest of these forces of evil and human unhappiness.

Man must discover new approaches to ease tensions among nations, and study to know himself. It is evident that by these great and wonderful scientific discoveries and inventions man has created a new earth, but he has not created a new spirit within himself that would reform and regenerate him and the society in which he lives, and thus make him a new creature, fit and capable to live in the world of his creation in safety, security, peace and happiness.

We have repeatedly urged reason, realism, tolerance and poise in matters of great national and international import. If we have maintained our sovereignty this long during a time when we stood as the only Republic in all Africa, we must certainly maintain it today, when the forces of imperialism are dwindling away and colonialism is fast beating its retreat. But more than this, we must determine with all our hearts and souls to win the battle for which we and others who have newly gained their independence have fought – the battle for democracy, freedom of the individual and the right of self-determination and provision for greater economic and social opportunities for all alike.

Changes of great political significance have occurred on our continent during the past few years, precipitating peaceful as well as bloody revolutions. The majority of the newly emerging states have already joined the comity of free nations, and the next few years will be exceedingly busy ones for them in their struggle to provide economic opportunities to support their political structures. Older nations have likewise turned to exploring newer possibilities to channel their hard-won freedom into more meaningful patterns. The need for a new emphasis is most compelling because the adequacies of yesterday have today proved woefully inadequate to cope with the demands of the new social order.

To this end APARTHEID in South Africa MUST go; the Congo crisis MUST BE RESOLVED: tension in Angola MUST BE EASED and the Angolans attain their freedom and independence; the Algerian question has to BE SETTLED: the conscience of those who still rule in Africa or any part of the world needs to be QUICKENED.

These imperatives MUST engage the attention of men of goodwill every-where.

There is a wise proverb of Solomon which says, 'a wise man foreseeth evil and hideth himself'; this, I opine, should be made to apply to the present threatening and dangerous international situation over Berlin, Ger-many. The great powers have all taken positive positions in this matter which has created a crisis of imminent danger.

Most wars and conflicts have been the results of nations manoeuvring themselves or permitting themselves to be manoeuvred into positions where negotiations and compromises were rendered impracticable because of national honour. They closed the doors behind them and therefore had no alternative in such circumstances but to plunge themselves into war.

The consequences that would necessarily follow in case a conventional or nuclear war were to erupt at present would be so tremendously devastating that no nation, great or small, could withstand their paralysing onslaught. In my opinion, it behoves all tribes, people and nations of the earth to express themselves strongly on the delicate issue of whether they are aligned with the Western or Eastern blocs or whether they consider themselves non-aligned, and thus prevent a head-on collision over the Berlin crisis, which would probably engulf the world in another global war, far more destructive than any war in history.

I am pleased to note that while some of the powers have stated in no uncertain terms their position on the question, they have not closed the door to negotiations but have expressly made known their willingness to negotiate. We appeal to those nations having any special interest and responsibility in Berlin and the German question, to avoid, in any case or circumstance, the resort to force or armed conflict and to settle that question within the bounds of rationality. Humanity deserves and demands that this be done; reason and common sense dictate it; religion, morality and materialism require it.

We appeal to the Secretary-General of the United Nations and to the Security Council to intervene immediately while the doors remain open for negotiations, and to take such actions as will lead to a settlement of this most provocative question by means of negotiation thereby enabling the great powers involved to find a just, reasonable and peaceful solution to the im-pending crisis.

The conferences held on the African Continent have all had the same objectives – striving to bring more and better understanding among African nations, creating a working formula and working toward world peace. These conferences showed in unmistakable terms the common concern of the participants for the problems which plague Africa and the rest of mankind, and the need to resolve them. Those who truly love Africa and are dedicated to the ideals of peace, prosperity and progress, need to combine their material and spiritual resources toward the attainment of these desired objectives. On this our national independence day we call upon the peoples of Africa to join in the epic struggle.

An interesting issue is currently debated in international circles. It is the question of alignment and non-alignment, for which, at present, we have so commonly accepted definition. While I am not certain of the precise inter-pretation, however, I affirm that Liberia will stand for the great pragmatic principle – the greatest good for the greatest number.

Liberia will always stand for the great principle and cause of justice, tolerance, liberty, equality before the law and regard for international treaties.

We will stand for the great principle and cause of universal peace and amity among men and nations.

We shall stand for the great principle and cause of the sacredness, the rights and dignity of the individual, and respect the sovereignty of all nations, great and small alike.

We stand for the great principle and cause of putting an end to any other global cataclysm which 'twice in a generation has brought untold suffering to mankind'.

These are some of the principles that guide us, and they are the principles with which we associate ourselves and not necessarily with special blocs or ideologies.

We are pleased on this occasion to extend felicitations and greetings to the members of the Diplomatic Corps accredited by their governments to us. The continued atmosphere of friendship and mutual understanding which has characterized our relations can be attributed to our yen for world peace and the formulation of realistic policies to implement this mutual desire, and to the statesmanship and devotion to duty of those filling these positions of great responsibility. May we ever continue to work assiduously so that harmony and peace may continue to prevail among us and all men.

Fellow citizens and friends, each recurring independence anniversary comes as a reappraisal of the contents and forms of our institutional processes, a day for a survey of both the past and the present with a view to increasing and implementing our contributions to the sum total of our national happiness and prosperity and the peace and security of the world. May the events of the past, the achievements of the present and the plans we continually envisage for the future security of our nation make us more appreciative of the blessings of liberty and freedom and create in us a greater urge to prepare ourselves more adequately for the solution of our own national problems as a preliminary to making greater contributions to the international situation.

Finally, let me remind you that Liberia is indeed our true inheritance. The ideals, government, laws and institutions were handed down to us in sacred trust. There must therefore be a continuity in her history and a progressive evolution in her advancement. The nation's continued progress in the future will depend upon what we do today with this inheritance. If we guard it wisely and zealously and thus improve the political, social, economic, cultural and educational opportunities, the country's future will be greatly secured. Only if we do well our part in carrying out these tremendous responsibilities with heart and soul shall we be worthy successors of those heroic souls who worked, suffered and died to achieve the blessings of liberty we enjoy today.

Second Annual Message delivered before the Third Session of the Forty-fifth Legislature

Monrovia, 9 January 1961

We of the continent of Africa are all inspired with the spirit of African nationalism with one accord to rise up and stand firm for the liberation of the territories and peoples of Africa and the attainment by them of that measure of human dignity and respect to which all men are entitled. It is imperative, however, that national patriotism be a preliminary to the achievement of the general ideal of continental nationalism.

Introductory Note

When President Tubman delivered this message to our National Legislature, the Berlin question and the Congo were the two major areas of crisis in the world. The idea of African Unity was just beginning to gain consciousness on our continent. It was the President's opinion that national unity should precede continental unity. This was further the first occasion when he spoke about subversion in Liberia and regretted that the youths of our land were being lured to consider this mode of action attractive. The future of Liberia would be endangered by their activities. It was also time that his programmes mentioned in his Fourth Inaugural Address got off the ground. Several new banks opened offices in Monrovia and the construction of several new public buildings was to be given priority. A Special Committee on Government Operations was set up, the writing of textbooks was to be encouraged, medical schools were to be built. Chinese rice experts came to demonstrate methods of increased rice production. The Bureau of Economic Research and Statistics was created. The major recommendations in this message concerned improved communications.

Monrovia, 9 January 1961

TIME IN its constant revolution has brought you together in your present session under the provisions of the Constitution and statutory laws of the country.

Many, varied and grave have been the problems that have arisen, both internally and externally, since your last adjournment but fortunately, threatening and apparently explosive though they were, they did not flare into a nationwide or global conflict; and this was due to the sober, patient and negotiating temper that characterized the handling of these delicate situations. While it is true that international tensions are still high, men of goodwill still see a gleam of hope for a possible statement of these conditions and for the creation of better understanding in the international arena.

We profoundly regret that it was not possible for us to make this Annual Report before now, but as you are aware, you granted permission and authorized us to accept an invitation from the President of the United States of America to make an official visit to that country in October of last year which necessitated our having to leave the country on the sixth of that month, three days before the convening of your present session.

Also, you granted permission and authorized us to accept an invitation from His Imperial Majesty Hailé Selassié I, Emperor of Ethiopia, to make a state visit to that historic empire.

We pray that the God of Nations Who guided and guarded our forefathers in the past and Who has always directed the affairs of this nation, will continue to shower His blessings upon your deliberations from session to session so that our country and all of its people may be beneficiaries of just legislations and wise statutes.

FOREIGN RELATIONS

Relations between this Government and the foreign governments represented near this capital, as well as member states of the United Nations, remain cordial and friendly and it is our earnest desire to retain such relations with all nations and people at all times.

In the process of the liberation of the African continent, new areas and territories have emerged and are still emerging into statehood and sovereignty. The territory of Tanganyika was the most recent of these states to whose independence celebration we had the pleasure of accrediting the Honourable Vice-President of Liberia as our personal representative.

It is both regrettable and deplorable that notwithstanding irresistible trends in international affairs to eradicate colonialism so that all men might be free, there are one or two nations that still cling to the old, archaic and obsolete policies of colonialism and apartheid; these nations are not wise, for there is a proverb that says, 'A wise man foreseeth evil and hideth himself but the fool rusheth on and is overtaken in his folly.'

The Berlin issue still remains an unresolved question and a threat to peace. However, there appear to be prospects for negotiations in an attempt to settle the crisis by peaceful means and it is our hope that these prospects will materialize for the benefit of world peace.

The Congo is still a centre of anxiety and the conduct of the Katanga régime, according to authentic reports received, has been such that United Nations troops and personnel sent to that area to preserve order, were constantly attacked in some sections of the Congo, murdered in cold blood in other sections and in others, beaten and imprisoned. This made it urgently necessary for the Secretary-General to take firm steps to restore the *status quo* and thus defend the organization's position and prestige.

STATE AND OFFICIAL VISITS

We believe that our visit to the United States was successful, not only in the interest of Liberia, but also of Africa. Our discussions with President Kennedy centred around national and international problems, particularly United States-Liberian relations and the acceleration of assistance to and expansion of our national development programme.

An outline of the nature of the assistance that the United States Government agreed to extend to the Liberian Government was expressed in general terms in a communiqué issued by President Kennedy and myself at the end of our discussions.

Great emphasis was placed by both of us on the necessity for the setting-up of a National Planning Council. The planning procedure will be forwarded to you during your present session. This procedure will embrace Economic Planning encompassing the planning of: (1) those government programmes and projects which are designed to increase national production and to improve the well-being of the people on the lines of nutrition, health, education, housing, transportation, communication and activities contributing thereto; (2) External assistance programmes designed to promote the purposes stated in (a) (1) above referred to; (3) Foreign investment programmes involving government concessions and/or government participation. The terms and extent of the general coverage of the communiqué are to be worked out.

Besides official courtesies, invitations were extended to us by various concessionaires and business houses operating in Liberia, led by Firestone Plantations Company, pioneer in rubber production, and Liberia Mining Company, pioneer in iron ore production.

Regrettably, our proposed visit to Ethiopia in response to the invitation of His Imperial Majesty Hailé Selassié I had to be postponed because of the sudden illness of Her Imperial Majesty the Empress. With all arrangements made for our visit to that Empire, we arrived in Paris on October 29th to fly to Addis Ababa on the following day, but at that moment we received telegraphic information of the Empress' illness and a request for the postponement of the visit. This necessitated the quick rearrangement of our itinerary, and we then decided, in lieu of the Ethiopian visit, to go to Zürich for a brief vacation and a physical check-up that had been previously arranged for Mrs. Tubman.

This re-arrangement delayed our return to Liberia by almost a fortnight and made the trip on the whole more expensive.

Arriving in Liberia on the 13th November, we had the distinguished pleasure and honour of receiving, on the 17th November, for a five-day state visit, His Excellency Felix Houphouet Boigny, President of the Ivory Coast Republic.

Following closely upon this visit was the visit of Her Majesty Queen Elizabeth II of Great Britain and her consort, the Duke of Edinburgh whom we had the pleasure, distinction and honour of receiving on the 23rd November. Although this royal visit was a one-day ceremony, the programme was compact and everyone seemed happy and enthusiastic in extending a joyous welcome to Her Majesty.

At the close of her visit, Her Majesty extended to us an invitation for a state visit in the summer of 1962. We request your permission to respond to this invitation.

In reponse to the invitation extended by His Excellency Leopold Senghor, President of the Republic of Senegal, we were to have made a state visit to that country on the 10th December but because we contracted chickenpox, we were compelled to request a postponement of the visit, which we hope to make some time this year.

Responding to the invitation of His Excellency Prime Minister Sir Milton

Margai of Sierra Leone, it was our pleasure to visit Freetown to witness the
independence ceremonies of that nation. The change-over ceremony from the
colonial régime to an independent government was moving and colourful.

At the kind invitation of His Excellency Felix Houphouet Boigny, President of the Ivory Coast Republic, we witnessed the first independence
celebration of the Ivory Coast in Abidjan on the 7th August which was
attended with impressive and imposing ceremonies.

Previous to these visits we had the distinguished pleasure and privilege of
receiving the sovereigns of two friendly nations who made state visits here
upon our invitations: His Excellency Leopold Senghor, President of the
Republic of Senegal and His Excellency Josip Broz Tito, President of the
People's Republic of Yugoslavia.

At the conclusion of each of the visits above referred to except that of the
Queen, official communiqués were issued.

THE CONFERENCE OF HEADS OF AFRICAN
AND MALAGASY STATES AND GOVERNMENTS

Nineteen-sixty has been called 'African Freedom Year' because of the
attainment of so many African states to sovereignty and independence.

With a burning desire for better understanding and the creation of a form
of unity among African and Malagasy states, and because we felt the need
for consultation on and discussions of the many problems that confronted the
African nations and peoples, we invited a number of African states to co-
sponsor a conference of African and Malagasy Heads of states and governments. Invitations were accepted by all of the states and governments
requested to co-sponsor the conference, except one, and the invitations were
issued in the name of the sponsoring states. Upon their unanimous agreement,
the conference was convoked in Monrovia on the 8th May 1961, and lasted
for five days. Twenty African and Malagasy states were represented.

A number of resolutions providing for cultural, economic and scientific
co-operation between the attending states was adopted. It was also agreed
that a meeting of specialists and experts in the above-mentioned field be held
in Dakar, Senegal, in the month of September last year. This conference,
convoked according to schedule, was successful.

The Monrovia Conference adjourned on the 12th May 1961, to reconvene
in Lagos, Nigeria in January 1962.

This conference declared that it was anxious and eager for all African
and Malagasy states to join in this great movement for universal co-
operation and unity between them, so that their discussions and exchanges of
views might tend to eradicate or clarify points of differences, wherever they
exist, in a spirit of 'give-and-take'.

INTERNAL AFFAIRS

We of the continent of Africa are all inspired with the spirt of African
nationalism to rise up with one accord and stand firm for the liberation of
the territories and peoples of Africa and the attainment by them of that
measure of human dignity and respect to which all men are entitled. Our
crusade in this direction has succeeded to a large extent, and we shall persevere until all Africa has been liberated and its people are enjoying, in

common with the people of other continents and all other races of mankind, the rights, privileges and benefits of free men, exercising the right of self-determination, independence and sovereignty. But there must be at some point a distinction between nationalism continental-wise and nationalism nation-wise, the latter of which involves patriotism, obligation to and love of one's own country. This is most essential to the safety, security, perpetuity and very existence of a state.

We maintain without hesitation that continental nationalism is a great ideal, that it represents the combination of several allegiances, and that its ultimate achievement will signify a great triumph for African political institutions, but we are also convinced that its strengthening will be possible only to the extent that national patriotism for the respective nations of Africa first becomes embedded in the heart, soul and very being of their people. It is imperative therefore, that national patriotism must be given basic priority in our planning and action programmes, as a preliminary to the achievement of the general ideal of continental or African nationalism.

Loyalty and devotion are obligations of nationalism which everyone owes first and foremost to his own country, and if these national duties and responsibilities conflict with other interests, the allegiance of the citizen to his own country must prevail. This concept must be taught in our university, colleges, schools and other institutions; it should be preached in the pulpits, promulgated in Sunday schools, social and political organizations and elsewhere in the nation.

A youth organization was recently discovered, designed to subvert the century-old stability of the Liberian Government by the introduction of ideas that seek to overthrow and create dissension among our population but appropriate action has been taken and special powers were requested of Your Honourable Body to enable the Government to cope with this and any other emergency situation; you promptly granted us these powers and vigilance will be exercised in this regard.

Earlier this year, a Commission on Government Operations was set up whose functions are to make a close study of Government's present operations and administrative system, and to make recommendations for reorganization where necessary, subject to your approval. This Commission is headed by the Honourable James T. Philips, Sen. with a number of specialists and experts in various fields from the United States of America, under the assistance programme between that Government and ours.

The Commission entered upon the discharge of its duties with satisfactory fervency, and has submitted its report on the Executive Branch of Government, which is being studied and which will afterwards be forwarded to you in due course.

It is therefore suggested that your consideration of recommendations contained in departmental and other annual reports submitted to you at this session respecting matters of reorganization in administration, be deferred until the Commission has completed its work.

The Commission authorized at your last session for a survey, and recommendations for a revision, of the political and territorial subdivisions of the country, has been constituted and it has entered upon the discharge of its duties. This Commission is headed by the Honourable Fitzroy Williamson and has been instructed to make its report within eighteen months, in keeping with the provisions of the act which authorize it.

There are several acts which were passed by Your Honourable Body in the past three years that have not been implemented. A special Commission has been organized under the chairmanship of the Secretary of State during the period under review to correlate and make recommendations for the implementation of all such acts.

The Treasury reports total revenue collections for the fiscal period under review at 32·7 million dollars as against 28·9 million dollars in the preceding twelve-month period, resulting in a net increase of 3·8 million dollars. Of this total the amount of 21·7 million dollars was derived from internal revenue sources including 8·5 million dollars from income tax collections. This reflects an increase of 2·7 million dollars from internal revenue sources as against 19 million dollars for the preceding fiscal year. Meanwhile, income tax rose by 1·2 million dollars above the previous year's collection of 7.3 million dollars, customs revenues added up to 8·4 million dollars, the increase being 1·2 million dollars over the preceding period; all other revenues accounted for 2·6 million dollars.

It is pointed out that it is important to bear in mind the fact that these figures include the January income tax and iron ore dividends based on the last quarter earnings of 1960. Because of the continued drop in the price of rubber during 1961, actual receipts are less than those for 1960.

Expenditures for the fiscal year 1960–61 were in excess of those of the preceding period. Total budgetary expenditures were 32·8 million dollars; this is 1·5 million dollars greater than the expenditures of 31·3 million dollars made during the fiscal period 1959–60. Total expenditure includes both capital and current expenditures and a sizeable portion of loans, invesment and debt retirement, but does not include Export-Import Bank Credit No. 1072 for power expansion, principal and interest, payment of which is now exclusively the responsibility of the Monrovia Power Authority.

THE NATIONAL DEBT

Short Term Loans	$24,232,505.24
Long Term Loans:	
(a) Development Loans	33,890,689.30
(b) Service Loans	37,994,794.78
(c) Claims	357,200.00
(d) All other Loans	11,902,988.54

making a total of one hundred and eight million, three hundred and seventy-eight thousand, one hundred and seventy-seven dollars and eighty-six cents ($108,378,177.86).

The major portion of this figure represents expenditure for development, public utilities, etc. and the National Debt will increase as the development programme of the country is expanded and accelerated.

It is not practicable to develop a nation solely from current revenues; there must be loans and other means of financing contracted to be amortized over a period of years, and it is a principle of political economy that future generations should be responsible for contributions for the liquidation and amortization of national debts incurred for developments from which they will benefit.

Both short and long term loans retired in 1961 amount to $19,776,269.74

(nineteen million seven hundred and seventy-six thousand two hundred and sixty-nine dollars and seventy-four cents).

On the 12th December 1961, treaties covering financial assistance and economic co-operation were signed between the Federal Republic of Germany and the Government of Liberia.

Under the terms of these agreements long term low interest rate loans will be advanced to the value of 50 million German marks, or roughly twelve and a half million dollars. Detailed agreements will be worked out for each project within the limit of this credit. However, the following priorities have been agreed upon: six and a half million dollars to construct the road from Greenville to Tappita via Duabo; two and a quarter million dollars for the Liberian Bank for Development and Investment; two million dollars to provide water facilities for hinterland towns, and the remainder to improve airfields and promote air safety.

In addition to capital aid, technical assistance will be provided to train the staff of the Liberian National Airways and to assist in city planning and forest control.

The European Common Market and its possible effects on the Liberian Economy

The European Common Market established in 1957 by the six members of the European Economic Community posed a serious economic threat to those African states not linked with the European signatories of the Treaty of Rome, and especially those states, such as Liberia and Ethiopia, which had no colonial links. Essentially, the threat was that the Common Market system of preferential tariffs, quotas and taxes would divert trade away from the non-associated African states to those African states associated by colonial or other ties with the European Economic Community.

These apprehensions have been somewhat allayed in the recent months by the steps taken to modify the organization of the Common Market by the admittance of Great Britain, by taking account of the independent status of former colonial territories of E. E. C. member countries, by making room for other African Associated States, and by providing special associate membership for those African states which have never had colonial ties with any European power as well as those African territories linked with non-member countries of E. E. C. Under the proposed modified structure, African states other than those already associated with the Common Market would be free to enter the Common Market club as they chose, while associated states would be similarly free to disassociate themselves from the club.

Some African countries regard the new proposal for modifying the Common Market as a disguised form of neo-colonialism. Political considerations apart, the opportunities of a wider market in the Common Market system and for financial aid are positive advantages for less developed countries. There is, however, the danger that the association of less developed with highly developed countries in a customs union arrangement may tend to retard the process of economic diversification and industrialization in the less developed countries, thus maintaining the *status quo* and retarding their rate of growth.

In the special case of Liberia, while the threat to the Liberian economy still remains, the country's trading experience over the past four years gives no clear evidence of any adverse effects resulting from the Common Market system.

Several factors must, however, be taken into account in determining the possible future effects of the Common Market on Liberian trade. Firstly, as projected improvements in agricultural productivity are successfully carried out, it is likely that traditional and other agricultural commodities will grow in importance in the country's export trade. Secondly, iron ore production is rapidly looming large in the nation's economy and will very soon take first place as an export earner. Thirdly, the large production of industrial raw materials and the expected large increase in production of these materials, coupled with the desirability of greater economic diversification in the interest of greater economic stability, points to the need for greater efforts at industrialization. Fourthly, to the extent that our efforts at industrialization succeed, and because of the smallness of the domestic market, we must depend heavily upon foreign markets as outlets for our products. Fifthly, the remarkable rate of income growth in recent years in Common Market countries, and the inevitability of a considerable growth income in African countries, suggest that there is a large and growing export market for primary and secondary products in Common Market and in African countries.

Taking into account all of these factors, any effective discrimination against our exports could have serious consequences for the future of Liberian trade and of the Liberian economy. It is therefore of vital importance that Liberia maintain the closest contact with developments in the Common Market and take appropriate action as and when necessary to protect its trading relationships with its traditional European markets and with its African neighbours.

The Monrovia Breweries Inc., received a Concession on the 27th day of May, A.D. 1957, based upon a Statement of Understanding arrived at between the late Robert F. Sulzer and H. Martin Hofer, Swiss nationals, and the Government of Liberia on the 6th of August, A.D. 1956.

The Brewery was formally opened on the 15th of November, 1961 and is already producing beer and various soft drinks in Monrovia. This represents an important step toward the eventual industrialization of our country.

In addition to certain tax concessions already granted to the Corporation, after satisfactory arrangements have been worked out, the Government, in keeping with its programme of encouraging the creation and growth of local industries, will take the necessary steps to give tariff protection during the infancy of this industry.

It is reassuring that we witness the advent of several new banking institutions into the country, which is evidence of our growing economy. In particular, during the year the Chase Manhattan Bank has opened offices here, and the Chemical Bank of the United States has vested interests in the Bank of Liberia. A word of acknowledgement is due to the Chase Manhattan Bank for the spontaneous assistance it has given to the Open Door Policy by encouraging foreign investments in Liberia by the issue of its pamphlet entitled, 'LIBERIA'.

This attitude of the Chase Manhattan Bank has had the effect of creating the kind of co-operation and mutuality which engenders faith and good relations, and it might be well for other institutions to follow the example of the Chase Manhattan Bank, for by increasing investment the economy of the nation will be advanced and the business and profits of the investors themselves will be increased thereby.

Another institution which opened its doors for business during the course of last year is the Commercial Bank of Liberia. There are already many indications that this bank will prove a boon to our economy.

Our increasing concern for equal educational opportunities for all of the peoples of our land demands consistent improvement in the quality of the educational programme, with special emphasis placed on qualified teachers. Progress in this respect is encouraging, but there is need for more intensive spurring of the programme with greater regularity and consistency. It is interesting to note that manuscripts for three textbooks were prepared during the year. Efforts in this direction must continue until textbooks for at least all elementary schools are specially produced by the Department of Public Instruction.

While the fundamental education programme is having some favourable results, there is a necessity for the strengthening of this type of education for the purpose of extending it throughout the country.

With the attainment of independence of nearly all the French- and English-speaking states of Africa, the use of French and English has become a vital necessity. It is therefore of the utmost importance that every effort be exerted to accelerate the teaching of French in our public school system, in recognition of our association with these sister African states.

For this programme to be realistic, it is necessary for French to become a functional language, not merely the learning of the rules of French grammar, and the Department of Public Instruction must take necessary action for its implementation. We ask for legislation in this respect.

In general, there has been peace and orderly administration throughout the country. However, there were attempts made by certain foreign agencies to undermine the Unification Programme by inciting basic prejudices aimed at creating dissension and subversion.

The unification of the people of any nation is evidently a great social triumph, and in particular the success and achievement of our Unification Programme can never be underrated.

In the Public Works phase of our development programme, there are now thirteen projects under construction, including the new Executive Mansion, the Law Courts building, administration buildings, interior schools, prison houses and low cost houses, costing a total of approximately twenty million dollars. These buildings are expected to be completed by 1963. Under the Rural Development Programme, fourteen elementary schools have been completed.

Agreement has at length been concluded between the Government and the Liberian National Electric Corporation for the construction of a hydro-electric plant at Mount Coffee. The activation of the provisions of this agreement has not proceeded satisfactorily; however in the event of further delay action will be taken, under the provisions of the contract, to abrogate the same.

Another significant step forward in our national development programme is the construction of the first twenty-five low cost houses by the Government. This project is being financed by the International Trust Company.

Liberia is essentially an agricultural country and therefore great emphasis must be placed on agriculture. The agricultural programme is administered under four divisions – research, forestry, extension and marine fisheries.

Poultry was given last year to farm services which included rice production, poultry and small animal production, vegetables and field crop production, tree crop production, large animal production and home economics. Under these divisions, marketing, farm credit, and youth organizations were begun, and some progress was made in these areas.

Because rice is the country's staple food, and inasmuch as this commodity has had to be imported into the country at high prices, the Government has sought to increase the yield by the introduction of swamp rice. At present, there are thirteen swamp rice planters in the provinces working with farmers and institutions.

During last year there also came into the country a team of experts in the growing of rice from the Republic of China, their main purpose being to explore the possibility of adapting Chinese rice-growing methods to Liberia. Should their experiments prove successful, they may help to further our rice production programme.

Although some progress has been made in this field, within the next three years there must be enough rice produced in Liberia to meet at least the demands of the population of the country. This is what we require of the Department of Agriculture.

The Government has concluded a concession agreement with the Hunt International Petroleum Company for the manufacture and/or processing of gasoline, kerosene, and diesel fuel. This agreement will be laid before you for appropriate action.

Plans for the construction of the Monrovia General Hospital and the proposed Medical School for the University of Liberia have been virtually completed. Work on these buildings is expected to begin within the first half of the present year.

Malaria remains the principal malady in the country and it is a problem of great magnitude. Although the WHO malaria control project terminated in August of last year, the use of a medicated salt programme was proposed, and an agreement drafted by WHO, ICA and the Government now awaits final approval.

During last year the vaccination programme for smallpox, a yaws eradication campaign, a quarantine surveillance at ports of entry, a leprosy control and tuberculosis control received special attention.

The Bureau of Economic Research and Statistics was established as the forerunner of a planning agency to be initiated after laying the groundwork in basic research and statistical data collection. The report of the Bureau, therefore, deals with the planning process, and to achieve the goals envisaged, the Government has committed itself to the establishment of a strong Central Planning Agency.

But by far the biggest project of this Bureau is the National Census, which is to be undertaken this year.

In the interest of making this national project a success, I appeal to everyone within our orders to co-operate enthusiastically in this undertaking.

The Liberian Information Centre serves as an agency for explaining and interpreting the Government's programmes and policies, and keeping it informed of public opinion. So important is this Bureau that we have made the Director a Minister Without Portfolio. The members are expected to be alert, aggressive within reason, and generally aware of the facts.

Iron ore mining in Liberia continues on the upward trend. The outlook for the 1961–1962 fiscal period envisages an export of 5,500,000 tons of ore. No new concessions were granted for minerals during the past year, but the present four (4) iron ore companies continue to make great improvement.

While some progress has been made in the nation's Civil Service System, the rapid rate of advancement in every area of our national life makes a review of this Service imperative.

The Supreme Court held its regular semi-annual sessions during the year, with the attendance of all members of the Bench. The Supreme Court continues to enjoy the full confidence of the public and it has improved administrative and procedural methods by revised rules and regulations.

RECOMMENDATIONS

The following recommendations are being made for your favourable consideration:

That the statute which gives stipendiary magistrates trial jurisdiction in embezzlement cases be repealed.

That because of the interpretation made by the Supreme Court that in cases of embezzlement, larceny and kindred offences where restitution is a part of the penalty imposed for the crime, convicts should serve the period of imprisonment specifically imposed by the judgment of the court and that restitution should be obtained by the private prosecutor in such cases by special suit to recover, the Act of the Legislature providing for restitution in the category of crimes above mentioned, be amended to provide that convicts in this class of cases, where Government's revenues are involved, shall, besides the term of imprisonment pronounced in the judgment of the court, serve an additional period of imprisonment sufficiently long to liquidate the total sum involved at the rate of fifty dollars per month.

That a change be authorized in the uniforms of the Liberian Army as described in the report of the Secretary of National Defence. Also that you authorize a re-organization and expansion of the Liberian Army and compulsory military service to meet the needs and requirements of this re-organization and expansion where voluntary enlistment proves ineffective and inadequate.

That legislation be made for the setting-up of a special commission to be composed of not less than three qualified persons to collect data, compile, edit and publish bi-annually a Liberian postal guide.

That the Act of the Legislature incorporating the Radio service under the Post Office Department be amended to incorporate and include the following: (a) The Telephone Exchange under the Post Office Department; (b) A change of the official title of the Commissioner of Communications to that of Commissioner of Communications for Telegraph and Radio or Commissioner of Telecommunications; (c) A change of the official title of the Chief Telephone Engineer and Assistant Commissioner of Communications to Commissioner of Communications for Telephone and Transport; (d) Creation of an office of Assistant Commissioner of Communications for Telephones and Transport.

That the Telegraph and Telephone Services be included under the Joint Commission Programme to be represented by the Postmaster-General.

That all agents and/or owners of airlines excluding those used by Government, be required to pay an annual fee to Government in the sum of $500.00

for the use of the operation of their aircrafts to and from all airfields in
Liberia except Robertsfield and that airline owners who have constructed
hangars for private use within the vicinity of these airfields be required to
pay $300.00 as annual rental to Government.

That the Bureau of Folkways be transferred to the Liberian Information
Service.

Fortunately we have endeavoured to instil national consciousness into the
hearts of the people of the country. We must now take measures to nourish
this national cohesiveness by the introduction of another element in our
political annals – the use of territorial and county flags to foster a deeper
county and territorial spirit. It is therefore recommended that you authorize the design of a county or territorial flag for each county and territory
within the Republic.

Certain changes which are necessary in the Labour Law of the country
should be made. These changes will be outlined to you in a special message.

The late Mr. Raoul Gauchy, Civil Engineer of French nationality, served
in the Department of Public works and Utilities for more than twenty years
and died leaving an aged widow in France. I therefore recommend that his
widow be granted an annuity for the duration of her natural life.

OBITUARY

Deep in the nature of all mankind is implanted an unconquerable aversion
to death. Reason cannot remove it, poverty cannot destroy it, wealth and
affluence cannot eliminate it. Every man, no matter how wretched, has some
ties that bind him to life. With many of us, including those who were called
from the terrestrial to the celestial realm during the year 1961, these ties
were and are many and strong and the surrendering of them forever can only
be done with painful contemplation. Nevertheless, a great number of our
fellow compatriots have been called and commanded to break all earthly ties,
to surrender all contemplation of life and to end all their earthly usefulness.

Among the many who have gone from us I mention:

Charles Dunbar Burgess King,
   Grand Old Man of Liberia, former Chief Executive and Commander-
   in-Chief, the last of our former Presidents which leaves that revered
   station in public service vacant. Eminent statesman, lawyer, jurist,
   practical philosopher, politician and churchman.

Dag Hammerskjold,
   Secretary-General, United Nations, apostle of optimism, courageous
   and dauntless servant of mankind regardless of race, colour, or clime.

His Excellency the Right Reverend John Collins,
   Internuncio Apostolic, representing the Government of the Holy See
   near this capital, prelate, and devout Christian imbued with Pauline
   zeal and missionary fervour.

Didwo Tweh and Boima Zinnah,
   legislators, statesmen and politicians.

John Lewis Cooper,
   advisor of communications, technician, pioneer in radiology in
   Liberia, farmer and churchman.

Colonel David F. Dean,
  soldier, strategist and veteran of many battles.

Thomas A. Weeks,
  director, Foreign Conferences, hard, ardent and efficient worker, progressive and liberal in outlook, passed suddenly while serving at his post of duty.

Captain J. P. Valentine,
  soldier.

Mesdames Sarah E. Harris, Charlotte Toomey, Amy Esther Jones, Annabel L. Walker, Sarah E. Dunbar, Anna Barbour, Maude Morris and Williette Jesena Payne,
  septuagenarians, social workers, church-women and musicians.

Mesdames Julia Elizabeth Page and Maria A. L. Dixon,
  nonagenarians and mothers in Liberia.

S. J. C. Davis,
  educator, author and administrator.

Major Victor Bowier,
  musical genius.

Major I. C. Steady,
  cleric and devout Christian.

I. Maxx Smith,
  private secretary whose sun went down while it was yet day.

James Alexander White,
  octogenarian, former commissioner of elections and churchman.

William N. Scott,
  Former District Commissioner and churchman.

C. H. Rennie,
  successful businessman, farmer and devoted Christian.

Ex-Paramount Chiefs Beda Beh and Cherwo Tarlu,
  seasoned experts in tribal affairs, culture and administration.

A number of Clan Chiefs whose passing we deplore.

A number of Public Servants in the lower echelon of the Treasury, Justice, Posts and Telegraphs, Defence, Public Instruction and Interior Departments:
  Faithful public servants who multiplied their talents even though they may have been only once in public service. Their departure we bemoan.
  We pray that they may have a 'calm and undisturbed repose unbroken by the last of foes'.

Finally, we commend and commit the nation, its Government and people to the safe, secure and peaceful keeping of the God of Nations and of our Father Who has extended to us in the past His beneficient kindness and mercy, and we pray that in these times of stress, anxiety, uncertainty and danger, He will continue to protect, defend, guide and guard us as a Nation and People.

Independence Day Message

At Sea, 26 July 1962

Let us resolve to put all the resources of our minds and energy, will and very being into the service of our country. If our nation is to reach her national destiny, we must act now and together.

Introductory Note

When Liberia celebrated the 115th Anniversary of its independence, the President was away from the capital on State Visits to the Republic of Israel, and the United Kingdom of Great Britian and Northern Ireland. The Secretary of State, His Excellency J. Rudolph Grimes, read a special message sent on this occasion to the people of Liberia from their President. The message was sent while at sea on his return journey home. It was the President's first absence from Liberia at the time of the celebration of her independence day. President Tubman spoke about Liberia's proud heritage and called upon all Liberians to give themselves in sacrifice for a continual blossoming of that heritage.

At Sea, 26 July 1962

IN THE process of time and things, and in the unlimited wisdom and perfect power of Him that ruleth in the affairs of men and of nations, we find ourselves absent one from the other on this one-hundred-and-fifteenth Anniversary of the Independence of our nation.

On that first historic and eventful occasion of the signing of the Declaration of Independence of the new State of Liberia on the west coast of Africa in 1847, the framers and signers of that sacred and immortal document forged a political instrument and a unique political entity in the comity of nations, that has survived, progressed and developed through 115 years. Theirs had been the noble task of conceiving the vision and making it blossom into reality; but the task of building a strong and progessive nation on the foundation they laid was left to succeeding generations, who were to direct, improve, perpetuate, nurture and supervise its growth. How well the inspiration was caught, how accelerated the tempo of developments has been, how productive, co-ordinated, and progressive the national endeavours have been, or even how well the sacred trust has been cherished, guarded and transmitted, can be seen on every side. Seen in our social and political institutions; seen in the leadership patterns of the men and women who guided the nation through those early turbulent years to the haven of social and political survival and development; seen in the consistent and persistent strivings of a people that continue to march confidently and work unceasingly for the welfare of a better and stronger nation that would serve their needs and aspirations; seen in the synthesis of careful planning and implementation – new building structures, serviceable roads and improved communications, better schools, new church edifices, increased job opportunities, new health facilities; seen in the determination of a people to be united in all things which pertain to the greater good of the nation. Today, as on every Independence Day, we have cause to thank God for the abundant outpouring of His manifold blessings on this nation, and to take new inspiration from the determination to dedicate ourselves to the unfinished work which lies ahead.

On this 115th Independence Anniversary Celebration when the imaginations of all Liberians should be alight, their wills fired and their hearts filled with joy over the nationwide strides which are taking place, let us resolve to put all the resources of our minds, energy, will and very being into the service of our country. And when I say all, let us judge not by whether we have given much, but by whether we have anything left. To achieve this objective we shall have to act and feel with a personal obsession and patriotic passion that we do not now feel.

You may remember the legend of how all the inhabitants of the earth agreed on one occasion that, at a given signal, they would give a mighty shout together to reach the ear of the inhabitants of Mars and at the given signal there was silence. Each man had decided to listen to the shout of the others. If our nation is to reach her national destiny we must ACT now and TOGETHER aware that the way of a successful democracy, in peace or war, must be for each individual to act as a personal trustee of the rest, so that its leaders may be the victorious incarnation of its spirit.

You who are in attendence at the official reception in the capital are aware of the peril which soon overtakes a nation if its people, forgetful of solemn obligations, permit selfishness, petty jealousies, personal ambitions and bitter rivalries to obscure the national image. You know the memory which this day should revive in you, and your inescapable obligations to see that the events of this day will not lose their true significance. You owe it to yourselves, your country, countrymen and countrywomen to accept your rôle in this national scheme of things, resolved to play a noble part so that our nation may grow from strength to strength in our time of progress and prosperity and the time of generations to come.

It is regrettable that we are absent from you on this momentous occasion which all Liberians welcome and enjoy with joyous anticipation.

Our state visits to the State of Israel in June and to the United Kingdom in mid-July have not permitted me to return home in time for an occasion which I have not missed for the past eighteen years. However, my thoughts, my joys, my hopes and my cheers are all with you today and I hope that the events of this day will remain with us during the course of another year and that the memories will inspire us to greater service in the interest of our nation, its people and God.

Because we are at sea on the return voyage from the United Kingdom, I salute you in absentio and after the fashion of the early Christians, I do so with a kiss to each of you.

To the Doyen and Members of the Diplomatic Corps I extend felicitations and express the hope that, as our relations in the past have been characterized by peace, cordiality and understanding, so the future will continue to make our associations and contacts, both official and personal, more friendly and productive of the results which we desire for our respective countries and peoples. I also express the hope that we shall be able to live in an atmosphere of peace and true friendship in this world, not only with our respective nations, but with the world at large; so that our work toward a just and lasting peace with all mankind may be greatly facilitated and enhanced.

God keep and save the State.

Third Annual Message delivered before the Second Session of the Forty-fifth Legislature

Monrovia, 23 November 1962

We have continued to exert our best efforts to keep our relations with the states of Africa and other nations of the world active and friendly.

Introductory Note

This year efforts to ban nuclear tests became a much discussed topic in international affairs, and in addition to news from the Congo, Cuba made headlines. The question of continental leadership in Africa became an important aspect of African diplomacy, and there was a tendency towards groups of regional blocks with common interests. At the same time African unity was considered desirable. The world leant an attentive ear to hear how Africa was making use of its new freedoms. In all of these matters Liberia took an active part. There was concern for the fall in world prices for primary products from developing nations, and for the effect of the European Common Market on our economy. The President reported that negotiations were being undertaken for the establishment of an African Development Bank, upon Liberia's initiative. The major recommendations in this message dealt with economic matters. The nation was warned of an impending period of austerity.

IT IS with deep and abiding gratitude to Almighty God for His mercies and benefits vouchsafed to us as a people and nation, and for His preservation of you, the nation and myself, that I am able to appear before you for the nineteenth time to render the Annual Report on the conduct of the affairs of the State required by the Constitution.

In the realm of international affairs, the threat of nuclear war was precipitated by the Cuban crisis. But high consideration, salutation and praise are due to the Statesmanship of the United Nations Secretary-General, the United States and the Soviet Union for the clear thinking, quick action, correct decisions and remarkable restraint exercised in the crisis in averting a major global nuclear war. To God we give thanks and adoration for His mercies in this crisis.

Efforts to ban nuclear tests have so far been unsuccessful. Although some progress has been made at the Geneva Conference on General Disarmament, the overall results have been disappointing; but there must be persistent, patient, relentless and continued efforts to effect agreement for general disarmament. If the attitude of the Nuclear Powers shown in the Cuban crisis is carried over to the disarmament discussions, greater progress will be possible.

FOREIGN RELATIONS

During the year relations between this Government, those with established diplomatic representations near this capital and with member states of the United Nations, have continued on an understanding and cordial basis. We have continued to exert our best efforts to keep our relations active and friendly with the states of Africa and other nations of the world. We have not failed to utilize every opportunity to exert our keenest endeavours to encourage and assist African peoples in attaining their independence, and have given substantial material and moral assistance to them.

FOREIGN VISITS

In January last that group of African States referred to as the Monrovia Group States met at summit level in Lagos, Nigeria. This was the second meeting of this group, the first having been held in Monrovia in May, 1961. At that conference a charter was presented and accepted in principle.

The conference was to be followed by another, composed of Foreign Ministers, to consider in detail the provisions of this proposed charter and to agree upon its final text for submission to Heads of State and Government at the conference scheduled to be held in Addis Ababa, Ethiopia, some time next year. The Foreign Ministers met in Lagos according to schedule, and their report awaits action by the Heads of State and Government Conference.

On February the first of this year, the day after the Lagos Conference adjourned, we flew to Yaounde, in the Camerouns, on a five-day State Visit upon the invitation of His Excellency President Ahmadou Ahidjo. The success of this visit was evidenced by the contents of the communiqué issued, which included a wide range of issues vital to our two countries, Africa and universal peace. We received many courtesies and the true spirit of friendship prevailed between us and the Government and people of the Camerouns.

Immediately after the Camerounean visit, we flew to Libreville, Gabon, for a three-day State Visit in response to an invitation of His Excellency President Leon Mba. We were accorded flattering courtesies and were greatly moved by the friendliness and hospitality of the people of Gabon.

On our return journey we made a brief stop at Lome, Togo, where we were warmly received by President Sylvanus Olympio and other dignitaries of the Government of Togo. Nearly all the people of Lome turned out to welcome us and thus honoured our nation.

After leaving Lome, we had the pleasure of making a day's stop-over at Abidjan, the Ivory Coast. Here we were extended a most hearty welcome and lavishly entertained by the Government.

In March last, we had the opportunity and pleasure of making a three-day return State Visit to Dakar, Senegal, upon the invitation of His Excellency President Leopold Sedar Senghor. The colourful receptions and the general friendliness of the Government and people of Senegal contributed greatly to the pleasure of that visit.

At the end of each of these visits communiqués touching upon economic, cultural and social co-operation were issued.

In consideration of the long-standing friendly relationship between the German people and the people of Liberia and as an act of reciprocity of the State Visit made to Bonn, Germany, by us in 1956, upon the invitation of President Theodore Heus, His Excellency President Heinrich Lubke upon our invitation made a State Visit to Monrovia, Liberia, in January last. We were most happy to have the visit of this great statesman, a representative citizen of a nation and people whose genius and ability for quick development, growth and resuscitation are unmatched in world history.

As a gesture of goodwill President Lubke announced that the Government of West Germany would staff and equip a vocational school in Liberia and send out ten experts to serve at this institution.

The already friendly ties between the State of Israel and Liberia have been greatly enhanced and strengthened by our visit to Israel in June last and the return visit to Liberia in August of His Excellency President and Mrs. Izhak Ben-Zvi.

These visits resulted in the signing of several important agreements between the two Governments in the fields of technical aid and other assistance and the Government and people of Israel went all out to shower honours upon us and extend us many special courtesies and, through us, to the Government and people of Liberia.

On the 10th of July this year we made a return State Visit to London, England, upon the invitation of Her Majesty Queen Elizabeth II of Great Britain whom we had the distinguished honour, privilege and pleasure of receiving on a State Visit to Liberia on November 23, 1961.

We were received by Her Majesty and Representatives of the British Government with the formalities, pomp and pageantry characteristic of British tradition, and not only were we the recipients of the warmest attention and consideration of Her Majesty and her husband, the Duke of Edinburgh, the British Nobility and the Prime Minister, but we were also warmly received by the Lord Mayor of London in the Guildhall and by Mayors of other cities through which we travelled, in addition to the courtesies and considerations we received from businessmen, industrialists, bankers and people in various walks of life. The Anglo-Liberian Society was very active and contributed greatly to the success of our visit. The Society continues to stimulate interest in Liberia and keep alive the friendly relations which exist between the two countries. These visits have made a considerable impact on Anglo-Liberian relations and the attentions we received were for the Liberian nation and people, we being only your representatives.

We look forward to the development of still closer and increased economic, industrial and other relationships between Great Britain and Liberia.

In response to an invitation extended to us by His Majesty King Gustaf VI (Adolf) of the Kingdom of Sweden we arrived in Stockholm on the 17th of September last for a State Visit. Our reception was royal and Their Majesties the King and Queen, the members of the Government and people of Sweden extended to us most generous attentions and considerations. Here again we witnessed a dazzling pageantry and saw colourful ceremonies known only to Monarchical Governments and Royalty. We were greatly touched by the warmth and friendliness we received everywhere in Sweden and at the close of this visit an agreement for the establishment of a trade school in Liberia was concluded between the two Governments.

THE SINO-INDIAN CRISIS

Awed by the frightful realization of the threatening hostilities between India and China over a border dispute and considering the ancient and historic background of these two most populous nations, together with our aversion to war and our implicit belief in the settlement of disputes by negotiations and conferences before actual fighting began, we addressed identical notes to Prime Minister Nehru of India and Premier Chou En-lai of China suggesting that they refrain from armed conflict, endeavouring rather to settle the dispute through negotiations by permitting the Afro-Asian group to exercise its best efforts to adjudicate in the matter; in the meantime we communicated the same proposal to all of the Afro-Asian States. Most of the leaders to whom we appealed indicated their concern and agreement, but although both Prime Minister Nehru and Premier Chou En-lai expressed their appreciation for the interest shown in the matter, each advanced his own firm terms as the only basis upon which negotiations would be possible. This somewhat complicated the matter and made it difficult to determine what further action could be taken; however it is gratifying to note that a cease fire is being observed all along the fighting lines and negotiations are ensuing.

THE CONGO CRISIS

The Congo crisis seems to be developing into a vicious circle. Thus far the general situation has been that whenever proposals were made and apparent agreements reached they seemed to culminate in nothing tangible or permanent. Because of this recurring intransigence the cost of the Congo crisis to the United Nations has been phenomenal in time, money, energy and blood. Clearly, it is time that the leaders and people of the Congo realize that rebellion, division and internal strife have militated against them, and that unity in essential and tolerance in non-essential things can make all the difference in the political and social growth of their young and promising nation; that the long struggle after independence has been costly and regrettable, and that it is in their own interest and that of their country that a quick settlement of the differences which now hinder unity be regarded as the only logical process; and that appropriate action be agreed upon by the Congolese themselves to implement their decisions. Thus we may hope that the bitter experiences of the past will bring the Government and people of the Congo to seek a new avenue to the enjoyment of their hard won freedom and liberty.

THE UNITED NATIONS

The United Nations as the citadel of international peace has experienced since its inception many great trials, tribulations, bickerings and oppositions; but it still survives and serves effectively, though not completely, the purposes for which it was founded. It has preserved peace not by force of arms, but through negotiation, meditation and arbitration.

Believing that mankind's hope for a peaceful solution to the world's ills lies with the United Nations, the Liberian Government will continue to support and defend that organization to the fullest extent of its ability, resources and strength.

INTERNAL AFFAIRS
THE SPECIAL COMMISSION ON GOVERNMENT OPERATIONS

After careful survey and study of the existing organizations of the Executive
Government, a new plan for the re-organization of this Branch of Government was completed and submitted in November of last year. The new plan
calls for the elimination of a number of autonomous agencies, and for the
concentration of Government activities under eleven Cabinet Departments.
Nearly all the recommendations submitted were approved, and an Act approving the reforms enacted by you at your last session is being implemented.

The Commission, in an effort to improve the budget system, has recommended the development of a modern system for implementation by 1963. A
Budget Officers Training Course of six weeks' duration was conducted, and
forty officials from Government departments and agencies were given training. By Executive Order a new budget process went into effect, and this year
a single consolidated national budget will be presented to Your Honourable
Selves for review and approval.

To provide for a better trained technical staff in the new reorganization
plan, arrangements were made through AID for several departments and
agencies of Government to send trainees to the United States for observation
in administration, administrative services, etc. A total of over 100 persons
has gone and more are expected to follow next year. The Commission is to
be complimented on its comprehensive and valuable work.

NATIONAL PLANNING AGENCY

The broad goals of development planning in Liberia are clear: higher *per
capita* national income, a distribution of income consistent with long-range
political stability and social justice, and richer and longer lives for citizens. In
May of this year when the National Planning Agency was established, the
step placed the nation's development on an appropriate footing, declares the
Director-General. The National Council is now actively operating under a
Director-General who also serves as Executive Secretary.

The new organization has already commenced its work by reviewing
capital programmes and projects in the 1963 budget, and has made a recon-
naissance study of current external technical assistance programmes. The
Director-General mentions the fact that the nation's transition to a modern
economy has been hastened by a combination of factors:

1. The heavy investments made by foreign capital, under which thousands
   of Liberians are receiving informal training in new skills.
2. The Government's own internal development programme.
3. The external technical assistance programmes provided by friendly
   countries and international organizations affiliated with the United
   Nations.

The great majority of the three hundred and fifty foreign experts now
serving in Liberia under technical assistance programmes is engaged in the
areas of general education, vocational training, public administration, agriculture, health and medicine.

The taking of the first National Census of population during the second
quarter of 1962 was a great step forward in our national planning. When the

results are tabulated and published, the census staff will be available for other studies which will assist the National Planning Council in determining economic policies and development priorities.

For almost two decades, Liberia has enjoyed a phase of unprecedented progress in the development of its natural resources. The Government is determined that the momentum of this development shall be maintained. However, like all countries which are major exporters of raw materials, Liberia has suffered from the general fall in commodity prices that has taken place all over the world. This unsatisfactory situation, which is not under our own control, must obviously increase the difficulty of financing the development programme of the country. We shall continue to do everything possible to attract investment from abroad as well as to resolve and overcome this present unfavourable situation.

It is essential that every dollar of available revenue and capital be applied in a way which will do most to develop our resources, provide employment, and give our people improved standards of living. For these reasons, the Government will ensure that the forthcoming budget contains only essential expenditure. This means that there must be some reduction in certain Government services, and that either special arrangements must be made for some projects or they will have to be deferred until more capital is available. By concentrating our available resources on essentials we shall do most to achieve the maximum rate of development.

To assure the speedy and efficient mobilization of our resources in overcoming the present economic squeeze, as well as to consolidate the progress in our Development Programme through the establishment of priorities and the comprehensive involvement of all facilities at our disposal, I have given instructions to the agencies concerned to develop a Five-Year Plan of Recovery and Advance. As soon as the necessary study and planning have been completed this Plan will be submitted to you for favourable consideration.

TREASURY DEPARTMENT

In spite of the great optimism which prevailed throughout the world as a result of the remarkable recovery from the 1958 depression, the Secretary of the Treasury points to the sudden crash in the New York Stock Market followed by violent downward movements in other parts of the world. And while the nation's economic activities in recent years show a sharp rise in receipts from eighteen million dollars in 1958 to an anticipated more than thirty-six million dollars in 1962, the rate of growth in 1961 and 1962 has sharply declined. Four reasons are given for this situation:

1. The world-wide recession.
2. The depression in commodity prices, e.g. rubber.
3. The fall in the price of iron ore.
4. The unavoidable delays in coming into production and early adjustment problems of the National Iron Ore Company.

To offset some of these realistic problems, the services of Mr. George Blowers and Sir Robert Jackson were engaged to consult with officials and economists at the Treasury to study the problems and make pertinent suggestions. After a ten-day conference in Monrovia the team recommended the following approaches:

1. Cutting down drastically on non-essential expenditures.
2. Seeking to create new sources of investment and income.
3. Improving revenues by improving revenue collection.
4. Developing an investment code for the nation.

Referring to the budget reforms, the Secretary makes the following suggestions:

1. All departments must adhere strictly to the approved budget.
2. There should be no budgetary transfers.
3. No official should be permitted to commit the Government for any expenses outside the approved budget.
4. Control by the Budget Bureau of all orders for supply and local purchases should be avoided.
5. Control of purchases in bulk with commission earnings to the Government should be required of all foreign orders.
6. The recommendation of the Special Commission to establish a Central Purchasing Agency should be implemented.
7. The entire procedure for handling of Government contracts should be reviewed to ensure competitive bidding and the most efficient use of public funds.

The Secretary of the Treasury observes that the Open Door Policy continues to be successful and has brought great benefit to the people of the country. However, the almost rash and uncontrolled influx and operation in the country of foreign based investment funds are likely to pose a crucial test. Alarming reports have been received that millions of dollars are being sent out of the country annually by Investment Funds which have been operating in the country in the past few years. Nevertheless, given pledges to maintain the free flow of capital and repatriation of dividends cannot be ignored, nor can we permit those operating under the economic protection of the Open Door Policy to destroy the very economy it seeks to preserve and keep free.

It is therefore recommended that all foreign based Investment Funds should be registered with the Treasury Department and be required to obtain annual operating licenses, and that all such Funds should agree to invest a portion of their total intake in projects of their own choice in this country. Where the law does not permit this, they should, by agreement with the Government, pay a tax rate, mutually arrived at, on such withdrawals as are made from Liberia and invested in foreign countries.

Revenue collections for the current year aggregate 36·1 million dollars as against 32·7 million dollars in the preceding 12-month period, an increase of 3·4 million dollars. Twenty-three point three million dollars was derived from internal revenue sources as against 21·8 million for the preceding period. Income tax suffered a decrease of 0·8 million dollars due to the fall in the price of rubber. There has been no perceptible decrease in 'other revenues'. Collections from the Division of Real Estate tax are 138·2 thousand dollars as against 118·5 thousand dollars for the preceding period; however, this is still disappointing because collections for the period ended September, 1960 were 153·2 thousand dollars which is a decrease of 15 thousand dollars in 1962. The Budgetary revenues of the Government for 1962 were estimated at 30 million dollars. Collections for the nine-month period ending September 30th totalled 26¼ million dollars which is 3¾ million dollars less than the total estimate for the year. Despite the decrease in income tax the overall picture is encouraging, because other sources of revenue produced substantial increases which served as an offset factor.

Expenditures were in excess of the corresponding period by 8·2 million dollars. Budgetary expenditures for the period were 41·0 million dollars compared with 32·8 million dollars for the previous period which include both capital and current expenditure. Principal areas of Government expenditure were the Department of Public Works and Utilities – 2·7 per cent – General Government 12·8 per cent – Foreign Relations 9·2 per cent – Education 8·2 per cent – Health 5·0 per cent – Travel 2·2 per cent – all others 59·9 per cent.

The total National Debt at present contracted for the Development Programme including interest is $181,827,860.02, of which $145,413,716.47 has been drawn and $32,669,616.18 has been repaid, leaving an outstanding balance of $112,744,100.29.

Negotiations are now under way for the establishment of a Development Bank for Africa, and a study was made by the Economic Commission for Africa which reported in favour of the project provided that necessary financial support could be obtained.

THE EUROPEAN COMMON MARKET

In our Second Annual Message we referred to our concern about the possible effects of the European Economic Community – now generally referred to as the Common Market – on the Liberian economy. The Government has continued to watch closely the evolution of this new economic association. Two developments of great significance can already be observed. First, it is anticipated that in the near future a new convention will be negotiated between the Community and the several African States, known as the Associated Overseas Territories, which already have a formal relationship with it. Second, it now seems likely that the negotiations for the United Kingdom to join the Common Market will be successful. Both these developments must ultimately have a profound effect on the political and economic relationships between virtually all of Africa and Western Europe.

Furthermore, the entry of the United Kingdom into the Common Market must have an equally significant effect upon the entire field of political and economic relationships between Western Europe on one side of the Atlantic and North America on the other.

These vast and historic changes in the relations between countries on three continents must obviously be of the greatest importance to Liberia, which occupies a unique position in that, at one and the same time, it is actively concerned with the political and economic development of Africa, the preservation of its export trade to Europe, and its special and historic relationship with the United States of America.

For these vital reasons, the Government will watch with greatest care all aspects of the development of the Common Market, and adopt policies which will do most to safeguard our existing position, and assist us in achieving our future objectives. We are happy to say that, in the short term, 90 per cent of Liberia's exports is not expected to be affected by the Common Market as it exists at present, but this does not mean that Liberia's position in the future may not be affected and the Government will therefore act when the necessity arises.

DEPARTMENT OF JUSTICE

The present method of probating title deeds in the Probate Courts of the country, under provisions of the Act of Legislature which require all deeds, agreements, conveyance and other Instruments in writing to be registered and probated, needs amendment. At present it is the practice for persons to go to the Probate Court and, within the space of ten minutes, probate a deed, thereby transferring title from one person to another without the benefit of notice to the public. By means of this loose practice, fraud, requiring long and costly proceedings in Chancery to cancel, may easily be committed. I therefore submit for your consideration the amendment of the above-mentioned Act, to provide that all deeds conveying title to real property and lease agreements offered for probation be retained for a period of fifteen days for notice to be given to the public through newspapers or the radio, describing by measurements and bounds the piece of property being transferred; if no objections are filed within the fifteen days, the instrument shall then be admitted for probation.

There was an increased volume of motor and automotive vehicular traffic in Monrovia and its environs, especially in the Central Province, resulting in the violation of traffic laws, rules and regulations. Corrupt practices were also discovered – such as chauffeurs carrying appearance bonds in their pockets before the commission of acts in violation of traffic laws. These practices generated a disregard for law and order and resulted in a tremendous number of accidents and injuries to persons and property, a great number of them fatal. Because of the inability of the Traffic Bureau and the Police to handle the situation, which had reached the point where people were afraid to get into their cars and move about, and because the Insurance Companies gave notice that unless the rate of accidents and destruction of vehicles were reduced they would either have to stop further insurance or greatly increase the cost of insuring vehicles, it became necessary in the interest of public safety to invoke the Special Emergency Powers granted by you, dissolve the Traffic Court and set up a Special Court to handle all matters involving traffic violations, and to suspend the Writ of Habeas Corpus for a period of six months.

This action was fruitful, in that the incidence of accidents and the violation of traffic laws, rules and regulations diminished instantly.

DEPARTMENT OF POSTS AND TELEGRAPHS

Another stride in the history of development in the Postal and Communication System has been achieved in the inauguration of mail vans serving the public and various departments of the Government, and the installation of mail boxes in Monrovia.

A long-felt need has also been fulfilled by the installation of a teleprinter press service between Monrovia and London on a trial basis. Extensive tests have been conducted for direct radio-telephone connection between Monrovia and Freetown, and a temporary link has been established. It is expected that the service will be extended to the public by the end of the current year.

DEPARTMENT OF NATIONAL DEFENCE

We have always been aware of the growing importance of the National Defence Programme for internal security. In recent years personnel training has been provided and intensified, modern equipment procured, the programme expanded and living facilities are being improved. It is clear that the National Defence Programme must be reliable, efficient and effective. The Government of the United States is making substantial contributions in this direction.

In its expanding programme for training officers for the Army, the University of Liberia and the Booker Washington Institute have reactivated their programmes under the advice and guidance of the ROTC Mobile Training Team.

DEPARTMENT OF THE INTERIOR

A state of peace and quiet has generally prevailed throughout the country and the Department of the Interior continues to function effectively.

The Rural Area Development Programme is indicative of the Government's concern to bring progress, prosperity and opportunities to all the peoples of the nation. Under this programme Gbarnga District has been selected for the initial project.

The Special Commission authorized by you to make a survey and study of the present territorial, political and administrative sub-divisions of the country and to recommend plans for the revision thereof which will tend toward the abolition of the present system of County and Hinterland Administrations, has submitted its report. However, there remain a few points of difference among the members of the Commission which are to be considered and a consensus sought before submitting the final report and recommendations to Your Honourable Selves for consideration during your present session.

The report thus far submitted recommends changing the Eastern Province into a county, the Central Province into two counties and the Western Province into a county, making a total of four additional counties to be administered under the Constitution, general laws and regulations governing county governments.

We observe that certain classes of foreign nationals are engaging in real estate business by leasing land, building houses and subletting them for enormous sums while paying to the Liberian lessors only nominal rentals, thereby profiteering and obtaining the virtual ownership of real estate in the country through long-term leases of three and four successive terms of twenty years each. This is in direct violation of the letter, spirit and intent of the Constitution, which prohibits foreigners from owning land or real estate in Liberia. I consider this practice an exploitation and disruption of the land economy of the country envisaged by the Consitution and a travesty of the Open Door Policy.

In my 1957 Annual Message I called attention to this growing practice and I quote the relevant portion thereof:

'The spirit and intent of the Constitution, which prevents foreigners from owning real estate within the country has to be very carefully guarded, and I note that some foreigners are now entering into lease agreements for realty and entering the real estate business by constructing and leasing houses and other buildings. This will create unfair competition for Liberians, because some of the firms and companies attempting to engage in this type of business are themselves construction companies, and can operate at greater advantage in this field than can Liberians.

I recommend that a law be enacted to prevent foreigners from entering into real estate business either directly or indirectly.'

You took no action on the above recommendation.

It is also known that some foreigners are engaged in transportation business and that Liberians organizing transportation companies hand them over to these foreigners who act ostensibly as their agents, but are in fact part owners, if not real owners. Such acts are against the interest of the protective measures adopted by Government in favour of Liberian citizens and are violations of the statute. A statute affixing a penalty of fine and confiscation of all such property should be enacted.

Furthermore, there are foreigners who are engaged in peddling. Since our commerce and trade is principally in the hands of foreigners, because Liberians are not in a position to compete successfully in trade and commerce at the present time, such foreign traders must be restricted to certain types of business and prohibited from peddling; and eventually they should be restricted to wholesale business only.

DEPARTMENT OF EDUCATION

Education for everyone in a democracy is a must if the people are to participate progressively and effectively in governing themselves. In Liberia education for the masses has always been a priority pre-occupation of the Government and people, although sometimes retarded by the lack of funds.

Along with Teacher Education, which the Department of Education is now stressing, priority must be given to the strengthening of the elementary school programme, since it is there that a real and solid educational foundation is laid. Unfortunately, quite a number of Liberian parents who are in position to do so, find it necessary to send their young children to foreign countries for schooling, thereby causing them to lose contact with their own country during the tender and formative period of their lives, and depriving them of the benefit of family life and the opportunity of growing up within the orientation of the Liberian way of life. In the interest of the culture we wish to develop and maintain, this state of affairs should not be permitted to continue. But before corrective measures can be brought to bear, there must be built up a strong and efficient elementary school programme of an unquestionably recognized high standard, and it must be the responsibility of the Department of Education to see that this programme is initiated and executed in the immediate future.

The Government's scholarship programme has borne abundant fruits and brought considerable satisfaction to the nation. The products of this programme are to be found in nearly all departments of government as doctors, engineers, economists, geologists, lawyers, school administrators and teachers, agriculturists, etc., contributing their knowledge, training and skills to the service of their fatherland. In a recent talk with some top-ranking international economists, they had nothing but high praise for the performance of some of our young men. We truly hope that this will be an incentive to those who are now holders of scholarship awards, and arouse in them the strong desire to utilize every available opportunity given them.

In the expanding educational programme the United States, through 'Crossroads Africa' and the 'Peace Corps', is rendering much assistance by sending teachers for assignment throughout the country. We need more and more of these. These contributions to the schools of the country are assisting in filling a void, and the Government is grateful for this assistance in its fight against ignorance.

Because I feel strongly that the change in the school year has complicated other areas of our national life and know that the best interest of our youth has always been uppermost in our national planning, a return should be made to the old school year; and I support this recommendation.

DEPARTMENT OF PUBLIC WORKS AND UTILITIES

During the year it became necessary to ask for the resignation of the Secretary of Public Works and Utilities. He was succeeded by Under Secretary M. Alexander Ketter as Acting Secretary of Public Works and Utilities.

Under provisions of an Act entitled, 'An Act to Amend the Executive Law to reorganize the Department of Public Works and Utilities' which became effective in June, 1962, this Department is being reorganized and sub-divided into three bureaux – Technical Service, Operational and Administrative Services – each headed by an Under Secretary.

The Acting Secretary of Public Works and Utilities reports on Government buildings as follows:

> November 1, 1963, target date for the completion of the Executive Mansion Building.
> May, 1963, target date for the completion of the Law Courts Building.

In this connection, I report with much regret that the Executive Mansion Building is costing much more than was originally anticipated, and has exceeded original costs by about seven million dollars. It is outrageous that any public building in Liberia, not excluding the Executive Mansion, should cost such an enormous sum of money, altogether out of proportion to the resources of the nation. Costs got out of hand in the pre-financing process, or by the inefficiency or condonation of responsible officials of the Department of Public Works. However, the evil had been done, and had gone so far when it was discovered that there was no alternative but to provide for the completion of the building. This situation is to be investigated.

An agreement for the construction of a hydro-electric plant near Mount Coffee has been concluded with a corporation headed by Mr. Arno Neumann. This concession agreement will be forwarded to you, and I request your favourable consideration.

DEPARTMENT OF AGRICULTURE AND COMMERCE

Repeated attention has been called to the fact that the principal responsibility of the Department of Agriculture and Commerce is to provide the proper technical and socio-economic basis of agricultural production. To this end efforts have been geared toward producing farmers, who will in turn produce commodities. The past trend has been in the production of tree crops and now, without restricting development of plantation agriculture, the focus is on the development of food crops.

During the past year the Department was fortunate in activating agreements with the United States, the Republic of China and the United Nations to provide, in part, two fundamental needs – credit and technical assistance.

Liberia is essentially an agricultural country and thus to ensure real economic progress and stability there must be increased production. This must be given priority over all other projects of the Department of Agriculture and Commerce, for only by means of an accelerated production will our balance of trade and of payment be favourable.

In his report, the Secretary of Agriculture and Commerce states that Government's policy for the encouragement of foreign investments on the basis of a partnership relationship and the granting of economic incentives continues to prove advantageous.

The regulation of Trade Union activities and the overall development of labour relations has engaged the interest of the Government. On the 22nd of August, 1962, I convened a conference of representatives of labour, management and Government to discuss the Labour Practices Law; the outcome of this was a newly proposed Labour Code entitled 'An Act to Amend the Labour Practices Law in Relation to the Rights and Duties of Labour Organization and Their Members Thereof.'

The proposed Labour Code represents a project of law, copies of which were distributed for study and for making such recommendations as may be deemed necessary in the best interest of labour, management and Government. While it is true that labour conditions have improved considerably within the last ten to fifteen years, further improvements are still necessary.

In some instances the wage scale and other facilities for the labouring man are below reasonable decent standards; in these instances consideration should be given. It must be realized, however, that labour, too, has corresponding responsibilities and should earn its wage. One of the conditions which still face us is the necessity of having overseers to see that a job is done well. Each worker should be conscious of his duty and responsibility, and should perform it for his employer as though he were doing it for himself. Clearly there must be the feeling of obligation on the part of management for labour and of labour for management.

The case brought before the International Court of Justice at the Hague by Ethiopia and Liberia against the Government of the Union of South Africa over the mandated Territory of South-West Africa entrusted to the Union Government by the League of Nations was heard in October last and decision reserved; this decision is expected to be forthcoming within the next few weeks. Representing Ethiopia and Liberia were Counsellors Ernest Gross and Edward R. Moore, Assistant Attorney-General; both of these legal luminaries made capable and impressive representations of the cause before that international tribunal; we are very proud of Counsellor Moore's performance.

In the implementation of an Act passed at your last session, authorizing the institution of a Produce Marketing Corporation, the Government has negotiated and concluded an agreement with the East Asiatic Company, Ltd., Copenhagen, Denmark to handle the purchase and sale of Liberian produce. This agreement was signed recently in Copenhagen by the Secretary of Agriculture and Commerce on behalf of the Liberian Government. Much credit for this accomplishment goes to the Commercial Adviser, Mr. J. D. MacRae, for his persistence in this matter.

NATIONAL PUBLIC HEALTH SERVICE

The health of the people of any nation should be of primary importance. In Liberia, while great progress has been achieved in the field of public health and sanitation, malaria and its effective eradication continue to challenge medical science. However, the fight against this insidious malady continues.

During the year under review a reorganization plan was prepared establishing the Bureau of Medical Services, Preventive Medicine and Administration, with the Deputy Director-General, the Co-ordinator and the Public Health Consultant heading these divisions respectively.

LIBERIAN INFORMATION SERVICE

The Liberian Information Service has taken on new dimensions, since it is the first time in history that people in all areas of the nation can turn on their radios and learn what is happening in the country.

With the assistance of the United States Information Agency, a Regional Information Centre was opened at Saniquellie, and it has so enriched the lives and widened the horizons of the citizens that the Rural Area Development Agency in Gbarnga has constructed a special building for another Regional Information Centre to cover its area of operations.

THE BUREAU OF CIVIL SERVICE

The Civil Service Bureau is one of the oldest in the nation and its service in the interest of the people of Liberia should never be minimized. The Director expresses dissatisfaction with the present system and feels that greater attention should be focused upon this Bureau in order to increase its effectiveness to our overall national programme. I recommend this for your favourable consideration.

PRESIDENTIAL YACHT

I note with appreciation the passage of an Act by you for the sale of the two old yachts because of the recent damage to the M/V *Liberian*, and the purchase of a new yacht. Even if these sales are effected, the funds accruing therefrom would not be sufficient to provide 25 per cent of the cost of a new yacht nor do I believe that it is possible at this time to get a yacht with the quantity of steel that the *Liberian* has. In my opinion, a new yacht would be much frailer. I think, therefore, that the M/V *Liberian* could be repaired and be of further service. I ask for your co-operation.

THE SUPREME COURT

The Supreme Court held its regular Semi-Annual Sessions during the year, but at the opening of its present term there was a bare quorum present, two of the Justices being out of the country, one on an official mission and the other for reasons of health. We are happy that both of these absent Justices have returned home and entered upon the discharge of their duties.

To improve the administration of justice, and to give a clearer insight and understanding to Justices of the Peace and Magistrates in the proper administration of justice and the application of the law as Courts of First Instance that come in contact from day to day with the masses of the people in adjudicating petty offences, His Honour the Chief Justice instituted a Seminar to assist these Justices of the Peace and Magistrates in the proper interpretation and performance of their duties.

We consider this an act that should improve and expedite the disposal of both civil and criminal cases coming before Justices of the Peace and Magistrates.

The Supreme Court still holds the esteem, high regard and confidence of the public and Government.

The Ministers have all discharged their respective duties and assignments excellently, some with five talents, some three and some two but none with one; they have all multiplied their talents and brought in their sheaves a hundredfold.

RECOMMENDATIONS

It is recommended that:

1. In view of the rapid development of Liberia, and in order to give more security and proper supervision to the recording and preserving of valuable data, the office of the Registrar of Deeds be located in the Bureau of Archives of the State Department, and a commission be set up to arrange for the proper care of records.

2. A tax be imposed on luxury consumer goods such as air conditioners, automobiles and accessories (other than for commercial purposes), and on alcoholic beverages.

3. The taxation system be reviewed so as to assure an equitable distribution of the tax burdens.

4. Detailed requirements for financial and statistical reports by concessions be insituted and enforced.

5. Authorization for compulsory free registration of births, deaths and marriages be given by legislation.

6. Legislation be provided to authorize the Bureau of Immigration and Naturalization to collect statistical data on all persons, aliens as well as citizens, who enter or leave the country.

7. A commission be appointed to draft a National Investment Code which, when approved, would be promulgated as the Investment Code of the Nation.

8. An austerity Budget be established.

9. The Budget Reforms outlined in the Secretary of the Treasury's report be approved and implemented.

10. Suggested expenditure (savings) and Revenue recommendations mentioned in the Annual Report of the Secretary of the Treasury be approved and implemented.

11. All foreign-based investment funds be registered with the Treasury Department and be required to obtain annual operating licenses.

12. The existing policy of collecting consular invoice fees be continued, but

in the case of expressed tax exempted concessions, only the cost of processing invoices at Liberian Consulates should be recovered.

13. Section 444 of the Revenue and Finance Laws be amended to provide for payment of Real Estate Taxes in two instalments – April 30 and October 31 of each year.

14. Closer co-ordination between Treasury and the Budget Bureau be authorized to facilitate the programming of budgetary expenditure in relation to anticipated cash flow.

15. A rigid minimum condition for renting of certain types of houses be established, and a review of assignment procedures instituted.

16. The Consultant Commission's recommendations on Foreign Concessions, particularly the Liberia Company, be implemented.

17. The Tariff on imported beer be increased and regulations made for an excise tax to be imposed on domestically brewed beer to offset the revenue loss.

18. Section 570 of Title 35 of the Liberian Code of Laws under Chapter 18: Stamp Duties, be amended to provide for Revenue Stamps on cheques, bills of exchange, transfers and other drafts.

19. The Supervisors of Customs and Internal Revenues be hereafter designated as Commissioner of Customs and of Internal Revenues respectively.

20. The State be granted the right to appeal in criminal cases on the question of mere law.

21. A Tax Court be established to have jurisdiction in all tax and revenue matters.

22. The status of the Radio Station be raised to a Bureau under the Department of Posts and Telecommunications, to be known as the Bureau of Radio Telecommunications.

23. The title of Commissioner of Communications be changed to Director of Communications and Director of Telecommunications.

24. The salaries of Provincial, District and Assistant District Commissioners be increased so as to ensure the procurement of high calibre persons for these positions, and an In-Service Training Course be inaugurated for the training of Commissioners and other administrative officers, the selection of this type of official to be by competitive examinations.

25. The scope of authority of the Department of the Interior be evaluated.

26. A Research Centre for effective planning in social, economic and cultural development be established.

27. All Government-financed schools of business in Monrovia on the elementary and secondary levels under the Division of Vocational Education in the Department of Education be consolidated.

28. Free textbooks for elementary school children from grades one to six and hired textbooks for secondary school pupils from grades seven to twelve be made available.

29. Legislative Authority for the establishment of a National Malaria Service be enacted.

30. The Act creating the Liberian Information Service be amended (a) to provide for the position of Assistant Director and (b) to change the status of the Divisions to Bureaux.

31. A National Cultural Centre be established.

OBITUARY

The body is the instrument by which men live, act, move and perform. The eyes, the ears, the hands, the feet and other organs of the body are the instruments by which men perform great, noble and historic deeds. It is by means of these identical organs that men commit evil, ignoble, wicked and disreputable deeds so that the body is thoroughly implicated in all the good and all evil that we do in life. Therefore the body must die and perish, but it is not the real self, merely the tenements of clay in which we live, our acts emanating from the inner, immortal part of us which is indestructible and undying.

The bodies or tenements of clay of our departed fellow citizens and officials have left us and laid down their mortality. We believe that in the realms above they shall reap the reward for the good acts and deeds they did during their lifetime.

These faithful public servants whose mortal bodies have put on immortality during the current year are:

Honourable John W. Pearson,
    cleric, educator and statesman.

Honourable Thomas E. Buchanan,
    engineer, builder and statesman.

Honourable Nathaniel V. Massaquoi,
    philosopher, author, orator, educator and statesman.

Honourable J. R. Crayton,
    lawyer, politician and statesman.

Honourable Momo Passawe and Honourable Deh Suah,
    specialists in native customary laws, legislators and statesmen.

Honourable Kedrick W. Brown,
    specialist in fiscal affairs and churchman.

Rev. Dr. Samuel D. B. Stubblefield,
    cleric and agriculturist.

Dr. Allen Burlic,
    physician and good samaritan.

Prof. Thomas F. Howard,
    educator, director of physical education.

Mr. John B. Delamey,
    merchant and soldier.

Prof. Howard B. Hayes,
    genius, accomplished musician and composer.

Mrs. I. K. Ferguson, Harriet A. Bailey, Eliza Writ and Yaidah,
    octogenarians.

Paramount Chiefs Boimah, Getombo, and Choami,
    statesmen and experts in tribal customary law.

Honourable J. T. H. Rose,
    administrator and agriculturist.

Mrs. Laura C. Woodson, Rose P. Cummings, J. Bunduka and Messrs.
P. O. Symboe, Isaac Fletcher and J. B. Kollie,
    school teachers.

Mrs. Sarah Horace,
  organizer and politician.

Mrs. Isabella W. Bruce-Gibson and Gertrude J. P. Greaves,
  mothers and devoted wives.
  and
  a number of prominent citizens, junior officials and soldiers.

Their earthly labours are ended; their tasks, sacrifices and duties for country, church and family well performed; may their eternal rest in silence be sweet and glorious.

May God, the Creator of all things, Who holds the rise and destiny of nations in His Hands, and whose Will all nature obeys, extend His protecting love, compassion and mercy toward this nation and its people, preserve and defend it and give to all nations of the world peace, unity and concord.

Independence Day Message
Monrovia, 26 July 1963

> *We endeavoured to fashion our hopes and ambitions around a free democracy, and not once has the body of the people, or any appreciable portion of it, felt the urge for any other form of government.*

> *Let everyone practise the gospel of hard and productive labour.*

Introductory Note

On the 116th anniversary of Liberia's independence, President Tubman's reflections on the period of calm and stability which exists in Liberia are an indication of the *status quo*. He further contemplates future expectations that *status quo* could bring. Independence Day is also an occasion when the citizens of Liberia are exhorted by new challenges for the greater development of their country, for, unlike the history of the development of many parts of our world, the inspiration and incentive given to Liberians to reach greater heights for their nation's advancement must come from within, and from their own recognition of their nation's needs. President Tubman often provides this inspiration in the guise of challenges. In 1963 he called upon them to engage in hard work and productive labour through the application of new scientific techniques and methods which have made other nations productive.

Monrovia, 26 July 1963

ONE HUNDRED and sixteen years in time, toil and planning; 116 years of anxieties, joys, felicities, woes, sorrows, sickness, death and life comprise the 116 years of nationhood of Liberia, the founding of which we celebrate to-day.

One hundred and sixteen years ago, the Founding Fathers designed a tapestry as the national fabric out of which this Lone Star State was to be made. Into it they put their dreams and aspirations; for it they built their hopes and because of it they laboured and endured bitterness and isolation at tremendous risks and costs to themselves. They underwent privations, endured physical sufferings, made great sacrifices in blood, and, when necessary, chose to eat the husk of swine, and even face death rather than surrender their freedom, sovereignty and autonomy.

In reviewing some of the difficulties which the early settlers experienced in their building of this nation, it is necessary to remember the warm and hospitable manner in which they were received when they first set foot on what is now Liberia. In the course of time the bonds between brothers and people of African descent would have been strengthened, misunderstandings resolved and a new nation formed without any of the costly sacrifices

which the pioneers and kinsmen underwent in internecine wars for
supremacy. But the indigenous population, becoming suspicious of their
new brethren, whom they began to regard as intruders, started to vacillate
in their attitude and policies.

The significant fact must be remembered that the early settlers who came
here, and the chiefs they met here, founded this nation together, thoroughly
convinced of the racial oneness and affinity between them. This fact was
borne out by an incident which occurred during the landing of the first
settlers who arrived in Maryland County. As one Anthony Woods jumped
from the boat to the land with a cutlass in his hand and began to cut bush,
some of the chiefs recognized him and embraced him exclaiming: 'this is one
of our sons who were taken away from us!'

In the organization of the new state, therefore, the pioneers did not undertake to seize any territories, but made concessions by 'honourable purchase'.
They negotiated for these territories with the Chiefs and tribal authorities,
and obtained deeds of cession which transferred the title not to the settlers
themselves as such, but to the new nation which was to be founded and in
which the indigenous people were to be equal partners. This act was followed
by another concession in the Declaration of Independence, in which the
tribal people were referred to as 'Lords of the Soil'. Thus, together the
settlers and their kinsmen were to build a nation, the Lone Star State of
Africa, wherein not only the tribal peoples and the settlers would have a
home, but all peoples of African descent.

On this anniversary observance, we do well to give thanks to the God of
Nations that their labours have not been in vain. Succeeding generations of
men and women have, through more than a century of nationhood, continued to carry on the tradition of the love of liberty by perseverance, hard
work, patriotism and a fierce determination to rear a yet nobler citadel than
that which was handed down to them.

In the history of social evolution, the goals which men set for themselves
and the ways and means by which they achieve them, have more or less
helped to shape their destiny. Our Declaration of Independence, the Constitution of the nation and the varied programmes which have been enunciated
over the years, give expression to our hopes and aspirations and contain the
structure of our preferred form of government. Thus have we endeavoured to
fashion our hopes and ambitions around a system of free democracy, and not
once has the body of the people, or any appreciable portion of it, felt the
urge for any other form of government. We have kept faith with those who
laboured to lay the foundations of democracy and who cherished the
hope that their posterity would maintain and perpetuate the sacred heritage
for which they gave so much. Nevertheless, we recognize the inherent right of
every nation to pursue and adopt that form of government which it feels will
best contribute to the safety and happiness of its people.

The democratic form of government which this nation adopted and whose
ideals we grappled to ourselves with hoops of steel has been predominantly
satisfying and has served our human and political interests. But new times
demand new changes, and never in the history of the world in general and of
our nation in particular have we faced so many new and grave challenges
than at present. Feeling that our democracy needed to be broadened, enlarged and perfected upon the principle of inclusion, the Government undertook to provide a more genuine and intrinsic form of social democracy by

making available opportunities for education and training on the basis of ability and merit, regardless of clan, class or tribe. In the practical application of the theory of economic democracy, the Government has endeavoured, in the creation of more opportunities of work, to abolish the glaring imbalance between the haves and the have-nots.

It has been the concern of this Government to do everything possible to round off this trinity of ideals in strengthening our political concepts, in the implementation of our social ideals, and in the realization of an economic upsurge which, when combined, would bring us safety, happiness and prosperity. The attainment of these objectives will make our struggles significant.

In recent years, no single political event has had such a resounding impact on the international scene as the liberation of Africa and the flowering into nationhood of so many independent and sovereign states. Perhaps a section of the history of African nationalism will be given over to exploding myths and dissipating old prejudices and misguided conceptions. Meanwhile, for those who were oppressed in Africa and other parts of the world, and who now have a new birth of freedom, there has been born a passion for the implementation of nationalism and with it a bold determination to keep the light of liberty forever burning on our continent. They are pushing ahead to the newer and higher levels which political freedom implies, and which human aspirations, ambition and endeavours can bestow. Not by their might alone, but by the maturity of the historical process, by the knowledge and reality of the conviction that all men are born free and endowed with certain inalienable rights, and by the practical benefits derived from pricking the moral conscience of the civilized world, can these be achieved.

The ideals of the United Nations and the work of its Specialized Agencies can no longer be regarded as highly impracticable or inopportune. Time and time again in the course of its almost two decades of life, it has vindicated its rôle as a veritable bridge between political idealism and practical realism, as the healer of the ills of nations, the guarantor of the fundamental rights of nations and the arbitrator in cases of armed conflict for supremacy between member states. The work of this international institution must be carried on at any cost at a time like this when world ideals and international actions are both desirable and imperative.

We know that it has taken centuries for the basic ideals of international law and procedure to develop and gain universal acceptance. In a similar vein, we of the present must assume our share of the moral, political, and social responsibility for the acceptance and absorption of some of the principles of international law, procedure and regulations in order to meet the changes and challenges which have taken place, and are still taking place, not only in Africa, but in Asia and other areas where millions of people once held in subjugation now enjoy political and social freedom and the rights of citizenship.

On the one hand, there may exist varying degrees of bitterness and resentment among peoples who have experienced the horrors of oppression, received shameful humiliations, and endured painful deprivations. On the other hand, it may not be easy to relinquish the rôle of master or abandon the *status quo*. But while human nature may preponderate, it is necessary for us to reflect that the interdependence of peoples is a present-day imperative. Certainly the injustices of the past may not fade away immediately, but time will obliterate the hard feelings and thus prepare the stage for re-adjustments in a world where to be isolated is indefensible.

During the recent Addis Ababa Conference of the Heads of African States, the ardent, sincere and untarnished desire of the African States to unite and work for peace, enabled us to reach agreement on a design for unity, to discover a formula for settling disputes, and to make provision for various arbitration Councils in the Charter which finally emerged. From our contacts and discussions together we were convinced that it is only when men and nations are sincere in what they profess, that they can easily reach agreement on fundamental issues, and subsequently work and persevere to implement and keep such agreements inviolate. This was the spirit which permeated the Conference at Addis Ababa.

But the Charter of African Unity is just the beginning. Herculean tasks remain to be accomplished. The needs of our own times and the demands imposed by the liberation of the majority of Africa's independent states, will prod and spur us on to the fulfilment and implementation of our political aspirations, and the realization of our economic, social and cultural responsibilities. Hereafter the Addis Ababa Conference will be a perpetual symbol of the culmination of a strong will to unite, and thereby strengthen the basis of our unity for concerted action. This Conference was, for all Africans, a rededication to the principles of unity in diversity, and to our determination to experiment on a continental basis.

In the enactment of the law which provided for a review of the political subdivisions of the country into counties, thereby abolishing the former dichotomy of jurisdictions, a great social and political revolution is taking place in the history of the nation. This significant step will give a greater rationality to the unification policy, and make for a more realistic approach to our political ideals. While it has taken a long time for this major step to be undertaken, due to pre-occupation with the struggle for survival and the demands in other necessary areas of development, which received priority consideration, coupled with the limited financial resources at that time, knowledge of necessity of this step and plans for its implementation have been part of the unscheduled programme. The time at length arrived when we felt that the historic hour had struck, and so we launched out on another political enterprise. Happily, the 1964 Independence Celebration, the first in the new administration, will see this act of the Legislature implemented, and the whole nation will celebrate the historic occasion.

Fellow citizens, it has again fallen to our lot in this generation to be the instrument whereby another milestone has been achieved in our nation's history. We are proud and grateful, and feel obligated to the people of the nation who have so consistently and loyally followed with understanding and supported the policies which were enunciated from time to time for the general welfare of the nation. May the future be always characterized by mutual understanding, and add to the enrichment of the spirit of devotion to duty in the interest of our expanding and growing nation.

In my remarks on the day of our arrival from Europe, I outlined some of the economic policies of the new administration. The root of the proposals is: hard work and productive labour. As a nation acquainted with the histories of great capitalistic countries, it is no secret to us that there is no magical or royal road to a nation's productive capacities and development. 'By the sweat of they brow shalt thou eat bread' is as true and imperative today as it was when it was first decreed by the Divine as a curse against man for his sins.

But labour must be construed to mean know-how, reinforced by a deep inner conviction of the necessity for the type of labour which accelerates development and provides a continuing support for progress. Let the gospel of labour become a national obsession and let it be preached from the pulpits of the nation, proclaimed in city and town halls, in the market places and on the streets; let it be recited around the family hearths, in the schools, colleges and universities until old and young, rich and poor are convinced that labour is the secret of our national stability and the only safeguard of our economic democracy. Let everyone practise the gospel of hard and productive labour.

The immense changes wrought by science and technology have given us a vision of dazzling vistas in terms of comfort and happiness. The wonder of mass production, the miracles of applied science and the tapping of nuclear energy have created for us a new world, and despite the fact that each generation must make its own struggle within the microcosm of its own problems, we face possibilities of a brighter era than was ever within the conception of our ancestors.

For us in Liberia the growing of rice, cassavas, yams, corn, the preparation of coffee, palm kernels, piassava and other products, in ways used over a hundred years ago, are an anachronism. The productive age of which we speak and which we envisage, is one in which the marvels of science must be harnessed to increase our productivity and thus satisfy our human needs.

In our continuing struggle to gain political stability, economic freedom and social progress, we have been greatly encouraged and materially assisted by friendly nations. On this Independence Day when we pledge anew our allegiance to our nation, we remember with gratitude all friendly nations and governments that assisted us first in our five-year plan and later in our nine-year plan by loans and grants for development purposes, and which opened the doors of their universities and technical institutions to our citizens for advanced specialized education and professional training. Foremost among these nations has been the United States of America. The granting of local and foreign scholarships, the awarding of fellowships and the provision for on-the-job training as well as the convening of seminars, have all helped to increase very substantially the efficiency and productivity of our citizens, which fact recalls to my mind the Chinese proverb: 'If you give a man a fish you feed him for two days, but if you teach him how to fish, you give him food forever.'

To the people of Liberia who have given unswerving support for about twenty years now, to our administration's policies (policies which we felt were necessary for progress and development), we express and extend our deep sense of gratitude. If these policies have brought political, economic and social advancement, it is because of your understanding, loyalty and willingness to comprehend the great issues which bind brother to brother in a nation, and nation to nation in the realm of international affairs. Of great importance has been your attitude of giving for the expansion of religious education in our nation. By turning again and again to the spiritual foundations of our democracy and by a deepening of our conviction that this is a nation under God, we seek indeed to be truly free, and in being truly free, we shall keep faith with our ancestors in their hopes and dreams, and by the labours of our hands Liberia will always remain a land of liberty by God's command.

For the past twelve days the world has been tuned in to Moscow with anxious anticipation, hopes, fears and yearning, as negotiations and discussions were being conducted in an effort to find a practical solution for concluding an agreement for the banning of nuclear tests.

On the eve of this 116th anniversary of our independence the echo resounded around the world of the announcement that the United States, Great Britian and the Soviet Union had reached agreement to ban all except underground nuclear tests. Mankind's optimism immediately returned and a ray of hope burst through the erstwhile dismal clouds which enshrouded the world.

We are happy that sanity has prevailed, evidenced by this agreement, and that it may not be said of this generation of Americans, Britons and Russians, that the world suffered from the perils of their lust for power or expediency. We salute and congratulate the United States, the Soviet Union and Great Britain for this epoch-making agreement, and I ask the American and British Ambassadors to be good enough to convey to President Kennedy and Prime Minister MacMillan respectively, and direct the Acting Secretary of State to convey to Premier Khruschev, the congratulations of the Liberian Government and people for the action taken in Moscow in reaching agreement to virtually ban nuclear tests. It is our hope that this agreement will become the nucleus for closer co-operation between East and West, and all nations of the earth, will lead to the abolition of the cold war, and will result in the solution of other problems involved in the tense international situation that has prevailed for almost two decades.

Mr. Doyen and gentlemen of the Diplomatic Corps, I extend to you our deep appreciation for your most cordial expressions of goodwill and friendship which you have so generously made concerning our nation, its people and us. I request that each of you, your Excellencies, be good enough to convey to your respective Chiefs of State and Governments our renewed assurances of friendship, goodwill, mutual understanding and co-operation. As our relations in the past have been cordial and harmonious, may they thus continue in ever increasing measure in the future, and may God shower upon all of us His bountiful blessings of peace, happiness and prosperity.

I recognize and extend felicitations to His Excellency the Foreign Minister of China.

Ladies and gentlemen, I offer you the health of the sovereigns, governments and peoples of the nations represented near this capital.

Fourth Annual Message delivered before the First Session of the Forty-fifth Legislature

Monrovia, 23 December 1963

We still hold the favour, respect and admiration of the people of our country.

Introductory Note

An imminent threat of nuclear holocaust hung over the world and a pall was cast over the peace of the world with the untimely passing away of a great man of peace, John F. Kennedy, thirty-sixth President of the United States of America. The interest of this world-renowned leader in our country was evidenced in his aid to our national industrial development programme in the construction of the Mount Coffee Hydro-Electric Plant. The President recommended for enactment by our Legislature the creation of new administrative posts in the Government, among them the positions of Special Assistant to the President and Under Secretary of State for Administration in the Department of State. The title of the Department of Interior was recommended to be changed to the Department of Internal Affairs, and a National Youth Bureau was to be created. The Copyright Act of 1911 was recommended for revision to provide for copyright privileges for the Library in the Department of Information and Cultural Affairs and the University of Liberia.

Monrovia, 23 December 1963

BY THE unbounded grace and mercies of God, extended to us through the propitiating advocacy of our Blessed Redeemer Jesus Christ, together with the unparalleled and undeserving preferment, support and spontaneous political generosity and affection of the people of the nation, I am privileged to appear before you in Joint Convention for the twentieth successive year to make the Annual Report required by the Constitution on the operation and administration of Government.

Twenty years, and we still seem to hold the favour, respect and admiration of the body of the people of our country; twenty years, and there is still a reasonable measure of prosperity, higher standards of living and a growing economy; twenty years of manifest loyalty, devotion, some political intrigues, disloyalties and disappointments; twenty years of successful planning and execution of these plans, correct decisions and judgments together with some mistakes and errors in judgment; and there still appears to be considerable progress, peace, unity and co-ordinated understanding throughout the country.

For all these we rejoice, give thanks and praise to God the all merciful and pray that His bountiful loving-kindness and tender mercies will continue to be extended to us in the present and future as in the past, and that the abiding presence of the Holy Spirit will remain with us as our guide, protector and defender. To the people we owe a most profound and lasting debt of gratitude for the manifestation of their consistent and continuous confidence and affection.

No man can but be completely overwhelmed and utterly subdued by the rare and extraordinary consideration which has come to us through the kind, staunch and continued support of the citizenry of this land. That we have not considered ourselves deserving of the many kindnesses, constant solicitude and consistent loyalty and devotion of our constituency is a fact which we have made known many times, both in private and in public. With utter reliance on God's unfailing grace and the strong and popular support you have given us, we have, through the years, tried to devote our best endeavours to the execution of the supreme responsibilities of the office you have entrusted to our care.

SOME WORLD EVENTS

During the year events of grave significance have rocked the globe, but due to the patience, sober understanding, realistic attitude and action of world leaders the unleashing of a global nuclear holocaust has been averted. Tensions still exist, it is true, but the negotiation and conclusion of a Partial Nuclear Test Ban Treaty between the Nuclear Powers has contributed to some extent to an improvement to the international climate. We reacted promptly to this new advance towards disarmament and became a signatory to the Instrument. Their Excellencies S. Edward Peal, George T. Brewer and J. Dudley Lawrence were accredited as our Special Plenipotentiaries to sign the Treaty on behalf of the Government in Washington, D.C., London and Moscow on August 8, 16 and 27 respectively. This agreement seems to have brought a gleam of hope in international relations, and may be considered the first stone in the foundation of what could become a formidable and impregnable superstructure of universal peace and understanding.

FOREIGN RELATIONS

In the general area of international relations we have maintained cordial and friendly relationship with member states of the United Nations, particularly those having diplomatic representation near this capital. In the general area of international understanding, while striving to make our stand known and maintaining our unwavering support of the fundamental human rights, we have at the same time, shown respect for the inherent right of all men to pursue the path considered by them best suited to the achievement of their political and social aims and aspirations, without outside interference or molestation.

FOREIGN VISITS

An important investment in the development of good human relations is the exchange of visits between heads of states and governments. These contacts have already been instrumental in improving understanding and engendering goodwill and mutual confidence, as well as substantially strengthening existing bonds of friendship.

It was thus that upon the invitation of His Imperial Majesty, Emperor Hailé Selassié I of Ethiopia, Mrs. Tubman and I left Liberia in May and flew to Addis Ababa arriving on the morning of the 15th instant for a State Visit.

The receptions, courtesies and hospitality extended to us during this visit were reported in our address to the nation upon our return.

The Summit Conference in Addis Ababa commenced two days after the State Visit ended, and it was our privilege to attend that historic meeting. This was the largest Conference ever convoked on the African Continent, and the atmosphere of calm and friendliness which prevailed throughout the session, the positive results achieved for African Unity and World Peace, and the new hope it raised in the hearts of all Africans made it not only significant but also historic. In addition to the Charter of African Unity which emerged at the end of the Conference, one great test has been met and overcome. I refer to the unfortunate boundary dispute which erupted into a border skirmish between Algeria and Morocco. Happily, with the timely intervention of Emperor Hailé Selassié I of Ethiopia and President Modibo Keita of Mali, and a subsequent meeting of the Foreign Ministers of member states, the situation was handled in keeping with the terms of reference of the Charter of the Organization. We therefore look with optimism to the future effectiveness of this Organization as a medium for the development, progress, peace and stability of Africa.

Upon invitations extended by Their Excellencies President Tito of Yugoslavia, President Scharf of Austria and President Habib Bourguiba of the Republic of Tunisia, Mrs. Tubman and I visited the Federal Republic of Yugoslavia and Austria in June and I visited the Republic of Tunisia, Mrs. Tubman being unable to accompany me, from September 30 to October 3.

The warmth of the receptions and hospitality accorded us on these visits were also reported in our address to the nation upon our return.

During the year we had the honour and pleasure of visits from three Heads of States, two Heads of Governments and other officials. His Excellency President Houphouet-Boigny and Mrs. Boigny of the Ivory Coast, and the President of the Federal Republic of Yugoslavia and Mrs. Broz made one-day stop-overs in Monrovia during August and September respectively, and in December the President of the Republic of the Phillipines and Mrs. Macapagal paid a State Visit to Liberia. His Excellency Ahmed Ben Bella, then Prime Minister of Algeria and His Excellency Dr. Hastings Banda, Prime Minister of Nyasaland, also visited Liberia in August and September. The usual warm and cordial feelings attended the visits and official receptions were accorded these State Visitors.

AN OUTSTANDING WORLD STATESMAN IS SLAIN

'Tell it not in Gath, publish it not in the streets of Askelon' that on November 22 a great tragedy struck the nations of the earth, from east to west, from north to south, and the peoples of the world stood aghast and bowed their heads in grief and sorrow, for John F. Kennedy, President of the United States, the embodiment of courage while serving his nation and the underprivileged people thereof, as well as the oppressed and down-trodden peoples of the earth, was viciously shot dead while he sought to forge additional links of friendship with the people of his native land. 'Tell it not in Gath, publish it not in the streets of Askelon' lest the deep, dark turpitude implicit in this vile act strengthen the arm of the enemy of the inherent right and privilege of all men to be equally free and independent.

Two of the last acts of the late President Kennedy towards the development programme of Liberia were the granting of authorization for the conclusion of agreements between United States financial agencies and the Liberian Government for the construction of a Medical Centre in Monrovia, at a cost of six million dollars, and the erection of a Hydro-Electric Plant at Mount Coffee, estimated at a cost of twenty-seven million two hundred thousand dollars, with a grace period of ten years, an amortization period of forty years, and an interest rate of three fourths of one per cent.

As a negligible and inadequate expression of the gratitude of the Government and people of Liberia to the memory of the late President John F. Kennedy of the United States, and as an indication of the obligation of our Government and people to the Government of the United States for these generous loans, conditions and provisions, I recommend that the Medical Centre be known and called the John F. Kennedy Memorial Medical Centre.

PEACE CORPS

The number of Peace Corps personnel rendering assistance in education and other fields of governmental activities in Liberia has been increased, and we are generally impressed with their approach, attitude and behaviour. As far as we have discerned and been able to gather, they appear to be sincerely interested in their work; they are not imbued with the complexes or ideas to be found in some of the personnel of other foreign agencies; they appear to have a simple desire to render service in the field for which they have volunteered and it is my belief that the Peace Corps is doing as much as any other foreign agency to create friendly relationships between its government and other governments.

INTERNAL AFFAIRS

For implementation of the several acts passed by you at your last session directing the creation of four additional counties out of the three provinces, we have taken the first step by ordering special elections to be held throughout the respective sections of the country on the first Tuesday in May, 1964, for the election of senators and representatives for each of these counties, in conformity with the provisions of the Constitution appertaining thereto.

We plan to take the next step in the organization of these counties by the appointment and qualification of superintendents on July 26, 1964, after the election of senators and representatives, and the appointment of other county officials we hope to effectuate towards the end of July or the beginning of August.

Because of the Unification Policy and the desire to unify the country, it appears appropriate that the titles 'Department of the Interior and Secretary of the Interior' be abrogated and substituted by: 'The Department of Internal Affairs' and 'Secretary of Internal Affairs' respectively.

A Treasury report reveals that it was realized late last year that the Government would face serious balance of payments and financial difficulties during the next few years, due mainly to the fall in the world price of Liberia's principal exports. Since this situation would affect the revenues of the country, the Government sought to re-adjust maturities of its external debt.

Accordingly, several procedures were undertaken in this direction: Firstly, the Government approached the International Monetary Fund to assist in a review of its critical financial position, help determine financial prospects and advise on necessary steps to meet the crisis. Secondly, it was decided to refrain from undertaking any new commitment which would have maturities of less than fifteen years, any major agreement not subject to bidding, or to obtain loans for any projects which did not have developmental priorities; thirdly, it was agreed that expenditures other than debt repayments be reduced by approximately ten per cent as compared to the budget approved by the Legislature; fourthly, to raise additional revenues, two measures were introduced – (a) the enforcement of existing collections and (b) the search for and development of new sources of revenue. To facilitate enforcement of tax laws a Tax Court was established and the services of a British auditing firm obtained to assist in the analysis and auditing of tax returns.

With such measures taken, the Government applied to the International Monetary Fund and subsequently signed an agreement on June 1, 1963, for a stand-by credit of 5·7 million dollars. This agreement assisted the Government considerably in the successful negotiations of the resettlement plan of debt with various creditors.

There can be no doubt, therefore, that the Government has emerged from the financial crisis strengthened in many ways. Further proof of this is revealed in the fact that revenues for the calendar year 1963 will be about three million dollars higher than those for the previous year.

Income for the fiscal period October 1, 1962 to September 30, 1963 was $36,154,694.87 as compared to $36,093,262.16 for the preceding period which indicates an increase of $61,432.71. The Financial Adviser considers this to be in sharp contrast to the amount of increase of the fiscal year 1962 over 1961 which was 3·4 million dollars.

The Bureau of General Accounting reports that Government's total expenditures for the fiscal period were $46,340,831.59, which figure includes the Export-Import Bank Power Project payment of $1,683,324.21.

The total budget for the calendar year as approved by the Legislature was $50,470,348.88. However, because of the introduction of the Government's austerity programme, total expenditures during the period January-September 1963 were kept down to $31,243,924.27. From the original 1963 Budget, the unexpended balance is $19,226,424.61; total allotments and expenditures other than debt service for the fourth quarter amounted to 7·2 million dollars. Consequently, there should be a total saving at the end of the year of approximately $12,000,000.00 from the budget as originally prepared.

If the anticipated debt service payments up to the end of 1963 are included, expenditures during the year will be roughly 42·1 million dollars as against an income of approximately 38·5 million dollars. The deficit of 3·5 million dollars will be met by drawings under the stand-by arrangements with the International Monetary Fund.

At the close of the last administration in 1959 total revenues collected were $24,552,443.40 and now in 1963 at the close of the present administration total revenues have increased to $38,500,000.00, which indicates an improvement in the revenue and financial position of Government since the coming-in of the present administration in 1960.

LIBERIAN STOCK MARKET

The Secretary of the Treasury states, that in view of the issuance and sale of stock by various corporations and the expected expansion of participation in equity ownership and the flotation of Government bonds thoughout the country, it is necessary that legislation be made to safeguard the investors. To effectuate this, the Secretary invites the support of all agencies of Government and private institutions.

DEVELOPMENT BANK OF LIBERIA

Negotiations for the Development Bank of Liberia suffered set-backs during the course of the year, according to the Secretary of the Treasury, so that the reorganization of the Bank now necessitates further changes in the charter. He states that negotiations are now under way with the United States Agency for International Development to supply top management for the initial period of the Bank's operation.

AUSTERITY

We enter 1964 still faced with a difficult economic and financial situation.

Our position may be compared to an army forced to adopt a defensive position. Earlier this year I explained to you the combination of circumstances that forced us to adopt stringent measures of financial control, and to enforce measures of austerity. Again, like any army on the defensive, our first duty and responsibility must be to ensure the success of our defences, and we are determined to do this.

First, we must live within our available financial resources. No one owes us a living, and our first duty is to do everything we can to help ourselves.

By this means we shall achieve our second objective which is to adhere rigidly to the financial plans worked out in co-operation with the International Monetary Fund.

This, in turn, will permit us to achieve our third objective, which is to honour our obligations to other governments, international institutions, and others who have loaned us money.

Like any Commander-in-Chief of an army I must talk to you frankly, and give you my confidence. Only by this means can leadership be effective, and the people of Liberia — who make up the Army — be expected to give of their best.

It is apparent that for some time to come, while circumstances force us to be on the defensive, there can be no alternative to a policy of austerity, and rigid financial control. For all of us, this must mean hardship in some degree, and postponement of some of the things that, as a Government, and as individuals, we should have liked to do. However, there is no escape from this situation if our defences are to be made secure. There are no easy answers and no quick solutions. But if our defences are made secure, we shall ensure the financial stability of our country, our international reputation will be preserved – indeed, our determination can enhance our international standing – as well as ensure that the savings of our people are protected.

An essential feature of our defences is our determination to adhere to the U.S. dollar as our currency, as it is our best insurance against inflation and for protecting our financial stability.

No army wins battles by remaining on the defensive. Therefore our strategy must be to get on the offensive as soon as possible. At a minimum, that means making every effort to maintain the momentum of development which has transformed the economy of Liberia in the past decade. For obvious reasons this will not be easy, but it can be done. Indeed, we hope that we shall be able to do even more, and as a result of real offensive over the entire field of development, we shall create greater opportunities for employment, better conditions for education and training, and, above all, continue to strive in our efforts to provide a better way of life for all.

It is appropriate to ask here, 'What is the purpose of this great effort to develop our country?' The answer is simple. By developing our country, we shall provide the resources to enable us to abolish poverty and illiteracy wherever they exist, to eliminate ill health and malnutrition, to provide shelter for all, and to ensure that our children shall go forward into a new world with equal opportunities available for them all.

This must be the fundamental objective for all of us, and as long as I am spared to be the Commander-in-Chief of your army, it will be the task to which, above all else, I shall devote myself. I should ask for no better memorial, than that the new generation of our boys and girls should enter a world in which they would fully participate as citizens as well educated and healthy in mind and body as youths from any other part of the world.

It may well be asked – 'How can we best set about achieving that absolute goal?' The first answer to that question must be that it is essential for us to have a clear cut plan of action. Hence our first task will be to produce a Five-Year Plan as quickly as possible. We do not expect to produce a perfect plan at once. Under present circumstances it will be better to produce a good, general plan, and to refine it as we go along, than to spend a long period doing nothing but preparing a perfect theoretical plan.

In this Five-Year Plan, 'Operation Production' must occupy a central position. Nothing is more important than that we should become self-sufficient, particularly in our food requirements, and export more than we import.

MONETARY FUND

The International Monetary Fund Mission which recently visited Monrovia on an inspection, as well as its representative assigned to the Government, have complimented and congratulated us upon the execution of the first phase of the standby agreement between the Fund and Government, and also for adhering to an austerity programme which has been instrumental in keeping expenditure down, and have intimated that strict adherence to the present policy will result in our experiencing a possible shorter period of economic difficulties. It is therefore imperative that we continue to persist in pursuing the strictest economy as an austerity measure.

OPERATION PRODUCTION

Upon my return from a European visit on July 13, I declared to the Nation
the policy which is to underscore our plan for a Five-Year Development
Programme — OPERATION PRODUCTION. Since that time, I have on different
occasions elaborated, emphasized, explained and stressed the importance of
such a national policy and indicated Government's concern for its vigorous
and speedy implementation.

It is worth noting the degree to which Liberians and some foreign residents
have reacted to the serious note of this policy and resolved to do something
about increasing national production. We shall continue to push this programme in every way until every man, woman, boy and girl has adopted it
as a personal responsibility which he or she owes to the nation's development; until everyone is acting in conformity with the national challenge and
obligation, and until practical results begin to be reaped in every city, town,
village, hamlet and household. Operation Production must be the national
priority number one programme in our Five-Year Plan of development.

The fact is inescapable that we must produce to survive; we must produce
to equal and excel our neighbours; we must produce to keep ourselves in the
race of the rapidly expanding African economy and the highly competitive
world market; we must produce and thereby open up new avenues and
create new opportunities for jobs which will help to improve our living
standards; we must learn to produce because it is the prerogative of a free
people in a free society.

In the industrial sector, we hope to prepare projects which will attract
local and foreign investment from both private and governmental sources.
We shall continue to adhere to the Unification and Open Door Policies, and
once more emphasize that these policies will always be based on the maintenance of a strong currency, and the preservation of financial stability.

As to infrastructure, we expect shortly to commence construction of the
Mount Coffee hydro-electric project, a scheme in which we have enjoyed
the fullest co-operation and support of the Government of the United States.
We are hopeful, too, that current negotiations with the International Bank
for reconstruction and development will be successful, and thus permit us to
embark on further road construction.

Nor do we forget the rôle of industries already established in Liberia. We
acknowledge the contribution that they have made to our economy in the
past, and feel confident that they will do more in the future.

These are the broad lines of the strategy by which we hope that it will be
possible for us to resume our offensive in the field of national development.
As the year ebbs and the new year comes, these tactical details will be
elaborated, so that each and every one of us may know what is expected of
him, and thus provide the opportunity of meeting the challenge.

THE EXECUTIVE MANSION

The Executive Mansion has been virtually completed and we hope to dedicate and move into it on the third of January, 1964. In my last Annual
Message I pointed out that the cost of this building had got out of hand and
that we ourselves felt it was too costly a building for a nation such as ours,
with the limited resources at our disposal. I now reiterate this feeling, but

also declare my belief that after one hundred and seventeen years of independence, the fates and the law of compensation would both seem to have
pre-ordained and justified that there should be such a beautiful, commodious
and imposing permanent edifice to be used not only as residence for Presidents and their families and for the entertainment of visiting dignitaries with
convenience and dignity, but also for the offices and bureaux of the Chief
Executive which were heretofore scattered over the city in six or eight
rented houses, making quick and easy contacts difficult. This is especially so
since it is the first Executive Mansion in the history of the nation that has
been planned and erected for this specific purpose.

It is not generally my propensity to take note of false and notorious statements but I feel obliged to resent and refute, without fear of the possibility of
successful contradiction, allegations that United States grants and aid funds
have been used in the construction of the Mansion; whoever said this made a
mendacious statement, because not a solitary cent of United States or other
foreign aids, grants or loans has gone into this building.

Another deliberate and malevolent assertion that has been expressed is that
the Law Courts building has been erected at a cost of between twenty and
thirty million dollars. This also is a diabolical untruth because the Law
Courts building has cost us less than five million dollars, which statistics will
prove.

We do not mind criticisms and attempts to ridicule us, as we have encountered these during the whole of our national life, but we do object to
deliberate and false representations designedly made against the Government
and people of Liberia by those who profess to be friends, who have enjoyed
our hospitality and consideration, and to whom we have gone all out to
prove our friendship. We cannot and will not continue to submit to this
practice of duplicity, for there is a limit to human endurance.

Foreign governments and international financial agencies have consistently
refused to grant loans for the construction of public buildings in this country;
yet their nationals have criticized the Liberian Government, alleging that all
of our public buildings were rented houses with tin roofs built on the pattern
of the old houses in the deep south of the United States. We were determined
that this condition should be changed, and now that modern public buildings
are rising in the capital and elsewhere throughout the country, they have
turned their criticism in other directions. We would like to make it understood that the type of building this Government shall have is a decision that
rests squarely with it and the Liberian people alone. This devious group must
be negrophobes who do not like black men to have anything decent that
they would have to respect.

Again, because the Government negotiated for the installation of a television unit, the same devious group that expresses no opinion but their own
(since we do not believe that their governments share these attitudes), suggested that if the Liberian Government could afford to produce a television
system she should be required to pay the ten per cent on all loans and other
projects negotiated for, and the consideration of a postponement of these
payments because of present financial difficulties should not be allowed. Be
that as it may, we must make it clear that grants, aids and loans are not like
the wrath of God which can destroy both soul and body, and if such grants
are intended as the golden calf or the brazen serpent set up in the wilderness,
or the golden image set up by King Nebuchadnezzar for all nations and

peoples to bow down to and worship at the sound of the trumpet, sackbut and psaltery, we shall not subscribe to, be led by, nor participate in such idolatry.

We have built the Executive Mansion and it shall be used for the purpose for which it was built; we are building the Law Courts Building, we shall complete it and it shall be used for the purposes for which it is being constructed; we have have negotiated for a television service and it shall be used to the best interest of the nation and its people, anything else to the contrary notwithstanding.

THE SUPREME COURT

The Honourable Supreme Court has had its regular semi-annual sessions during the year, and at those sessions disposed of a record number of criminal and civil cases appearing on the docket of the Court.

The Chief Justice inaugurated a plan of instruction for Justices of the Peace and Magistrates in the performance of their duties and the speedy administration of justice, particularly since they are Courts of first instance and the great majority of the people come in contact with them.

The Supreme Court continues to hold the confidence and respect of the public.

LIBERIA NATIONAL YOUTH ORGANIZATION

I attach great importance to the National Youth Organization and pay special tribute to the Israeli Specialists and the Liberian Director who are rendering a great service to the country by the physical and vocational training being given these youths.

Boys and girls whose energies may have been so mis-directed as to intensify the problem of juvenile delinquency are now being re-orientated, and, through training, will emerge with healthy minds and bodies to take their places in the march of progress towards our common heritage.

As appropriation permits from year to year, we intend to expand this movement throughout the country.

RECOMMENDATIONS

The following measures are projects of law that I will submit and for which I respectfully request your favourable consideration:

1. That the outline of Operation Production as priority number one, advanced by us since your last adjournment be approved and authorization given for its maximum and speedy implementation.
2. That the Vagrancy Act be revised so as to respond to the present-day requirements and needs of the country particularly in respect to the implementation of priority number one Operation Production.
3. That due to the increased nature of work of the Chief Executive there be created in the office of the Chief Executive a position under the style and title 'Special Assistant to the President'.
4. That there be created in the Department of State a position under the style and title 'Under Secretary of State for Administration'.

5. That the title 'Department of the Interior' and 'Secretary of the Interior' be abrogated and substituted by 'The Department of Internal Affairs' and 'Secretary of Internal Affairs' respectively.

6. That the Statute relating to admission of Lawyers to the Bar and the disciplining of Lawyers for malpractice and ungentlemanly conduct should be revised and the provisions thereof vigorously enforced.

7. That Government should authorize the floating of a local bond issue which should be limited to assure full subscription and its income be tax free.

8. That the Investment Code which has been prepared for presentation to you be given due and favourable consideration and be enacted into law.

9. That legislation be enacted to grant Customs Officials authority to ground and detain all aircrafts delinquent in the payment of landing and other fees.

10. That legislation be enacted to require all Courts to furnish the Revenue Service with copies of all probated wills and trust indentures.

11. That the Honourable John E. Dennis, Deputy Postmaster-General, who has attained the age of seventy-five and has served the postal service for fifty-five years, Mrs. Mary Benson McClain, Parcel Post Clerk, who has served for twenty-five years and Mr. Frank G. Cooper, Collector of Customs for Sinoe County, who has attained the age of seventy-one and who has served in the Customs Service for forty-one years, be honourably retired with annuities of fifty per cent of their present salaries.

12. That the postage rates be revised.

13. That the establishment of a special delivery service be inaugurated throughout the country.

14. That to accomplish its primary objectives the work of the Special Commission on Government Operation be extended for another two years.

15. That the Act reorganizing and expanding the Bureau of Mines into the Bureau of National Resources and Surveys approved January 31, 1959 be amended to include a Cadastral Survey, replacing the former Bureau of Lands, Surveys and Titles of the Department of Public Works and Utilities in keeping with Executive Order No. 7 and I recommend that the title of the Chief of the Bureau of Natural Resources and Surveys be changed to 'Director-General'.

16. That legislation be enacted requiring all public land surveyors to submit their field notes after survey of all private and/or public land for checking to the Cadastral Survey before probation of deeds are permitted and that no deeds be offered for probate until a release has been issued by the Cadastral Survey.

17. That the Copyright Act of 1911 be amended to provide copyright privileges for the Library of the Liberian Information Service and the University of Liberia. Such a copyright privilege will make it obligatory under penalty of law for authors of books, pamphlets, booklets, maps, music and all other scientific and artistic literature, newspapers and translations, to deposit one copy in each of the specified Libraries, as part of the copyright procedure.

18. To offset the confusion that has resulted in the contradictory spelling of Liberian geographic names, the Board of Geographic Names be reconstituted to finalize the matter for further action by Government.

19. That there be a National Youth Bureau headed by a Director who will be responsible to the President and a permanent committee be established to consist of the Departments of Education, Defence, Agriculture and National Planning. That the Harrisburg Youth Centre be open as a centralized youth village for vocational training, that state agricultural camps or co-operative villages, be founded by youths and that model farms be established in agricultural areas throughout the country. That the Liberia National Youth Organization be incorporated as a distinct and specialized agency of Government and appropriation be provided for this purpose.

20. That the Debt Law be repealed and a new law appertaining to debt be enacted to provide that should a debtor fail to meet his obligation or repay a debt on due date, after seven days of grace his creditor may enter action against him and may at once move for attachment against his property, real and personal, his credits or income of any kind to the extent of the debt plus fifty per cent; the additional fifty per cent to take care of cost and expenses that may be involved.

All actions of debt shall be heard and determined expeditiously upon the filing of a complaint and an answer; no further pleading shall be necessary. Actions of debt shall be given priority on the dockets of all civil law courts and in the courts of Justices of the Peace and Magistrates.

The jurisdiction of Justices of the Peace and Magistrates in actions of debt shall extend from one cent to two thousand dollars. Upon obtaining judgment against a debtor the creditor may move for execution which shall be granted unless the case is appealed and upon the issuance of an execution in any action of debt the Sheriff, Police or Constable shall be authorized to proceed and attach the lands, goods, chattels, credits or other properties of the debtor and expose same to sale at public auction after publication in one or more newspapers or otherwise giving notice of the aution sale for fifteen days. Should the debtor have no property, or the Sheriff, Police or Constable be unable to find any property, credits or valuables of the debtor capable of being converted into money he shall arrest the debtor and take him before a court that would order his imprisonment in a room or place that shall be provided for the purpose, for a time sufficiently long to cover the debt at the rate of $50.00 a month and the debtor shall be responsible for his own subsistance while in prison.

When a case of debt is tried by a Justice of the Peace or Magistrate and lands are inserted in the Writ of Attachment or Writ of Execution such writ shall be made returnable before a court of record.

HONOURABLE MENTION

There are a number of Ministers and Officials of Government who have rendered outstanding services in their respective positions and I have referred to these officials in several of my statements on various occasions. Now, I pay compliment to these officials and public servants for their outstanding ability in their respective fields of specialization, their patriotism and achievements in the interest of their country, particularly to those who have handled the most delicate and difficult negotiations for the re-setting of our international debts, negotiating the Stand-by Agreement with the Monetary Fund and the inauguration of the Austerity Programme.

OBITUARY

In the realm of human life and existence there is no point where there is such a vast difference to be found as between life and death. In life there is activity, there is action, there is thought, there is invention, there is growth and development. In death there is exactly the reverse; there is inaction, decay, stillness and muteness. Therefore it is recorded that there is hope for a tree if it be cut down that it shall sprout again, but as for man he lies down and dies and rises not again until the heavens shall be no more.

This difference between life and death is apparent even between the city and abode of the living and the city and abode of the dead. Walk along through the streets of the city of Monrovia, or ride around in a car and see the hustle and bustle and activities of those moving up and down, to and fro; hear the sound of music; the ringing of bells, the noise of the city, and walk into the quiet surroundings of our cemetery and witness the stillness of life. And so we ask God's gracious blessings upon the souls of our revered dead.

As in the past we looked to none other for guidance and protection than He who has kept our nation under His wings of loving care. May God continue to prosper the work of our hands.

Fifth Inaugural Address
Monrovia, 6 January 1964

The nation has come a long way since the Policy of Unification was first enunciated. What was perhaps regarded as impracticable, undesirable, or even untimely, has brought great blessings to the country. The time has come when integration should be practised in all phases of our national development.

Our nation's commitment to free enterprise and the Open Door Policy is whole-hearted, emphatic, and enduring.

Introductory Note

By 1964 President Tubman had spent twenty consecutive years as President of Liberia. The nation was in the throes of an austerity period, and in spite of it was called upon to proceed undeterred with its programme of industrialization and social welfare. Out of this address came a Five-Year Development Plan for the execution of the nation's priority number, Operation Production Programme; a Free Trade Area Association with Guinea, Sierra Leone and the Ivory Coast; a telecommunications network linking Liberia with the world; a hydro-electric plant; an increased educational fund drive; a city school system for Monrovia; and the John F. Kennedy Memorial Hospital. The President was further pleased with the success of the Unification and Open Door Policies. A new day dawned in Liberian democracy. Nineteen hundred and sixty-four witnessed the completion of the great task of National Unification.

Monrovia, 6 January 1964

IF THE wealth of treasured memories of the courageous deeds of the founders of our country, the national aims, hopes, aspirations and achievements that our nation represents were an individual responsibility, this solemn and high commission which I have just received by the administration of the constitutional oath of office to which I have just subscribed for the fifth time in succession, would impose obligations and restrictions much too onerous for me to bear or fulfil. But as I have been sustained and strengthened in the past by the strong arms of the Almighty, the examples of enormous strength of character evinced by my stalwart and illustrious predecessors in office, together with the unswerving support and loyalty of many of those who have associated with me through the twenty-year period which passes into history today, as well as the tremendous support of the body of the people of the country, I rejoice in the fact that there has been kept actively alive in the bosoms of the people the burning desire for freedom and liberty and the constant determination to keep its torch forever burning on our shores.

No less reassuring, as the Chief Magistracy of the nation passes from one to another in an orderly and constitutional process, is the satisfaction of the continued maintenance and perpetuation of the same political philosophy which has guided us in our onward march, and in our determination to hand down a better and richer heritage. We remember today with admiration and deep gratitude the sacrifices of love and devotion of all those who, since the birth of this sovereign state, have given themselves to her guidance in political wisdom, wise and unselfish statesmanship and loyal and devoted service – the sung and unsung heroes of the past and present.

You have today, in this memorable, sacred and historic edifice where other Presidents before me have been inaugurated for more than a century, on the very spot where the Constitutional Convention was held and the Declaration of Independence adopted, witnessed the administration of the Oath of Office to your humble and grateful servant for the fifth time as President of this Republic.

That God through His bountiful mercies accorded me a reasonable portion of health and strength to have endured the various and varied rigours implicit in this office, carried on the tremendous responsibilities, and with earnest and honest effort resolved the momentous, viable and difficult problems that have arisen ever and anon, convinces me beyond doubt that your spontaneous and persistent requests for our continued service have been inspired by the will of God. I dare not enter upon the duties of this high and responsible office for a fifth term without exercising my religious freedom by kneeling in an attitude of prayer, and ask those who have no scruples against it to join me in silence:

Great and eternal God, Father of our Lord Jesus Christ, by Whom all things that are were created and made, Thou that art without beginning and without end, that reignest eternal in the Heavens; Thou great God of our Fathers by Whose almighty power and tender mercies the foundation of our nation was laid and whose wisdom and power imbued with knowledge, wisdom and understanding the men and women that bore the toil, endured the pains, made great sacrifices of themselves, their talents and their lives from the incipiency of this nation in 1847 to the present, we give Thee thanks; we adore and praise Thy Holy Name for the blessings which Thou didst vouchsafe to our fathers and all those who assisted in any way towards the founding, perpetuity and growth of our country.

Now, most merciful Father, look down in pity upon Thy humble servant who kneels before Thee in humble humility, meekness and contrition and pray for the forgiveness of the sins and iniquities of our nation, collective and individual that we have committed from time to time against Thy Divine Majesty, provoking most justly Thy wrath and indignation against us, but through the mercies of Thy Son, Jesus Christ, who is the propitiation for our sins we confess, acknowledge and bewail our transgressions and iniquities and earnestly and fervently pray for forgiveness; and that Thou wouldst extend to us Thy sustaining grace to keep us from sin and to improve us in all righteousness and godliness. Great God, we humbly beseech Thee that as Thou didst in the past guide, guard, defend and protect this nation and its people from foes within and without, Thou wilt grant unto us now and hereafter the same merciful kindness and consideration as Thou didst to them and of which we stand in need.

Bless, we humbly beseech Thee, all nations and people of the earth; in a particular manner we invoke Thy Divine help towards those who endured the painful experience of tyranny, deprivation and oppression. Give to them endurance and perseverance in their struggle and fight for liberation and freedom and bring peace, Heavenly Father, to this strife-torn world. Thou, Great God, that wroughtest the reconciliation between God and man we most earnestly pray that Thou will bring reconciliation and understanding between man and man and extend the reign of universal peace upon earth, and we pray that Thou wouldst grant us the ever-abiding presence of the Holy Paraclete.

All this we ask, though unworthily, through the mercies of Thy Son, Jesus Christ Our Lord. Amen.

It is twenty years since we first took office, two decades of varied and varying experiences; periods of peace, co-operation, a measure of prosperity, progress and happiness; also, to a lesser degree, vicissitudes, conspiracies and lately austerity; but we laboured on in the belief that our cause was just and that 'our nation first, and our nation always' was the consuming passion of our life as a public servant. The errors to which the natural sequence of human foibles subject us, have been subordinated to the successes which we hope have accrued to the nation in the broadening and strengthening of our national and international relations, by the peace which has prevailed at home, and the degree of progress and prosperity which has come to us. Having witnessed some of the visible results of our labour during this long and unprecedented period, we approach another administration with the hope that utter reliance upon God and your continued support, loyalty and sacrificial labour will be the instruments through and by which we may carry to completion the plans and policies that we are placing on the trestle board, in the nature of political guide lines and propositions for demonstration and execution.

We cannot ignore the vast transformations which have taken place – the material growth all around us, the many indications of a new life of personal dignity, economic security, political stability and broadened social perspectives. We have indeed entered a new era in which MORE AND BETTER are bound to become catchwords whose impact on our way of life promises to be revolutionary.

And so fellow citizens, let us step boldly and fearlessly into the future with courage, fortititude and indomitable resolve to effectuate policies and projects which will be further attempts to actualize in our society the principles of liberty, equality, justice and progress. Let all Liberians realize that the nation needs their services, so that the world may become convinced of our determination to work hard and conscientiously for the advancement of our country in things political, social, economic, scientific and spiritual.

Let the vision of a new Liberia in a continent of transition be the framework of our national goals and aspirations.

To these ends and to the noble ideals of freedom and democracy I rededicate myself today; I renew my services for the advancement of our common country in all phases of its development; I redirect my efforts to the pursuit of permanent world peace, and I resolve to work towards the realization of greater mutual understanding and friendship with all nations. I dedicate myself anew to serve my God, my country and my fellow men. God helping me, I shall not fail.

FOREIGN POLICY

In the realm of international relations, our policy remains fundamentally the same as that which we advanced in our 1944, 1952, 1956, and 1960 Inaugural Addresses. We have endeavoured to contribute to world attempts at diminishing the causes of war, and we shall continue to pursue such policies as we think will tend to the best interest of the government and people of this country and the cause of world peace.

A large number of African states has gained independence since the enunciation of the international policy outlined in our 1960 Inaugural Address, which has resulted in increased leaders and leader relationships. The contacts between officials of different nations at international conferences, on delegations, missions, councils and at the United Nations have increased understanding and heightened our respect each for the other. As in the past we shall continue to pursue a policy of friendship and comity with all states, particularly member states of the United Nations.

However, as long as the African Continent remains partly free and partly under foreign and minority domination, the fight for total liberation must continue to be waged until the peoples of South Africa and of the Portuguese and other territories in Africa have also achieved the inherent right to self-determination, and until the shackles of tyranny and oppression have been shaken off, and all men stand on the pedestal of freedom, with the right and privilege of exercising the inherent quality of men to conduct their affairs in a manner of their own choosing.

Specifically, it will be the goal of the new administration to advocate and advance an African Co-operation Policy in our foreign relations. We have in the past participated with enthusiasm and some satisfaction in the movement towards African Unity and co-operation which culminated last year in the Conference at Addis Ababa. Our foreign policy remains committed to the success of this endeavour. We are particularly anxious for the generation of greater efforts to achieve closer, more constructive and productive co-operation in the fields of trade, economic development, science, education, health, communications and transportation.

In a specific attempt to maintain the momentum toward African Unity and Co-operation, in recognition of the close historical ties and the common problems which tend to unite our peoples, and in a move to give added assistance to our efforts under Operation Production, I propose the following programme of economic co-operation and association with our neighbours, the Governments of Guinea, Sierra Leone and the Ivory Coast with whom we have contiguous frontiers, in the hope that in the very near future it will serve as the nucleus of a much larger group of co-operating states.

I suggest that negotiations be undertaken as soon as convenient with the Governments of Guinea, Sierra Leone and the Ivory Coast to establish immediately the Guinea-Sierra Leone-Ivory Coast-Liberia Free Trade Area.

Much of what is proposed will mark sharp departures from the past and will serve to blaze new trails. It is our belief that these joint efforts should and will attract the interest, support and participation of other nations, international agencies and private institutions.

THE PARTIAL NUCLEAR TEST BAN TREATY

Our concern for world peace and our willingness to support and contribute to
the success of all attempts designed to secure for mankind the best conditions
of living, made us hail as a forward step the signing of the Partial Nuclear
Test Ban Treaty negotiated and concluded in Moscow by the Governments
of the Union of Socialist Soviet Republics, the United States and Great
Britain. Along with other nations, Liberia became a signatory to this important instrument which, while not a panacea, can be regarded as a significant
approach to the easing of tensions in the world. The Government of Liberia
will continue to give moral and material support to all such endeavours for
peace.

However, we opine that peace can only be expected to dawn and prevail
when men and nations realize that it cannot be attained or achieved by the
sword, nuclear bombs or missiles, but by deliberate, sober and human statesmanship based on the principles of right and justice. Nations and their
leaders must think straight and avoid the odium of a double standard of
diplomacy, one form for display and another for use, and we must in all
earnestness set our hearts and wills completely against war.

INTERNAL AFFAIRS

Unification and Integration — The nation has come a long way since first the
policy of Unification was enunciated. What was perhaps regarded as impracticable, undesirable or even untimely has brought great blessings to the
country.

If, therefore, these concepts have been overworked and overstressed, it is
not only on account of the importance and absolute essentialness which we
attach to them as such, but also because of the benefits which have been and
are still to be derived. We have striven to have them become a part of the
national consciousness and to see their manifestation in the daily life and
activities of the people and nation.

However, it is not for Liberians alone that integration should have a
meaning. For those foreigners within our borders, the time has come when
integration should be practised in all phases of our national development, and
just as Liberians must learn to live and work together in an atmosphere of
mutual respect and equality, so too must the foreign residents learn to
accept Liberians as equals and work and live with them under a government
which gives them protection and which is exerting its endeavours to afford all
citizens and foreign residents equal protection and security under the law.

During this administration, therefore, positive steps will be taken to ensure
that integration takes place at all levels regardless of race, creed or station,
in order to implement realistically and fully the intents and purposes of the
Unification Policy.

The Open Door Policy — Our nation's commitment to free enterprise and
the Open Door Policy is whole-hearted, emphatic and enduring. Already incorporated into our laws, this commitment forms the basis of our economy
and is the foundation upon which our domestic and foreign policies rest.

In this connection we make two bold but reassuring declarations:

(a) We will not nationalize or confiscate private business or private
property.

(b) We are firmly committed to the maintenance of a sound currency and to freedom from currency restriction.

The numerous concessions in the country, the influx of small businesses, and increased trade and commerce attest the extent to which advantage is being taken of the Open Door Policy. It is obvious, however, that this Policy must grow and change in order to evolve with the nation's growth, although it must not be weakened or undermined; and it must be based on mutuality of interests, reciprocity of obligations and benefits. Priority of employment for Liberians must be provided, but we shall insist that Liberians justify that consideration by hard study, conscientious and productive work and the acquisition of competence. Correspondingly, we will continue to protect management from the unreasonable demands of untrained or unproductive labour. However, we shall require management to begin an active training programme at every level of employment.

The end of government being to evolve a better standard of living and to insure the happiness, peace and security of the people in whatever political or economic system obtains in a nation, the socialist governments, reserving for themselves the factors of production, provide all training and other facilities for their people, assuming the dual responsibility of government and management to labour. To attain this end in a free enterprise system such as ours, where the overwhelming portion of the ownership of the factors of production is in private hands, it is the obligation of private enterprise and business to assume this responsibility and Government will require management to provide the facilities implied with such ownership to supplement and complement those provided by Government.

In our efforts to improve public administration, to plan for the future, and to insure enforcement of tax and other legislations, our agencies will request information and co-operation from private business, both foreign and Liberian. We expect all those who have prospered with us during the years of affluence, profits and gain, to contribute and share in times of adversity and austerity.

Although we must continue to encourage additional large, multi-million dollar investments, we must recognize that there are important areas of investments barely touched, which could be equally beneficial to our economy in the long run — the manufacture of products and materials consumed by these great enterprises, the provision of services required, the substitution of Liberian products for imported goods — foods and manufactured supplies. Here we must attract investors with expert knowledge and experience, but perhaps with less capital to invest.

The encouragement and growth of such investment is one of the central goals of Operation Production. It is our desire and intention that all the appropriate resources of the nation be concentrated on this programme, and to this end, I am directing that the following steps be taken:

First, that the appropriate authorities complete for immediate adoption an Investment Code which should reflect, in the concessionary rights envisaged, the priorities established under Operation Production.

To attract small investors (both Liberian and foreign) the code should be aimed at clearly establishing priorities, eliminating any confusion of authority and ensuring the speedy and expeditious conclusion of agreements with Government.

Second, I propose that anti-dumping legislation be drafted and adopted so as to protect Liberian industry from unfair competition and predatory practices.

We especially want this legislation to reflect the fact that most Liberian production must be based upon sales to the large enterprises here. While we must oppose any practice or policy which would increase the production costs of big business or hamper their ability to compete in world markets, it is our express intention that Liberian products should enjoy every protection and advantage which Government can provide.

Next, as a part of our overall policy of African Co-operation, particularly economic co-operation, we will strive to negotiate bilateral as well as multilateral agreements providing for the free entrance of Liberian products into other African nations the reciprocal rights for the products of those nations.

Realizing that one of our greatest handicaps, and one of the greatest handicaps of most African nations, is the relatively small market which we represent, we will direct major attention to pushing back the trade barriers facing our products, and provide constantly increasing markets for Liberian goods.

THE AUSTERITY PROGRAMME

No Liberian needs to be reminded that our nation is today in the throes of a period of austerity. However, all of us need to keep in mind the cause, the purpose and the goal of that austerity. Only when seen in its true perspective can our 'Austerity Régime' be accurately assessed; only then can its challenge and its promise be fully appreciated.

The dictionary defines austerity as: 'rigorous self-denial or asceticism; enforced or extreme economy'. Who would dispute the work when we see our budgets cut, our plans postponed, our hopes deferred? We are proud but not surprised that our nation and its people have exhibited the fibre, the fortitude, 'the rigorous self-denial' demanded by the times. In these circumstances our task is not to enforce self-denial but to evoke from it, and from this austerity, new horizons, larger plans and greater hopes.

In retrospect, the past year has been one of a tightening of the belt. Out of these experiences, however, it is gratifying to know that the nation has emerged strengthened and wiser in many ways. We shall approach the new year with wider horizons and enriched understanding of the obligations which we owe to the nation and its people, in the days of prosperity as well as in the days of stringency.

At the beginning of this new administration and in spite of austerity, the nation must employ all its human and natural resources, all its energy, and dedicate itself to the final assault on ignorance, want, disease and social injustice.

The Five-Year Plan. To boost our economy, stimulate production and pave the road to national self-sufficiency, I enunciated, a few months ago, the nation's priority number one programme OPERATION PRODUCTION which will serve as the axis of the new Five-Year Plan mentioned in some detail in the Fourth Annual Message to the Forty-fifth Legislature. I have declared on several occasions that this administration will not relent until all available manpower is actively engaged in the programme of Operation Production.

Again, I call on all Liberians and foreigners to co-operate with might and main, and push the proverbial battle for Operation Production to the very gates and over the top. This is positive, this is imperative; and all departments, bureaux and agencies of Government must participate to the fullest extent of their power and ability without excuse, without failure and without diffidence or reticence.

EDUCATION, HEALTH, ROADS AND COMMUNICATIONS

The strengthening and expanding of our educational system will remain an important consideration in the Five-Year Plan. To this end elementary and primary education will be made compulsory throughout the nation and a general system of mass education vigorously pursued.

Simultaneously the best standards must be demanded for secondary and higher education in all their ramifications.

We shall continue to encourage the progress of Agriculture, Public Health and Sanitation, Roads and Communications until there is an abundance of food and other agricultural products; until health and sanitation standards are greatly improved, and the people of the nation enjoy good health and practise up-to-date sanitary methods; until a network of roads links the various counties to facilitate transportation and communication.

While we have in the past executed these programmes to some degree, the gap has not been sufficiently bridged, so that they must be pushed at a faster and more satisfactory pace in order to bring the results which, we are convinced, will synthesize all our national activities into a sounder and more realistic economic position.

The Youth of the Nation. The availability of local and foreign scholarships, and increased corps of professionally trained teachers, and the political consideration and patronage extended to the young people today are indications of the abundant opportunities, improved facilities and higher educational standards this generation enjoys over previous generations. Despite all of these considerations the results in improved mental, physical, spiritual and moral achievements have not been sufficiently significant.

The Boy Scout and Girl Guide Movement in Liberia, the National Youth Organization, the YMCA, YWCA, and other related organizations are designed to capture the imagination of the young and sublimate their energies and abilities into creative and useful channels. As gratifying as the results of these organizations have been, we need to push these programmes forward more vigorously during the coming years at all levels of our society so that whatever talents, contributions and skills the people possess may be discovered and put to practical purposes.

There is at present a growing group of intellectuals in the nation, many of whom have earned advanced degrees from colleges and universities both at home and abroad upon Government's patronage in the nature of scholarships. I would like to see these academic and technical talents unfolded productively for the advancement and enrichment of the people of the country. We would prefer to see this class of intellectuals demonstrating their knowledge and their education, rather than talking about it.

Much of what is written about Liberia has been the opinion and ideas of foreigners who see things from their own viewpoint, often unaware of their true meaning or implication. The time has come when we must be awakened to our responsibilities, and make recognized contributions to literature and art, writing books, becoming authors, artists and sculptors of national and international repute like Edward Blyden, Abayomi Karnga, Edwin Barclay, F. A. Price, Ernest Yancy, Doris Banks Henries, C. L. Simpson, Roland Dempster, Nathaniel Richardson, Emanuel Erskine, Bai T. Moore, E. O. Fahnbulleh and others, men and women who have contributed to the fields of literature and art. The intelligentsia of today should excel those of yesterday, because they have had greater opportunities and 'Much is expected from those to whom much is given.' Insitutions of learning must search for students with talent of whatever kind, and having discovered them, provide the atmosphere to corral and nurture these talents and make possible their eventual use in the service of the nation.

As a further implementation of some of these ideas, I propose the establishment of C.O.P.E., to be known as COPE – LIBERIAN CORPS FOR PRODUCTION AND EDUCATION, as a pilot project. The general structure of the programme could have two parts – Agricultural and Industrial – whose objectives will be to provide at minimum cost, a means to:

(a) Capture the energy, enthusiasm and ambition of trained youths – such as engineers, agricultural specialists etc., whose services are not being fully utilized in the nation's development.
(b) Provide employment, training and opportunity for further development to those with high school or similar education.
(c) Provide useful employment and basic training for truants, drop-outs, unemployed, loiterers, etc.

The details of this programme will be submitted to the Legislature for enactment of a provision of law for its implementation.

LAND TENURE

The practice has grown in recent years for citizens to approach and obtain the consent of tribal authorities, by the payment of nominal sums of money denominated 'Cold Water' to acquire enormous quantities of land to the extent of fifteen to twenty thousand acres, and some of the chiefs themselves indulge in the same practice of acquiring twenty-five and fifty thousand acres of land for themselves and their families. While it is true that they can afford to pay the meagre purchase price of fifty cents per acre for this quantity of land, we hope that with the expanding national education programme, the political developments all over the country and the spreading concentric circle of the Open Door Policy, the centres which are now predominantly rural will develop into strategic industrial and urban areas. What is to become of the growing educated population of young men and women who may be eager to remain in their country seats and develop new communities, if the lands in and around them are all appropriated?

I realize that there is more than enough virgin land throughout the country, but we expect our population to grow, we expect industries of various kinds to expand, and we must look forward to the future and see that adequate reserves of public lands are maintained for the benefit of future generations.

DISTINGUISHED GUESTS

We note and observe with pride the presence at these Ceremonies of a number of Chiefs of African States and Heads of Government, foreign dignitaries
representing friendly nations, and distinguished citizens and friends. Particularly happy and honoured are we to have with us His Excellency Sekou
Toure, President of the neighbouring Republic of Guinea, who has always
consistently shown genuine and fraternal regard for the Government and
people of Liberia; His Excellency Joseph Kasavubu, President of our Sister
African Republic of the Congo who has shown himself a pillar of strength in
the great and many ordeals to which he and his country have been subjected; His Excellency Sir Milton Margai, Prime Minister of the neighbouring State of Sierra Leone, with whom Liberia was closely identified even
before that nation attained its independence, and between whose people and
ours a personal relationship subsists; His Excellency the Premier of Northern
Nigeria, Alhaji Sir Ahmadu Bello, the Sarduana of Sokoto, a true champion
of the African liberation movement, representing the largest and most populous of African States; His Excellency Auguste Denise, Vice-President of
the neighbouring State of the Ivory Coast, representing President Houphouet
Boigny, our longtime friend and a great African Statesman; and His Imperial
Highness Crown Prince Asfa Wossen Hailé Selassié of the oldest independent
African nation, the Empire of Ethiopia, all of whom we welcome with
warmth of heart and spirit.

We salute and hail the Sovereigns of Governments and Heads of States
represented here through Your Excellencies, their special diplomatic representatives to these ceremonies and extend to you and to all of our foreign
friends and well-wishers a warm welcome and our sincere wish for a pleasurable and enjoyable stay in the nation's capital.

THE UNITED STATES DELEGATION

The most moving and touching experience that I have had during this
Inaugural season was the presentation handed to me by Her Excellency Mrs.
Helen Gallagan Douglas from the Honourable Lyndon Johnson, President of
the United States, which I consider of the utmost importance and of great
historic significance. This invaluable presentation consists of a letter written
to me on November 21, 1963, by the late President John F. Kennedy which
was the day of his departure from Washington on that fateful visit to Texas,
and it is said in official Washington circles that this was one of his last
official acts.

I consider this deserving of incorporation word for word in this address so
as to become part of it; the letter reads as follows:

'THE WHITE HOUSE
WASHINGTON
November 21, 1963

Dear Mr. President:

'It gives me particular pleasure, in extending warm greetings on the
occasion of your Inauguration as President of the Republic of Liberia, to
commemorate also the one hundredth anniversary of the establishment of
diplomatic relations between our two governments. As a token of the
significance which the American people attach to these historic ties, I

have had prepared a special portfolio, containing facsimiles of some documents, now in the Archives of the United States, which I trust you and the people of Liberia will find of interest.

'They include copies of the instructions addressed by President Abraham Lincoln to the American Minister at the Court of St. James, Mr. Charles Francis Adams, empowering him to negotiate a Treaty of Commerce and Navigation with the Republic of Liberia; the Treaty itself, signed in London by Mr. Adams and President Stephen Allen Benson of Liberia, together with the documents pertaining to ratification by the United States Government; the Letters of Credence of the First United States Commissioner and Consul-General at Monrovia, Mr. Abraham Hanson, and of the first Liberian Chargé d'Affaires at Washington, Mr. John B. Pinney; and, finally, reproductions of portraits of the then President of Liberia, Stephen Allen Benson, and of the United States, Abraham Lincoln, and of their Secretaries of State, Edward W. Blyden and William H. Seward.

'Mr. President, in a world which is marked by constant crisis and continual change, it is gratifying to consider the close and cordial relations that have now existed officially between our two governments for over a century, as well as the special and friendly ties that have linked us unofficially for an even longer time.

'May I take this opportunity, Mr. President, to extend to you and to the Liberian people the warm good wishes of the Government and people of the United States.

Sincerely,
(Sgd.) John F. Kennedy

His Excellency
William V. S. Tubman
President of the Republic of Liberia
Monrovia'

In keeping with the above letter he had assembled all of the historic documents and despatches mentioned, and His Excellency President Lyndon Johnson, in a letter delivered by the hands of Mrs. Helen Douglas, his personal representative, transmitted the portfolio containing these documents of history.

President Johnson's letter evinces the identical active and warm interest in the future of Africa and deep concern for the people of Liberia, and therefore I am impelled to incorporate it into this address so as to form a part of it for the benefit of history. President Johnson's letter reads as follows:

'THE WHITE HOUSE
WASHINGTON
December 19, 1963

'Dear Mr. President:

'One of the last official acts of President Kennedy was the signing of a letter transmitting this portfolio. I have had the late President's letter, together with an engraving of him, made an integral part of the portfolio.

'John F. Kennedy had an active interest in the future of Africa and a deep concern for the welfare of the people of Liberia. As a symbol of the continuity of the traditionally close ties of our countries, I am pleased to send his collection, together with my personal greetings, on the occasion of your inauguration.

'May I also extend, Mr. President, the warm good wishes of the Government and people of the United States to you and the Liberian people.

Sincerely,
(Sgd.) Lyndon B. Johnson

His Excellency
William V. S. Tubman
President of the Republic of Liberia
Monrovia'

President Kennedy's letter, written a day before his assassination, cannot but evoke the deepest feelings of emotion, grief and sorrow and deepen the feelings of affection and the ties of friendship subsisting between the United States, his great country, and Liberia.

President Johnson's letter is reassuring and stimulates confidence. We cannot but be tenderly and affectionately touched by the spontaneity of these attitudes of great men of a great nation toward our country, and register our appreciation for the solicitude, interest and ties of friendship that have subsisted for more than a century, and will, in the words of Shakespeare, 'bind them with hoops of steel' and nurture them so as to cause this relationship to grow in ever-increasing measure through the years.

It gives me especial pleasure that these were entrusted to the gentle hands of an outstanding American lady, Mrs. Helen Gaagan Douglas, former Congresswoman from California for delivery.

CONCLUSION

Finally, always trusting the direction and guidance of the God of our Fathers, will continue to save the State, I enter upon the execution of the sacred task to which I have been called for the fifth and, I earnestly hope, the last time.

Independence Day Message

Monrovia, 26 July 1964

> *On this eventful occasion ... the 117th anniversary of the independence of the nation, four additional counties have come into being as integral and indivisible parts of the nation.... With this phase of national undertaking thus far established, we have reached another level in our political and social thinking and achievement. It will mean the enlargement of our political framework, the expansion of our social, educational, economic and cultural opportunities; and, what is more, the broadening of our democratic concept and outlook.*

Introductory Note

President Tubman's Independence Day Message on the occasion of Liberia's 117th anniversary is another historical document. The creation of the four new counties was the final act in the nation's long drama to ensure the inalienable rights of man — life, liberty, and happiness to all of its citizens. There was to be one law for all of the people of Liberia, irrespective of cultural origin or geographic location. Hinterland jurisdiction and administration were altered to accommodate county governments, in harmony with the five Atlantic seaboard counties. The President was pleased that it became the lot of this generation of Liberians to undertake a task so noble and heroic. He further exhorts Liberians to the execution of an Operation Production Programme, and invites all citizens and residents to participate in a drive for the Emergency Fund For Education.

Monrovia, 26 July 1964

THE ANNOUNCEMENT of the Declaration of Independence to the Nations of the World by the Founders of the Republic after the transition from Commonwealth to Republic on that first Independence Day, July 26, 1847, has been resounding in increasing degrees since that momentous occasion up to to the present. Today we gather in every county, city, township and village to observe and celebrate with grateful hearts, thankful prayers and modest pride the 117th Anniversary of our Independence and commemorate the valour, indomitable and unconquerable will and spirit that inspired, characterized and sustained the noble founders of this country, and that have been passed down through succeeding generations of Liberians. We salute them, revere and hold sacred their devotion to the cause of democracy, freedom and liberty and their struggle for survival, progress, development and unification which have brought us together under such unique and inspiring circumstances.

Realizing that a new chapter in our political and social history unfolds itself today, we have come not only to express our belief in the fundamentals of freedom in the Declaration of Independence and the Constitution but also to re-dedicate ourselves, our services and our lives to the great cause of freedom and liberty which our progenitors moulded with such skill and fashioned with such soundness at a tremendous cost; and to reassert our determination to demonstrate that those who made this heritage of freedom a reality did not labour in vain. They are with us today; they hover around us as a cloud of witnesses attesting their approval and their imprimatur or their disapproval and malediction: We feel assured that it is the former-approval and imprimatur. Let us therefore lift ourselves out of our purely material existence to the spiritual, and unite with them in communion of spirit, mind, hope, aspiration and determination for the continual growth, development, perpetuity, integration and solidarity of this 'Land of Glorious Liberty by God's Command' and regard this 117th Anniversary of our Independence as 'National Progenitors Day'.

If we can today visualize the struggle of the pioneers, or learn to appreciate the nobility of character and the statesmanship which they displayed; if we can feel the intensity of the fervour which motivated and kept them alive when living was, at best, a series of excruciating experiences; or will to the young of this nation the priceless heritage of freedom and teach them the lessons which this and other anniversaries cannot, they would constitute a pathway on which our present and future steps may rightly be guided, toward the promise of a better and brighter future. The achievements of the past century, no less than the lessons of today, should make us humble, grateful and prayerful, lest in the midst of our rejoicings we forget the Eternal Source that sustained our fathers; that has continued to be its guiding Providence over us through the years, and to Whom we give glory, honour, praise and adoration.

Only a few historical accounts of Liberia point to the fact that those who returned here and founded this nation came, not as masters or lords of those they met here, but rather as their kinsmen and kinswomen. The former group, although having been subjected to the thraldom of the most iniquitous human traffic of the time, were exposed to some refining influence of civilization, religion and culture, and brought back with them new ideals and ideas, new skills and new ways of life which would aid in the establishment of the new society they intended to organize. Recognizing the latter's rights, they referred to them in the Declaration of Independence as 'Lords of the Soil'; they were resolved to work and strive together and thereby build a homogenous society which would be impervious to further inroads of the devastating traffic in human lives and suffering, which had torn mother from father, wife from husband, brother from sister and become a blight in the history of mankind.

Lofty ideals motivated the early fathers, for they were pioneering, patriotic and religious men to whom freedom and independence carried sacred connotations; they were determined to work hard towards its realization. They belived that in time their dreams, their toils and the work of their hands would be realized in the emergence of future generations which would know the reward of honest labour, enjoy the freedom of the free, give their children the kind of educational opportunities that had been denied them and finally build a new home by the agglutination of the old and new, eventually giving rise to a new society; a glowing fulfilment of the dreams and purposes of the philanthropic institution in the United States known as the Colonization Society of America, that was imbued with the great moral, spiritual and physical principles of freedom for mankind, regardless of race or colour.

It was to be expected, and it is understandable, that the 'Lords of the Soil' who had remained for centuries living their own primitive way, knowing nothing of payment of taxes, content with their primitive methods and ways of life and administration, without any desire for change, development or progress, and who had accepted their fellow kinsmen as brothers and children when they returned home, should resent and rise up against them and consider it an effrontery and demagoguery that these their sons and daughters, whom they had welcomed and to whom they had ceded land, should demand of them payment of taxes and subject them to laws and regulations incompatible with their century-old primitive customs and methods of life.

Besides these, there were foreign traders established in the country selling their wares, good and merchandise without customs control or the payment of dues on their merchandise. This foreign element encouraged and even assisted the Chiefs and Tribal People to struggle against the exercise of Government authority over the territory, and the foreign traders, on their part, refused to pay taxes or customs duties or to recognize the authority of the Commonwealth over them, alleging that the Commonwealth was not a sovereign entity. This position of the traders was supported by their Governments. Because of this the Commonwealth, upon the recommendation of the Colonialization Society of America, declared itself an Independent State only twenty-five years after it had been established; but there was a destiny for Liberia – a destiny that would ensure to all peoples inhabiting these territories and to Negroes, people of African descent and black men wherever dispersed the world over, a home where, as they used to say, 'They could worship God under their own vine and fig tree where none dare molest or make afraid.' Therefore it has been correctly said that 'Liberia is a child of Providence.'

How significantly have the years changed conditions in our national design; beginning with three original counties at the signing of the Declaration of Independence in 1847, adding another, Maryland County, in 1857, ten years later, and another, Grand Cape Mount County in 1922, seventy-five years later. And now on this eventful occasion which is also the 117th Anniversary of the Independence of the Nation, four additional counties have come into being as integral and indivisible parts of the nation. Thus the political structure of the country has been changed, the principles laid down in the first sentence and Article of the Constitution that:

'All men are born equally free and independent, and have certain natural, inherent and inalienable rights; among which, are the rights of enjoying and defending life and liberty, of acquiring, possessing and protecting property and of pursuing and obtaining safety and happiness.'

The decision of the Supreme Court and the Unification Programme are being implemented and fulfilled.

With this phase of our national undertaking thus far established, we have reached another level in our political and social thinking and achievements. It will mean the enlargement of our political framework, the expansion of our social, educational, economic and cultural opportunities; and what is more, the broadening of our democratic concept and outlook.

THE LEGISLATIONS OF THE FOUR ADDITIONAL COUNTIES

It is said that commitments to great causes make men great. May those of
you whose fond privilege it has been to become associated with the great
events of today, accept unconditionally the obligations implicit in your preferment, so that you may dedicate and re-dedicate yourselves anew to the
bigger tasks awaiting you, you who received the singular honour a week ago
of representing your consituents in the National Legislature, thereby becoming members of the first Co-ordinate branch of Government. May you
be worthy proponents and defenders of the great and eternal principles for
which this nation has stood for more than a century and for which her sons
and daughters have fought and died, that have survived through the century
in the fight for freedom and liberty, justice and equality, unity and brotherhood and that have kept the Lone Star, our National Flag, gloriously afloat
at staff top.

THE EXECUTIVE OFFICIALS OF THE FOUR ADDITIONAL COUNTIES

You have today been preferred and honoured by Commissions which have
been handed you as Vice-Regents in your respective countries and as Judges
of the Circuit Court of these counties with the Judiciary of the County.
Along with this honour, however, go tremendous responsibilities; you Superintendents are the official exponents and Representatives of the Chief
Executive of the Nation, you are the Representative of each of the Executive
Departments of Government in your respective Counties and the watch-dogs
of the nation's frontiers from south-east to north-west.

It will be your responsibility to look after the constant safety of the borders
within your jurisdictions, while your colleagues on the littoral will exercise
similar duties. It is expected that you will be vigilant, devoted to duty, loyal
to your country and possessed of a high sense of honour and integrity; you
must strive to be true leaders in every sense of the word. In the discharge of
your duties as guardians of the territorial integrity of your sections of the
country, you are to seek to develop cordial relationship between border
states and your own country, Liberia. This is all the more essential because
they are all African.

Superintendents are Administrators whose official Council as advisers com-
prise the Senators, Representatives, County Attorney and the highest Military
Officer in the county, all of whom stand in a similar relationship to the
Superintendent as the Members of the Cabinet to the President; but the
Superintendent is solely responsible for the effective and successful admini-
stration of his county, and he is not obliged to accept all advice given by the
Members of his Council if in his judgment they will not be in the best
interest of administration.

May I admonish you to strive to be men of clear thinking, sober understanding, correct judgment and positive action. Let nothing destroy the
effectiveness of your high office, but rather let the service you will perform
for your county be more eloquent than words. May you be strong, vigilant
and alert to your duties and responsibilities, thus reflecting credit upon
yourselves, your respective counties and our common heritage.

I express thanks and appreciation to the members of the Legislature who
unanimously voted for the Constitutional changes and the necessary repeal

of the Act which divided the country into county and hinterland jurisdictions. Although the Constitution required a two-third vote by both Houses, there was not a negative vote in either the Senate or the House of Representatives on this question.

The greatest acclaim, however, goes to the people of Liberia who were enfranchised at the time of the recommendation for the change in the law, and who voted unanimously for its adoption while about one thousand votes were cast against my election at the same time.

We cannot refrain from praise of his Honour Chief Justice James Jerome Dossen who in 1918, along with his two concurring colleagues, delivered the opinion that declared the relevant Act unconstitutional.

It is therefore self-evident that this change which has taken place today is not the act of any one man or person; it is the act of the whole Government and body of the people of Liberia.

The world today provides fertile background for revolutions in thought and action amidst the transformations which have come into the limelight, in one of the greatest political dramas of history. To strive to keep the equilibrium, to be discriminating in our sense of values, to keep up with the momentum of events, and to act like men of sober thought and determined action are some of the challenges which today's observance imposes upon us. The heritage of freedom is the opportunity to aspire, to achieve and to reach out into new directions, so that democracy may survive the onslaughts of other ideologies; since indeed we believe that it alone excels in extolling the dignity and privilege of the individual. Fellow citizens, this is your heritage of freedom; cherish it, guard it and maintain it so that it may be handed down improved and enlarged.

Liberia today, with its nine political subdivisions, crosses the threshold of a new history. Those who will play the dramatis personae in this act will become the heroes and heroines in the new chapter which the nation now enters and will write in its political history. May each of you be worthy of the rôles you will be called upon to play.

We return tomorrow to our daily vocations and avocations. The words and events of today will soon be enshrouded in the mist of human memory; but our cities, our counties, our people, our nation, raintime and harvest, work and leisure and life and death will remain with us every hour, every day, every week, every month and every year. The problems of human existence will continue to press for practical solutions; world peace will become more and more urgent; mankind will be irresistibly drawn closer and closer to the vortices of universal brotherhood, and science and religion will become extensions one of the other. Unless we resolve to face the facts surrounding our nation and the world, become responsive to the lessons of history, strike the better chords within our higher natures, and bring to our tasks all our ingenuity, all our human and material resources, our patriotism, loyalty and dedication, we step into the future with uncertainty and blindness. But let us be men and women, Liberians, people who are loyal and devoted to the highest dictates of the supreme law of God and man. Let honour to God, service to our country, a closer kinship with our fellow compatriots be some of the considerations with which we can today enter upon this new threshold of history.

I commend the enthusiastic reception and the favourable comments and energetic action upon Operation Production on the part of the people. General

interest has been sparked, some plans initiated and serious work has commenced in many areas with the ultimate objectives of increasing the nation's
productive capacity. Seriously, there can be no greater dedication to a
nation's cause on this Independence Day Anniversary than a commitment to
make realistic in every way such a vital programme in the interest of our
national well-being. May we all, therefore, on this day, renew our pledges
and resolve to go to work on every level and in every way, doubly inspired in
the knowledge that with each stroke of the hoe, the cutlass, the axe, or the
digger, and with each acre of land planted, we help to bring nearer the era
of abundance.

EMERGENCY RELIEF DRIVE FOR EDUCATION

There is today a greater yearning, anxiety, urge and quest for education by
the young people of the nation throughout its length and breadth, and because of the demands of the age in which we live for highly trained men and
women in science, technology, literature and the arts, with the addition of
the four new counties that will require a greater number of trained and
capable men and women and the emergence of sister African States which
has increased the demand for better, higher and more efficient level of education, a challenge greater than ever before is thrust upon the Government
and people of the nation.

Our austerity programme has of necessity slowed down some of the vital
national development projects, and nowhere has this been more keenly
felt than in the field of our expanding programme of education. Notwithstanding the fact that appropriation for education in this period of austerity
has been increased (including that of the university), our plans for expansion compel us to make greater and more commitments, and because education is the key to the future of our continued progress and development and
the secret of our stability and success in this highly competitive age, we cannot permit postponment and delay in so important an area.

The adequate training of the youth and people of the nation is so imperative that even in time of austerity this field should not be changed to any
significant degree. The education we need and seek should be based not on
mere idealism, but used as a practical instrument in the daily lives of men
and women so that they may learn to live fully, produce abundantly, create
and contribute usefully to their country and to the world of peoples and
things. There is not a single citizen throughout the country who has not
been benefited by the progress that has been made economically and politically; there is not a citizen, nor even a foreigner residing within our borders
whose income and standard of living has not been raised; all of which has
come about because of the era of prosperity.

From the Open Door Policy Liberians have been privileged to invest in
different enterprises and concessions; these privileges and opportunities were
offered to every citizen throughout the country, and most of those who took
advantage of them have already begun to receive dividends; those who have
not yet begun to receive dividends will do so in the near future, and this ensures a future of economic safety.

Notwithstanding the austerity programme, salaries have not been decreased; regular monthly payments have been made and, as mentioned before, there have been increases in the appropriation for education in most

respects. However, we must boost and push forward our educational programme of expansion in a more rapid and effective manner; which will understandably require additional revenues. Our responsibility to the young people of the nation compels us to provide up-to-date and additional facilities for their training and education.

I therefore propose a special three-year emergency relief drive, within which period we must raise six million dollars for education by the levy of a tax of ten dollars *per capita* to be known as an emergency relief fund tax for education. Revenues accruing to this special fund will be applied solely for educational purposes and will become a part of the proposed five-year over-all development plan. We shall immediately send forward to the Legislature a message on this proposal, and ask for its approval by Legislative Enactment, but we are appealing to every man and woman from the age of twenty-one upwards to pay this tax willingly and promptly, not only because it is a taxation, but because we feel it is an obligation which we owe to this special effort in time of emergency.

This tax shall apply also to foreign residents within our territorial confines, except those who by special agreements previously made are exempt or have immunities in this respect.

I would prefer to have the people make voluntary contributions rather than refer to this as a tax, but for the benefit of efficient collection and strict accountability, as well as for the purpose of creating an educational fund, I call it a special emergency relief tax.

The question might arise in the minds of some as to why it is suggested that every citizen pay the same amount for this tax rather than create it on a graduated basis according to the financial ability of the citizen. There is one main reason, which is that you cannot impose a greater *per capita* tax on one class of citizens rather than on another, without its becoming class Legislation which would involve a Constitutional issue. It is only in cases of income tax that a graduated scale of taxation may be set. What I ask of you – the poor and poorest – is that you make a sacrifice and pay this tax for three years at ten dollars per annum so that you may have the satisfaction of having contributed as much as any other citizen in your country, whether high or low, to the education of your children, your brother's children, your grand children, your friends' and relatives' children.

To those of affluence, for the same reasons that I have mentioned to the poor and poorest, I appeal that because of your better financial situation you do not restrict yourselves to the payment of ten dollars per annum for this great purposeful drive but make contributions within these three years as your financial ability will permit. Some of us have numerous buildings and housing projects on lease; some of us have healthy bank accounts both at home and abroad; some of us are engaged in developing profitable industries and businesses with Government agencies such as the Credit Corporation, the Development Corporation, and even the Government itself has assisted by guarantees to banks and other institutions. This class of us should remember that 'much is expected from those to whom much is given', and Mrs. Tubman and I will lead in response to the call for greater contribution than the mere ten dollar tax per annum.

Conditions have temporarily changed and things are not as good as they used to be but we know that within a relatively short period of time the *status quo ante* will be restored and there will be a greater measure of

prosperity. Nevertheless, the great urgency to push forward without interruption the educational programme and insure our ability to meet the contributions which the Government is required to make as its share of payments
for grants and loans offered and negotiated for education, also to construct
schools, promote vocational, scientific, technological and other branches of
education which the country is in dire need of at the present time, will become greater with each passing month and year.

I appeal to the people of the country, to every citizen in every walk of
life, to realize the critical need for expanding and raising the levels of our
educational standards, and our responsibility to accept and overcome the challenge and make great sacrifices to attain this end. Therefore, in the interest of
the young people of the nation who are clamouring for more schools and
better facilities, and to ensure the future of the nation, I urge and appeal to
you to rally and respond to the new programme for education mentioned
above.

There are concessionaires operating in the country that are exempted
from taxation under the provisions of their concession agreements, but because they too have received considerable if not enormous benefits from the
low taxation rate that they are required to pay and from the still lower rates
that they paid in the past, we would like to feel assured that they will as an
act of goodwill voluntarily respond and give financial contribution in this
educational crisis.

UNIVERSITY OF LIBERIA

Liberia College served the needs of the nation during the past century.
However, the birth of the University of Liberia now demands a greater
obligation and that imposes a heavier responsibility. The University must
receive special consideration so that its standard may be raised – dormitories
built, and equipment and facilities for science laboratories obtained. To this
end let us determine anew that the University will receive special attention so
that its programmes for development, strengthening and financing will be
formulated and implemented on the most realistic and modern basis. Because
it must now cater to a wider community in the new Africa, the University of
Liberia must seek to create and develop a Faculty strong enough and excellent enough for students from all over Africa to be attracted by it and draw
nourishment from its fountain. Let us begin now!

THE CAIRO SUMMIT

The recent meeting of the Heads of African States and Governments was
most certainly a success in advancing the ideals of the African continent for
freedom, unity and solidarity, and has undoubtedly made more significant
another important impact on the history of mankind, contributing to the
insistent demands for world peace and human brotherhood. No one attending that conference could fail to comprehend and appreciate the success
achieved in arriving at practical solutions to problems which had erstwhile
been viewed from national perspectives, and satisfactory conclusions were
reached in record time; to say nothing of the gains made in good human
relations, the engendering of more sympathetic understanding, the flowering of deep and genuine friendships and the blossoming of goodwill. Certainly all of our problems were not solved, nor did we discover a panacea.

But, this we do know: As we have met from time to time, we have had greater faith in ourselves and in the Organization of African Unity as an effective and lasting instrument which will bring us closer and closer to our goal of African Unity and Co-operation and become a positive contribution to world peace.

THE UNITED NATIONS

This organization is the world's greatest and best hope of human survival and brotherhood. Our faith in it must remain unshaken, our support unceasing, and our hope for the consummation of its worthy ideals must continue to receive encouragement and nourishment, so that the day may not be too far distant when all nations will become member states of this great world organization and thus be guided and governed by its lofty moral principles for all.

DISTINGUISHED GUESTS

It is a great honour and privilege that we have with us at the festivities His Excellency Nicolas Grunitzky, President of the sister Republic of Togo. His presence enriches and adds lustre to the uniqueness of the 117th anniversary observance! We extend warm felicitations to him, the members of his party and to the Government and people of Togo, wishing for the President good health, and prosperity, peace, happiness, unity and solidarity for the Government and people of our sister Republic of Togo.

THE DIPLOMATIC CORPS

We are deeply touched by the remarks of the Doyen of the Diplomatic Corps on this occasion, assuring us in particular of the happiness of the Diplomatic Representatives accredited here and of their proud association with us in this observance.

We are happy and fortunate that our relations with the Governments represented near this capital have been most cordial and that peace and cordiality have dominated all our official and social contacts. We congratulate you, Mr. Doyen and Members of the Diplomatic Corps and assure each of you of the continued wish of the Government and people of Liberia to live in peace and friendship with all nations and to work and live together as equal partners in the pursuit of permanent world peace and brotherhood.

Please convey to your respective Sovereigns and Chiefs of State my personal felicitations and those of the Government and people of Liberia.

CONCLUSION

May God ever keep and guard the people of this nation, save our state and lead us in the future, as He has done in the past, in this new step that we have taken in broadening the basis and expanding the concept of Liberian democracy.

First Annual Message delivered before the Second Session of the Forty-fifth Legislature

Monrovia 24 November 1964

The foundation stone of the execution of your enactments changing the three provinces into four counties was laid on the 27th day of July, 1964. It is with great pleasure that I extend to you the profound appreciation and congratulations of other branches of the Government and of your constituents for your vision, discernment and patriotism in these acts whereby you have deepened, broadened and established a new basis of Liberian democracy.

Introductory Note

On the international scene the Congo continued to make news headlines. On the domestic scene four new counties were to be carved out of the old provinces and districts. Agricultural expansion was made a national priority programme. The President further launched a new plan for mass education in the form of an Emergency Relief Levy for Education. Certain measures were to be instituted to raise the standard of the legal profession in Liberia. The Liberian Information Service was recommended to be made a Department of Government. The creation of new ports of entry was also recommended. Business competition and certain excesses in this competition were becoming a national concern. The President considered these excesses as an abuse of the Open Door Policy. The Government and people were called upon to consider ways in which adjustments could be made to a period of austerity and our economy made more productive.

Monrovia, 24 November 1964

ORGANIZED LEGISLATURE in Liberia, which had its genesis after the Declaration of Independence in 1847, has continued successively through the century and brought you together in 1964 in attendance upon the Second Session of the Forty-fifth Legislature. It is a source of happiness that your assemblage is being held in an atmosphere of internal peace and stability, the happy lot of our nation, as well as in the conscious pursuit of understanding among nations and peoples in the urgent quest for universal peace. I welcome and extend to you sincere greetings and felicitations.

FOREIGN RELATIONS

Relations between this Government and member states of the United Nations, particularly those represented by the diplomatic corps near this capital, continue to be harmonious and cordial.

THE INTERNATIONAL SITUATION

International tension over the past two years appears to have relaxed somewhat as a result of several acts and agreements concluded between some of
the great powers and adhered and subscribed to by most nations. As a result
of the basis laid for better understanding and agreement on the controversial
subjects of disarmament, the partial banning of nuclear tests, peaceful co-
existence, the cold war and other subjects that foment misunderstanding and
prevent the attainment of peace by most nations, a certain degree of hope has
been raised in the hearts of mankind.

However, the state of affairs between nations, even the smaller and developing countries, does not present a satisfactory picture, nor does there appear
to be evidence of a genuine desire and determination for peace; for in Asia,
Africa, the Americas and Europe there are conflicts which, although considered as local, could flare up and become global. These are a decided
menace to international peace and security and result principally from subversive activities and interference in the internal affairs of states by other
states.

These uncertain conditions are multiplied and intensified by the greater
number of nations that have procured and possess atom and nuclear bombs
and weapons. Unquestionably, unless a universal agreement between not only
the nuclear powers but all nations can be negotiated and concluded, outlawing and banning nuclear tests of every kind and prohibiting the production of
nuclear bombs as well as subscribing to an agreement or convention not to
contrive, procure or possess nuclear bombs, missiles or weapons, the number
of nuclear powers will increase progressively with time. It is clear that should
one nation possess nuclear bombs or weapons, every other nation that considers it a rival or a potential enemy will seek to develop or procure the same
bombs or weapons in the interest of its own national safety and security.
This is a matter which concerns all nations and peoples and it seems to me
that there is no other way or means to prevent the spread of nuclear weapons
and the increase of nuclear powers.

In such an international situation, we declare and avow our aversion to the
possession or use of nuclear weapons in every form and our adherence, in
theory and practice, to non-interference in the internal affairs of other
states, to the rule of law, to constitutional democracy under the free enterprise system of government and to the right of all nations to determine and
pursue the system of government of their own choosing without molestation
or interference from others, directly or indirectly.

THE CONGO

The peoples of Africa cannot but be bewildered and horrified at the tragic
course of events in the Republic of the Congo (Leopoldville). Since her
advent to independence that nation has been beset by turmoil and strife.
Internal dissensions and bitter rivalries have erupted into civil war with
enormous loss of life and property. Individual and national progress has
been retarded and the future of the nation presents an anxious picture. That
all this has been, and still is, attributable to the machinations of foreign
agencies and nations who refuse to allow the Congolese to work out and
create their own national image; that interference in the internal affairs of

the Congo has come from various parts of the world, including ourselves in Africa; that some blame rests on the Congolese themselves who have invited other nations to enter into their internal affairs in one way or another, assisting one side against the other thereby causing untold suffering, bloodshed and destruction of property, are all facts which continue to bedevil and besmirch the national stature of this African State and thus render its future uncertain and precarious. Only the Congolese leaders and people can provide the answer to this enigma and bring to an end this tragic situation.

We appeal to the Congolese Government, the rebel régime and to all the people of the Congo, to envisage the picture of a whole and unified and strong country, to forget the things that are behind and to 'let the dead past bury its dead'. Only then will the people of the Congo nation regain the confidence and courage which aroused in them the noble sentiments of nationalism that motivated their demand for freedom and independence.

We advocate, support and stand for the liberation, freedom and self-determination of all peoples and nations; we stand against oppression, apartheid, racial segregation and deprivation of peoples and nations; we stand for the settlement of disputes by peaceful means and against the use of force, except in extreme circumstances where all peaceful efforts to remove injustice, oppression and malevolence have failed.

We stand against any policy aimed at exterminating or intended to liquidate any nation that is a reality; we adhere to and support the Charter of the United Nations, the principles it represents and for which it was organized.

FREE TRADE AREA

In our Inaugural Address of 1964 we recommended the organization or institution of a Free Trade Area. In pursuance of this policy, invitations were extended to Their Excellencies the Presidents of Guinea, and the Ivory Coast and the Right Honourable the Prime Minister of Sierra Leone for a conference to discuss the proposals and to endeavour to work out formulae for the practical implementation of this policy. Our invitations having been accepted by these Honourable invitees, the Conference was convoked in Monrovia on August 20 where in an atmosphere of cordiality and understanding, agreement was reached which laid the initial premise for the implementation of the proposal. Copies of the communiqué will be forwarded to you for your information.

STATE VISITS

During the current year we responded to an invitation extended in 1960 by His Excellency President Philibert Tsiranana to make a State Visit to Madagascar, the Island Republic which is almost a continent, situated in the Indian Ocean in South East Africa, and to another invitation from His Excellency President Julius Nyerere to make a State Visit to the Republic of Tanganyika and Zanzibar, now the Republic of Tanzania. We had also accepted invitations to make State Visits to Kenya and Uganda, but unavoidable circumstances necessitated a postponment of these visits.

Returning to Monrovia on the 13th of July we were obliged to leave the country again for Cairo, Egypt, on the 17th to attend the Conference of the Organization of African Unity from which we returned on the 22nd. In less than two months thereafter we again left the country on the 17th of September for Cairo to attend the Second Conference of Non-aligned Nations and returned on the 30th October. Reports on these visits were made to the people upon our return and will be forwarded to you officially.

This Government was honoured this year by the visits of President and Mrs. Diosdado Macapagal of the Philippines, Prime Minister Sir Eric Williams of Trinidad and Tobago and President Nicolas Grunitzky of the Republic of Togo. These State Visits by Chiefs of State and Government of African and Caribbean nations, together with our visits mentioned above, will have the tendency of creating better understanding and co-operation between our respective governments and peoples.

During our visit to the United Kingdom in 1962 we extended an invitation to Lord Mountbatten of Burma to visit Liberia; this invitation was accepted and the visit made in September of this year. I regret my absence from the country at the time of the visit which was necessitated by my having to attend the Second Conference of Non-aligned Nations. However Mrs. Tubman and my eldest son, assisted by the State Department and other officials of Government, received and entertained Lord Mountbatten and his party. We have received complimentary expressions from his Lordship concerning the warmth and enthusiasm manifested by the Government and people of Liberia.

DEPARTMENT OF STATE

The Secretary of State in his Annual Report, reviews the conduct of foreign affairs and relations between this Government and foreign governments. His report will be submitted to you, in keeping with the usual practice.

INTERNAL AFFAIRS

The foundation stone of the execution of your enactments changing the three provinces into four counties, was laid on the 27th day of July, 1964, the day on which the 117th anniversary of our National Independence was celebrated, the 26th being Sunday. On this occasion the chief administrative officials of the four counties were inducted into office and a proclamation declaring the four new counties legally instituted was issued and promulgated. Copies of this proclamation will be sent forward to Your Honourable Bodies.

It is with great pleasure that I extend to you, Honourable Gentle Ladies and Gentlemen of the Legislature, the profound appreciation and congratulations of other branches of the Government and of your constituents for your vision, discernment and patriotism in these acts, whereby you have deepened, broadened and established a new basis of Liberian democracy.

Already there are gladdening signs of improvement and effectiveness in the administration of these new counties and the four superintendents are giving evidence of their co-operation and resolution to see their counties and country grow and progress.

We extend to the Senators and Representatives of the new counties who have recently become a part of the National Legislature of Liberia a warm and genuine welcome into the national fabric of the first branch of Government and feel assured that they will join their colleagues in seeking to promote and insure the welfare and safety of the State by wise and progressive legislations.

OPERATION PRODUCTION

Ours is a nation whose basic economy is embedded in the agricultural potentialities and possibilities we possess. With the application of modern science and technology by an alert, enterprising and determined people, our virgin forests, the productive soil and the evergreen flora can be transformed into a great granary of production, principally for home consumption and to provide surplus goods for world markets. Experience has already proved to our satisfaction that there is every justification for a programme of this kind, geared to the stimulation and maximum tapping of our agricultural resources, to be given priority consideration in our national planning and implementation.

The steps which were taken in explaining and initiating Operation Production, the media set up for implementation, the great enthusiasm engendered and the success already derived, have naturally led to a strengthening and expanding of the year-old plan, conceived and launched to insure maximum exploitation, on a concerted basis, of the agricultural resources in order to accelerate production in the grand design to bring to the nation a period of prosperity.

Generally, the response to the Operation Production programme has met with more spontaneity than we envisaged, to the extent that people in many areas have moved forward more rapidly than the Government's arrangement for organizing and handling the disposition and sale of products. This, more than any other factor, has brought great satisfaction and the Government is determined to continue to stimulate, lend assistance to and advance the programme of Operation Production in all its conceived and possible ramifications.

The future for which we work is one based on freedom from want, where the creative genius of our farmers and technicians can be successfully applied to the utilization of the agricultural resources we possess to yield abundant returns for all our people; and industrial progress, under Operation Production should be accelerated by proper planning and implementation so as to speed up our programme of transition from subsistence agriculture and primary commodity production to secondary production of processed and semi-processed commodities. No undertaking holds greater promise for the vigorous and stable economic growth of the nation; no situation of the present or future challenges us more truly.

EMERGENCY RELIEF LEVY FOR EDUCATION

The breadth and depth of our educational programme, the quality of the educational opportunities and the pursuit of desirable educational goals are imperatives of our development programme and impose on us greater obligations than ever before. Any investment made in education, therefore, is an investment designed to produce a better and more productive type of future citizen, who we hope will be better educated and more responsive to the ideals of true citizenship. But educational objectives and achievements are ineffective when available facilities and opportunities do not lend themselves to the development and maintenance of a favourable learning climate.

Therefore, at a time like this in the nation's history and in the midst of emerging African States, when unity and co-operation in important areas have been envisaged and discussed, and in some places are already taking root, no effort should be spared to make our educational programme strong, effective and capable of holding its own with other comparable systems. It must be a system capable of retaining and enriching the soul of our national dreams and aspirations, thus transmitting to posterity the vital force that we are convinced is implicit in education.

But worthwhile objectives in themselves, however well conceived and constructed, cannot be effectuated unless undergirded by practical applications which make them living forces in our creative and advancing human community. And so, because the government's austerity programme imposed restrictions due to limited resources we recommended the imposition of an Emergency Relief Levy for Education to help our expanding programme with emphasis on teacher education, vocational training, the raising of the levels and standards of our institutions of higher education.

The Secretary of Education provided justification for this Emergency Levy when he mentioned in his report: 'through it the Government expects to deal more adequately with the foundation of progress – education. In this way citizens and friends of Liberia will participate in supplying the country with essential qualified manpower to cope with our rapidly advancing economy.' He concludes by stating: 'The Republic of Liberia will reap returns in young people better prepared to enter colleges and professions and in an increased number of qualified citizens to supply the manpower demanded by our rapidly advancing nation.'

Again I appeal to the people of this nation and to all who see in quality education the flowering of the best values in our present and future societies, to respond to the patriotic call by contributing willingly and generously to a project which promises greater security and better and more educational opportunities for those for whom the thirst and quest for knowledge still provide unlimited challenges to the human mind and spirit.

REVENUE COLLECTIONS AND THE AUSTERITY PROGRAMME

Despite the Austerity Programme, Government revenue for the fiscal period under review was almost three million dollars in excess of the 1962–63 collections so that the revenue for the 1964 fiscal year is expected, for the first time in the history of the nation, to reach the record figure of between thirty-nine and forty million dollars by December 31, 1964.

However, some fundamental steps must be taken to insure against stagnation of the country's economy and we should emerge from the disciplines taught by our Austerity Programme greatly strengthened, to move forward to newer heights and greater endeavours. In this connection, a Portfolio of Priority Development Projects for the consideration of external financing sources was completed on August 31, 1964. It was felt that these outstanding projects, which would undoubtedly be included in the Five-year Development Plan, should not await the completion of the plan itself, and that every effort should be made to obtain early financing for as many of them as possible in order to contribute to the maintenance of economic activity and the cushioning of the effects of the tapering off of large-scale private enterprise construction projects with which the country is now faced.

DEPARTMENTS OF GOVERNMENT

The Secretary of the Treasury in his report, referred to and submitted the following projects:

A Three-point Programme for economic stability,
A Tax Treaty,
A Banking Act,
Outlook on International Monetary Fund and World Bank Meetings,
The African Development bank,
Agreements with other concessions and Banks,
Agricultural and Engineering Projects,
Loans,
Revenue collections and disbursements,
A Debt Resettling Plan.

and other suggestions and recommendations, a number of which will be included in the recommendations that will be made to you later in this Message.

It became necessary to effect a change in the Department of Justice and the Honourable James A. A. Pierre, Associate Justice of the Honourable the Supreme Court, was invited to accept the position of, and to serve as, Attorney-General. Notwithstanding the life-tenure nature of the office of Justice of the Supreme Court, his patriotic consciousness moved him to tender his resignation as Associate Justice and to accept the position of Attorney-General. He entered upon the duties of this Department about two months ago and has brought with him in his new assignment his usual zest and devotion.

I respectfully request that you give special study and consideration to:

The Postmaster-General's Plan for the organization of an initial and intensified training programme for telecommunications technicians to upgrade their standards and skills;

The Secretary of Defence's insistence upon raising the standard and efficiency of the Liberian Army and Coast Guard so as to insure greater preparedness, efficiency, effectiveness and better protection to our sea coast, and his recommendation that a lighthouse tax be levied for ships using Liberian ports;

What the Secretary of Education in his report terms 'an Education Policy';

The new plan of the Secretary of Public Works and Utilities for the establishment of an annual highway fund to assist in defraying maintenance costs of public highways;

The new agricultural programme set out by the Secretary of Agriculture;

The Director-General of National Public Health's new plan for community health workers and national health planning projects;

The special references made by the Secretary of Commerce and Industry with regard to price control as a result of the high cost of living, the institution of a port and harbour authority and a commission to study the type of port authority that would be best suited for this country, as well as his suggestion for finding appropriate means by which industries in the country can be expanded and promoted;

The new plan set out by the Director-General of Information Service for the dissemination of information and the efficient operation of his Bureau which he has called 'The Nation's New Image'.

The Director-General of the National Planning Agency's summary of economic conditions and trends which points out:

The general level of economic activity,

The necessity for continued stringent economic and financial measures,

The employment prospect for the immediate future,

The increase in the tempo of industrial research activities, and

The census data which is now substantially ready for printing.

The Departmental Secretaries will be forwarding to you their respective annual reports which will expose the detailed operation of their departments for the last fiscal year in response to the requirements of the Statute.

In Section Two of Article Two of the Constitution under the Title 'Legislative Powers', it is stated:

'The representatives shall be elected by, and for the inhabitants of the several counties and provinces of Liberia and shall be apportioned among the several counties and provinces as follows: The County of Montserrado shall have five representatives, the Territory of Marshall shall have one representative, the County of Grand Bassa shall have four representatives, the County of Sinoe shall have four representatives, the County of Maryland shall have four representatives, the County of Grand Cape Mount shall have three representatives, and the three existing provinces of the Republic situated in the hinterland thereof shall each have one representative, and all counties which shall hereafter be admitted into the Republic shall have one representative, and for every ten thousand inhabitants one representative shall be added . . .'

It is apparent that the Constitution does not contemplate that the original number of representatives of counties should be predicted upon the ratio of 10,000 inhabitants, but specifically names the number of representatives for the respective counties; for new counties it designates one representative and provides that for each additional 10,000 inhabitants there shall be an additional representative, until the number of representatives reaches thirty. Thereafter, an additional representative shall be added for each 30,000 inhabitants. It is interesting to note that the Constitution does not provide for electoral districts or constituencies but simply states the number of representatives for each county. Heretofore, the political parties have made distribution of the representatives in the counties in such a manner as would best serve their purposes and interests.

Since these constitutional provisions affect the Honourable House of Representatives, I am loath to make a specific recommendation, but suggest that perhaps you may consider creating electoral districts or constituencies in the various counties.

THE SUPREME COURT

The Supreme Court held its regular semi-annual sessions during the current year. The resignation of His Honour Justice James A. A. Pierre to accept the portfolio of Attorney-General, created a vacancy on the Bench, and at the opening of its October Term, the Court met with a bare quorum present because of the illness of Mr. Justice Harris. However, the vacancy was filled by the appointment and induction into office of Counsellor Clarence L. Simpson, Jun.

In his opening address, His Honour the Chief Justice reported that the several Circuit Courts in the country had held their regular quarterly sessions.

We share with His Honour the Chief Justice and other Justices of the Supreme Court what we believe is modest pride for the completion of the magnificent edifice to house all of the Law Courts in the country, to be named 'The Temple of Justice', which is scheduled to be dedicated on Pioneers Day, January 7th, 1965. We pray that the transaction of business, the administration of justice, the interpretation and expounding of the principles of the law upon which the life, liberty, rights and privileges of citizens and foreigners rest, may correspond to and justify the name given to this structure – 'The Temple of Justice'.

There is a tendency among a certain class of foreign nationals to enter into businesses and become competitors with Liberians, and, because of their access to greater business facilities, ability to procure capital and to live cheaply, these foreign nationals create unfair competition which Liberians find difficult to match. The Government has been most considerate and liberal towards some members of this class of foreigners, and I have personally spoken to the diplomatic representative and leaders of this particular foreign element advising against their entering the motion picture, ice cream, peddling, hawking and other small businesses that should be left to Liberians. Despite assurances given by these foreign nationals that they would desist, they still persist in carrying on these types of businesses, thereby putting Liberians out of business by unfair competition. In the case of the motion picture business, foreign competitors obtain the monopoly of films, which places them at a post of vantage and enables them to operate their motion picture businesses to greater advantage than Liberians, thereby creating unfair competition. Again, although foreigners are forbidden to engage in transportation, this same class of foreigners violates the statute by devious means and methods, not content to live under and within the provisions of the laws of the land. This constitutes a vile and unscrupulous violation of the Open Door Policy and must be checked.

This situation cannot be permitted to continue and specific recommendations will be communicated to you by Special Message.

The following measures are being presented for your consideration at your present session:

That the Statute relating to the admission of Lawyers to the Bar be revised to provide that Lawyers shall be admitted to the Bar only upon graduation from the Louis Arthur Grimes School of Law or some other recognized Law School; that in addition to this, candidates for admission to any of the Legal Bars within the country who may or may not hold a Diploma from a recognized Law School, shall be subjected to examinations by a Bar Committee of five, three of whom shall be professors or teachers in a recognized Law School in Liberia; that a penalty be imposed for any disregard and violation of the provisions of this statute or for the admission of Lawyers to the Legal Bar in any manner or form contrary to the provisions thereof.

That the Income Tax Law be revised, particularly with reference to corporations, and income tax to be paid by corporations be assessed on a graduated scale up to forty-five per cent for those earning more than a specified amount of profits.

That the Liberian Information Service be made a Department of Government and the title and style of the administrative Head be Secretary of Information and Broadcasting, and the positions of an Under Secretary of Information for Folkways and Culture, and an Assistant Secretary of Information and Broadcasting be created in this Department.

That streets, public buildings and other public works undertaken and completed at the expense of Government within corporations, cities, municipalities and commonwealth districts, be maintained at the sole cost and expense of such corporations, cities, municipalities and commonwealth districts; and that an Act be passed requiring all city, municipal and commonwealth districts to allocate seventy-five per cent of their budget for development purposes.

That because of the change made in the political structure and subdivision of the country by the creation of four new counties, the statute creating the Department of Internal Affairs be revised so as to have the duties and functions of this Department correspond to and efficiently cope with the new order thus created.

That patents, trademarks and copyright concerned with the protection of Industrial property be transferred from the Bureau of Archives to the Department of Commerce and Industry.

That the Liberian Government's monetary arrangements for honorary consular remunerations be amended to eliminate budgetary allowances for honorary consular missions.

That the Investment Code and Banking Act when presented, receive Legislative approval.

That because of their growing commercial importance, Mano River, Toe Town and Konjo be declared ports of entry.

That because of the Mano River Iron Ore Operation, which has resulted in an increase in population, trade and revenue in that area, the Mano River be declared a Revenue Agency.

That the Bureau of Government Housing be reorganized and a technically trained staff procured to conduct a proper inventory of Government property to avoid the many abuses now obtaining. In this regard, penalties should be attached to wilful misuse of Government property; also that after an occupant has been requested and given ample time to leave, summary eviction proceedings be entered against persons occupying Government houses unlawfully.

That officers of the Militia be required to attend the Liberian National Guard Officers Candidate School as regular active Officers and upon successful completion be allowed to attend overseas service schools.

That appropriation be provided for barracks and pier facilities to be constructed at the Coast Guard base to minimize maintenance cost and to prolong the life of the Coast Guard vessels.

That arrangements be made for the purchase of two corvettes and two 75-foot cutters with steel hulls for patrol purposes along our sea coast.

That because of the opening of additional Postal Exchanges two junior Postal Inspectors be authorized.

That a manpower commission composed of Government specialists, educators, and representatives of private industry be established to determine the present and near future requirements of the country in the various categories of managerial, professional and trade skills in agriculture, forestry, fisheries and other industries.

That the programme to classify and evaluate Government positions be accelerated and that salaries be appropriately adjusted and equalized.

That special action be taken to intensify research and extension requirements, and in allocating resources.

That priority be given to the co-operative credit programme as a means of providing financial assistance to farmers.

That the public be protected from exploitation and unscrupulous practices by restricting the importation of vehicles, radios, television sets and other products requiring servicing to such local companies or commercial firms that import spare parts and are equipped to maintain and repair such vehicles, radios, television sets and other products, and have qualified technicians employed for adequate repairs in keeping with international standards.

That all radio announcers, disc-jockeys and news-casters be required to operate under a licence obtained from the Bureau of Revenues after passing an examination to be administered by the Liberian Information Service; that Government review and revise its present Tax Policy on the Motion Picture Industry in Liberia which is considered by them to be unfair in relation to other local industries; and a National Advisory Commission on Cultural Affairs consisting of representatives from each of the nine counties be created for the purpose of advising and assisting the Bureau of Cultural and Touristic Affairs in the promotion and popularization of the cultural heritage of the nation.

That action be taken on the proposed tax legislation to revise penalty provisions; that a general Services Agency be created to provide central services, such as supply and procurement, and mobile equipment management; that legislative authorization be given for the complete evaluation of the equity and effectiveness of the Produce Marketing Corporation; that the proposed Bureau of Local Government be activated in the Department of Internal Affairs to provide leadership for generating interest and support for community development on a self-help basis; and that the Commonwealth of Monrovia be strengthened as a municipal institution through its assumption of certain local responsibilities now on an unsatisfactory basis.

OBITUARY

The most dreaded and most tremendous event in human experience: when the day closes, work ceases, darkness covers the earth, a strange drowsiness steals over us, the eyes close, we pass into a state of oblivion and all is mute and silent about us; this is death! When our human limitations have been removed and we have been stripped of our human habiliment, when the human part of us disintegrates and decomposes and the spirit enters into its limitless and illimitable sphere; it is then that gravitation, the most powerful force in nature, which attracts and holds us to the earth and prevents our flying into space, loses its power over us and we move without restraint from the ranks of mortals into the shining portals, from the terrestrial to the celestial and on into the Elysium Fields, the Paradise of God.

This has been the fate of a large number of public servants, statesmen, administrators, parliamentarians, clerics, soldiers and citizens in every walk of life during the year and we will pay them this last tribute of respect by standing in one minute unbroken silence.

May peace serene pervade their tranquil slumber and may they rise to the haven of just men made perfect at the general resurrection of the dead.

CONCLUSION

Into the keeping of the omnipotent God we commend the State and the people of this nation.

Independence Day Message

Monrovia, 26 July 1965

We have been able to develop the stability of our political admini-stration.

The people of this vast continent of Africa must continue the for-ward march of freedom for all; they must pursue the battle to the very gates without respite or compromise until a new dawn is em-blazoned upon the world's horizon.

Introductory Note

Under the guidance and direction of President Tubman, Liberia by 1965 had reached a state of political equilibrium. Liberia now had to consolidate her internal gains politically, economically, socially, and to work for the further expansion of those gains. Her gaze upon the African scene became wider, and she desired for the new independent states what she had her-self successfully accomplished in the field of political experimentation.

Monrovia, 26 July 1965

THE PROGRESSION of events which started with the constitutional Convention that culminated on July 26 1847, with the presentation and adoption of the Declaration of Independence, reaches today the 118th Anniversary of the Independence of the Republic of Liberia, our native land.

We celebrate this anniversary in a world which, from a political, social, scientific and religious angle is so different from that of 1847 that should any-one living during that period return to earth today, he would be lost in won-der, astonishment and praise. The cataclysmic and revolutionary changes which have occurred and transformed the earth and the thinking of its peoples have not, however, shaken the fundamental principles of this nation – a nation dedicated to God, democracy, human freedom and individual dignity. In this our fathers did not err and we have endeavoured to keep their faith.

Standing upon a pyramid of vantage constructed by 118 years of toil, affliction, disappointments, losses, achievements, failures and successes, we view the future from the known past and, considering present-day circum-stances, determine what the future could hold, indeed, what the future must hold for us as a nation.

When the nation had its beginning in the Commonwealth period, about 135 years ago, the world was pre-occupied with the philosophy of *laissez faire*, which evidenced itself in its most cynical form – the expansionist move-ment in Africa. Before this time, in fact even prevalent at this time though somewhat abated, slavery was an accepted practice throughout the world. The founding of a State which would obviously become a threat to colonialism was therefore looked upon with disfavour. The odds that the nation faced in her incipiency were almost imponderable. The only independent Republic in

135

Africa, her laws were disregarded with impunity by foreign nationals both private and official; her territorial sovereignty and integrity were time and again violated and in many instances her territory forcibly seized; her international policy was invariably formulated with apprehension and the knowledge that 'gun-boat diplomacy' and 'might makes right' were the prevailing order of the day. There was no international forum to which the nation could appeal for redress, nowhere that she could utter her complaints and be heard. It was like the law of the jungle – a predatory era!

We can look at the events of the early years of our nationhood and thank the God of our Fathers for the spirit, the will and determination to persevere, with which He endowed them and their successors in spite of the overwhelming odds which affected but did not deter them.

During the past 118 years of Independence, we have been able to develop the stability of our political administration; some of the valuable natural resources of the land are being explored; major government programmes have been undertaken; we have seen, during this period, an improvement of our transportation and communication systems to the point where the hazardous mode of travel from coast to coast has been abolished and the many inaccessible parts of the country made accessible; the standard of education has been raised and the number of schools throughout the country multiplied; specialized training has been insisted upon and students to whom scholarships have been awarded have returned and are now actively participating in the political administration of government and in many fields of industry and technology. We continue in the orderly and peaceful enjoyment of our hard-won freedom and independence, in the pursuit of happiness and security, and in strengthening our international relations.

The changes which have taken place, and which have raised the hopes of leaders and citizens alike have not always been a continuous steady progress and development, nor have they come about by easy methods. Consciousness of the ideal of freedom in all our political and social endeavours, hard work and determination have supported our national aspirations, ambitions and achievements; and in these difficult times, we must continue this hard work and this determination, as well as keeping before us the ideals of freedom for which we have sacrificed all these years as we try to solve the problems which beset us.

THE AFRICAN SCENE

Plenipotentiaries and representatives of the Liberian Government participated in and were associated with the founding of both the League of Nations and the United Nations as well as with all movements designed to liberate the people of Africa, and men everywhere, from the thraldom of oppression and servitude and place them upon the eminence of free men. We still stand today in the vanguard as advocates of the doctrine of self-determination and universal freedom for all men, regardless of race, colour or creed.

Africa Freedom Year brought into being a new political order on the Continent; new states were born which gave freedom and independence to millions of Africans; from being the ruled they became the rulers. Heretofore accustomed to thinking in terms of narrow tribalism, they broadened their vision and instituted a new social consciousness, social cohesiveness and political equality. Political independence had brought with it economic, educational, social and other responsibilities and obligations together with the increased burden of national development.

The people of this vast continent must continue the forward march of freedom for all; they must praise the battle to the very gates without respite or compromise until a new dawn is emblazoned upon the world horizon. We must remove the baneful pangs of apartheid, social injustice, racial malignance and political bigotry wherever it is found so that all nations and peoples shall live on an equal plane with mutual respect for each other in brotherhood, fellowship and love.

We must not permit *coups d'état*, internal warfare and subversive activities to spread distrust, suspicion and misunderstanding among us, for we are brethren whose concerted efforts should be directed towards upholding the Charter of the Organization of African Unity and building a free Africa, united in purpose and dedicated to a new and better life for all its peoples.

It is encouraging to note that the situation in the Congo (Leopoldville) has improved during the past year, and that this state, which has experienced hardships, turmoil and civil war, appears to be stabilizing. We congratulate the leaders and people of this state and hope that they will persevere in overcoming the difficulties which still divide them, thereby being able to concentrate on the development of their country, even though some of their fellow Africans support rebels against constituted government, when it is certain that he who spoils, after having spoiled, shall himself be spoiled.

THE INTERNATIONAL SCENE

We are today encompassed by a new world order, entirely dissimilar to that which prevailed 118 years ago, and we find ourselves in the midst of un-settled and bewildering world conditions.

As we celebrate here today, people are dying in many parts of the world from wars, earthquakes, floods and other violent natural phenomena. In other sectors there are internal dissensions, unrest, oppression and hunger. These are some of the conditions that plague mankind and continue to recur.

We believe and stand for the settlement and adjustment of national and international differences and understandings between men and nations at the Conference table, in the Conference hall or at some national or international forum. In any case where one party to a dispute, or one of the parties engaged in war *sua sponte* offers to negotiate for peace unconditionally, it appears an anomaly evidencing a peculiar mentality for the other party to persist-ently reject efforts for peaceful adjudication, especially when to co-operate in talks for peace does not involve a compromise of the national honour and prestige of the rejecting party.

Such an attitude or course of conduct conclusively evinces an innate love or preference for war and an abhorrence for peace.

More than 150 years ago, when the steam engine was invented, it was intended for commercial purposes and transportation. Similarly, when the aeroplane was invented by the Wright Brothers, it was intended for trans-portation. In later years, the steamboat was converted into battleships and navies and the aeroplanes into bombers, fighter planes and air forces. In the atomic age, however, when the atom was split it was originally intended and utilized primarily as an instrument of war and destruction, with nations rivalling each other for the mastery.

From this trend we see that research and invention for purposes of war comes first, and use of the invention for peaceful means follows, which would indicate that as we advance in these various fields of endeavours our ability and desire to destroy ourselves increase disproportionately.

Today, one finds it difficult to know or determine what are the principles and regulations by which nations may be guided in their intercourse with each other. The fineness of the art of diplomacy formulated by international conventions and agreements, concluded and correlated for centuries between governments and made the basis for international intercourse between nations, sometimes referred to as international law, is either wantonly disregarded and violated or has become outmoded. In either case some action should be taken to ensure respect for the law of nations. If they have been outmoded, a review and careful re-examination of what is known as international law protocol and procedures should be undertaken under the auspices of the United Nations, or some other appropriate international agency. This might contribute towards international peace and better understanding among nations.

We in Liberia from our incipiency adopted and pursued a democratic free enterprise system of government. We do not contend that this system should dominate the world except by the voluntary will of its peoples and nations. We become suspicious and apprehensive when any nation, group of nations, or any political system entertains as a part of its basic philosophy and aim the concept of world domination by force, subversion or any other artifices, and adopts this as an instrument of national policy, declaring that the flag representing that ideology and government shall be unfurled throughout the world, on every hilltop and valley, in every clime, coast and nation.

I prophesy that there will never be another single world power exercising domination over the whole world, and there will never be one system of government or ideology pervading the world, for history has proved that all the great world powers of the past, the last being the Roman Empire, which were founded upon military might, force and conquest, have fallen and disintegrated mainly because people cannot be perpetually kept in subjection and exploited for the benefit of others.

THE EMERGENCY RELIEF FUND FOR EDUCATION

The general response of the people, foreign friends and business men to our appeal for an Emergency Relief Fund for Education has been inspiring. That education is regarded by the people as the yeast of our democratic society and the safeguard of our freedom and independence is evidenced by the enthusiastic reception and active co-operation which the appeal has received. Let us remember that this is a three-year project and, as we have done in the first year, so let us continue to the end.

I tender grateful appreciation and thanks to my fellow citizens and foreign friends for this practical demonstration of the importance which they attach to our educational programme.

OPERATION PRODUCTION

The people of the various counties have seemingly realized the benefits to be derived from increased production and are working hard to implement the

Operation Production Programme. In some areas the work has not only been a great success but also of marked economic advantage to the people.

Our first attempt at evaluating the extent of the success of the Operation Production Programme will be at a National Fair to be held in Grand Bassa County in conjuction with the National Unification Council which is scheduled for 1966. We ask that all farmers, business men, concessionaires and artisans of every class participate in this national exhibition and show to the nations and peoples of the world what progress we are making in agriculture, industry and other fields of national activities, with particular emphasis on increased production.

SERVICE AND LOYALTY

The Founding Fathers of this Republic were dedicated to the cause of democracy, a belief which they transmitted to succeeding generations. On this 118th anniversary of our Independence it should be the responsibility of every citizen to rededicate himself or herself to the principles of democracy, and to pledge continued loyalty and service to these high and lofty principles, not permitting ourselves to be moved or traduced by strange, untried and untested ideologies and philosophies, which are basically and entirely founded upon materialism, and opposed to religion and belief in God.

THE DIPLOMATIC CORPS

The gracious remarks made by the Doyen on behalf of the Diplomatic Corps reassure us of the happy relations which exist between the respective governments represented in the Corps and our Government.

We esteem it an honour and privilege to be associated with you, Mr. Doyen and Members of the Corps, because of our mutual respect for each other, our willingness to function in our relations with each other upon a high plane of honour, truth and the faithful regard for treaties and agreements.

In the settling of the Corps in Liberia and its representation, Mr. Doyen, there has rarely, if ever, occurred a single diplomatic incident that would affect, in any degree, the fine relation of comity and amity subsisting between your respective governments and ours. There appears to be mutual confidence and understanding between each and all of you and this government to which you have been accredited, but this happy state of affairs has its source in the extra-territorial residence of each of you in your Embassies here. The great source from which this spirit of amity and friendship emanates and flows is the policy, philosophy and attitude of your respective governments at home. We assure you, Mr. Doyen and Gentlemen of the Diplomatic Corps, of the safety of your properties, your persons, and your lives. We on our part shall exercise our utmost endeavours to maintain and promote this fine spirit of co-operation.

We request that you be good enough to convey to your respective Sovereigns and Chiefs of State our personal best wishes for their personal well-being and happiness and for the peace, prosperity and cohesion of their governments and peoples.

SPECIAL GUESTS

It is our pleasure to extend to our special guests from Sierra Leone, Israel, Las Palmas and the President of the Anglo-Liberian Society, London, a warm welcome and wish that their stay will be pleasant and fruitful and that they will enter into the feeling and meaning of these festivities with us as friends and brothers.

CONCLUSION

To the perpetual protection and guidance of the God of our Fathers we commit this nation now and in the years to come. May He bless and save the state and keep us firm in our determination to maintain and perpetuate in this land the choicest fruits of democracy.

Annual Message delivered before the Third Session of the Forty-fifth Legislature

Monrovia, 16 November 1965

> *We rejoice and give thanks and praise to God for the benefits of peace, unity and understanding which seem to prevail throughout our country. Let us continue in our way of life, recognizing God as the beginning and the ending, as the Author of our faith, security, defence, progress and stability.*

Introductory Note

In 1964, the Vietnam Question was beginning to become of world-wide concern. At home, despite the shadow of austerity, calm and prosperity were in the air and the President devoted considerable discussion to a review of the health of our economy. Recommendations were made for stringent economic measures. Pioneers' Day was to be known henceforth as Founders' Day so as to perpetuate the ideals of patriotism and unity. The President observed that the Emergency Relief Fund for Education and Operation Production were beginning to become popular national self-help programmes.

Monrovia, 16 November 1965

IN A world rent and torn with discord, racial hatred, ideological conflicts, amazing scientific and technological advances and discoveries, you have convened according to law in the third session of the 45th Legislature.

It is with pleasure that I extend to the Honourable Members of both Houses of this Honourable Body a warm welcome to the capital, in the name and on behalf of the Executive Branch of Government, and pray that your deliberations and activities will be characterized by the high quality of unselfish and patriotic service which characterize the standard heretofore set by you.

The usual gala aspect of your meeting this year has been marred by the sudden and lamentable death of one of the outstanding members of the Honourable House of Representatives, the Honourable Roland T. Dempster, whose natural life was brought to an unexpected and sudden halt in the prime of his existence and at the apex of the fulfilment of the promising quality of service the nation expected of him. We deeply deplore his passing and pray for the peaceful repose of his soul.

FOREIGN RELATIONS

We have maintained cordial relations with all nations, especially with member states of the United Nations.

STATE VISIT

On March 30th of this year, in response to an invitation from His Majesty King Hassan II of Morocco, Mrs. Tubman and I paid a State Visit to the Kingdom of Morocco and were accorded royal courtesies, entertainment and consideration.

King Hassan II, although young in age, impressed me as a man of mellow experience and sound judgment. We returned from this visit with deep admiration for him and the people of Morocco.

INTERNATIONAL SITUATION

Relations between several member states of the United Nations continue to be strained and in some instances an actual state of war exists. In other areas, diplomatic relations between some states have deteriorated to the extent that the niceties, common decency and regard for international regulations and principles have been disregarded. Embassies and other premises, which in international law are considered extra-territorial (the territory of the nation whose diplomatic mission it is), have been violated and in some instances des-troyed, and these acts may be considered as acts of war. I am happy to report that these practices have not been indulged in by the people of this country and we should never permit history to record on its pages any such behaviour by citizens of Liberia.

Strenuous and continuing efforts have been made during the current year to seek agreement on the total banning of nuclear and underground tests for the prevention and spread of nuclear weapons and other related matters in the interest of world peace, but little progress seems to have been made. We must persevere until our goal for ensuring peace among nations and men has been attained.

The Indo-Pakistan conflict and the war in Vietnam are nerve centres of threats to peace. In the case of the Indo-Pakistan hostilities, the United Nations has succeeded in arranging a cease-fire, and continues through the Security Council to seek a settlement of the crisis which has been long stand-ing and deep seated. We appeal to both contesting parties to permit reason and good judgment to prevail and on no account to allow strife between them, for they are brethren.

The war in Vietnam has occasioned accusations, charges and counter-charges, each side maintaining that the other is the aggressor. I shall not attempt or undertake to judge or declare who is the aggressor. I do know that one of the parties in this war has asked for a negotiated peace at the conference table and has evidenced its sincerity by efforts to effectuate this in different ways and by diverse means which have been ignored or rejected by the other party. I hope that all parties to this unfortunate conflict will renounce the further use of force and effect a negotiated peace which is of the utmost importance to themselves and to the world.

THE UNITED NATIONS

There appears to be a growing tendency among nations to think of and treat the United Nations with indifference and as a nonentity, flouting its decisions with impunity, ignoring the fundamental principles of the Charter and refusing to meet their obligations as member states. In this generation in which the United Nations was founded and where numerous conflicts which flared up and threatened to become global have been localized; in this period when so many nations have emerged and been brought into being by the influence, power and effectiveness of the United Nations; in this age in which the United Nations offers a forum where all nations great and small, nuclear and non-nuclear, rich and poor may meet on a level to measure their forensic ability and debate upon the floor of this great organization, we must not and cannot afford to permit this Institution to degenerate and dwindle into the status of a helpless creature, limping on crutches.

Upon our return from a brief leave of absence which we took in Zürich earlier this year, we commented on the situation that exists in the United Nations today and emphasized *inter alia* that the United Nations Charter is an obligation voluntarily concluded between nations pledging most sacredly and solemnly to observe and execute the provisions contained therein. The fundamental and organic law of the United Nations and its primary and principal aim and objective is to prevent and avert war, so that men and nations may live together in peace, understanding and friendship. Nevertheless, because of human nature and its foibles, misunderstandings and disturbances will ever and anon arise, but in all such cases the United Nations will seek to bring us to a realization of the spiritual and nobler element of our nature as against the animal part of us in an effort to resolve all such differences peacefully.

I am prone to believe that the institution of a Special Commission within the United Nations might be helpful in reviewing its Charter and insisting upon the conformity of member states to the conditions and provisions to which they have already subscribed, in addition to seeking out the reasons and causes for the apparent irreconcilable breach between nations, especially between East and West.

It has been suggested that East and West could exist together peacefully under what has been called the principle of co-existence. Acting upon this principle we could try to investigate how this might be effected; because East and West were placed on this planet by God (or we may say by nature, if the materialists or atheists object to saying God), and neither can exterminate or destroy the other without exterminating or destroying themselves and the Earth. An international protocol or agreement defining the term 'Co-existence' and outlining the principles of peaceful co-existence between differing and vying political ideologies, philosophies and systems of government, without resort to force or subversion, might be presented to the United Nations by this Special Commission, to be approved and subscribed to by member states.

An important achievement of the General Assembly was the establishment of the United Nations Conference on Trade and Development as a permanent organ. This institution should promote sound action in the fields of trade, and of trade as related to development. From the outcome of the last conference held in Geneva, we are pleased to report that there appear to be better prospects of trade relations between the developed and the developing countries, even though at the present time statistics reveal that the developed countries are still benefiting disproportionately to the developing countries who supply primary products. This creates a serious imbalance which requires correction.

The Secretary-General of the United Nations indicated in one of his reports that the rate of expansion of economic structure continues to be slow and that international aid to developing countries had 'virtually ceased to increase', while the population explosion calls for urgent action. Thus it appears that the developing world would get poorer in the second half of the development decade unless governmental policies which aim at perfecting education, public health, and such other services are implemented, and action is taken to decrease the birth rate, increase long term investment, etc.

With a majority of the people in the world living in substandard conditions, the economic picture looks bleak for developing countries. That is why we still hope that developing countries will undertake policies on a regional and sub-regional basis that will increase income from the exports of primary commodities and enable us to earn our way.

With reference to birth control we need and seek increased population and at the present time do not subscribe to birth control in this country.

THE ORGANIZATION OF AFRICAN UNITY

The Annual Summit Conference of the Organization of African Unity met in Accra, Ghana, from the 21st to 25th of October. I consider the Conference very successful. Although there were some misgivings about its success, several important decisions were made that should tend to the liberation of the Continent and to greater unity and understanding.

President Nkrumah and the Government of Ghana have to be congratulated for the magnificent edifices that they have constructed within a relatively short period of time; they are monumental.

RHODESIA

The blatant and unconscionable act of the Ian Smith régime in Rhodesia in declaring unilateral independence for that country under its present minority rule cannot be more correctly described than has been done by British Prime Minister the Right Honourable Harold Wilson as 'rebellion and treason.' The statement by the British Premier that he does not intend to use military force to condemn the illegal and unconstitutional declaration of independence, but will do so by imposing economic sanctions and other means, and the declaration by the British Government that the Governor-General of Rhodesia is the lawful representative of the British Crown and will be protected against violence or any attempt at unlawful expulsion, appear to me to suggest that force will be used if it becomes necessary, but only as a last resort, and that economic sanctions and other means are the preliminary steps being taken. If my conjecture is correct then I agree with the position of the British Government; if my conjecture is wrong then I join those who contend for harsher measures.

INTERNAL AFFAIRS

We rejoice, give thanks and praise to God for the benefits of peace, unity and understanding which seem to prevail throughout our country. Let us continue in our way of life recognizing God as the beginning and the ending, as the Author and Finisher of our faith, our security, defence, progress and stability.

While we have enjoyed the benefit of peace and a reasonable amount of prosperity in austerity since your last session, I profoundly regret to report to you that a new type of crime appears to be infiltrating into our country. I refer specifically to the cold-blooded murders of Madame Korlu in the Township of Kakata, a virtually civilized community, and of Gabriel Diggs in Harper City, Maryland County.

As both of these matters are at present *sub judice*, I shall endeavour to refrain from making any statement that might be prejudicial to either of the accused, but I must state, in the interest of morality and a civilized society and on behalf of the Government and people of this country, that crimes of this nature must not under any circumstances be condoned. While Madame Korlu lay sleeping in her home in the peace of God after a hard day's labour by which she earned her living, her home was broken into by a number of persons against whom she had committed no offence and to whom she had done no wrong. Her throat was cut and her life ended as if she were a swine. This would seem to indicate a complete disregard for human life and property. A similar thing happened in Harper, Cape Palmas, Maryland County where Mr. Gabriel Diggs, after having entered his house, is alleged to have been cajoled out by those he considered to be his friends, driven off to an obscure place and murdered while in the peace of God, and his body carried to the shores of Shephard Lake and left there. This type of crime is attended with the deepest stain of turpitude and wickedness – their blood was shed not because of any controversy or hatred between them and anyone, or any wrong that they had committed against their assailants. This is the kind of crime that the Bible, in which most of us believe, calls 'The Shedding of Innocent Blood' and the Prophets uniformly declared that the shedding of innocent blood without punishment brings disaster unto any people who condone it. I do not mean by this that any innocent person should be punished: rather that no guilty person should go unpunished.

Each of us must unite in a concerted effort to stamp out this new inclination to disregard human life and to shed innocent blood.

Liberia's adherence to the free enterprise system, with the fair competition that it encourages, accounts for the presence of a large number of foreign investments in the country. Besides tapping the natural resources of the nation, manpower is being increasingly utilized, and it is gratifying to note that a programme of training is either expressed or implied in several concession agreements. The present rate of production strengthens our faith in the future, and in the better results accruing to participating partners.

While the austerity period necessitated a set-back in the economy because of fluctuations in the market and other unavoidable factors, the Liberian Government notes, with thanks and appreciation, the gesture of the concessionaries who readily agreed to negotiate a revision of their agreements, to provide increased royalty in some instances and profit tax in other cases. This attitude on the part of our business partners cannot but generate a true spirit of partnership, which we feel should be reciprocal.

With the development that is taking place in the country at the present time, the old restrictive measure which provides that a foreigner cannot lease land for more than twenty years should be revised; because at the time that this restriction was placed, foreigners were not considering the construction of buildings costing more than one hundred thousand dollars. Nowadays, foreigners are interested in investing in construction for their business to the extent of millions of dollars and to restrict leaseholds to twenty years seems to be too short a period for even the amortization of such a huge investment. It appears to me, therefore, that it should be made legal for foreigners to lease land from Liberians for forty-five to fifty years.

Adverse comments on the celebration of Mathilda Newport Day are being made but I see no objections to the celebration of Mathilda Newport Day, because, according to history, she saved the Commonwealth in a unique manner which made her a heroine. If the defenders of the Commonwealth had lost the day in the battle of Fort Hill there would have been no Liberia, and so it seems to me that the saviour of the day, especially because she was a woman, should have a place in the galaxy of our great men and a day dedicated to her would appear to be most appropriate.

The Legislature has set aside the 7th of January as Pioneers' Day, to do honour to the Pioneers who returned home from the United States of America. In my opinion, it is not sufficiently clear whether this is intended to include the Chiefs and people whom they met here and who had remained here when they were taken away into bondage, and with whom they negotiated for the territories that comprise the Republic of Liberia. The Pioneers' Day Act should therefore be changed and the day denominated 'FOUNDERS' DAY' so that it may include the pioneers who landed here as well as the Chiefs and people whom they met here and with whom they signed treaties ceding the land for the benefit of all concerned.

The economic development of a country usually brings with it problems of various kinds which in some cases may involve tragedies and loss of property, limb and life.

Within the past ten years the quantity of motor vehicles plying the highway has increased tremendously, with a resulting rise in the accident rate.

The Government has endeavoured to enforce stricter traffic regulations to reduce this, but it now seems imperative that other measures be adopted to afford greater protection to the average citizen, his life and his property, and it is therefore recommended that an Act be passed imposing the compulsory insurance of all motor vehicles.

The Development Corporation will continue to function and have close but separate association with the Development Bank. The Development Corporation should be made an autonomous institution with a General Manager or Secretary-General, as the case may be, charged with the responsibility for its operation.

The Agricultural Credit Corporation should be merged with the Development Corporation.

DEPARTMENTS OF GOVERNMENT

During the course of the year changes were made in the Departments of Education and Agriculture while the Senate was in recess, and the Honourable Augustus F. Caine was appointed Acting Secretary of Education and the Honourable John W. Cooper Acting Secretary of Agriculture.

The Secretary of State has submitted a comprehensive report narrating in some detail the conduct of the Department and the Foreign Service, for which his Department is responsible under the direction of the President. He made several recommendations, some of which will be mentioned later in this Message under the title 'Recommendations'.

In his Annual Report under the title 'General Economic Survey' the Secretary of the Treasury points out:

'The two principal export commodities of Liberia, iron ore and rubber, have shown a continuous decline since 1960. From a high point of sixty cents a pound on the New York Market, natural rubber prices dropped in 1961 to around twenty-five cents. Although during the Korean crises and since that time it rose; it has continued to move each year in a downward trend. In the New York Market it is now below twenty-five cents and the domestic price is fifteen cents.

'Iron ore similarly dropped from the highest peak in 1952 of about fifteen dollars and ninety cents. It has constantly, with the exception of 1957, moved downward. Present prices have dipped below eight dollars a ton.

'In the case of the Liberia Mining Company, despite the fifty per cent increase in net profit participation in 1965 from thirty-five per cent to fifty per cent, net earnings have declined by approximately three million dollars.

'Also implicit in this is the need for long loans for financing not only short falls in export earnings but also for long term capital growth.

'Despite the great and alarming decline in iron ore and rubber prices the Government revenues for the period under review rose from 39·06 million dollars to 41·8 million dollars: an increase of 2·74 million dollars. If we also consider the previous increase of 1964 over 1963 which was near the same magnitude, there is a total increase in revenue of over 5·6 million dollars in the past two years of austerity.

'Expenditures in the reporting period totalled forty-three million, three hundred and thirty-five thousand, eight hundred and eighty dollars.

'Thus there was incurred an operating deficit of one million, four hundred and ninety-nine thousand, six hundred dollars. This has been met by drawings under the Standby Agreement with the Monetary Fund. Operation deficit of the previous reporting period was about three million dollars. Consequently there is a marked improvement in our financial position.'

There is still a visible decrease in the level of employment, but with the beginning of the construction of various projects it is expected that this situation will improve.

It appears to me that Sheriffs, while being ministerial officers of the Courts, and Clerks of Court, while assigned and attached to the Court, are not Judiciary Officers but Executive Officers. We have tried both systems, placing them under the Executive and under the Judiciary, and experience has shown that better results are obtained when Sheriffs and Clerks of Court are placed under the Executive, because the Department of Justice operates daily while the Courts do not necessarily meet in session daily.

It therefore seems necessary that all Clerks of Court and Sheriffs be retransferred to the Department of Justice for greater efficiency and better administration.

The Postmaster-General's report indicates that telecommunication facilites are being installed throughout the country and postal officials have been surveying and analysing the requirements of the four new counties, with a view to establishing improved postal facilities in these areas. Trained staff and equipment are being procured for these areas.

The Secretary of Defence has made several important recommendations intended to improve the efficiency of the Liberian National and Coast Guards. These will appear in the Secretary's report.

The Department of Internal Affairs, according to the Secretary, has operated smoothly and effectively during the year and administrative officers of the Department have discharged their duties faithfully. There is marked improvement in the administration of the various counties and outlying districts.

Despite the austerity programme the Government's educational plans for 1965 have proceeded as outlined and we look forward to a much more encouraging year with regard to increased facilities for schools throughout the country.

The Secretary of Public Works has indicated that the administrative services of his Department have operated satisfactorily, despite the problems and drawbacks which the austerity programme created.

The Secretary of Agriculture expresses concern for the drop out of students from the School of Agriculture and Forestry of the University of Liberia, and advises that a Special Committee is studying this problem with a view to increasing the number of Agricultural and Forestry students. This is of the utmost importance in our advancing economy.

The Report of the Director-General, National Public Health Service, indicates an upward trend in the health situation throughout the country.

The Secretary of Commerce and Industry has advanced several ideas for improved and increased trade and industry during the next year, which will be submitted to you in his annual report.

The nation's image as presented by the Secretary of Information and Cultural Affairs continues to be favourable and he has expressed the hope that broadcasting, television and reporting may soon be so improved as to compare with the best in the world.

In his annual report the Director-General, National Planning Agency states that:

'It is clear from the experiences of other countries, and from sober analysis of Liberia's needs, that the growth of effective planning is intimately tied to a parallel growth of certain basic pre-conditions. The most important of these can be summarized as follows:
1. improved procedures for co-ordinated and soundly-based economic decision making;
2. an improved budget system, and increased effectiveness of expenditure control;
3. the establishment of a close relationship between planning and budgeting, mainly by providing an institutional link between annual programmes contained in any plan and Government's annual budget;
4. the generation of more and better designed projects and programmes;
5. the generation of more extensive and systematic information about the economy, especially with respect to such basic matters as financial relationships within the public sector, and data required for proper presentation and justification of the development projects;
6. the availability of trained and experienced manpower to administer and guide the planning process.'

The Chairman of the Special Commission on Government Operations in his Annual Report points out the necessity for relieving the President of the heavy burden he carries, with particular emphasis on interviews, and makes certain recommendations in this connection, which will be submitted to you in his report.

THE EMERGENCY RELIEF FUND FOR EDUCATION

The Emergency Relief Fund for Education has received a ready response from the people of the country, as well as from foreign friends, who have also contributed liberally towards this scheme.

Total collections as of September 30, 1965, were one million, four hundred and ten thousand, eight hundred and one dollars, fifty-one cents and we expect that next year's collection will exceed this figure. It is hoped that Revenue Collecting Agents who have been vigilant in this respect will put their spurs on to make this a reality.

OPERATION PRODUCTION

On the whole, production throughout the country has increased under the Operation Production Programme by a large percentage.

As this is the first year since the programme for the competitive production was instituted, I shall not mention names, but unless some of the counties step up their production there will be no alternative but to make public comment on their laziness and lethargy.

THE SUPREME COURT

The Supreme Court has had its regular Sessions in keeping with Law, but unfortunately Mr. Justice Dessaline T. Harris has been unable, because of physical disability, to perform his duties to the Court as in the past and having recently suffered a stroke he is now incapable of continuing to perform his duties as Associate Justice of the Honourable Supreme Court.

I therefore recommend that he be honourably retired and, because of his long tenure of honest, faithful and honourable service in the Judiciary of this country as County Attorney, Circuit Judge and Associate Justice of the Supreme Court over a period of fifty years, awarded a special annuity.

RECOMMENDATIONS

The following measures are being presented for consideration at your present Session:

That the Naturalization Law be revised so as to meet the changes that have occurred universally within the last ten years.

That the comprehensive fiscal recommendations comprising a new tariff, new taxes togther with new administrative procedures and regulations be enacted into law.

That Section 50 of the Revenue and Finance Law be applied (as for Customs) by the Attorney-General deputizing at least two members of the Income Tax Division for the summary attachment of a tax delinquent's goods where the tax involved does not exceed fifty dollars and that the Tax Court be regularly used to collect arrears in excess of that amount.

That the existing appeal procedure in Section 163 of the Revenue and Finance Law be amended by substituting a Tax Review Board for the present cumbersome references, first to the Commissioner of Internal Revenues, then to the Financial Advisor and finally to the Secretary of the Treasury. The Tax Review Board should consist of the Secretary of the Treasury or his Deputy, Chairman; a representative of SCOGO; the Attorney-General; President, Chamber of Commerce; and the Financial Advisor. The taxpayer may appeal to the Circuit Court under Section 180 after payment of the due amount.

That the principle of Section 164 (2) be implemented vigorously, and that for this purpose the section be amended to specify that the advance payments to be made shall, in the case where the business was in existence during the previous year, be not less than forty per cent of the actual tax assessed for that previous year.

That an Assessment and Evaluation of Real Property Committee comprised of representatives of the Treasury and Public Works Departments and the Bureau of Natural Resources and Surveys be established and commence work as early as possible but not later than the first quarter of 1966.

That the rate of commerce registration fee be one hundred dollars for a business wholly or partly carried on in Monrovia, and twenty-five dollars for a business wholly carried on outside Monrovia.

That the tax inspectors make a random sample survey of the number of huts and families in tribal areas anually to provide a control on the accuracy of town chiefs' returns, and to create, over a period, a more accurate record of potential yield and that study and consideration be given to the total burden of existing *per capita* group taxes.

That no case be passed to the Tax Court without an adequate indentification of the name and address of the defaulter.

That provision be made in the Budget to provide the Tax Court with one or more Bailiffs to the Sheriff in serving summonses, and with adequate transportation to enable seizure of goods to be made as soon as execution is granted.

That a co-ordination procedure be established between the Department of State and Treasury regarding Concession Agreements, taxation, and other Acts of Legislature to the effect that the Treasury Department will be timely notified of the publication of such acts and the proper Customs Officials advised of the tax provisions involved.

That arrangements be made for the handling of all local unpaid bills of merchants and other persons and payment thereof provided.

That all Clerks of Courts and Sheriffs be re-transferred to the Department of Justice for administrative purposes.

That the Act which provides for a Change of Venue in Criminal cases be amended.

That the law controlling the non-support of illegitimate children be amended, to provide reasonably enough for the child until he reaches his majority.

That the premises now occupied by the Monrovia Post Office be expropriated and just compensation paid to the owners.

That the rate of domestic telegrams be reduced from ten cents per word to five cents per word so as to be comparable with published inter-urban telephone rates.

That the National Examination System now in vogue be legalized in order to develop a real Liberian Educational System based on the condition and needs of the Liberian society and to raise the standard on a par with other African Countries.

That a five-year National Agricultural Programme be authorized and a committee organized to prepare and present a programme.

That by legislation making chest X-rays be made obligatory for army recruits and, once yearly, for teachers and for school children from the first to the fifth grade; and for food handlers such as waiters, cooks, etc.

That legislation be made for the creation of a Pharmacy Board within the National Public Health Service for the control of drugs and narcotics in the country.

That the registration laws and requirements be amended so as to provide stricter controls to curb existing bad business practices by unscrupulous businessmen.

That a General Services Agency be created.

That a Counterpart Training Programme be established within the Special Commission on Government Operations for the training of Liberians.

That a physical property inventory survey be authorized to commence in January, 1966.

That a Committee on Transportation be established to study the cost and utilization of Government-owned vehicles and to make recommendations to regulate these.

That legislation be made to govern the supply, connection and usage of facilities to be provided by the Public Utilities Authority.

OBITUARY

The record of mortality for the year 1965 shows that a large number of our fellow citizens and compatriots have passed away since the last Annual Message. Among them were statesmen and public servants who had rendered invaluable services to church and state and from your ranks, Ladies and Gentlemen of the Legislature, went the Honourable Richard Stanley Wiles, Former Speaker, and the Honourable Roland T. Dempster, active member of the Honourable House of Representatives. Among them also were Prophet Samuel Odwole, priests, doctors, jurists, soldiers and women some of whom were octogenarians.

I make special mention of the Honourable Lester A. Walton, former United States Minister Extraordinary and Plenipotentiary to Liberia, who held this post when the administration first took office, and the Right Reverend Bravid W. Harris, Bishop of the Protestant Episcopal Church in Liberia, long-time pilgrim for the infinite, who have passed away.

'It passeth away' is written upon every living thing here on earth. We look, we love, we desire, we possess — but no matter how dear and how cherished the object, we soon trace upon its fragile form this melancholy inscription, 'It passeth away.'

Our pleasures, what are they doing? Our afflictions, what are they doing? Passing away; they have all but a moment. Where are the companions of our childhood? Where are the associates of our youth? Our fathers and mothers, where are they? Where are they who once inhabited the houses in which we dwell and who occupied the chambers in which we will sleep tonight? Where are those who once strode these hallowed streets and filled the chambers of the state? Where are they – gone! They have finished their course; they have passed away. And we are following them. We, too, are accomplishing our assignments. And everything around us is changing, consuming, vanishing as a cloud passing away. A few months ago, this year 1965 was new, but it is passing away – almost gone. The seasons, the sun, the opportunities, all, all are fleeing and passing away – hastening to be gone.

These colleagues, friends, brothers, sisters and partisans who have preceded us to the great beyond to try the recesses of another world, have accomplished their tasks here as mortals and now inhabit or exercise themselves in the spirit world that is without length, breadth, height or form. May it be a grand reunion when, at the mystery of the sounding of the trumpet and the rising of the incorruptible dead at the last day, as foretold by the apostle, we shall all be changed in a moment, in the twinkling of an eye; and become just men made perfect.

CONCLUSION

Into the tender and unerring power and guidance of God I commit you, the Government, the people of this nation and myself praying that, unworthy though we are, He may continue to extend His mercies and loving kindness to us as a nation and people and that we will confess our sins, turn away from wickedness and herald the truth and righteousness now and hereafter.

Independence Day Message

Monrovia, 26 July 1966

The interest of Africa and its people demands that we rise above individual nationalism. We are now creating and developing the African image.

Introductory Note

An angry message: President Tubman made a survey of the international situation and did not like what he saw happening, especially in Africa and to Africans. Borne out by the 119th Independence Day Message were certain unpalatable realities confronting Africa and the world. Several *coups d'état* had occurred which threatened to undermine Africa's newly won independence and democratic governments; the rebel racist government of Rhodesia had not been toppled in the time specified by the Labour Government in Britain; there was universal dissatisfaction over the World Court's Decision in the South West Africa case which denied that the applicants, Liberia and Ethiopia, had a legal interest in the case, thereby reversing a previous judgment which acknowledged the legitimacy of their interest; the war in Vietnam had escalated to new proportions. The world, in short, was far from achieving even relative peace. President Tubman hoped and prayed for the peace of the world.

Monrovia, 26 July 1966

THE INTERNATIONAL skies are dark. Storm clouds, driven by the rising winds of selfish nationalism, revolutionary philosophy, greed, propaganda, falsehood, ungodly principles of materialism, religious fanaticism and wanton disregard for right and justice, portents of war, obscure the sun. Flashes of lightning across the skies reveal bewildered leaders of peoples and nations whose voices are lost in the thunder of confusion.

In this universal state of affairs we are meeting throughout the nation to observe and celebrate the 119th Anniversary of our Independence. It is to the great and eternal God, Creator and Absolver that we must turn for guidance, wisdom, patience, tolerance and reliance, to be able to penetrate the denseness of these clouds and find a gleam of hope and light. And so let us in prayer implore for peace with a hymn written by the Russian poet, Alexis Lwoff, and I ask and invite all who have no religious scruples to join in repeating the last line of each verse which is: 'GIVE TO US PEACE IN OUR TIME, O LORD.'

> God the all terrible! Thou who ordainest
> Thunder Thy clarion, Lightning Thy sword;
> Show forth Thy pity on high, where Thou reignest;
> Give to us peace in our time, O Lord.

God the all merciful! earth hath forsaken
Thy ways of holiness and slighted Thy word;
Let not Thy wrath in its terrors awaken;
Give to us peace in our time, O Lord.

God the omnipotent! mighty avenger
Watching invisible, judging unheard
Save us in mercy, oh save us from danger:
Give to us peace in our time, O Lord.

So shall Thy people, with thankful devotion,
Praise Him Who saved them from peril and sword;
Singing in chorus from ocean to ocean
Peace to the nations, and praise to the Lord.

As we observe this Anniversary of our Independence with befitting ceremonies, we reflect upon the uncertainties and imponderables that surrounded
and beset those stout-hearted men and women who brought freedom and
democracy to these shores, and those eminent sages, the Chiefs and people
whom they met here and who in the Declaration of Independence are
referred to as the 'Lords of the Soil'. These rediscovered kinsmen welcomed
and accepted them and their new political philosophy of democracy, and
joined with them in creating and establishing a lone Negro state on the
African Continent during those days of the virulent onslaught of colonial
expansion. Their efforts were crowned by a Constitutional Convention which
culminated in the presentation of that immortal and historic scroll, the Declaration of Independence, which was subsequently referred to referendum,
adopted and made the sheet anchor of our freedom, liberty and democracy.

There were concomitant sources of opposition and irritations at work—
the last vestiges of the slave trade, the inimical and cancerous climatic conditions, the intrigues of foreign forces opposed to the principles, aims and
objectives of this Negro political experiment, and the meagre financial and
other resources. However, their tenacity of purpose, the justness of their
cause and the inherent principles that this experiment represented so fired
their determination that failure was not possible.

I quote from an address delivered by the Honourable Edward Everett of
Massachusetts, to the Fifth Annual Meeting of the American Society for
colonizing the free people of colour:

'Sir, when men have a great, benevolent and holy object in view, of
permanent interest, obstacles are nothing. If it fails in the hands of one,
it will be taken up by another, if it exceeds the powers of an individual,
society will unite toward the desired end. If the force of public opinion in
one country is insufficient, the kindred spirits of foreign countries will lend
their aid. If it remains unachieved by one generation, it goes down as a
heritage of duty and honour to the next; and through the long chain of
counsels and efforts, from the first conception of the benevolent mind,
that planned the great work, to its final and glorious accomplishment,
there is a steady and unseen, but irresistible co-operation of the Divine
influence, which orders all things for good.

'Am I told that the work we have in hand is too great to be done? Too
great, I ask, to be done when, too great to be done by whom? Too great, I

admit to be done at once; too great to be done by this generation perhaps; but not too great to be done. Nothing is too great to be done, which is founded on truth and justice ... Sir, I may ask without irreverence, in a case like this, though it be too great for man, is it too great for that August Providence, whose counsels run along the line of ages and to Whom a thousand years are as one day?'

These were the principles and spirit that stimulated and inspired the pioneers of this nation and have characterized succeeding generations of Liberians and administrations of Government from 1821 to 1847 and from 1847 to the present.

Following this tempo of events, every passing year has added greater lustre of renown to the history of this heroic nation. Every passing year has made more sacred the tabernacles of peace, freedom and justice which inspired our Pioneer Fathers to venture into the unknown amidst raging winds to establish the first Democratic Republic across a tempestuous ocean.

The interest of Africa and its people demands that we raise ourselves above individual nationalism, political mysticism, and inglorious ambitions for continental domination, and remain vigilant against the imposition on the African people of systems of administration more gruesome and oppressive than colonialism has ever been, or neo-colonialism can ever be. It demands that all African States be left free from the interference of other states; that each state, without let or molestation, be left alone to pursue the course it feels to be in the best interest of itself and its people and that African States be permitted to choose their own system of Government, be it fascism, communism, socialism, free enterprise, democracy or republicanism, to ensure for themselves peace and growth upon solid foundations rather than upon foundations of shifting sand. To do otherwise would destroy even the prospect of unity and create a spirit of enmity, hatred, and war, and would bring reproach upon us as Africans and substantiate the pronouncement of our enemies that the African is not capable of governing himself.

I must repeat: We are now creating, forming and developing the African image; there are incidents and events taking place that do not present a hopeful or honourable image of which we and the world can be proud. African States are maligning, conspiring and intriguing against other African States and leaders; African States are threatening war and carrying on border invasion raids against sister African States; others are planning the overthrow and downfall of sister States, encouraging and participating in *coups d'état*. These are some of the current events that are becoming a part of or being welded into the African image that we are creating, which will bring disrepute and ignominy on ourselves and our posterity when the history of this era is written.

I earnestly plead for a different and more realistic approach, better logic, a greater sense of justice, a deeper sense of real, genuine affection and brotherhood — not from the lips but from the heart. I plead for well-planned, well-considered and rational decisions in matters of great moment; I plead against hasty and rash decisions and actions in all matters affecting African and other states and the Organization of African Unity. If we continue and persevere in the mood and trends that we seem to be pursuing it may cause the disruption or at least the retardation of the Organization of African Unity which we have striven so hard and relentlessly to organize and found upon a Charter that should be made the anchor and foundation of our actions.

In its transition from colonialism to nationalism and independence, Africa has become an influential factor in changing the tempo of power diplomacy among the world community of nations.

In the past, nationalism in Europe and the Americas did much to change the history of the world. Today nationalistic movements in Africa and the world are bringing phenomenal transitions on the continent and throughout the world, thus inscribing the African image on the pages of history. Africa has become a centre of attraction in the past decade and there is every indication that she will escalate to higher stages of progress with greater momentum, depending upon the course we pursue in the interest of freedom and justice.

THE RHODESIAN QUESTION

Like South Africa and the Portuguese African Territories, Southern Rhodesia has become a nightmare that seeks to degrade and ridicule the African and relegate him to a place in the internal and international society of men and women similar to that of an ape or an animal of the lowest species. The wilful, bold, vicious and contemptible attitude and practice of the Ian Smith régime in Rhodesia bespeak their contempt not only for Africans but also for all black men and peoples of colour wherever dispersed the world over.

In this Rhodesian drama we have advocated and exercised patience and even tolerance. We believed in the Declaration of the British Prime Minister that the imposition of ecnomic sanctions on the Smith régime in Rhodesia would have a salutary effect and change the ugly picture that existed there within a matter of weeks and not months. This has not happened, and the régime seems to be growing stronger, more persistent and defiant. It seems now that while we wait and continue to be tolerant and patient, Rhodesia is becoming a furnace heated seven times hotter with oppression, depression and murder; and this, in an era of civilization, with an international organization called the United Nations and its Charter which guarantees the right of all men to freedom and the inherent right to self-government and self-determination — a Charter that guarantees to all men freedom of speech and expression, freedom to worship God in his own way, freedom from want and freedom from fear, but which is being disregarded and violated with impunity by Portugal and South Africa, member states of the Organization. Resolutions condemning them have been passed, one after another, but they seem impossible to implement because of what appears to be the insincerity and double-dealing of some member states.

In this connection I cannot emphasize too strongly the very grave responsibility which the United Kingdom has, in the unfortunate situation that has developed in Rhodesia. A crisis involving confidence has been created among all African States as a result of what is considered an attitude of irresolution in this all-important matter, which can lead to unfortunate consequences. The fundamental rights of four million Africans should not be sacrificed for about a quarter of a million whites by policies which appear to be wavering and half hearted. The cause of justice will prevail in the long run, because it is right.

THE DECISION OF THE INTERNATIONAL COURT OF JUSTICE

In addition to the Rhodesian situation there is the decision of the International Court of Justice, before which was brought an action against South Africa for mismanagement and violation of its obligations of the mandate of the League of Nations to the mandated territory of South West Africa.

The decision of the Court that applicants had no legal interest in the case, and its refusal to go into the merits of the case after its previous determination in December 1962, that applicants did have a legal interest and the Court had jurisdiction to determine the case on its merits, savour of casuistry and legal pyrotechnics which is, to say the least, most surprising and puzzling. In fact it generates unpleasant suspicions about the Court.

I believe in due respect, regard and submission to the final decision of a Court of Justice, because I believe in the rule of law; but a decision or judgment of a Court, such as this one by the International Court of Justice in the South West Africa case cannot admit of assent because it is unclear as regards law, justice, equity and morality. It is so unclear that it cannot borrow light from any legal or moral sun to illumine it, but it is tinged by racism and the old régime of colonialism; and it leads one to wonder whether it is not the handiwork of men still imbued with bias and race prejudice.

The one thing to the credit of the Court in this case, and I am happy that one thing does exist, is that it has proved that all Members of the Court have not bowed their knees to Baal, that an equal number of the judges on the Bench of this International Judicature were opposed to, and did not assent to, this unjust and sinister decision, and that it required a casting vote from one of the judges who is President of the Court and had already voted in favour of the decision, so that this double vote was necessary to establish the decision as the judgment of the Court. These circumstances render the Court's decision weak and untenable beyond compare. However, we salute and congratulate those seven noble men with a high sense of justice and rectitude for their stalwartness in saving the Court from total and universal disgrace and ridicule.

In this matter we believe that there is victory in this temporary defeat and the people of Africa, Member States of the United Nations, will coalesce and join forces to eradicate these injustices and malpractices of South Africa, Portugal and Southern Rhodesia, both in the United Nations and by other appropriate means that will effectively retrieve the present ignoble status of the International Court of Justice and give relief to the victims of South African, Portuguese and Rhodesian oppression.

After careful study and analysis of various possible alternatives the Liberian Government will determine, in consultation with other African governments as well as friendly governments of other continents, the new course to be pursued in these matters. Nevertheless I wish to reassert that, because all men are created equal and on the basis of human rights should be treated equally, the arbitrary and abominable policy of apartheid is iniquitous and unjust. The principle of self-determination at present denied by the Portuguese Government to the inhabitants of the territories under Portuguese administration is an inherent right. Peace on this earth cannot be achieved until the international community not only recognizes these principles but also gives full effect to them. The Liberian Government will therefore use all means within its power to seek this goal.

THE INTERNATIONAL SCENE

The world seems to be at war with itself. Wrongs are in army against rights. The dangers of the tragedy that may result from the present trend in international upheavals cannot but arouse great concern in rational people throughout the world. The people of the world seem to be split wide open by ideological differences with very little, if any, prospect for compromise or reconciliation. These two divisions of international society appear to be each so convinced of the righteousness of their own system and the evil of the other, that they seem to be intent not merely on the maintenance of the *status quo*, but on the possible abolition and destruction of the other system. There are those who advocate co-existence and frankly speaking, since the pronouncement of co-existence as a policy, some Communist Countries have evidenced sincerity in the demonstration of this policy. Others reject it and assume a negative attitude towards every proposition, action or movement proposed, in an effort to find solutions, ameliorations, compromises, or even exchanges of views or intercourse of any kind in the interest of peace.

On the other hand, some of the Western Democracies, in the interest of their own national life and the preservation of their democratic system and way of life, seem determined to defend their liberties and their political institutions at whatever cost. Consequently, scientists, factories, laboratories and other research centres are continuously engrossed in a search for new technological inventions and discoveries that will put them in a position of preparedness to cope with the situation. The other side is equally active in these respects.

Preparedness is necessary but it should not be regarded only as a matter of military force able to repel aggression and preserve liberty. Preparedness should involve more than military force, might and power. It involves also the removing of injustices suffered by people throughout the world because of race, religion, political and social affiliation and adherence; the eradication of prejudices that stalk arrogantly in a nation because of class, heredity, race, creed, colour and other considerations, sometimes made manifest in demands of freedom for oneself but denial of freedom to others, the understanding of people's desire for better and abundant living and the initiation of appropriate action to attain this goal. We should not forget a general belief that it is ignorance and selfishness which stand between the common man and the use of productive machines that will produce all that is necessary, useful or beautiful, and will distribute such productivity so as to be possible for all the physical basis of life; but we should remember that world peace will be more greatly enhanced if satisfactory solutions can be found for these urgent and pressing problems.

Wise political leaders will see that their nation is properly prepared to protect itself against aggression and to maintain its existence and freedom. They will seek increasingly to find security in an ordered world; they will co-operate with other nations in the United Nations until world law and order shall supplant international anarchy, the sword shall become the ploughshare and the scorched earth become the fertile earth. Such men should also see that true preparedness lies in example and not only in precept. There is no fifth column, nor any subversive elements, as potent as the fact of liberty alive, justice practised, brotherhood revealed; there is no power in a slogan that does not possess reality. Ideologies cannot be conquered only by force of arms. Victor Hugo emphasized this when he said:

> 'You can defeat an army of soldiers,
> but you cannot defeat an army of ideas.'

We know that within the framework of democracy we can build a just and brotherly society in which creative talents may be truly evoked and man may live in security, enjoy leisure and fruitful labour; in which the impulse to creative action and service will be stronger than the acquisitive impulse. We need to recruit the youth as well as all the citizens of the nation and acquaint them with the thousand-year-old struggle for political freedom, fire them with passion to preserve it and, still more, to use it to bring equality and fraternity to their fellows; we need to impress upon their minds that they must do more than sing and yell the lines and verses of the National Anthem and National Hymns; to teach them that they must launch out with a firm determination to work, to face the problems that beset their nation and the world, with cool and resolute minds, ready to live and to die, so that the society in which freedom and justice reign supreme may emerge in that condition which makes it fit to be called a democracy.

To have peace, nations should pursue policies that really mean peace; each nation should make its own democracy so just and so brotherly as to be impregnable and attractive. What can be done for nations all over the world that are suffering and experiencing economic and financial difficulties and failures? What can be done for developing nations that produce primary produce? What can be done for nations and peoples who still carry the yoke of slavery, oppression, segregation, civil and political privations and injustices?

Modify unconscionable sharp business practices based on the policy of ALL FOR ME AND AS LITTLE AS POSSIBLE FOR YOU! Pay the producer of primary products fair and just compensation for his products! Consider every person to be a human being entitled to enjoy the same inherent rights and privileges as yourself without let or hindrance.

At International Forums, let the soft voice of conscience dictate the application of the principle of honour and fairness and not only of expediency; let Judges designated to dispense justice, but who render perverse and wrong judgments, thereby making justice a travesty and by-word, be removed. We should desist from seeking to impose one nation's system of government and way of life upon another nation, for if we indulge in this practice we are not winning but alienating them. It should be the high privilege of great, powerful and industrialized nations to co-operate and maintain the conditions of freedom, acting upon that principle and abiding by decisions of freedom.

THE WAR IN VIETNAM

At the centre of the trouble spots throughout the world stands the war in Vietnam, a volcanic crater towering above all others, erupting and sending forth lava around and into many parts of South-East Asia. This eruption is threatening to flow into other parts of Asia and the war may perhaps escalate into one involving the world in a third global war. Without specifically expressing any opinion on the rights and wrongs or on the question of who is the aggressor, there is one indisputable and outstanding fact in this struggle that cannot reasonably nor rationally be discarded or ignored if one is to think correctly and express a just and fair opinion. That is that, no matter what the situation, when nations are engaged in war and either of the belligerents suggests peace talks, but the other flatly rejects the offer not only of the party seeking compromise but also of disinterested parties repeatedly interposing and pleading for the cessation of hostilities and negotiations for peace, then the attitude of the belligerent party which rejects every approach and effort, even for a meeting to talk about peace and seek an end to the war, cannot but be judged as opposed to peace.

BACK HOME

Service, loyalty and national consciousness are indispensable characteristics of the members of any democratic society. Our thoughts are much like our inclinations; our writings and speeches are affected by our learning and our preconceptions; but our daily actions bear an imprint of our real selves. At work we tend to fear that if we do too much, there will be little or nothing left for tomorrow – and so we slow down in order to keep pace with the past. This is an invidious fallacy which must be completely eradicated from the Liberian Society, and we must move forward with ever-increasing momentum and intensity in our development programmes.

At present we are receiving technical and economic as well as industrial assistance from several friendly nations. We have experts, specialists and technicians from these countries in our offices, our schools, colleges, universities and other Governmental agencies. We must seize the opportunities presented by such assistance and utilize them to the best and fullest possible extent, for these assistance programmes must end. They cannot continue indefinitely and we should not desire them to, for we ought to have an eternal yearning to stand on our own feet as men and citizens of a sovereign and independent nation capable of conducting and administering our own affairs in every avenue and phase of our national life.

It is not enough merely to read in our history books of the broad sweep of forces that have shaped our nation, without making any realistic contribution towards the further progress and development of our common Country;

It is not enough to peruse the Holy Bible and the Koran and then act inhumanely towards our fellow man;

It is not enough to expend money to earn a College or University degree through tedious study and hard work and then remain utterly indifferent to the constructive activities of our communities;

It is not enough to render less service than duty requires, and attempt to justify this as balancing the equation between labour and reward;

It is not enough to seek a stately funeral with wealth and power, without showing the slightest concern for the pain and agony of destitute peoples, far and near;

It is not enough for seven cities to claim a Homer dead through whom a living Homer begged his bread;

It is not enough to be 'Up Yonder' when the roll is called to give an account of our stewardship when there has been no stewardship;

It is not enough to compose the most brilliant literary manifestoes and to deliver persuasive rhetorical orations on 'Disarmament', 'Atheism', Racialism', 'Communism', and 'Capitalism', when virtually all our minds and hearts are not dispossessed of the intrigues of these controversial issues;

And it is not enough to engage in the intricate complexities of diplomatic see-saw at summit conferences on the solution of international problems when in essence the answers to these provocative issues are within ourselves and more often have been left behind in our respective home countries.

But it is diligent and faithful service that spells confidence, trust and respect through administrative channels of authority in public service;

It is national consciousness and devotion that illustrates useful citizenship;

It is unselfish personal sacrifice in the national interest that shows patriotism;

It is hard work, earnest toil and vigorous labour that demonstrate honour and the dignity of manhood;

It is Operation Production, increased productivity and a diversified agricultural economy under a carefully planned national agricultural programme that generate national prosperity;

It is a good-neighbour policy and practice that spell a good worldly brotherhood;

It is courage and perseverance to uphold the Constitution, with undiminished resolution to respect, protect and defend the laws of the Republic that evince undaunted loyalty, patriotism and devotion to the State; and

It is a good Liberia, a good Africa, a good America, a good Europe, a good Asia and a good Australasia that will provide a good world for all of us.

THE DIPLOMATIC CORPS

Touched by your kind and gracious remarks, Mr. Doyen, we are gratified that our relations with the governments represented near this capital have been most friendly and that cordiality and understanding have prevailed between your respective governments and ours, and are being maintained in our official and social intercourse. On this 119th Anniversary of our Independence, I salute and extend felicitations to you, Doyen, and Members of the Diplomatic Corps and through you to your respective Sovereigns and Chiefs of State and governments in the name of the Government and people of Liberia and on my own behalf. I assure each of you of the continued determination of the Government and people of Liberia to live together with you and all nations as true counterparts in the pursuit of permanent world peace and the brotherhood of man.

To nations as to individual persons, there come great moments, spring tides for revolutionary changes and for good or for evil when mysterious great moments are impending! The world picture in the present crucial hour, as seen from current events and scientific and technological strides, looms dark and perplexing indeed; yet there is in the hearts of those who have discovered the eternal and inexhaustible resources of faith an ineradicable conviction that we are about to witness another striking and arresting epoch in the cycle of evolution. I believe that God is behind human life and in it, that He will not allow the human race to be overpowered or destroyed by materialism, atheism or agnosticism; neither will He allow human nature to lie idle, to waste itself in trifles or be content with low ideals. But Nations that profess belief in God must demonstrate it by thought, words and deeds, knowing that as sure as night follows day those nations that forget God or deny his existence shall be utterly destroyed, and that without remedy, in fulfilment of Biblical Prophecy.

Fellow Citizens, a great moment is upon us that requires action – purposeful action, courageous action, determined action. It is a moment in which we can accomplish great things for our own country and its people as well as for the peoples of all the earth, regardless of race, colour, creed, nationality or system of government. Let all of these be tolerated alike, for in dictating to others or trying to interfere with the course they set for themselves we would be attempting to deprive them of their right of sovereignty and independence and doing to them what we have complained about and fought against for centuries.

What we pray for ourselves we pray for all Africa, for all Europe, for the Americas, for all Asia, for Madagascar, for Australasia and all the isles of the seas wherever man is found.

May God extend to Liberia and its people His strong arm of protection, His merciful attribute of forgiveness and His majestic power to sustain and save us.

Third Annual Message delivered before the Fourth Session of the Forty-fifth Legislature

Monrovia, 15 December 1966

The high hopes that we entertained for African unity and for the development of a new entity in international affairs that might bridge the gap between existing political and ideological warring groups have not yet been realized.

Introductory Note

The year 1966 was a time of great upheavals in Africa. The Rhodesian question was not settled and there seemed to be no solution in sight. The issue was considered to be the responsibility of Britain but African states were not satisfied that Rhodesia should remain solely the concern of Britain. They began to reflect and plan for ways to end the white racist régime in that country.

On the domestic scene, austerity became every citizen's concern, since it unexpectedly followed upon the heels of a period of prosperity. The President called upon all Liberians to assume responsibility and to make contributions toward providing relief. An austerity tax was recommended and immediately put into effect. The central issue in this message therefore dealt with various forms of remedy for our austerity and how to effect their implementation. The President further recommended the creation of a National Library and the annual observance of a National Festival of Arts. Based upon our latest census report, provision was made for additional representation from the four new counties in our Legislature and an increase of one representative for Montserrado County.

Monrovia, 15 December 1966

CIRCUMSTANCES BEYOND our control have occasioned the delay in making this Annual Report to you as required by the Constitution.

I ask your tolerance and pardon for the lateness of this Message.

FOREIGN AFFAIRS AND FOREIGN RELATIONS

Although international affairs and relations are clouded by political, racial and ideological strife and feuds, although the achievements and development of codes, conventions and protocols relating to international procedures and intercourse between nations, formulated by experience gained over centuries, are flaunted and disregarded, and recklessness to the extent of anarchism is practised, nevertheless world leaders and men of thought in the United Nations and elsewhere have kept their equilibrium, asserted the greatest virtue – patience – and thereby averted a global or local nuclear holocaust. But relations between nations still swing like the proverbial pendulum of danger and uncertainty as a result of vying political ideologies, one seeking world domination by revolutionary processes such as inciting disloyalty, treason, rebellion and *coups d'état*; the other generally defending and protecting the principles, hoary with age, that the sovereignty of all nations should be respected and non-interference in the internal affairs of other states maintained. Thus peace seems to be as far away as it was during World War II.

The solution to these vying and conflicting political ideologies and processes seems to lie with the principle of peaceful co-existence, because there will never be another world government or power. Rome was the last. This has been declared by the Prophets and all of the revolutions in the world cannot change it.

Relations between this Government and other governments remain cordial and friendly.

The high hopes that we entertained for African Unity and for the development of a new entity in international affairs that might bridge the wide gap between existing political and ideological warring groups have not yet been realized. Most of us, although claiming to be non-aligned seem to be influenced by either one or the other of existing political and ideological groups; we may deny this but our actions in this respect speak so loudly that our words cannot be heard. Perhaps in time this will change.

The Rhodesian question is one that has baffled our assessment and understanding of the procedures being pursued by those responsible for handling it. While we could tolerate a peaceful settlement without bloodshed, if that were possible, we cannot understand how an open, blatant and persistent rebellion which is treasonable in character can be palliated and handled with such gloved hands, such soft actions. Nor can we understand how a defiant rebellion which is an infamous crime can be disposed of without the imposition of deserved and legal penalties, at least against the instigators and leaders of the rebellion. To fail to impose penalties would mean that those responsible for handling the rebellion convict themselves of the crime of compounding a felony.

REVIEW OF THE OPERATION AND ADMINISTRATION OF DEPARTMENTS, BUREAUX AND AGENCIES OF GOVERNMENT

The reports on the administration and operation of the various Departments, Bureaux and Agencies of Government during the current year will be submitted to you by their respective Heads for your information, study and disposition.

According to the report of the Treasury, the overall state of the economy is sound. The total estimated revenues for the fiscal year 1965 to 1966 is forty-six million, eight hundred and forty thousand dollars and revenues collected during that period totalled 47·6 million dollars. Details of estimates collected and disbursements are contained in the report of the Treasury Department.

According to financial circles, the international economic future throughout the world looks dark and grim, and warns of the necessity for caution. A review of the present economic trends indicates that the developing nations are being deeply affected by the problem of filling the gap between the price structure of raw materials and finished products. The high interest rates which add to the already unavoidable public debts of developing nations do not give much hope with regard to loans, and there is a general feeling of extreme caution in respect of spending among peoples and nations all over the world who fear either inflation or deflation.

Due to the decline in the prices of rubber and iron ore, two of our main sources of revenue, as well as the recent United States quota imposed for coffee imports – from which we hope there will soon be some relief – the situation looks even more gloomy, and revenues for the next four years are expected to fall below production, unless we take immediate measures to offset it.

This means that we must be still more austere, cutting back and saving on both recurrent and non-recurring items, as well as reducing expenditures for new development.

In our Opening Address at the recent Unification Council at Buchanan, we pointed out that in an effort to meet and avert this financial crisis, we had requested all foreign concessionaires to increase their profit tax and sharing agreements with the Government to assist in the attempt to avoid a financial slump. They had responded so favourably that no demands were made on us Liberians for any contributions or sacrifices to the Government's austerity programme by the relinquishment of any of the emoluments and financial benefits of which we have been the recipients for more than twenty years; nor had there been any special taxation imposed for the benefit of the austerity programme.

The time has come, is even now upon us, when we Liberians must assume full responsibility and make our contributions toward providing relief from the universal depression that has been predicted by the international financial and economic prophets. I therefore submit the following Economic Plan for which I earnestly request your favourable and speedy approval:

DEBT SERVICE RESERVE

It is the desire of the Government, beginning in 1967, to take measures to assist in meeting increasing debt service payments in future years, especially in 1969 and 1970, and to meet Budget deficits.

For this purpose, a special Debt Service Reserve account should be established and beginning in 1967, one and one-half per cent of collected revenues should be set aside and deposited in this account.

REDUCTION IN ALLOWANCES

There is a need to reduce lower priority Government expenditures in order to concentrate resources on basic services and development activities. It is proposed that all allowances for all purposes be reduced as follows: All Presidential allowances reduced by fifteen per cent, all other allowances by ten per cent. This includes all allowances except subsistence, rental, security, local travel and military allowances.

AUSTERITY TAX

There is an urgent need to increase Government revenues to provide for public services and to support development activities. Although a number of other revenue measures are being recommended as projects of law, these will not be sufficient to cover necessary requirements. The alternative would be to reduce expenditures on public services and development projects with corresponding retrenchments. Rather than increasing unemployment and making retrenchments it would seem preferable for citizens earning incomes to assist in meeting the cost of government operations and thereby avert unemployment and retrenchment.

An annual tax on all monthly earnings or fixed compensations of citizens in both the private and public sector is proposed. This tax should be imposed for a period of three years beginning January 1, 1967.

The tax should be equivalent to one-half month's earnings or fixed compensations *per capita* of persons earning $6000.00 per annum or over. For persons earning less than $600.00 per annum the tax should be the equivalent of one-fourth month's earnings or fixed compensations. In the case of salaries and wages, the tax should be withheld monthly at the rate of 4·2 per cent of the citizen's monthly salary or wage.

The employer or party shall be authorized to withhold said tax and shall make such filing and payment of the tax withheld, as shall be required by regulations relating to the collection of this tax.

IMPROVEMENT IN COLLECTION OF EXCISE TAXES

It has been extremely difficult to collect excise taxes imposed on certain local manufactures in order to offset the loss in revenue resulting from the decline in imports of these manufactured products. First of all, there is difficulty in determining the level of production and sales of these products in order to calculate the amount of excise taxes to be paid. Secondly, although in some instances, it has been possible to assess the amount of excise taxes to be paid, the manufacturers have been delinquent in their payments to the Government. Under the present circumstances, it is in the interest of the Government to adopt those measures which would offer the best control and lowest collection costs.

It is recommended that the equivalent of the excise tax should be applied as a special tax on the imported raw material components of the products to be manufactured. The tax should be at a level which will produce revenues equal to the existing excise taxes and should be paid by the manufacturers at the point of entry of their raw materials along with their customs duties. The tax would be imposed on, for example, emulsion for paints, syrup for soft drinks, malt for beer, etcetera. The administration and collection of the tax will be the responsibility of the Bureau of Customs instead of the Bureau of Internal Revenues.

TARIFF ADJUSTMENT

The recent change in Customs Tariff classifications created increases in tariff rates on certain items of general consumption as well as other items. In general, these increases have caused the retail prices of some of these items to rise; and it is reported that, for some items, imports have actually fallen with the corresponding reduction in customs revenues from these sources.

We recommend the adaption of a specific tariff revison submitted by the Commissioner of Customs through the Secretary of the Treasury.

The intent of this measure is correspondingly to reduce sale rates of such items as may fall within the above mentioned categories.

DUTY EXEMPTION

It would seem necessary at this time to

(a) limit duty exemptions to include only items essentially necessary for the operation of schools, hospitals and such businesses as are specified by agreement or legislation, also materials for, the specific use of Government.

(b) limit exemptions granted contractors for Government projects to machinery and raw materials to be used exclusively on the project and

(c) modify and confine duty free exemptions to religious organizations to building materials, church and school supplies as well as imported food for boarding schools, colleges and other educational institutions.

Liquor, cigarettes and other consumer goods imported by these organizations for use of their personnel should be dutiable.

COMMERCIAL REGISTRATION FEES FOR TAXI-CABS, BUSES AND TRUCKS

Each commercial transport company pays an annual registration fee of $100.00 irrespective of the number of vehicles owned. It has been evidenced that many such registrants are permitting other owners of taxi-cabs and transport buses to register under their names, thereby avoiding the payment of additional registration fees.

It is therefore recommended that commerce registration fees for each fleet of taxi-cabs, transport buses and/or trucks be changed from $100.00 per firm to $25.00 per vehicle.

Other matters requiring legislation I submit and list hereunder, craving your favourable consideration and action.

To co-ordinate Government's present programme of revising the Immigration and Naturalization laws, I ask that you give consideration to liberalizing the requirements for tourists' visas so as to make it easier for tourists to enter the country.

In view of the additional departmental responsibilities such as the appointment of the Secretary of State as Chairman of the Commission on the Coordination of Technical Assistance, it is recommended that an assistant to the Secretary of State be appointed to assume some of these responsibilities, the rank of Assistant Secretary of State.

There is considerable lack of efficiency in the collection of certain classes of taxes, principally the Real Estate Tax. Immediate steps are hereby recommended to be taken for a countrywide assessment of all real property and for the purpose of facilitating the efficient collection of outstanding and future Real Estate Taxes.

We also recommend that an amendment be made to the Real Estate Tax Law to provide a penalty of fifty per cent for failure to pay this tax when due, as the present penalty of three per cent has had little effect.

In connection with the payment of excise taxes, it may be interesting to point out that during the period under review a total of only 770 thousand dollars were collected of which amount the Monrovia Brewery paid 403 thousand dollars, more than fifty per cent. The Treasury points out that this Company has been commendable in meeting its obligations regularly and without argument and I wish to record the appreciation of Government for this type of business management, which lends credit to the organization, and inspires the confidence of the country in which it operates.

To ensure that all individuals and businesses meet their filing dates, it is recommended that a comprehensive income tax filing and collection programme be initiated.

It is also recommended that the Motor Vehicle Inspection and Registration Programme be extended to areas outside Montserrado County.

A Port Authority Law giving specific consideration to revising Port Rate Structure will be presented for your consideration.

Because of the increase in volume of work in the Bureau of General Accounting it is suggested that an additional Deputy Director be appointed, and that authorization be given for the engagement of a Pre-Audit Expert to be attached to this Bureau.

In view of recent trends it is strongly recommended that urgent consideration be given at your present Session to the Banking Code already submitted to Your Honourable Body.

In a free enterprise economy such as ours, one of the most important stimulants for the development of commerce and industry is the availability of credit and other banking facilities. We have been rather disturbed not only by the declining level of such facilities in the country, but particularly by the extent to which these facilities are becoming more and more inaccessible to Liberians. We consider this to be an unhealthy situation and, in our desire to find solutions to the problems, held discussions with representatives of the groups concerned: business, commerce, banking, labour, etcetera. These discussions have afforded us the opportunity of determining some of the actions which the Government itself could take to improve the situation where it is reported that Liberian and foreign businessmen fail to meet their obligations and creditors are unable to recover their debts expeditiously, because of complicated legal procedural practices which delay the disposal of these causes, and mortgage foreclosure proceedings which are protracted because of the complicated system of pleadings. To try to relieve and obviate these conditions we propose the following measures for your consideration:

1. That you authorize the preparation of a Commercial Code for enactment into law. This Code should establish the rules and procedures for all types of business transactions including letters of credit, bank deposits and collections, commercial papers, etcetera.

2. A special Debt Court should be established to handle only debt matters and thus eliminate the long delays in concluding court actions on debts. Pleadings in such cases should be restricted to a complaint and an answer without the necessity of filing an appearance. All debt actions before the Debt Court should be decided on issues of fact and not of law.

3. Legislation designed to provide for voluntary or involuntary bank-

ruptcy should be enacted and an appropriate agency established to administer the affairs of a bankrupt.

4. Some foreign businessmen are in the habit of obtaining credits, entering into business and then absconding, leaving their creditors without the means of recovering their advances thereby adversely affecting the flow of cash and impugning the name and reputation of the country. It is therefore proposed that every foreign-owned business to be established in Liberia be required to post a cash bond of not less than ten thousand dollars. Evidence of the deposit of such a bond with a bank in Liberia would be required before the registration and licensing of the foreigner or firm to do business. The bond would not be negotiable nor available as collateral.

   Concessions and other businesses which have special arrangements with the Government for the issuance of similar bonds will be exempt from this requirement.

5. The penal law against the issuance of worthless cheques should be strengthened. We therefore recommend an amendment to the law which will be forwarded to you for your consideration.

6. Because of mounting storage rates which often exceed the value of the goods stored at the Free Port of Monrovia over a period of time, and to obviate the loss of shippers and importers of these goods and of revenues to Government, it is recommended that Bonded Public Warehouses be constructed in the Free Port Area where goods may be transferred at a standard rate, to enable importers to clear them within a reasonable time, failing which they may be sold.

The Development Corporation continues to function and to have close but separate association with the Development Bank.

As indicated in my Annual Message last year the Development Corporation should be made an autonomous institution with a General Manager or Secretary-General, as the case may be, who will be charged with the responsibility for its operation. To this effect legislation is respectfully requested.

With the intention of reorganizing the Militia, arrangements were made with the Swiss Government for three Liberian officers to proceed to that country to observe and study the Swiss Militia System. The three officers were despatched to Berne, and, having completed their observations and study course, they returned and have submitted their report, which will be sent forward to you for appropriate action. In the meantime we recommend that the Liberian Militia be re-organized after the general pattern of the Swiss Militia System.

It would seem reasonable that lighthouse dues be paid to Government by all shipping companies operating in Liberia since this is a policy practised throughout the world. We ask for legislation to this effect.

During the year the Department of Defence activated the 11th, 13th, 14th, 16th and 17th Militia Infantry Regiments, Armed Forces of Liberia and the report of the Secretary of National Defence indicates that personnel of the new regiments are actively engaged in the performance of their duties.

Special compliment must be paid to the regiment at Nimba County which staged a March Past during the recent birthday celebrations in that County. They were most impressive, outstanding and soldierly in their performance. This regiment impresses me as being among the best in the country and I congratulate the Superintendent, its Officers and men on their soldierly bearing and discipline.

Realizing the responsibility of Government for the welfare of the citizens, especially for the rising generations who will assume leadership and conduct of national affairs, we recommend the establishment of an office in the Department of Education that would be responsible for social welfare. This office would serve the nation by making essential research into the causes of certain social problems, and by recommending measures for prevention and remedy, as well as co-ordinating all welfare groups and organizations to avoid waste and duplication.

Because of the value of records and literature in national development, planning, research and history, we should now consider the establishment of a National Library where all important government documents, books by and about Liberians and other literature would be deposited.

In the selection of textbooks for our schools other than those prepared in the country, great care must be taken, since some editors and publishers are prone to present African Countries in a ridiculous manner, to vent their veiled racial antipathy. Therefore all textbooks to be used in our schools and colleges must be carefully examined and scrutinized.

In an effort to cope with the increased demands for educational facilities, it is recommended that appropriation be made in the 1967 Budget for additional furniture for public schools.

It has been brought to my attention that the high schools throughout the country are collecting a tuition fee of $1.00 from each student, but that this amount is not paid into the Bureau of Revenues; also that other educational institutions collect substantial revenues other than from school fees which are not reported or accounted for.

In relation to Government expenditure for secondary education throughout the country, a fee of $1.50 is nominal and it is recommended that the tuition fee charged be increased to $1.50 and that all monies collected by public high schools or other public schools, for any source whatever, be deposited directly into the Bureau of Revenues.

Because of the importance that Agriculture holds in the development programme and our desire to speed up Operation Production Priority Number One, it is recommended that the Agriculture Credit Corporation be reorganized along lines recommended by the Treasury Department, the Planning Department and the Department of Agriculture, in co-operation with the USAID Experts on Co-operatives and Farm management.

The Operation Production Programme must be accelerated and made more effective. This programme being essentially agricultural, we recommend that it be transferred to the Department of Agriculture so that it may be co-ordinated with the total national production effort.

The Department of Agriculture is preparing an Overall Agricultural Programme which will be submitted to Your Honourable Selves and we pray your approval of it.

Within the past fifteen years Government expenditures for health and sanitation have increased by more than 200 per cent. Health services have been established with clinics and hospitals constructed throughout the country. During the past fiscal year under review expenditures for health were more than 2·5 million dollars.

A total of 200 births a month was reported at the Maternity Centre in

Monrovia and patients treated at the Government Hospital here averaged about 10,000. Despite the substantial expenditure for this service and the number of persons treated, total revenues collected from hospitals and clinics throughout the country during the 1965–1966 fiscal year amounted to only $4,000.

This amount is negligible when compared to the services extended and the money spent for them, and, while health services and hospitals are not profit-making institutions, yet the Government cannot afford to permit such financial conditions to continue. Measures will be introduced to regulate clinical calls, payment for drugs, and treatments at all Government clinics and hospitals, and stricter accounting must be made of all drugs supplied and monies collected and spent.

The Director-General of the National Public Health Service will submit, for your consideration, a plan to obviate the situation reported above, entitled 'Payment Plan for Medical Services'.

Because of the increasing manufacture and use of radioactive material, it is important that precautions be taken with regard to its importation into the country and it is suggested that the Public Health and Safety Laws be amended to include a section dealing with the importation and use of radio-active materials.

The high and mounting cost of living has reached such proportions that the Government must take action to give some measure of relief. Because of our free enterprise system we are loath to regulate and control prices of general commercial businesses or place restrictions thereon, yet when business shows an attitude of recklessness and total disregard for the rights of the individual by the imposition of price rates that are prohibitive, it is Government's obligation to step in and prevent this exploitation.

I recommend therefore that the Department of Commerce and Industry be authorized to take appropriate steps to curb the rise in prices of essential commodities other than luxury items.

In order to awaken greater interest and encourage the continuing production of our arts and handicrafts, it is recommended that a National Festival of Arts be held yearly when artists throughout the nation will be invited to participate and prizes will be awarded for the best work of art, whether it be an oil painting, a pencil drawing, a wood carving, a raffia or bamboo object, needlecraft, a piece of sculpture; or an original musical composition, a poem or a local story.

Because of the many archaeological discoveries made this year which show that there is a gold-mine of valuable treasures within our territory, authorization is respectfully requested for engaging the services of an experienced archaeologist to evaluate these discoveries.

It is recommended that a National Statistical Commission be established which will be attached to the National Planning Council as the highest policy and co-ordinating body of Government in the field of statistics.

The Department of Planning and Economic Affairs has prepared a Development Plan for the years 1967–1970 which is designed to increase the pace at which the nation is to achieve its social and economic goals, for the consolidation of the gains obtained and initiated and the process of continuing growth in the economy and a broader distribution of the fruits of economic progress. This will be submitted for your appropriate action.

In order to re-organize the system followed at present with regard to the leasing of houses, it is recommended that a Rental Board, the membership of which be determined by the President, be established. The primary responsibility of the Board would be:

(a) to relate rentals to be paid by Government for leased property to the housing market generally and

(b) to establish equitable rentals among the various lessors for property leased to Government.

The Bureau of Natural Resources and Surveys submitted to Your Honourable Selves a Survey Project of Law to which we hope you will give attention during the present Session.

As a result of the census, which was recently completed and published, it is apparent that each of the new counties is entitled to additional representation in the Legislature, and since the General Elections are due to be held in May 1967, and the census report may not have been approved by you before that time, it is recommended that you authorize by legislation the election of two additional representatives in the House of Representatives from Loffa, Bong, Nimba and Grand Gedeh counties, and since the census report reveals an increased population of over 100,000 inhabitants in Monrovia, it is recommended that one representative be added to the present representation of Montserrado County in the Legislature.

During our recent visit to Europe by permission of the Legislature, we had talks with a number of businessmen and industrialists. These discussions resulted in the formation of a Consortium consisting of Salzgitter Industriebau of Salzgitter, Germany, Motor Columbus of Baden, Switzerland and EDESCO of Zürich, Switzerland, who have agreed to act as economic, industrial and investment consultants and promoters for the development of industrial and other economic activities.

Final details in connection with the operation of this Consortium are to be worked out and presented for your consideration and approval.

Because of the still unsettled conditions in the world today, it would seem necessary that the Emergency Powers granted to the President of Liberia be extended for an additional twelve months.

In my Second Annual Message before the Third Session of the Forty-fifth Legislature I recommended legislation to impose compulsory insurance of all motor vehicles plying the Liberian highways. To date no action has been taken and I respectfully renew my request in this regard.

UNIFICATION COUNCIL AND OPERATION PRODUCTION FAIR

Returning from the Unification Council and National Fair two days ago, I came away with faith, hope and assurance in the coherence and national unity of the Liberian people.

Special mention must be made of the general interest manifested in the Council and Agricultural Fair by the people throughout the Country including foreign concessionaires and businessmen as well as the most generous and hospitable entertainment of the delegates and visitors to the Council and Fair by the Superintendent, Members of his Council, the people of Grand Bassa and foreign residents there. There was nothing but welcome and friendly embraces from all to all. We record our abiding thanks and appreciation for all of these courtesies.

The Secretary of Commerce, the Secretary of Agriculture and the Secretary of Internal Affairs, in whose hands were entrusted the preparation and arrangements for the Council and the Fair, rendered officient services and were principally responsible for the success of both the Fair and the Council. We extend our thanks and congratulations to them. May their performances be kept at the mark they set themselves in the preparation and arrangement of the Unification Council and National Fair of 1966.

EMERGENCY RELIEF FUND FOR EDUCATION

Because of the increasing demands from several counties for additional school buildings and educational facilities, it is hereby recommended that the Emergency Relief Fund for Education be extended for another three years to assist in meeting these very pressing demands, which we cannot ignore.

THE LIBERIAN NATIONAL YOUTH ORGANIZATION

The Liberian National Youth Organization shows signs of promise in developing the youth of this country into useful, strong and co-operative citizens. According to the Director of this Organization there has been considerable expansion in the Organization's programme during the year, and youths are taking greater interest in it and its work. Youth camps are being established throughout the country and youths trained according to a programme that is geared towards rehabilitation.

We hope that this important phase of our national development programme will continue to reflect credit to its Director, Staff and particpants, especially the Experts from Israel who initiated it, and who have rendered invaluable services in connection with the implementation of this programme.

THE SUPREME COURT

The Honourable Supreme Court held its regular semi-annual Sessions during the year. Because of the resignation of His Honour Dessaline T. Harris, due to ill-health, with the advice and consent of the honourable Senate, the Honourable H. Augustus Roberts, then Assistant Attorney-General, was elevated to the Bench of the Supreme Court as Associate Justice in succession to His Honour Dessaline T. Harris. This Court still holds the respect of the people of this country.

His Honour, the Chief Justice, reports that peace and harmony have characterized their Sittings during the year.

In our Development Programme over the years the Government of the United States has been most generous and helpful in making loans on easy terms of payment, giving technical assistance, making grants and other contributions to this programme. Other nations such as the Federal Republic of Germany, the Governments of Israel, Britain, Italy, Sweden, China, and France, and other friendly states, have made contributions in different degrees.

These acts of beneficence we appreciate, and we record our thanks, because we feel that they were not under any obligation to be helpful, and that at least they are entitled to our gratitude, which we gladly and sincerely extend.

OBITUARY

Life is the beginning of man and death is his end; life begins and continues to generate existence over several decades but finally the end comes which we call death, and this is the fate of all the living. To live, inevitably means to die; there can be no life without death, neither can there be death without life and so at this time we pause to commemorate, pay homage, tribute and honour to those of our colleagues, fellow citizens, friends and acquaintances who have predeceased us during the current year and have been translated from the scene of the living into the realm of the spirit.

Among them were legislators, jurists, executives, businessmen and women, politicians, clerics and soldiers who have finished their sojourn, ended their labours, and have been removed from the rank of mortals into the shining portals of Divine Providence. Through the habiliments of death they have transcended the terrestrial and now are within the Elysian fields, the Paradise of God. We regret and mourn their loss, and the end of our association, exchange and interchange of thought, ideas and work with them, but we will ever cherish and remember their great contributions, their labours and sacrifices in the interest of our common country, the nation they served so faithfully. May they live forever in the bliss and joy of Paradise where all is peace and God is Love.

CONCLUSION

Fellow citizens and foreign residents, as we enter the octave of the Christmas season I extend to you on behalf of Mrs. Tubman and myself, warm and joyous greetings of the season, and pray that the New Year will bring brighter hopes of peace and love among all men and that nations will hush the noise of war and strife, and hear the Angels sing.

Let us pray earnestly and fervently for the peace and goodwill of the world, for the peace of our country and its people, and for unity and concord, for plenty and prosperity – the results of hard work and toil. May God grant our prayer.

Speech delivered at the Executive Pavilion in reply to Speeches of Welcome by Leaders of the Three Branches of Government

Monrovia, 6 November 1960

> *Whatever the future may hold for mankind, however secure we may be in our own ideologies, whatever plan of action the peoples of the world may adopt, I have come to believe in the ability and willingness of men of goodwill everywhere to approach world problems with a new spirit and new heart.*

Introductory Note

President Tubman in 1960 was granted leave of rest by the National Legislature which took him to Switzerland. In his reply to the speeches of welcome, when he returned to Liberia, he noted a new liberalism in the world. The admission of fifteen new independent African states as members of the United Nations further heightened his realization of that liberalism. Because Liberia, in her own way, had fought to see Africa liberated, the President rejoiced at the fulfilment of the hopes and aspirations of Africans to be free from foreign domination. He saw a new world order in the making, which carried hopes for the peace long sought for by mankind.

Monrovia, 6 November 1960

IT IS with a sense of great joy and happiness that we give thanks to God for having guided and guarded us during our absence and now for having brought us back home, safe and well, to participate in this happy reunion. In deep and grateful humility we acknowledge His abiding presence with us throughout the course of our travels. It is, therefore, with very great pleasure that I, on behalf of Mrs. Tubman, the members of my party and myself, express our feelings of genuine joy and happiness to be back home after a period of two and a half months' absence on a health and rest trip granted by the Legislature. To the members of that august body I express my grateful thanks for their foresight and generosity in authorizing this vacation without even an application or request from me, an act dictated solely by their sense of loyalty and goodwill.

All modes of travel involve certain risks and hazards – whether by air, sea, or rail. While we did not use the first means, we did utilize the latter two. I am aware that your solicitude and prayers in the interest of our safety while away, added to our own entreaties, sustained us during the months of our absence. Fortunately we were not subjected to any major illnesses, nor were we exposed to the mental anguish of any impending danger. We return to you with the grateful recognition that while we were physically absent from you, our souls and spirits often communed together in our common aspirations and pleas for a happy reunion. God has granted our wishes and we are both grateful, thankful and happy.

Travelling as we did through many foreign countries to our destination, we were overwhelmed by the many courtesies extended to us by the officials through whose territories we passed. I express to their several representatives in our city our deep appreciation for kindnesses which were bestowed on us, and for the security measures provided for our safety wherever we went. These gestures will go a long way toward cementing the links of friendship which already exist between us and them.

One of the principal objectives envisaged by the Legislature in authorizing this vacation was to afford me an opportunity for a health check-up and a period of rest. While it is true that we did have some rest, it was not as much as we had contemplated or thought desirable. Events both at home and in the international setting rendered this objective impracticable. Thus it was that while away we engaged in state business day and night – very often until late at night. There were urgent state and international matters which required immediate analysis and action, and therefore had to be attended to.

After arriving in Zürich I underwent medical examinations by the world-renowned Professor Löffler and other universally acknowledged specialists, such as Drs. Schinz and Brunner and others known to some of you. Both Professors Löffler and Schinz came to Liberia at the invitation of my attending physician, Dr. Meyer. These examinations showed good health and no necessity for clinical treatment. But as a precautionary measure, the performance of a surgical operation was recommended. I therefore entered the hospital on the 18th September, underwent the operation on the 19th and was discharged seven days thereafter.

It has been remarked that a President does not escape his office. Thus it was that during the period of our absence we received several delegations, including the Trade Delegation to Yugoslavia, the Rubber Delegation to Malaya, the Delegation from Holland in exploratory talks on the future of a ship-building project, the Delegation in connection with the establishment of a Medical College at the University of Liberia, etc. On the decision of the independence of the Federation of Nigeria, I attended and addressed the club of Nigerian students in Zürich when it celebrated its nation's independence. Then, as if to round off our activities, we paid a three-day unofficial visit to The Hague at the invitation of Her Majesty Queen Juliana and His Royal Highness Prince Bernhard of the Netherlands. This visit was a source of great pleasure and satisfaction to Mrs. Tubman and myself, because it afforded us the opportunity to renew old acquaintances at The Hague, where we had been four years earlier.

The present session of the United Nations General Assembly is significant because of the attendance thereat of a number of Chiefs of State. Issues of world significance emerged which were fundamentally designed to alter, to a large extent, the framework, form and organization of that great world parliament which has been the instrument by which wars have been averted, and many nations, including African States, have achieved and retained their nationhood.

We are aware that, after fifteen years of existence, there may perhaps be certain constructive changes deemed necessary in the Charter to meet the demands of present-day developments, for conditions have changed considerably since the formulation and adoption of that instrument. Both organic laws, constitutions of nations, charters of international organizations and even the constitutions of clubs and ordinary social orders are not changed or annulled by spasmodic or impromptu suggestions and demands of individual members. The organic law of any state or organization is regarded as sacred, and changes are only made with the greatest care and after careful consideration and deliberation, requiring the appointment of committees to study the instrument and any amendments which may be offered. One of the amendments which is necessary, and which has been suggested for many years, is the veto power, but no mention was made of this at the present session of the United Nations.

Most organic laws of nations and of other organizations provide that no amendments or changes should be made at the same session at which the amendment is offered, since such action requires deliberate thought, careful study and painstaking review, and a vote of at least two-thirds is imperative.

Conceived in this light, the Liberian Delegation to the present session of the United Nations General Assembly was directed to oppose any arbitrary changes in the Charter of the United Nations or any subtle attempt to affect adversely the proper character, power and influence of the United Nations by any manoeuvre no matter how subtly or carefully planned. That was where we stood a few weeks ago and that is where we stand today.

I did not attend the United Nations General Assembly when a few distinguished personages both at home and abroad thought I should have done so, because I felt that I should not have gone to the session, and I did not; nevertheless, it was as well that I was in Switzerland, where I could be in constant contact with the UN headquarters in New York by radio and long distance telephone about the day-to-day activities of the Assembly.

My message to the newly admitted African States at a luncheon tendered them by our Secretary of State in New York evinced clearly my deep concern, growing interest and general happiness for the rapid independence of the African States and their membership of the comity of nations. I believe it is generally known that our faith in the United Nations and all that it stands for remains unshaken. To me it is still the greatest bastion of fundamental human rights and the ultimate hope for permanent world peace.

The United Nations is a Delegated Body and each member state is entitled to send a delegation. I could not delegate myself as a delegate to the United Nations General Assembly. I could have gone as Chief of State and addressed the General Assembly on any issue I thought involved sufficient magnitude. There was but one matter, one question that I considered enough to have required my presence; that was the Congo crisis. However, that question had been settled by the Security Council, and an appeal taken to the General Assembly, which was heard in a special and extraordinary session of that body before the opening of the regular session. The decision of the Security Council, having been sanctioned by the General Assembly, closed the question.

Liberia has always been, and I pray God, will always be a law-respecting and law-abiding nation. Therefore when the Security Council took that action and the General Assembly sanctioned it, the matter was settled and I considered my attendance unnecessary, and, in the final analysis, I am responsible for the administration of Government.

In 1954 upon invitation, I visited and addressed the General Assembly of the United Nations. I believe the newly admitted chiefs of state were well advised to attend the session and to witness the admission of their respective countries into the comity of nations.. I also think that any chief of state of any nation had a right to attend if he wanted to, and I congratulate all who found it desirable to attend. For myself I have the satisfaction in my own mind and conscience of having acted in accordance with my better judgment, which I have not yet regretted.

I express great satisfaction at the trend of events at the General Assembly, for the fifteen new African States which were admitted to the United Nations General Assembly had the support, aid and advice of the Liberian Government. I am indeed happy that Liberia played some rôle in the struggle for the liberation of all African States that have attained their independence since the great nationalist movement commenced.

At that time Liberia stood virtually alone in the United Nations for the liberation of Indonesia, Tunisia, Morocco and all the other African States. At the meeting of the General Assembly, whenever our Government took a strong and positive position in the interest of the liberation of Africa and Africans, certain of our colonial neighbours reacted by invoking the right bank treaty provision of the rivers as boundaries between us. There were other innumerable difficulties imposed on us by rigid customs formalities, closing of borders to Liberian visitors, etc. All these we endured for the emancipation of Africa, remained undaunted and persevered in the defence of our people's freedom.

Similarly, during the entire period of the colonial expansionist movement in the nineteenth century Liberia, like Daniel of old, in accordance with the courage of his convictions, never yielded to colonial influence and force. We believe in the principle of daring to be a Daniel, daring to stand alone, daring to have a purpose firm, and daring to make it known.

We will ever stand and support unswervingly the total liberation of Africa and Africans; we have dedicated ourselves to this objective. But we will not indulge in extremist activities calculated mainly to satisfy our personal ambition and to win us personal or national notoriety or fame. In the past we fought, and we are still fighting, for the cause of African liberation and redemption. No insidious propaganda or diabolical demagoguery or coercion can intimidate us.

In 1868 the Legislature of Liberia created the Order entitled the Humane Order of African Redemption, an Order which successive generations and administrations of Liberia have worked to maintain and perpetuate. We may not be as bellicose or as loquacious as some, but we have been effective and loyal to the cause.

We stand at the threshold of a magnificent opportunity for African peace, progress and prosperity if we are indeed to play a vital rôle in the political, social, economic and cultural history of our Continent. This objective can be achieved only by consultations, free discussions and deliberations in all matters affecting our common welfare. All African States should therefore be respected, and placed on an equal footing with each other. This is the objective for which we have fought; this is the objective for which we shall fight, and we will remain dedicated to this ideal.

I express my grateful thanks and appreciation to His Excellency the Secretary of State and the Cabinet who conducted the affairs of Government during my absence. The Under Secretary of State also deserves commendation for his contribution in holding over in collaboration with the Cabinet during the absence of the Secretary of State.

Finally I extend my heartfelt congratulations and thanks to all who have in any way contributed to facilitate the smooth functioning of the machinery of Government, and to all the people for their loyalty and patriotism displayed during our absence.

Whatever the future may hold for mankind, however secure we may be in our own ideologies, whatever plan of action the peoples of the world may adopt, I have come to believe in the ability and willingness of men of goodwill everywhere to approach world problems with a new spirit and a new heart. Only in this framework can the staggering task which confronts us be minimized. And, despite the ominous signs of the times, perhaps we can learn to look with Justice Holmes beyond the vision of battling races and an impoverished earth, beyond confused ideologies and conflicting philosophies, to catch a dreaming glimpse of peace.

May you, my friends, citizens and residents in Liberia, come to a clear recognition of this dreaming glimpse of peace and so bring a new approach, a new spirit and a new heart to the national and international problems which confront us.

Coming back home, our hearts throbbed fast and high with delight this afternoon as the ship sailed into port and finally dropped anchor in the beautiful port of home, and thus our absence and our travels have ended; our joys of travel for the present time have been consummated because we have reached home, home, sweet home! For there is no place like home.

At the Dedication of the Unification Monument

Kolahun, Loffa County, 5 January 1961

> *My ardent prayer has always been ... that all the people of this nation may remain devoted, loyal, and dedicated to the principle of unity and solidarity so that our great patrimony of democracy may grow stronger and greater as the years go by.*

Introductory Note

The erection of a national unification monument in Voinjama, Loffa County, was a hallmark signifying the success of our National Unification Policy. President Tubman spoke of his belief in that policy and of certain national issues which led to its implementation by him and the people of Liberia. The monument, he believed, would tell its own story to succeeding generations of Liberians in whose hearts and minds the meaning of the noble and heroic efforts and deeds to achieve national unity would never be forgotten.

Kolahun, Loffa County, 5 January 1961

THE UNIFICATION PROGRAMME, in honour of which this monument has been erected by authorization of the Legislature, in response to the appeal of the people of the three provinces, has indeed been a source of very deep satisfaction to me. I know that my fellow citizens share with me a kindred feeling, for in my view the monument speaks more pertinently than words can of the success of the efforts which have been made in the direction of unification.

At this time I am tempted to follow the example of the eminent British sculptor who, after a national committee had unveiled one of his latest masterpieces was asked to make a speech. The already famous man rose slowly to his feet, and pointing to the sculpture said, 'That is my speech' and sat down. Citizens and friends ... the Unification Monument is our speech.

But I will not sit down. I shall go further by referring to the fact that the Unification Programme started many years ago in the administration of the late President William D. Coleman. At that time I was a fledgling, and thereafter had the privilege of being a Collector of Internal Revenues of Maryland County, and, travelling extensively throughout that part of the country, I experienced very intimately some of the former barriers and hindrances against the success of the Unification Policy.

In 1930 the International Commission of Inquiry from the League of Nations, at the invitation of the Government, came to Liberia and published to the world its biased *ex parte* investigations in which high Government officials and common citizens were charged with heinous crimes. Against these indictments the people had no opportunity of appeal, or of being heard.

Thus the ideal of unification remained dormant for many years thereafter, and a situation of estrangement developed.

In 1944, when by the vote of the constituents of the nation I was elected President, one of the first acts of the adminstration was to tour the interior from the Western Province to the Eastern, right through to Cape Palmas. On all of these journeys I had to be carried most of the time by hammocks on the shoulders of the tribal people. I saw the misery, hardships and oppression which this means of travel imposed; I saw men with hammocks and loads on their heads knock their toes against stones and the stumps of trees; I saw them fall from under the hammocks, receiving bodily injuries; I saw some of them faint; I saw the wearied, tired, and resentful throw down their loads and hammocks and escape into the bush; I heard the labourers who were carrying hammocks and loads sing, and when I asked what they were saying some of them explained that they were telling of their woes and of the hardships which they encountered, the burdens of having to carry hammocks on their shoulders, the rigours of travelling through dense forests, of being bitten by scorpions and snakes, wounded by stones and stumps of trees. We saw hundreds of people infected with yaws, sleeping-sickness and diverse diseases; we saw the interior cut off from the littoral and tribes isolated from tribes because of the lack of roads, transport and communication; we saw the urgent and imperative need of hospitals, clinics and schools; we saw soldiers routing the people and the resultant enmity between them; we saw commissioners receiving monthly supplies of food for the subsistence of soldiers, messengers, and other interior personnel without giving just compensation for the same. At Executive Council Meetings we witnessed influential, noble and self-respecting chiefs rise and present goats, cows, rice, chickens, palm-oil, sheep, skins of animals, and elegant country cloths woven by them, their wives and children, and receive nothing in return. I was shocked, and declared as a matter of policy that no official of Government, from the constable, the private soldier to the President of the nation should accept any gifts without giving just compensation, or value for value. I became completely convinced that talking merely of unification was getting us nowhere. Besides that, the Constitution guarantees the right to all men to be equally free and entitles everyone to equal justice before the law, equal privileges and benefits under our free system of government. And because this state of affairs involved fundamental principles of humanity, it became necessary to make a diagnosis of the situation precipitated by frequent inter-tribal and governmental conflicts, acts of disloyalty and resentment of governmental authority. These manifestations, understood to be effects of deeper underlying causes, had to be identified as a preliminary to the unification programme. We, therefore, set ourselves to the task of trying to benefit from the results of our experiences by deciding to seek a more realistic, vigorous and satisfactory solution.

As is universally required and voiced in our own Declaration of Independence, taxation without representation is oppressive, and contribution without participation is iniquitous. We, therefore, sought legislative approval, as well as that of the people of the country, for constitutional and legislative reforms to remove these objectionable aspects of the organic laws of the state, so as to provide for such legislative provisons that would enhance and sustain the unification programme.

We were most agreeably surprised when the new programme received unanimous support in the Legislature instead of the two-thirds required for constitutional amendments. Similarly at the referendum these amendments received the unanimous vote of adoption throughout the country. Thus these acts on the part of the entire citizenry at that time upheld the banner with great magnanimity, and history will certainly record this outstanding event in the annals of a people who had the ability to see, and the wisdom to understand and feel, the need for such historic reforms.

It is with deep appreciation that I express my personal gratitude for the spirit evinced by the voting population of the country at that time and the enthusiastic response of the tribal people throughout the country in favour of a step which has thus unified the nation and integrated its population. Feeling proud of this accomplishment and grateful for the general satisfaction which has ensued, let us all chant joyfully a loud AMEN.

This monument has been erected of stone, mortar, and iron at the request of the tribal people inhabiting the hinterland, as a memorial to symbolize the union of all the elements of our population, and has received the concurrence of the body of the people in the nation through their representatives in the Legislature. May it remain eternally *in perpetuam memoriam*.

Let each of us throughout the nation re-dedicate ourselves to the essentially fundamental principle of unity and co-operation so that all sections, sectors, elements, tribes, political entities and subdivisions of the nation shall be completely fused into one great political and national union genuinely represented as indivisible.

It is to be remembered that the petition presented to the Legislature by our citizens inhabiting the hinterland prayed and insisted that one such monument might be constructed in each of the provinces, as a hallmark of the concurrence of all the people of the nation in the principles and intentions of the Unification Conference, first convened in Maryland County on May 24, 1954 and subscribed to by all. However, the Legislative body in its wisdom has deemed it wiser to erect only one monument in the Western Province at this time. Perhaps that body may later see the wisdom of having a similar monument erected in each of the remaining two provinces and in each of the counties, so that in the future these monuments, towering skyward, shall become the symbol of Liberian Integration and Unity, and be looked upon forever in the same manner as the ancient oracles of Delphi, to bear testimony to the solemn obligations and vows which we have made.

My ardent prayer has always been, is now, and will ever be that all the people of this nation may remain devoted, loyal and dedicated to the principles of unity and solidarity so that our great patrimony of democracy may grow stronger and greater as the years go by.

To the Men who returned from Services in Congo, Kinshasa

Monrovia, 23 January 1961

Tramp, tramp, so firm and strong, They made a name in history. And that's why we are so proud to see Our own boys were marching there.

Introductory Note

During the early months of the Congo crisis a contingent of the Liberian National Guard, formerly known as the Liberian Frontier Force, was deployed to actual service in the Congo. It was the first time in the history of Liberia that any section of the Liberian army had been deployed outside of their home base. They made a name for Liberia and for themselves and brought home honour. No lives were lost. The President proudly welcomed them home.

Monrovia, 23 January 1961

GENTLEMEN, OFFICERS and men of the contingent of the Liberian Frontier Force recently returned from service in the Congo:

As I see you today, my mind goes back to the last time that I saw you at Robertsfield, when you were about to depart from this country to the Congo to do service there. Your morale was very high at that time; your soldierly bearing and experience inspired confidence, and I am happy to say that the confidence that you inspired in us and in your country at that time has been justified, and that your services in the Congo have merited every bit of the confidence that we reposed in you, and more too.

Before you went to the Congo you, like most of the officers and men of the Liberian Frontier Force, had only seen active service. Every soldier who enlists in an army is engaged in active service, but when you went to the Congo and encountered attacks and became combatants you not only saw active service but you saw what we call in military parlance, actual service.

I am very happy, and I am sure that the turn-out today to welcome you evidences the appreciation of the Government and people of Liberia for the invaluable services which you have rendered your country, and not only your country but your race and the entire continent of Africa.

We have heard and we have read of some of the charges that were levelled against you; we have heard and we have read of your good report, and we are happy that investigations revealed that you were not guilty of those charges. Therefore you have come out with honour.

History will record you as the very first contingent of any section of the Liberian army, or of any of the services of the Liberian army, to have been sent out of the country for any kind of actual service, and upon your conduct very largely depends the credit and respect which the Government of Liberia may receive from foreign governments and foreign people. We are, therefore very pleased that you have reflected credit upon your nation, upon your families and upon yourselves.

As I saw you march past this morning, looking well and hearty, strong and apparently ready to run through troops and leap over walls, my mind went back to an old soldier song that we used to sing when I was a young soldier, and I think it is very appropriate. If you were one of us then I could ask you to join me in singing it but since you do not know it I presume I could recite it:

> There go our soldier boys
> Our pride our only joy
> Their regiment out in fine array
> And the soldiers make a grand display
> In the uniforms they wear.
>
> Tramp, tramp so firm and strong
> They made a name in history
> And that's why we are so proud to see
> Our own boys were marching there.

Finally, I am directing the Secretary of Defence to make payment to you on one month's salary as a bonus. The Legislature will be requested to authorize and approve a special military award or insignia for those who served in the Congo, and when that has been approved by the Legislature, each of you shall receive that award, as well as all of the rest of those who have gone to the Congo for service.

Those of you who received wounds incapacitating you for further service will be provided with a special pension. We are happy that none of you lost your lives (I suppose you would rather be living than dead, so that your relatives might receive a pension!)

Other details in connection with your services in the Congo will be communicated to your headquarters through the Secretary of Defence.

I congratulate you, and welcome you home.

Responding to the True Whig Party during a Demonstration in His Honour for the Convening of a Conference of African Leaders

Monrovia, 30 May 1961

The Monrovia Conference of Heads of African and Malagasy States was an expression of a long recognized belief that Liberia and other African states are interdependent parts of a single community which must be bound together by a network of transportation and communications, public facilities and common economic and cultural interests.

Introductory Note

The people of Liberia, particularly those residing in Montserrado County, on 30 May 1961 organized a mass demonstration and called upon President Tubman to say how pleased they were with the successful results of the Monrovia Conference under his leadership, which had seen the largest gathering of African Heads of States and Governments in the history of Africa. This meeting was followed by the Summit Conference of African Heads of State, held two years later in Addis Ababa, Ethiopia, when the Organization of African Unity was born. The Monrovia Conference was organized with the sole objective of arriving at a united front to solve problems common to Africa. Having acknowledged this demonstration of appreciation by the True Whig Party, the President then spoke to his people about certain internal conditions, specifically matters affecting our National Unification Policy.

Monrovia, 30 May 1961

I AM touched, very deeply touched, by this extraordinary and unprecedented demonstration which you have staged today in the nation's capital. To you, my fellow partisans, citizens and friends, young and old, participating in this mass exhibition, I acknowledge, with great humility and deep gratitude this mark of your loyalty, love and devotion to the great cause with which we have always identified ourselves. As on previous occasions I have questioned myself incessantly and scrupulously to ascertain the true reason for the continued and most flattering confidence which inspires these recurring ovations tendered me through the years, your confiding trust and faith in our leadership, and your consistent and persistent private and public solicitation for the continuity of that leadership; so now I ask myself again whether I am deserving of all the encomiums, congratulatory expressions and sentiments heaped upon me. I must consider myself as totally undeserving and unworthy, but through the mercies and grace of God I am what I am, and therefore perhaps deserving of your tribute.

Whatever the future may hold for our nation (and we believe that greater and better things are in store), may we all continue to implore Divine Providence for a greater measure of love of country, devotion to service, loyalty to our God, fortitude, strength of character and a deepened sensitivity within ourselves, as we continue our struggle for the maintenance and perpetuity of the lofty ideals of a true democracy.

I have noted with profound interest and satisfaction the numerous references made concerning the conference of the Heads of African and Malagasy States and Governments held here recently, and the contributions made to the success of that historic gathering. Of even greater significance was the fact that all of us throughout that meeting were conscious of one overwhelming desire — the liberation of all Africa and the establishment of unity, peace, understanding and prosperity for all. The unity to which I have referred is not the kind which is a subterfuge or mysticism — saying one thing and meaning another; not the kind of unity that means more for me and less for you; not the kind of unity that is contrived under the pretext of nationalism and devotion to a great cause which, in point of fact, is fraught with selfishness, personal and individual nationalism. The unity I have in mind is the one which, like love, is long-suffering and forbearing, which is not puffed-up and which recognizes in each and all the same rights, privileges, opportunities, respect and regard as we have for ourselves.

We knew from the beginning of our deliberations that we were not in search of a panacea *per se*; nevertheless, we were greatly optimistic that with the gathering of representatives of twenty-one African and Malagasy States, comprised of the best brains and minds, most of whom are Heads of States and Governments — a gathering unprecedented in Africa, and for that matter, in the whole world, we were afforded an opportunity to look at our problems objectively and take stock, with a view to tackling those which were common and uncommon to us. Our unanimous agreement on the issues raised exceeded our expectations. You, my fellow citizens and friends, were witnesses of our combined endeavours to bring peace and understanding, and to establish friendship among the peoples of Africa. We believe that time will justify the results which emerged.

My concern and that of the Liberian people is what it has been since this administration took office in 1944 — that in all matters of national and international affairs, we must never lose the substance for the shadow, but rather that we must be realistic and truthful and keep our feet on the ground. Hence all our efforts regarding Africa and Africans have been without fanfare. We have, over the years, waged a firm, consistent and persistent war against all forms and aspects of subjugation, domination and discrimination. We have condemned, fought and waged wars against colonialism and imperialism for more than a hundred years, at a time when they were rampant and functioning in full force and vigour, at a time when all Africa was over-run and partitioned by them. Liberia alone stood four-square, challenging the onslaught of colonialism and imperialism, and although we received many hard knocks, bruises, wounds and setbacks we were never subdued nor conquered by them, nor did we ever become tools or stooges in colonialist hands but maintained our independence and sovereignty, fighting against imponderable odds through those dreadful years of colonial expansionism. Now that colonialism is dying and imperialism is ashamed of its name, by what stretch of the imagination could Liberia be considered a stooge in the hands of imperialism or colonialism? No, never! But the truth is that Liberia recognizes that colonialism is dying, and we have agreed to join hands with all others to hasten its death in every corner of the earth where its life is not ebbing fast enough. But we do not believe in pretending to be doing more than we are; we do not believe in lifting a sledge hammer before the world and pretending that we are killing elephants, bush cows or lions when in fact we are merely killing a mosquito, thereby pretentiously seeking world renown and thus rendering ourselves notorious.

We have provided an asylum for Africans from all the colonial countries in which they were subjugated in the colonial days; we have shared our material resources with our brethren to the limits of our capacity; we were indeed the pioneers in the battle of Africa against exploitation and serfdom. The Monrovia Conference of Heads of African and Malagasy States was an expression of a long recognized belief that Liberia and other African States are interdependent parts of a single community, which must be bound together by a network of transportation and communications, public facilities and common economic and cultural interests. The decisions of the Monrovia Conference are facts for history and they have brought about a change in African affairs. No amount of vituperation, slander or false accusation by mortified, chagrined sources, smarting under their abject failure to sabotage and adversely affect the success of that conference, can change the facts or the effects of it. We are not unmindful to answer such aspersions, but rather in the manner of Zerubbabel when he was building the walls of Jerusalem; all of the Sanballats and Tobiahs in the world cannot detract, alter or deflect our determination to build our own walls: we will not come down from them or be moved. We are not interested in answering our detractors in anything they may say, because we realize and sympathize with the universal and international shame which is theirs at this time, and we extend brotherly sympathy, forgiveness and tolerance.

You will recall, and I am sure those who have followed our thinking on the subject of a United States of Africa will attest, that my views are the same today as when the proposition was first mooted and proposed upon the attainment of independence by the Republic of Ghana. It is a matter of schools of thought. I told newsmen who interviewed me as to the probability of such a Union when they returned from that celebration, that the idea, though desirable, is as remote as a Federation of Europe. The idea of a United States of Africa was the pet theory of Mr. Marcus Garvey, a concept which served to arouse those in whose bosom the flame of nationalism was already burning. But Pan-Africanism only remained a concept; and even though times have changed and the majority of the nations of Africa have become independent, with the responsibility of guiding the destinies of whole peoples, reason and contemporary events dictate that African leaders should take a realistic rather than an academic approach to the questions which plague us and mankind.

Reverting to the question of African leadership, the position I maintained even before the emergence of other independent African States is, that it would require the aggregate of the best elements in all the African States compounded in such a manner as to represent the divisibility of an indivisible Africa, and that no one nation could assume the leadership of Africa. In the same frame of reference, I still maintain that a United States of Africa or even a United States of West Africa is Utopian and devoid of any political realism. Let us wait and see; time will tell.

I am particularly happy to observe the interest with which the people of all walks of life in this Republic followed the Monrovia Conference. I have listened with glee and joy to the sentiments and expressions you have made indicative of your appreciation, and which you have requested me to transmit to the co-sponsors and participants of the conference. They are well deserving of all the high praises which you have bestowed upon them and the people they represent, for they are truly the harbingers and proponents of a changed Africa.

So far as the conference itself is concerned, my part in the success of which you have spoken was only to guide its deliberations against tangential polemics, which is the responsibility of any Chairman. Happily this was not necessary at this conference, for everyone worked with a singleness of purpose. The credit of its success is therefore attributable not only to the sponsors, but to all the delegates who participated; to the several Departments and their staffs, the police and security authorities, the conference secretariat, the translators, the stenographers, the servants and anyone who so much as served a glass of water. In short, everybody and every citizen contributed to the success of the conference.

We should all rejoice in the fact that for the first time in the history of our continent twenty-one African States and Governments met in Monrovia, Liberia, to decide upon new approaches to their problems and to ameliorate their difficulties and disabilities.

THE NEW LEGISLATION

I am extremely happy at your endorsement of and special reference to the Act of the Legislature authorizing the President of Liberia to set up a Special Commission to make a complete comprehensive survey and study of the territorial and political sub-divisions of the Republic. The timeliness of this Legislation cannot be more appropriate, nor over-emphasized.

I observe that there are still a few people who frown upon this Legislation, and who were, I believe, the principal cause of the attempt to assassinate me in 1955. However, before I embarked upon this policy, I consulted the leaders of our country. Most of them agreed with me, while some opposed the suggestion but dared not say so at the time. And because I was convinced of the justice of the cause, I pursued and requested legislation for it. The voters in a referendum supported the idea unanimously. I cannot therefore bring myself to agree with anyone who may think that Liberia should have continued in the same divergent social categories as when we assumed office in 1944, with the population divided into Come-heres, Country-men and Americo-Liberians. I believe and will always believe, that Liberia belongs to all three groups, and all the people of Liberia working as an integral team in the great enterprise of building a sacred, undivided, free and sovereign state.

I am a full-blooded descendant of those who came here from the United States. Maryland County where my people and I live had been the scene of more blood-battles and internecine wars than any other part of this country; and in those wars the Tubman family was always foremost, lost and sacrificed more blood, sustained more sufferings and deaths than any other family.

These facts date back to the earliest history of our nation and continued until my own time and generation, and I too participated in these internecine wars. If I now declare a new day, so that we may forget the things that are behind and reach forth to the things that are ahead, letting bygones be bygones, and letting the dead past bury its dead, I fail to see why anyone should linger and cling to the past. I am happy, therefore, very happy indeed, that God has caused my line of descendants to participate in this pleasant phase of national reconstruction and rehabilitation and in particular afforded me the opportunity to have initiated a programme of unification and integration, not only in words and in theory but in vigorous and successful action, so that all segments of our population are being welded together. We are thereby causing a rebirth of a greater degree of respect for the innate worth and dignity of all human personalities, and the activation of a genuine sense of national consciousness as a means of saving the nation from disintegration and annihilation.

TRUE WHIG PARTY HEADQUARTERS

Concerning the construction of a True Whig Party Headquarters, it is a source of extreme pleasure that you have approved my recommendation for these headquarters to be constructed on the site heretofore known as the Old Court House and Old Senate Chamber on Ashmun Street, the place where Edward James Roye, the first True Whig Party President, was taken from the sea by his enemies, more dead than alive, carried to the jail house at the rear of the building and there thrown on the ground like an ox from a stretcher, where they said he must die in jail. We must raise on that spot buildings that will be a monument to his memory, to his statesmanship, to his patriotism and courage and to the invaluable contribution that he made to the True Whig Party and the nation.

TESTIMONIALS AND RESOLUTIONS

For the testimonials and resolutions which you have this evening presented to me I am grateful beyond my ability to express my deepest appreciation. I cannot understand the loyalty, continued affection and enthusiasm of my fellow countrymen who, after their preferment of me for twenty years still insist upon drafting me for another term of four years. But I am impelled to employ the rhetorical figurative hyperbole used by Paul in one of his Letters in the Bible when he said, 'O, to know the love of God that passeth knowledge,' I say, 'O, to know the love and affection of the people of Liberia that excel my understanding and knowledge.'

THE LIBERIAN FLAG

The Lone Star Banner of Liberia represents the first attempt of an African State at a Republican form of self-government. The flag is therefore a link between the past and the present. It is essentially different from any other flag in Africa. It is different because of the varied adventures which it has undergone. It connotes or signifies age, experience, and maturity. It has stood the test of time for more than a century of struggles against colonialism, imperialism and many other forms of subversive and intriguing devices. In many respects it is the Lone Star Republic of Africa that has endured throughout the years gone by, because it represents the only nation in Africa which was able to stem successfully the tide of colonialism and imperialism, at a time when there were none to assist her.

A Panegyric to the Memory of the Late President of Liberia, Charles Dunbar Burgess King

Monrovia, 8 September 1961

As a hero, as a statesman, as a patriot, he lived nobly and died regretted.

Introductory Note

It is believed that Charles Dunbar Burgess King, Liberia's sixteenth President, was one of President Tubman's political mentors. This panegyric was an indication of that popularly held belief. President King resigned the presidency of Liberia under a cloud, after having served his people as President for ten years. In this memorial address President Tubman made a real effort to remove that cloud, and we are asked to behold the man as he was, as he lived and died. For many years President King, when he had left the Executive Mansion, stood in the same lonely and greatly maligned political category as did President Edward J. Roye. While time has borne out the validity of President Roye's activities, thanks to President Tubman, President King's position during the most critical period in our national history has only gradually begun to be revealed. President Tubman, champion of lost honour and leadership, gave an historic discourse on the times and circumstances during which President King served as President of Liberia.

Monrovia, 8 September 1961

AGAIN, A Great Leader of the nation has passed from time to eternity, and while this is the ultimate end of all life and natural existence, there are some deaths that bring to families, peoples and nations a different degree and magnitude of sorrow and loss.

The removal of former President Charles Dunbar Burgess King, Elder Statesman, the last link between the past and the present at such a time as this, when the world is in commotion, when the forces of nationalism (especially on our continent, Africa), are asserting themselves, when nations and varying ideologies are contending for international supremacy, when the fate of men, nations and even the earth itself appears to be swinging in the balance and when the counsel, admonition and advice of the most mature, practical, realistic, calm, unperturbed and sober minds are of extreme importance; the loss of such a noble, experienced, tested and tried statesman as he whose remains lie before us, and to whom we now pay our last tribute of respect, cannot but be considered as one of the first and highest magnitude.

191

Therefore, I am constrained to exclaim with the Prophet Isaiah in his apocalyptic vision:

'For behold the Lord, the Lord of
Hosts doth take away from Jerusalem
and from Judah the Honourable Man
and Counsellor.'

Former President King's name will survive throughout the centuries because it is indissolubly connected with some of the greatest events in our national history. His presidency of eight years was filled with events of such magnitude that even if he erred in judgment at times, as all of us do, his patriotism was always conceded to be beyond reproach and doubt.

He entered upon the duties of the office of President at a time when there were considerable uncertainties threatening disasters to the nation's very existence. I remember distinctly, during the political campaign of 1918, at the convention which was very strongly contested to ensure his defeat, a plank was written into the platform of the True Whig Party which demanded that before any candidate was nominated at the convention for the presidency, he should subscribe to what was called the American Programme. Normally, at national conventions, the aspirants, or those who seek nomination, do not attend. At this particular convention, however, there was a rift between the machinery and leadership of the party concerning the two principal candidates: the late Chief Justice Dossen of Maryland County and the then Secretary of State and now late former President King.

The contest at the convention became so tense that an attempt was made to exclude our honoured dead's name from the presidential candidacy of the convention unless he appeared before the convention and subscribed to what was called the American Programme. He came to the convention, and I see him now as vividly as I saw him then, standing as in review before me, young, handsome, dignified, firm, and making the following statement *inter alia*:

'It has been suggested that I subscribe to the American Programme. Delegates to this convention: I do not know what the American Programme is and if you, Mr. Chairman, or the delegates to this convention will apprise me of what the programme is to which you refer I shall then be able to decide whether I can subscribe to it or not; but until that is done, I will not and I cannot subscribe to an obscure proposition. I pause until I receive an answer from this convention that has required my presence here.'

He sat down. There was silence; no one could immediately answer. Eventually the Standard Bearer of the Party interrupted and declared that the American Programme meant that Liberia regard the United States as her best friend and that any candidate for election then should subscribe to that proposition. Secretary of State King then replied as follows:

'If that is what you call the American Programme, I have been subscribing to such a programme from the time that I entered public service first as County Attorney, then as Attorney-General and now as Secretary of State. I fail to see, therefore, any justification for your requiring me to suscribe to a programme that I have supported throughout the years and will continue to support.'

He then took leave of the convention and retired.

He received the nomination but was sent out of the country on a diplo-matic mission to the United States to negotiate a five million dollar loan. The election was approaching and he was still in the United States attending upon the negotiations. Some of his friends felt that his absence at that parti-cular time would adversely affect his election; they therefore communicated with him and demanded that he suspend the negotiations and return home until after the election. He replied that his first duty to the State was to execute the obligations imposed by the office he held under constitutional oath and he could not subjugate nor violate that trust to ensure preferment or election to another situation, even though it be the presidency. He there-fore rejected the demand to return home, remained in the United States and continued the negotiations until they were concluded. The election was held during his absence and he was elected by an overwhelming majority. He was a patriot; he was an honourable man and not merely a politician or job seeker.

Now let us revert to his character and life service prior to his election. President King often told me how he entered public life; how, as a clerk in one of the mercantile stores in Monrovia, he was earning fifty dollars per month and how, not feeling himself adapted to the petty processes of mercan-tile or commercial life, he resigned and accepted a position in the State Department as clerk with a salary of eighteen dollars per month; notwith-standing the disparity in emolument, he made the sacrifice so as to be of greater future service to his country, his family and to himself.

Starting off thus at the foot of the ladder in public life, he reached the peak of that ladder, rising from the lowly earth to the vaulted skies, mounting to the summit rung by rung.

There is another incident in the public career of the revered deceased that I consider deserving of special mention: it is the rôle that he played at the Versailles Conference as Liberia's Chief Plenipotentiary. There in Versailles he had the pleasure of meeting and associating with the delegates and partici-pating in the discussions that resulted in the Treaty of Versailles, and he was one of the signatories to that Treaty together with men like President Wood-row Wilson of the United States, Georges Clemenceau, known as the Tiger of France, and Lloyd George of Great Britain.

In those days it was not normal to give preferment for positions of promi-nence to young men. Age and maturity were generally the standards by which preferment was made, but President King changed the pattern.

The illustrious subject of our remarks, pursuing a policy of attracting foreign investment to the country, especially from Americans, directed his Secretary of State, the late former President Edwin Barclay, to proceed to the United States for the purpose of negotiating a loan of five million dollars with the Finance Corporation of America.

The negotiations were concluded and Secretary of State Barclay returned to Liberia with the agreement, establishing a five million dollar line of credit and a rubber planting agreement of one million acres of land for a period of ninety-nine years between Government and the Firestone Plantations Com-pany. There was tremendous opposition to both of these projects. In the parlours of the Mansion during a council of state convoked by the President for a discussion of these matters, one of the objectors declared that to give one million acres of land to Firestone would be depriving the people of Liberia of their inherent and God-given heritage. Another said, 'I left the United States, running away from these white folks, and now the President has gone and brought them here to follow us and take away from us our country, which we have successfully defended against the colonial powers who tried to squeeze us out.' And so the largely negative discussions of that evening went on and on.

After everyone who desired to had spoken, President King replied, 'Gentlemen, I am happy to know that now I am charged with causing the Americans to come to Liberia to deprive the people of Liberia of their sacred heritage and bringing white Americans here to chase those who had run away from oppression in the United States. When I was a candidate for the presidency, some said that I was pro-British and therefore demanded that I subscribe to support the American Programme. Now I am supporting that Programme and some of you say that I am giving away the country to Americans. But I am not perturbed by these adverse comments. These are some of the inconsistencies that one must experience in public life.'

With the conclusion of these two agreements for foreign investments, internal stability was established, and respect for our territories was shown by the colonialist powers of the day. Thus, his wise and efficient statesmanship called a halt to the encroachments, border incidents and other threatening events which had plagued us from the colonial days in 1822 until 1926. By this action alone, he can be said to have rendered more valuable service to this nation than anyone else.

He was re-elected in 1927 for a third term. After two years of that term had expired the campaign of 1931 began to loom and political intrigues were set afoot by some of the leaders of the True Whig Party. The opposition, on the other hand, charged that there was forced labour and slave trading in Liberia.

President King then directed that an International Commission of Inquiry should be invited to come to Liberia to investigate these charges on the spot. The Commission made its advent and although in their findings, and in a special letter written to President King, they stated that he had not been implicated in either of the charges, he was nevertheless requested by the House of Representatives to tender his resignation as President.

He took the position that he would resign only if the House of Representatives expressly and unequivocally stated in writing that he was not being requested to resign because he was implicated in the charges investigated by the International Commission of Inquiry, or because he had committed any act of malfeasance, misfeasance or nonfeasance, and that if this condition was not complied with he would prefer that articles of impeachment were presented against him and he be given an opportunity to vindicate himself. The House of Representatives prepared such a statement and presented it to him. It was only at this point that he tendered his resignation as President.

It was during his administration that a development programme was inaugurated and demonstrated; it was during his administration that, by wise and successful legislation the revenues of the country reached the million dollar mark for the first time; it was during his administration for the first time in the history of the country, that radio facilities were introduced and a modern lighthouse installed; it was during his administration that electricity and street lights were considered by Government and introduced into the capital; it was during his administration that Booker T. Washington

Institute, the first technical and industrial institute in the country, was founded, and it was he who first inaugurated a telegraphic system extending as far as Bassa.

Generations of Liberians will be further eternally grateful to this beloved and great leader, during whose administration the plan for the observance of the Centennial Celebration of the nation was conceived. Two other accomplishments adorn that administration: I refer to the erections of the Pioneers' and the Matilda Newport Monuments, two national memorials, which stand proudly on the grounds of this Centennial Pavilion.

To me, he was a benefactor, a counsellor and an adviser.

His patriotism did not permit him to become embittered against any administration, no matter how much he differed from and disapproved of its policies, nor to withhold the benefit of his experience and advice even when he felt that the administration had oppressed him. He was always willing to give all he had and all he knew, under any circumstances, for the benefit of the State. As long as his health permitted he was never absent from any public function, ceremony or council of state to which he was invited, and his presence indeed gave encouragement, inspired hope and confidence and made assurance doubly sure.

He was witty and had an admirable sense of humour and a great store of anecdotes and wise sayings. He would often give utterance to expressions like these: speaking of men in office who happened to get out of office and of life and death he would say, 'The only way not to get out of office is not to get in and the only way not to die is not to have lived.' In political matters if a partisan or group of partisans deserted the party he would observe, 'That is all right, the planks fall from the house, the house never falls from the planks.' Another of his anecdotes was, 'If rats are in a house the first one that comes out is a rat, any other is just another one.'

I recollect that although seized with the malady that resulted in his physical removal from us, and lying in his bed when I called to see him, he said to me, 'Shad, I am ill. I feel strong enough to get out of bed and walk around but as Independence Day is approaching, I shall remain in bed for the present so that I may recover my strength sufficiently to attend the Independence Day Celebrations,'; he did so and was able to be in attendance at the celebrations, but I observed a considerable physical weakness in him and after the ceremonies he, with Mrs. King, accompanied us to the Executive Mansion whence we sent him home. That was his last public appearance, and from that time on, his health began to deteriorate.

I suggested that a concilium of doctors diagnose his case and determine whether or not they considered him strong enough to be taken to Switzerland for specialized medical examinations and care. The report was in the affirmative. About to leave for Switzerland, he asked me to come near his bed; when Mrs. King left the room he said to me, 'Shad, I hear what the doctors say and I respect their professional knowledge and opinion; but I am going to Switzerland not trusting in nor depending on what they have told me but resting and leaning on the Rod and Staff of Him Who is able to comfort me, to restore my health or to call me hence to His Divine Abode.' He went to Switzerland and shortly thereafter he returned home, his condition still unimproved, and although he realized that the end was near, he remained composed, undisturbed and patiently awaiting the inevitable.

At last, on the fourth day of September, 1961, the end came, and his soul moved out from earth into limitless eternity where he now knows the real meaning of infinite love and perfect power.

He was blessed with the benefit of a long and fruitful period of natural life and 'he has come to his grave in a good old age like as a shock of corn cometh in its season'.

I cannot think of him as dead; he was so much and in so many ways amazingly alive that I know not how to think of him in terms of death.

Life being universally good in his all-beholding eyes, he insisted on order in days and seasons and things, in order to achieve long life.

I can never allow my mind to dwell upon those strange days of his preparation for mortal departure without remembering his calm confidence. His was not a sudden departure. He went about the removal of his temporal tent, for the repitching of it on immortal shores, with slow, calm steps.

He was the man on whom nature seemed to have impressed the stamp of greatness, whose genius beamed from his retirement from school with a radiance which dazzled and a loveliness which charmed. The hero, called from a sequestered retreat, whose first appearance in public service was as a clerk in the State Department, although a stripling, won the esteem of President Arthur Barclay who appointed him County Attorney for Montserrado County and subsequently Attorney-General, the duties of which later position he executed so fearlessly and zealously that he made an impression on the then Secretary of the Treasury, Daniel E. Howard. When Mr. Howard assumed office as President he promoted Attorney-General King to the position of Secretary of State.

Live! Thou Statesman, the correctness of whose principles and strength, and whose mind, are inscribed on the records of the Executive and on the annals of our councils of state. The Legal Counsellor who was always and until his death, the pride of the Bar and the admiration of the Court; whose apprehensions were quick as lightning and whose pursuit of truth was luminous as its path; whose argument no change of circumstance could embarrass; whose knowledge appeared intuitive, and who, by a single glance, could survey the whole field of controversy – see in it what way truth might be most successfully defended and how error should be approached; and who, without ever stopping, ever hesitating, by a rapid and manly march, led the listening judge and the fascinated jury step by step through a delightful region, brightening the way as he advanced, till his argument grew to conviction and all other eloquence was rendered useless even by demonstrative evidence; whose talents were generally employed on the side of right; whose voice, with its peculiar tone, whether in the councils of state or at the Bar of Justice, was virtue's consolation, and at whose approach oppressed humanity felt a secret rapture, and the heart of injured innocence leaped for joy.

Wherever President King was, in whatever sphere he moved, the friendless had a friend; the fatherless a father; and the poor man, though unable to reward his kindness, found an advocate. It was when truth was disregarded or the eternal principles of justice violated – then it was that on these occasions he exerted all of his strength; it was on these occasions that he sometimes soared so high and shone with a radiance so transcendant.

The patriot whose integrity baffled the scrutiny of inquisition, whose manly virtue never shaped itself to circumstances, who, always great, always himself, stood amid the varying tides of party and political strifes and intrigues like the Rock of Gibraltar; the friend, who knew no guile, whose bosom was transparent and deep, in the bottom of whose heart were rooted tender and sympathetic virtues, whose worth various opposing parties acknowledged while alive, and on whose remains and tomb they unite with equal sympathy and grief to heap their honours.

As a hero, as a statesman, as a patriot, he lived nobly and died regretted!

His widow, his children, his family, who have been stricken with grief and loss by his transition, have a claim on the good offices of the Government and people of Liberia.

We condole, we regret and we express our co-ordinated sympathy with him.

> His carven scroll shall read
> Here rests the valiant heart
> Whose duty was his creed
> Whose choice the statesman's part
> Who when life's fight was done
> The grim last foe defied
> Naught knew safe victory
> Surrendered not but died.

Broadcast on the Eve of his Departure on State Visits to the United States of America and to the Kingdom of Ethiopia

Monrovia, 4 October 1961

This nation has been lifted in the eyes of the world.

Introductory Note

All was not calm on the home front. Subversive activities and elements were seeking to establish roots in what they considered a favourable environment. Ever vigilant, the Government soon discovered the source of subversion and took certain legal and disciplinary measures to curb its influence. The President was especially saddened to see subversion make its way among the youth of the land, who, as he correctly said, had received better and more opportunities to achieve fruitful lives than any other generation of Liberians in our history. Since it was obvious that subversion was aimed at disrupting our National Unification Programme, the President was equally determined that this influence would not succeed nor undermine his labour for the realization of so important and vital a national endeavour as national unity. This unpalatable intelligence was brought to his attention amidst preparations to embark upon state visits to two friendly nations.

Monrovia, 4 October 1961

WE LIVE in a period of great transition, generally of orderly evolution and sometimes of peaceful and bloody revolutions. Various political forms of government, social doctrines and philosophical and scientific theories manifest themselves in the affairs of men and nations. Perhaps the world has never been simultaneously a more beautiful and yet a more dangerous place in which to live than now. It appears that man's supremacy over the forces of nature will become both a barrier and a threat to his peaceful existence should his wisdom fail to give the needed equilibrium to his creativity and action.

Each age, each generation, has its peculiar opportunities and corresponding problems and responsibilities in which some rise above, while others cling to or sink beneath, the *status quo*. This generation of Liberians must face the challenging opportunities of the present – opportunities which are fraught with grave and great responsibilities and in doing so, rise above, not cling to or sink beneath the *status quo*.

It is gratifying to me that these challenging opportunities and grave responsibilities have fallen to my lot as leader of our nation in this age of transition. Our predecessors had their own national and international problems, difficulties and trials which flanked them on all sides; problems which erupted from within and those which arose from without. World sentiment frowned upon them, the lack of technical know-how was a barrier, the unsettled world condition a deterrent to progress, and the cynical attitude of those who looked upon Liberia as a mere philanthropic experiment became a psychological block. However, those leaders lived up to and surmounted the difficulties and thus made possible the continued existence of this nation. Those were different days, we say, and the challenges they had to face were in a different category from those which we encounter today. Those days and those challenges had to do with nation-building and maintenance. Today we have the problems of subversive activities, a condition which is rampant throughout the world and is the diabolical activity of the age.

For more than a year now, we have been following, investigating, and gathering evidence on subversive activities in our country. These evidences accumulated to sufficient probative value for us to have taken certain initial steps nine months ago, but we refrained from doing so in order to be more certain that these *sub rosa* movements were a reality determinedly bent on changing the democratic society in which we have lived for more than a century into an unknown, outwardly attractive, but spurious form of government which we have always considered dreadfully dangerous.

Our democratic way of life has served us in the past through a long period of several generations, amidst acrimonious opposition, opprobrium, ridicule and the consistent and perpetual tendency to squeeze us out. But guided by the concept of the democratic way of life and spurred on by our determination to succeed, we have survived for more than a century.

There are many indications in our history which convince us that we have not merely survived, but that a planned, steady and satisfactory pace of development and progress has been in evidence all along. While our dreams of a true democracy may not have been fully realized, they are certainly not in the direction of a new form of government destined to deprive other generations of Liberians of everything for which their forefathers fought and died. We are obligated to rise above, not sink beneath the things for which our forefathers fought, bled and died.

In recent years, and I say this with every degree of modesty and with diffidence, this nation has been lifted in the eyes of the international world. Our hegemony has been maintained successfully, and the entire world has noted with gratifying comments some of the changes which our nation has undergone. Liberia's voice is today heard in the high councils of international parliaments. Our economic, social, and political status has been improved tremendously, and every man and woman, every boy and girl, not excluding a solitary person and stranger within our domain has been a recipient and beneficiary of the products and results of the progressive policies of this Government. Our economic opportunities, the increased number of concessions in the country, county and nation-wide road programmes in addition to the county-development programmes, have all come into being because of the Government's desire and determination to provide its citizens with the blessings of the new day which has ostensibly dawned in the world and in Liberia, and to provide for the common man more and equal opportunities. Certainly the ultimate in all this has not yet been achieved, not by a long shot, but the positive evidences are not difficult to find. We must continue to forge ahead with purpose and determination and renewed faith in our vision of a true democracy. When that vision fails then indeed will Liberia be doomed to the ravages of traducing ideologies or any other isms.

In the midst of all the upheavals, the rumblings, and the uneasiness of the times, it is heartening and reassuring to know that at least ninety-nine per cent of the population of the nation has approved our policies as enunciated, demonstrated and executed for over seventeen years. This fact is evidenced by the recognition that the people of this nation have not only requested but have said that they require the return of this administration at the end of the present term of office. They have gone further to assert and affirm that they are definitely drafting us, that they want no reply from us and that their decision will be implemented at the convention and the polls.

It is well to remember what I said before, at the end of my second and third terms, that I would prefer to retire to private life after having served the nation in the capacity of President for such a long period. Nevertheless the citizens, without any coercion, subtle suggestions or influence of any kind from me came forward spontaneously and voluntarily, in mass demonstrations, insisting that the present administration continue in office.

I am aware that there are some who are as capable and deserving, and who could administer the affairs of government at least as well as I have done, if they were given the opportunity. I do not claim for myself superiority over any other person, least of all have I discredited the ability and capability of any person to carry on the responsibilities of government. In a democracy there is no limit to a citizen's aspirations. But the call must emanate from the people. Let the people call those who have said that they would like to have a chance of coming into this pulpit and preaching the sermon that they feel they can preach and thereby correct the errors which, according to their interpretations, I have made. But even here I have not claimed perfection for myself. I realize that I have committed many errors, made mistakes and blunders common to all men. But they have not been designedly done in any case, since I have always been guided by the greatest good to the greatest number.

If in my approach to the problems which have faced me, the greatest good has come to the greatest number, I feel further justified that my obligation to my country has been fulfilled. If I have failed to achieve this objective then let our detractors and our competitors whet their weapons with what they choose. But let not malice, greed, self-interest, chauvinism, diabolical scheming and narrow-minded patriotism be used as arguments to beguile the citizens of this country in a matter which concerns the destiny of a people.

As I have said on other occasions, I shall indeed welcome an opposition, another aspirant to the Presidency of this nation, and as I affirmed in the campaign of 1955, any opposition will be extended the same rights, privileges and benefits as the True Whig Party which we lead, and that any opposition candidate would be granted the same rights, privileges and protection as I myself enjoy. I stand by my declarations and commitments.

In the 1955 campaign which we have mentioned, we wrote to the opposition on matters concerning their rights and protection, and when they had their first demonstration we granted them the use of the Frontier Force Band and extended them the benefit of the use of the Antoinette Tubman Stadium and the Executive Pavilion. They were permitted to register their party under the election laws of the country, and when it became officially known that their printing press had been damaged by bandits, we offered to purchase a new printing press for them. This attitude we continued to show and exemplify openly until it was found that the opposition was not loyal to the Government of Liberia, but that it was proceeding and operating under methods deleterious to the organic laws of the country, and bent on pursuing revolutionary and destructive policies calculated to destroy law, morality and decent government.

Unworthy motives, in whatever form conceived, the rule of passion, malice and unpatriotic contrivings, do not mix well with love of country. True love of country, to be seen and recognized, must be made of better ingredients. The life of every public servant is an open book to the people of our country, and it is common knowledge that citizens know and appraise correctly all leaders in public offices.

Such were the circumstances surrounding the campaign of 1955, so that even when the assassination attempt was made upon my life, only then was the Government forced to take measures to secure the safety of the state. Furthermore as an outgrowth of the then threatening state of affairs, emergency powers were granted to the Government by the Legislature, yet not a single man, not a single culprit, not a single person was tried by a special court set up for the purpose. Those who became involved were arrested, prosecuted under normal and due process of law and subsequently convicted to be hanged. All these persons, except one, have since been pardoned. If such a spirit of tolerance and mercy can be defined and described as demoniac, then I rejoice in being this kind of a demon.

As a result of recent investigations into planned subversive activities in this country, aided and abetted by external agents and internal insurgents, we alerted the nation to the gravity of the situation, and, under a mandate of the Legislature, we have apprehended some of the local agents, three of whom have voluntarily exposed the plot and its ramifications to overthrow the constituted Government by force. Some of these agents are still in hiding, but we assure you that no efforts will be spared in ferreting them out and thereby destroying root and branch this insidious political malady from our soil.

Any form of government may be suitable for those who desire it as a way of life, but I know I am expressing the view of the overwhelming majority of our citizens when I say that we will stick to our concept of democracy and, therefore, do not want and will not have any strange ideology imposed upon us.

Our democracy advocates evolution and the adaptation to circumstances in a constitutional manner. Other ideologies advocate revolution and the use of force to attain their objectives. Their chief characteristics are, inciting a minority of ne'er-do-wells against the majority, inconsistencies, falsehoods, propaganda, riots, strikes, perpetual tensions and utter disregard for personal liberty, life and the pursuit of individual happiness. Such a system in Liberia will destroy not only our independence but everything that we and our forefathers have striven to accomplish over a period of 115 years of freedom. Subversive influence in this country must be rigorously exterminated.

Although the methods we have pursued over the years and the instruments which give validity to our actions may reveal some shortcomings, many of them have worked reasonably well. The effectiveness of all politico-legal instruments do not depend upon the written word alone but also on the intentions and deeds of men.

It is indeed fatuous for any foreign agents to conjecture for a moment that they can divide our people by the outmoded propaganda of telling the indigenous elements that the country belongs to them; and thereby engender conflict and chaos to facilitate the achievement of their aim of an African Imperium under one absolute leadership.

These agents and their sources are grossly mistaken. They have missed the bus. In Liberia today there are no natives, Americo-Liberians, or come-heres. All are citizens of the Republic of Liberia with equal rights and privileges for all.

Under our Unification Programme, whose tentacles embrace every segment of our population, and which is now too deep-rooted to be affected by the propaganda of men whose political experiences just suffice to make them bores even in their own countries, the indigenous people of the Republic will be the first to rise against these agents of subversion and disorder. Already we have received messages, letters and personal calls from the tribal elements and groups in all parts of the country, condemning and deprecating such insidious and invidious propaganda. Together we are striving to promote freedom of expression and religion and to attain a society free from disease, crime, ignorance and unhappiness.

THIS IS OUR CRUSADE

It is needless to repeat that but for the Unification Programme, the progress we have made in all areas of our country would have been imposssible. It is reflected in the policies enunciated by our administration and, by their successful implementation, peace has reigned throughout the country. There has been no armed conflict between the Government and the tribal people, or between the tribal peoples themselves. On the contrary, each tribe has taken advantage of the opportunity for progressive development afforded to it by the Government – schools, roads, transportation, medical services, business facilities, franchise rights, representation, and full participation in government.

The present situation in Liberia does not involve partisan politics as such. To my mind it is a movement aimed at deliberately destroying our Government and everything which we have cherished in our democratic institutions. To the end of combating these evil influences and thus saving our nation from perils, I call upon all Government agencies, all parties, all persons, either as individuals or in groups to act as agents to track down, discover, and reveal any plans aimed at subversive activities in our nation. In the name of the love which you bear for your country I ask this favour of you.

Fellow citizens, we have invested too much toil, sweat, tears and blood in this heritage to indulge now in catastrophic political experiments. Divorce your actions completely from alien doctrines and isms, and, with closed ranks, scale the pinnacle of continuing progress guided by the sure hand of God. Those persons, however, who are not susceptible to verbal persuasion will be convinced otherwise.

If our ancestors had heeded and followed the call of all of the political obstructions that beset their pathway, they would not have perpetuated this government as our inheritance. They would have made Liberia a pawn on the chess-board of world history. Our chief political problem on this continent is to survive as an independent and democratic state; but in order to survive and escape foreign domination this state must grow and grow in oneness of purpose.

In a world of decaying cultures, crumbling empires and ideological conflicts, our task in Liberia and for all Liberians is to develop a new sense of reality and responsibility in order to walk upright upon the path of justice, brotherly love and national peace. It is to this sense of responsibility and dedication that I challenge all the citizens of our nation.

To the National True Whig Party expressing Gratitude for its Loyalty and Devotion against Subversion

Monrovia, 16 November 1961

Whether we wish it or not, the hands of the clock of history cannot and will not be turned back.

Introductory Note

President Tubman did not like rumours and reports of subversion in Liberia. It was the duty of the Government and of every citizen of Liberia to destroy any form of subversion as a civic and patriotic duty. The National Unification programme seemed especially to be the target of subversion. The True Whig Party demonstrated their allegiance to the President's policies and pledged to assist the Government in destroying all subversive elements. The President thanked the Party for this act of devotion and patriotism, and further condemned subversion as an evil means which aimed at uprooting our national heritage, so painstakingly preserved and handed on to succeeding generations of Liberians.

Monrovia, 16 November 1961

IT IS with very deep gratitude that I rise to acknowledge this spontaneous demonstration, and to thank you with all my heart for the expressions you have made as a pledge of your loyalty and devotion and to register publicly your disapproval of the action of certain political groups of irresponsible, prejudiced and inexperienced fledglings. These would-be leaders, acting under the indoctrinating influences of certain foreign agencies, are determined to divide and segregate the country into sectional groups in order to set one element against the other and thereby undermine the constituted Government.

Among the policies which we outlined at the beginning of our administration seventeen years ago, was the Unification Programme. We explained, pointed out and emphasized the importance of unification and its beneficial results in the life of any advancing nation. Since then we have pursued this policy unflinchingly, and, in a large measure, it has achieved great success, united and integrated the people and brought peace and progress in its wake. Both by provision of laws enacted by the Legislature and constitutional amendments approved by that body, and by a referendum submitted to the people of this country, the programme has won nation-wide acceptance. And so, encouraged by this achievement, the Legislature, after a long and careful study in which the constitutional basis was thoroughly reviewed, authorized the revison of the territorial and political sub-divisions of the country. Consequently, upon the authority of that act, we set up a Commission to study and make recommendations for its implementation. I entertain no doubt that this has been a very significant advance and one which will, I hope, be acclaimed as a vital step forward in our national and political history.

One hundred and fourteen years ago this country was founded by men and women of vigorous minds, stout hearts and stern determination, who when they came here in search of freedom met men and women with equally sturdy characters and brave souls who loved and guarded their liberty zealously. Together they joined forces in the interest of establishing a nation that would become a beacon-light to the entire world and be a proof of the ability of the Negro at self-government. And although the tribal people and those who came were all of African descent, there were misunderstandings, internecine wars, and armed conflicts against the Government from time to time, but in each case there were tribal fightings with and alongside of Government troops. In the course of the long history of these quarrels, disputes, and wars, neither side has been able to exterminate the other; it was God's plan that those who came and those who remained here were to be equals, to unite to form a stable Government, and that this nation was destined to be an asylum for black men and women as a shining example of the love of liberty.

Subjected to scathing criticisms by our detractors, faced with the partition of our territory, undaunted by the unwillingness of some of our foreign friends to help in developing the natural and human resources of our nation because we were determined to rule and not to be ruled, startled by the easy propensity to capitalize the internal and external unsettled conditions in the new nation, everything seemed to be against us. But leaders and people bore all with patience and a strong determination. Times have now changed and a remarkable evolution has been made in the direction of an orderly Government. We have stoically weathered and survived the political storms, battled successfully the internal and external warfare, and achieved a tolerable degree of peace and harmony, progress and prosperity.

For more than seventeen years now there has not been a single conflict between the Government and the tribal people, or even between tribe and tribe. We have enunciated and pursued a policy of equal opportunities for all throughout the length and breadth of the nation. We regard the Unification Programme as one of the highly successful achievements of our administration. The results are far too numerous to recite. The judgment of history will, I am sure, be on our side in this achievement. Our great objective has been to preserve the peace and make the people one in loyalty and allegiance to the great ideal of constituted government.

The situation which presently prevails in the country, as a direct result of the Unification Programme, is one in which the indigenous population is taking full advantage of the opportunities for self-development and advancement afforded by their Government. Schools have been built in strategic areas, roads have been constructed, communication facilities established, medical services offered, business facilities given, franchise rights bestowed and representation and full participation in government enjoyed. Certainly, with such a degree of success, it should be unthinkable that anyone would want to revert to a state where the position would be reversed, and thus prepare the grounds for tribal feuds, armed conflicts, aggression and living under a form of government that would restrict all that the nation's founders and leaders have tried to achieve by way of national unity, progress, solidarity and orderly government.

Let us not be deceived by vain political promises or the logic of the demagogues, nor should we trust our destiny to those who dabble only in theories and speculations. No one section of our population has priority in the nation's wealth and opportunities, but all segments of the nation's manpower are entitled to share alike in the rights and responsibilities of citizenship. History has provided abundant examples of the benefits to be gained when people live as equal partners in any progressive society, and advance in an orderly manner to a fuller life. Whether we wish it or not, the hands of the clock of history cannot and will not be turned back. The idealism that needs to be inculcated is one that will make people more sensitive to the national consciousness. The work that needs to be done now is one that will unify all sections of our people more and more into a political and cultural awareness, so that a better and greater Liberia may emerge.

Finally, I verily believe and am absolutely convinced that your action today is not the result of any undue influence exercised over you by some of the youths of this country, who may have been misled because of their lack of experience and knowledge of the unwritten history of our nation and what it meant to all Africa when there were only two independent states. And because of the liberal attitude of the Government towards foreign diplomatic missions to this country, some have sought, perhaps without the approval of their Government, to sow seeds of discord with the design of disrupting the unity and concord created and established in the nation. But such a state of affairs will not be permitted to continue. We have stood upon our own feet as a nation for more than 114 years, and met the challenges, conditions and circumstances of each age. We shall do it again and again, and each time that it becomes necessary we will fight to the death in defence of our liberties until all obstacles have been overcome, our way of life made secure, and peace and happiness assured to all our people everywhere.

We say like the Miller of the River Dee that we envy no man or nation; we thank the River Dee that turns the mill to grind the corn, but we envy no man or nation and we think that no man or nation should envy us. We thank the Gods, we thank our friends and, like the proverbial Miller, thank the River Dee because it turns the mill that grinds the corn and feeds our babies and us. But we ask to be left alone. Should future interference be made in our affairs by any foreign country, we shall be compelled to break off diplomatic relations and sever all friendly intercourse.

The Government and people of Liberia have not been deceitful, and are not deceitful. We are forthright and what our hearts feel we express in unequivocal terms. Liberia and the Liberians have not been an enigma. We seek no expansionist movement, we have no wish for territorial aggrandizement nor do we possess any inordinate ambition for African or world leadership. We want to live only upon our merits and there is no force on the entire earth that could intimidate or deter us; for we are not experimenting at government or taking undue risks; rather, we have always pursued the policy of acting cautiously.

Gravitation is the most powerful force in nature, but it is unseen and unheard. And so we move quietly along, certainly not like the most powerful force in nature or among world governments, but as a powerful, moral and spiritual force without bellicosity or loquaciousness. Our responsibility has always been to preserve the peace of the nation. We are determined to do this at all hazards.

Let me close by quoting the last paragraph of my remarks made on 5th January 1961, at the unveiling of the Unification Monument:

'My ardent prayer has always been, is now, and will ever be that all the people of this nation may remain devoted, loyal and dedicated to the principles of unity and solidarity so that our great patrimony of democracy may grow stronger and greater as the years go by.'

I challenge you to the opportunities of believing in this ideal, working for it and making it a true national achievement for all times in our social and political history.

Again, I thank you, one and all.

A Broadcast on the Eve of his Departure on a State Visit to Israel

Monrovia 1 June 1962

The turbulent speed of events in recent years behoves us to set new goals and values in our society.

Introductory Note

President Tubman made state visits, when invited in the interest of peace and friendship, between Liberia and other nations of the world. Subversion had raised its ubiquitous head in Liberia and aimed to attack the nation where it was most vulnerable – in the schools and institutions of higher learning. This inroad made by subversive elements made the President angry. Unless action was taken to eliminate subversion and its causes and effects by those institutions of learning mentioned in reports he had received, the Government would intervene in the interest of the preservation of the state. The schools were further infected with certain alien practices which were unwholesome, and which in one instance caused the death of one student. It was time to set new goals and values for the youth of Liberia, who would later be entrusted with the task of building a better future for all Liberians. The President gave examples of some of the goals and values which should be taught in our institutions of learning.

Monrovia, 1 June 1962

DURING THE COURSE of a 114 years' evolution as a state, successive administrations of government have worked unceasingly to strengthen our ties with other nations. To this end, we of this administration have, through a guided policy of moderation and active gradualism, endeavoured to preserve that stability which, in our opinion, is necessary for a true well-blanced national progress. Beginning from the very bottom of the ladder of nationhood, we had few precedents to guide us in an international society, little wisdom or adequate knowledge to avoid failures, pitfalls and fumbling. We stood virtually alone on the brink of the unknown. But with determination, courage and abiding faith in God, we countered the tide of human events, entered into agreeable policies of alignment in the early years of our nationhood, devised new methods to meet shifting political relationships, and, with a measure of sagacity and maturity, eventually evolved a meaningful and indispensable partnership for all the segments of our population by the policy of Unification and Integration.

The turbulent speed of events in recent years behoves us to set new goals and values in our society, to work for a realistic understanding of the pressures between rival institutions, forces, groups and individuals, to become more sensitive to the things that maintain, preserve and foster our national heritage with its freedoms, social and political institutions, lest we become lost and confused in the rising tide of irresponsible conduct and strange, erroneous, subversive propaganda outbursts.

Over the years our strivings have been motivated by certain tenets:

1. Team loyalty to a common homeland;
2. Common dominant social institutions;
3. A common history;
4. Love and esteem for our fellow citizens and things Liberian;
5. A common and modest pride in our national achievements;
6. Hostility to any group that attempted to divide us or undermine our national solidarity;
7. Devotion to the nation with its common territory, culture, social, economic, religious and political institutions;
8. A sublime hope and aspiration for a great and glorious national future.

These are some of the noble sentiments to which we are dedicated and we will not relinquish them, lest we betray the faith and hopes of the founding fathers, those of future generations as well as all who gave their lives for the perpetuity of this nation.

In our efforts to transmit a mature political, social and cultural heritage to posterity, and to save our sons and daughters from the influence of irresponsible and reckless actions, the adminstration has endeavoured to put greater emphasis on, and give new impetus to, the educational programme.

Notwithstanding, there are yet among our student population some who apparently ignore the significance and meaning of general education. I refer here to the recent regrettable and misguided student incident on the campus of Booker Washington Institute, on the night of April 12th when one of the promising freshmen students became the innocent victim of an initiation brawl and was struck down unconscious with a dangerous instrument by another student. Since that date, student Charles Ledlum's fate has oscillated between hope and despair, life and death. The impact of this despicable, brutal, regrettable and outrageous crime, conceived and inspired, no doubt, by some malevolently minded persons, came as a great shock to the nation's leaders, its people and educational authorities, cast a sad reflection on our institutions of learning and completely dumbfounded the grief-stricken family. For this was educational practice at its ugliest, a vile misrepresentation of some foreign institutional practice whose philosophy has not yet been fully imbibed, and whose significance has not yet been altogether comprehended and hence not understood. As a result of this unfortunate incident, the student who dealt the deathly blow is imprisoned, the Dean of Men dismissed, the Assistant Dean suspended indefinitely, the senior students suspended for a period of a year for their complicity, all initiation rites banned and sterner disciplinary measures introduced.

All of these measures are necessary and maybe helpful, but they are not enough; for they do not strike at the core of the criminal propensities made evident by these acts of certain students. Practices and notions are developing which have apparent attraction for some of the young people and students of our land, which stem from the influence of the radical and extremist philosophies now prevalent in some parts of the world. This attraction for students seems to be extending its influence into Liberia.

At present there are graduates of the University, the colleges, high schools and other institutions of learning imprisoned upon charges of sedition for alleged engagements in criminal acts of subversion aimed at overthrowing the Government of our country by the use of force. Although those charged have not yet been convicted, the very fact that an inquisitional forum has, in its opinion, found sufficient evidence to charge them and a Grand Jury to indict them is an index pointing to the insidious danger inherent in these activities. More than this, it has been brought to our attention that during the episode at Booker Washington Insititute when young Ledlum was nearly murdered, and sustained injuries from which he still lingers between life and death, a senior student was heard to remark 'let us get a spike and drive it through his head'. If this is the mind and spirit with which Liberian students are possessed, and the kind of attitude or behaviour pattern which the institutions of learning in our nation are encouraging and inculcating, where is the hope for the retention of our century-old national and international record and traditions of the stability of our government, and the law-abiding and peace-loving character of its citizens? Does this mean that the right kind of training is not being given to our students in our schools? Are the students responsible or are their preceptors? Is it because of the weakness of the system which has been adopted and which is being pursued which is responsible for this state of affairs, or is it the result of the influence of the atomic age or even the predominantly materialistic culture in which we live which has led to a lessening of those values which have been held dear to us in the past? For there have been student strikes in our colleges, revolts of students against teachers, disregard and disrespect of young people for their elders, and a glaring lack of reverence for things sacred, all of which paint a dismal picture indeed.

I am not fully informed about the causes of these incidents but I do know that one or two things contribute greatly towards this new condition – the inhibition against reading and studying the Bible, the Koran, the Bund Avesta or other holy writings which are at best literature in themselves, and the outlawing of the use of the switch in our schools, especially in the elementary grades. These, I believe are the largest contributing factors to this appalling situation which prevails through the world and which has now infiltrated our social and political institutions.

I insist upon putting back into our schools the sacred records and the use of the rod which, the wise man declares, if spared, spoils the child, and which was made for the backs of fools. It is an acknowledged fact that all of us of advanced years were subjected to this kind of training, and consequently such practices as are now being experienced where young people and students assassinate parents or companions, and commit numerous other crimes, were unknown.

Educational institutions exist to explore, develop, transmit knowledge; to advance man's thought and action to new areas of learning and discovery; to keep alive the sense of continuing intellectual curiosity and research and to prepare the student to live a fuller, a more comprehensive, unique and successful life by his effective participation in, and valuable contributions to, his society. And to the extent that school authorities play this rôle with sober imagination and enlightened guidance, to the same extent will progress ensue to enrich human understanding and experience and guide life through useful channels of constructive endeavours and accomplishments.

The schools should always be harbingers of great ideas and ideals, for each society looks to its educational institutions to safeguard to a great extent its human liberties and needs, solve its persistent problems and lead the way to new levels of human happiness and creativity. Those therefore who enter these institutions are bound to leave behind them the heritage of a richer and greatly improved social order of things.

Booker Washington Institute was founded after the ideals of a great American Negro Educator and Emancipator whose philosophy is still reflected proudly in the educational programme of Tuskegee Institute in Alabama, United States of America. The acquisition of needed marketable skills and the development of the potentials of youth have been the guiding principles in the education and training programme of that institution. And now in order to enable this school to achieve more significant and far-reaching results, not only has it been made a part of the University of Liberia's larger programme, but its own offerings have been greatly enriched, enlarged and strengthened to provide greater and more productive service to the nation. The students who pass out yearly from this institution are bound therefore to cherish these noble ends, and to strive unceasingly to contribute to the creation of a suitable and wholesome atmosphere in which these ideals will flourish.

This history of revolutions throughout the world has been a history of faction, treachery, rapine, bloodshed, propaganda and the suppression of freedom. Revolutions once begun must continue in an endless series, with benefits to no one. We in Liberia have always regarded revolutions as dangerous to our national existence. We expect our students and citizens alike to do all in their power to adopt a similar attitude and refrain from toying with their destructive influence. For student revolutions and revolutions of any kind may be likened to the ripples of a lake which spread and spread *ad infinitum*.

Our nation needs responsible men and women, responsibility conceived in its entirety and in a larger framework. Unless you bring into your educational environment an enlightened vision, a magnanimous spirit, and a guided sense of objectivity, all our strivings will be in vain.

Finally, I appeal to the educational authorities of our nation, to all parents and guardians, to everyone entrusted with the care and nurture of the young, to take an increased interest in, and responsibility, for the education and training of the future citizens of our nation.

I appeal to every teacher, man or woman, as leader in the community of every school in the Republic, from the most elementary up through our colleges and university, to act as if the response of the community was to be the response of the entire nation, and hence a decision of the whole world.

May the painful and disappointing experience of the past renew in us the will to forge ahead in the direction of a new and saner educational philosophy, through which a free, and only a free, people can hold their purpose steady to a common goal, not only in their own interest but in the interest of all mankind.

Response to the County Branch of the True Whig Party of Grand Cape Mount County after holding a Mass Demonstration in which the Citizens of that County pledged their Support to President Tubman

Monrovia 31 October 1962

The people of Grand Cape Mount County have always been noted for their conservatism.

Introductory Note

One factor which determined the popular esteem for President Tubman on the part of his people was the call to succeed himself in office, generally only three months after he had been sworn into office for a new term. While the President appreciated this gesture he often took a long time to reply to a new call. The partisans of the True Whig Party of Grand Cape Mount County were seldom afforded the opportunity to demonstrate their own esteem for their President during this early period due to barriers to transportation not affecting partisans of other counties, who enjoyed and were provided an easy access to reach Monrovia and show their loyalty to him. The partisans of Grand Cape Mount County had further won the political description of being conservative in all matters affecting local or national politics. President Tubman observed that this characteristic of Cape Mountainians and their leaders was a positive and constructive force — one which enabled them to consider carefully any direction in which Liberia was headed before giving that direction their support. Because of that quality in their mental outlook, they have always supported the policies of President Tubman. The President thanked them for their loyalty in the common task of building a democracy in Liberia.

Monrovia, 31 October 1962

THE COLOURFUL and impressive demonstration which was staged this evening is one which undoubtedly carries with it the love and loyalty of the people of Grand Cape Mount County to the common cause, for which others before them have subscribed by their participation in similar gatherings. The expressions which have been uttered, the resolutions which have been read and presented and the careful planning and work which have gone into all this, do credit to you, the partisans of the True Whig Party of Grand Cape Mount.

It is because you believe in the cause of democracy that you have co-operated in making this meeting a success, for I understand that many of you came here on your own, to join with your leaders and officials of the local party in this demonstration. I congratulate you for your fine spirit, enthusiasm, participation, contribution and support which you have so generously given this move.

The people of Grand Cape Mount County have always been noted for their conservatism. And that is why other counties with the exception of my own home county, Maryland, provinces, and territories have already presented resolutions asking me to accept the fifth term. Cape Mount has waited until this time. The leaders are known to weigh, ponder and assess issues before taking action. This peculiar characteristic has made Cape Mountainians politically shrewd, always steering a middle course. May you continue to be what you have professed to be all along, so that the national party will always have in you a dependable and strong local support.

We are engaged in a great task, that of maintaining and perpetuating this nation which was bequeathed to us by those who made supreme sacrifices, so that we, their successors, might enjoy the blessings of freedom and liberty. Generations of men and women have contributed their quota to the enriching and strengthening of the national structure, and their memories will always live in the hearts of their fellow-men and women. But more than this, we are also engaged in building a better and stronger nation with greater and better economic opportunities for all citizens. It is incumbent upon us that we bring to our task a wider vision of service and dedication to the cause we have always believed to be just.

In the midst of the national and international situation to which we are exposed, we need to reappraise our social and political institutions, manifest a greater interest in them to justify the belief that these institutions shape and mould the future of the citizens of succeeding generations. It is my profound belief that democracy must be made to work pragmatically; that we must believe in it with all our heart and soul and work for it with all the energy that we possess. In the fulfilment of these matters I have appealed to the citizens and partisans of other counties, provinces and territories. I wish to reiterate the same sentiments to you at this time.

And now the fifth term. Having already been presented with resolutions, petitions and requests which have hailed from nearly all the counties, provinces and territories, I am bereft of the will to refuse such an overwhelming sense of public loyalty and affection. My gratitude to you, the people of Liberia, knows no bounds; your faith in me, your loyalty and devotion to me and your support of our policies have touched me greatly. We are grateful and indeed humble and can only ask that you continue to pray for us so that God may grant us a greater measure of wisdom and understanding, grant us physical courage and fortitude and give us mental health to bear with efficiency and fervour the responsibilities which increase from day to day.

We thank you, fellow partisans of the local True Whig Party of Grand Cape Mount, for your loyalty and support in the past, for the demonstration which you have staged today and for the future promises you have made to work with us in the maintenance and perpetuation of this national trust. I hope that those of you who travelled long distances from the interior of Cape Mount will return and meet your families well; to them I send my personal best wishes for their welfare. I look forward to seeing you in the future when the big day comes for the many expressions and resolutions which have been presented to take final shape and form.

Until then, God bless you and your loved ones.

A Response to the National Convention of the True Whig Party endorsing him as Candidate for the Presidency of Liberia for a Fifth Term

Monrovia, 7 February 1963

I dedicate myself to the national struggle to make our country the haven it was meant to be.

Introductory Note

We have in this major address not only President Tubman's response to the True Whig Party and his acceptance of their selection of him for another term of office, but also a revealing history of the True Whig Party and its ideals, and a refutation of the allegation that Liberia has always represented itself as a one party state. President Tubman further rededicated himself to serve his people and expressed his gratitude for their faith and trust in his leadership.

Monrovia, 7 February 1963

I APPEAR before you in response to your call that I attend the Convention grounds to receive the announcement that I have been nominated by you as the True Whig Party's Candidate for the Presidency of Liberia.

The National Convention of 1963 will hold a unique place in the political annals of the nation and of the True Whig Party, because it is the first time in the long history of public service of members who have figured prominently in the affairs of state and the Party, and the growing strength and popularity of the Party attest to the useful functions it has rendered in our political machinery, and the effectiveness of the wise policies and principles which its members have generally followed. We are proud of these accomplishments and look forward to the future with great hope and optimism that the ideals of democracy will continue to flourish, and that deeds and not words will become an important social and political reality in the life of our people. Indeed, it is for the implementation of ideas and ideals into reality that political parties are formed. Men having similar views and ideas join a union or political party whereby they aspire to inspire popular support through elections, so that their ideas may see fruition through action. It is important to be cautious however, and to remember that in an election, only one person or party can emerge victorious. Thus all *bona fide* political parties should be good sports and, having lost an election, settle down to support or constructively criticize the administration in securing the best for the majority of the people of the country. Plans should then be made for the next election when the people will again register their choice. This is democracy.

It is an insult to the idea of government by the people that in many areas of the world, including Liberia, bands of ambitious men form so-called political parties which, when they are rejected by the people in free elections, resort to force and subversive practices. Citizens who resort to these practices are infidels to society, as they desire, not that the will of the people prevail but rather, that their own ambitions obtain whatever the cost or whatever the will of the people. Perhaps this inordinate ambition is best explained by John Milton when in *Paradise Lost* he has Satan say:

> 'To reign is worth ambition though in Hell:
> Better to reign in Hell, than serve in Heaven'

Democracy says, however, and I feel that this is right, that the people had rather live in Heaven than in Hell, and so democracy advocates free elections that thereby the people may prescribe their own Heaven. The True Whig Party has never compelled anyone to remain in its ranks, and the laws of the nation explicitly provide for the formation of political parties.

Under the laws of Liberia, any three hundred citizens have the right to organize a political party, which must be recognized. In the past, whenever the people of this country have felt it necessary, they have exercised this right and formed political parties to contest the True Whig Party. Personally, I welcome an opposition party, and I have always done so. In every instance where there has been an opposition formed since my incumbency as President, I have accorded to it every right, privilege and function guaranteed under the constitution and laws of the Republic.

In the contested campaign of 1955, when the Independent True Whig Party announced that its printing office had been broken into and the printing press damaged, I offered a new press to carry on its political press activities, and when the leaders asked for the use of the military band for their parade I directed that the request be granted; and again when they asked for the use of the Executive Pavilion for their meeting, it was made available. In every reasonable way, we have endeavoured to encourage an opposition. However, a victorious political party in power cannot be expected to hand over the reins of government to an opposition party. To do so would be to admit that it has no faith in its own ideas and ideals. Besides, the people must decide which person or party should lead them. But we insist that all political parties, including the True Whig Party, exercise their political rights and privileges within the scope, provision and authority of the will of institutions; rather such institutions must be subject to and governed by the law.

Ever mindful of the magnanimity of your preference for us, constantly grateful for your faith, loyalty and devotion, and deeply appreciative of the popular support you have always given our administration, let me say with all the emphasis and sincerity at my command that I am profoundly thankful to you, the leaders and partisans of the True Whig Party and the citizens and people of Liberia, for your approval of what we have striven to do in the interest of our nation and its people.

No one not in my position and not having been the beneficiary of so great material and spiritual opportunities and blessings can fully comprehend the depth of my emotion at this hour. Suffice it for me to say that having envisioned the Liberia we desired twenty years ago, we planned and toiled for its realization. Together we waited for results in terms of an economic upsurge, better educational opportunities, improved health and high sanitation standards, improved roads and communications, technical development, progress along all lines, and above all, a unified and happy people, friendship with all those who desire our friendship and the maximum development and utilization of the human and natural resources of the country.

We can look around and see some satisfying results to commend our collective efforts. They stand sometimes as mute and sometimes as eloquent witnesses of the determination, careful planning, devotion and dedication to the ideals of democracy, and the willing co-operation of you, the leaders and peoples, partisans and citizens of this True Whig Party. I congratulate you for your vision and commend you for your loyalty and support.

I stand as I have stood in the past, to serve further the best interest of the people, and I again invite you to labour more productively and creatively with me, so that our nation may become better and better in a world where differing political and social ideologies vie to engulf each other. In the days and years which are ahead, your loyalty to service, your adherence to the principles and policies which have under-girded our party, your love of country and your constant vigilance will be instrumental in keeping the light of liberty burning on our shores. I appeal to your patriotism; I rely upon your loyalty, I need your constant support and prayers and I have faith in your love for your sons and daughters, and your desire for a better social and educational experience for them. I adjure you to join hands with us by giving a fuller measure of your devotion and service, in building a nation towards which you have already contributed so much. In thus accepting your participation in our nation's programme, you will be making a more significant contribution and thereby extend the dimensions of the love of liberty, without which no true democracy can survive.

Every age has its own peculiar challenges. Living at a time like this and surrounded by forces which are determined to engulf all mankind into a maelstrom, we indeed face a series of alternatives:

To enlarge the national vision, or to allow provincialism to close our minds to the happenings in the world of peoples and things;

To continue with our policies which have stood the test of time, or to abandon them for less definitive and untried ones;

To continue to explore new fields of national interests, or to be conservative in our outlook;

To close our ranks and march as a great phalanx, or to allow personal ambition to confuse our ranks.

In the light of what we have always desired for the good of national progress and stability, I can only ask that you choose an alternative in keeping with the spirit of true love of country and a correct sense of purpose and direction. I ask that you be responsive to the historic opportunity.

I thank the officers and members of the Party for the painstaking planning and efficient execution which have gone into today's activities. I trust that the same spirit of harmony and concord which has prevailed at this Convention will characterize the remaining events of this year's political activities. I feel sure that the best interest of the state and its advancement will always be foremost in your consideration.

And now having listened to the many petitions, having received resolutions from all of the people of our nation, having had verbal and written appeals from you, my beloved partisans, fellow citizens and friends, I have already indicated that I have no alternative. In spite of my own personal reasons which stood in the way, I have been conquered by your goodwill, your solicitude for my welfare, your love and affection and the great support you have given me. I cannot be ungrateful to the people, citizens and friends and partisans who, for nearly twenty years, have reposed implicit faith in me, supported my policies and followed me in practice by assisting to implement the policies of the administration – many of which we have had the opportunity and joy of seeing come to fruition. In our common concern for our native land we have done everything humanly possible to bring the nation a reasonable degree of progress and prosperity. Any measure of success which has been achieved must be attributed to your loyalty, devotion and faith: first of all, in the principles of democracy, and secondly in your willing co-operation to see them work in reality. The part which you have played cannot therefore be minimized in any way.

I am greatly attracted by your nomination of the Honourable William R. Tolbert, Jun., to be the Vice-Presidential Candidate for the True Whig Party for another term of office. In him I have found a man conscientious, patriotic, devoted, trustworthy and reliable; a man who has convictions and the courage to make known these convictions; a man imbued with the ability to make prompt decisions which almost invariably are found to be constructive and objective.

After long years of planning, work is to commence on the construction of the National Headquarters for the True Whig Party on Ashmun Street in Monrovia. The building is to be constructed on the very spot where President Roye, elected by the True Whig Party, was cast into prison and there died the death of a martyr. No more fitting memorial, I believe, can be erected to the memory of so illustrious a personality and so brave a fighter and leader. Generations of Liberians in general, and True Whig Party leaders and partisans in particular, will undoubtedly derive strength and comfort from the lofty principles for which President Roye stood and for which he died.

We call upon every loyal partisan to support the decision whole-heartedly and contribute generously to make the headquarters a living monument, one of which we can always be justly proud.

The City of Clay-Ashland is the place in Liberia where the True Whig Party had its birth under the leadership of the dynamic John Wallace Good. I recommend for your consideration the erection of a monument in that city on the grounds where the Party met and was formally organized. I think that this would be a deserving memorial to those great souls who conceived and promoted the Party.

The platform which you have adopted at this Convention today shall have our support and we subscribe our assent to the principles and policies laid down in each plank.

And now having consented, or should I rather say, yielded to the insistent and repeated requests of you, the partisans of the True Whig Party, to be your candidate for the office of President in the ensuing elections for the fifth time, I can only say, in humility and gratitude, that I shall dedicate myself to still greater service in the true development and forward march of the nation we all love so well.

I dedicate myself to the national struggle to make our country the haven it was always meant to be.

I dedicate myself to join others in Africa and in the world to fight tyranny and oppression, and to be instrumental in freeing those still deprived of their human rights.

I dedicate myself to African Unity and solidarity and to peace and prosperity with all in Africa and in the nations of the world.

I dedicate myself to the service of the God of Nations Who has never forsaken His people and to strive always for the maintenance and perpetuity of our Lone Star Republic, to the end that the challenges from which our forefathers never shrank may find us ready to fight, and if necessary to die, for the ideals which we have always cherished.

May God bless and prosper the True Whig Party and the State.

At the Opening of the Third Biennial Unification Council

Kolahun, Loffa County, 14 February 1963

We are determined to continue the various programmes of social, economic, cultural and political reform which we enunciated and began implementing upon our induction into office.

Introductory Note

When the Third Biennial Unification Council was convened President Tubman took the opportunity to announce plans for the abolition of the political sub-divisions of Liberia. Before he made this revelation, however, he discussed at length the path and progress which our National Unification Policy had followed and achieved. It was a most propitious moment for this new political development, especially when seen in terms of African nationalism, which was then rampant. The fly in the ointment, however, was subversion, and this claimed the President's attention; especially when it was conceived as a deliberate effort by some citizens to retard the political advancement of Liberia – National Unification being the keystone of that advancement. His thoughts were again and again turned to this new turn of events which required much effort to be rooted out of the national consciousness, and especially out of the nation's institutions of learning. Loffa County, formerly of the old political division of the Western Province, had always been a test ground for the implementation of national unification. The President was pleased with the favourable response which the citizens of that county gave to this national policy and challenge.

Kolahun, Loffa County, 14 February 1963

NINE YEARS ago we embarked with faith and determination upon a programme of unifying and integrating the people of the country into a united whole. The policy which has led to the observance of this programme today is referred to as the Unification Policy.

Twelve years earlier we repudiated publicly any idea that any section or segment of the nation was entitled to political and social preference or right over any other, and we declared that it was impossible to build a powerful and progressive nation with divided loyalties, suspicion and fear. This was in our statement of policy when we first stood for election to the office of President in 1944.

In our first inaugural speech we outlined our social philosophy, declaring that we would take little or no pleasure in being called President of a nation of vassals and sycophants, and calling for an educational programme for all the people of the nation, in order that they may be better prepared for the

responsibility of intelligent government. We then avowed that all Liberians
are entitled to the same rights and privileges.

Immediately we embarked upon a programme which brought universal
suffrage to the people of Liberia, and nine years ago the first unification
council was convened in Maryland County, where we challenged those who
had constantly believed or entertained the idea that one segment of the population should live apart from, rather than as a part of, the whole people of the
nation. In thus establishing this policy we also threw out a challenge to all
sections and elements of the nation to unite and contribute to building a
strong and progressive nation.

That the people have picked up the gauntlet and accepted that challenge
is indicated by the progress that has been made.

Two years ago, a monument was erected here commemorating the national
endorsement of the Unification Programme. You may recall that the resolutions presented to the Legislature by you advocated the erection of a monument in each of the provinces as a mark of concurrence in the unification
policy and programme by all the people, but the Legislature decided to erect
only one monument in the Western Province, the first to petition it with
such a request.

It is our hope that the idea for which the Unification Monument stands
will perpetually endure, and that, so long as all national elements hold together, the monument will be a constant reminder and covenant symbolizing the concurrence of all elements and sections of the population, and that
through the unification of the nation we stand in strength and justice.

Today, the Unification Programme is near the end of one era, and the
beginning of another era, which we hope will be greater and nobler. It is our
hope that this present Council will be the final one held whilst the nation is
divided into counties, provinces and territories. At our next convocation the
nation should be divided principally into counties, with all rights and privileges which go with county administration under our system of government.
This is the new era to which we look hopefully forward in the immediate
future – an era which will call upon all of us to share an even greater responsibility in the day-to-day life of the country. Whatever the task therefore we are to perform for the national progress, we should happily give our
best.

We feel gratified that all sections of the country, and the people have co-
operated in making the Unification Policy a success. During the last twenty
years there have been no inter-tribal wars. All tribes, segments and elements
of the country have stood together in support of the nation and the Unification Policy. No better, or greater or more eloquent testimonial to the support
of this policy could be demonstrated than by the approval the people have
given to the policies of the administration, or by their constant demand that
we remain their National Leader, often over and above our objections, and
re-inforced by their unanimous nomination of us a week ago today.

There is no question that the Unification Policy has been successful, and
that it has brought manifold benefits to the nation. This gives much satisfaction to all those who had anything to do with the inauguration, the shaping
and execution of the policy as well as to every citizen who has co-operated in
making the practical application of the policy a reality.

This policy could not have been successful without the Open Door Policy
and vice versa: the Open Door Policy could not have succeeded without the

Unification Policy. The Open Door Policy brought about better and numerous roads to almost every part of the country, airfields and other means of communication and transportation which made the remotest parts of the country accessible to traders and businessmen and thereby activated development in these areas, as well as affording to the people in different sections of the country the means whereby they could communicate with, visit and get to know more about each other. The Open Door Policy also brought greater advantages in education, health, social and other benefits to the citizens of the country. It made possible the coming of various concessions, such as the mining and agricultural concessions, which enable more of our people to be gainfully employed and to receive practical on-the-job training, higher wages and other benefits.

Moreover, we felt that not only should the Government and the concessionaires share in the profits of these concessions but that the people themselves should also obtain direct benefits therefrom. In this connection we enunciated the policy that wherever possible Liberian citizens, without regard to station, tribe or clan, inhabiting the littoral or the hinterland, be offered the privilege to purchase stocks in these concessions. Many of the chiefs and the citizens living in their chiefdoms are holders of share certificates in one or more concessions.

In the case of the LAMCO stock when the people of the hinterland and remote parts of the littoral failed to purchase shares on time because of the distances to be traversed, the Government saw to it that the time was extended, so that all might benefit by participating in the wealth of their nation.

I, personally, as President, made a broadcast to the people throughout the country trying to persuade them to invest in this enterprise.

The purpose of all of these ventures has been our wish to raise the standard of living of the people of the nation, and to develop a middle class, which is so necessary in a democratic and free-enterprise system of government.

However, there is no doubt or question that human nature in its various aspects and propensities manifests itself in different ways under almost any circumstances. Indeed, sometimes these human frailties even invade the realm of the deities. The story is told of Lucifer, the angel of light in heaven, who not satisfied with this high station became a traitor, causing confusion and war in heaven itself and having to be hurled into the bottomless pit of hell.

Traitors have arisen again and again in society, the church, in nations and in the family, which is the smallest unit of the state. Whatever the man, whatever the institution, whatever the people may decide, treachery at some time will show its monstrous head. And so just at the time when the nation and people are seeking to conclude arrangements for the review of the territorial sub-divisions of the nation, as when the sons of God appeared before the throne, Satan also appeared in their midst and attempted to challenge God, so also at this time did Satan appear in our midst and attempt to challenge the Unification Policy, all that it stands for and has accomplished, to disrupt the peace, unity and stability with which this Government has been credited through the Unification Programme.

It is perhaps interesting, and even necessary, to mention that even when there were internecine wars, uprisings and rebellions within the country, they were not aimed at the assassination or murder of the Chief of State, nor at a change of the frame and system of government, but were waged in opposition to some wrong which the belligerents believed to have been committed against them, whether right or wrong. What is not generally known is that most of the wars and uprisings which occurred in the early history of our country did not have their origins in disputes and disagreements between the Government and the tribes, but amongst the tribes themselves, and often one or several of them brought their complaints to the Government for investigation and decision. Generally, these complaints were over boundary disputes and the tribe against whom the Government rendered a decision objected, and refused to submit to the decision of the Government, which, being the supreme authority of the nation, was compelled to enforce its decisions. And in such cases the tribe in whose favour the decision was rendered generally became an ally of Government in executing the decisions.

Now, a new, strange and traducing concept seems to be attracting some of our people, particularly some of the young, impressionable and irresponsible ones who seem to be still obsessed with the idea of tribalism and have fallen easy prey to the propaganda and indoctrination that is secretly and stealthily being disseminated amongst them – that the land and territory of Liberia belong to them and that they have been deprived of their heritage; that the only way to retrieve the situation is to engage in subversive activities, treason and sedition and overthrow the Government by force and murder, establish a socialist system of government, expropriate the properties of those who by their many years of labour, sacrifices, toil and sweat acquired their possessions and then distribute these properties among themselves.

We have no quarrel; we wage no war against socialism if it is kept within the territories of, and among the people who are socialistically inclined and who desire it. Each nation has the right to pursue the way of life it prefers and we will never attempt to impose our way of life on any other nation or people. But we shall fight to the death any attempts to impose and force upon us what we consider a mystical illusion. Our democracy has stood the test for almost a century and a quarter. Let us wait and see what reward socialism will bring to socialistic countries within a century or half a century, and then draw up the balance sheet. Perhaps at that time what now seems attractive to some of the young in this new, flashy ideology may prove itself.

This doctrine is being disseminated by certain foreign agencies and it is finding its way into some of the schools of our nation, particularly Cuttington College, the College of West Africa, the University of Liberia and other schools. The authorities of these institutions are, or should be, aware of the infiltration of this ideology, and unless they take appropriate action, the Government will be constrained to do so. I must in fairness, however, state that Bishop Harris of the Protestant Episcopal Church has sensed this situation and has been very active in trying to trace and stamp it out; but even that is not enough, it must be completely exterminated. But from the University of Liberia and the College of West Africa no official intimation or action has been forthcoming. On the contrary, we get the impression that Nelson's eye seems to be turned on these activities in the University of Liberia and the College of West Africa, and unless it is stamped out completely, the management of these two institutions will be changed; if that is not enough, then they will be closed down at any cost.

That some of the youth of our nation seem to be attracted by these traducing ideologies is somewhat astounding, for never before in the history of the country have the young people of Liberia had such splendid opportunities for education in many and various specialized fields without regard to tribe or origin as at this time, including scholarships (both foreign and local), medical facilities and other necessities of life.

But, to be more specific, less than two weeks before the convocation of this Unification Council, the hydra-headed plot to assassinate the President and other officials of the Government and thereby overthrow the Government by force was unearthed, the designated executor of the plot being the Acting Commander of the National Guard, Colonel D. Y. Thompson. This officer, not being able to induce a sufficient number of officers and men of the Army to join in the conspiracy, moved arms and munitions from the arsenal kept by Lieutenant Jenkins, and organized a civilian group called 'the club'. This was composed principally of Klemoweh Greboes, some Vais, Krus, and a few citizens of Arthington whose son, Booker T. Bracewell, was convicted of treason but pardoned. Immediately thereafter he committed the identical crime for the second time, whereupon he was again arrested, imprisoned and is now awaiting trial.

The present plot is a survival and revival of the one discovered about eighteen months ago by a number of young men, principally students, such as Appleton, Thompson, Sherman and others who were arrested, indicted and imprisoned and are now awaiting trial for treason.

The fact remains, nevertheless, that with the trial of that case not yet begun, the same sources from which that movement started found fertile soil in Colonel D. Y. Thompson, whose brother was involved in the above mentioned plot by students, and who has been indicted and imprisoned for trial. Colonel Thompson was further an old criminal suspect in the 1955 assassination attempt, an adversary of democracy and orderly government and a natural miscreant, unable to move the army or even the unit that he commanded without resorting to the organization of a civilian movement to activate his designs. He and Lieutenant Jenkins, also a suspect of the 1955 conspiracy, together with Lieutenant Joseph T. Gibson, all of whom had been charged with and convicted of larceny, but had been permitted to find their way back into the Army, becoming officers of the Liberian National Guard having access to the Government arsenal, undertook to provide these men with arms and destructive weapons to execute their despicable plan.

When intimation of the organization of the plot was received, action was at once taken to penetrate it and sufficient evidence having been accumulated, arrests were made. The inquiry and penetration continue, and if convicted, everyone involved in the plot, whether as principal, accessory before or after the fact, shall receive the full penalty of the law, because from little acorns great oaks grow.

Notwithstanding all this, the Unification Policy will go on and the development of the nation will move forward in ever-increasing momentum, and nothing can or must stop or retard it, because it has your support, you, the people of the nation.

We are determined to continue the various programmes of social, economic, cultural and political reforms and progress which we enunciated and began implementing upon our induction into office. And why have we pursued these programmes? To see them dissipated through the efforts of a few irresponsible and treasonable persons, and a few vain and ambitious men? Have we invited foreign capital into the nation to have the sacredness of contracts and obligations violated and abused and make the nation the object of the

ridicule and scorn of the civilized world? Shall our promises be words of
expedience with no more value than the paper on which they are written?
This cannot be! It shall never come to pass!

The Government, I, and others, owe a special debt of gratitude and tribute
to the chiefs and people of the interior and hinterland, some of whom having
heard of this plot almost at the same time as I did, came down to the Capital,
assured me of their support and of their condemnation of this subversive
movement and took certain actions on their own to ensure the safety of the
state as well as my personal security.

The Unification Policy is founded on our sincere belief that all citizens
are entitled to the basic guarantees of the Constitution. It is in our opinion
axiomatic, that if I demand respect from every man I should respect myself;
but I cannot respect myself if I do not respect my fellow-man since to
demand respect from someone I do not respect is meaningless and does nothing for me, as it is no honour to be thus respected. But to be respected by
someone for whom I have respect is to be honoured. Thus I honour myself
when I respect my fellow-man and am in return respected by him. It follows
that the nation must be composed of men who are equal under the law and
have the same rights and privileges. This is fundamental to the Unification
Policy.

And so as we are about to embark upon a new era in the political life of
the nation, when counties will comprise the basic sub-divisions of the nation,
this step will demand that an even greater sacrifice be made by the citizens in
order that our nation may continue her forward march. We must be vigilant
and ever watchful, that we do not fruitlessly chase mirages and utopias. We
should remember that there is much to be done if our country is to grow,
prosper and retain the fundamental principles of the love of liberty and
respect of the individual.

Clearly, this is a time for firmness in resolution, a time for the enlargement
and deepening of our national vision and dedication to the things which we
cherish most. For a nation which has always believed in, and subscribed to,
equality and justice, freedom and independence must always be our priceless
heritage. This will require every man and every woman, every chief and
official, every boy and every girl to be eternally vigilant and an individual
watchdog against subversion and traducing ideologies and intrigues, to make
immediate reports and trace any who may be engaged therein.

Within the past few years, very significant changes have taken place on the
continent of Africa. The new nationalism which sparked the emergence of
many nations, the phenomenal developmental strides now taking place, the
comprehensive programmes for economic expansion and greater educational
opportunities, and the insistent talk of African unity and solidarity are
issues upon which the fate of 250 million African peoples may well depend.
Everywhere I travelled in or outside the continent, in discussions with African
and world leaders and peoples, my conviction has been strengthened that in
unity of purpose and action lies our greatest hope. The greatest challenge,
therefore, which confronts us in this country and in other African nations is
our ability to comprehend the nature of our responsibilities and our willingness and readiness to shoulder the tasks which will lead to the solution of
these problems.

The experiences through which our nation has gone, the lessons of history
we are eager for this generation to learn, and the indivisibility of a unified

Liberia which we have tried to convey to the people of the nation, express more than anything else, our determination that we will stand ready to fight for and die for these cherished goals of liberty and freedom which have always been encouraged and taught in our social and political institutions. To these ends my faith in you, the people of the country, has always been unshakable and unshaken, and in spite of actions which have recently brought shame and infamy to the history of our nation, I urge you to set your gaze on a united Liberia, the realization of which will bring us more happiness, greater prosperity and peace within our borders and with all mankind.

I offered my life upon the altar of my country in three or four battles, and therefore, being used to alarm, I declare that 'none of these things move me, neither count I my life dear unto myself if it is necessary that my life be offered up again in the interest of the principles and ideas for which our nation was founded and for which it stands'.

When the new arrangement for the territorial sub-division of the nation that we envisage materializes, and additional counties are established, and if this new arrangement tends to the best interest of the nation, the possibility exists for still another step to be taken for the benefit of greater and more effective integration and as a measure of decentralization of Government. States could be established within the Republic with a certain amount of sovereignty in each. As a tentative or arbitrary suggestion, for instance, Montserrado County, Grand Cape Mount County and the new Lofa County could comprise one state; Grand Bassa County and the New Bong County, another state; Sinoe County and the new Nimba County, still another and Maryland County and the new Grand Gedeh County, a fourth state. This arrangement is only hypothetical and may not comprise the actual combination of counties to form states in the order that I have suggested, should it become desirable to do so. This, however, I expect to be after my day and generation.

Fellow citizens of the Western Province, what great transformations have come to your province because of your foresight, your hard labour, your loyalty and devotion to the ideals of yourselves and your fellow men! For you, your children, your wives and those surrounding you, life can never return to what it was heretofore. The new day of prosperity and progress of which you dreamed, worked for and fought for has begun to come to you. By your splendid co-operation and constant loyalty, you have blazed the trail to national unity and progress. The congratulations of the Government and people of Liberia go to you today and always for the great pace which has been set in the history of your province and in the annals of our nation.

In the light of these accomplishments, one might be tempted to suggest that the objectives of the Unification Programme have been achieved and therefore that other national goals need to be set and pursued. But the end is not yet in sight; we are just beginning. For while appreciable gains have been made, there are psychological barriers which must be overcome; Unification is a thought process as much as it is a coming together of peoples of different elements, sections and tribes as part of the constitutional requirements of the nation. More than this, it must become a thought pattern, since it is in the hearts of men that ideas originate, be constantly nourished, so that it will spread to all areas of our national life. This policy must continue, until even our critical foreign critics can no longer discern differences among the peoples of this nation.

Unification must become a way of life deriving its greatest support from the innermost conviction that the strength of all societies is resident in the contributions which are called from all classes and levels of the society. It is with this thought and this conviction, that we continue to work towards a more prosperous nation and a happy and enlightened citizenry.

Fellow citizens, after everything we will say and do at this Council is forgotten, the ideal and idea of unification must become a part of us and remind us continually of our united will and determination to become one people, Liberians.

Remember that a stronger and greater Liberia of tomorrow will depend upon your share and my share, now and in the future, in the great political programme which has served the nation so well and which has greater possibilities for the future of the country.

We have all been tremendously thrilled by the wonderful reception and demonstrations accorded us since our arrival here. Thank you for your continued interest and unflinching loyalty to our administration and the state, and we hope that the same spirit which marks our joint efforts, and which has borne abundant fruits, will continue in the future for the benefits of our common country, Africa and the world, even when we have passed away.

May we from this meeting and from this day adopt a new frame of mind towards our country's future, its progress and development and thereby take greater courage for its continued welfare, safety and perpetuity in the comity of nations, and may the vision of a united Liberia be perpetually before us so that we may all work constantly and conscientiously towards the fulfilment of our true destiny as a nation and people.

At the Closing of the Third Biennial Unification Council

Kolahun, Loffa County, 19 February 1963

In this great task of uniting and integrating our people, we have nothing to fear except the fear that we shall relax our vigilance.

Introductory Note

Unification Councils were held every two years to assess the progress and success of our National Unification Policy as a positive force for national unity. At each Council the President and people of Liberia were delighted to observe the good that was derived from this policy in every area of national development. President Tubman, though especially grateful, took further notice during this Council of a plan by certain conspirators, including certain officers of the Liberian National Guard, to destroy the Policy of National Unification, a plan further serving as a nucleus of an opposition party. There was nation-wide condemnation of this conspiracy at this Council, where many political leaders seized the occasion to let their views be heard and to demonstrate their support for President Tubman. The President acknowledged with gratitude the overwhelming support he received.

Kolahun, Loffa County, 19 February 1963

AFTER FOUR days of delightful and free association in an atmosphere of mutual understanding and working together as one people and one nation in this rapidly developing town of Kolahun, we have come to the end of the Third Biennial Unification Council. The crowded hall from day to day, the intense interest manifested by everyone, the patience exhibited in sitting through the many lengthy addresses and discussions, the high degree of participation seen and, above all, the reassuring remarks made by individuals and groups concerning the Unification Programme, testify to the huge success achieved by the Unification Policy. Surely, the visible gains of nine years of national experimentation with a programme which still challenges us, provide positive proof of the deep roots the programme has taken and the permanent benefits which have already come to the nation and people.

In this great task of uniting and integrating our people we have nothing to fear except the fear that we shall relax our vigilance and determination, that our enthusiasm may become cold and that we may lose sight of the purpose and objectives we have set before us. But, knowing that every aspect of our national life has been touched, improved and benefited, we are inspired and encouraged to move forward with greater enthusiasm, vim and courage until unification and integration become part and parcel of every man, every woman, every boy and girl in our nation; until all parts of our country are linked by a network of roads and communication; until human creativity and productivity yield us manifold material and spiritual blessings; until we are all one and can march proudly hand in hand in defence of our common country.

Characteristic of this Council were the various resolutions presented, decisions taken and recommendations made which covered practically every aspect of our national life. When we reflect upon the conditions which existed several years ago and compare them with those we see all around us, we have cause to be proud of our accomplishments. But we cannot rest; we must never rest, for to rest is to rust. I have abundant confidence in you, the people of this country, that together we shall all put our shoulders to the wheel of fortune, which will turn to greater and still greater national progress and prosperity.

Only too well am I conscious of the problems which faced you in the past, the ones which face you now and those which will confront you in the future. But because you have worked so assiduously with your Government and because the plans we have worked out together are gradually coming to fruition, you do not stand alone and you will not stand alone in the solutions of the issues which lie ahead. As you have reposed implicit confidence in your Government, as you have relied upon the assistance afforded you and as you have tapped gainfully your own creative genius, so now do I exhort you to bestir yourselves more vigorously in the days ahead when greater sacrifices will be required of you, to the end that you may reap the corresponding rewards from the Unification Programme. May you keep constantly before you a comprehensive picture of a unified Liberia, a happy and a prosperous people, and having had this picture may you work always towards its realization and eventual enjoyment.

Ostensibly out of gratitude for the great success of the Unification and Open Door Programmes which we enunciated and which together we have pursued, you have from time to time, even at this Council, given me all the credit as President. It is true that I enunciated the general policies of the administration, but the Legislature and you the citizens have co-operated very splendidly towards the achievement of our desired goal, so that it was not I who accomplished it alone but all of you and others who contributed. For when it came to the time of the granting of universal adult suffrage to the people of this country, which required legislative action when the matter was presented to that law-making body, instead of the mere two-thirds majority required, it received the unanimous approval of both Houses. When it became necessary for a referendum on the subject, the people who held the suffrage unanimously voted for extending the suffrage to everyone in this country. It is understandable, therefore, that without the approval of the Legislature and the citizens I could have done nothing to effectuate these programmes in the manner in which they have been so successfully executed.

Let me mention, in passing, that the Unification Programme was enunciated and vigorously enforced not as the result of the formation and organization of the United Nations and the general idea of human rights contained in the Charter of that universal body as some people are apt to believe. Let it be said that these social reforms in Liberia were started long before the birth of the United Nations in 1945.

With reference to the recent discovery of the assassination plot against my life, of which so much has been said in this Council, I have been greatly heartened by the many statements of condemnation and denunciation by the people of the nation, individuals and groups of this Council who demand that these culprits be brought to justice so that they may receive the just reward of their labours.

Believe me when I say, that since this information was divulged I have not spent a sleepless night nor have I brooded over the matter to any great extent. I know fully that I have always given my best in the interest and welfare of the country and people and that God and you have been solidly and whole-heartedly behind me in the Unification and other programmes. If assassination and death shall be my reward, then God shall judge between me and them.

This plot I liken to a military operation in which Lieutenant-Colonel D. Y. Thompson and the men who have been apprehended and placed in custody represent the tactical unit of the plot; they are the men who were designated to carry out the design of the conspirators. Those who contrived the plan are the strategists who have not yet been arrested, but evidence pointing to them has begun to come in, and the net is fast closing in on them. Feel assured that we shall comply with the demands of the people that these culprits be brought to justice and punished when their complicity in this crime has been established.

How vile is inordinate ambition! By and because of it Satan and his hosts fell; so too will the ruthless ambition of these strategists. Certainly Lieutenant-Colonel Thompson did not want to be President, even if he and his collaborators had killed me and all other officials who may have been in the line of succession. Neither would Lieutenants Gibson and Jenkins have contended for the Presidency. That choice spot was to be reserved for the strategists who contrived the plan and offered forty thousand dollars for its execution. What a woeful day and what devious times we have entered upon, my fellow citizens, when mean and vile men begin to scheme thus! But God shall confound them and bring their wicked thoughts and actions to naught.

I am very happy that the authorities of the University of Liberia and the College of West Africa have taken immediate and positive action to inquire into and grapple with the situation in their institutions. We have vowed that our schools must never become breeding places for new-fangled, insidious and invidious ideologies. Let us resolve that every man, every woman, every boy and every girl from east to west, from north to south, shall become a watchdog against subversive actions against the State or the Unification Programme.

And now to return to a more cheerful topic. Again I thank and commend you for your pledges of loyalty and fidelity. I rejoice with you that peace and an era of prosperity are with us; I swear in eternal fealty to you that I shall never, never, betray your trust and confidence, and, God helping us all, may we depart to our various counties, territories, provinces and homes, in the firm conviction that our cause is just, and so may we continue to fight until we win the battle for the unification and integration of the people of this generation and succeeding ones. May you be strong, loyal and dedicated to God, your country and your countrymen in this national undertaking.

God bless you and save and prosper our State.

Broadcast on the Eve of the 1963 General Elections

Monrovia, 6 May 1963

> *We have endeavoured throughout the years to practise the motto of the True Whig Party: 'Deeds, not Words.' Congratulations on a job well done. Three cheers and a hip, hip, hip, hurrah for the continued success of the Grand Old Whig democracy as it leads the march of our nation successfully forward to newer and nobler heights.*

Introductory Note

President Tubman was pleased with the success of the policies of his administration. In this address he gave his reasons for standing for re-election, and further engaged in an historical discourse on some of the forces and incidents which had affected his decision to serve his nation as President. It was indeed an historic challenge and he was pleased to have been afforded an opportunity to respond to that challenge.

Monrovia, 6 May 1963

I AGAIN acknowledge with a keen sense of appreciation your desire to have me stand for election to another four-year term of office as Chief Executive of the nation. After twenty years of service, I feel that the opportunities, challenges and problems I have faced and your unflinching and dexterous support of my adminstration deserve some reflections on the eve of this general election.

Truly, we live in a great age and three great phenomena characterize our time. First, the great scientific marvels, the veritable triumph of the mind of man over matter and space. But despire these advances in science, these are also times to try men's souls, for fear that their vision of the eternal verities of life – love, beauty, truth, justice and righteousness – might be overshadowed and they pursue vain shadows instead of substances.

Secondly, the division of our world into two opposing camps. I refer to the ideological struggles between East and West. The non-aligned nations, representing a third bloc, came into being, and with their emergence, there was hope that they would be a stabilizing factor to bridge the widening gap between East and West. However, in the Geneva disarmament talks that have now been going on for almost two years in an attempt to arrive at some workable solutions, not much success seems to have been achieved, even though there appears to exist cause for some optimism that eventually a solution may be found.

Thirdly, the realization of freedom and liberty, which has been the watchword of millions of peoples the world over. The right of self-determination has been achieved by many, and while others still smart under the yoke of foreign rule, the independent peoples of Africa and the world continue to press their demand for the liberation of all and the removal of the last vestige of tyranny and oppression. Thus, those nations which have gained their independence have taken their places in the galaxy of nations and by becoming members of the United Nations and other world organizations, are continuing to make their contributions to the progress of the African continent and nations of the world.

In retrospect, much has taken place since I took office in 1944. I came into office in the shadow of World War II, one of the most destructive catastrophies mankind has yet experienced. Despite the difficulties of those years, both nationally and internationally, under God's guidance and protection, we have been able to maintain our autonomy, secure a measure of development and progress, and promote the hegemony of the nation.

The Local Scene: You will recall that at my first inauguration we advanced policies which we have consistently endeavoured to pursue through the years. I am sure you are agreed that the Open Door Policy and the Unification Programme have done a great deal towards the political, economic, social and educational advancement and development of the nation and has helped to lay a more enduring foundation of national stability, economic emancipation and true national integration and progress.

And so, after I had served you for the first eight-year term, exercising your suffrage, you requested my return for three successive four-year terms, during which period we laboured together to bring peace, progress and prosperity to the nation and its people.

This call for a fifth term was no less surprising than it was dramatic, for it was a new experiment in the annals of our political history. Never has so much been conferred upon one citizen by the great majority of the nation and yet never has so much service been demanded of one citizen by the great majority of the people. After lengthy deliberations and prayerful considerations, I felt a strong conviction, a sacred obligation and a profound sense of duty which constrained me not to shirk such an historic and singular challenge.

Meanwhile, on the physical side, the attendant strain and stress of the duties inherent in the office of the Presidency had taken their toll and common sense dictated that my advancing age might not endure the increasing and heavy continuing responsibilities implicit in a re-election for a fifth term. But you, the people, had made a solemn appeal and I felt confident that God would guide me through the strain, stress and uncertainties of the years ahead; for it is only He Who could have sustained, encouraged and strengthened me to grapple and overcome the myriads of problems which I have had to face and resolve in the past. To Him, therefore, let us give unbounded praise and thanks for all that He has done for us during those times and the present. I make bold to say that this God Who has always guided and guarded me, and Who continually watches over me and our nation will lead us unceasingly to the full consummation of our nation's ultimate aims and destiny.

I have repeatedly said during the presentations of testimonials, resolutions and petitions offering us the fifth term, that I would personally prefer to retire to private life and do some of the things that I have always wanted to do; that having given the greater part of my life to public service, I would prefer to rest and devote what time remains to me in quiet retirement; and, that finally, because of my advancing years, I would welcome a change from the rigours of office routine with its manifold ramifications, over-crowded schedules and matters that press for momentous decisions and im-mediate action and solution.

Behind these rationalizations, however, stood the realization that there was a cause greater than my own and an interest more impelling than my own; so that I was obligated to the nation by virtue of the fact that I am one of its citizens, bound to it by ties of blood and a common allegiance; bound to it by the work of generations of Liberians who before us laboured and sacrificed themselves for the perpetuity of the state; bound to it by the bonds of the past, by our knowledge of the present, our faith in and aspirations and hopes for the future.

There were two other attendant circumstances which contributed greatly to my decision in yielding to and accepting the nomination and election for a fifth term. I knew fully well that this was unprecedented, but I was also aware that in our constitution it is declared that all power is inherent in the people and that the will of the people must prevail.

I know that there are others of my fellow citizens and compatriots who too are capable of executing the duties appertaining to the office of the President with equal credit and dignity to themselves and the country. Yet you, the people have continued to call upon me, and my high sense of patriotism and love for the people of the nation of every class, creed and kind, left me no alternative but to submit to your call and, like Esther, when the very existence and life of her people was in danger, declare: 'I will go in unto the King even though it is not in accordance with the law and if I perish, I perish.'

Other factors which influenced my decision to accept the nomination and election for a fifth term of office included:

(1) My desire to see effectuated the acts of the Legislature which pro-vide for placing on the copestone of the Unification Programme, so vital to national unity and solidarity; to further strengthen this Programme by recommending to the Legislature, and approving after their passage of it, an act re-defining the political sub-divisions of the country, repealing all laws and legislations which divided the country into county and hinterland juris-dictions.

(2) Unfortunately, just at this time we encountered financial and economic difficulties due to reasons made known and explained in a nation-wide broadcast, when I also informed you of the action which the Government anticipated taking to relieve the situation. I would have felt unable to retire under such circumstances when you, the people, were demanding my continu-ation in office, especially so since I had yielded to your requests at times previously when the financial and economic position was more favourable.

Having acquiesced in your request, if by your suffrage tomorrow I am re-elected, I shall expect that all of us will coalesce and participate to the fullest extent of our abilities by making maximum contributions, by hard work, increased production, meeting our national obligations, paying taxes of every kind, as well as by purchasing Government interest-bearing bonds, should it become necessary to issue such bonds.

The crisis through which the world is passing at this time, and particularly the African continent, requires the united effort of every individual. The co-operation of every citizen in all walks of life is needed for the perpetuation of our society and the security and stability of the state. Personal ambitions and predilections should give way to the national interest and we should unitedly put our shoulders to the wheel, never faltering, never looking back, until our goal is attained.

In all of my public utterances and speeches, I have tried to refrain from making references concerning my parents, my family or myself. But at this time I am persuaded to make known some incidents which I think may be interesting, and I do so with every degree of modesty.

As is well known, more wars, tribal uprisings and conflicts have occurred in Maryland County, the county whence I hail, than in any other county of our Republic. These wars and conflicts, between the Greboe Tribe and the Liberian Government, have been more costly in blood, lives and money than any other conflicts, and my family from the earliest beginning of our national history has given more in terms of life, blood and service to these conflicts than any other family.

My grandfather, William Shadrach Tubman I, was beaten to death by tribal people, because when visiting one of the towns he found four or five tribesmen tied together for the ceremony of administering sassywood, a trial by ordeal by which accused persons are convicted or acquitted of dealing in witchcraft. He walked into the group, kicked over the bowl of sassywood and tried to prevent them from administering the concoction. He was beaten to death.

The following year, 1875, his son, William Shadrach Tubman II, my uncle, was killed in battle at a place called Wrukeh and left on the field by the retreating Government forces. His body was dissected and divided amongst the tribesmen. Alexander Tubman, my father, and the next in age to William Shadrach Tubman II, and his younger brother, John Hilary Tubman, also fought in the battle. The youngest brother, John Hilary, was wounded. My father was greatly distressed, he later told me, by the death of his eldest brother and the wounding of his youngest brother, so that while the Government troops were retreating, he lingered behind them musing over the tragedy of the battle of that day with his gun slung over his shoulder.

It was while he walked slowly along communing with himself, that a friend of his named Dyne Weah, one of the young tribal warriors at that time which the Greboes call the Kineboes, accosted him. As my father was passing near a large tree and a bug-bug hill, he was hailed by his friend Weah who called to him, 'Alex, Alex' and when he looked and took his gun from his shoulder to fire, he saw that it was his friend, Weah, who urged him to hurry up in order to catch up with his people for the enemy was hot in pursuit and would surely catch and kill him. My father then ran, and later was able to join the retreating Government forces.

A very intimate friendship developed between my father and Dyne Weah thereafter, and when I reached manhood my father called me one day in the presence of his friend Weah who had saved his life and said to me, 'Shad, as long as you live do nothing against Dyne and his wife, Wree. Should you survive them, bury them. See that they do not suffer in any way if you can help it.' He continued: 'The Greboes are a savage, stubborn and war-like people, but they are not given to savagery or ferociousness.' He admonished me to do everything within my power whenever I could, to stop the conflicts between the tribes and the Government since neither could exterminate the other. 'You are Shad,' he continued, 'and during your lifetime I want you to do all you can to work for better understanding between the tribal people and the Government, should ever an opportunity present itself.'

I myself have been involved in three of these wars, and in every engagement it has not been an easy thing for victor or victim. I am, therefore, very happy that God has cast my line of ancestors in such a pleasant phase of national endeavour and to be a descendant of this family of Maryland County that has produced so great a number of outstanding soldiers; that being the direct descendant of a family who fought and sacrificed so much blood in tribal conflicts, I have been able to enunciate the Unification Programme, recommend its Legislation, get Legislative enactment, and see it executed and bear fruit in the nation to such an extent that within the twenty years of my administration as President there has not occurred a solitary incident of tribal or inter-governmental uprising and wars. But in all this I can only exclaim, 'Not by Might, nor by Power, but by My Spirit, saith the Lord.'

The True Whig Party: While for over ninety years our indomitable True Whig Party has exercised great leadership in the Government and country, it was in 1877 that the Grand Old Party gave a crushing defeat to the Republican Party.

Since then, there has not been such a battle fought against the Whigs, nor has the True Whig Party encountered any major defeat. The True Whig Party, in its victory of 1877 abrogated and crushed the stigma of a type of segregation prevailing at that time, and has since then adhered to policies which have attracted the people of the country. This achievement was effected by and with the approval of the vast majority of the electorate.

I now have the pleasure and honour of paying a very high compliment to the Honourable William R. Tolbert, Vice-President of the Republic, with whom we have been associated for three administrations. His services as Vice-President of the nation have been invaluable and his assistance and support given to all Government programmes and policies for the advancement and development of our nation is noteworthy and praiseworthy. It is with pride that I record the genuine and selfless nature of this great man's contributions and the patriotic sense of devotion with which he has served his country and people. He has unquestionably given a creditable account of his national stewardship.

We have endeavoured, through the years, to practise the motto of the True Whig Party: 'Deeds, not Words'; and we feel that we have kept our promises, fulfilled our commitments to all members of our constituency at all levels. We have kept the faith, hoping to build, with the loyalty, dedication and devotion of all True Whigs, a true and progressive nation of which any people may be proud.

I feel sure that every leader and member of the True Whig Party is proud of the rôle they have played and the contributions they have made to the body politic through this time-honoured political entity. It is my ardent hope and prayer that the future of the True Whig Party will become brighter and that its accomplishments will continue to be cherished in the annals of our nation. Congratulations to all on a job well done; three cheers and a hip, hip, hip, hurrah for the continued success of the Grand Old Whig democracy as it leads the march of the nation continually and successfully forward to newer and nobler heights.

Tomorrow, you will be exercising your franchise at the polls. I trust that order and peace will prevail so that you may continue to demonstrate the spirit and intent of our Party's motto, 'Deeds, not Words'.

May God bless every one of you, may He let the State prosper, and may He preserve us all for greater service to the nation we love so well.

Reply to the True Whig Party following his Re-election for a Fifth Term of Office as President of Liberia

Monrovia, 13 May 1963

I feel assured that the people of the new counties, under the impetus of the Unification and Open Door Policies, guided by the experiences of the older counties, and, above all, grateful for the political, economic, technical and other benefits, will rise magnificently to this historic challenge.

Introductory Note

Of all the presidential terms of William V. S. Tubman, his fifth term of office will be remembered as the most historic and significant. This term saw the completion of the National Unification Programme of Liberia under his guidance. The act was peaceful and without bloodshed, notwithstanding the tendency of some citizens to undermine that programme by subversion. The political division of Liberia for administrative purposes was affected by this term of office, which brought complete equality to every section of the nation. The President, in this speech, spoke about the significance of this national transition, and the growth of our country towards political maturity.

Monrovia, 13 May 1963

A FEW days ago we were exceedingly thrilled and greatly moved by the scenes we witnessed at the different voting precincts in and around the limits of the City of Monrovia. Today, we are completely overwhelmed, and understandably so, by this mammoth demonstration, with resolutions in support of the Legislative action taken in unifying the country politically, thereby abolishing the former county and hinterland jurisdictions. The demonstrations also inform us, the Vice-President and myself, of the results of the elections held on the 7th day of May which apprised us of our election for a fifth term as your President and Vice-President respectively.

In our broadcast to the nation on the eve of the general elections, we dwelt to some extent on the new political sub-divisions of the country and pointed out, among other benefits, the great political triumph this step signified. We are now happily convinced that this step is indeed the copestone of the Unification Policy. To me the Unification Programme is the execution of a deep-rooted conviction I have held for as long as I can remember, and it is therefore very, very dear to me. We are pleased that these changes which have come about can now probably be construed as the *Quod Erat Demonstrandum* and the *Quod Erat Faciendum* of this conviction.

237

Perhaps there are some who think and feel that this action has been preci-
pitate and that it should have taken a more evolutionary trend. We differ
from such thinking, if there be any such, because these legislative changes,
coming as they do after 115 years of nationhood, make the period they have
taken to come to fruition a true evolution, despite the fact that they may
have been only recently effectuated.

You will recall that, as a preliminary to the execution of this advanced
phase of the Unification Programme, we recommended to the Legislature,
first, the granting of adult suffrage to the people of the hinterland and also
the granting of representation in the House of Representatives to the interior
people in the Legislature. These actions were whole-heartedly supported by
the Legislature and the people who exercised the right of suffrage at the
time. We feel it highly significant that within six days after voting the
administration back into power for a fifth term, you, the people of the nation,
should gather to give full approval to these political and administrative re-
arrangements of the country, without any manifest dissent from any quarter.
We interpret this gesture as an indication of your whole-hearted approval of
this latest step in the Unification Programme of the nation and of the administration.

But let me emphasize that this step is the only just, honourable, correct
and constitutional course that we could pursue. The Constitution of our
country opens with this declaration, the very first thought in the very first
chapter: 'All men are born equally free and independent, and have certain
natural, inherent and inalienable rights: among which are the rights of
enjoying and defending life and liberty, of acquiring, possessing and protecting property, and of pursuing and obtaining safety and happiness.'

Indeed, what impelled and re-dedicated us unceasingly to pursue this
policy to fruition was our conscience, which told us that this was the only
right and just thing to do. Again, the Constitution and the dictates of the
founding fathers emphasized and demanded its fulfilment. Liberia, they tell
us, was founded as a haven where black men may find peace and equality
under the law. Equality imposes the obligation that government be representative of the whole people and not of one segment of the people only.

It is therefore my feeling that this new political advance will remove all
barriers, restrain tendencies towards tribalism, sectionalism and all other
types of parochial and elemental divisions. This will be possible, however,
only if all citizens on both sides fully accept this concept, and resolve to work
unitedly in pursuing it. Only thus will the attendant results which we envisage yield their lasting benefits. There may be those who will oppose the
smooth operation of this new *modus operandi* for one reason or another, for,
as with all new legislation of like magnitude, it must undergo the rigours of
testing, and we must prepare ourselves for the resulting difficulties which
may arise.

The implications of this historic advance in our political organization can
in no way be minimized. They are far-reaching, and their ramifications will
touch and affect every phase of our national life. It is left to all patriotic,
loyal and unpretentious citizens to believe genuinely in unification, and to
see in it that justice which should be a restraining force and which will
further enable that policy to facilitate the practical functioning of these
changes. It will be left to the good judgment and sincerity of men and
women, fellow citizens, partisans and everyone who can and should play a

part, to accept and implement these changes, not with mixed emotions, but for the greater good of the nation, and with the welfare of its people as the paramount objective. You have pledged to do this by your resolutions presented today.

Because apprehension may exist in the minds of some people regarding the new counties, some clarification may be necessary on certain issues which have been raised.

Firstly, paramount, clan and town chieftainships will not be abolished in the predominantly tribal areas. Under the old county and hinterland administration and jurisdiction these officials performed their functions effectively. Therefore, as long as a part of our population lives after a tribal manner and under tribal authority, they must be governed by the customary tribal laws. The fear that these tribal officials may lose their status is unfounded. On the contrary, the tribal people in these areas will live and be governed by the customary tribal laws, so long as these laws do not conflict with the organic and statutory laws of our country.

Secondly, there will be County Commissioners in the new counties, who will be responsible for carrying out, expeditiously and effectively, the policies of government just as they are in the present counties on the littoral, under the superintendents of the respective counties.

Thirdly, I have heard it remarked in some quarters that the creation of the new counties is bound to upset the political equilibrium of the country, and that as a prerequisite the inhabitants of these areas should have been exposed to more educational and civilizing opportunities before the bestowal of such an important national privilege and responsibility. I differ from this view.

These new counties may need guidance just as the nation needs technical advice and assistance, but it seems to me that this is a necessary phase through which all developing nations and peoples must pass. I am strongly convinced that the political structure of our country will be strengthened by the creation of these new counties because this act on your part is just, right and deserving.

More education, a greater literacy programme, better health and sanitation, improved living standards are some of the 'musts' of the new counties as well as of the old ones. But once the pace is set, I feel assured that the people of the new counties, under the impetus of the Unification and Open Door Policies, guided by the experiences of the older counties, and, above all, grateful for the political, economic, technical and other benefits which will follow in their wake, will rise magnificently to this historic challenge. More than ever I feel that this step will integrate more securely the people of the different sections of the country into a strong and homogeneous nation.

Fourthly, the abolition of the dowry under customary tribal laws, and with it the creation of a new status for women, has been pointed to as a *sine qua non*.

But in this connection I have held the position that to legislate forthrightly the discontinuance of a social practice which dates from time immemorial and which constitutes an important foundation of a people's social, moral and economic philosophy, is too radical a step to take. However, allowing for the transforming influence of more education and civilization, exposure to the saving grace of religion and the penetration of roads into remote areas of the nation bringing cultural, trade and other contacts, the thoughts and habits of people in these areas are bound to change. In short, time must be allowed to play its evolutionary rôle in this important social question.

We cannot be too far wrong if our motive in taking this forward step is designated to unite the people of the nation and accelerate the rate of progress and development in the country. We cannot be greatly in error if we are resolved to work hand in hand to make this new political venture practicable and worthwhile in the life of the people of the nation. We will not be wrong if we significantly enhance the spiritual, educational, economic, political and technical elements of the new era in our nation's history.

Finally, after twenty years in the Presidency of this nation, it appears that your enthusiasm, loyalty and devotion have progressively grown with the years. On election day we visited all the voting booths in Monrovia and other areas, and everywhere we went the spirit of entertainment was wonderful, the enthusiasm great and atmosphere tumultuous but orderly. Never before have I witnessed an election of this order.

Let me thank you from the bottom of my heart for your deep and abiding loyalty and devotion, your love and affection and for your faith and confidence in our leadership. As long as we live we can never forget these acts which constantly assure us that together we shall continue to work with one heart and hand for the maintenance and perpetuity of our country. God helping us, we will not waver in this determination.

On the Occasion of the Formal Announcement by the Legislature of Liberia of his Re-election to a Fifth Term of Office

Monrovia, 14 August 1963

Despite my realization of the tremendous responsibilities and their implication, as well as the toll which they will take on me physically as I advance in age from year to year, I shall assume the duties and obligations of the task implicit in my re-election with all the vigour and resources I possess.

Introductory Note

In this address in which he responded favourably to his people's request to serve a fifth term as President, President Tubman took a long look at his tenure in office and what his administration had accomplished, and what he considered as unfinished business which needed his direction. As on other occasions, matters affecting the peace of the world, especially Liberia, brought out the serious side of his nature. He asked simply that peace should prevail in order that he might conclude his unfinished task. The absence of peace, especially at home, he saw as a set-back to this task. He thanked the people of Liberia for the renewal of confidence in his administration and in his leadership.

Monrovia, 14 August 1963

NINETEEN YEARS ago, time in its orbital flight began the first eight-year tenure of office to which the people of the country had summoned me to serve as Chief Executive Magistrate. Continuing its evolution, the year 1952 began for me a four-year term in consequence of the second summons; and, with the years still rolling onward into time, came still the call for a third and a fourth tenure of office consisting of four years each. Yet, all these did not end the dramatic, spectacular and astonishing manifestation of affection and confidence, and it was with greater political fervour and an unmatched enthusiasm, that the demand came again from my constituency and the people of the land to serve a fifth term of office. In each case, I felt that I had no alternative but to respond favourably for the reasons set forth in my respective acceptance speeches when the aggregate demands were summed up.

In my broadcast to the nation on the eve of the last general elections, I outlined the main reasons that impelled me to concur in your demand for a fifth term. Even though I would have preferred to retire to private life and

241

would have welcomed a change from the rigours of office routine after enduring the pressure for twenty years, I felt bound to adhere to the will of the
people which I believe was also the will of God, and see the further effectuation of certain programmes that had been enunciated.

The high esteem, consideration and incomprehensible favour which the
electorate has demonstrated, by its continuous and consecutive preferment of
myself, have been overwhelming and over-awing, and I declare and avow my
complete surrender and loyalty to the Constitution and laws of the country as
well as to the will, welfare, peace, prosperity and solidarity of the people and
the development, progress and security of the state. Unworthy though I have
felt myself of these considerations, I have throughout the years endeavoured
to give my best, in all sincerity, in the execution of the duties, responsibilities
and obligations implicit in the high office of President, as God has given me
the vision and ability to comprehend and the guidance to perform these
onerous tasks.

Because of the human foibles common to all men, I have erred and made
mistakes. I have been guilty of sins of omission, commission and self-indul-
gence. I have never professed perfection because it falls within the realm of
divinity. Whenever I was convinced of an error or wrong judgment, I have
always condemned myself, sought to retrieve such errors, and tried to make
amends. If, therefore, I have been able to achieve any success for our nation
and its people, it has been by virtue of your tolerance, your understanding of
the nature of the great national and international issues involved, and the
courage, faith, loyalty and co-operation which you have manifested and
given most freely through the years.

At the beginning of my first term of office, I set out in pursuit of certain
policies which I felt were essential and integral to the building of a strong
and united state. Because I was deeply aware of the justice and necessity of
this policy, I advocated firstly the Unification Policy. It was a bold political
and social attempt to obliterate any sociological or political division amongst
our people and a further attempt to create national consciousness and prepare the grounds for absorption of the various human elements forming part
of the body politic.

In this crusade I realized that education and specialized training were the
key to the nation's future. I therefore commenced my crusade by holding
Unification Councils, providing more educational facilities for the people
regardless of cultural origins, tribe or location and granting scholarships for
specialized studies abroad and at home to our citizenry so that they could
acquire the professional and technical skills which are indispensable to the
development of any country. I made available hospital and clinical services
to those who live in isolated as well as in other metropolitan and coastal areas,
and forged ahead with road and communication programmes to facilitate
travel and communication in an effort to improve living standards. With
these physical contacts and increased opportunities bringing to the people
the awareness that the Government was concerned about the health, mind
and material welfare of every citizen, whether living on the littoral or in the
hinterland, a new chapter was opened in the political and social history of the
nation. It has given me great satisfaction to realize how intelligently, conscientiously and enthusiastically most of the people have responded to Unification and Integration.

Secondly, I introduced the Open Door Policy whereby foreign investors and concessionaires were invited and induced to come to Liberia to explore and exploit those natural resources and other potential investment possibilities existing within our nation. Despite the scathing criticisms and unfavourable demonstrations which this policy initially evoked at home, with your support I stood undeterred and with determination and perseverance set out to initiate and implement the policy already outlined. Providentially, I had the good fortune of receiving invitations from several Chiefs of State to visit them. These were happy responses to my desire to acquaint foreign investors with the many investment possibilities available to them in Liberia.

Beginning in 1952 with a visit to Spain, I continued this programme with other visits to the United States, Haiti, Jamaica, Italy, France, Germany, the Netherlands, Switzerland, Israel, Great Britain, Sweden, Yugoslavia and Austria, advertising and presenting the Open Door Policy to foreign investors.

Following the attainment of independence by many African States, with a view of strengthening the already existing friendly ties and creating strong relations of fraternity, better understanding, unity and identity of views, objectives, business, cultural and other relationships, I also made State Visits to the following sister states of Africa: Ghana, Guinea, Sierra Leone, Nigeria, Cameroons, Senegal, Mali, Gabon, Togo, Ethiopia and the Ivory Coast.

That our country has been opened up for further development, that our economy has advanced from a stage of mere wage-earning to a higher level, and that many Liberians have, by their own initiative, created considerable economic progress, are all facts familiar to you and avenues from which a large proportion of the people have benefited. Because of the national benefits that have accrued, we should cast behind us all unpleasant experiences of the past and resolve to march forward with greater confidence, determination and intrepidity to the achievement of the ultimate goal of the Open Door Policy, the wisdom of which history has already vindicated.

In retrospect, I now feel more convinced than ever that the Unification and Open Door Policies have been deeply established in the thinking and action of the people of the nation. With the successes thus far achieved in the demonstration of these two policies, we must persevere in our efforts to further promote, and strengthen and consolidate them so that they may remain embedded in the national consciousness and will of the people. Recognizing these achievements, I have the abiding conviction that it is now opportune, expedient and necessary for us to launch out into new directions, and advance other policies that will lead to greater economic development and expansion.

In my remarks upon our return from Europe almost a month ago, I outlined some of the new economic policies which we should pursue within the perspective of a five-year development programme. The basis for these proposals you will, I trust, have the opportunity to study and enact legislations for their implementation.

Taking into consideration some of the things I mentioned in this respect, an Agricultural Development Programme or Plan should provide for:

1. Increasing the production of goods already locally produced, by the introduction of improved methods, facilities and equipment, and by research and experiments.

2. Introducing, where practicable, new products that can be economically produced in the country.
3. Increasing the production of as many products as possible to meet domestic demand and in the case of certain products, for export.
4. Inaugurating small industries to can, dry pack, refine and otherwise preserve our products, in keeping with the highest international standards.
5. Conducting continuous research and experimentation into new areas of agricultural production and looking into ways and means of improving the current methods of production.
6. Constantly and properly disseminating valuable new information among farmers and training them in the best and most advanced methods of farming.
7. Operating the Agricultural Credit Corporation in a business-like, fair and objective way in order to bring the greatest good to the greatest number of serious and eligible famers.
8. Working closely with the farmer as a friend and adviser, and doing everything possible to encourage and protect him.

From these considerations, it is clear that we and other developing nations like ourselves would derive great benefits from our industrial enterprises. Some of these benefits are:

1. The severe drain on our foreign exchange would be discontinued, because import cost would fall.
2. Our foreign exchange would rise and we would quite likely maintain a more favourable balance of payments as a result of exporting manufactured goods to neighbouring countries and to non-African countries.
3. The Liberian people would acquire greater skills, earn larger incomes and enjoy a much higher standard of living.
4. The Government would then receive substantially increased revenues by virtue of the expansion in the gross national production of the country.
5. The Government would be able to float more bonds in the local money market, the proceeds from which could be used for further economic development.

Lastly, there is an immediate and practical consideration which lies in the construction of hydro-electric power plants. The justification of the Government's undertaking of the financial commitments involved in building such plants, would be the supply of cheaper power to a larger number of people that can now afford to use this commodity, and the belief that this would encourage the establishment of local industries, which may require a considerable quantity of electric power.

It may interest you to know that a line of credit for $27,200 is at present in the last stages of negotiation, and an agreement is expected to be concluded shortly with the United States Government for the construction of a hydro-electric plant on the St. Paul River, the conditions being a 10-year grace period, a 40-year amortization period and an interest rate of three-fourths of 1 per cent. But this single hydro-electric plant cannot satisfy the demands of the country for cheap power. We must seek means and sources for financing the construction of additional plants to increase the pace of our agricultural and industrial developments as well as provide cheap power for the whole nation.

Ratification of the Charter of African Unity by the Governments of the participating countries, the signing of the Partial Nuclear Test Ban Treaty by the United States, the Soviet Union and Great Britain, and the decision of the Spanish Government to grant independence to Fernando Po and Spanish Guinea, are three recent events which have aroused universal interest and raised the hope of nations. Because they basically affect the destiny of mankind and relate to human happiness, freedom and world peace, these events are of great importance to us.

Some comment should be made on the decision taken by the Spanish Government to give independence to two of its colonial territories, Fernando Po and Spanish Guinea. It is of special significance that Spain, whose colonial possessions at one time covered a large part of the surface of the earth, having given up or lost a major portion of its colonies should now be willing to grant freedom and independence to two of them. This act should attract the attention and admiration of all nations, especially those which cling to colonialism and apartheid with the fervour with which Naaman's leprosy clung to him, until he was healed by several dippings in the River Jordan, by direction of the Prophet Elijah. Apartheid and Portuguese colonialism are tantamount to leprosy to all intents and purposes, and those who practise them are lepers, and should be treated as such.

At this stage, I deem it necessary to mention the question of freedom of religion and religious tolerance in Liberia, which is being attacked by a sect of Christians called Jehovah's Witnesses. Our Constitution declares that no religious sect shall enjoy exclusive privileges over other religious sects and that there shall be religious tolerance in the nation. The Jehovah's Witnesses were welcomed into the country as a religious sect and were extended equal privileges such as are given to every other religious sect. They enjoy every benefit and privilege of the law. Their persons and their property have been under the protection of the law just as those of every other religious sect. Their missionaries in Liberia have been granted the privilege of bringing into the country, duty free, all of their equipment, stores and supplies for missionary work, in common with other religious groups. They have had eleemosynary grants of land for their evangelical and educational work. They have received the courtesies of the Government and people.

There is, however, a penal statute which requires all persons, regardless of race, creed, religion or sect, to salute the Liberian Flag when they are in sight of it's being hoisted or lowered with ceremony, and which affixes a penalty for failure to do so. A refusal to conform to this regulation constitutes a violation of the statue, for which the penalty is a fine or imprisonment for Liberian citizens, and deportation for foreigners. Any person or persons who refuse to obey the laws of our land are subject to the penalty provided by law. This is no departmental or military regulation, but a part of the penal statutory laws of our nation, and any action taken against those who refused to conform to this statute was taken not because they were Jehovah's Witnesses, but because they disobeyed and violated the law of our land and were therefore subject to the penalty provided by the law.

It was reported and established that certain atrocities and brutal treatments were inflicted on some of the violators of the law in March of this year when they refused to salute the flag as it was being hoisted with ceremony in their presence. The Government deplores, abhors and deprecates brutal mal-treatment of people under any circumstances, and when the matter was brought to its attention, and the guilt of those involved was established, they were punished because they violated the law in manhandling and brutalizing citizens and foreigners. No report has been received to date of any deaths occurring as a result of the mistreatment by the culprits. Having meted out punishment to those who mistreated and maltreated these violators of the law, Government can do nothing more with regard to punishment.

I am to hold an Executive Council beginning on the 26th day of August to investigate the conduct of affairs in both the Gbarnga and Salala Districts which is now overdue. Rumours and reports that people who violated the law by refusing to salute the flag died as a result of maltreatment and mistreatment by soldiers will be personally investigated by me.

The Jehovah's Witnesses, as a sect, are welcomed in this country, but they will be required to conform to the law requiring all persons to salute the flag when it is being hoisted or lowered at ceremonies in their sight, or keep away from such ceremonies. There is another statute which requires the flag to be hoisted at school houses daily, during which ceremonies the students are required to salute and pledge allegiance to it. Under our Constitution this does not infringe religious liberty.

I have received numerous letters from the United States, Great Britain and Canada claiming that to require people who are Jehovah's Witnesses to salute the flag is a deprivation of freedom of religion. This may be true according to the laws of the United States, Canada or Great Britain, but the law of Liberia is *lex loci* and must be enforced and respected within our territories.

It is claimed by some that this sect of Christians maintain that to salute a flag is idolatrous. The question then arises: Is their refusal to comply or submit to the law of the land in which they reside in harmony with the law and ordinances of God? In the 13th chapter of Romans, it is written: 'Let every soul be subject unto the higher powers. For there is no power but of God: the powers that be are ordained of God. Whosoever therefore resisteth the power, resisteth the ordinance of God: and they that resist shall receive to themselves damnation. For rulers are not a terror to good works, but to the evil. Wilt thou then not be afraid of the power? Do that which is good, and thou shalt have praise of the same: For he is the minister of God to thee for good. But if thou do that which is evil, be afraid; for he beareth not the sword in vain: for he is the minister of God, a revenger to execute wrath upon him that doeth evil. Wherefore ye must needs be subject, not only for wrath, but also for conscience sake. For this cause pay ye tribute also: for they are God's ministers, attending continually upon this very thing. Render therefore to all their dues: tribute to whom tribute is due; custom to whom custom; fear to whom fear; honour to whom honour.'

Finally, I acknowledge with grateful and sincere appreciation the official announcement made to us of our re-election as President and Vice-President for another four-year term.

Twenty years in office is an unusually long time, and an election for four additional years, which may amount to twenty-four years, is still longer. It means that children who were not born when this administration came into power have become men and women; it means that those who were children when this administration came into being have seen but one person inaugurated as President while they attained adulthood; it means that those of my age group or within its octave, who may have had aspirations for the presidency, have been unable to see their ambitions realized. It also means that for twenty years a single individual in the office of the President has had varied experiences, confronted manifold difficulties, suffered disappointments, encountered disloyalties and treacheries by friends – men in position, men in whom he confided. It means that he has had to take action against those who had been dishonest and had betrayed their trust. It has also meant that I have enjoyed the pleasure of the confidence of the people, the benefits, emoluments, privileges, immunities and honour which the office accords. However, these veritable varieties make up and constitute the exigencies of life, and I do not believe in musing over the past, except to correct errors and retrieve wrongs. I believe in, and have tried to practise, the principle of 'forgive and forget', and 'let the dead past bury its dead'.

In a country like ours, where virtually everyone knows everyone else, it is not a pleasant thing to be out of favour with authority. I know this, because I have had this experience, and for anyone to fall into disfavour with authority for five, ten, fifteen or twenty years may not be very helpful because, in general, every Liberian wants to be free to visit his President, Vice-President, cabinet ministers and other officials of Government and mingle socially and politically. Therefore I present the olive branch of peace to all of the 'outs', extend the hand of fellowship to them and, as Abraham said to Lot in Holy Writ, when they were battling over the right of possession: 'Let there be no more strife, I pray thee, between thee and me, and between my herdmen and thy herdmen, for we are brethren.'

Despite my realization of the tremendous and vast responsibilities and implications, as well as the toll that they will take on my physical being as I advance in age from year to year, I shall assume the duties, obligations and responsibilities of the task implicit in my re-election with all the vigour and resources I possess or that I can marshal.

Together with my election has come the re-election of Vice-President William R. Tolbert, jun., a man of talent and keen perception, with unusual creative ability for building and administering with understanding; a man with a keen sense of justice and righteousness; a man diligent in his duties, reliable, resourceful, intelligent and dependable. What great joy and satisfaction to any man as President to have associated with him one such as the Vice-President whom you have declared re-elected to office today; one who can be trusted in the dark as well as in the light, in peace as well as in war, in joy as well as in sorrow, in prosperity as well as in vicissitude – that man is William R. Tolbert, jun.

It is fascinating and rejuvenating that there are two members of the Honourable House of Representatives still in harness, who started out with me when I first came into office. They are the Honourable Richard A. Henries, Speaker of the House of Representatives, a towering political figure, outstanding historian, jurist, educator and scholar; an eminent personality whose keen intellect, depth of understanding and unstinted patriotism have enabled him to make invaluable contributions to our nation which he has served so long and well. It has indeed been a distinguished privilege and rare pleasure to have been associated with him during the past nineteen years. The other is the Honourable Samuel D. George, a politician to the manner born, a vote-getter, an orator and staunch Christian. To these two gentlemen who are as old in service to the Government as I am, I adjure 'much is expected from him to whom much is given'. Let us labour on, spend and be spent, no matter what the cost.

The Senate: When I took over the administration of our nation this Honourable Body was composed of men who were physically fit, virile and devoted to public service. Today, although these stalwart men have been replaced by others who are equally virile and imbued with love of country and devotion to duty, not one of the original members remains with us, all having journeyed to the undiscovered country to which I myself am travelling.

The Cabinet: In like manner I recall the coming into office of this administration and the members of the Cabinet who were first chosen to serve as my advisors, and administrators of the respective departments of Government; men of ability and high qualification. All of them have been retired by the revolutions of office tenure, resignation, and one by death.

The House of Representatives, by the return of the ballots cast at the last General Elections has a number of new members who were qualified and sworn into office two days ago. We extend to you, gentlemen, the congratulations of the Executive for your preferment by your constituencies and feel that you are given, by virtue of your election, a great opportunity to join with your colleagues to work and to make your maximum contribution towards the development, maintenance and protection of our common heritage. A great challenge is yours, to have been elected to the Legislature at such a time as this, when the whole world seems to be in a state of transition. This is an opportunity for you to join with those you have met in the Legislature and by wise, useful consultations and planning, strengthen the efforts of this and other branches of Government to build a strong, progressive and respected nation.

May the God of our Fathers give you divine direction and endow you with wisdom so that peace and happiness may characterize this called session. As you have in the past proved your love of country by your keen sense of duty, so now I call upon each of you to continue to exert your best efforts in the interest of our nation, our common heritage, the Republic of Liberia.

GOD SAVE THE STATE!

On the Occasion of Accepting the First Executive Mansion built by the Government of Liberia

Monrovia, 3 January 1964

We have succeeded in erecting a permanent structure which we hope will be the pride of generations to come.

Introductory Note

After a period of 117 years of independence, the Government of Liberia finally succeeded in erecting a home for its Chief Executives. Planning for the construction of such a home, after long years of residing in temporary dwelling-places, was not an easy task. All offices attached to the Executive Mansion would be given accommodation under this plan, and at the same time become a symbol of architectual beauty. The Government succeeded in both of these aims. President Tubman gratefully received the Executive Mansion, becoming the first Chief Executive to reside in it. We have in his address of acceptance a revealing and important historical discourse, since on every occasion of national significance he took the opportunity of discussing in detail a great deal of the unwritten portion of our national history. The acceptance by him of our first Executive Mansion afforded him such an occasion.

Monrovia, 3 January 1964

MR. SPEAKER, you have on this historic occasion presented to us the first Executive Mansion built by the Liberian Government and people after 117 years of independence, to be used as a place of residence for Chief Executives and their families, as well as for the offices of the President, Presidential Assistants, Bureaux and the various Divisions and Sections appertaining to the Chief Executive. We accept this palatial, commodious and imposing structure with gratitude to the Legislature for authorizing the appropriation for its erection, and for its co-operation which has made the project a success. We who will live, work and perform our duties within this exquisite building expect to do so in a new atmosphere and under conditions different from our former dwellings, and further inspired by its attractiveness, its convenience and the facilities which it affords, we hope to render better and more effective service.

The Vice-President, who was a member of the House of Representatives when the idea was first conceived, and the older members of the Legislature, will recall that where the Capitol is now situated was the site originally selected by the Executive for the Executive Mansion, in preference to the present site; the Capitol was to be located West of where it stands at present and its cornerstone had already been laid, but the Legislature, exercising its legislative authority, removed the cornerstone from where it had been placed in due and ample form, and the Capitol Building took over from the Executive the site that was selected for the Executive Mansion. Being an old former Senator myself, and knowing what extreme action by the Liberian Legislature can mean, I would not be drawn into a fight, nor did I raise any question concerning their action in this respect, but rather began immediately to ponder and use any resourcefulness which I possessed to find another site for the Executive Mansion, and I soon reached a decision that the site on which the Mansion is at present constructed, and where we are now assembled, would be the ideal place, even better suited than the site they had taken away from us, because of its great historic, sentimental and reminiscent significance.

It was on this very spot, in February, 1909, where a military garrison called Camp Johnson then stood, that the authority of the Liberian Government was challenged and its autonomy was threatened and hung in the balance. A certain British Officer, Major McKay Cadell, who had been engaged by the Liberian Government to organize a Police Force for service on the Liberian Frontiers, with Captain Dinneu, his Adjutant, and the Quarter-Master, Captain Blythe, both British officers, occupied this area, where officers and men were encamped. The expatriates encouraged them to mutiny, on the pretext that they had not received pay for four or five months, and further urged them to refuse to accept or obey orders from the Liberian Government, the Commander-in-Chief, President Arthur Barclay or the Secretary of War, George S. Padmore; and the troops were ordered to march through the streets of Monrovia, in front of the Executive Mansion and the War Department, uttering threats, before returning to camp. ·

Major Cadell was ordered to evacuate the camp and hand it over to the Liberian Government. He refused. In the meantime diplomatic negotiations ensued between the Liberian Government, the United States Legation and the British Consulate-General. The late Honourable F. E. R. Johnson was then Secretary of State, and former President C. D. B. King, Attorney-General. Dr. Ernest Lyon was American Minister and Captain Braithwait-Wallis, British Consul-General. The Government then made a decision to take over the garrison by force, and declared a state of emergency in the capital. The Legislature and Supreme Court were in session; every able-bodied man in and around Monrovia, including Legislators, Cabinet Ministers and Judges, were armed and equipped with such arms and equipment as were available, and pressed into service. This was on the quarterly parade day of the First Regiment, commanded by Lieutenant-Colonel Isaac Moart, with Major Joseph Dennis as Second-in-Command; the entire regiment with all other available manpower was mobilized and held in readiness for any emergency. The First Regiment was a military unit of the Liberian army, not as professionally trained and armed as were the troops entrenched in Camp Johnson behind concrete stockades. Among these professional soldiers in Camp Johnson were expatriate soldiers from the neighbouring British colonial territories.

Notwithstanding these untoward and disadvantageous circumstances the die had to be cast, the honour and autonomy of the nation and its sovereignty over its territory had to be exercised and maintained, and soon the issue became a case of sink or swim, live or die, survive or perish, and a contingent of the First Regiment under the command of Lieutenant-Colonel Isaac Moart, with Major Joseph Dennis as Second-in-Command, was sent with an order from the Commander-in-Chief through the War Department, for Major Cadell to withdraw from the garrison and surrender to Colonel Moart all arms, equipment, accoutrements and other property belonging to the Liberian Government that were in his possession or in the garrison.

Upon arrival near the garrison, the contingent was challenged by sentries and ordered to halt. Colonel Moart, who was in command, knew that it was correct for his men not to proceed further until he had made attempts to contact the Commander of the garrison and inform him of the order he had from the Commander-in-Chief through the War Department. Therefore he ordered his men to halt. Major Dennis attempted to countermand Colonel Moart's orders and commanded the troops to continue the march against the garrison, but Colonel Moart exercised his authority as Commander and ordered his troops to remain stationary. He ordered the sentry to require Major Cadell to report and receive a despatch from the Commander-in-Chief through the Secretary of War, which required him to evacuate and hand over Camp Johnson immediately, or he would storm the garrison and take it by force. Major Cadell at first refused to heed these orders, and a fight seemed inevitable. In the meantime diplomatic negotiations continued.

The Capital City, Monrovia, was in a state of excitement, but finally Major Cadell indicated his willingness to comply with the orders of the Liberian Government (obviously upon the advice of the British Consul-General), and marched out of the garrison together with the expatriate British troops and, according to the records of the Department of State, with a great number of British subjects including men, women and children, who were with him. Colonel Moart and his men entered the garrison and took it over, and the day was saved. The emergency ended, peace and order were restored, the honour of the Government preserved, and the exercise of its sovereignty over its territory effectuated. Most of the people of this generation cannot appreciate the implication and gravity of a situation like this in the old days of sabre rattling and gunboat diplomacy.

This is a bit of the history of the grounds upon which we now stand and which at the ground-breaking and cornerstone-laying ceremonies we declared to be hallowed ground; ground made hallowed by the courage, patriotism, loyalty and fervour of the Liberian Army and people through the mercies of God.

Four years ago we broke ground to begin the construction of this building. The late Honourable Thomas E. Buchanan was then Secretary of Public Works and Utilities. Plans, specifications, drawings and models for an Executive Mansion had been presented by various firms upon the invitation of the Department of Public Works for tenders. The plans, specifications and drawings submitted by the Stanley Engineering Company were accepted and approved. Construction was begun, the cornerstone was laid and today we have met together to dedicate this building to the service of the nation and its people, and to the memory and honour of the long line of my predecessors — Roberts, Benson, Warner, Payne, Roye, Gardiner, Russell, Johnson, Cheeseman, Coleman, Gibson, Barclay, Howard, King, Barclay — men whose intrepidity, patriotism, resourcefulness, honour and integrity were unimpeachable and unmatched. They lie in their graves, their flesh and bones returned to ashes and their souls to the God who gave them. But, as we are taught to believe that we are encompassed with a great crowd of witnesses, I know that each and all of their spirits hover over and associate with us here, at these sacred ceremonies today, and they evaluate, more than we, the strides that this nation has made from 1847 to the present. May the ideals for which they lived and died, and the work of their hands in laying the foundation for building this national superstructure which has been handed down to us, be kept unimpaired, and remain an imperishable memorial and testimony to the endurance and greatness of their bodies, minds and souls, and as a bold and perpetual reminder to us of our obligation to the present generation and to posterity.

This should be one of the glories and pride of all Liberians, for after a century of pre-occupation with the preservation of our economy it has now been possible to direct attention to the construction of public buildings in the order of constitutional sequence; first, the Capitol, followed by the Executive Mansion, then the Judiciary of Law Courts Building. The Capitol has been completed. The Mansion is now completed and is being dedicated. The Law Courts Building is nearing completion, and we hope to dedicate it when the Honourable Supreme Court opens for its November term in 1964.

In this area on Capitol Hill will also be constructed, with Legislative approval, a Department of State building, and here on Capitol Hill will be the central focus of the three great branches of our Government.

Since the time the construction of this building began, several events have taken place which interrupted and delayed the building operation. There were necessary changes in the plans, labour strikes took place, unfortunate accidents occurred which took the lives of some of the workmen, and many other unforeseen circumstances. While it had been hoped that the building would be ready in time for the 1964 Inauguration, with these developments hope began to fade, and it appeared to many that the objective could not be achieved. However, work continued steadily after the initial difficulties had been overcome, so that at the beginning of this year it was possible for the contracting agencies to give assurance that the building would be ready by November, a date which was subsequently changed to December. They have made it!

The Government, people of Liberia, our foreign friends and residents are, I am sure, infinitely glad that this hope has been realized and that the new Executive Mansion is virtually completed. This indeed is a great feat in architectural design, and in imaginative and skilled craftsmanship. It is a work of beauty and artistry, and a distinctive achievement in modern architecture which reflects credit to the planners, builders, decorators, workers and the nation itself. We heartily congratulate all those who planned and executed the building plans, the workmen who have undergone so many difficulties and taken numerous risks at the peril of their lives and all others who have contributed to make this a happy occasion and a truly fitting climax in the history of public buildings in our nation.

We have succeeded in erecting a permanent structure which we hope will be the pride of generations to come. We hope that here on Capitol Hill will develop, in time, the central nerve fibre of all governmental operations, and that it will become a place of natural beauty and great intellectual, moral and spiritual attraction. This mansion must become a symbol of the great ideals for which this nation has always stood. It must be the embodiment of the sacrifices which we have made, and which future generations will also undergo, to maintain and enjoy its possession. It must be the pride of our nation. Every man and woman must come to revere the history of our national endeavours, and the children of our institutions of learning must be taught their future obligation as they mature to full citizenship status and assume their own responsibilities in helping to carry on the government and perpetuate the social and political ideas of the nation.

For over a century of struggle, the people of this nation have endeavoured, with their available resources, the gradual opening of the country and the exploitation of its natural resources, to direct their affairs so as to bring happiness, stability and a better standard of living to all. With the emergence of the new African nations, the need to make our position secure as the oldest independent African nation has become imperative. We accept the transformation which has taken place throughout the African continent.

In the age in which we live and through which the world is passing, every area of this vast continent has become susceptible to change, progress and development. Long ago we opened our country through the Open Door Policy to stimulate industries, activate business enterprises, and in the sum total to ensure living in a land of liberty, where freedom and protection would be guaranteed to all Liberians alike and to the foreigners who chose to live here. In all this, we have tried to offer our friendship and to assure everyone of our good intentions and our desire to work so as to keep pace with the vast developmental strides going on in Africa and throughout the world.

And now, I quote from my remarks made at the laying of the Cornerstone on May 15, 1961.

'May the significance of the laying of this cornerstone of our new Executive Mansion not be soon lost upon us, either today or in the near future, but may it become the pride of this generation and succeeding ones in the purposes for which it shall serve the nation. Just as this hillside is being developed to be the central point of our governmental activities, so may the men and women who shall serve here and elsewhere be true to the best ideals of service for their country, in their work and devotion.

This new Executive Mansion will be more than a beautiful architectural structure. It must be the living embodiment of the hopes and aspirations of the people of this nation and a pride to future generations. Let it become one of the national shrines of our country, in our hearts and in our lives, now and hereafter.'

Since we have reached another milestone in our nation's history, it is fitting that on this day we re-dedicate ourselves to the service of our country in all its true significance. Other equally important national goals remain to be achieved, and during the next administration, the Government will give priority to projects which, we are convinced, will accelerate our national progress and development. But only in unity, and with the constant vision of a united and happy people, can the years ahead contribute to the results we desire for ourselves and our posterity.

At a time like this we need to lift ourselves, become selfless and acquire greater patriotism and love for our country. The people of this nation must look within themselves to determine anew what the ideals of liberty and freedom still connote for us and the part each citizen will effectively play in making the nation greater and better.

We must make this a greater nation of people whose concepts of justice,

254

integrity, fair play and professional ethics have been broadened and deepened, and whose public conscience is ever sensitive to the highest dictates of the moral law; whose nationalism transcends individualism. We must create a better nation where unity, concord, friendship and love of country will prevail; where the old will hand down to the young the pristine virtues of honesty, decency and a sense of striving hard to earn a living by honest labour; a nation of abundance, made better by ideals of service; by a people free to develop their political, social, religious and educational institutions for the maximum benefits of all.

That Liberia must be a greater and better place in which to live is an injunction placed upon us who have received so much of the bountiful goodness of God and enjoyed the goodwill and friendship of many nations. Let us remain ever conscious of our national and moral responsibility and rise with a singleness of purpose to the future development and progress of our nation and its people.

May God continue to extend to us the omnipotence of His blessings and mercies.

On the Occasion of the Laying of the Cornerstone of the Edward T. Roye Memorial Headquarters of the True Whig Party

Monrovia, 8 January 1964

The facts of our history prove that Liberia is not a one party Government, but a Government of as many parties as the people of the country may desire.

Introductory Note

In this unique address on the history of the True Whig Party, President Tubman traced the long road the Party had travelled, its attempts to establish itself as a positive factor in Liberia's advancement, the opposition it encountered during past years, and the ideals for which it stands. In particular, the occasion was one to honour the founders of the Party, and to remember the first successful and martyred President of the Party, Edward J. Roye, in whose honour and in whose memory the Party's Headquarters would be named. This was further the first major effort of the True Whig Party to build its Headquarters after nearly a hundred years of existence and power. The occasion was therefore one of great political and national significance.

Monrovia, 8 January 1964

IN THE history of men and nations there are times when one is deeply reminded of past events, their relation to the present and the high ideals they inspire within the hearts and minds of the nation's people.

Today, the True Whig Party of Liberia, one of the greatest democracies of political history, makes a great forward step in laying the cornerstone of a building which will answer some of the needs of this great True Whig political entity. We are reminded of the first meeting of this party, 104 years ago, in the home of John Henry William Goods in Clayashland, the hardships the organizers had to endure, and the struggles they encountered and had to overcome to make the kind of Party of which we, their fellow compatriots, could be proud.

We remember today Mr. John Goods, Samuel David Richards, James David Simpson, Augustus Houston, Dr. Edward Blyden, George Freeman, Alexander Burke, the Reverend Debric Simpson, Captain Severin George, the Eskines, the Ashes, Mr. Henry Ricks and a host of other political leaders from the Counties of Montserrado, Grand Bassa, Sinoe and Maryland who made great contributions towards building up the strength of the True Whig Party.

To Mr. Goods, the chairman of the Party, and to all of the others

255

who contributed their energy and political acumen and dexterity towards laying the foundation of this great democratic entity with which we are proud to be identified, the Party is greatly indebted.

For many years, the political party known as the Republican Party and the True Whig Party were competitors in the political arena of the nation. The Republican Party, composed mainly of the élite of the nation, men of affluence, was predominant on the political scene. But the True Whig Party never relented in its attempt to gain political prominence. Finally, in 1869 after a decade of failures at the polls, the political sway, influence and power of the Republican Party was successfully challenged, and they were defeated by the True Whig Party in the election of Edward James Roye, the first dark-complexioned Liberian candidate of that party to be elected to the Presidency.

Mention must be made of the great historic significance of Hilary Richard Wright Johnson, who served as Private Secretary to President Benson, was elected a member of the House of Representatives, and later became the first candidate to be unanimously nominated, carried to the polls and elected by both parties as President of Liberia in May 1883. When the question arose as to which Party his administration would belong, since both had contributed to his election to office, President Johnson declared unhesitatingly, 'The True Whig Party'.

Another thing that boosted the influence of the True Whig Party and possibly led to President Johnson's identification of his Government with this political group was the Party's consideration of the tribal people and the common man, and its denunciation of the odious caste system that prevailed at that time, simultaneously declaring its belief in the right of all men to be free.

The True Whig Party has grown in strength and numbers, in vision and outlook, and has made such contributions to the moulding of the new Liberia that it has been able to withstand and defeat all other parties that have risen against it during the past ninety-five years.

This does not mean that the Whig Party has had things all its own way. In 1911 there was a strong opposition staged by an opposition party formed by the late Chief Justice J. J. Dossen against the Whig Party candidate, Daniel E. Howard. In 1927 another hotly contested campaign was waged against the Whig Party when former Vice-President S. G. Harmon and T. J. R. Faulkner contested the Whig Party candidate, the Honourable C. D. B. King; and again in 1938 when the True Whig Party candidate, Edwin J. Barclay, was contested by an opposition party with former President C. D. B. King as its candidate. In 1943 our own candidacy was contested by an opposition party with the Honourable James F. Cooper as opposition candidate. In 1952 our candidacy was contested by the Reformation Party, with the Honourable Richard Holder as candidate; and in 1955 by an opposition party with former President Edwin Barclay as opposition candidate. But in all these political campaigns and upheavals the True Whig Party, because of its principles and tenets of equality and privilege for all alike, the high ideals for which it had stood since its organization, and its recognized reliability as expressed in its motto: 'Deeds not Words', has been impregnable for the past ninety-five years. It has been able to withstand the on-slaught of conspiracy, attempts at assassination, plots and other vile and low-bred political intrigues.

I recall that at a National Convention of the True Whig Party, one of our most astute politicians in a speech made before the convention declared: 'This great Whig Democracy has grown and grown, and become so big by virtue of the people's confidence in it and its regard for all its adherents, that nothing can break it up. It will just have to fall to pieces by itself, if it should fall at all.'

These facts of history prove that Liberia is not a one party Government, but is a Government of as many parties as the people of the country may desire.

Like many other things in Liberia, the True Whig Party has had to make haste slowly because of the peculiar circumstances that have attended the nation and its institutions since its founding. Having to rely for its support mainly on contributions from its partisans, who were mostly within the low and average income brackets, the Whig Party has been unable to amass any significant wealth or make any substantial investment. However, we have been privileged to share the devotion and loyalty of a vast majority of our constituency, and this in some instances has meant more than material gains.

When we recall that the history of political parties in years gone by was punctuated by bitter rivalries, which many times erupted into open fights and murders, particularly on election days, and at a time when our election laws and voting methods were not well regulated, it is understandable that there were many obstacles which had to be overcome. Happily, during the course of the years, the True Whig Party has been able to surmount many of these difficulties, and thanks to the vision, zeal and determination of the leaders and partisans, the Party has gained popularity, power and prestige to such an extent that many of those who originally belonged to other parties have now joined the ranks of the True Whig Party. We appreciate this development and look to the future for greater political achievement for the True Whig Party, its leaders and members.

The history of the True Whig Party cannot be recorded without mention being made of the fact that Edward James Roye was the first candidate on a Whig ticket to defeat the Republican Party, as well as the first dark-complexioned Liberian of the Party to be made President. President Roye, during his administration, pursued liberal policies with the intent to develop trade, expand commerce and improve the economic condition of our people and country, for which purposes he negotiated a loan with British businessmen, he himself being a prosperous businessman. But the old Republican die-hards who, although defeated, were very strong and influential, both financially and intellectually, opposed his policies with great vehemence and, under the pretext that he was an impostor and was attempting to remain in office without being re-elected, started an uprising. President Roye, realizing the danger that confronted him, attempted to escape, but on his way to board an Elder Dempster Ship then in port, the canoe or dugout in which he attempted to make his way to safety to the ship was fired at from the shore and capsized. Successful efforts were immediately put forth to capture him. So bitter was the opposition against him that he was imprisoned; they took him from the water languishing and dying, brought him on a bier to the jailhouse which was situated on this identical spot where the True Whig Party Centre is to be built, and threw him into prison, where within a few hours he languished, and languishing, died.

Therefore, this Centre shall hereafter be known and called the Edward

James Roye Memorial Headquarters of the True Whig Party. May it ever be an inspiration to us and generations unborn to fight for the high ideals for which he lived and died.

This building will contain offices for the National and County Party officials, and will have office space to let, which will provide a source of income for the Party's increasing functions, responsibilities and other purposes. The auditorium, capable of seating about 3,000 people, will be used for conventions, convocations and other general purposes. It is our hope that this building will stand as a perpetual memorial to the only martyred President of the nation and Standard Bearer of the True Whig Party in our history up to the present.

While the Edward J. Roye Memorial Centre will be an expression of the Party's appreciation of a great statesman, we hope that it will also be the pride of all True Whigs and serve as a symbol of the sacrifices and achievements of our Party.

May the ideals we have always cherished find their greatest challenge, growth and expansion within these walls and may the love of country, service to the nation and loyalty to the ideals of the Party always keep its membership together. God bless the labours of our hands and hearts this day and for all future times.

On the Occasion of the Dedication of the Temple of Justice

Monrovia, 7 January 1965

Let justice be done to all men.

Introductory Note

In the effort of our nation to construct public buildings, priority was given to the erection first of an edifice to house our National Legislature, second, an Executive Mansion for the home of our Presidents, and third, a seat for the Judiciary. President Tubman in this address emphasized the significance of law and justice in Liberia, and the rôle of the Judiciary, which is to ensure their application fairly to all men. Of added significance was the plan for the construction of a building which would accommodate the Supreme Court and all lower courts of the nation's capital, Monrovia. President Tubman was pleased with the success of his building programme and saw an end at last to the hardships which our nation had undergone in past years to provide suitable accommodation for the Legislature, the President, and the Judiciary.

Monrovia, 7 January 1965

THE DEVELOPMENT programme of government today takes another step forward with the dedication of this edifice, the object and purpose of our presence here. It is pleasing to note the welcome presence of representatives from Sierra Leone, Guinea and the Ivory Coast, as well as people from all parts of the country, participating in these ceremonies.

Upon the assumption of office, we found ourselves in dire need of public buildings and therefore set upon the task of arranging for their construction as an important part of our development programme. Every effort to procure financing by loans was rejected, but as we considered this project of the utmost urgency and involving national pride, respectability and honour, we resolved that public buildings had to be constructed. Therefore, after all other efforts failed, we engaged in negotiations for the construction of some of these buildings by pre-financing, which proved to be very expensive; but, choosing between not having them and having them at high costs, we chose the pre-financing way, which met with the approval of the Legislature.

As a result of this, the Capitol Building, the first in the history of this country, was completed, dedicated and occupied in 1956, housing the National Legislature, the First Great Branch of our Government. Following that, a little over a year ago the Executive Mansion, another first in the history of the country, was completed, dedicated and handed over, housing the Chief Executive, the Second Great Branch of Government. And now today, on this eventful, happy and historic occasion, the home of the Judiciary, the Third Great Branch of Government, is being dedicated for service.

This symmetric and aesthetic structure, standing majestically and elegantly on Capitol Hill, abutting the Capitol Building, adjacent to the Department of Information and diagonally opposite to the Executive Mansion, has been denominated the Temple of Justice.

These three buildings – the Capitol, the Executive Mansion and the Temple of Justice – symbolize the ideals, aspirations, hopes and determinations of the people of this nation. They have been made commodious principally because of our desire and policy that each of them shall contain all the bureaux and agencies appertaining to these respective branches of Government. Thus, here within this shrine of justice are the Supreme Court, the representative symbol of the judiciary of the nation, and all of the Subinordinate Courts and the Courts of First Instance within the Capital City. This is a system particularly and peculiarly Liberian, for perhaps nowhere else are all of the functionaries of each of the great branches of government centralized in one building and under one roof.

Under circumstances and conditions different from those which prevail today, the members of Government gathered, more than fifty years ago, for the dedication of what was then called the 'Supreme Court Rooms'. The same building housed the House of Representatives on the second floor and the Treasury Department on the third floor. It would be well to remember, however, that the total annual revenues of Government available for its appropriation and expenditure at the time when the old Supreme Court Rooms were provided, was approximately only between 500,000 and 600,000 dollars. While modestly proud of our accomplishment in providing this fabric for the courts of the country, relatively speaking our achievement gives us nothing more creditable and memorable than theirs.

As we rejoice and are happy for the progress made, we give thanks and praise to God for His Blessings vouchsafed to and bestowed upon us, so that we have been successful in expanding the work begun in 1914 by our predecessors – from Court Rooms of the Supreme Court to a Temple of Justice for all of the courts of the capital city.

Since those years, although the nation has undergone many political changes, the Rule of Law has become more and more a stabilizing and significant factor, indeed the life-artery of our society. Current world events, the increasing number of independent states in the world and the new forces which the demands of the time have created, force upon us the necessity for a new look at the increased emphasis on the restraining power of the law. Therefore, the courts of this nation, the justices and judges who constitute the courts, the jurors who attend upon the court to determine the guilt or innocence of those charged with crimes or offences, and the lofty ideals which we hold for our nation as well as the intents and purposes of the law, form the great bulwark for the safety of our democratic society and the safeguard and assurance of equal rights, liberty and privilege for citizens and strangers alike within our borders. The Rule of Law must be our sheet anchor, and a guide line by which to measure our social, legal, moral and political conduct.

So great was the significance which the justices and judges of those days placed on freedom, liberty and the privilege of the individual that in a case of contempt brought upon appeal to the Supreme Court by the late Counsellor A. D. J. King against His Honour Judge Joseph R. Moore, Mr. Justice T. McCant Stewart laid down the principle that 'The liberty of the citizen is above the dignity of the Judge.'

The anxiety of the Liberian Government and people of days gone by for justice and righteousness was so great that when the Supreme Court was composed of three Justices, invariably one was a Methodist preacher, another a Baptist preacher and the third a lawyer, who was the Chief Justice: the theory being that the two Ministers would by prayer, supplication and righteous living promote and dispense justice while the Chief Justice, the lawyer, would guide them along the path of correct legal procedure.

It has been the practice of different administrations of the Supreme Court of Liberia to adopt various slogans as mottos for the dispensing of justice, one of which was:

'LET JUSTICE BE DONE THOUGH THE HEAVENS FALL';

another:

'LET JUSTICE PREVAIL THOUGH THE HEAVENS FALL AND THE EARTH BE MOVED'.

The motto which the present administration of the Supreme Court has chosen is emblazoned on the outer wall of this Temple:

'LET JUSTICE BE DONE TO ALL MEN'.

Justice which knows neither East nor West, North nor South; Justice which recognizes neither rich nor poor, high nor low, foreigner nor citizen; Justice which is transparent and untrammelled; even-handed Justice which when necessary invokes the doctrine of equity which is righteousness; where any injury or wrong finds no remedy in law, there is equity which requires him who flees for relief to come with clean hands.

In the evolution of the history of law in this nation, the idea of justice has survived through successive stages, from the courts with inquiring and trial jurisdiction – the Justices of the Peace, Magisterial and Circuit Courts – to the highest court of appellate jurisdiction – the Supreme Court. From time to time it has been asserted that our confidence in that body remains unshaken and that it continues to dispense justice after the manner for which its members are named, and to which they are dedicated. God grant that His Honour, the Chief Justice, the Associate Justices, Judges, all Magistrates, Justices of the Peace, lawyers, officers of the courts and all who function and attend at the altar of justice in our courts may, in honour, integrity, honesty and unselfishness, bring to their tasks a new and enriched vision, a new determination and re-dedication to service, so that by their wise, sound and the lofty juridical opinions and judgments, our nation may have peace and the people remain confident that at the Bar of Justice, which means so much to the stability and contentment of any nation or people, justice is assured.

We have chosen to dedicate this building on this date which carries such great significance in the history of our country, being the anniversary of the day on which the pioneers and founders of the nation landed on Providence Island – the 7th of January, A.D. 1822. We dedicate this building not to ourselves but to God, and the ideals of liberty, freedom and democratic ideals which safeguard the individual and extol his human dignity and worth. We dedicate it to future generations who will in turn, we hope, continue to cherish the ideas of freedom, justice and democracy, and hand down to succeeding generations of Liberians the tradition of the Rule of Law under an enlightened, progressive and God-guided Government and people. We hope that future generations of Liberians will honour the name and memory of those who today have striven to make this building a contribution to the adornment and progress of the nation.

Your Honours, Mr. Chief Justice, Associate Justices of the Supreme Court, and Judges of the Subordinate Courts, as you work in this new atmosphere and this inspiring environment, equipped with modern facilities and natural beauty of terrain, it is our hope and prayer that you will be granted grace, knowledge and wisdom from above, and that by your knowledge and application of the law, your ability to distinguish between truth and falsehood, right and wrong; your courage and strength of character to withstand all evils that may tend to reproach and affect the administration of unsullied justice, you may be able and willing to be judged by such judgments as you may render.

It is my distinguished honour, privilege and pleasure, Your Honour, Mr. Chief Justice, by the authority vested in me by the Legislature which authorized and appropriated the funds for the construction of this Temple of Justice, to present it to you, that you may take authority to execute the laws of the land and interpret the Constitution fairly when issues arise, so that this edifice may become a haven of protection for the wealth of the wealthy, a safeguard for the rights and privileges of the distressed and needy, the widow and orphan; a bulwark of protection for the foreigner and a national shrine of justice for the nation.

May God guide and guard the Courts, bless and prosper the State and lead us continually to the reign of peace and justice in this land and throughout the world.

A Broadcast to the Nation on the 153rd Birthday Anniversary of Joseph Jenkins Roberts, Liberia's First President

Monrovia, 15 March 1965

Let us resolve to honour those who saved our nation from territorial harassment, eased our social and political pangs, relieved our economic inconveniences and brought us to a new day of freedom and independence and to all that glorifies and adorns the dignity of the individual and spurs him on to newer fields of creativity and productive endeavours.

Introductory Note

In this tribute to President Joseph Jenkins Roberts, President Tubman spoke of the high ideals our first head of state which he considered to be desirable qualities that every Liberian should emulate. He then spoke further about national issues and the Government's policies affecting those issues. National Unification, Education, Austerity, and Operation Production claimed his attention, and in this address he informed the people of Liberia of measures implemented by their Government, and what he considered to be the citizen's own responsibilities for the success of those measures. President Tubman then discussed African matters, defined in terms of alignment and non-alignment with the great powers of the world, and Africa's moral responsibilities in choosing discriminately its position *vis-à-vis* these powers.

Monrovia, 15 March 1965

EIGHTY-EIGHT YEARS after his death, the memory of the man who was popularly regarded as a fearless and courageous fighter, generally recognized as an erudite statesman, an eminent scholar and a renowned educator, and who has been affectionately dubbed 'Father of his Country', still lives evergreen in the hearts of the people of his country, with as great veneration and admiration as ever before.

President Roberts loved his country with great compassion; he represented his nation's cause with astounding brilliance, sincerity, boldness and success; he constantly sought his people's welfare with unceasing solicitude, and when he knew that his earthly mission was drawing to a close, made provisions for the establishment of a foundation by and through which future generations of young Liberians would benefit from the educational facilities to be provided. In thus thinking of, and making provisions for, the needs of others, this great man left a legacy of love and gratitude in the hearts of future generations and an opportunity to follow knowledge like a setting sun.

On this memorable occasion of the 153rd anniversary of the birth of this outstanding personality, our minds go back to the early days of the infant nation: to the effects of the great expansionist movement in Africa; to the heinous human traffic; to the birth of the American Colonization Society – a voluntary association formed for benevolent purposes, national in scope and character; to the founding and settling of Liberia; to the political and social vicissitudes and great wars of affliction encountered during the colonization, commonwealth and Republican periods; to the accomplishments of the first century of our national existence, and the unfinished work which the nation faced after the centenary celebration of 1947.

Only those who have experienced the ravages of poverty, the scourges of disease, the blight of ignorance and pressures from within and without can appreciate the trials and tribulations which our forefathers faced, suffered and endured. By their unconquerable wills and the true pioneering spirit with which they were possessed they remained undeterred in their noble purpose, aspirations and ideals. They were absolutely, utterly and passion- ately convinced that what they envisioned and had already achieved was worth fighting for, living for and even dying for; hence they have today be- queathed to us, the people of this nation, of every clan, tribe, element, creed and class, an organized, progressive and developing nation and a form of government which we are proud to call our own. In their moments of sor- row and distress they often prayed this prayer out of the deep recesses of their souls, evincing their reliance upon God as their mainstay in a weary land and as a shelter from every storm: 'We thank God for this land of liberty, where we can worship Him under our own vine and fig tree, and where none dare molest or make us afraid.'

May we of this and future generations be ever imbued with these identical political, social and spiritual ideals, and spurred by these same principles, so that by our accomplishments we will continue to hold aloft the torch of liberty which must never be extinguished upon our shores; a torch in the hearts and imaginations of all Liberians to burn ever brightly till all our people – every man, every woman, every girl, every boy, and every child – are invigorated with its glow and until the entire continent of Africa basks in the light of liberty, freedom and independence. For these ends did our forefathers pray and labour, and we their descendants must continue to maintain, enjoy and perpetuate these ideals and join with others of like-mind to hasten the day of the reign of peace and goodwill among ourselves and all nations of the earth.

THE AFRICAN SITUATION

From day to day we face the painful reality that the optimism we shared for greatly improved conditions on our continent since Africa Freedom Year is waning, and we are bound to admit that interpersonal relationships among African leaders have been far from the best that could be desired; that the impact of the United Nations Charter and the Organization of African Unity has not been significant enough to have activated full co-operation and sympathy so that these institutions could be the guiding principles of our conduct on national and international levels.

Respect for the noble concept of freedom and independence, emphasis on the inherent rights of all men, the belief that all nations, great or small, should be permitted to live under the form of government which best seeks their welfare, fulfils the aspirations of their people and meets the requirements of their citizens for living in a world in which there is equality, co-operation and respect one for the other – are ideals which are becoming accepted norms among the members of the comity of free nations. The attainment of these ends could be delayed unless mankind is willing and ready to re-evaluate aims and objectives, look for objectivity and practical results, and implement decisions which are the outcome of free and dispassionate discussions.

We in Liberia have always believed that every nation should be free to follow the system of government that tends to its own interest and welfare, be it Socialist, Communist, Constitutional Monarchy, Free Enterprise Democracy or Republican. We believe that there should be no interference in the internal affairs of one nation by another, nor should there be any attempts, by subversive manoeuvres or by intrigue and stealth to force any form of government of one nation upon another. Frankly, there appears to be a determination in Africa on the part of some Socialist states to impose Socialism upon other states not socialist in form or principle, by inciting revolution, disloyalty and vicious propaganda to effect this end, but the proponents of such malignant practices seem to forget the old, wise and faithful saying that 'what you sow, you shall reap and when thou hast finished spoiling thou too shalt be spoiled'.

There is need for heart-searching and soul-searching, retrospection and introspection. All the human and spiritual resources of mankind must be brought to bear upon the great issues which today face the world. The cause of peace is imperilled; it has become a universal concern, a desired goal which is no longer confined to one nation alone. Our world has become 'one world' in the sense that media of communication and transportation have made the free flow of ideals, goods and peoples possible on a scale never before imaginable, and what now affects one nation in any part of the world is likely to affect other nations as well. We can no longer take refuge behind geographical isolationism or impenetrability.

We say invariably that we are non-aligned. However, some of our actions speak so loudly that what we say with our mouths cannot be heard. As a matter of fact we appear to be widening the breach between East and West and among each other by the slanderous statements and invectives hurled against one another and by libellous expressions and statements made against even the great world powers. We must remember that if a nuclear war should erupt, we in Africa will be the greatest losers, even more so than the great powers, most of whom have enjoyed the benefits of liberty, freedom and self-determination for centuries. Some of these nations can literally be said to have reached old age, and some to be in middle age; their development is marked by great progress and prosperity, while we in Africa and in other parts of the world are under-developed and developing.

Some of us are even in infancy and others in adolescence, seeking aid by means of technical assistance, loans, grants and gifts, and we say we accept these with no strings attached. At least one string is attached to every assistance given, every grant, loan or aid rendered, by the eternal principle of morality, the string of gratitude; any man, any nation or any people who receives assistance of any kind – grants, loans or aid from any source – and repays with ingratitude or slander, commits an outrageous crime of malevolence. Such an attitude is unconscionable, depraved and unscrupulous. My fellow countrymen and women, young and old, I exhort you to guard against such unprincipled practices. Do not ask for, nor accept any gifts, grants, aid or assistance from any source to which you cannot feel free to say 'Thank you' or pay a debt of gratitude.

UNIFICATION AND INTEGRATION

No nation or people can successfully ascend to the summit of national greatness and unity if the components which make for coalition, cohesion, fusion and national consciousness and identification are lacking; if common ideals are not discovered, valued and shared. As eloquently expressed in one of the lines of our National Anthem 'In union strong, success is sure', if the concept of one people, one nation and one aspiration is not made a part of the conscious life of the nation, our efforts may be in vain.

Even in those early years of the country's existence, the principle of national unity was conceived and accepted as the sheet anchor and pillar of strength of the state, where unity of purpose and action would be instrumental in stemming the rising expansionist movement and withstanding the inroads and incursions of unfriendly harassing enemies. Over the years and by repeated attempts the stage was reached whereby internecine wars disappeared, the rule of law was established, the various elements were brought gradually together into the body politic, and pride in being called Liberians and working together like a team in the march towards peace, progress, friendship and solidarity filled each breast.

That tribal rivalries and feuds have been resolved without recourse to war; that all elements of the nation have learned to respect one another and to live together in peace and harmony; that education is being accepted as an effective tool for nation building and that the feeling is becoming stronger and stronger that we shall reach political and social maturity only when we emphasize and utilize the similarities which bind us rather than capitalize on the dissimilarities which divide us; that we have come to accept fully and without reservation the obligations which citizenship bestows as blessings capable of transforming us into a happy forward-looking, hardworking and progressive people and a nation with a manifest destiny, are all happy outcomes of the Unification and Integration Policies.

Encouraged by these results, we face the future with hope and determination that in unity and with faith in ourselves our nation will be saved from internal ravages, dissensions, petty jealousies, rebellions, bitterness, confusion and war. Always cognizant of these facts, and having already benefited from the fruits of past and present experiences, we shall resolve that never again will misunderstandings, greed, littleness of mind, and strange ideologies be permitted to destroy our faith in the ideal of Liberty and Freedom. Let us resolve to honour those who saved this nation from territorial harassment, eased our social and political pangs, relieved our economic inconveniences and brought us to a new day of freedom and independence in all that glorifies and adorns the dignity of the human individual, and spurs him on to newer fields of creative and productive endeavour.

AUSTERITY

We entered the austerity period because of the Government's simultaneous involvement in the construction of public buildings, schools, hospitals and clinics, roads, power and water supply, communications and transportation facilities and other development projects, which normally are undertaken by long-term loans and other special financial arrangements. But because of the Government's inability to obtain such loans or make other financial arrangements for roads, public buildings and airstrips in some of the cities, we were forced to arrange for these development projects on a pre-financing basis, payment of which had to be met from current revenues on a year-to-year payment plan.

This situation may last for five, ten or even fifteen years, but even so it is the rule and principle of political economics that it is normal and reasonable for future generations to share in meeting the costs of projects from which they too will benefit. Thus fifteen years, if it should last that long, would see the settlement of these obligations within the life span of this present generation, even if not within the present administration.

Generally, the first President of a nation is recognized as the Father of his country, for he is usually accepted as having laid the keel and started the ribs for the superstructure of the ship of state. And so we on this occasion, salute and commemorate the day that gave birth to our first President, Joseph Jenkins Roberts, of immortal memory.

It is a regrettable fact that in the liberation of the continent of Africa national leaders who led the liberation movement and became the first Chiefs of State and representative citizens of their country have been imprisoned, overthrown, and detained; one of them brutally murdered and others threatened with assassination and the overthrow of their governments. Is this the price that we Africans are willing to pay for national leadership in the first phase of our national independence? I am prone to exclaim in the lines of the poet, 'O judgment, thou art fled to brutish beast and men have lost their reason.'

In the wake of enjoying the freedom which has come to the majority of African nations formerly under colonial rule, we in Africa are also making history and when it is written, these things will be mentioned and will certainly constitute a paradoxical episode in its dismal pages and a blight on the reputation of our continent. May we now bring ourselves together to reason and consider how we think, how we act and how every action has consequences, not only in terms of the present, but also of the future.

It is our hope that as a result of the bitter experiences of the past the peoples of Africa, and African leaders and statesmen will seek a juster understanding of the issues involved in nationalism and refrain from actions which future historians will term blind and unnecessary; for freedom and independence can only flourish in an atmosphere of peace and security, not of fear and bloodshed.

EDUCATION

No sounder foundation can be laid for the preservation of the freedom and happiness of a people than a system of mass education. From the founding of this nation to the present, faith in education has been an over-riding consideration, and constant and consistent efforts have been made to provide quantitative as well as qualitative educational opportunities. Certainly the history of education in Liberia has not been without its drawbacks, disappointments and hazards, but the results which have been achieved encourage us to push vigorously ahead to improve, strengthen and expand our system so as to make the diffusion of knowledge available to a greater number of people than ever before. We must continue to forge ahead until the blight of ignorance is removed and the literacy level of the nation compares favourably with that of other progressive states.

Statistics from the Department of Education show that since 1944 the number of schools multiplied fourfold, enrolment rose by 450 per cent and the number of teachers increased almost five times. These are very impressive figures and impose obligations and conditions of the most urgent nature upon us, which must be fulfilled to meet the rising challenge. They mean that more schools have to be built with adequate facilities, prospective teachers encouraged, a Future Teachers of Liberia Club introduced, and the training and education of these teachers fostered to a greater degree. And if education must take new dimensions, teaching must be made as attractive as other professions.

The provision for vacation schools for working teachers, the recommendation of a Pension Scheme for teachers, the scaling of teachers' salaries and the introduction of a Provident Fund for teachers are some of the measures which we hope will serve as fringe benefits for those who devote their time, energy and life to teaching as a time-honoured profession.

OPERATION PRODUCTION

The response to and participation of most Liberians and many foreign residents in Operation Production have been most encouraging. We have received reports about increased production of rice, vegetables, citrus fruits, pineapples, and other farm commodities. It is interesting that some journalists have commented on the inability of the people to sell their products rather than on the fact that the nation has experienced increased productivity. When there is more productivity, more food available than is required, this is progress, and that is the primary objective of our priority number one programme, Operation Production. Because this is only the first year of the introduction of this programme we cannot judge with any degree of certainty that these products represent surpluses or that they will even be enough for home consumption. Our first concern, therefore, should be increased production.

Another revealing development is the fact that many people have moved faster with the programme than the machinery which the Government has been able to set up. We are optimistic that conditions will gradually improve and that the system will become more efficient. And so we think that this year the importation of rice should be reduced by fifty per cent, and, as more farm-to-market roads are constructed, many more commodities will find new markets.

We promised, as an incentive to Operation Production, to award a prize to the county or territory producing the greatest quantity of rice during the past year. To this end the Secretary of Internal Affairs has been instructed to gather statistics of rice produced, distributed and sold or disposed of by each county or territory. A prize of $10,000.00 will be given to the county or territory reporting the greatest yields. I hope that this will be a yearly feature of our agricultural programme and that it will encourage the holding of agricultural fairs to give impetus to competition, not only in terms of quantity, but also in terms of quality.

To the Nation on his return from a State Visit to the Kingdom of Morocco

Monrovia, 12 April 1965

The determination to make Operation Production the foundation of our national programme for progress and economic stability is realistic, and is the outgrowth of a realistic national need.

Introductory Note

Once again Pesident Tubman enthusiastically brought home what he learned abroad – this time from the Moroccan way of life; and once again he received greater incentives to do all in his power for the success of Operation Production.

The war in Viet Nam further claimed his attention at this time, and he thought he saw hopes for an end to that war in the proposition of the United States at this time for unconditional talks with the other parties to the war in Viet Nam.

The President further lamented the passing away of a reputable African apostle at the hands of an assassin. Again he congratulated the officials of Government upon the peaceful conduct of the affairs of state in his absence.

Monrovia, 12 April 1965

AS USUAL, the President and members of the Christian Ministers Association have conducted a Thanksgiving and Intercessory Service for us upon our return from the State Visit to the Kingdom of Morocco. It would seem particularly befitting at this time that such a service takes place because our return home falls within Holy Week and the octave of the queen of feasts – Easter, which signifies the resurrection and proves the Messiahship of Christ, preceded by Good Friday, which commemorates His suffering, crucifixion and death.

Muslims throughout the world also at this time celebrate the feast – Tabalski – commemorating the faithful patriarch Abraham who, in obedience to the command of God, offered his son Isaac as a sacrifice upon the altar.

We are happy that our return home coincides with these religious festivals, and extend our thanks to the President and members of the Christian Ministers' Association for this service.

It has been our distinguished honour and pleasure to be received as guests of monarchs, kings and queens in various parts of Europe and of the only Emperor in Africa: but our recent visit to Morocco was the first time that we had the privilege and distinction of being the honoured guests of an African King, His Majesty Hassan II of the Kingdom of Morocco.

Leaving here on March 23, our visit to a nation long reputed for its military exploits, ancient culture and civilization, where the new has been fused with the old, filled us with great admiration and wonder. Looking back at the historic relics and trying to assess the present-day advancement and progress, one must admire the phenomenal cultural and material achievements this nation has made. Morocco is today a great and attractive tourist centre, a land of indescribable beauty and contrasts: a country possessing a distinctive civilization and culture, an invigorating climate and a virile, ingenious and enterprising people with a great future.

The ship taking us to Morocco docked at the port of Casablanca on the morning of March 30. His Royal Highness Prince Moulay Abdullah, a committee of honour and other officials of the city of Casablanca boarded the ship and after the customary exchange of greetings escorted us to the quay where military and official ceremonies took place. We then boarded a special train and reached the gaily decorated railway station in Rabat, the Capital, after an hour's journey from Casablanca. Here His Majesty King Hassan II, high-ranking Ministers, Members of the Court and Diplomatic Corps and a tremendous crowd of people showered their welcome upon us. For two days we remained in the flag-bedecked city of Rabat enjoying the hospitality of the King, the Royal family, the Government and people of that city.

At the end of the two-day stay, a communiqué was issued which has already been made public and it is therefore not necessary for us to reiterate it here.

On Thursday, April first, we left Rabat for Fez via Meknes, fourth of the Imperial cities and one of the important centres of the nation where may be seen the vestiges of one of the most glorious epochs in the history of Morocco: our sightseeing here took us to the tomb of Moulay Ismail, the great king, second Alourite Sovereign who had transformed the city and devoted great attention to the construction of his palaces and grounds, comparable to those in Paris and other places, and to the National School of Agriculture at Hadj Kaddour. These palaces, built centuries ago, remain impressive works of engineering, architecture and art.

We arrived at Fez, once the capital of Morocco, which was and is still the intellectual centre of the nation. Built by rulers of many historical eras, here the past and present merge, and because of this it is commonly admitted that Fez is a city of great contrasts. Our stay there included official engagements and sightseeing trips to the Fez Arsenal, the Cofitex (textile factory), the Sidi Harazem, an ancient hot spring frequented, we were told, by the Romans, and which has now become a traditional spot for visiting tourists and Moroccans. The Governor, local officials and people of this historic city accorded us many courtesies and we came away impressed not only by the history and progress of the city, but also touched by the friendliness and hospitality of the people of this cultural and intellectual centre.

Having been the beneficiaries of their unbounded hospitality, having talked with friendly officials and people, listened with rapt attention to historic accounts of their nation's past and seen some of their centres of interest and attraction, it was time for us to say good-bye to Fez. And so on Saturday morning we set out for Casablanca via Ifrane, a well-known summer and winter resort. Here His Majesty the King met and received us at his private residence in the mountains, where we had the unique experience of seeing snow fall in Africa for the first time. Later we took leave of His Majesty and resumed our journey, arriving in Casablanca at seven o'clock the same evening. On the following afternoon, after departure ceremonies and official leave-taking, we boarded the French liner *Ancerville* for Dakar, spent three nights there and embarked on the *General Leclerc* on the tenth instant, arriving home today with the joyful feeling of being back and receiving this warm welcome and enthusiastic reception.

We have just visited a country with a great civilization where the shadows of the past still cast their reflections on many aspects of modern day living and from which the people derive constant inspiration and a deep sense of national pride. The palaces, the mosques, the walled cities, the arts, crafts, the rich traditions and the people themselves, with their reverence for the great past, make Morocco a nation with a magnificent history.

The fertile northern coastal plain along the Mediterranean and the rich plateaux and lowlands lying between the rugged Atlas Mountains make Morocco a great agricultural country. The extensive fields under cultivation, and the abundant crops seen everywhere, could not but lead us to the conclusion that imagination, hard work and modern know-how have combined to make this country a great nation. The Agricultural College at Hadj Kaddour where we saw a modern programme is the great power house for the future agricultural possibilities of Morocco, a vital factor and source of strength of the nation's economic growth and stability.

In Morocco, as in many nations of Africa, education is a prime necessity. In 1956 the Government launched a national Literacy Campaign and since that time their programmes for national education have been revitalized, improved and expanded. There is a greater need for education than ever before and the Moroccan Government is faced with the gigantic task of providing more educational opportunities for young and old.

Launching out on our Operation Production Programme was a forward step in the interest of increased production with emphasis on agriculture. Everywhere that we have gone within the last two years has convinced us that agricultural production is and must be the basis of our national economy. The determination therefore to make Operation Production the foundation of our national programme of progress and economic stability is realistic and is the outgrowth of a realistic national need.

As the response of the people to increase production last year was so effective, we again appeal to everyone, in all lines and kinds of businesses throughout the country, including agriculture, to boost, expand and increase their production so that it may far exceed last year's production and successively increase throughout the years ahead.

Agriculturists of the Government of the Republic of China from Formosa have been rendering us great assistance in our Agricultural Programme, even prior to the promulgation of Operation Production and continue to do so in increased measure. This kind of technical assistance has introduced new types of high-yielding rice and a greater number of crops per annum. We appreciate the assistance thus rendered and express thanks to the Government of China and the Chinese Agriculturists for their contribution to our Agricultural Programme.

In education we must meet the challenge of the present times. We cannot be complacent about the yearning for quantity and quality education. New institutions must be built to take care of the rising school population; more teachers must be trained, particularly for elementary and secondary teaching assignments; increased educational facilities must be provided; courses must be strengthened and present programmes enriched. The true progress of our educational system must have its roots deep in the culture which we are anxious to develop, and thus be compatible with our willingness to face the realities in our schools today with a determination to weave objective patterns into programmes which will make education a noble pursuit in creative endeavour, enriched living and productive skills.

VIET NAM

The conflict in Viet Nam has reached such proportions that it has now become a matter of international concern and a threat to world peace, due to the possibility of the conflict spreading. In the midst of our concern, like a peal of thunder out of a clear sky, came the appeal of President Lyndon Johnson of the United States for unconditional discussions with a view to restoring peace in South-east Asia and the offering of economic assistance, to be administered by the United Nations, as well as the soliciting of other governments to join in this attempt to bring peace to that war-torn area. The offer for peace talks without pre-conditions by the President of the United States has raised his stature in our eyes, and it seems to us that all lovers of peace should be willing to give this request a trial, proving thereby the sincerity of the proposition. At least it is our opinion that any offer of peace at any time, on any conditions, should be given study and consideration because we all profess to be yearning for peace.

When it comes to the offer of economic assistance made by the President, it would seem that this is a question entirely up to the parties concerned to accept or reject, as in our opinion it stands in a different category from the appeal to discuss peace.

As we arrived in Casablanca to start the state visit, we received the sad intelligence that Ambassador David who had been accredited *ad hoc* Ambassador to the Kingdom of Morocco for our visit was motoring from Rabat to Casablanca to meet us, when the rear tyres of his car had blow-outs, causing the vehicle to skid and collide head-on with an on-coming car. The driver of Ambassador David's car was killed and Ambassador David, his secretary who was to have served as our French translator and interpreter during the visit, and the three occupants of the other car were wounded. Mrs. David and one of their daughters were at the Ambassador's bedside for two days following the accident and Senator Isaac David has since joined his brother. We are profoundly grateful to the Moroccan Government for its sympathetic concern and the co-operation shown in this unfortunate accident, by providing the services of its hospitals, doctors, nurses, medicines and medicaments without cost; we are also grateful to the United States Embassy in Morocco for their solicitude and assistance rendered the Ambassador and his family in Rabat and for the arrangements made by them for Ambassador David to enter the American Hospital in Paris upon his return from Morocco. We are also happy to report that we have received information that the Ambassador has returned to Paris.

One of the greatest tragedies in the history of this country occurred when an assassin, moved and instigated by the devil and his own wicked heart, or in a strain of mental unbalance or insanity, struck with a hand-axe the body of Apostle Oduwole of the Church of the Lord and felled him as one would a tree, thereby taking away the life of a great and useful man, who had given his services to the people of this country in prayer, healing and fasting and in prophesying to those who believed in him. His prophecies extended to the nation and to the world; he was an attendant on occasions like this and his seat is empty today; he established in this country a new creation, a new faith and constructed one of the most elegant church edifices that we have in the country. The late Prophet Oduwole, while praying for his assailant, was smitten by him. So also his Master Jesus Christ, who while hanging on the cross, prayed for those who did Him wrong.

Our sympathy and condolence go to the widow, fatherless children and immediate relatives of the late Apostle and we commend them to God and to the charity and benevolence of the people of this city, whom the Apostle served so faithfully and well.

Our hope is that the work which he commenced will not deteriorate or fail, but move steadily forward and grow in strength and grace. Let not the members and adherents of the Church of the Lord which he established be scattered; let them continue the good work, relying upon the strength of Him Who is able to do all things.

May the soul of the Apostle find rest and peaceful slumber in the realm of bliss beyond this vale of tears.

For conducting the affairs of government during our absence from the country, we congratulate the Vice-President, the Secretary of State, the Speaker, Members of the Cabinet and all other officials of Government, and record our deep gratitude for this repeated evidence of patriotism and loyalty.

God save the state.

To the Civic League of Crozerville, Liberia

Crozerville, 10 May 1965

> *They came, these men, women and children, and founded this settlement.*

Introductory Note

Early in the modern period of its history, Liberia, under the supervision of the American Colonization Society encouraged immigration as a national policy. The great majority of immigrants who organized a democratic state in Liberia came from the mainland of the United States. Upon the attainment of self-government in 1847, the leaders of the new Republic continued to pursue this policy but now with the emphasis on receiving immigrants from Barbados, who settled in Crozerville in May, 1865 as the first major effort of the National Government. The local centenary of Crozerville was therefore given proper recognition by the Liberian Government in 1965. A tribute was paid by President Tubman to its founders and their descendants, many of whom had rendered outstanding service to the state.

Crozerville, 10 May 1965

THE HONOUR, pride and glory of human adventures and endeavours find a place in the annals of history through the success and benefits achieved for the advancement of peoples and nations and the good of society. The strength of such endeavours is measured by the results which attend them through all time.

Upon this basis we meet today to observe and celebrate with national pride the landing on these shores, 100 years ago of 346 emigrants of great daring, intrepidity, determination, faith and courage from the West Indian Island of Barbados, many of whom were farmers, mechanics, traders, shoemakers, wheelwrights, printers and teachers. They had come to find a new home, to seek new political and economic opportunities and to identify themselves with the destiny of their brethren who had founded Liberia, and who were already, by dint of perseverance, struggling, together with the tribal people whom they met here, to maintain and develop an African State that was a beacon of hope to all of their fellows and brethren of Africa. This emigration from the Island of Barbados in the Caribbean was the result of the Legislative Act of 1864, which authorized President Warner 'to adopt measures to encourage emigration to Liberia from the British West Indian Islands'.

The Reverend Dr. Edward Blyden, himself a West Indian, was chosen and accredited with the responsibility of conducting this mission, and his appeal, inviting the people of Barbados to aid in building up a Negro nation of freedom and Christianity on the continent of their ancestors by migrating to Liberia, caught the imagination of many who had felt the need for freedom, expansion and adventure. But while the response was most enthusiastic, the consent of the Liberian Government was necessary to assume the supervision of and responsibility for the expedition, since under the terms of the charter of the American Colonization Society, its funds could only be used to repatriate to Liberia Negroes residing in the United States of America. If the plan was carried through, it would represent the first group of emigrants which the Liberian Government was to sponsor.

Because the Society had some experience in sending emigrants to Liberia, it willingly accepted the Government's request for help, and, together with the Pennsylvania Colonization Society under the Presidency of Mr. John P. Crozer, whose younger brother, Dr. Samuel A. Crozer had been the first agent and physician for the Society and had sailed with the first company of emigrants to Africa, the plans began to take shape.

The American Colonization Society accepted the responsibility, and despatched Mr. William McLain, Financial Secretary of the Society, to Bridgetown, Barbados, where he met with deputations from two organizations, The Barbados Company for Liberia, and The Fatherland Union Barbados Emigration Society for Liberia. Thus it was that after preliminary arrangements had been made, on April 6, 1865, the brig *Cora* set sail for Africa with a human load of 346 persons, and arrived in the harbour of Monrovia on May 10, 1865, exactly 100 years ago.

They came, these men, women and children and founded this settlement. The generosity of Mr. John Crozer and other Philadelphians who had advanced the needed funds to undertake the project was not forgotten, and as a token of gratitude to him the settlement was named 'CROZERVILLE' in memory of him and his deceased brother Dr. Samuel A. Crozer. And so, forty-three years after the landing of the Pioneers and eighteen years after the Declaration of Independence, this group, which was to make significant contribution to the history of the nation, found a home here.

Despite the difficulties of those years, when lack of adequate supplies plagued them, when tropical disease invaded their ranks, and when their morale became low due to other circumstances, they stayed on and endured pains, trials, tribulations, hardships and deprivations. No greater testimonial can be given to the determination and success of those settlers than the following excerpt which appeared in the *African Republic,* a Monrovian newspaper, of March, 1867.

'The West Indians. — Fears were entertained a year ago that the immigrants from Barbados in the *Cora* were not going to prove much of an acquisition to Liberia. It was thought that when compared with the same number of labourers, mechanics, and agriculturists from the southern portion of America, these Barbadians would lose vastly by the comparison. Indeed some were of the opinion that as a general thing they were shiftless, wanting in industry, and willing to continue to live on the aid which was so nobly reached out to them by the generous Liberians when passing through their period of acclimatization. But time has proved beyond all doubt that those fears were groundless, and those opinions so hastily formed, were not well founded.

'Now and then we see beautiful pieces of furniture carried through our streets made of unrivalled wood of Liberian forests. These are made at Careysburg by a Barbadian, a first-rate cabinet maker, and would not shame a furniture warehouse in any city in the United States.

'Go to the man's brother's shoe shop in Monrovia and see him make as neat and nice a shoe or boot as ever came from the hand or from the last of any of his trade. He is a Barbadian.

'Who in the world raises those fine yams, my friend, why we never saw any like them for the many years we have been here? The Barbadians up the river, sir.

'So too in Krootown, as we are informed, may be seen as good a tailor, cutting and finishing as neat a work as any man of the shears and needle ever made in any community. He too is a Barbadian.

'And so we might enlarge. But let it suffice to say that the major part are agriculturists, have formed a Barbados and Liberia Agriculture Society, and are going to concentrate their efforts, and send their sugar, coffee, arrowroot, ginger and cacao to the United States in quantities. Success to the enterprise.'

How I wish these performances could be re-enacted today in Crozerville, and spread to all the other settlements along the St. Paul River, as well as to all the territories and counties of the Republic. Should this happen, a greater force and reality would be given to Operation Production and soon the nation would be out of the clutches of the austerity period.

Special reasons prompted the decision to seek to obtain emigration from the West Indies. Islanders are universally noted to be hardy, dexterous and pioneering. The people of the West Indian Island in the Caribbean were known to have been trained in skills, small industries, trades and professions that were ideal for the type of emigrants that were needed and required to accelerate the economy and development of Liberia at that time. This is shown by the record that each of these emigrants, except the children, was a craftsman or an agriculturist. Also, most of the West Indian Islands were over populated and under colonial rule, the people were anxious for freedom, and their hearts and yearnings were for liberty in the land whence their forebears had been carried away as captives.

An outstanding and noteworthy characteristic of these emigrants was that they were able to adjust themselves and assimilate with the Government and people of Liberia almost immediately, and did not segregate themselves into a separate and distinct class, nor evince any spirit or attitude of superiority. They realized that their desires, their aims and their great objectives and purposes were the same as the people of Liberia – freedom, self-determination, social and political justice and equality.

Several of these emigrants of the first generation, because of their outstanding ability, achieved unparalleled renown and consideration, both political and social. Arthur Barclay, who landed here at the age of ten, became President of the nation; J. W. Worrell, an Associate Justice of the Supreme Court; James T. Wiles, the first Postmaster-General of Liberia; George Stanley Padmore, Secretary of War and Major-General of the Army.

But many others among them, and among their descendants (most prominent among whom was Edwin Barclay of the second generation who also was preferred as President), attained eminence and made great contributions to

Church, State and Society, and if we look among our ranks today, even here in this place, we see many of their descendants.

We honour today the memory of these pioneers, who fought to keep the light of liberty burning in this settlement and who gave their lives to make it possible, leaving behind a proud heritage and a tradition of perseverance and achievement. We applaud the zeal of those who have carried on where they left off, and we congratulate all who contributed to the constant building and improvement of Crozerville, and who have, for this occasion, erected enduring monuments which the sands of time will not obliterate.

One hundred years ago these stalwarts, fired and filled with a spirit of patriotism and love of liberty, landed here. To us, who gather to honour their handiwork and to memorialize their illustrious deeds, it is as yesterday because it is past. But what were their anxieties, their afflictions, disappointments, toils, sufferings, deprivations; what were their joys, aspirations, achievements, progress and contribution to the national superstructure during these 100 years? They were many, great, and varied. And where are they, those eminent men and women? The tide of time has carried them away as a flood, to the inevitable realm of our commonalty, and they sleep the sleep of death, but their works follow them; and on this historic occasion, we salute, revere, pronounce and declare them to be among the famous men and women of the nation's history. We crown them with glory and declare the labour of their hands to be creditable and memorable, because it has withstood the ravages of time.

A 100 years have passed as yesterday, but Crozerville, the settlement of their founding, survives as an integral and integrated part of the national fabric.

The churches in this community, the Centennial Monument which was unveiled yesterday, and the Antoinette Tubman Community School which was dedicated a short while ago, will hereafter speak of the faith, the vision, tenacity of purpose, the accomplishments and hopes of the people who lived here, those who now live here and those who will live here in the future. They will stand for the sacrifices of the early settlers and their devotion to the ideal of liberty; they will stand as a testimony of our belief in education as the true emancipator of the whole man – body, mind, spirit. The Centennial Monument will ever remain a bridge between the first century and the second, and a solemn reminder to keep faith with those who made this bold beginning and bequeathed to us this heritage. The Antoinette Tubman Community School will stand as a symbol to dispel the light of ignorance and offer a challenge to all who will knock at its doors. What is more, we hope that the church and school, the greatest social and civilizing agencies, will bequeath to all the traditions of faith and education to make us lovers of freedom and religion, and patriots of our nation, and to give us instruments by and with which we shall aspire to nobler heights. Mute as they are, these memorials will re-assert themselves over and over in our daily affairs, and will always remind us of the courage, patriotism, devotion and faith of those we honour today.

May you, the descendants of those valorous souls who have gone before, inherit their vision, their perspicacity, their patriotism and all of the qualities in breadth, height, depth and length that fitted them for the great task assigned to them and which they so nobly performed. It is fitting that on such occasions as this we stop to ponder some of the great ideals that must have motivated their thoughts and led them to positive actions.

1. Those men and women were conscious and proud of their rôle as *Homo Sapiens,* not of their identification with an inferior race. They performed so well that the colour of their skins was quite forgotten.
2. Those men and women were individuals, who never wavered in their determination to succeed, and to found a new and better approach to a life of happiness and safety.
3. Those men and women were uncompromising in their stand for liberty and justice, and they worked unceasingly to demonstrate, by their lives and actions, the principles which they were convinced would stand them in good stead at any bar of justice.
4. They were willing and ready to face fearful odds and displayed great courage and greatness of soul at all times.
5. They were creative geniuses who always extolled the dignity of labour and achieved by their labour and toil what they did not possess in talent.
6. They practised their religion and lived their education. To them religion was the mainstay of their entire life; to them education was the acquisition of knowledge for its own sake – to enrich the soul and to learn to be free and wise individuals in a free society.

These are some of the attributes which your forefathers possessed, which they used in the service of the nation they loved so well and for which they made costly sacrifices.

What about your moral and civic responsibilities to the momory of those who once lived here and whose descendants many of you are? Crozerville was once a booming settlement where many useful industries were carried on; it was a community from which many stalwart characters hailed; it was a settlement which had a proud history. What is going to be your moral and civic responsibility at the turn of this century, the beginning of the second? Let all of you find it in your hearts to resolve that you will face the challenges of this century and thereby emulate and eventually surpass the achievements of the first century. Thus only will this centennial observance have a real and abiding significance and meaning for you and the nation.

These valiant men and women of the past had their problems; they wrestled and fought hard against doubts and fears; against intrigues, treacheries, subversion, battles, wars and death from within and without; but because their cause was just and right and because they had self-confidence, determination and reliance upon God, the only true and living God, they prevailed over the artifices and contrivances of their enemies.

THE AFRICAN SCENE

We today are cumbered with tremendous loads of care, threatening and subversive ideologies which declare that the whole world must be dominated by a single ideology, and that through this sole ideology all Africa must become a single state with a Union Government.

We are confronted with the open declarations of revolutionary governments and policies. The continent of Africa, by our joint and concentrated fight against colonialism, has been virtually liberated, except for some territories held by the Union Government of South Africa and the Salazar Government of Portugal, and we in this era are fighting with might and main to liberate these remaining areas of the continent.

We believe that the principal aim of developing countries is the search for a better life for their peoples, by a quest for modernization, so that the dignity of man can be apparent. In this search there may be different paths to be chosen. We believe further that each country has a right to a free choice of the path it wishes to take, whether it be what we might term the traditional-liberal philosophy, the Marxist-socialist philosophy, a mixture of the two or any other philosophy or system.

We do not believe, however, that any country has a right to impose its choice on any other country or group of countries by subversion, assassination or force.

The question naturally arises, what are the aims and purposes of further revolutions? Against whom are they directed? This must be made clear, or otherwise those who do not accept this warped ideological theory, in their own interest and for their own safety, must organize, and see that no Union Government of Africa or any other system of Government is forced upon them in derogation of and against a system of their own choosing.

Then there is the question of the allegations and charges made by some African States of the setting up of institutions in other African States for tutoring and training people for subversion and murder.

We have always been and will always be proponents and advocates of African unity, but mere verbal and written tributes to unity can never achieve it. Besides, peace and harmony are the strength of all institutions, particularly political ones. Interference in the domestic affairs of other states, no matter how much stealth, cunning and devious means are employed, have never created or sustained unity. Therefore, we maintain that if charges are made by one African State against another, or by any group of African States against any other group of states, these charges should be disposed of and not ignored, especially if they suggest or allege threats to the life of Chiefs of State and the overthrow of the government of a sister state.

To ignore or treat with indifference declarations of revolution as an instrument of national policy or the training of saboteurs and bandits for any purpose whatever could be suicidal, and I appeal to all African States to be watchful, to organize and prepare against the day of reckoning, when states which are accumulating large concentrations of arms, equipment and accoutrements of war may unleash them, lest we die the death of Abner – as a fool dieth.

Already an African Chief of State has been brutally murdered; this is history. Others have been overthrown by *coups d'état*; an assassination attempt in public was levelled against another less than two months ago. These are facts of current history. There have also been cases of subversion in the attempted overthrow of African States by other African States and the culprits have been apprehended, tried and convicted under the laws of that state. Some African States have jointly declared that they will support rebels against a sister African State that has been recognized by the Organization of African unity. These are also facts of current history and we have done nothing to condemn these wrongs, not even to speak out against them.

To maintain the unity that we sought to establish at Addis Ababa would require the removal of all of these unprincipled, wicked and baneful tendencies, threats and practices from among our ranks: otherwise we shall have no alternative but to pursue a course that would seem in the best interest of those who do not adopt revolution as an instrument of national policy, or the doctrine that the whole world must subscribe to one ideology of socialism or communism or to a Union Government of Africa. Men should be left free to eke out such a way of life as seems to them suitable and in their best interest.

Let the events of this day, and the inspiration which we shall receive, arouse in us a greater measure of patriotism to contribute our share to an even greater extent than did those before us for the peace, perpetuity, security and safety of the state. Let us close our ranks more than ever before in the unfinished tasks before us in this settlement and in this nation. Together let us take up the challenge to make this nation truly united, free, happy, prosperous and strong in the things which make a nation great.

Speech made during the Presentation of Resolutions to President Tubman by the Women's Political Movement of Liberia

Monrovia 5 August 1965

We must be particularly interested in people.

Introductory Note

The emancipation of the women of Liberia by President Tubman was a major contribution to Liberian democracy. For this act he won their gratitude which they renewed at the polls every four years. The President's unusual tenure in office was the result, in a large measure, of his political reforms, from which the women of Liberia and the citizens of Liberia's four new counties (Bong, Gedeh, Loffa, Nimba) were the greatest beneficiaries. He thanked the women for their resolutions and gave a brief history of his attempts to win suffrage for them as citizens of Liberia.

Monrovia, 5 August 1965

I MUST apologize for the absence of Mrs. Tubman because of her bereavement, and offer regrets on my own part because I am ill. I have been suffering from 'flu for the past four days.

I am reminded of an old Militia Officer who came from America but lived on Immigrant Hill in Cape Palmas. We used to start drilling at about half-past five in the morning when I was a young soldier in the Army. At times during the drilling some of us fellows would misbehave in line. One morning the old soldier shouted at us, 'now, young men, behave ... behave yourselves this morning. I am sick. I just took a dose of blue mass from the massy, and I have got no business out here this morning.'

Well, I too, have no business out here today because, as I said, I am ill. But I could not refuse or disregard the command of the women of the country to come and meet them.

Here today I note for the first time and with great satisfaction that everyone joined in the singing of our National Anthem. I first observed it being done in this manner in Sweden where everybody joined in singing the National Anthem whether it was performed by band, orchestra or in any other way. And I must congratulate you.

The times in which we live have changed and are rapidly changing. Today, people think differently from what they thought yesterday. The attitudes of men and women are vastly different today from what they were the day before yesterday. The actions of people are also different. To get along, and to move in and out among the people of this day and of this age, to govern

281

them, to advise them, to have them understand you and you understand them, requires a great amount of almost daily re-examination, re-assessment, and re-adjustment of thought, policies, and action.

You have referred to the benefits which the women of our nation have received from this Administration. I remember that at the National Convention of the True Whig Party, when I was first nominated, I suggested that female suffrage be made part of the platform of the Party for that election. I wrote it in my outline of policies; the Convention turned it down, it would not approve it. At the first meeting of the Legislature, after the inauguration, I recommended this same programme to the Legislature and stated that it was iniquitous and immoral to deprive some citizens, because of sex, of the rights of suffrage and every other privilege guaranteed other citizens, in spite of the fact that those deprived are required to pay taxes and to make other contributions. The Legislature approved the recommendation and passed the Act. The Act was put to the people through a referendum, and they adopted it.

At the first Executive Committee meeting of the True Whig Party thereafter, there was a vote of censure proposed against me for having violated the decision of the National Convention of the True Whig Party. That failed.

This proves that I was not the only one who worked for the granting of female suffrage; every member of the Legislature also worked, because there was not a 'Nay' vote cast. Every citizen of our country also did his part, because there was not a 'Nay' vote cast in the adoption of the constitutional amendment granting the women of Liberia the rights of suffrage.

So, it was the True Whig Party, and the men of this nation who extended this great courtesy to you.

As for me, I believe in people. I believe in men, I believe in women; I believe in boys, I believe in girls; I believe that every living person is entitled to the same rights and privileges and benefits from our nation as any other citizen. I believe in the eternal principle enunciated and declared by our Constitution: 'All men are born equally free and independent – all men – and have certain natural, inherent and inalienable rights among which are the rights to acquire and defend property and so on.'

'All men are born equally free and independent.' The term 'men' as used in the Constitution is generic. It means men, women, every living individual.

That is the basis of our free enterprise system of government. Every man and every woman are equal. The only thing that makes the difference between men in the eyes of our Constitution is their ability to work, to develop, to acquire, and to pursue. In the pursuit of these things, some men acquire more than others in one respect; other men acquire more than others in other respects. Some men have the benefit of political advancement and preferment, while others do not. That does not make the man who has political preferment necessarily better than the other fellow. For there are men who have no political status at all (or a very little of it, if any) but are more honourable or as honourable as the man who wears the highest political toga. There are men who acquire great wealth, which does not make them more honourable than those men who are paupers and who own nothing. There are men possessing nothing, or very little, who are honourable or often more honourable than men who own great wealth.

Thus has God made all the people of the earth, and we must be particularly interested in people. By people, I mean the masses, not the classes. The classes can more or less take care of themselves. It is the masses that need the help of classes.

Man is given power. He can utilize that power to destroy, to defeat, and even to kill, both politically and physically. I do not believe in killing politically, nor otherwise. It becomes necessary in politics to fight, but I believe in being on the defensive. I have said, and I repeat here today, that I challenge any man or any woman in this country to assert truthfully that I have ever started a fight with him or her. I do not fight aggressive political battles. I believe in fighting defensive battles.

Now, when I attack politically, knowing that the position you have given me carries a considerable amount of influence and power, I do not believe in striking back the first time. There must be two or three offences and attacks before I start a fight; and when I start to fight I fight hard and long enough only to subdue the enemy, not to kill him. And if I am successful in subduing him, and he leaves me alone, I am always prepared to try to restore him and to put him back on his feet.

That is the kind of politics that I believe in; not destructive – but constructive, keeping uppermost in view the safety of the state.

If you have a people who is impotent, cringing, weak and frail, you have that kind of a nation – for that is the same way they represent the state. The people represent the nation, and the kind of people you have indicates the kind of nation you have. You cannot have a weak, unprogressive, nonchalant, indifferent mass of people as citizens, and then expect to have a strong, progressive state.

Therefore, I believe in the individual dignity of a person and the free enterprise system of government, but not in the system of government where the Government controls everything, where one has only what the Government wants one to have, and where one's action and every movement is watched by the Government.

These are some of the principles for which our country stands and in which our forefathers believed, and in which I know that we believe. These principles have carried us through 118 years of great difficulties and troubles, and will still carry us onward.

When I entered this room and saw all of these ladies, I thought of the tremendous battle in which Sisera and Deborah engaged in the old days of Israel. During my visit to Israel, I was particularly attracted by what I saw when I visited the old battle grounds. I saw the hill upon which Sisera stood, and the hill upon which Deborah stood; and the vast fields over which the battle was fought. It is recorded that the stars in their courses fought against Sisera for Deborah. Now, when I see all of you here this evening, I know that even the stars in their courses will fight for your cause.

Whatever this Administration has done, or whatever you consider I may have done, for you has been doubly repaid, so that you owe me nothing. I consider your demonstration here today as 'interest' because the 'principal' has been paid. If you keep on this way it will accumulate and it will become 'compound interest'. I thank you very much.

I like the tone of your resolution; it is unique. I have had the pleasure of beginning to learn the aspirations and ambitions of the Liberian women. At a similar affair in Bassa a few months ago, the lady who spoke for the Bassa women said, 'We are demanding a fifty-fifty representation in the Legislature.' That is what the Bassa women want. Now, according to the statement made here today, all the women of the country want representations not only in the Legislature but also in the Cabinet and in the Foreign Service. I think they are entitled to it.

I shall keep under consideration your request for unlimited terms of office, which would mean a lifetime in the Presidency. But you know that there is danger in that course of action. It is a very uncertain and dangerous thing for a man to die in office as President. A man who is President must have some enemies, because he has to disappoint some people. He has to encounter jealousy and all that sort of thing. Now, if he dies in office he leaves his family and children behind. The minute he dies another man has to be declared President. The family of the deceased have to survive and do the best they can. With kings it is different: kings can afford to die as kings because they know that if they die as kings, their sons or daughters will reign in their stead.

Notwithstanding all these facts, ours is a democratic and republican form of government, and we cannot pursue a policy to make any man President for life, or to make any man king. We must maintain our democratic form of government. We must do no act that would tend to do away with our democratic form of government.

In closing, I wish to say that I noticed how the Master of Ceremonies referred to the assistance you received from friends and supporters. I, too, express thanks and appreciation. I am overwhelmed, for I cannot understand how you did all these things without costing me a penny. This kind of love and affection is the kind which the Apostle Paul refers to in the phrase that he pronounced: 'Oh to know the love of God that passeth knowledge.' And I say 'Oh to know the love of the women and people of Liberia, for me that passeth my understanding!' Thank you very much.

Speech of President Tubman to the Liberian National Guard

Monrovia, 5 February 1965

I call upon and command you in the name of the Republic, and in the interest of the service to which you belong, to remain constant and resolute as becomes a good soldier, for upon your proper behaviour depends the safety, perpetuity and security of your country, its people and their liberties.

Introductory Note

Towards the end of 1965 and early in 1966 the armies of several African states seized power. As Commander-in-Chief of the Liberian Army it was the duty of President Tubman to call the attention of our army to the dangers of what appeared to be a contagion, and he admonished the enlisted men of their responsibilities in defence of our liberties, in the maintenance of internal peace and security, and as a bulwark against aggression. The army of Liberia must be above reproach and true to the record which it had set for itself and had followed since the beginning of our history.

Monrovia, 5 February 1966

ATTENTION!

World history shows that great nations have risen because they possessed a lucrative economy backed by a strong and powerful army; that nations have fallen for want of a flourishing economy and stable military leadership. In the event of industrial, social and political development every army has two primary rôles to play: to maintain law and order in the internal affairs of the state under constituted legal authority, and to protect the country against external agression. There is still a third function which some armies have been known to perform, and that is to expand their country's territory by predetermined illegal, undiplomatic, immoral and destructive irruption and acquisition.

Even in our own day and time, evidence of interference by inspired and encouraged subversion in the internal affairs of states by other states is rampant, as well as the overthrow of governments by force, through devious means, and in most cases against the will of the majority of the people, with a view of establishing upon their ruin systems of government of their own likeness and kind, contrary to and in violation of the Charter of the United Nations, the Charter of the Organization of African Unity and all principles of International Law and morality. Liberia will maintain the *status quo*, remain loyal and faithful to her obligations under the provisions of the Charters of the United Nations and the Organization of African Unity and the principles of International Law and morality by meticulously administering its own affairs and leaving the legitimate affairs of others to themselves.

Today, nations in quest of peace have adopted varying measures for its attainment, but most of their efforts have failed because of inordinate ambitions and extreme individual nationalism with a disregard for the rights of others and for international social justice. In view of these circumstances, the importance of an army for the defence of a nation and for the maintenance of peace within its borders cannot be over-emphasized. The army and all other arms of military service are essentially necessary to withstand aggression and to preserve internal peace and security. I am pleased that the Liberian Army throughout its history has consistently performed the rôle natural to it with fortitude, intrepidity and honour, thereby establishing a decent and glorious record for you and future generations to emulate.

Every soldier has a grave responsibility and is unconditionally obligated and constrained to fulfil the provisions of the oath upon which he was admitted into the army; his honour, faithfulness, devotion, steadfastness, watchfulness and loyalty to the state and the Commander-in-Chief must be uncontrovertible, unquestionable and beyond suspicion. He must be a bulwark and model of the courage, perseverance and fidelity which were the proud and honourable possessions of the soldiers comprising the army of this country from its incipiency, of those who lived, fought, bled and died to maintain our patrimony.

I call upon and command you in the name of the Republic and in the interest of the service to which you belong, to remain constant and resolute as becomes a good soldier, for upon your proper behaviour depends the safety, perpetuity and security of your country, its people and their liberties.

God sustain, make noble and strong the army and save the state.

To the Nation on the 154th Anniversary of the Birthday of Joseph Jenkins Roberts

Monrovia, 15 March 1966

Every Liberian, every African, has a golden history of which he can be proud. But his real pride must rest upon the strongest conviction of his life — that he will continue to advance to a nobler destiny the great cause of nationalism and patriotism so ably initiated and carved with pure and valiant hearts.

Introductory Note

The anniversary of the birthday of the first President of Liberia, Joseph Jenkins Roberts, is one of Liberia's national holidays. Further it is an occasion to pay homage to the early fathers of our nation, to be reminded of the trials of those early times when they lived, and to resolve to follow their noble footsteps. President Tubman in this message spoke about those early times in our nation's growth. But the situation prevailing in Africa in his own time equally engaged his thoughts. He denounced the overthrow of legally constituted governments by subversion, and prayed for the peace of Liberia, Africa and the world. Uppermost in his mind was his concern for the preservation of our national heritage, which had been transmitted unimpaired to Liberians of the twentieth century.

Monrovia, 15 March 1966

THE HISTORY of Liberia records today, March 15, 1966, as the 154th anniversary of the birth of Joseph Jenkins Roberts and the 119th year of his election and inauguration as the first President of our Republic. We observe this day with ever-increasing veneration, reverence and hallowed deference for the gift by God of this great patriot and statesman, the father of our nation.

It is a cherishing and inspiring opportunity to pause for a moment and reflect on the unfolding events, conditions and circumstances under which President Roberts and his gallant associates laid the foundation for the development of these territories from commonwealth to nationhood, with liberty and justice for all.

A comparative study will reveal that the issues, thoughts and universal attitudes of today differ from those of the Roberts epoch. Then, there was the slave, gold, guinea and spice trade; now, there is trade in iron ore, rubber and timber. Then, there were the colonial expansionist and exploitationist movements; now, there is cultural and ideological warfare. Then, there were the colonies and protectorates; now, there have emerged independence and sovereignty for most peoples of the earth, particularly Africa. Then, there was gunboat and sword-rattling diplomacy; now, there are underground and subversive techniques. Then, there were cannons and conventional weapons; now, there are nuclear and atomic missiles and other implements for mass destruction. Then, there were individual and national rivalries and now there is complex co-operation and diversity. And so from year to year, man's problems would seem to change upon the principle of elimination by substitution.

President Roberts and his courageous and stout-hearted associates boldly faced the problems of their age and time with miraculous effectiveness, and guided the nation and its people through many perilous crises. Upon us in our day and generation have fallen the tremendous and complex problems that plague, not only our own country and Africa, but the world, and we must stand up to them, not with bellicosity and loquacity, but with calm, well considered analytical or deductive reasoning rather than subjective or inductive reasoning, thinking like men of action and acting like men of thought.

Removed from the colonial cycle to that of the liberation of Africa, we stand on an entirely different plane from that of our forefathers, and our decisions and actions may well spell out the weal or woe not only of our respective countries but of the whole of Africa and of black men everywhere. What a momentous responsibility; a responsibility so involved that it does not admit of rash, hasty, extremist or violent thought and action.

The changes which have taken place in Africa within the last decade have moved over the face of this continent with hurricane velocity, and hitherto subject and colonial territories have been brought into nationhood and sovereignty with an amazingly limited amount of bloodshed and wars. The colonialists seemed to have recognized their untenable position, and in the great majority of cases not only robed their colonial possessions with the toga of independence but invited them into their commonwealth and community. Some of them have accepted the invitation; in other instances some offered to become themselves a part of these commonwealths and communities. Now, all of Africa, with the exception of the so-called Portuguese territories, South Africa, South West Africa, Rhodesia, and a few other places, enjoys the benefits and privileges of free men.

After such a rapid sweep from colonialism to independent status, it would seem advisable, in the interest of caution and stability, that we consolidate our positions, and not over-stretch our supply lines before obtaining understanding for ourselves and creating a climate conducive to friendship, brotherhood and unity by deeds and not by words. We need to realize that people who have borne the pains and anguish of servitude and slavery are naturally sensitive, and the change-over from colonial servitude to independence imposes the necessity for great care in the political administration of government in relation to the members of society which we call citizens.

We in Liberia have always been and must always be opposed to *coups d'état* and the overthrow of the Government through violence. As our Constitution provides, we believe that 'all power is inherent in the people and that theirs is the right to meet and consult upon the public good, to require those vested with authority to return to private life when they think that their peace and happiness demands it, and even to change their form of government should they desire'. But this is the right of the people and of the people only, and must be done in an orderly and peaceable manner.

The Liberian Constitution states further, that in time of peace armies are dangerous to liberty and the military must be kept in direct subordination to civil authority. When armies are promoted to the first place in civil administration and become the instrument by which an administration is kept in power, the army then realizes that it is not the will of the people that maintains and sustains civil administration but its own force and might, and the stability of any form of administration may become endangered.

It is regrettable that we in Africa, having been blessed by God with the precious gift of religious freedom and civil liberties, should embark upon policies of subversion and interference in the affairs of African and other states, and design the overthrow of government through youth movements, unions, and military operations, thereby imposing dictatorial régimes of our own invention. How can we expect not to reap what we sow? How do we expect to engage in the overthrow and murder of our colleagues of sister states and not expect the same thing to happen to us sooner or later? It has been said, 'the Adzes of the Gods grind slowly but surely'; therefore we who, as Chiefs of State and Government, live in glass houses should not throw stones. When these things occur we cry out that this is the work of the imperialist, the colonialist and the neo-colonialist, but we fail to realize that most invariably it is our own reckless actions and attitude towards the people that has brought on the disaster.

We cry 'African Unity'; we greet each other with a warm handshake and a kiss on both sides of the cheek and at the same time we carry a dagger in our hand to stab in the back those we kiss, bent on their assassination, the overthrow of their government and the destruction of their people. Can we expect to sow coconuts and reap bananas?

In less than a decade we have witnessed over a dozen *coups d'état* on the continent of Africa, and should the present trend continue, it is not difficult to predict the outcome. Africa has witnessed the attainment of independence by most of her peoples, but unless we live up to the high standards of equality, justice and liberty for all alike, and adhere to the Charters of the United Nations and the Organization of African Unity, we shall become frustrated and confused, and usher in the dawn of a reign of terror and chaos more baneful and destructive than the colonial period.

In my opinion, we should at this time do stock-taking and make an analysis of conditions in Africa today, with a view to ascertaining the cause or causes of these repeated and recurring *coups d'état* and overthrow of governments, because these are the symptoms and not the disease. It is only when we find the cause that we will be able to treat the disease and provide a remedy.

It would appear necessary for us to devote our time to the development of our respective countries, assisting each other whenever we can, developing our economies and improving the structure of our respective political administrations and not undertake to remake the world, or carry the continent on our shoulders. We do not have the strength, the ability nor the competence, individually or collectively to carry such a load. It is too heavy, it will crush us.

Every Liberian, every African, has a golden history of which he can be proud. But his real pride must rest upon the strongest conviction of his life — that he will continue to advance to a nobler destiny the great cause of nationalism and patriotism so ably initiated and carved with pure and valiant hearts.

Finally, my fellow citizens, let us continue to be imbued with the high principles upon which this nation was founded, the principles of democracy, tolerance, patriotism, sacrifice and faith in God. Let us realize that every nation has the right to choose its own form of government without hindrance from others, and no matter what others may do, let us not be tempted to do evil. I adjure you in the words of the Psalmist, as recorded in the 37th Psalm:

FRET not thyself because of evildoers, neither be thou envious against the workers of iniquity.

FOR they shall soon be cut down like the grass, and wither as the green herb.

TRUST in the LORD, and do good; so shalt thou dwell in the land, and verily thou shalt be fed.

DELIGHT thyself also in the LORD; and he shall give thee the desires of thine heart.

COMMIT thy way unto the LORD; trust also in him; and he shall bring it to pass.

AND he shall bring forth thy righteousness as the light, and thy judgment as the noonday.

REST in the LORD, and wait patiently for him: fret not thyself because of him who prospereth in his way, because of the man who bringeth wicked devices to pass.

CEASE from anger, and forsake wrath: fret not thyself in any wise to do evil.

FOR evildoers shall be cut off: but those that wait upon the LORD, they shall inherit the earth.

FOR yet a little while, and the wicked shall not be: yea, thou shalt diligently consider his place and it shall not be.

BUT the meek shall inherit the earth; and shall delight themselves in the abundance of peace.

THE wicked plotteth against the just, and gnasheth upon him with his teeth.

THE LORD shall laugh at him; for he seeth that his day is coming.

THE wicked have drawn out the sword, and have bent their bow, to cast down the poor and needy and to slay such as be of upright conversation.

THEIR sword shall enter into their own heart, and their bows shall be broken.

A LITTLE that a righteous man hath is better than the riches of many wicked.

FOR the arms of the wicked shall be broken: but the LORD upholdeth the righteous.

THE LORD knoweth the days of the upright: and their inheritance shall be for ever.

THEY shall not be ashamed in the evil time: and in the days of famine they shall be satisfied.

BUT THE wicked shall perish, and the enemies of the LORD shall be as the fat of lambs: they shall consume; into smoke shall they consume away . . .

MARK the perfect man, and behold the upright: for the end of that man is peace.

BUT the transgressors shall be destroyed together: the end of the wicked shall be cut off.

BUT the salvation of the righteous is of the LORD: he is their strength in the time of trouble.

AND the LORD shall help them, and deliver them: he shall deliver them from the wicked, and save them, because they trust in him.

To the Nation on his return from State Visits to the Republics of Togo and Dahomey

Monrovia, 7 May 1966

If all the leaders of Africa work in concert and close communication with each other, utilizing their energies in calm judgment, we can give Africa decisive and effective leadership.

Introductory Note

President Tubman's visit to the Republics of Togo and Dahomey was undertaken at a propitious time. He met several African leaders besides those of Togo and Dahomey, and discussed matters affecting the tranquillity of Africa – matters which aroused their mutual fears and concern for the future of Africa. The year 1966 was one of *coups d'état* in Africa, and in those nations adjacent to Liberia, border warfare was imminent. The President was a successful mediator in this dispute. He had always encouraged good principles of neighbourliness between Liberia and her neighbours. His visit gave him added incentive to push his Operation Production Programme at home, and he outlined in this speech the way in which increased production could be effected. The emphasis was again on increased agricultural production. But the speech itself is a significant economic document, well planned and tending more than ever towards the successful execution of certain basic objectives, which he painstakingly outlines.

Monrovia, 7 May 1966

YOU KNOW that we left the Capital by air on the 25th of April, 1966 on State Visits to the Republics of Togo and Dahomey, in response to invitations extended to us.

En route to Togo, we made a transit stop at the Ivory Coast to meet and talk with His Excellency President Houphouet Boigny. Upon our arrival in Abidjan, cheering crowds lined the route from the airport to the Palace, and the people danced and clapped hands to the charming tunes of typical African drums, horns and other musical instruments.

Had we been making a State Visit to the Ivory Coast, there could have been no greater outburst of enthusiasm or welcome. Upon our arrival at the Palace we were accorded a most sumptuous and palatable luncheon. Thereafter the President and I held discussions on the world situation, and the African scene in particular, with special reference to the Ivory Coast–Guinea dispute. The President assured me that within two days thereafter all Ivory Coast troops would be withdrawn from the Guinea border, but upon my arrival in Lomé, I received a telephone call from him, telling me that there had been a border clash which made it impracticable for him to carry out his promise. I immediately sent telegrams to him and President Touré urging them not to permit this incident to cause a further rift between them but to endeavour to settle it by the peaceful means provided either by the Charters of the OAU or the United Nations. Ending our brief transit visit through Abidjan we took flight for Lomé, Togo and after ninety minutes our plane landed safely upon the airfield at Lomé where we found ourselves once more upon terra firma. His Excellency President Grunitzky, members of his Government, members of the Diplomatic Corps and thousands of Togolese from all walks of life welcomed us while students lined the route from the airport to the Palace – cheering and waving Togolese and Liberian flags in the brightly decorated city of Lomé. Before going to the Palace we were ushered into a special religious service at the Salem Methodist Church in Lomé, held under the auspices of the Protestant Episcopal, Presbyterian and Methodist Churches. The edifice was packed to capacity, crowds stood outside, echoes of trumpets blended with the majestic choir whose voices resounded in clear and persuasive melody. We were very impressed with the religious attitude of the Togolese people.

In Togo we visited many places of interest, amongst them the old German and French Colonial settlements, including an Agricultural Experimental Station at Clidji, a Hospital, the Lycée University College, the new port being constructed and a phosphate mining plant, where we were particularly impressed with the extraordinary care taken in preserving the top soil of the mining area, which is replaced after removing the phosphate. In this way the subsequent utilization of the soil for agricultural purposes is not wasted.

We had the pleasure of meeting a number of Liberians who are resident in Togo, some of whom migrated there as early as 1902; as well as the families and relatives of many Togolese resident in Liberia. In this way we found that the sharing of citizenship between the two countries has strong and fascinating historical roots in the culture and traditions of our two nations.

Our visit was timed to coincide with the Togolese Sixth Independence Celebration which afforded us the unusual opportunity of participating with President Grunitzky in the lighting of the torch of Liberty and Independence and in witnessing President Grunitzky decorate the Togolese Flag with the highest order of the country, after which the flag was turned over to the Army for safe and secure care and keeping.

We were tenderly touched by the genuine feeling of friendship and hospitality accorded us by the people of Togo everywhere we went. After four full days of engagements, inspections, sightseeing, discussions, feasting and decision-making, as appeared in the communiqué issued at the termination of our visit, we departed from Togo with feelings of satisfaction that our visit had been fruitful, and had opened new potentialities for closer and more effective co-operation between our two countries.

We were very happy to visit Dahomey, because we had, over the years, developed some belief in and appreciation for the glorious history and effervescent culture of the ancient kingdoms of that state. We were not disappointed in our search for this treasure island, because what we had read and heard about Dahomey from childhood days was verified as relics of the traditional culture and ritualistic civilization still exist, honoured, revered, venerated and preserved.

Our first contact with this rich culture was in the city of Porto-Novo which represents the cradle of Dahomeyan antiquity in arts, crafts, industry, relics, and artefacts.

Last Sunday, after worshipping at the Bethel Methodist Church in Cotonou, Mrs. Tubman, Mrs. Soglo and other members of the party visited the lake city of Ganvie – the Venice of Africa; while President Soglo and I remained at the Palace for an exchange of views on various problems of common interest.

The following day we toured Ouidah (Weedah) city which is particularly characterized by the snake culture, the sacred totems and fetish mysticisms. Historic d'Abomey is another city of kings dating as far back as the tenth through the eighteenth centuries. One of the most notable things about the Dahomeyans, is that in spite of all the impact of Western civilization and European influences, including Christianity, the people of Dahomey have succeeded in preserving their native culture, traditions and animism. From what we have seen we think it is necessary for us to preserve our Liberian culture and undertake new initiatives in this direction.

We extended President Soglo an invitation to make a State Visit to Liberia, which he accepted. Thus we ended our sojourn in Dahomey, bringing away with us many impressions of the great work which the people of this country have done through the years. We boarded the Presidential Yacht M.Y. *Liberian* and sailed homeward.

The National Liberation Council of Ghana extended us an invitation to make a transit stop in Accra, which we gladly accepted. We were received by the Council, Government and people of Ghana with great warmth and wild enthusiasm. The Chairman and members of the National Liberation Council, Chiefs, members of the Administrative Committee and the Ghanaian people shouted loud cheers with the special slogan 'Freedom and Justice! Freedom and Justice!' There were thousands of people on both sides of the streets as we drove from Tema to Christianburg Castle where after discussions and talks with the members of the National Liberation Council we were guests at an elaborate luncheon with members of Government and Diplomatic Corps, members of the Clergy and high ranking military officers, civil leaders, paramount chiefs and their wives.

We found the people of Ghana apparently very happy. Business seemed to be normal. There was no unusual appearance of soldiers, police or military forces in sight. Those whom we met expressed hope for the improvement of economic conditions in their country.

The Liberian Government assumed the position that the recent occurrences in Ghana were the internal affairs of the Ghana Government and people, not of any outsiders, and that since the present Government of Ghana had met the requirements of the principles of international law governing the recognition of states we extended it both *de facto* and *de jure* recognition.

General Ankrah and other members of the Administrative Committee showered great courtesies upon us during our brief stop over, and offered us two corvettes of their Navy to escort the M.Y. *Liberian* from Cotonou, Dahomey, to Tema, Ghana and from Tema to Monrovia – a very great act of friendship on the part of the Ghanaian Government which we and, I am sure, you the people of Liberia, greatly appreciate.

Our brief transit stop in Ghana thus ended, we embarked again on the yacht and continued our journey homeward.

On Friday we interrupted our voyage to stop at Cape Palmas, Maryland

County for the purpose of meeting old friends and relatives, which we greatly enjoyed.

THE INTERNATIONAL SITUATION

In my discussions with President Houphouet Boigny, President Grunitzky, General Soglo and General Ankrah, we shared a community of views on the problems of Africa. It is our belief that if all the leaders of Africa work in concert and close communication with each other, utilizing their energies in calm judgment, we can give Africa decisive and effective leadership.

I was particularly interested in an observation reported to have been made recently by my colleague, President Modibo Keita. He is reported to have said that the Organization of African Unity may become the laughing-stock of the world. I share President Keita's views.

I myself feel that too much power politics has been introduced into that body. Some delegations have often met secretly, determined certain rigid courses of action and, by power politics, attempted to force these upon the other members of the organization.

I believe the Organization of African Unity should be careful in its eagerness to prepare and give hasty approval to resolutions which are easily drafted, but difficult to implement. It is my considered opinion that, should this practice continue, it will bring discredit to the Organization and probably endanger its existence.

Here I must refer specifically to the resolution approved early this year by the Council of Ministers, which called upon Member States to sever diplomatic relations with the British Government within two weeks if that government had not undertaken military and other means to destroy the illegal régime of Ian Smith in Rhodesia.

It must have been apparent to the Council Ministers that it had no right either by the Charter or by the Heads of State to pass a resolution which only the Council or Heads of State could approve. It should have been equally apparent that it was illogical for that body to give an ultimatum of two weeks – a time limit in which a nation was being asked to undertake military preparation and military action, and achieve a military victory.

I have great confidence in the ultimate victory as well as the justice of our cause, but rash action, faulty thinking and power politics will never secure for the people of Africa the rights to which they are entitled.

OPERATION PRODUCTION

Liberians must primarily depend upon agriculture as their mainstay through the years. It was because of this that we initiated the Operation Production Programme. While this has had some success in an unprofessional and perfunctory manner, it cannot meet the urgent and pressing demands or requirements which must be met in order to enable us to support ourselves, live at home and board at the same place.

We therefore invited the Secretary of Agriculture to accompany us on this visit which, we believe, has been revealing, inspiring and instructional. Our Agricultural Programme must be professionally formulated so as to modernize and improve our agricultural productivity.

In this regard the Secretary of Agriculture advises that in keeping with earlier directives the National Development Programme is under review and construction. The plan calls for undertaking the Agricultural Development Programme in five stages so as to have the maximum impact on each stage, with resources in hand, before moving forward to the next stage.

The first project is the expanded rice programme, whereby approximately 1,000,000 acres of swamp rice, which would otherwise be lost, are expected to be brought into production. The second project is tree crops, where efforts will be directed to improving plant materials; improving management efficiency where rubber is concerned; and developing further the oil-palm and coffee industries as a counterbalance to the one export commodity – rubber. The third will be livestock, with all relating and supporting projects. Others include fruits and vegetables, and mapping, testing and analysing the soil.

The five-year agricultural programme, as being developed, provides for four agricultural development areas to be organized into co-operatives. Crop production will be the main activity but the economic living standard or condition of the population through co-operative effort should be raised across the country. The objective of the co-operative should be composed of health, social, and religious activities, so that along with economic development, the whole life pattern of living is improved.

We expect two experts to arrive shortly: one in Agricultural Co-operation and the other in Farm Credit Management, with a view to organizing the counties into agricultural co-operative districts.

I suggest that revenues for the support of this new National Agricultural Development Programme be provided by the levying of a modest tax on our export commodities such as coffee, oil-palm, cocoa, etc., the working out of the details of which will be referred to the appropriate fiscal experts. The Secretary of Agriculture has been notified concerning this matter and we expect greater impetus on agricultural production.

Again I must repeat what I said before. It is vitally important to re-emphasize the grave significance which a functional and diversified agricultural programme bears to the economic stability of any nation, be it large or small, strong or weak. The basic necessities of life which may be obtained from tilling the soil should and must be given high priority consideration in our national development programme. The first in the sequence should include the nutritive or edible commodities such as carbohydrates, vegetables and other such products. The second should comprise the vegetable products such as rubber, cocoa, coffee, oil-palm, piassava, and others of similar classification. The third category which may be considered a rather short-range type of economic commodity, includes forest products and the like.

Sooner or later our iron ore, diamond, and gold resources may be depleted. Sooner or later our timber and ivory resources may become exhausted and extinct. With the rise of synthetic industries and the concomitant fall in the prices of natural products or raw materials, it may be expected that rubber, cocoa and coffee, which depend upon world markets, may not yield profitable economic returns sufficient to cover adequately the minimum operational costs. This we have already experienced.

This nation must therefore strive toward a self-sufficient and self-sustaining economy if it is to keep pace with other advanced and advancing nations. The first step in this direction is the increased agricultural production of indigenous commodities. This nation must foresee these eventualities and plan for them in sufficient time to meet the critical and challenging circumstances which lie ahead. This nation must seize every opportunity to build the economic foundations upon which true freedom, justice, and the principles of democracy may abound and prosper.

I wish to express my sincere thanks and deep appreciation to the Secretary of State and Cabinet with the assistance and co-operation of the Vice-President, Speaker, and people of this country, for the able manner in which they co-operated as one family unit in administering the affairs of state during my absence from the country. This is a further manifestation of the loyalty, devotion and confidence which you have shown in this Administration, because you, as well as I, feel and know that it is your Administration — it is our Administration.

Speech on his return from Zürich, Switzerland

Monrovia, 1 October 1966

Let us continue our national race in pursuit of constitutional democracy; keep to the even tenor of our course and not be beguiled or deceived by any new language.

Introductory Note

It became customary for our National Legislature to grant President Tubman annual periods of rest, and he often went to Switzerland for a vacation and in the interest of his health. On this occasion while he was away, he was informed about the near occurrence of a *coup d'état* and urged to return home. He did not return, and was even annoyed that his rest period should be disturbed by such rumours. Eventually he returned, in good health, after having also made contacts in industrial relations for the co-ordination of all industrial activities in our country. A good deal of his attention was turned to the international scene in these remarks upon his return home.

Monrovia, 1 October 1966

AFTER ABOUT two months' absence we have today returned and are happily and deeply moved by the very warm, loyal and stimulating welcome you have extended to us. We are grateful to the clergy and to the religious people of the country for their constant prayers for the safety, progress, solidarity and prosperity of the nation. We also extend our deep gratitude to officials of Government at every level, the body of the people and the armed police, security and intelligence services for their patriotism, loyalty and invaluable services during our absence, and above all to God, the Eternal Source of Life, Inscrutable Wisdom and Perfect Power.

Our travels began on the 7th of August; we arrived in Zürich, Switzerland, on the 17th of that month and Mrs. Tubman and I started medical examinations and tests of many and varied kinds, which were performed with great efficiency and care. After Professor Doctor Loeffler, our chief physician, reported that we were in excellent health, we received many kind and thoughtful radiograms of congratulations. I would like however to point out that 'excellent health', and the Professor's statement that my health is as good or even better than it was when he first met me ten or twelve years ago is relative, considering my age. I have deemed it expedient to make this comment because I do not want to fool myself and undertake to do things that I did twelve years ago, thereby misinterpreting the Professor's statement, disappointing you and injuring myself. However, I do feel reasonably and relatively well, having lost a few pounds. I do believe, primarily, in preventive medicine.

As had been our usual practice, we extended invitations to a number of persons from various sections of the country to accompany us when we felt they were in need of specialized medical services. Most of them were in good health and required treatment for only minor ailments. Three of them had major operations. When northward bound one member of our suite had an miscarriage on board ship. All returned well and in apparent good health.

THE UNITED NATIONS

International crises seem to increase, loom larger and become more difficult with time. The Twenty-first Session of the General Assembly of the United Nations, that world forum organized and instituted for the benefit of unity, concord and brotherhood among men and nations, organized and instituted for the promotion of peace and the settlement of disputes arising among nations and peoples, met a few weeks ago enshrouded in uncertainty and virtual bewilderment. The choosing of a Secretary-General in succession to U Thant, because of his announcement that he will not stand for re-election, has imposed a problem that adds to the crucial conditions obtaining in and confronting that great organization. Let us hope that delegates will find a solution to these intricate and delicate problems.

THE ORGANIZATION OF AFRICAN UNITY

The Organization of African Unity is scheduled to meet in its Fourth Annual Session in Addis Ababa on the 5th of November this year, to deal with the difficulties and problems that confront it and threaten its very existence and survival. A large number of member states advocate a postponement of this Summit Meeting until next year. Until now, it has been claimed by some that a sufficient number of states have concurred in having the meeting in November to constitute a quorum, while others maintain that a quorum has not yet been obtained. Even if there is a quorum and this large number of objectors fail to attend, and although I am in favour of holding the meeting in November, more harm could be done by proceeding with it than by a postponement. Sometimes it becomes necessary for the majority to give serious consideration to a potent minority. This creates a problem.

THESE TIMES

Thoughtful men and nations cannot remain impervious to the wide swirl of mighty forces let loose upon the continuing life of free and democratic people and nations. The sanctity and sacredness of freedom, civil liberty, justice, right, religion and even the resting places of the dead are no longer considered as hallowed, and are violated and desecrated with ruthless impunity by newly rising human tides of unscrupulous truculence. Every age forms a bridge between that which preceded and that which follows it. This age in which we live is obviously and unquestionably an epoch called upon to deal with the unanticipated and unforseen problems of a revolutionized and new society, thrust upon it by fantastic scientific discoveries.

1 The Administrative Building, Sanniquellie, Nimba County

2 The Administrative Building, Gbanga, Bong County

3 The Temple of Justice

4 The Administrative Building, Voinjama, Loffa County

5 *The Unification Monument*

6 *The Executive Mansion*

7 *The Monument of Joseph Jenkins Roberts,
the first President of Liberia*

8 *The Walker-Faulkner Hydro Electric power plant at Mount Coffee*

Life today is surrounded by conditions and forces which have sprung up so suddenly and swiftly as to take it unawares. The tempo of modern life has been so accelerated that it has become difficult to condemn it, or even understand exactly what are its ultimate goals. Spiritual values are either denied and relegated to the gallery of fogyism or given away to materialism. For more than a decade the world has been passing through a period in which such forces have been particularly numerous and powerfully active.

As a result, *coups d'état*, subversion, treason, rebellion and wars are extant in different parts of the earth; all of them, though temporarily localized, show signs of possible expansion that could escalate into a global war. Viet Nam in Asia, Rhodesia in Africa, South West Africa, Portuguese African colonial administrations and South Africa's apartheid policy – all tend to retard or prevent the rule of law and peace on earth.

In this connection, I am prone to repeat a question asked in agony many centuries ago: 'Shall the sword devour forever?' This question has been heralded down through the ages and the relationship of man with man today seems the same if not worse than when this question 'shall the sword devour forever?' was first propounded. My answer is, yes; unless and until the nations and peoples of the earth resolve that they will no longer be governed by selfish ambition, but will in all things strive to love their neighbours as themselves and do unto others as they would others do unto them; unless and until individual nationalism and greed for power and world domination by traducing ideology, force and might be abolished; then, and only then, will the sword cease to devour.

Although a ray of hope appears when we consider the progress made by the rising tide of nationalism that has liberated approximately ninety per cent of the people of this continent and the breaking down of old barriers of racial discrimination, segregation, serfdom and slavery in various parts of the world, yet still the newly liberated nations and peoples are not left free to pursue their way of life and enjoy their well-earned freedom in peace and tranquillity; for they find themselves, like the rest of us, caught up in this tremendous swirl of subversion which adds to their difficulties in becoming adjusted as new nations.

We cannot stand aside and see ourselves and the world led to destruction without protesting or at least uttering a groan.

No sane person can deny that one of the crucial and fateful hours of human history is now upon the world. It has been remarked that: 'We are at both the end and the beginning of an age.' Only time can reveal the truth or falsity of this assumption, but even the most obtuse person is aware that in this epochal period the days and the weeks have the fullness and significance of years and of decades. The furnace of life seems to have been heated seven times hotter than ever, and into that furnace the ideals and institutions current in this testing moment of history have been poured. They are at present in molten form. It is our task to help draw them off into new moulds, and thus determine the shape of things to come.

The war in Viet Nam seems to be the most imminent threat to international peace, and there seems to be no question that the South Vietnamese people have become the subject of aggression and oppression. All peoples and nations should rally to the call for a settlement of this devastating conflict and bring peace to Viet Nam, and thereby to the world.

The policy of the Government of Liberia towards Rhodesia and South

West Africa as given in my last Independence Day Message still stands, and on the question of Rhodesia we look with great anticipation to the overthrow of the rebel régime in Rhodesia by the end of this year, in keeping with the communiqué issued by the Prime Minister of the British Commonwealth of Nations at their last meeting. In connection with South West Africa we look forward to the acceptance and implementation of the terms of the petition submitted to the United Nations by certain African and Asian states, requesting that this Organization take over the administration of South West Africa.

In dealing with the question of Rhodesia we have generally overlooked the tremendous sufferings, deprivations and hazards of the people of Zambia who have borne the baneful burden, the pains and the brunt of the repercussions of the vile policy of the rebel Government of Rhodesia. I hail and salute President Kaunda as a man of great courage, intrepidity, wisdom, good judgment, patience and patriotism, and I send to him, on behalf of the Government and people of Liberia, our congratulations and assurances of our support and admiration for him, his Government and people in their struggle against the onslaught of tyranny and injustice.

As an expression of our identity with them, we will make a contribution of fifty thousand dollars to him and his Government, as our widow's mite to assist them in such a manner as they may see fit. To the people of South Viet Nam who are fighting and dying in the struggle for the preservation of their sovereignty and liberty we donate fifty thousand dollars in coffee for the purchase of medical and hospital equipment to be utilized for the benefit of the sick, wounded and dying.

DISCUSSIONS WITH INDUSTRIALISTS AND FINANCIERS

Even though the leave of absence granted us by the Legislature was intended for health and rest we have been forced in the national interest, to devote most of our time abroad to discussions and negotiations with businessmen, financiers and industrialists. The result of these discussions is expected to attract additional investment in both the agricultural and industrial sectors of our economy. Details of these discussions and agreements, leading to their implementation, are now being worked out by our technicians in the Department of Planning and Economic Affairs.

One particular case of special interest and importance is the result of discussions held with Swiss and German industrialists and financiers, and culminating in the formation of a consortium consisting of Salzgitter Industreabu of Salzgitter, Germany, Motor-Columbus of Baden, Switzerland, and EDESCO of Zürich, Switzerland, to act as economic, industrial and investment consultants and promoters for the development of industrial and other economic activities in Liberia.

As part of these negotiations and upon the conclusion of an agreement, we were invited to visit the head offices of Motor-Columbus in Baden, Switzerland and Salzgitter, Germany, where we were most cordially received. The executives of these companies are due to arrive in Monrovia shortly, to establish offices and work out final details of their activities.

ECONOMIC AND FINANCIAL SITUATION

It has been reported that at the present meeting of the Board of Governors of the World Bank Mr. George Woods, President of the Bank, indicated that the proportion of aid from donor countries in relation to their economic prosperity has steadily declined over the last five years. This trend, he stated, arises at a time when the terms of raising loans for developing purposes by the primary producing countries are becoming more and more difficult.

We in Liberia must take immediate action to meet these financial and economic pressures, as in the words of the motto of the Congo Progressive Association in Liberia: 'Prop your banana trees, storms are coming.' We cannot remain indifferent to the circumstances of our times. Therefore, like other nations which have taken measures to protect their economies, recommendations will be made to the Legislature in support of the 1967 Budget. The objectives of these recommendations will be to avoid future financial crises and to remedy some of the errors in the 1966 Budget. To this end, while we do not contemplate any salary reduction, we will institute several economy measures which will include a cut in certain allowances and the creation of no new positions except those patently in the national interest.

On the revenue side, we must express our concern with the stagnation, and even reduction, in the collection of real estate taxes over the last five years. Those revenue officials responsible for the administration of these taxes are expected to show increases in collections over the last year by the end of 1966. In this connection, the Treasury Department is authorized to withhold further payment of salaries, rentals and claims to anyone in default of their real estate taxes.

It is our firm and earnest hope that all public servants, both in the Executive and the Judicial Branches of Government, responsible for the implementation and enforcement of the real estate tax legislation and collection will prove their mettle and loyalty in the discharge of their functions so as to avoid the arduous and unpleasant task of being charged with negligence of official duties.

In our Annual Message to the Legislature details of these financial and economic policies will be given and we crave your support for them.

OPERATION PRODUCTION

Three years ago we announced the Operation Production Policy aimed at and intended to increase production and improve the standard of products and commodities. This has had the co-operation and support of most of the people, but it has not yet progressed sufficiently to meet the purpose and intent of the scheme. We shall now embark, with new energy and greater intensity, upon the increase and the improvement of production in every field of national endeavour. During World War II an emergency was declared, and for a period of time there was double panel tapping for rubber throughout the country. We do not propose to suggest this at the present but should the necessity arise during this period of austerity, and if the downward trend in the price of rubber continues, we may have to come to this. At the moment, we urge all concessionaires and producers of rubber and rice to increase their production as a matter of national emergency. Iron ore concessionaires are requested also to increase their production and not to permit their interest in mines elsewhere, if they have any, to restrict the volume of production and sale of iron ore, particularly at this time of national and international economic and financial problems and of the falling market price for iron ore.

THE UNIFICATION AND INTEGRATION POLICY

The Unification and Integration Policy has been most effective and successful over the past twenty-four years. The old inter-tribal and internecine wars between tribe and tribe, and between tribes and Government have been non-existent. Unquestionably, the Unification and Integration Policy thus enunciated, pursued and demonstrated, is responsible for this happy condition. It is worthy of note that this policy was enunciated in 1944 when the administration first took office, which was before the universal upsurge of nationalism swept the continent of Africa and the world; and because the Unification and Integration Policy was not merely a matter of theory but actually demonstrated in practical terms, peace has prevailed throughout the nation and there is unity among all elements and sections of the country.

But the policy has not been completely demonstrated. It must have due and speedy implementation. The national census has just been completed and published and this requires consideration of representation in the Legislature in consonance with the Constitution and the census report. Recommendations concerning this will be made to the Legislature in our Annual Report.

Ending these remarks, let me leave with you the moral of a story of the hound and a cat. A hound was in full pursuit of a cat determined to destroy it; the race went on. The hound failed to catch the cat, then he mewed like a cat: m-e-e-o-o-w! The cat looked back but continued to run; the hound then the second time mewed louder: M-E-E-O-O-W! The cat attracted by this deception turned around and ran into the claws of the hound and the hound then declared: 'What a great advantage there is in strange and new languages.' Let us continue our national race in pursuit of Constitutional Democracy; keep to the even tenor of our course and not be guiled or deceived by any strange or new languages of M-E-E-O-O-W-S.

Speech at a Dinner held in Honour of the Forty-fifth Legislature

Monrovia, 10 October 1966

We enrol you; we draft you.

Introductory Note

When President Tubman addressed the Forty-fifth Legislature of Liberia, he directed the attention of the legislators and those present to matters peculiarly Liberian and particularly affecting national politics and policies. He further made a passing reference to reports of plans to overthrow the Government of Liberia which he had heard while abroad in the interest of his health, but which caused him no alarm, being confident of his own record as President and his people's own confidence in that record. The unsettled conditions prevailing in the world generally, however, further claimed his attention and caused him some anxiety for he feared that whatever the big powers did, for good or ill, was sure to affect the little nations of the world, Liberia being one of those little nations.

Monrovia, 10 October 1966

AS HAS been our custom, upon the convening of the Legislature in regular session, we have met the honourable members on the evening before their first regular session for a general tête-à-tête, and exchange of views, a kind of reunion of views, expressions and feelings.

For three successive convocations of this honourable body in annual session, we have been absent from the country. Tonight then is the first time in three years that we have had the pleasure of being with you at the beginning of your session. We are very happy to be with you this evening and to extend to you again, as we did at the Executive Mansion when you paid your courtesy call, a very warm and hearty welcome.

As usual, this is an important session. It precedes the general elections which are due to be held in May, 1967. The political boat will be capsized. The President, Vice-President, Speaker, all the members of the House of Representatives, and one half of the Senate's membership will be in the water swimming, trying to save themselves. According to our famous seamen, the Krus, when boats capsize all heads are equal on the water. It is then, to use a local expression, that the people have the privilege of drawing their salaries for at least five or six months. After that they leave you and you draw your salaries. But during a campaign salaries belong to the people. Now, I hope and trust that those of us who are in these boats that will be upset and who want further consideration for another term, will be fortunate enough to have the favourable consideration of their constituents. If they do not give you the consideration you desire, well, it is their free will, and a free gift of the people; and no one has any right to become chagrined or mortified or annoyed, because it is a free gift of the people.

Now, the people of Liberia have asked us to accept another term of office. They have gone so far as to say, 'We enrol you, we draft you.' They have further asked the Vice-President and the Speaker to accept another term, and have brought several resolutions incorporating their request.

For my own part, although this request was made three months after the last inauguration, I have not yet given a reply. I have said to the people that I will consider this matter, and in due course communicate to them my views on the question, so that they themselves may judge it. In due time I will do that.

Well, the Vice-President has been in office as Vice-President eight years less than I have been in office, so I am sure you can depend upon his returning. The Speaker has presided over the House of Representatives as its Presiding Officer eight years less than I have been President. He succeeded the Honourable Benjamin Green Freeman; I am sure the people of Montserrado County will consider him for re-election.

Well, there are members of the Legislature who have had only one term; there are others who have had two terms. Under the rules and regulations of the True Whig Party from its inception, the Party ensures members of the Legislature who serve loyally at least two terms. Thereafter, if they are politically popular or strong enough to carry three, four, five or six terms, that is up to them; but it must be upon their own initiative and appeal to the people. But for those with only a first term, the Party ensures support for a second term if they have been loyal. For the other terms, it is up to the people. I think that is fair. If a man has been in the Senate or in the House of Representatives, or if he has been Vice-President or President or Speaker for two terms but has not made good enough to be able to maintain himself with the people whom he has served for additional terms, then he should not expect the Party to insist upon his re-election by the people lest he becomes an incubus. That is the old policy of the Party, hoary with age.

And so you find yourselves this year under these conditions. I am sure that in each of the counties the Party will, in due course, decide and determine whom they will have to represent them. This has reference to the political phase of the present time. Now, there is the national aspect which involves the very life and existence of our country, the age and time in which we live. I have called it epochal because things which are happening have such strange, rare and singular perspectives that all mankind everywhere, and all world leaders are puzzled and perplexed. No certainty exists anywhere about things that are happening because of the rapidity with which they move.

I do not know why, but sometimes I feel rather apprehensive about international and world conditions. I remember then a remark by one of our most outstanding statesmen and politicians. He was a man with whom I had associated in the Senate; we were both Senators. He subsequently became Vice-President of the Nation in the administration of our late President, Edwin Barclay. Later, I was elected to the Presidency. When he received his first annuity cheque and observed that it was bigger than the cheque he received as Vice-President, he returned it to be changed. I then invited him, as an old Senatorial colleague, to spend some time with me at the Mansion, and he accepted.

While we were conversing one evening, he said to me, 'Shad, before the turn of this century there will be an epic' — he didn't say 'epoch' but 'epic'. 'I will not be here to see it; you may be here and you may not be here. But if you are here, you mark what I am telling you, that there will be an epic — a radical and complete change on the earth.' He added, 'Next year I will die.' Then I asked him, 'Brother, how do you know?'

He said, 'Well, the late Chief Justice Dossen, Dr. Fuzzet and myself once visited Germany and went to a place where we were told that Dossen would die in 1924; he died; that Fuzzet would die in a certain year, and he died then; and I too was told the year in which I would die; and so I know I will die.' I told him that I would not like to go to such a place, for I do not want to know when I will die. I only want to die when I cannot help it.

The gentleman of whom I speak died the following year. He was the late Vice-President James S. Smith from Grand Bassa County. I have been watching what he said about 'epic', but I have not found sufficient implication in the word to portray or adequately explain what it is that would change the whole world. And I did not think then to ask him what he meant by 'epic'. He has gone, and the chance to ask him is lost, so I have substituted 'epochal' for 'epic'.

It appears as if things are changing; everything in the world is changing. I have often said that man has created a new earth. This is a new earth. People think and act differently from the way they used. Here we are, in these old bodies, living in a new earth without a new spirit within us. We need a new spirit, a new understanding to be able to live peaceably on this new earth. I do not know who will convert us or regenerate us and implant within us this new spirit which I suggest is necessary for us to live together peaceably in this new world.

The clergy is mainly concerned with spiritual things. They are making some changes — talking about ecumenity and all that sort of thing. But there is no change of spiritual things. The physical changes that are taking place in the earth are so rapid that the spiritual changes are not keeping up with them. The spiritual is intangible and generally moves faster than the physical; but in this case the physical seems to move faster than the spiritual. Now, what will happen I do not know; but there is no need for us to be timorous or fearful, we have got to live in this world just as other people are living. We have got to make up our minds to confront the new rising tide of revolution, nationalism and other things that are disturbing the world. Fortunately for us, in this part of Africa, we are not yet plagued to the same extent and degree, by the things that plague people in other parts of the world and in other parts of Africa. I refer to natural phenomena such as earthquakes, floods, volcanic eruptions, and also to the overthrow of governments, murders, and all of those things.

When it comes to the question of natural phenomena, that is beyond our authority, capability or capacity. That is nature's doing. I hope they never come our way. However, it seems from what I have heard and read recently that floods do seem to be coming our way. I understand that there were several flooded areas in the country this year. Thank God they were no worse than they were.

Rebellion and the overthrow of governments are the order of the day in many places. But I have been trying to make an assessment of the attitude and mentality of the Liberian people. I think of the years and times when we had annual uprisings, internecine wars, and rebellions in different parts of our country. The Government was invariably successful in all of these wars. Government troops razed and burned towns and ordered the inhabitants not to return to them any more. But, immediately after the war, the Government offered to reconstruct the towns it destroyed.

The Liberian mentality is not one of destruction, massacre and death as it is in some countries. You know this is the case. If the people are dissatisfied and want the retirement of the Government, they say constitutionally that they want such an administration to be changed, and then it is done.

Now, when I was away the other day there was a great excitement in our country about a plot or a plan to overthrow the Government and establish a new one. When I heard of the circumstances, I was never perturbed or restless for one single moment, because I knew that the people of Liberia were in favour of my Administration.

I say that with every degree of modesty, humility and thanks to God and to the people. More than that, I know that the people of Liberia have confidence – implicit confidence – in the leaders of our nation in this Administration. I refer to the Vice-President, the Speaker, the National Chairman of the True Whig Party, the General Secretary of the True Whig Party, the members of the Cabinet and, of course, the Courts who have no power in themselves but must depend upon the confidence of the public. I am sure that the people of this nation have implicit and utmost confidence in the leaders of the Government at the present time. We are very grateful to you, and we shall, as we have in the past, whether in office or out of office, bind ourselves to you, as Shakespeare said, 'with hoops of steel'.

Our critics have said that Liberia is a one-party government. But Liberia is NOT a one-party government. No administration, no President in Liberia, nor any Legislature could enact a law to deprive the people of their right to form another party if they wanted to, without a revolution starting here immediately. If I recommended the Legislature in my next message to pass a law that there should be but one party, you would see trouble in the country immediately.

If you know a one-party government, you know how to be a one-party government. But, if by wholesome laws, and by the administration and application of those laws, the people of the nation are satisfied to the extent that dissident and disgruntled elements are unable to organize a sufficient force to challenge an administration, I think that is to the credit of the administration.

Therefore, let us try to look after the interest of the people. Let us gain their confidence. Let them believe that when they are distressed and in trouble, the leaders of the country are with them, think of them and share with them their sorrows and their sufferings – not a bunch of men, who, during campaigns when they want something to be done by the people, go into the little nooks and corners and into houses where they never went before and will never go afterwards, and try to fool the people in order to get their votes and to promote them to high positions, and then after the election put on a bold front and stalk up and down the street. That is why I have advocated and still do advocate, as a matter of political philosophy, that a public servant should live every day as if elections were tomorrow – not stalk up and down as a peacock with three tails during pre-election time, and when elections come, go here and there, under cover of night, ashamed of having the people see him in those places even during the day. For, as Abe Lincoln said, 'you can fool all of the people some of the time; you can fool some of the people all of the time; but you cannot fool all of the people all of the time'. They will soon pick you out.

Now, the American politicians, when they have been in office for fifteen, sixteen or twenty years, they talk among themselves saying 'Oh, haven't they found you out yet?' Well, here, it has taken somebody a long time to find us out – you, the Speaker, myself and some of these legislators of eighteen and twenty years' standing. The people have not yet found us out. I do not think they would find us out any more than they have already done, because I believe they know that we are sincere and genuine.

Above all, let us safeguard this sacred heritage that has been handed down to us by our forebears. I am not afraid of a revolution, *coup d'état* or the overthrow of government because I know that there are a few disgruntled and dissident people here who would do it if they could, who would have done it but do not have the confidence or support of the people of the country because the people know them.

I am not afraid of the Army or of the Police undertaking a *coup d'état* or the overthrow of Government, because I know that the Army knows the difference between what the Army is today, what they receive, what they stand for, and what they did yesterday.

So, when I heard that an ambassador – some foreign representative – had called somebody and offered him a certain amount to get the Army to overthrow our Government, I said, 'Well, that is all right, let them try it. I am not at home.' Then some people cabled me saying, 'Come immediately, fly!' I said 'I am not coming home immediately. I have confidence in the people whom I left in charge of the Government. I have confidence in the Army – the Liberian Army!'

And on this I would say like the Apostle Paul, 'But none of these things move me.' I am sure that no weapon of the devil can be effectively formed against this Administration nor against the Government of Liberia by inordinate and ambitious people who want to rise by violence or force, because they cannot carry the people and the people have no confidence in them. I am not afraid of what they may do, or of anything, because they are nothing but themselves and one or two disgruntled people.

I know I have been President longer than any of my predecessors; and I cannot understand why. The people accord me this singular honour of their own volition each time. I have never asked anyone to vote for me. When I was first nominated, I was told to go out to meet the people of Montserrado County, and to know them so that they could see me. In all of my speeches that I made – the Vice-President, General Secretary of the Party, and the Speaker were there – I said, 'I have not come to ask you to support me as President. I am not come to ask you to vote for me. I throw myself before you. If you want me, you will vote for me; if you do not want me, you do not vote for me.' I never prayed to God to help me to become President. After the choice of my name was intimated to me my prayer was, 'Lord, if it is thy will that I come into power as President of Liberia, let it succeed; if not, foil it.' That was the prayer that I prayed. And in each succeeding election I have had no occasion to ask anyone to vote for me because three months after each inauguration, the people would come back with resolutions saying, 'Come again!' 'Come again!' 'Come again!' I remember what

Chairman Jonathan Goodridge said at the elections: 'Now, we will ride the willing horse to death.' I agree with him; I am almost dead.

I want to thank you very much gentle ladies and gentlemen of the Legislature and fellow partisans, for listening to my harangue for so long. But I welcome you, and I hope that you will have a fruitful session. We have to rush this session because you want to get back home and look after your own interests in politics. We will try to help you; we will push and you will push. I think you should try to adjourn by the end of January or early February. We thank you very much and extend a warm welcome to you again.

Speech made at Barclay Training Center

Monrovia, 30 October 1966

Every soldier, every citizen of our nation owes allegiance and loyalty to his country and his Government.

Introductory Note

The independence of African States gave the armies of several of these states a new sense of importance in the form of vying for political power or as mediators in disputes among politicians. Their intervention in politics was often encouraged from without and from within. On a few occasions there were rumours and speculations that the Liberian Army would become disaffected, and evidence to support such an eventuality was at times not lacking. Realizing the demoralizing effects of such speculations on the character of the Liberian Army, which had always been above suspicion, the Defence Department and officers of our Army and the enlisted men presented President Tubman with resolutions expressing trust and confidence in him as their Commander-in-Chief and as President of our nation. We have President Tubman's response to these resolutions.

Monrovia, 30 October 1966

THIS IS a strange and novel procedure. When I heard of it and as I sat there listening to the resolutions that were being read, I wondered what had occasioned it. It has been said that to everything there is a cause and effect. The preparation and reading of the resolutions, and the presentations of them are effects of a cause; and I have been thinking and wondering what the cause is. I am convinced, or at least I am inclined to believe, that it is the unsettled conditions in the world today and particularly in Africa, which have caused the Army of Liberia to have taken this course of action.

In the first place, I must express my appreciation for the assurance of loyalty. I would like to point out that every soldier, every unit of the Army, every citizen of the nation inherently and naturally owes allegience and loyalty to his country and his government. That loyalty should be unquestionable, unimpeachable, unchallenged. Under our form of Government, the Constitution declares that all power is inherent in the people, that they have the right to meet in an orderly and peaceable manner, to consult upon the public good, to require those who are vested with authority to retire to private life, and even to change their form of Government when they feel that their peace and happiness demand it. These are the provisions of the Constitution of Liberia.

Therefore, the people of the nation, not the Army, have the right to require in an orderly and peaceable manner – when they feel that their freedom, their liberty, their rights and their privileges are assailed – that those vested with authority like the President, Vice-President, Legislators, and constables — retire to private life.

Major-General George Washington, while reading the resolutions, very correctly stated that this is a Government of, for, and by the people. The primary and principal interest and object of this Government must always be in the best interest of the people. When any administration or any government fails to recognize this fact, that government should be required to retire to private life.

I have never thought, I have never imagined, I have never believed, and I do not believe now (for I believe it is impossible) that any individual, any internal group or external group, could move the Army of Liberia to commit or stage a *coup d'état* or a rebellion against the state. Occasionally, there may be inroads or attempts made by politicians ambitious to take power; they may attempt to move the Army of Liberia to such action. That was tried not so long ago, but the Army has remained immovable and steadfast. And I believe that this will always be the case.

Now, governments and people in authority should realize the rights and privileges that are inherent in the people, and that the government is for the people and not for a few; that justice, equality, and privilege must be accorded and extended to all alike. Any other course is iniquitous, is wrong. The people under such circumstances have the right to rise up in an orderly and peaceable manner to demand that government to retire to private life.

I thank you again and ask you to convey these expressions to the officers and enlisted men of the Army.

Yours is the responsibility to defend and protect with your own lives the Government and the people of your country.

No justification can be found for a betrayal of this trust. Any betrayal of this trust is treason. And I am sure that there will be no treason among you *now* just as there has never been any in the past. I thank you again.

At the Fourth Biennial Unification Council and Unification Fair

Lower Buchanan, Grand Bassa County, 8 December 1966

Every segment of world society, no matter how small, seeks some means for strengthening its own cohesion.

Introductory Note

National solidarity is a most desirable goal and the ultimate objective of every nation of the world. The stimulus for its achievement can come either from within or from without. In Liberia's own history the stimulus has been provided from within. A fitting tribute to the long years which William V. S. Tubman spent as President has been the title of 'crusading President'. He often seemed to lead a one-man crusade, initially a lonely task for him. Educating and winning people to his views took more of his energy than the actual execution of our national programmes of development. By 1966 he could rejoice in the triumph of all of his policies. In this address the nation's austerity programme was provided with a certain degree of remedy. He spoke further and at length about the new space age and pondered about its achievements and their relevance to human values.

Lower Buchanan, Grand Bassa County, 8 December 1966

IN DEMONSTRATION of the expression 'United we stand' we meet today in the Fourth Unification Council which is combined with a National Fair, as an indication of the progress made towards improving the economy of our country by the united efforts of all its citizens.

History and experience have taught us that the very nature of mankind, and the evolution of his long and varied cultural traditions, make it imperative that every segment of world society, no matter how small, seeks some means for strengthening its own cohesion, creating its own solidarity, establishing its own avenues of mutual understanding and setting the pace for its own rate of progress. It was toward this end that we enunciated the Unification Policy, one of the oldest policies of Government in this Administration.

What fixed this idea in my mind most were two incidents which occurred shortly after my name was passed at the Whig Party Caucus as a possible candidate for the Presidency. A few days after the Caucus a group of partisans from a certain settlement, which was composed mainly of partisans of the Congo element, came to Monrovia to see me. They stated very bluntly: 'We have heard about you, and some of us have known you, and we think that you are a good man, quite capable of being a great President; but we hear that you have Grebo blood in you and we could not support any man for the Presidency who is Grebo, so we have come to find out if it is true that you have Grebo blood in you.' I replied that I did not think that the type of tribal or other blood that one had in one should determine one's qualifications for the Presidency of Liberia or for any other public office; and that the Constitution does not set this consideration as a requisite qualification for the Presidency.

A short time thereafter, a few partisans from another settlement asked to see me, and I granted them audience. They met me and mentioned that they were willing to support me for the Presidency because they knew of the contributions made by me when I was in the Senate and on the Supreme Court Bench, but they had heard that I had Congo blood and they could not support any man with Congo blood for the Presidency of this nation. I answered them in a manner similar to that which I answered the previous group.

These interviews and the attitudes of the two groups struck me forcibly, making me fully conscious of the great danger we were in by our 'unhappy division', and I realized more than ever the necessity for bringing our people together in fellowship and brotherhood, working as Liberians in a united country, with singleness of purpose, for the advancement and perpetuation of our common heritage, rather than as a class, tribe or element.

We believed then as we do now, that when our ideas and aspirations are guided and guarded by unquestionable patriotism, loyalty and devotion, and dedicated to the safety and security of the State, we pledge ourselves to be defenders of the great cause of the nation and the principles for which it stands.

We in Liberia believe that if we work together in unity we will create and build a formidable bulwark for ourselves, and throw an impressive image upon the international screen, thus setting the foundation and the pace for greater prosperity among our people. The fathers of our nation realized this fact and in the National Anthem which they gave to us they sang it, and handed it down to us to sing:

'IN UNION STRONG SUCCESS IS SURE, WE CANNOT FAIL.'

It is irrefutable that unity as a result of unification, and unification as the forerunner and integral part of integration, is the surest foundation of our democracy, which consists of different tribes, elements, cultures and traditions, representing our national superstructure as divisibility indivisible.

Many changes have occurred since the last Unification Council in Kolahun three years ago. Many have been the changes not only of a material nature but of the understanding by the people of what it takes to maintain and operate a united, strong effective and progressive government. Even the very site upon which we now stand, and on which this Council is being held, together with the buildings, pavilions and general layout and accoutrement bespeak these changes more articulately than words. Extending our examination beyond the confines of this Council, to the county of Grand Bassa, it is not difficult to note the transformation that has taken place within the past few years, the physical development, industrial progress and growing economy of the County of Grand Bassa.

It must, therefore, be admitted that this policy has attained a considerable measure of success and has brought substantial benefits to the country and to ourselves. The credit for this great achievement goes not only to those who participated in its formulation and pursuance, but also includes every citizen who has co-operated in making its objectives a reality. So may we always, now and in the future, broaden our vision and extend our horizon beyond the limited and narrow ideas of tribe, race, colour and element to the universal kinship and brotherhood of all the inhabitants of our country, as fellow citizens of a united and indivisible nation.

Liberia is mainly agrarian, and it is therefore essential that we increase our agricultural productivity in order to meet local demands as well as supply foreign markets, and thus improve the economy of the country. The Operation Production Programme, launched four years ago, has had some measure of success, but the ball has just been kicked off, and it is only in the first stage of the national production game. Some action has been taken in this direction but this is not enough, there must be a continuing and intensified action in the implementation of this programme, because any nation that fails to give special attention to its agriculture, even though its soil may be barren, invites poverty and want. We therefore re-emphasize our appeal and call upon each and every male citizen from the age of sixteen upwards to roll up his sleeves, get out in the open, till the soil and work to improve and expand the agricultural products and by-products of this nation. We must produce more rice, improve the breed of our cattle, increase the supply of fresh vegetables, tree crops and fruits and, in short, render ourselves a nation that is able to produce more than is required for the consumption of its people. Only when this is verified by statistics will we realize full economic independence and stability.

The present session of the Unification Council will present discussions on the National Development Programmes in the areas of Education, Health and Operation Production throughout the country. We hope that these discussions will acquaint us with the progress and advancement made in each of these fields, and will point out the areas which require improvement, so that adequate steps may be taken to correct the errors and enable us to upgrade our presentation at the next Council and Fair.

In these days of unrest and tension, it is satisfying to note that peace and stability remain our happy possession, as a result mainly of the pursuance of the Unification Policy. So may we always keep it, so may it always be and so may it always bind us with hoops of steel.

There is a great amount of scepticism in the world today concerning the present economic and financial situation. How far this mood will continue before there is a reversal, as there must be, is hard to determine, but these developments are with us and while we hope that we are now seeing the worst, and that the dawn of a brighter world will soon break, we must take definitive action to offset any unfavourable effect on our economy.

From a review of the present economic trend it would seem that the developing nations are being squeezed dry by the decline of primary commodity prices on the one hand, and increasing prices for manufactured goods on the other. The present money market does not give much hope with regard to loans, as interest rates and carrying charges would be onerous. A feeling of apprehension in Europe and America has been reported, and people are becoming more cautious about spending and have a fear of either inflation or deflation.

Due to developments beyond the control of Government, namely the decline in the price of rubber and iron ore, revenues for the next four years will be considerably less than projected and we must take measures to offset this. This means that on the expenditure side we must be still more austere, cutting back and saving every possible penny both on recurrent and non-recurring items, as well as some reduction in expenditures for new development.

If great developing countries find themselves in economic and financial difficulties, it is obvious that we must expect to encounter the same thing, and to a greater degree. I believe in the admonition of Solomon in the Proverbs that:

'A wise man foreseeth the evil and hideth himself but the simple pass on and are punished.'

We foresaw this and sought to take measures to offset the approaching danger, we negotiated with foreign concessionaires to increase their profit tax and the sharing of arrangements with the Government, to which they responded favourably. During this period no demands have been made on us Liberians for any contributions or sacrifices to the austerity programme, nor have we been requested to relinquish any of the emoluments and financial benefits received by citizens from all over the country, in both the public and private sectors in which there has been an economic boom, and we have been able to build houses, open bank accounts and travel abroad for the past twenty-two years as a result of the Open Door and Unification Programmes. Now we have reached the stage where we Liberians must assume our share of the responsibility and make our contribution, as the foreigners did, upon our earlier request, during this period of austerity. We are therefore submitting a financial plan to this Council with the request that it be referred to a committee for study and submission, and that on the day that this Council resolves itself into a True Whig Party Caucus, it should transmit its approval and recommendation to the Legislature.

The Plan we suggest is that:

1. One and one-half per cent of the estimated and collected Revenue be set aside each year, commencing 1967, as a reserve to meet the rising cost of debt service.

2. A ten per cent reduction be made in all allowances for all purposes including the attendance upon foreign conferences by officials and other persons, as well as Legislative, Presidential and Judicial travel and other allowances.

3. That an annual austerity tax equivalent to one-half month's salary *per capita* on salaries of $600.00 per annum and over, be imposed by the Legislature on all citizens, male and female, in government or private businesses for a period of three years.

This plan is aimed at preventing a depression, thus obviating general retrenchments, as well as for the benefit of meeting budgetary deficits.

Superintendent Williams together with the Chairman, Co-Chairman and Members of the Fair Committee have been most diligent in their efforts to complete arrangements for this Council and Fair, and I am sure that all of us are pleased with the results of their concerted efforts. I therefore take pleasure, in this public manner, in extending to each and all of them my personal congratulations and thanks, as well as that of the Government, for these elaborate preparations. If this type of co-operation, planning and work were practised in every phase of our national activity the results would be far-reaching and most pronounced.

While these exercises are being held at a national level, we cannot be impervious to the record-breaking period in which we live and the great scientific and technological standards and achievements that are being accomplished by man, and since we are a part of the universe and of international society, we must naturally be subjected to, or be the recipients of, the weal or woe of mankind. Therefore I now leave the national and proceed to the international, some aspects of which give cause for grave concern, almost to the extent of alarm.

Apart from the instinct of man's self-preservation and the perpetuation of his kind, no emotion so pervades the history of man as his remarkable thirst for knowledge. From the moment we first glimpse man's activity on earth, we see him engaged in a persistent, daring and often dangerous preoccupation with the world about him — always striving to control another of its forces, always aspiring, it would seem, to wrest power over the universe from the hand of God.

We cannot doubt that man was indeed meant to grow in knowledge and understanding. Given, from the first, 'dominion over the earth and everything that moveth on it', man has also been urged since time immemorial to expand his understanding of the universe and of his rôle in it.

The Proverbs of Solomon ring with the praise of learning:

'. . . a wise man will hear and increase learning . . .'
'. . . teach a just man, and he will increase in learning . . .'
'. . . the heart of the wise addeth learning to his lips . . .'

Homer and Sophocles sang learning's praises. Euripides warned that 'whoso neglects learning in his youth, loses the past and is dead for the future'.

This theme echoes down through all of human history. We heard it from our own fathers; we are passing it on to our own children.

We are surrounded by proof that knowledge can enhance our lives, that learning can lessen suffering, broaden horizons, and enrich our days. We are the beneficiaries of mankind's unquenchable thirst for knowledge. We can only join the sages of the past in praising knowledge and in appreciating those who seek it and use it.

And yet man's history gives rise to doubts. We question whether it is knowledge alone that we should seek. We cannot, after all, be blind to the fact that it was for tasting the fruit of the tree of knowledge that our first parents were banished from paradise! We do not believe that God would have man live in ignorance, but we do believe that man's goal should be wisdom and understanding, rather than mere learning or knowledge.

We are not the first to question the worth of untempered and undisciplined learning.

Sir Francis Drake reminded us that 'The desire of power in excess caused the angels to fall; the desire for knowledge in excess caused man to fall.' The Apostle Timothy spoke of men '. . . ever learning and never able to come to the truth'. And it is truth which we are told will set men free — not knowledge.

'Knowledge comes,' says Tennyson, 'but wisdom lingers.'

So, it is our desire at this time to draw the subtle but essential line between an unbridled, unthinking, hollow quest for knowledge and the purposeful, thoughtful, creative search for understanding.

History readily demonstrates how easily, how often and how unhappily man's knowledge outstrips his understanding. Man's discoveries have repeatedly liberated some, only to enslave others. Man's imperfection is never more clearly seen than in this inadequate and painful employment of the fruits of knowledge.

The Pharaohs advanced the frontiers of engineering knowledge, creating monuments which are admired down to our times — but their discovery cost the lives of tens of thousands of their fellow-men.

The gin made possible the cultivation of cotton on a scale never known before — and the resultant demand for slaves has scarred the history of our continent.

The spinning jenny and flying shuttle brought mass production of cloth and clothes to people who could never before afford them but the machines consumed the lives of children, as the cotton fields did the lives of Africans.

The bow and arrow, the cross-bow, the firearm, each made it easier for man to obtain food — and to kill himself in ever greater numbers.

The energy of the atom has been released and controlled with still unimaginable promise for the good of men — but its principal use is still to hold in terror most of mankind.

Now, we watch in awe and apprehension as man reaches into the very heavens with the same imperfect hands and inadequate understanding that have marked his progress throughout the ages.

Just as King Canute could not sweep back the tides with his broom, we cannot, and would not want to impede the thrilling tides of man's progress. But we can and would cry out like Solomon: 'With all thy getting, get understanding!'

Man's knowledge is awesome, but what of his understanding? Does man understand adequately the forces which he believes he now masters? Has man's wisdom kept pace with his learning? It would not seem so.

We do not think that man is yet mature enough, disciplined enough, wise enough to lay his hands on the very secrets of the universe. When we think of the suffering which has so often accidentally and blindly followed man's past advances in science, we can only believe that man now owes it to himself to pause and reflect before plunging wilfully on the path he has chosen.

We are told that one apparatus has transmitted so many thousands of photographs of the moon that it will take months simply to develop; not to study, just develop them. We were told that man in a weightless state could accomplish prodigies of strength; but we see a brave man forced to renounce his efforts in space because he is exhausted by less than an hour's work. We hear that men in space now sight man-made objects which none can identify and that two such objects circling the earth recently collided in all that expanse of space.

In short, we must concede that once more man's reach has surpassed his understanding. Would not all mankind and all human progress benefit from a pause for study and assimilation of the information that man has accumulated but has not assessed? Would not the dangers of unsuspected catastrophes be reduced if man refrained from throwing new objects into space until he understands better the meaning of those he has at present circling there?

It would seem so, and we believe that all men would be benefited by an international agreement to refrain for a given, reasonable period, five years perhaps, from engaging in any experiments in space not specifically accepted in advance by international agreement. We believe that such a period could be used to collate, to study, to evaluate, to understand the data already collected.

Ample provision could be made in such an agreement for the launching of such internationally useful and apparently benign objects as communication satellites. Provision might also be made for internationally sponsored and controlled weather observation satellites.

Whatever the approach to details, the substance of the agreement would be the same – to remove the element of competition, of haste, of heedlessness from man's exploration of the heavens, and to oblige man to take the time to arrive at a mature understanding of the forces with which he is dealing before he risks plunging himself and all humanity into a cataclysm which none could foresee, took the time to look for, or could remedy.

There is no need to dwell on the collateral benefits which could result from such a moratorium. The senseless waste of manpower and money which results, not from the quest of knowledge itself, but from the haste and urgency with which these experiments are undertaken, could be reduced, if not eliminated. Even if only one-tenth of the sums we see mentioned for such activities were devoted to the alleviation of hunger, disease and ignorance on earth, what miracles could be worked.

We know that an agreement of this type would not be easy to reach. It might affront national pride, anxiety for self-defence and the sacred cows of science and progress. The chance for man's understanding in this field to keep pace with his knowledge would surely make the effort worthwhile.

Liberia and its neighbours are, of course, not direct participants in the 'space race' today. But no matter how small the struggle, no matter how poor we may be, we share the same heavens with the greatest powers. Their catastrophes are usually ours; their failures of understanding affect our lives as intimately as their own; their concentration of money, imagination, scientific endeavour and national ambition on a headlong, impatient and wasteful race for knowledge, which they cannot even take the time to study, affects our lives, our hopes, our future, just as it does their own.

In this context we do not think it inappropriate, and we hope that none takes it amiss, that we should propose in this manner, to commence an effort to obtain an agreement to halt, or at least limit and control, the space race for a period of five to ten years; that we should call upon our sister African states to join us in developing specific steps leading toward the negotiation of such an agreement; that we should, further, look to the co-operation and assistance of all those who share with us a compulsion to take every step necessary to assure that man's lust for knowledge is not allowed to ravish his wisdom and understanding.

We may, I think, rightly paraphrase Alexander Hamilton in comparing knowledge to a great river; 'kept within its bounds it is both beautiful and useful, but when it overflows its banks, it is then too impetuous to be stemmed; it bears down all before it and brings destruction and desolation wherever it comes'.

Let us then use daring and imagination and wisdom and understanding to curb the excesses, and keep this glorious quest for knowledge within the bounds of man's ability to understand and to employ its forces intelligently.

Having thus commented on and expressed our great concern about the present day's ambitious, unrelenting and continuing quest for knowledge without understanding, not only of the things around us but of the things above and beyond us, in this epochal era, which rationally and of necessity form a part of the very life and existence of the present, the hope and prospect of the future; we commit our country, ourselves, all nations and people to the one eternal God and pray for guidance and deliverance from suicidal destruction and annihilation.

May God out of His bounteous mercy forgive and save us.

Acceptance Speech for a Sixth Term of Office as President of Liberia

Monrovia, 21 February 1967

> *We have now reached the point of no return.... I merely ask of you all that you have; I will give to you all that I have in the staggering task you have assigned to me.*

Introductory Note

A sixth term of office signified for William V. S. Tubman twenty-eight years as President of Liberia. The decision to accept still another opportunity to serve his people was not taken lightly by him. He was forty-eight years old when he became President of Liberia for the first time in 1944. Upon the completion of a sixth term in office he would be seventy-six years old. But, such was the pattern of national events which he himself had fashioned, that he now placed the life of the nation and its interests above his own. His policies of National Unification and the Open Door, which had revolutionized Liberia in every sense, while overwhelmingly successful, were still in need of a steady, guiding hand. There was to be no turning back of the clock. The *father* of his people still felt the need to see his children reach adulthood; and there were signs that the National Unification and Open Door Polices might receive a set-back if their architect were removed from the national scene at this time. After much reflective thinking in terms of personal sacrifices, President Tubman yielded to the overwhelming acclaim of his people to continue as their leader.

Monrovia, 21 February 1967

I APPEAR before you at this time in response to your summons served on me by your Special Committee that escorted me here; I salute and greet you on this momentous and noteworthy occasion with a heart overflowing with gratitude and a mind and being overwhelmed by the mystery of your continuing support and preferment for such an unworthy and humble fellow partisan as myself.

Our history and traditions, from the earliest incipience of the True Whig Party, record and show that never before has a single citizen and partisan been called upon to serve as President of the nation, or in any other position of trust, for a duration of twenty-four years. At the end of that time a spontaneous call has been made for further preferment, for an additional four years of service, which would make an unbroken and successive period of twenty-eight years.

As I look back over the twenty-three years already past and gone, I declare, like the Psalmist, that they are but as yesterday; but when I meditate, muse and cogitate on the events crowded into those years; events of

319

good and evil, failure and success, danger and set-back, I cannot but feel a sense of gratification that your support has been the keystone and sheet anchor to our victory over the forces of a darkness and perfidy.

But above all this stands the eternal verity and truth that God, the source of all power, strength and might, has been with us. To Him we ascribe glory, honour, praise and thanksgiving, and to Him we attribute the impelling and motivating force that has maintained peace within our nation, and brought such success and progress as may have been attained in this administration to the benefit of the nation, its people and ourselves. Besides this, we have enjoyed reasonable good health throughout these twenty-four years and have not been constrained to be away from duty for more than a fortnight because of illness. We know that as surely as God is God, He has extended to us His guiding and protecting arm.

The True Whig Party won its spurs and took over the political administration of this nation because of the soundness, fairness and justness of its policies, which appealed to and convinced the people of the progressiveness and democracy of the Party. The True Whig Party was successor to the Republican Party that operated on the principles of segregation and discrimination from the founding of the nation in 1847 until 1869, when Edward James Roye was elected to the Presidency by the True Whig Party. Segregation and discrimination were so rampant under Republican Administrations, that the people built up a resentment to it and elected Partisan Roye to the Presidency, the first man of dark complexion of our Party to hold this office. By the strength, intrepidity, perspicacity and astuteness of the leaders and partisans of the True Whig Party, the nation has been maintained, has survived and progressed through the years, and on this Convention Day the people have been so moulded together that notwithstanding the statutory law that permits any three hundred citizens to form a political party, they have not sought to exercise the privilege and benefit of this statute because of their satisfaction with the Whig Administration.

In my last acceptance speech I mentioned among other things that: 'The City of Clayashland is the place in Liberia where the True Whig Party had its birth under the leadership of the dynamic John Wallace Good. I recommend for your consideration the erection of a monument in that city on the grounds where the Party met and was formally organized. I think that this would be a deserving memorial to those great souls who conceived and promoted the Party.'

I regret that nothing has yet been done in this respect and I renew my recommendation that this monument be erected.

I postulate that politics is perhaps the most hazardous of all professions and one that requires regularity of action, eternal vigilance and alertness, to the extent that the heart of the politician must never miss a beat; that he must prove himself to be a man with hardened and unshakable nerves that can withstand the pangs and arrows of sudden disappointment and unexpected misfortunes without wavering or squealing. I say to you on this memorable day, in this public manner, that risks, even danger, are the inseparable companions of honour and, with all the uncertainties involved, politics still remains the noblest career that any man may choose.

This National Convention of the True Whig Party is the ultimate result of a movement started by the SINOE WOMEN'S SOCIAL AND POLITICAL MOVEMENT under the leadership of Partisan Delsena Draper – a movement that was commenced almost immediately after we took office in 1964 and gained such momentum that it spread like wild fire throughout the country and has resulted in the nomination, on this Convention Ground today, of party candidates for the Head of the ticket for the May 1967 General Elections.

We of this party should not rest on our laurels, always bearing in mind the political axiom that 'the price of liberty is eternal vigilance'; but as we sit in this delegated Convention of our Great True Whig Democracy, we should feel justly proud of the advances that have been brought about in the country by the policies of the True Whig Party in broadening the basis of our Liberian democracy.

Comparing the strength of the delegations attending upon this Convention with that of the 1963 Convention when there were present five counties and four territories, we now have within this enclosure delegations representing nine counties and five territories. This evinces the soul and spirit of the True Whig Party in its determination to demonsrate and fulfil the provisions of the Constitution of Liberia, that:

'All men are born equally free and independent, and have certain natural, inherent and inalienable rights; among which are the rights of enjoying and defending life and liberty, of acquiring, possessing and protecting property and of pursuing and obtaining safety and happiness',

a fact indicative of the True Whig Partisans's unswerving effort to provide a realistic political superstructure of just representation, the forerunner of internal cohesion and stability.

I tell you, fellow partisans, that not one of you can fully know and understand the propulsions and emotions that possess me at this time. You know very well that I have not sought or encouraged the extraordinary and enviable honour and encomium that you have heaped upon me. Because of the duration of the patronage which you have given me over a period of twenty-four years, I dare not, nor could I have the cheek, to intimate, in any form whatever, a desire for further patronage from you.

That my heart has been troubled, that I have not sought this nomination, that I could not seek it in good conscience, that I would not seek it in honest self-appraisal, is not an indication that I value it the less. Rather, it is symbolic of the reverence that I hold for the office of the Presidency of Liberia.

I have been heartened by the harmonious conduct of this Convention. There may have been disagreements and contentions concerning some of the issues that have arisen, but this was the surest avenue to agreement, especially since you did it without spoiling our best tradition in a naked struggle for superiority or power within the Party.

You have written a platform that does not equivocate, contradict or evade our national issues. You have unmistakenly and positively restated our Party's achievements and held forth its principles and its purposes, with a firm confidence in transparent justice, untarnished and unshackled freedom, and utilization of our best endeavours for universal freedom, and utilization of our best endeavours for universal peace on earth, that would raise the hearts and hopes of mankind towards the day when no one rattles a sabre or drags a chain. To this platform I subscribe without reservation.

At this point I ask that you join me in gratitude and respect for those great and stalwart True Whigs who are enjoying the resourcefulness and fertility of the 'Land of No Return', who founded the Party, passed through the crucible as a minority Party, and maintained the political struggle until the victory was won and the banner of the True Whig Party, with its glowing motto 'DEEDS NOT WORDS' emblazoned upon it, was unfurled and illuminated the political skies. We also express thanks and appreciation to those leaders of our generation whose vigour, character and devotion have won the respect of the Liberian people and the world and have enriched the high and noble traditions of this Grand Old Party that never grows old.

In this epochal era of the earth and the inhabitants thereof, we are eyewitnesses to the constant mounting of national and international tensions between nations and peoples. We are now in the stream with its heavy undercurrents, whirlpools and quicksands; we must therefore swim with undaunted courage or else we shall sink, but sink we never shall. We must realize that there are no gains without pain, that we are in an age requiring grave decisions, not easy ones. We must also be aware that the victory to be won in this twentieth century mocks the pretension of individual acumen and ingenuity. For it is a citadel surrounded by thick walls of ignorance, mistrust, subversion, treachery and malevolence, which do not fall before the trumpets' blast or the politicians' imprecations, or even before a General's baton. They are, my fellow partisans, walls that must be directly stormed by courage, morality and vision standing shoulder to shoulder, unafraid of ugly truths, contemptuous of lies, half-truths and demagoguery.

I vividly recall that while making one of my acceptance speeches at a previous National Convention, you were reminded that during this period when Africa is regaining her pristine glory and the eyes of the world are upon her, it will become a challenge to Liberia to consolidate her position and fortify herself to play more ably the rôle of an Elder Sister which she so nobly performed, almost single-handed, in the past. But now I say to you that the world is using its bi-focal binoculars to penetrate and unveil the activities on the African continent and nothing escapes its scrutiny. We of Africa are part of a great world society and are expected to observe and practise, like the people of other continents, the rules of justice, fairness, morality, law and honour. We must therefore act with caution, and square our actions, whether they be political, moral or social, with the universally recognized principles of right.

Let us strive with all our might to build up a great African cultural heritage that will be free of tensions, for during our time we have seen that tensions breed fear; fear breeds repression; and repression breeds injustice and tyranny. Let us reject the prophets of fear; let us move ahead modestly, proud and unafraid – confident of our capacity to meet the challenge of today and to realize the infinite possibilities of tomorrow.

We cannot forget those who have been associated with us during the period of our service, nor the many, varied and valuable contributions they have made to the successful implementation of our programmes, for without the continued loyal and devoted services of the Vice-President, the Speaker, Members of the Legislature, Members of the Cabinet, past and present, Officials of Government in all categories, Civil Servants and the body and mass of the people who stood beside and behind us like the rock of Gibraltar, this Convention and the many achievements of which we are proud, would not have been possible.

To all of you who have contributed to the achievements that are responsible for our success, and who must now share the pride that we feel at such spontaneous evidence of approval, we can only pledge our undying thanks, continued affection and resolute endeavours.

We have now reached the point of no return. The die is cast! I realize, and my wife and family agree, that for me to retire at this time would be wisest from the point of view of my health. But then, how can one put 'self' before country, especially when one's constituency over and above one's objections, perseveres with its demands for one's continued service?

Knowing very well that your prayers and supplications and those of our Sainted Mothers and Fathers have already gone up to the Throne of Grace on our behalf, and being assured of your whole-hearted and solid support, I feel safe in submitting myself AFFIRMATIVELY TO YOUR CALL.

Finally, my compatriots, regardless of the consequences, you now have my 'AYE' to enter the political arena of the ensuing campaign, and through the next four years. I merely ask of you all you have; I will give to you all I have, and in the staggering task you have assigned me, I shall always try TO DO JUSTLY, TO LOVE MERCY AND TO WALK HUMBLY BEFORE MY GOD.

To the True Whig Party upon his Election to a Sixth Term of Office

Monrovia, 5 May 1967

You have conferred upon me honours of every kind: you have extended to me your patronage in a manner that exceeds the highest magnitude: you have given me your confidence to a greater degree than to any other of my fellow citizens or statesmen of the past, from Roberts down to Barclay.

Introductory Note

On May 2, 1967 President Tubman was elected to succeed himself in office for a sixth term – an aggregate of twenty-eight consecutive years. During that period he had been re-elected thrice opposed and thrice unopposed. The victory of the True Whig Party thus evidenced in his re-election he saw as the whittling away of the major dissenting forces in our society, and as an indication of the popularity of his administration and its programme.

Monrovia, 5 May 1967

THE POLITICAL machinery of our great and grand old party in the exercise of its political obligation and responsibility was put in motion and summoned your patriotic and partisan fealty to choose and elect candidates for the Presidency, Vice-Presidency, and House of Representatives for a tenure of four calendar years, and one half of the Senators for a tenure of six calendar years. In fulfilment of these obligations, on the 21st of February 1967 you, assembled in the National Convention, nominated the Honourable W. R. Tolbert, Jun., and my unworthy self as your candidates for the Vice-Presidency and Presidency respectively. On February 28th 1967 in your County and Territorial Conventions, you nominated candidates for one half of the Senate and the House of Representatives, and in the true spirit and tradition of the True Whig Party you elected these nominees to the positions required by the Constitution, to become your representatives in the Legislative and Executive branches of Government.

The resilience, enthusiasm and national support that characterized and attended the elections throughout the country, without incident, testifies to the national popularity and approval not only of the candidates themselves, but also of the time-honoured and revered Party which they represent.

The voting is over, you have elected us and upon our honour and integrity we pledge our patriotic loyalty to the Constitution and laws of the Republic, our fealty to the True Whig Party and to its traditions; our adherence to the platform adopted by you and presented to us as a guide to the execution of our respective duties through our several Constitutional Oaths of Office and by our profound, abiding uniform and even-balanced interest in the welfare and well-being of the people of the country, regardless of element, clan or tribe.

Six consecutive times you have successfully carried us as your candidates for the Presidency – one eight-year term, and five four-year terms, and each time I have hesitated. In some instances I have virtually rebuked you for your affection and patronage, but you have persisted and now leave me no room for suspicion or doubt of your sincerity.

As you will recall, the present campaign was a typical example, I refused to run for re-election and asked you publicly to find another candidate, but in Bassa you urged me to such an extent that I had no alternative but to accept your mandate.

You have conferred upon me honours of every kind: you have extended to me your patronage in a measure that exceeds the highest magnitude: you have given me your confidence to a greater degree than to any other of my fellow citizens or great statesmen of the past, from Roberts down to Barclay.

These are some of the things that happen in one's lifetime that are above and beyond comprehension, and I feel this evening, as I believe the Apostle Paul felt on one occasion, when he was constrained to utter the phrase: 'Oh, to know the love of God that passeth knowledge!' and so, I am led to exclaim: 'Oh, to know the love of the people of Liberia that passeth my understanding!'

Reviewing the past and present consistent demonstration of your loyalty and affection, we find ourselves with mixed emotions, of happiness that with your co-operation we have been able to achieve as much as we have, and of regrets that our human limitations do not enable us to repay you as fully as you deserve.

Bleak as the prospect seemed when we first took office, we have been bolstered by the unique courage and loyalty displayed by you, the people of Liberia, whose support and co-operation has increased in velocity over the years. It was courage of a special type; courage of a man to whom the stygian darkness of despair cannot spell surrender, that inspired you to urge us on. In the darkness that seemed to engulf us we espied the light beyond the horizon and struggled ahead.

As we launched one project after another, the nectar of success began to replace the bitterness of failure and despair and we persevered until today we can say gladly that we are not the least among the Princes of Judah.

We observed with pride the orderly manner in which the Campaign and elections were conducted throughout the country, and our appreciation goes to the Superintendents, County and Local Chairmen, Officials and Partisans of the True Whig Party, and all the people, for their able administration, conduct and support.

At this point we would like to make special mention of the rapid political progress demonstrated by the new counties, as evidenced by their performance during the last campaign. When we consider that this is their first experience in the management and direction of a national campaign, of which they are carrying the total responsibility, it is both noteworthy and creditable and we register our special admiration and thanks to them.

It is in Montserrado County that the Chief Executive resides and it is from this County that the greatest support and success of any administration stems; it is also here that the central machinery of the Party operates. Therefore we express our appreciation to the people of this county and of the other counties for their co-operation and continuing loyalty to the administration, and their support of the policies which have characterized the conduct of the affairs of state for the past twenty-three years.

The politicians have wrought well, they designed the campaign with remarkable skill and applied political tactics and acumen to the execution and implementation of that design with perfect and apt ability, bringing to the Party one of the greatest and generally approved victories in the history of the True Whig Party.

ECONOMIC AFFAIRS

To a Business Club

New York City, U.S.A., 13 October 1961

Buttressed by long years of close relationship and guarantees of continued confident collaboration, Liberia may become the bridge between the United States and the rest of Africa.

Introductory Note

Perhaps no other group of businessmen have had a warmer welcome in Liberia than American businessmen, historical ties notwithstanding. President Tubman, in this address to a New York Business Club, assured its members of the protection which Liberia accords all business enterprises under a free enterprise system, and further invited them to explore new business opportunities in Liberia in fields other than the traditional ones – rubber and iron. His attention was focussed on the encouragement of agricultural industries.

New York, 13 October 1961

LADIES AND GENTLEMEN,

To meet here so many distinguished heads and representatives of business enterprises of this great nation, where seven years ago it was also my privilege to meet and address a similar gathering of American entrepreneurs of this city, is one of the highlights of my present visit and one for which I am indeed grateful.

Since then, much has taken place, both in my country and yours, as the outgrowth of the invitation which, at that time, we extended to business and capital; and also because of the renewed interest in my country by those who have always had faith in our endeavours, tenacity of purpose, stability and reliability, and who have given encouragement and help at critical points along our national pathway.

I said at that time, 'My people and I are dedicated to the purpose of expanding friendly relationships between you and ourselves. You possess technological know-how and capital and we, considerable natural resources which we are willing to share. Working together can be of immeasurable benefit to both of us.'

Today, the Liberia Mining Company (Bomi Hills Iron Ore Concession), LAMCO (The Nimba Mountain and Bong Range Projects), the National Enterprises, Ltd. (The Mano Iron Ore Project), the B. F. Goodrich Rubber & Tyre Company, the Chase Manhattan Bank of New York, the International Trust Company, the Business and Commercial Bank of Monrovia, the beer and cement factories, and other companies soon to begin production – to name only a few, The Liberian Construction Company, the African Construction Company and the National Construction Company –

have all found in Liberia promising and profitable business possibilities as a
medium of strengthening our friendly relations while bringing to each other
the mutual benefits of combined economic enterprises.

Those of you who are already participants in these greatly satisfying and
rapidly expanding business projects in Liberia, are well acquainted with the
liberal policies of the Liberian Government, which lend incentives to business pursuits and encourage the investment of foreign capital in that country. I refer to the Open Door Policy and the Unification Programme, which
have been and continue to be vigorously pursued and are still vehemently
prosecuted in Liberia until every one of its citizens has become convinced of
their validity and accepted them as a way of life to be cherished and
defended by present and future generations of Liberians as a prized heritage.

Through the Unification Programme, the people of our nation have been
integrated; peace and progress have been facilitated and the sense of identification has made accomplishments possible even in areas where the inhabitants were formerly suspicious of and hostile to constituted Governmental
authority. But once the premise of unity was laid down, the pathway by
which the indigenous people travelled was followed without fear and suspicion and they have, since then, participated whole-heartedly in the progress
and development which now characterize our way of life.

Increased educational facilities, the raising of health standards under the
aegis of the Rural Development Programme, better economic opportunities,
the right of representation, the emergence of the indigenous people to positions of trust and respectability – these are all the results of the successful
prosecution of the Unification Programme. Together we are firmly resolved
and dedicated to make our nation happy and prosperous.

Already, the Open Door Policy, by which foreign investments have been
invited into the country, has yielded appreciable dividends to investors and
citizens alike and we look forward to greater strengthening of the foundation laid for understanding and friendly relations between us and foreign
investors.

But encouraging and beneficial as the results of these enterprises are and
may be, I wish to direct attention to the present necessity for industrialized
enterprises in the country, which are so vital to accelerate and support our
rapidly growing economy. Under the Open Door Policy, opportunities are
afforded for foreign investors to explore possibilities and confer with government agencies directly concerned, and to make decisions only when both
parties will mutually benefit and when the conditions for the enterprise have
been studied, reviewed and assessed.

In particular, I wish at this time to invite discussions about the possibilities
for local industries in such commodities as piassave, palm-oil, sisal, citrus
fruits, pineapples, avocados, all of which are native to Liberia and which
constitute possible commodities for foreign trade. There are other areas, too,
which I am sure afford opportunities for similar explorations.

America has always been noted for leadership in commercial enterprises.
We therefore look to you to provide the leadership in industrializing Liberia
for our mutual benefit.

The life of nations is characterized by periods of growth from infancy to
manhood; from hoe culture to machine civilization. The greatness of the
United States is attributable to its expanding industrial progress since the
end of World War I. History records that those nations which are most

9 *The Treasury Department*

10 A typical new highway

11 The Department of Information and Cultural Affairs

12 The Telecommunications Building

13 The University of Liberia

14 The Ducor Intercontinental Hotel

15 The St Joseph Hospital

16 The Tubman Center of African Culture

talked about are those which have made some contribution to the industrial progress of the world.

Self-determination has made Liberia free for one hundred and fourteen years with an agricultural economy, but to remain independent requires resources in an industrialized society. The 43,000 square miles of our territory confer many precious gifts which we hope to develop with your advanced resources, investment and skills, the revenue from which we hope to apply to the eradication of poverty, ignorance and disease in our midst.

We offer you a cohesive, viable, secure and profitable field of investment.

Our economy needs good husbandmen with skills, experience, faith and integrity. Buttressed by long years of close relationship and guarantees of continued confident collaboration, Liberia may become the bridge between the United States and the rest of Africa.

'When minds are the same, that which is far off will come.'

I thank you.

Address at Dinner in His Honour tendered by the American Business Leaders

New York City, U.S.A., 18 October 1961

Liberia may become the bridge between the United States and Africa.

Introductory Note

In this important address to American businessmen by President Tubman, we have a review of Liberia's economic activities, and of new areas of economic co-operation and development through the Open Door Policy of our Government, and an invitation to participate in investing in these areas.

New York City, U.S.A., 18 October 1961

IT IS a great pleasure to be here with you tonight, especially since I see before me so many friends of Liberia, men whose foresight, effort and resources have contributed so much to the growth of my country.

Seven years ago it was also my privilege to meet and address a similar gathering of American entrepreneurs. Since then, much has taken place both in my country and yours as the outgrowth of the invitation which we extended to business and capital to participate in the development of our economy.

What I have to say tonight is in the nature of an economic report to you and, through you, to the entire American business community. But I cannot talk about economics alone, because in order to discuss economic matters intelligently, one must also take account of the political and social spheres. They cannot be separated from one another.

When I spoke to you in 1950, I said that my people and I were dedicated to the expansion of friendly relationships between you and ourselves. You possess technological know-how and capital. We possess considerable natural resources which we are willing to share. Working together can be of immeasurable benefit to both of us.

We in Liberia believe that business is entitled to an equitable share of the profits it makes. In inviting business investment in Liberia, we want you to make money because we know that this will help build Liberia.

Our Open Door Policy is recognition that we need business investment and will welcome it, consistent with Liberian economic aims. In the seventeen years since this policy was promulgated, some of the greatest names of the business world have invested in Liberia. The results of our economic partnership have exceeded the expectations of each of us.

This year the value of our iron ore exports will exceed the value of our rubber production. This is due to the continually-rising output of the Liberian Mining Company in Bomi Hills which began production in 1950, and the start of production later in the year of the National Iron Ore mine at Mano.

Last year we exported almost three million tons of iron ore. Within two to three years the National Iron Ore Company alone will be producing five million tons annually.

Development of the Mt. Nimba mine of the LAMCO Joint Venture Enterprise is going forward, a gigantic development involving an investment of $200,000,000. LAMCO will start production in April of 1963 as the third great Liberian mine. By 1964 this mine alone will be turning out four million tons annually.

A fourth great mine is in the process of development in the Bong mountains. This is the Delimco operation, and beginning in 1963–64 the output will be from three to five million tons of iron ore concentrates.

Thus, by 1964 Liberia will be one of the largest ore exporters in the world.

The large-scale coalitions of know-how and financing which are carrying through these projects include such names as Bethlehem Steel and Republic Steel, in addition to leading firms of West Germany and Sweden.

The tremendous expansion in iron ore development does not mean that Liberia's primary agricultural export is getting smaller. On the contrary, rubber exports increased in value by fifty per cent from 1958 through 1960. This represents the production of the great Firestone plantations and the 6,000 Liberian growers. Soon – beginning on a token basis next year – the rubber trees of the extensive Goodrich plantation will begin to yield. Thereafter, rubber production in Liberia will continue to climb annually at an accelerated rate.

Other well-known firms sharing in our economic growth include several banks: Chase Manhattan, First National City, Chemical Bank New York Trust, Bankers Trust, the International Trust and the Business and Commercial Bank of Monrovia. The new beer and cement factories will soon begin production. Numerous construction companies – the Liberian Construction Company, the African Construction Company and the National Construction Company, to name but a few, have all found promising and profitable business possibilities in Liberia.

Increased production has brought increased government revenues. When I took office seventeen years ago our national income was less than a million dollars a year. In 1950 government receipts were about four million dollars. In 1958, we collected more than eighteen million in revenues and the following year, 1959, this had grown by one-third to twenty-four and a half million. Last year there was another one-third increase to thirty-two million and I think we will have a substantial gain this year.

It has been estimated that by 1970 Liberia will have an annual export of between two hundred and two hundred and fifty million and Government revenues of about 100 million dollars annually. This is the estimate of Mr. George A. Blowers, until recently a director of the Export-Import Bank. He said further that this would mean that Liberia is destined to enjoy one of the most rapid increases in gross national product in the world in the years ahead.

It is no small tribute to the opportunities and prospects in Liberia that the Export-Import Bank has granted more loans for Liberian enterprises than to any other country in Equatorial or North Africa.

More than seventy million dollars in credits have been made available by the Export-Import Bank for Liberian development; for highways as well as iron mines; for electric power, and for harbour construction.

The private banks have been equally enthusiastic. More than four hundred million dollars from abroad has been invested in Liberia.

I am happy to say that in my contacts with businessmen I have encountered many altruistic men, and they have been among the most competent and most successful. They, at least, would want to know what we have been doing with the increased revenues which Liberia is realizing from the greatly increased pace of investment and development.

We are increasing our onslaught on illiteracy, poverty, and disease. Last year we built a new school every week, on the average. This year we are building two schools a week. Next year we will increase the pace.

A national health programme has already made great strides against malaria and other ills. New clinics and hospitals are going up constantly. Sanitation is not being neglected.

Our rising standard of living is bringing more goods and services of every description within the reach of our people. With the years, more and more of our expanding income will go towards education, health, a better diet, better communication, a better life.

Those of you who are already participants in these greatly satisfying and rapidly expanding business projects in Liberia, are well acquainted with the liberal policies of the Liberian Government, which lend incentives to business and encourage the investment of foreign capital in the country. I refer to the Open Door Policy and the Unification Programme. These policies will continue to be vigorously pursued until every Liberian citizen is convinced of their validity and accepts them as a way of life to be cherished and defended by present and future generations of Liberians as a prized heritage.

Through the Unification Programme, the people of our nation have been integrated; peace and progress have been facilitated and the sense of identification has made accomplishments possible, even in areas where the former inhabitants were suspicious and hostile.

Once the premise of unity was laid, our people accepted Governmental authority without fear and suspicion. They have participated whole-heartedly in the progress and development which now characterize our way of life.

Increased educational facilities, higher health standards, better economic opportunities, the right of representation, the opening of job opportunities to all peoples on the basis of initiative and ability alone – are all the result of the successful prosecution of the Unification Programme. Together we are firmly resolved and are dedicated to make our nation happy and prosperous.

Already the Open Door Policy by which foreign investments have been invited into the country has yielded appreciable dividends to investors and citizens alike. We look forward to a greater strengthening of the foundation laid for understanding and friendly relations between us and foreign investors.

But encouraging and beneficial as the results of these enterprises are, I wish to direct attention to the necessity for further industrialized enterprises which are vital to accelerate and support our rapidly growing economy.

Under the Open Door Policy, opportunities are afforded for foreign investors to explore possibilities and to confer with the Government agencies directly concerned. They can then make decisions to invest when the benefits to both sides are mutually satisfactory and when the conditions for the enterprise have been studied, reviewed and assessed.

In particular, I wish to invite consideration of possibilities for local industries based on such products as piassava, palm oil, sisal, citrus fruits, pineapples and avocados. These are other areas, too, which I am sure afford opportunities for similar explorations.

Gold and diamonds exist in significant quantity and are mined, but there is room for more activity, more exploration, more development of these resources.

Field surveys indicate that we have other mineral riches: lead, manganese, mica, graphite, corundum, and columbite-tantalite. There is opportunity here.

Also, we are the most heavily-forested country in Africa. Our soil, our climate and our rainfall give us a quick re-growth cycle. There are 235 native species of trees with more than 100 species which attain suitable size for first-class commercial exploitation. We could support a major timber industry with fine woods, many of which are now unknown on the commercial market. We could support other tree crops on millions of ideally suitable acres.

The waters off our coast are among the richest fishing grounds in the world, as the Japanese have already discovered. Here, too, there is plenty of room for development.

We also need small businesses of every description: small engineering and contracting firms, light manufacturing, repair shops of all kinds, service enterprises, home-builders, sawmills. The small investor is no less welcome than the large.

And in the Free Port of Monrovia there is a base of operations for development of the whole West African market, that sleeping giant which has just begun to stir.

The world has much to contribute to Africa – in its own interest, I may add, since nowhere in the world will there be greater return in terms of world enrichment for each technician 'invested', each dollar, each school, each mine and factory.

For it is also true that Africa has much to contribute to the world.

Before World War Two, Liberia was one of only four independent countries in all of Africa's 11½ million square miles. Today there are nearly thirty independent nations.

Now, for the first time, with their governments in their own hands, millions of Africans have the freedoms which have been denied to them for centuries – all those freedoms which add up to the freedom to develop.

It is important for Americans, no less than for Africans, that Americans understand Africa in this era. It is important that the United States – the man-in-the-street as well as the official – understand the striving as well as the strife; the achievements as well as the failures.

We know we can expect this understanding from the United States because there is in your tradition a great man, one of the greatest Americans of all time; indeed one of the greatest men the world has ever produced.

His portrait hangs on the wall of my office. His face and his words and

his deeds are a daily inspiration to me. This man who died a century ago
would have understood Africa today. This man who said his country could
not endure half-slave and half-free would know how we feel about Angola,
South West Africa, and the Union of South Africa. This man who strove to
preserve the Republic against the deep-running currents of feeling which
set brother against brother would understand the Congo today.

And finally, as the signatory of the Emancipation Proclamation and as a
human being, Abraham Lincoln would understand the temper of Africa's
millions whose aspirations have been too long dammed up.

Self-determination has made Liberia free for one hundred and fourteen
years in an agricultural economy. But to remain independent requires
resources in an industrialized society. The 43,000 square miles of our territory confer many precious gifts which we hope to develop with your
advanced resources, investment and skills. We hope to apply the returns to
the eradication of poverty, ignorance and disease in our midst.

We offer you a cohesive, viable, secure and profitable field of investment.

Our economy needs good husbandmen with skills, experience, faith and
integrity. Buttressed by long years of close relationship and guarantees of
continued confident collaboration, Liberia may become the bridge between
the United States and the rest of Africa.

'When the minds are the same, that which is far off will become near.'

Remarks at Luncheon in His Honour before the Washington Press Club

Washington, D.C., U.S.A., 20 October 1961

Liberia, founded as an asylum for all people of colour, extends the hand of fellowship to advance its political, social, educational and economic history.

Introductory Note

On the occasion of his second state visit to the United States of America, President Tubman made these remarks to the American Press on the achievements of Liberia's development politically, culturally and economically; its prospects for further development, and its excellent relationship with foreign businessmen through the Open Door Policy of the Government of Liberia.

Washington, D.C., U.S.A., 20 October 1961

I AM overwhelmed by your indulgence for this opportunity to appear before you and to speak through you to the American people. Before doing so, however, let me express my grateful appreciation, and that of the Government and people of Liberia, for the gracious invitation extended me for the second time by your distinguished President and members of Government to visit this great world capital. These contacts, beneficial as they are on the national level, contribute substantially to all our efforts to bring peoples and nations together into a better, more co-operative and more respectable relationship, and to create thereby the desire to live and work together as free and equal partners in a world society.

The scientific shrinking of the world in which we live and the uneasy situations to which peoples and nations are subjected from day to day, have rendered peaceful existence ominous if not perilous. Yet it is clear that we must live in and not outside of the planet Earth, and just as man has conquered many of the things of his environment, so too, it appears that he must eventually learn to subdue and overcome the things which now give rise to tensions – threats to peace, quarrels, acts of aggression, selfishness, lust for power and the my-country-and-my-country-alone complex.

The study of the history of nations, ancient, medieval and even modern, should serve as a constant and solemn reminder of the fate which befell the great empires and kingdoms of the world. Nor can we so quickly forget the lessons of contemporary times. Mankind must build upon the achievements of past generations and so rear yet more beautiful cities, develop the great world cultures, render man more deeply appreciative of the eternal verities of life, and make him truly responsive to the spiritual stirrings of his soul. If scientific inventions have taught any lesson, it is that we are neighbours,

337

even if we are not brothers, and that each one's welfare is inextricably bound up with the other's.

How then shall mankind live in such a relationship with his fellowman? The fate of humanity hinges on his willingness to seek this relationship and work towards its materialization in true human perspective.

Independence has been the magic formula for the African continent, for in the year 1960 alone, popularly called the Africa year, over fifteen states won their independence and since then the number has increased. These states have already taken their places in the comity of nations. Our participation in the United Nations and its specialized agencies, our attendance at international, financial institutions, have all tended to change the complexion of our continent. We hope that these have also exploded the racial myth and so opened up a new chapter in race psychology.

We ask men of goodwill to look for the facts, and when they find them all, to examine and appraise them for what they are worth, so that together we may work hand in hand toward the new day of human relations and brotherhood.

But as yet the fight for the independence of Africa is not completed; self-determination for all the peoples of Africa has not been achieved. Unless and until this is done, leaders and peoples of the continent must continue to lift their voices in courts of justice, international councils, at the United Nations, in an appeal to world and public opinion in the interest of the dignity and the right of self-determination for all the oppressed peoples of the earth. We indulge the hope that you, the people of America, who have always shown sympathy for the cause of Africa and lent your moral support and financial backing, will continue your support for the cause of freedom for all men. To this principle, indeed, your own history provides a parallel. The peoples of Africa and the world assuredly look to the leadership of democracy for a way to man's freedom and independence and for an end to the conflicts of ideologies for supremacy. You must not fail Africans and the rest of mankind.

It is wishful thinking to suppose that any area, however small, will remain a colonial possession in this era of change. The way may be long and the fight bitter, but the end to tyranny and oppression is bound to come.

The idea current among Africans is that they are entitled to a share in the comforts of civilization—that they should be able adequately to house, clothe and feed themselves and to manage their own affairs. They know that there are people in your country, the United States, who share their desires for a better life and are set on helping them to realize it. It is against this background that I address you today.

Gentlemen, you will agree with me that it is a divine right for people to manage their own affairs in their own way; that self-government, whatever its shortcomings may be, is more satisfying and ennobling than non-self-government no matter how efficient. I should make it emphatically clear that there can be no universal peace, and I see no prospect of any, so long as some people arrogate to themselves the right to govern without the participation and consent of the governed.

In recent years greater diplomatic representations, more cultural and trade exchanges and large concessions to our country from yours have proved mutually beneficial. Many Americans are happily contributing to the progress, prosperity and national stability we have achieved. The people of Liberia continue to welcome all races and peoples of African descent who wish to make their home in Liberia. Thus we have continued to show the world that Liberia, founded as an asylum for all people of colour, still extends the right hand of fellowship to those who would welcome the opportunity of helping to advance the political, social, educational and economic history of the nation.

The time has come when the basis of these relationships must be made stronger, by concrete proposals for co-operative endeavours on a long-term arrangement. Our natural resources, the upsurge in our national economy, and the developmental pace of progress support the feasibility of such endeavours. We therefore invite business entrepreneurs to explore and exploit the possibilities of industrial enterprises in Liberia.

Finally, our hope for a better world order is derived from our basic belief in democracy, as a way of life compatible with human inclinations. We are proud of the history of our struggle to maintain the heritage of freedom which our forefathers bequeathed to us. We shall continue to fight, to defend and, if necessary, to die for it.

Our belief in the work of the United Nations as man's greatest hope for survival is reflected in our institutions of learning. We shall continue to support unswervingly the fundamental tenets of this world organization.

Our belief in men of goodwill and the eventual fashioning of a world based on the brotherhood of man and the Fatherhood of God makes our struggle for survival significant.

Our desire to strive for closer collaboration, to strengthen the basis of our friendship and co-operation and to dedicate ourselves to the solidarity and prosperity of our nation, are ideals which provide motivation to our thoughts and actions. To all men of goodwill who desire our friendship and co-operation we extend the right hand of fraternity, wherever you may be.

Gentlemen, you are the harbingers of fair play, truth and justice. May you be the torch-bearers to the new frontiers of peace and human brotherhood.

A Radio Broadcast to the Nation on Austerity Measures

Monrovia, 15 April 1963

We hold in trust for our children the new Liberia of the future.

Introductory Note

This message was President Tubman's first announcement to the people of Liberia informing them that Liberia had entered a period of austerity. Here he gave the reasons for that austerity, and outlined the measures which the Government proposed to take to ameliorate the situation. His appeal to his people to accept a change of fortune was positive and generated hope for a new and better day for all Liberians.

Monrovia, 15 April 1963

I MUST talk to you tonight about a serious problem that affects every man and woman in our country.

Liberia, as I shall explain to you, now faces serious financial problems and the Government is determined to take effective action to deal with them. The Government's actions must affect all of us, and I am making this broadcast so that everyone may know clearly what the problem is, and how we are going to solve it.

The root of our financial problem is this. In recent years, as our income from the sale of rubber and iron ore and other goods increased, the Government seized every opportunity to accelerate our national development. That development, as you know, is aimed – like that of all other countries in Africa – at eliminating poverty, disease, and illiteracy and giving our people, most of all our children, happy and useful lives. This is a vast task and we have done everything in our power to tackle it. With those basic objectives always in mind, the Government initiated a programme of national development that has stretched our financial resources to the limit.

Some people may say we have tried to do too much. I do not agree. The truth of the matter is that Liberia, like all the other developing countries, has only started the bare minimum of work to create for our people conditions that could be considered as reasonable in the modern world. No Government, certainly not the Government of Liberia, could ever accept conditions in which all our people are not properly fed and housed, provided with reasonable medical facilities and good educational opportunities for their children, and where jobs are available for all. These are no more than the minimum conditions which can be expected politically, socially, and morally in the modern world. Naturally, we must do everything in our power to provide them.

In our efforts to create these basic conditions, we have undertaken many projects all over the country and naturally these have to be paid for. Our income from rubber and iron ore has been of vital importance in paying for this development, and, in addition, the Government—like every other country—has raised loans so as to increase the rate at which essential projects can be carried out.

Recently, the world price of rubber has fallen and we have not exported quite as much iron ore as we had hoped. Beside this, new iron ore mines that had been scheduled to be in production before now have not materialized. As a result Government revenue—or you could call it income—has not been as large as we anticipated. At the same time our expenditure—mainly on development—has increased, and we have also discovered that some of our loans from abroad are more costly than we thought.

Our financial problem as a Government is thus very like that which faces many families. Like a father, we have been trying to provide all we can for our family. Now the father finds his wages have dropped, but somehow he must still provide for his dependents.

What would the father do? First of all he would consider what expenses he could reduce. That is exactly what the Government will do—I have given directions that the purchase of certain supplies and equipment is to be reduced, and the cost of certain services will also be cut. Other measures to reduce Government expenditure will also be taken.

However, I am glad to tell you that there will be no terminations of employment. The present Government staff will keep their jobs—but there will be far fewer new posts in the future until we have overcome our present financial problem. We in Liberia are fortunate that it has so far not become necessary to dismiss people from Government employment to any extent—as has happened in so many other countries when faced with a major financial problem.

Having reduced expenditure substantially, the Government, like the responsible father, must see if he can earn more money from any other source. For the Government that means collecting more revenue. First of all, I appeal to all loyal Liberians to pay their taxes. More and more people, I am glad to say are paying their income tax. I hope that all companies trading in Liberia—both national and foreign—will also ensure that they, too, pay the proper taxes. At the present time, the Government is owed considerable sums of money—mainly in the way of taxes—from individuals and companies, and I have given directions for special action to be taken to ensure that these debts are paid. It is intolerable that honest people should be asked to make more sacrifices while dishonest people and companies continue to avoid paying their debts. I am determined that this shall not any longer happen in Liberia.

Second, the Government must get more revenue from other sources. The fairest and most effective way to do this is to increase duties on our imports. Accordingly, duties will in the future be levied on the cost of the imported goods plus insurance and freight, but there will be one vital exception.

There will be no increases in the duties on those things which are essential to the basic life of every family—by this I mean such things as staple foodstuffs, simple clothing. I repeat, there will be no increase in the cost of these things, which are essential to the basic life of every family, and if any trader attempts to increase his charges—at the expense of the ordinary family—I wish the circumstances to be reported immediately to the Department of

Commerce so that the offender can be prosecuted. Special legislation will be asked for against profiteering.

While the general increase in duties will not be applied to the basic necessities of family life, there will be further increases in the duties paid on all luxury articles such as big motor cars and large radios. I am sure that everyone will agree that this is right. Basically, it is the application of the old philosophy 'to each according to his means'. The less fortunate of our people will be expected to make the smallest sacrifices; it is only right and proper that the better endowed should make the greatest contributions. There will also be an increase in property taxes.

If we can demonstrate to the world that we are doing everything within our power to put our financial house in order, I am confident that we will then receive effective co-operation from abroad. To do this we must cut out all unnecessary expenditure and waste, and we must increase Government revenue to the maximum. At the same time we must ensure that that revenue is put to the best and most productive use.

If we undertake these unpleasant tasks of genuinely cutting expenditure and increasing revenue, I believe that the International Monetary Fund — one of the great institutions of the United Nations — will be willing to help us to overcome the next difficult phase. Furthermore, I am confident that the Government of the United States — with which Liberia has always had a special relationship — will be sympathetic to our problem. But before we can expect co-operation and assistance from abroad we must first clearly demonstrate that we have done everything possible by our own efforts.

Just as we in Liberia are affected by events overseas, such as those that have reduced prices for our rubber and iron ore, so what happens in Liberia will also affect people and companies from overseas who have investments in our country, and who have trading relations with us.

To our friends overseas I say this: First of all, we trust that the determination we are showing to deal effectively with our financial problem will reassure them as to the soundness and stability of Liberia in every way. Secondly, we will honour our international obligations, as we always have done, and we will adhere only to sound financial policies. Thirdly, I would remind them of a fact which must never be forgotten. Liberia is in the almost unique position of using the United States dollar for its currency, and has every intention of continuing to do so. The United States dollar remains the strongest currency in the world, and all our financial policies and operations are directly related to that fact.

To my fellow countrymen and countrywomen I say this:

We are faced with a serious financial situation.

It can be overcome by resolute and well-thought-out action.

The Government of Liberia will take that action and I, as your Chief Executive, pledge you my word that I myself will ensure that the right decisions are taken, no matter how unpleasant they may be.

We must all prepare ourselves for real sacrifices from now on. We must tighten our belts — both as a Government and as individuals. There is no easy solution to our problem — but as I have just said it can certainly be resolved if we take resolute, determined action. We will take that action.

There is another important point for us to remember. Our financial problem can also be likened to a physical illness. It can be cured; there is no doubt of that. But the cure will be more effective and less painful if the medicine is taken sooner rather than later. It is for that reason that the Government of Liberia is taking strong and effective measures now, rather than being forced to take much more drastic and harsher measures later.

I call on every man and woman in Liberia to give his and her full support and assistance to solving this national problem. The sooner we can restore our financial position the more we can do to achieve the effective development of our country, and to give everyone a better way of life.

It has not yet been given to Liberia to enjoy all the advantages of a fully developed state, but God has been good to us in many other ways. We possess many precious assets, and one of them is the unity of our families, and the love shared by parents and their children. Just as our forebears did their best to provide for us, so we today hold in trust for our children the new Liberia of the future. Already we know that many of them will be able to enjoy greater advantages than we did: it must be our most cherished ambition to provide first-class opportunities for every one of our boys and girls in Liberia.

To do that we must do everything in our power to develop our country.

First, however, we must overcome the present financial problem as a means of achieving effective national development.

Together, a Government and people united in a common effort, we can do this job. Therefore let us work together, make personal sacrifices appropriate to our circumstances, and persevere in all our efforts until we achieve real success.

And in all our efforts and sacrifices let us never forget that what we are doing is for the national good of our beloved country, and especially for our children who will become its citizens of tomorrow and will guide its destinies to further and greater achievements and triumphs.

God bless you all, and prosper your efforts for the common good.

At the Dedication of the LAMCO Joint Venture

Nimba County, Liberia, 15 November 1963

The dedication of this vast project represents the beginning of a new economic era in the exploitation of the mineral resources of this nation.... We wish to count upon the continued help and co-operation of our foreign friends in bringing to reality our dream of a land of liberty and plenty in deed and in truth.

Such a large number of various nationals representing industry, finance and business, betokens the new day that is dawning on our planet, when race, language ... no longer keep men from uniting in enterprises for their mutual benefit and the benefit of mankind.

Introductory Note

The Liberian American-Swedish Minerals Company (LAMCO) was an innovation in investing large capital in a developing nation. It was bold, daring, full of calculated risks, and signified an act of man's conquest over nature. It was man's ability to forge ahead through what appeared then to be insurmountable barriers that brought to Liberia a joint venture in business cooperation undertaken by three governments. President Tubman was pleased with the success of this undertaking.

Nimba County, 15 November 1963

AFTER ABOUT ten years of disappointments, set-backs, large-scale planning, intensive investigations, negotiations and stupendous technical construction, the LAMCO Mining Project has come into production and is today a reality.

A few years ago the surrounding area was an uninhabited mountainous region, dangerous and inaccessible, infested with reptiles of all sorts, considered the home of demons by some of the indigenous inhabitants; where some of the country's most savage fauna roamed in dense forest. The transformation of this area, and the realization of what technical know-how and perseverence have brought about, fills one with admiration for what man can do, and has done in this case.

We congratulate upon their foresight, ingenuity and stick-to-itiveness, those who have shared in this great undertaking and we honour the memory of those who gave their lives that this venture might be made possible. We share, in common, the excitement and pleasure which this happy moment brings to us, and pay homage to those who have remained with the enterprise from the early beginnings up to the present. Equally do we salute those who entered later and made their contribution to the success that has attended this project.

The coming into production of the LAMCO Project is the story of a great engineering feat, imagination, intrepidity and hard labour in which man, as always, pitted his faculties against nature and disease. Perhaps the initial difficulties, problems and disappointments of those years and the anxieties of the future of iron ore will be easily forgotten. But the telegraphic message received on the day before Christmas Eve of 1955 reporting the discovery of the main ore body will long remain in the memory of those undaunted pioneers in whose work romance and legend happily combined to give birth to a project, the economic and social implications of which will have far-reaching repercussions for the participants.

It is gratifying to reflect on the satisfactory degree of mutual co-operation which has characterized the relationship between the partners in this venture, and the Liberian Government will continue to lend its support and give full co-operation to the furtherance of this project. It is my hope that there will develop among the entire personnel of these operations the *esprit de corps* so essentially necessary to make the LAMCO operation a living example in Africa of the possibility for success of such huge multilateral operations.

The dedication today of this vast project represents the beginning of a new economic era in the exploitation of the mineral resources of this nation and we look forward to a future where social development will advance hand in hand with this great project, because we have always considered the maximum development of human potential of equal importance. The vast housing projects already undertaken by LAMCO to accommodate the new community will contribute greatly towards this end and we are proud of the facilities which are being provided to make living and working conditions healthy, safe and pleasant.

The presence here of such a large number of various nationals of the first magnitude representing industry, finance and business, betokens the new day that is dawning on our planet when race, language, coast and clime no longer keep men from uniting in enterprises of industry and other businesses for their mutual benefit and the benefit of mankind in general. To all of you gentlemen I extend a warm, genuine and happy welcome.

With the new national campaign underway to make Liberia a producing rather than merely a consuming country, I solicit the co-operation of the more than two thousand five hundred employees of LAMCO, both management and labour, in this great challenge of OPERATION PRODUCTION by resolving to produce something out of the soil. By doing this we will not only accelerate the realization of a future of true progress, stability and prosperity, but also bring a greater measure of economic security and happiness to the entire inhabitants of the country, including those with vested rights in the LAMCO venture.

We look forward to the day when this nation will have a network of industrial enterprises operated largely by Liberians, and wish to count upon the continued help and co-operation of our foreign friends in bringing to reality our dream of a land of liberty and plenty, in deed and in truth.

At the Ground-breaking Ceremony for the Walter F. Walker and Thomas R. Faulkner Hydro-Electric Power Plant

Mount Coffee, Liberia, 29 January 1964

We will be tapping gainfully a source of national power which promises to revolutionize our way of life and bring untold blessings to our nation.

Introductory Note

Man's mastery over the forces of nature is often an indication of his march of progress, and of the industrial growth of any nation. For a long time Liberians have experienced difficulties due to an inadequate and unreliable supply of power to serve the basic functions of daily living. The St. Paul River was harnessed to rectify this situation. The dam on the river further fulfilled an old dream and wish of President Tubman.

Mount Coffee, 29 January 1964

FILLED WITH emotion at the realization of one of my highest hopes for the development of our country since I first took office, I am prone to exclaim in my own characteristic fashion: 'Thank God!' Thanks to the financial institution of the United States that granted the loan for the financing of this project on such generous terms and conditions; thanks to the designers of the plans and specifications; and to the Liberian negotiators who conducted the negotiations and concluded the agreements that have enabled us to meet on this area upon which is to be constructed the largest and most enormous Governmental project ever undertaken.

Today, one of my loftiest dreams and ambitions for the development of the country is being realized. Taking office in 1944, I vividly recollect proposing to the Legislature two major projects of law; one to provide for the payment of income tax which hitherto had been unknown in the country; the other to seek for the construction of a Dam that would give hydro-electric power which would be cheap and within the reach of all classes of our citizenry, as well as for industrial operations. Four separate and distinct explorations and surveys were undertaken and made to ascertain the feasibility of the project, and each report was favourable, though in some instances different sites were recommended.

Negotiations for financing this project, based on the feasibility study and recommendations made in several reports, met with little or no success until a few years ago, when an agreement was reached between the Government and the Liberian National Electric Corporation for the construction of this hydro-electric plant. Then, world market prices for some of our principal exportable products declined and dropped. Other projects that were expected to go into operation and create new sources of revenue did not materialize for various reasons. The Government being therefore unable to meet the terms and conditions of the agreement with the Liberian National Electric Corporation, negotiations for a review of the contract ensued, but no agreement for better terms or for any substantial revision of the contract was possible; whereupon by mutual agreement between the parties concerned, the contract was cancelled upon conditions stipulated in the agreement of cancellation.

Following this, approaches were made in the United States for the financing of this project and negotiations begun with the United States Agency for International Development. Notwithstanding the enormity of the amount involved, about 24·3 million dollars, agreement was reached and concluded, and the loan granted within a shorter period of time and on more favourable conditions than any other loan ever negotiated by this Government.

I have vivid recollections of a letter that I addressed to the late President John F. Kennedy on the subject of this project in which, among other things, I gently hinted that the consideration of rates of interest on loans extended by his Government to some governments of three-fourths of one per cent had never been extended to the Liberian Government. I wondered if some such consideration could be extended to us, and indeed the loan was granted at an interest rate of three-fourths of one per cent, with ten-year grace and forty-year amortization periods.

This action on the part of the United States Government is a further indication of its goodwill toward and interest in our development programme, and I wish to record once more the gratitude of the Liberian Government and people for this consideration, which will reflect favourably on the economic life of the nation and its people.

With this ground-breaking ceremony today, we launch out in another significant direction convinced that the undertaking will add immeasurably to the nation's economic advancement and improve living conditions considerably.

The availability of cheap and adequate power means the establishment of more industries and the expansion and improvement of existing ones; it means that as a result of the stimulus of scientific methods a bigger crop of agricultural products will be realized, thus enhancing our Priority Number One Programme – OPERATION PRODUCTION; it means that all areas where power is used will benefit.

Harnessed power provides unlimited potentialities to turn the wheels of gigantic machineries for industries that in turn will transform raw products into semi-finished, finished and marketable commodities. Because this source of power is inexhaustible, we are optimistic that the project will bring to the people of this nation a greater degree of peace, happiness and prosperity than ever before. This power will be utilized in the homes, in offices, in business establishments, on farms, and in other areas. Cheap and abundant power will create a climate for conditions which will stimulate and increase production in every way. All in all, we will be tapping gainfully a source of natural power which promises to revolutionize our way of life and bring untold blessings to our nation.

In the many anxious months and years from 1944 to the granting of this loan, and to the present, I have had no one more solicitous and persistent in pushing and urging for arrangements for hydro-electric power in the country than the late Honourable Walter F. Walker, the first Secretary of Public Works and Utilities in this administration. Even after he retired to private life, he continued his interest in encouraging, assisting and advising on the feasibility of the project and up to his death we seldom met without his mentioning the absolute necessity for cheap power.

It has been stated before and officially confirmed today that this plant is to be named after me; while I greatly appreciate this high consideration, I would prefer, and do hereby suggest, that the name of this plant be Walter F. Walker Hydro-Electric Power Plant.

With this beginning today, we are about to launch out on another significant project which we know will add immeasurably to the economy of the nation as well as improve living conditions by providing cheap power. We are optimistic that with the completion of this momentous project, the people of this nation will enjoy in a greater degree the blessings of peace, prosperity and happiness. Let us congratulate ourselves upon this forward step and pool such resources as are necessary for the project to be carried to a satisfactory completion.

While we are happy about this project, which is the largest that Government has ever undertaken, yet we must construct additional and larger dams that will be required for agricultural and general development purposes, to harness the waters of the many rivers and waterfalls with which God has so generously and bountifully blessed our land.

We are, my fellow citizens, on the threshold of another administration. What the future holds for the nation and its people, we cannot with any degree of certainty predict; but I feel confident that if we join hands with each other, march boldly and confidently forward and dedicate ourselves to the supreme task of building a stronger and better state, we shall eventually have a nation where liberty and justice will continue to prevail and where happiness, plenty and prosperity will abound for all.

To the International Labour Conference
Geneva, Switzerland, 26 June 1964

*Labour and management are interdependent . . . Government must
have great concern for the equities between labour and management.*

Introductory Note

President Tubman was probably the first Head of State to address a
meeting of the International Labour Organization in Geneva. That was
not the purpose of his visit to Switzerland in 1964. He had gone there for
reasons of health. At home he had often been called upon to intervene in
matters affecting labour and management and had kept a watchful eye
on their activities. Though he was at first reluctant to address the International Labour Conference, he finally consented, after some persuasion,
to accept the invitation to speak which was extended to him by the
President of the Organization. He spoke about the inter-dependence
between labour and management which was vital to industry and the
progress of the world.

Geneva, 26 June 1964

I AM highly honoured by your invitiation to come here and meet you. I
cannot bring myself to agree to make a speech, because I have not prepared
one. I have been twenty-one days at sea and landed this morning at
Marseilles. There I joined a train and travelled here by rail. Not being very
well, I sought through the leader of the Liberian delegation, Mr. Horton,
to find an excuse, but he and my old friend, Mr. Jenks, got hold of me – and
I am reminded of a story in the Bible (I am a Christian) about a man
named Jacob wrestling with the angel – and they would not let me go. So
finally I find myself here, and I am very happy to be here.

I am overawed by the history of this building in which you are gathered.
Here was the first international forum intended to solve human problems,
differences and misunderstandings, without the shedding of blood. That
organization was short-lived, but the spirit, the purpose and the intent
survived.

Next came the United Nations, that great bastion of liberty, the advocate
and symbol of peace and equality for all men and nations, which has not
been content to concern itself merely with the political matters that arise
between nations and people, but has extended its interests beyond these
engagements to concern itself with the economic welfare of the world.

It takes into consideration the benefits and privileges of education and
then reaches down and sees the labouring man and realizes that labour and
management are interdependent, one on the other, and that governments
must have great concern for the equities between labour and management.

349

I have always held and believed that there is no necessity for labour and management to be enemies. They should be friends, because one is dependent upon the other.

I have read and heard broadcasts about some of your work done here, in these sessions of the International Labour Conference. Yours is not an easy task, but I am happy that there appears to be a coming together, a meeting of minds, a better understanding between delegates on the issues and matters that arise in this assembly, and that you are gradually adopting the policy of give and take and putting the greater and wider interest above individual, national or personal interest. I congratulate you and I hope that this session will be one of the most outstanding sessions of this Conference yet convened. I congratulate you, too, on the election of your President.

A great change has come about in the world, where great and powerful nations meet in the assemblies of international organizations such as the United Nations, I.L.O., W.H.O., U.N.E.S.C.O. and all the other specialized agencies, where one representative has the same rights as another and is given the same opportunity to express himself and state the views of his government. This is a great step forward. Before the organization of the United Nations such a thing was unthought of, unheard of. It was force, it was might, it was power. Although these things still exist, yet such a disposition has reflected and manifested itself in these organization – in the international forums provided by the United Nations, and in the specialized agencies to which I have referred.

We must not, we cannot, we shall not permit the United Nations nor any of its specialized agencies to become disrupted or fall to pieces. We must keep them alive in the interest of humanity, in the interest of peace and in the interest of equality and brotherhood among men. I thank you for the opportunity given to me to address this Conference.

At the Opening of the Conference of State and Governments of Guinea, the Ivory Coast, Liberia and Sierra Leone on the Free Trade Area

Monrovia, 20 August 1964

Contemporary events ... should impress upon us the utter necessity and importance of co-operation and exchanges in cultural, economic, trade and commercial activities. The proposal for the creation of a Free Trade Area between our four countries appears to me to be sound. Let us accept the challenge that this opportunity affords ... for the establishment of closer economic co-operation, achievement of mutual development and accelerated advancement of our countries.

Introductory Note

The Free Trade Area was envisaged by President Tubman as a positive step toward the achievement of African unity. Guinea, Ivory Coast and Sierra Leone, being Liberia's immediate neighbours, were first invited to participate in this enterprise. However, the invitation was also extended to all African countries who desired to join them. President Tubman personally led this drive for economic co-operation.

Monrovia, 20 August 1964

IN THIS changing world, with its high degree of competition in society, ideology, trade, commerce and politics, the purpose of our meeting at this time is self-explanatory and offers an opportunity for the exchange of views, the expression of opinions and the study of economic problems. We also propose to seek solutions to problems affecting the growth and expansion of trade, commerce, industry and other businesses in our respective countries in their relation to each other. In the context of mutuality, it is my distinguished honour and privilege to say to you, my worthy colleagues, brothers and friends, on behalf of the Government and people of Liberia, and of myself, that we welcome you in the spirit of brotherly affection out of the deep recesses of our hearts.

We need not be reminded that contemporary events bring us hourly nearer to the realities of the world situation and to trends on our own continent which should impress upon us the utter necessity and importance of co-operation and exchanges in cultural, economic, trade and commercial activities. These ends are the more justified because of the common ties and interests among us; because we share the same social philosophy for the development of our peoples; because on international forums we have stood

351

together in the interest of world peace, human freedom and brotherhood, and because we have dedicated ourselves to the fight for the total liberation of all Africa. The ends we seek, therefore, are geared to contributing to bigger objectives and we act on the basis of the demands of the present and future for economic security, social progress and political stability.

Africa has experienced an unusual renaissance, which has made us more optimistic about the progress and development of this continent than ever before. The political stability achieved by the majority of the African States which gained independence within the last decade, the coming together of African leaders at different international conferences, their appearances before that great international forum of human rights, the United Nations, the frequent visits between Heads of States and Governments and the emergence of the Organization of African Unity as an instrument for peace, unity and brotherhood, are clear demonstrations that old myths have been shattered and that the gates of opportunity have been opened for the creative genius of the African to unfold.

How quickly and effectively we have grasped the opportunity and how well our focus as been set on the maximum development and utilization of all our potentialities, can be seen in the gradual disintegration of the ideological groups which once were a threat to the march of progress on our continent. This frequency of contacts among us has led to the development of mutual understanding and sympathy, appreciation and respect for each other's views and the discovery of more similarities among us; thus our goals have become more definitive and our progress more assured. May we now and in the future continue to join hands in the spirit of true brotherhood and march bravely and confidently forward to achieve our desired goals.

The proposal for the creation of a Free Trade Area between our four countries appears to me to be sound, and lies in the realization that if industrialization and overall economic progress is to be achieved, the size of the market of our four countries should be considerably broadened, and tariffs and other governmental barriers either eliminated or relaxed, to facilitate the movement and sale of goods and services produced. To this end, it is proposed that we consider the desirability of organizing ourselves into a Free Trade Area.

In order to derive maximum benefits from the proposed Free Trade Area among us, it would appear that the generally accepted nature and concept of a Free Trade Area might not be quite appropriate. I think that schemes limited to freeing intra-regional trade from artificial and other quantitative restrictions would not produce the desired effect or provide opportunity for a rapid overall development of the combined region. On the other hand, it must be recognized that the different existing international economic relationships of our four countries make it unrealistic to expect that in the immediate future we could form ourselves into a traditional customs union with identical external tariffs leading eventually to an adoption of common fiscal and monetary policies. Consequently, the Free Trade Area which is envisaged here would lie somewhere between these two extreme concepts. The exact nature and form of our future co-operation will be for our technical experts to study and recommend. It is proposed, however, that the present conference endorse, in principle, co-operation in the areas of industrial development, transportation and communications, agriculture and trade.

In the area of industrial development, we should agree in principle to finance, either jointly or singly, industrial research with a view to identifying feasible projects which would be suitably established within a tariff-free and externally protected area. Such studies should also determine the most economical location within the Free Trade Area for each feasible industry, so long as a balanced regional development is assured, and regional discrimination or concentration of industries is discouraged. In the agricultural sector, it is not the size of the market that is the major impediment to development but rather poor soil conditions, pests, outmoded methods of production, inadequate irrigation facilities and poor marketing techniques. We can jointly do much to facilitate research into the means of increasing the production and distribution of many agricultural items.

The feasibility of various future industrial and agricultural projects will depend largely upon the availability of adequate transportation and communication facilities to bring centres of production and consumption into close contact with each other at the least possible cost in time and money. Hence it is proposed that we jointly consider the desirability and feasibility of developing coastal shipping and an inter-state highway system, co-ordinated and integrated as fully as possible with existing and proposed national road systems that would best meet the national and regional interests of our respective countries, with due consideration given to the economic aspects involved and without imposing any undue financial strain on any one member country.

In view of the existing trade patterns and policies of our countries the expansion of trade itself may prove the most difficult and complex problem, although greater intra-area trade is implied in my proposal for a Free Trade Area. This is because any removal of official obstacles to trade within the proposed Free Trade Area invariably raises the question of ways and means to be used, with a view to avoiding discrimination. Here again, a jointly sponsored expert-study group is called for. While these studies are being conducted the Governments of the four countries may examine the possibilities of voluntarily taking steps to remove those restrictions on intra-regional trade that do not violate their existing international trade agreements, and explore the methods that would best facilitate the establishment of industries indicated by the feasibility studies.

The merging of our limited national markets into a larger regional one will encourage greater specialization and a more efficient division of labour, resulting in more readily attainable economies of scale. Existing investment could also be examined and exploited on a co-operative basis, leading to a more rational use of our resources. Investment decisions would be based upon an interplay of economic forces within our entire region and not limited to undue restrictions or competition within extremely small national markets, thus enhancing the prospects of investment in the region as a whole. In this connection, serious attention should be given and studies conducted into arrangements for the joint financing of industries and intra-regional development projects. I recognize that there are other areas in which co-operation is desirable and feasible, but considering the probable cost, and since it is entirely conceivable that we might have to solicit the assistance of international organizations to work with our technical experts in conducting these studies, I recommend at the present time that we restrict ourselves to the areas suggested herein.

I recognize also that for any selected area of co-operation to be acceptable, meaningful and efficient, it must of necessity provide the greatest possibility for such trade exchanges as do not conflict with the present international relationships of our four countries while at the same time giving stimulus to industrialization and economic diversification in our countries. Lastly, any co-operation should be complementary to the expansion of trade and development among our countries on an equitable basis.

Colleagues, I have attempted here to summarize what I think the purposes and aims of this conference should be, together with some of the advantages that will accrue to our four countries. The formation of a Free Trade Area would bring some problems which would have to be resolved if the principle and concept of the proposed Free Trade Area is generally accepted. The most outstanding problem would seem to be that of payments. I realize that co-operation in the fields of industry, agriculture and transportation would certainly raise intricate financial problems, to which careful attention must be given. These problems would be particularly complicated in view of the fact that our four countries have different currency systems as well as varying restrictions on international payments. In this respect, it would seem to me that the most important problem is that which relates to the provision that must be made for the possibility that an increased level of trade between us might not balance, even though certain safeguards designed to prevent a concentration of industries in one country to the exclusion of another might be provided.

By and large, it is my thinking that none of the countries concerned is likely to have an abundance of foreign exchange and therefore would scarcely be in a position to accumulate non-convertible balances without adversely affecting its overall development programme. However, in order not to impede the growth of intra-regional trade, consideration should be given to devising some machinery for granting temporary mutual credits to one another to finance at least part of any trade imbalance which might occur among member countries. No one country should be expected to grant credits to another, so long as the latter country has a trade surplus with other countries outside the region.

In view of the limited time at present at our disposal and of the highly technical nature of the problems involved, I suggest that a commission be organized to examine the intricacies of these problems and to make relevant recommendations.

I submit this statement, and the proposals contained therein, for your consideration to such an extent and in such a manner as you may deem appropriate.

To each of you, I again extend a hearty welcome. In the same spirit which has always characterized our meetings, let us accept the challenge that this opportunity affords and let us enter upon our tasks with confidence that our deliberations will be blessed, so that a plan may be evolved for the establishment of closer economic co-operation, achievement of mutual development and accelerated advancement of our countries. Let us not permit the decisions taken at this conference to remain mere written words on scrolls of paper, not effectuated by implementation nor made real by concerted action.

A Broadcast to the Nation upon the Establishment of a National Development Bank

Monrovia, 19 October 1964

> *The National Development Bank of Liberia is both an opportunity and a challenge to all Liberians. . . . We must by our own efforts . . . advance the cause which we have undertaken. The Government needs your assistance to enlarge its national prosperity. . . . No public cause has ever offered greater benefits or profits.*
>
> *In the name of your children and your own future, for the advancement of your nation in the enlargening concept of a sounder economic future, I ask you to rally to the call of the nation at this time and make the Development Bank a successful national and international investment.*

Introductory Note

Perhaps no other phase of Liberia's growth is worthy of such sympathy and understanding than its long and tortuous search for a viable and sustained economy. The National Development Bank was an outgrowth of the Open Door Policy, which was intended to encourage Liberians to undertake business enterprises, thereby enabling them to participate directly in the economic growth and expansion of their country, and at the same time accelerate the nation's industrial development. Liberians were urged to look upon this Bank as a true Liberian enterprise in which their participation and co-operation was needed.

Monrovia, 19 October 1964

ONE OF the principal considerations which has guided the Liberian Government, and particularly this administration, in the continuing struggle to make our nation a truly unified, strong and progressive state has been the philosophy of self-help; the endeavour to help ourselves to the fullest extent of our abilities first of all, and to seek outside assistance only when we were unable to accomplish unaided what we wished to achieve.

From small beginnings therefore, we have gone on to bigger things in our political, social, educational and technical planning; from ideals we have approached the realm of ideas and from the fruits of our own efforts we have achieved co-operative results in planning and accomplishment. It is encouraging to remark that as leaders have from time to time initiated programmes for development, the people of the nation have become conditioned to this doctrine of utilizing their own resources to the fullest extent before turning their gaze outward. By acting on this principle we have

355

been able to fulfil some of our national ideals and aspirations; we shall rely upon it to carry on in the present and future convinced that 'heaven helps those who help themselves.'

The steadily changing phases of our development projects, increasing both in number and in complexity, and the high priority we have decided to accord to programmes which accelerate growth and lend themselves to greater stability, give us the satisfaction that we are moving in the right direction to an era of increased peace, progress and prosperity. There can now be no turning back, no relenting of our efforts, but rather a continued process of study and analysis with a view to strengthening and improving our existing programmes. To achieve these ends we must push ever onward by bringing to the task all our human and natural potentialities. The task which lies before us is one which will demand all our patriotism, all our loyalty and all our devotion.

Following in the wake of this self-help formula, and after lengthy discussions and planning in which the pros and cons were fully weighed, the Government decided to sponsor the organization of a National Development Bank to accelerate the era of progress and development upon which the nation has happily entered. We are hopeful that the establishment of this Bank will be another great step forward for our nation, one which will be of great benefit to all enterprising Liberians, and we hope that it will arouse others to useful activities in the direction of progress and development.

It is gratifying to state that since the making of this decision a friendly government and a number of foreign corporations and companies have welcomed the idea and contributed substantial sums to the capitalization of the Bank. This is indeed a great incentive and should provide the pace which all can follow, with pride to themselves and credit to the realization of a plan of action which is bound to have an impact on the overall development of the nation. The National Development Bank of Liberia is both an opportunity and a challenge to all Liberians. We rely upon you to play your part in making it an effective instrument for social progress and economic stability.

In my remarks at the Cabinet meeting held on Tuesday, the 17th instant, I stressed the fact that inasmuch as God had blessed the nation and its people with a certain degree of economic growth, Liberians should become responsible for the capitalization of this Bank, and I voiced the hope that every Cabinet member would become responsible for popularizing the idea so that interest may be aroused and action initiated in support of this new venture. I am happy to report that as a result of this appeal the Cabinet responded by promising to invest in the sum of $15,000.00, and both the Vice-President and the Speaker have indicated that they will invest in this worthwhile endeavour by contributing $5,000.00 each. I hope that the truism 'like leaders, like people' will operate to advantage in this instance. Your leaders have taken the lead, and so I appeal to and invite the citizenry of this nation, in this public manner, to invest in this laudable undertaking.

We should be constantly aware that the development of this nation is our responsibility and while we shall always be glad to share with others the enjoyment of the blessings of up-to-date developments and the amenities of twentieth-century civilization, we must by our own efforts impress and invite others to throw in their lot with and assist us to advance the cause which we have undertaken. In this particular case, the Government needs your assistance to enlarge its national prosperity, to make investments and contributions by investments which will later be mutually profitable to both Government and investors. No public cause has ever been more needful or offered greater benefits of profits, and no appeal has ever contained so much of the quintessence of national progress and prosperity as the National Development Bank. No matter how small the investment, all can take part in this venture and make it one of the greatest achievements of this generation. Let us therefore act now in the interest of a better and stronger Liberia.

Those of you who have already invested in the Liberian enterprises, LAMCO and other Concessions and Companies, by buying shares, must feel the satisfaction which a future financial security will provide for you and your children. The Development Bank of Liberia is to be the outgrowth of your own capital and the result of your interest and faith. A brochure containing detailed information on the organization, operation and investment policy of the Bank has been prepared, copies of which are available at the office of the Honourable Lafayette Morgan, Under Secretary of the Treasury for Fiscal Affairs.

Finally, I want to commend you for the response you have in the past given to my appeals in such matters. Your understanding attitude and your willing co-operation have greatly and substantially assisted in effectuating the programmes which we placed before you and for the support of which we appealed to your sense of loyalty and patriotism. In the name of your children and your own future, for the advancement of your nation in the expanding concept of a sounder economic future, and in the interest of a greater order which we all envisage for our nation, I ask you to rally to the call of the Government at this time and make the Development Bank a successful national and international investment.

Thank you and good night.

At the Opening of the National Industrial Relations Conference

Monrovia, 27 January 1965

It is people who count; it is they who create and help to maintain the factors of production.

Introductory Note

The Open Door Policy has brought not only the foreign investor and investment to Liberia, but has created problems of industrial relations as well. This industrial conference, the first of its kind to be held in Liberia, was convened for the purpose of enabling labour and management to become better acquainted and more informed as to what rights were accorded and guaranteed to each under the protection of the labour laws of Liberia. President Tubman defines these rights, and also the responsibilities and obligations of labour and management to the Government. The Government's own responsibilities and obligations to labour and management are also stipulated.

Monrovia, 27 January 1965

THIS CONFERENCE, given the title ascribed to it, could become one of the greatest, most unique and effective conferences in the history of human relations between management, labour and Government, particularly labour and management, depending upon the objectivity of their approach to the problems, subjects and questions inscribed on the agenda and their adherence to the principle of the golden rule: 'Do unto others as you would that they should do unto you.' I would emphasize that this rule does not suggest that you do unto others as they do unto you, but that you do unto them as you would like them do unto you. Conversely, if labour and management, in the debates and discussions that will be held here, become obsessed with subjective, irrational and unrealistic attitudes, the results could be disastrous to both management and labour. It is interesting that along with labour and management the Government is represented as a go-between, a mediator intended to see that fairness, justice and right prevail.

I approach the task of addressing you at this opening session with a certain amount of diffidence and yet with a greater amount of pleasure. Perhaps something I may say may serve a useful purpose and help to influence either or both parties to reach correct decisions. I hope to avoid the plight in which the late revered President of the United States, Franklin D. Roosevelt, found himself when management and labour were engaged in a fierce conflict; he was so greatly annoyed that he declared, 'A plague on both your houses', and John L. Lewis, one of the great labour leaders of that time came back with this scathing philippic against the President:

'Labour, like Israel, has its sorrows, her women weep for the fallen of the race and it behoves him who has supped at labour's table and lived in labour's house, to curse with equal fervour both labour and its adversary when they are locked in deadly embrace.'

You, the representatives of labour, management and Government, have come together to take part in this very important Industrial Relations Conference; to discuss labour-management problems and the labour law administration involved in expanding domestic and foreign business enterprises; to seek practical and just solutions to these problems; and to map future plans designed to stimulate progress and development. I congratulate those who conceived the idea and planned the conference, extend a cordial welcome to the participants who have come to share in this business and social experience and wish them an enjoyable and rewarding stay in the capital. May all that you will do and say here throw added light on the significant relationships which should exist between labour and management, and engender closer understanding and a sympathetic appreciation of the rôle which each group is capable of playing in enhancing the status of the rapidly expanding industrial development enterprises in our nation.

Andrew Carnegie is reported to have been asked which was the most important of the three factors in modern industry – capital, labour or management. Smiling, the great steel magnate replied, 'If you can tell me which is the most important leg of a three-legged stool, I will answer you.'

It may not be easily attainable for management and labour to lie together in the same bed and become bed-fellows; it may also be difficult for them to agree with each other completely on every issue. It may appear impracticable for them to take the same point of view on questions of work, wages, salaries, labour legislations, social security, workmen's compensation, pensions, retirement benefits, housing conditions and related matters, but with a resolute, dispassionate and unselfish approach, and with determination and perseverance, all of these questions can be settled. There will sometimes be differences between management and labour, strong differences that may occasionally be fundamental. Periodically, there may occur threats from labour or management; threats of strikes, sabotage and reprisals, but in every case, each, while insisting upon what he considers his rights, should also give consideration to the merits involved in the dispute and the rights of the other party.

We in Liberia believe strongly in and encourage a free economy. As this requires a stable government, an intelligent and hard-working labour force, and enlightened and scrupulous investors and management to constitute an economy based on the system of free enterprise, we support private initiative.

We hope that neither management nor labour will by any act attempt to adversely affect, disrupt or destroy this system, but will lend their efforts to improve the national economy in support of the free enterprise system and the implementation of the Operation Production Programme.

This Government believes in the wisdom and value of collective bargaining and is opposed to violence, whether between political parties, citizens, corporations, tribes, counties, townships, families or labour and management. The Government will see that neither management nor labour take advantage of, destroy, over-ride or rule out the other, because both of them are symbols of the free enterprise system, which we support both in theory and in practice. No economy can become really sound without an active and free labour organization; by the same token, without the private element of management, employers and investors, no economy can be free or even exist.

It is of interest to discover, in reading the history of great industrial leaders that most of them came from the ranks. A foreman is generally chosen because of his ability to lead and influence people. If as a foreman he exemplifies the same ability, he may become a superintendent, a department manager, a general manager or a top executive. A real leader of men should never, therefore, lose sight of the fact that neither management nor labour should be concerned with things so much as with people. It is people who count; it is they who create and help maintain the factors of production. If both sides come to realize that good human relations can be achieved and maintained, not so much by legislation but by attempts at fair play and co-operation, their organizations will have gone a long way in attaining one of the vital levels in industrial enterprise.

One of the things that might be accomplished at this conference is that labour will know more clearly at its close where management stands on certain issues. On the other hand, it will be clear to management what labour thinks, seeks and expects. The Government should have learned with greater certainty what the basic aims and objectives of both parties are and thereby be in a better position to adjudicate, conciliate and arbitrate when necessary. Labour and management should have a valid interpretation of the Government's policies, programmes and position. This conference may not bring about complete agreement on all points or subjects, but it should certainly bring understanding and a full disclosure of the position of all parties concerned. On the basis of these disclosures and this new acquaintance between the Government, management and labour, the Government should be able to improve legislations, procedures, regulations and policies in the interest of management, labour and national development.

We are at this time passing through a period of austerity when the flow of capital is not increasing. A large portion of Government revenues is being applied to debt settlement. In these circumstances, the Government is considering a short and a long range solution to this problem.

The short range solution is geared to enabling the Government to meet its operational requirements, to continue some of its development programmes and meet debt obligations under the resettling plan.

The long range solution will increase the Government's revenues by creating more working capital for business institutions, by bringing in more investment capital and by generating additional investments from within. The long range solution is to provide more employment, better job opportunities, insistence upon vocational and technological training; therefore, we have proposed Operation Production as priority number one.

For Operation Production to become a successful reality, the private sector of the economy must share most of the responsibility and take the leading rôle, because ours is an economy of free enterprise, private initiative and rugged individualism. Productive activity must rest predominately in the hands of the private sector if we are to be truly a private enterprise nation.

Within the private sector of any economy are two principal forces: labour and management – the employee and employer. These are the forces responsible for the progress or stagnancy, the failure or success of a nation whose economy is based on the private enterprise system.

In such a system, the Government's rôle is mainly to protect property, ensure liberty, life and privilege; to defend the weak, the strong, the minority and the majority alike against injustices to the same degree; to ensure the enactment of reasonable and efficient laws, and stress their correct interpretation and effective enforcement. However, the problem of production, distribution, consumption, savings and investment rests principally with the private individual, the private corporation and private initiative.

It is the responsibility of the Government to stimulate private initiative, to provide public utilities and services that will encourage and assist private enterprise, corporations or individuals in their productive efforts. It is also the responsibility of the Government to ensure political stability, and to maintain a climate conducive to investment, progressive economic activity and national development.

The Government is endeavouring to fulfil these obligations. If then, Operation Production is to be a success in Liberia, if the crises of austerity are to be quickly overcome, if the people of the nation are to enjoy a more prosperous life, labour, management and all forces of the private sector of the nation must assert themselves to the maximum in this struggle, and in the fulfilment of their obligations to Operation Production.

It has been observed that this is the first National Industrial Relations Conference to be held in Africa and that the effort has received compliments from the International Labour Organization and friends around the world. One of the most important aspects of such a Conference is to note how much understanding can be reached and implemented. It is not so much the decisions and their faithful execution; for in principle and despite all differences, management and labour should always join hands, have a common motive and offer a united front when it comes to the national interest, the solution of the present problem of austerity and the execution of our programme for Operation Production.

From these considerations we arrive at the conclusion that Labour and Management must co-operate since both are mutually interdependent entities – two partners on a three-legged stool, and what affects one vitally affects the other.

Finally, I congratulate you, the delegates gathered here today, for the work you are to undertake. It is my fervent hope and prayer that as a result of your deliberations and decisions at this conference, you will close your ranks, set a new pattern and raise a new standard for the conduct of labour and management in their attitude toward each other, which will become the basis for an eventual peaceful revolution in the history of industrial enterprise in Liberia and elsewhere, and that the nation may continue in the continuum of peace, progress and happiness. As William Green, President of the American Federation of Labour, once said: 'With labour and management working together in common cause, and not against each other, we can build, produce and prosper. We can defeat any threat from whatever source against our security and the peace of the world.' And so may it be.

To the Board of Trustees and Officers of the National Iron Ore Company

Monrovia, 13 May 1965

We are forging ahead with the struggle to give to our people a greater measure of freedom, prosperity and happiness.

Introductory Note

The National Iron Ore Company owes its existence to the foresight of Lansdell K. Christie, an American businessman and a benevolent friend of Liberia. Liberia, at the time of the creation of this Company, was witnessing a period of great industrial boom, the first of its kind in its history of more than a hundred years. Liberians from all walks of life were invited to participate in this economic boom by the purchasing of shares on liberal terms. President Tubman appreciated this unique business trend as an act of philanthropy rare in the world of business.

Monrovia, 13 May 1965

YOU, THE officials of the National Iron Ore Company, have done us a unique honour by giving this sumptuous dinner on our behalf. Not only are we profoundly grateful for this gracious gesture, but deeply touched by the expression concerning the humble efforts we have endeavoured to exert to serve the nation. Whatever measure of success and satisfaction may have been achieved must also be attributed to those who have helped in the process of providing the guidelines and bearing the burdens implicit in such ventures and operations.

We live in an era largely dependent on business and industry, the success of which contributes to the peace, progress and prosperity of the world. It is a recognized fact that the output of industry and the distribution process of business make possible high standards of living. Those nations, therefore, that have made great development in business and industry, through what is known as the process of expanding production and the improved processes of distribution, have made greater progress than other nations that have not risen so high in the scale of industrial process. But this is human progress, and it is toward this goal that every nation, particularly the developing states of Africa, is striving. We continue to look to our friends and well-wishers to lend their support and co-operation.

It has always been the concern of the leaders of this nation to help the citizenry achieve a higher standard of living through education and the provision of better health methods. However, the barely tapped resources of the nation have not made this goal easy to achieve; but as the country has gradually opened to free enterprise, as the stability of our political structure gained greater recognition and as investors became more and more attracted by the Open Door Policy and tax regulation within the last decade, our economic position gained in strength and vitality. This is a responsibility which we are determined to continue, so that more and more investment capital may be attracted and investors, Government and people may benefit. Constant research, surveys and studies predict for the nation and its people an era of increased economic opportunities and a brighter and more encouraging future for business and industry.

In this upward trend, we are pleased to state that the National Iron Ore Company set a new pattern in the business world when it made provision for opening new avenues for participation by Liberians in its mining project. By this plan Liberian citizens were offered twenty per cent of the shares of the company. Nor was this the only new liberal dimension. Mr. Lansdell Christie, President of the Liberian National Enterprises, worked out a payment plan whereby any Liberian citizen desiring to invest in the Company would pay twenty per cent of the purchase price of the total twenty per cent of stock owned by him, the remaining eighty per cent being advanced by him to be repaid only out of future dividends at the rate of fifty per cent of earned dividends per annum.

This generous plan, by which Liberians purchased twenty per cent of the total shares and the Government fifty per cent, makes the Company in reality almost wholly Liberian-owned. We consider this to be not only an unusual business approach, but the unselfish act of a man with a great and generous heart and conscience.

Because of the very helpful rôle which the mine management associates are playing in stimulating the economy of the country, confidence has been established and a sense of mutuality and identity created. To all credit and banking institutions, all individuals and firms which have in any way provided assistance, especially during the crucial years of the Company's operation, the Government and people of Liberia will always be grateful. Your confidence in the nation's future for economic advancement and industrial and business possibilities are good business assets, and will be instrumental in reaping large dividends for all.

If you are one of those who have worked in Liberia and participated in activities designed to stimulate growth in business and industry, then you have perhaps experienced the satisfaction of seeing some of the seeds that you have sown burst into fragrant blooms. Or, if you came to know of Liberia through informed sources and are here for the first time, we hope that the contacts already made have impressed you about the trend of events in this nation and the direction in which the Government is going. But, if you are an old friend of Liberia, then you are aware of its history and the path it has travelled from its incipiency to the present, and we hope that you will continue to show interest and sympathy in our development programme. We are forging ahead with the struggle to give our people a greater measure of freedom, prosperity and happiness. If you have been all these, then you may be aware of the pace of development here and the response of the people themselves to the opportunities of history for national growth and advancement.

I know that the shareholders of this Company will be happy when they learn that dividends are to be paid at the end of the current year. Certainly,

Mr. Christie is relieved of the anxiety he entertained when, because of certain difficulties and other disappointments, the Company was unable to keep its production schedule. We hope that the venture is now in calm waters and its future assured, and that its success and prosperity will bring happiness to investors and shareholders alike.

Speech at Dinner in Honour of A. G. Lund, President of Firestone Plantations Company

Monrovia, 28 June 1965

Our relationship with Firestone has been long and enduring.

Introductory Note

Not only has the relationship between the Government and people of Liberia and the Firestone Natural Rubber Company, an American business enterprise, been long and enduring, but so has the personal relationship between President Tubman and the leaders of this company. In these brief remarks we have an indication of the type of amicable co-operation which exists in an atmosphere of mutual confidence and trust between Government and private capital.

Monrovia, 28 June 1965

MRS. TUBMAN and I and representative citizens of our country seek by this ovation to express gratitude and thanks to two of our friends, Mr. A. G. Lund, former General Manager of Firestone Plantations Company and now President of the Company, and Mrs. Lund, for their co-operation, their contributions and the services they have rendered to the Government and people of Liberia, as representatives of the oldest concession in Liberia.

I had always thought that the President of Firestone Plantations Company would be a lawyer. I knew Bill Hynes who came to Liberia in 1925 to negotiate the Firestone Plantations Company's concession. He was a lawyer (and I became a lawyer for Firestone here at that time). Following Hynes was George Fisher who became the legal representative of Firestone Plantations Company, virtually in charge of the operations of the company in Liberia while he was in Akron, Ohio. George Fisher was succeeded by Mr. Byron Larabee, who was also a lawyer. Later, Larabee became President of the Company and he retired. Now, our friend, Mr. Lund has become President of the Company. It is either Saul among the prophets or the prophets with Saul.

Sometimes I become afraid of lawyers because Christ told them, 'Woe unto you lawyers, for you have taken away the key of knowledge.' I do not know what He meant by that; we might need some theological or ecclesiastical explanation of Christ's statement. But I feel a certain amount of satisfaction when I read that, for that was the only condemnation Christ made of the lawyers. But He certainly condemned the Scribes and Pharisees. He said unto them: 'Woe unto you Scribes and Pharisees, hypocrites; for you gather burdens grievous to be borne and lay them on men's shoulders, but you will not touch them with the tip of your fingers. Woe unto you Scribes and Pharisees, hypocrites! for ye devour widows' houses and for a pretence make long prayers. Woe unto you Scribes and Pharisees, hypocrites! who say that he that sweareth by the temple is nothing but he that sweareth by the gold that is on the temple is a debtor. Thou blind guides! which is greater? the temple that sanctifies the gold or the gold that is on the temple.' And Christ went right on condemning the Pharisees.

However, we have now one that is not in that category; a plain business-man. I have known Mr. Lund approximately for the past ten years, and I have found him to be a straight, honest-to-goodness businessman; a person who knows what he wants, knows how to go about getting what he wants, and knows how to get what he wants.

We are exceedingly sorry to lose his constant and intimate association with us in Liberia. But although removed, he is not so far because with modern facilities like the aeroplanes, the radiograms, and now telecommuni-cations, he is closer than he was while up there at Harbel.

You carry with you, Mr. and Mrs. Lund, our very fondest wishes and our prayers for your success in your new position. Having taken on this new position and leaving the old, you are in the position to look back and see with satisfaction the successes you have made. It is a great thing to be able to take off the armour, to serve and then retire honourably and peacefully. For as long as you are in service you are on the front line, you are on the firing line and you cannot tell when your feet might slip and your soul get lost. Therefore, having risen first to the managerial position which you held here in Firestone and now to the position of boss of Firestone in Liberia, we are very happy. We are sure that your administration in the new position will be as successful as, if not more than, it was in your past position.

As you leave us, we ask you to convey my thanks to my friends (from 1925 to the present) Harvey S. Firestone, Jun., Raymond Firestone, Mr. Byron H. Larabee – men who have made great contributions to the economic growth and success of our country. Tell them that we believe in saying 'thank you' for blessings, benefits and gifts bestowed.

You succeed a man like Mr. Larabee, during whose tenure of office the Government of Liberia, by negotiations, received the first income tax pay-ments from your company. Later, the amount was increased. And in recent years, when the Government of Liberia ran up against austerity, we asked all of the concessionaires who have recovered many times their capital expenditures, to increase their income tax, to increase the Government's participation in profits. Not a solitary one of them failed or refused to do so. They all acquiesced, and they are all our dear friends; we regard them as patrons of the Republic of Liberia.

I would like you to tell Harvey Firestone, Jun., that we are a crowd of boys and I would like to see him come here at least once more before he retires and before I retire. We do not have much time; he must come quickly. Also Raymond Firestone; well, he is a young blood; he is just getting into the business and is becoming adjusted. Raymond was a little fellow when I went to Akron in 1928; the other brother Roger was a young fellow in the Navy.

While we were at a luncheon given in my honour by Mr. Firestone, Roger was a little slow in coming. Mr. Firestone was very conerned about the whereabouts of Roger. But when Roger finally came in, his face was all red. He reported to his father that someone had run into his Lincoln car and damaged it, almost killing him. Firestone told Roger to sit down and get another Lincoln. Before we left the luncheon Roger had another Lincoln car.

Our relationship with Firestone has been fond and enduring. It is true that people who live far apart are in less danger of misunderstanding one another than those who live together as neighbours, where they come into contact with each other every day, know each other and their failures better, and all that sort of thing. So that with Firestone, with you Mr. Lund, and all of the other fellows in the United States – although the old man Firestone and some of the fellows have gone to the great beyond – we want the same relationship to exist now and in the future between the leaders and people of Liberia and Firestone as has existed between us in the past and in the present. Convey to all of them this message.

Before I ask you to join Mrs. Tubman and me in wishing Mr. and Mrs. Lund our final bon voyage, I would like to note the presence here with us of a Minister from the Federal Republic of Nigeria, the biggest and largest State on the African Continent; more than that, an African State that we can understand, that we think is understanding and understandable. We extend to him our very hearty welcome.

Then, we have here also a Minister of the Israeli Government, a very friendly state; a minister whom I met at a peculiarly and singularly Israeli institution called a Kibbutz, where Mrs. Tubman and I were invited to enjoy the Israeli communal system – where the interest of one is the interest of all. It is an organization which wonderfully illustrates Psalm 133: 'Behold, how good and how pleasant it is for brethren to dwell together in unity!' We had a good evening there.

We also have with us as our guest at the 118th Independence Anniversary Celebrations His Excellency the Civil Governor of Las Palmas, where any Liberian visitor is made to feel as much at home as in Liberia. Our guest and his consort are with us. Also we have the Lord Mayor of Las Palmas and his consort. We have been their guests more than once and expect to be many more times, as often as we make stop-overs in their lovely island. I recall the time we visited Las Palmas in 1952, when we were the first to lodge in the city's newly constructed, beautiful but then undedicated 'Catalina' Hotel. We were especially honoured. That I remember well.

To all of our guests here we extend a very hearty and warm welcome.

At the Formal Opening of the Bong Mining Company

Bong Mines, Liberia, 12 November 1965

In the execution of the Open Door Policy we have sought to diversify investors so that here would exist a multi-national investment of different nations and peoples contributing and effectively participating in the economic and technological development of a country which practises democratic principles and believes in the free enterprise system.

Introductory Note

The Germans have a long-established business tradition in Liberia. Following the interruption of this contact due to two world wars in which Germany was actively engaged, they returned and renewed their economic ties on a mutual basis, especially in the area of mining. Active in war, active in peace, they have contributed substantially to Liberia's industrial growth. President Tubman expressed gratitude for this resurgence of German interest in Liberia and the new dimension it has taken.

Bong Mines, Liberia, 12 November 1965

AFTER TRAVELLING in comfort over the rails on a modern locomotive, after enjoying the beauty created by earth-moving machinery which has carved out the bosom of Mother Nature's hills and filled in her valleys, and after watching the wonders of engineering that bridged her waterways and penetrated through silent jungle, we arrived at this site of impressive industrial activity which the Bong Mining Venture has established on these hills.

This is indeed one of the few occasions on which one cannot but be filled with mixed emotions, of undaunted faith in God and at the same time of pride at the achievements that have been made in so short a time. This is especially true when the sown seeds begin to germinate, unfold, blossom and bring forth good fruit — not only to assuage the appetite of financiers but, most important of all, to benefit humanity, directly and indirectly. A decade ago one would never have believed that we could today have reached such a stage of advancement as to be present here for these memorable ceremonies. This ceremony today is the outgrowth of an idea and a principle which, through processes of synthesis, brought about the Open Door Policy, whereby we ventured to invite and induce interested foreign businessmen to invest in this country on a fifty-fifty assessment basis.

In the execution of the Open Door Policy we have sought to diversify investors so that there would exist a multi-national investment of different nations and peoples constructively participating in the economic and technological development of a country which practises democratic principles and believes in the free enterprise system.

There is no doubt that in an investment of this magnitude and quality there are countless benefits to be derived, both for the nationals of this country and for nationals of other countries. While we know these things to be self-evident, we cannot predict the extent of the benefits which nationals other than Liberians may derive from these operations.

We foresee that your concession will reduce the number of out-of-school youth by providing adequate elementary education facilities; it will reduce our unskilled manpower population by a sound vocational educational programme including apprenticeship and on-the-job training; it will reduce our infant mortality by efficient and broadly-based medical services; it will reduce the incidence of poverty and disease by equitable compensations and liberal health programmes; it will raise the economic lot of its employees, their immediate families and dependents; it will intensify the Government's programme of Unification and Integration by bringing citizens from different elements of the country to work together with a common purpose – to serve humanity in a peaceful and thoughtful atmosphere of human rights and the dignity of the individual, with loyalty and respect for the state and supreme reverence to the God of our Fathers. All of these and many more such co-operative endeavours will go a long way in cementing our individual, corporate, national and international interests and understandings.

I am particularly pleased and highly impressed with this first German industrial investment project of such magnitude. The Germans hold an international business reputation and usually whatever they undertake to do, is carried to completion with thoroughness and exactness. In the past when the leasing of houses from Liberians by foreigners was one of the lucrative factors or aspects of our economy, Liberians believed that for many reasons it was to their advantage to deal with the Germans. The same attitude prevailed with regard to German commercial business, which earned for them an enviable record that has been maintained through the years. I mention these attributes to remind ourselves of the fertile soil which lies ahead for German businessmen and enterpreneurs for sowing seeds of greater prosperity in the future. Of course, this is not meant to imply that the Germans are better concessionaires than anyone else; it is yet to be proved.

I cannot over-emphasize the dynamism with which Dr. Plotzki, President of this venture, has brought it to this stage of development in spite of strong discouragements and adversities in difficult times and conditions. It may be that he also is from the same stock as the heads of other German firms who have made such an indelible mark for themselves in the commercial business of this country.

I would like to revert to the ideal which is responsible for all of these efforts and deliberations – the Open Door Policy. Through this policy we advanced the formula of joint ownership, which seems to have caught the consideration of some other countries, to the extent that they have also adopted the same policy, perhaps under different forms and styles.

The world climate today indicates a strong need for concerted efforts towards narrowing the gap between the highly industrialized nations and the less developed countries; between the capitalists and those who possess the raw materials of technology; between the investors and the receptors. *We believe that a healthy partnership, in which joint interests are shared to the mutual benefits of the parties concerned, is a wholesome one. We believe in the principle of 'give and take' which is an inherent element of the Open Door Policy.*

The Open Door Policy has benefited many Liberians and Liberia itself; but up until now it has perhaps benefited more greatly, those of our foreign partners whose pockets are too deep for us to plumb. However, we are not in the position to contest this issue. We can only rely on those concessions which have preceded you, for they have established a tradition of which both of us are equally satisfied and proud.

In paying our compliments to the several groups with vested interests in this project, I express my thanks and appreciation to the many dedicated and hard working people, both present and absent, who have made these ceremonies possible and contributed to the Bong Mine Operations up to its present stage of development. I thank the planners for their ingenuity and the bankers who made available the necessary loans to get this joint scheme on a sound footing. I sincerely hope that all vested interests will receive the innumerable benefits they expect from their respective investments.

I extend a special and warm welcome to Mr. Schmidt-Hornix, Special Representative of the German Government, and the many foreigners holding interests in this joint operation and hope that their stay here will be both pleasant and rewarding.

Tribute on the Passing Away of Lansdell Christie, Friend of Liberia

Monrovia, 24 November 1965

We should think of Lansdell Christie as a lover of men.

Introductory Note

Lansdell K. Christie came to Liberia as a philanthropic businessman. Whatever economic benefits he derived from his mining investments in Liberia he saw to it that the people of Liberia also received an appreciable share of those benefits. He was further reported to be the first foreign investor in Liberia to invite Liberians to own shares in the exploitation of their natural wealth. President Tubman deeply mourned his passing. Lansdell K. Christie risked his fortune in investments in Liberia at a time when few foreign investors saw little, if any, future in investment possibilities here. The rich dividends which accrued to him encouraged many foreign investors to come to Liberia. Lansdell K. Christie was probably the first foreign investor to believe and have faith in the future success of Liberia's Open Door Policy. He was besides a great admirer of President Tubman.

Monrovia, 24 November 1965

LANSDELL CHRISTIE, pilgrim to the Infinite after sixty-one years, eleven months and twenty-six days of pilgrimage on these hallowed grounds of sorrow, has left us. A few of those who loved him and knew him are gathered here to pay their tribute to his memory. A few, I say because the great host of friends and acquaintances who sorrow and mourn at his passing are scattered throughout many continents of the world.

To those who did not know Colonel Christie, except as he appeared upon special occasions, the first impression of him would have been that of a rather severe dignity which discouraged any approach. In reality, Mr. Christie was of the broadest sympathies and appropriately companionable in almost every sphere of association. Like a friend, father or brother, he had fitting words for the house of sorrow but was also able to bring his contribution of cheer to the marriage feast. He was at home in the flashing exchange of brilliant conversation or in the companionship of common people. He was the genial comrade of those who experienced pain, disappointments and difficulties, but he could be a brother among young people and a playmate even with children. Such was the unconstrained range of his comradeship.

In the world of general literature there were few masters with whom it might be truly said he was not acquainted. If the contents of their thoughts were really of value, obscurity of style was merely a challenge to him. He was not to be turned away from his quest for the treasure because the way of its possession seemed difficult, and he was at home with the greatest of the masters. Let us think of Colonel Christie today principally as a lover of men.

I cannot bring myself to write a memorial tribute to one whom I feel to be so very much alive with the Infinite, after sixty-one years of pilgrimage with the Finite. It would seem better, at this sombre service, for us to sit in silence and if we might visualize the composite picture, wrought of our recollections and affection, such a gathering together of tender memories would be far more eloquent than the words any one of us might be able to speak. However, I wish to point out as clearly as possible to the people of every class and range of Liberia, the unselfish, deep and immovable love and interest that this great man, Lansdell Christie, entertained for the development of this country, and prosperity of its people, particularly its common people; and his unexcelled and unparallelled sacrificial contribution to every phase of national, civic, educational and industrial life of the nation and its people.

His interest and friendship could not be challenged, it was above and beyond question. He was as much a Liberian as a Liberian could be and this interest he carried and manifested by word and deed from the time that he entered business in this country. He often gave public utterances of his gratitude, claiming that he felt that the material benefits he earned from the country demanded of his conscience acts of benevolence and charity to his fullest ability. Mr. Christie did not stop here. He negotiated another iron ore concession for the Bie Mountain Range and began exploration this year.

His last visit to Liberia was in May of this year, his final adieu to the land he prized next to his own country. I have tried to portray the real, genuine interest of Lansdell Christie in Liberia and its people but let me now permit him, though dead, to speak for himself. Mr. Christie appeared to have realized the seriousness of his illness when on August 19th of this year while I was in Zürich, Switzerland, he wrote me a letter, excerpts of which I will read in verification of my opinion of his attitude toward Liberia and Liberians as well as the extent of the warm personal relationship between the two of us:

'Dear Shad:
    'I reproach myself for not having written to you much sooner, but I will defer the reason until later in my letter.
    'Garland tells me he is going to Switzerland to see you in September, so I am calling him a little later in the day to review matters of moment.
    'Knowing of your great dedication to the welfare of your country, I know you will be interested to know that the geological work in the Bie Mountains continues to be very promising. Chuck is spearheading that matter and while I should not talk out of school, I do get the impression that he is very optimistic. As you perhaps recall, the Bie Mountains are estimated about a billion tons. This then would transcend any other deposit within the confines of Liberia and of necessity would have a wonderful impact on the country. Another year will elapse before all the geological information is amassed and by that time it is within the realm to hope that the course is clearly outlined. Chuck really has his teeth in it and I get the feeling he is loaded for bear.

'And now again I refer to my first sentence and feel it is necessary to explain why I have been remiss in writing. About six weeks ago I grew to realize I was not in good health. I checked into my old stamping grounds and put myself into the hands of those old veterans Baldwin and Aranow. They, in turn, called in specialists and apparently they found cause to make them uneasy. As a result I am at the present time scheduled for an operation on Monday. Only Vernon, Ceil and Ben Greenberg, along with, of course, my immediate family and now yourself, will know about it.

'I have watched your amazing career and would I could wish I were to emulate you in some small way. Now I can only wait and see what fate holds in store.

'My association with you has been an exciting one and we have many warm memories. Mayhap fate will deign to smile on me and I will be back in harness once again. One great incentive to carry on is always the keen memory of all the good times we have had together.

'All the best to you, Shad, and grace be to you and peace be with you.'

To this I made a reply which I will also read during these remarks:

'My dear Chris:

'It has been a great relief to have Garland here as he speaks with you over the telephone occasionally and tells me how you are getting along, of your improvement...

'Notwithstanding this gratifying information your illness has caused me constant concern, worry and distress and I thank God that you are now improving, as reports received suggest that you will be out of hospital within three weeks. What good and glorious news it is!

'Your physicians' skill, your nurses' faithfulness, the prayers of your family and friends and your own personal fortitude crowned by the blessings of God have brought this to pass and will restore you to normal health and strength again.

'Let His name be praised!

'It has occurred to me as due to you from me as a friend and brother that I should send Shad over to see you and Mrs. Christie, to express to both of you Mrs. Tubman's and my own deep and sincere regrets for the illness that has befallen you, to also make known our joy and happiness that your health has been recovered and to rejoice with you and your family for this great act of mercy extended to you.

'Please believe me, Chris, when I state that your illness has cast a great pall over me but now that you are recovering the morning light breaks in and the darkness disappears.

'Shad will hand you this letter in person if he is permitted to see you but if your illness does not permit his seeing you then he will hand it to Mrs. Christie for you.

'With intent solicitude and affectionate regards I remain now and always,

Sincerely and cordially yours,
Shad'

This was the last exchange of letters between us. Fate was not as kind to him as he had hoped and as I had prayed, but this act of fate, this removal from the transcient and the mortal to the celestial and immortal, from the

Finite to the Infinite was the kindness of kindnesses; and so today in the midst of the Finite Lansdell Christie, father, brother and friend, lives eternally. Our condolences and sympathies go out to his widow, children, brother, sister and all of his relatives, each of whom has a claim on the good offices of the Liberian Government and people.

I have said previously that we should think of Lansdell Christie as a lover of men. He was the quintessence and embodiment of the kind of man that the poet, Leigh Hunt, showed Abou ben Adhem to be.

> Abou Ben Adhem (may his tribe increase!)
> Awoke one night from a deep dream of peace,
> And saw — within the moonlight in his room,
> Making it rich, and like a lily in bloom —
> An Angel writing in a book of gold.
> Exceeding peace had made Ben Adhem bold,
> And to the presence in the room he said,
> 'What writest thou?' — The vision raised its head,
> And, with a look made of all sweet accord,
> Answered, 'The names of those who love the Lord.'
> 'And is mine one?' said Abou. 'Nay, not so,'
> Replied the angel. Abou spoke more low,
> But cheery still; and said, 'I pray thee, then,
> Write me as one that loves his fellow men.'
> The angel wrote, and vanished. The next night
> It came again, with a great wakening light,
> And showed the names whom love of God had blessed,
> And lo! Ben Adhem's name led all the rest.

A Nation-wide Broadcast on the Firestone Strike

Monrovia, 12 February 1966

*Let every citizen regard it a sacred trust to be watchful, patriotic
and loyal to his own country, refusing to be persuaded by the mysticism of unrealistic ideologies that are illusions.*

Introductory Note

Organized labour in Liberia has a brief history. It has, however, established contact with several international labour unions. The result has
often been exposure to various ideologies permeating these unions, to
which labour unions in Liberia have won recognition or become affiliated.
The Liberian Government under the Tubman administration has won
international reputation for stability, and because of it, has attracted
many foreign business concessions. Organized labour in Liberia has on
several occasions made attempts to undermine business confidence and
the stability of the Government. A case in point was the strike of labourers
on the Firestone Rubber Plantation. The Government has laid down rules
for the conduct of a strike and has in no way denied labour this freedom
of action. On the other hand it will not permit nor tolerate labour's
propensity to undermine its stability. The President here reminds labour
of its responsibilities and obligations to the Government, and warns it
against the danger of the infiltration of foreign ideologies within its ranks.

Monrovia, 12 February 1966

FELLOW CITIZENS:

The obligation and responsibility of Government to maintain law and
order and to execute the laws of the Republic in preservation of the safety
of the state is its highest and most solemn duty.

Laws are not enacted or made for idle show, and while they remain the
guidelines by which the cohesion of the nation is assured, the Government
would be derelict and remiss in its duty and obligation to the body of the
people in allowing any segment of the population to violate the law with
impunity.

It is therefore regrettable that a large number of workers on the Firestone
Plantations instituted, have organized and staged a strike in violation of the
labour laws of the country. The labour laws provide that any person or
persons, union or unions, group or groups of workers have a right to strike
but the same laws also outline the procedure to be followed before the
staging of a strike. One of the basic provisions laid down in the law is that
if employer and employee disagree representation should be made to the

Grievance Committee, Department of Commerce and Industry, for its review and action before a strike may ensue.

The Government received no notice from the Firestone workers that disagreement existed between them and their employer. They went on strike in violation of this provision of the law. Word was received that the strike was in progress and moreover that the strikers were laying waste large quantities of latex, thus destroying property, and further that they were beating up other workers who desired to work.

I received a delegation of five of the leaders of the workers and pointed out to them their violation of the law in not first reporting this matter to the Grievance Committee and that the destruction of property was a crime; but I assured them that notwithstanding their violation of the law, no penal or punitive action would be taken against them if they retrieved their error by returning to work and submitting their grievances to the Grievance Committee as the law requires. I intimated that should they comply with this suggestion their complaint would be immediately looked into and duly considered, and a settlement of the dispute sought. These five men presented themselves as representatives of the workers who were on illegal strike and gave assurance that in compliance with law, they would see that the strikers returned to work the following day and submitted their grievances.

With this understanding I wrote a letter to the workers outlining the procedure to be followed in case workers desired to strike, just as I had explained it to their representatives, and gave it to them to take to the workers. I assured them that they were Liberian citizens and that Government would see that *their* rights were protected and preserved, as well as the rights of their employer. They left, and the machinery was set up by the Government for an inquiry into their grievances immediately after they were received.

Immediately after this, it was authentically reported that these five leaders, upon presentation of the letter to the strikers, were nearly mobbed and accused of having been bribed by their employer, Firestone, and of not having seen the President at all. Hence the letter was returned. They further stated that the type of stationery on which the letter was written was not the President's, as all letters from him have an imprint of the Liberian Flag.

Upon receipt of this information I wrote a second letter and sent it to the strikers by one of my Aides-de-Camp, General Samuel Johnson, along with the Secretary of Commerce, pointing out that they were persisting in violating the law and requesting them to return to work and refer their grievances or any dissatisfaction that they may have had to the Grievance Committee, as the law directs. One of the strikers stated that he had been to Monrovia to representatives of the CIO and showed them this letter and they had informed him that the signature was not the President's; therefore they ignored the second letter. They further alleged that General Johnson, by whom I had despatched the second letter, was not an Aide to the President.

By that time it had become evident that their representation in the above respect was mainly a pretext and a ruse, and that the men were determined to take the law into their own hands. Notwithstanding this I sent my son, because he is known to be a great labour sympathizer, to repeat to them what I had written in my two letters and impress upon the strikers that if they did not comply with the law they would not, under any circumstances, be permitted to continue its violation. They paid no attention to him but said that it was an impersonation.

Conditions worsened. Police and other security and peace-keeping officers were sent on the scene, but the strikers would not listen to anyone, nor would they submit to the majesty of the law. They insulted the officers of the law, disregarded them and threatened them. After two days of this lawless, riotous and unsettled situation, the Government felt obliged to take strong enough measures to compel their compliance with the law, and to prevent the commission of other and further crimes. A riot squad was therefore despatched to the area to protect those who desired to work, to prevent the destruction of property and to safeguard and protect life. They informed the strikers that anyone who did not wish to work would not be forced to, but on the other hand, neither they nor anyone else would be permitted to prevent and obstruct others from working if they desired to do so. This had no effect.

The strikers continued to threaten and assault workers who desired and attempted to work. An additional riot squad was then ordered to the scene with identical instructions. In their effort to protect workers who were willing to work, to prevent damage and destruction of property and to ensure the safety of life, the soldiers and police were attacked by strikers in groups of between five and six hundred. The soldiers used tear gas in the first instance but it proved effective only in some areas.

Reports received at this stage revealed that the strikers persisted and persevered in their attacks against the workers, soldiers and law enforcement officers and one soldier was wounded in the arm. In compliance with orders issued them, the soldiers fired over the heads of the advancing mob, but this did not deter them and they continued to advance on the troops. Whereupon, in obedience to further orders issued regarding such a situation, the soldiers fired at the rioters intending to disperse them. One rioter was wounded.

That night the strikers rioted and attacked with shotguns some of those that had returned to work, as well as the soldiers, and shot and wounded four of the workers. The soldiers again used tear gas and fired over the heads of the strikers, but still to no avail. A shot was then fired into the mob and one rioter was killed. Following this, workers on thirteen Divisions returned to work and revealed that they were instigated by certain persons on the plantations and others from outside the plantations, members of the CIO, who visited them at night immediately preceding the staging of the strike and encouraged and incited them to strike.

Laws are made for the protection of society and to ensure the stability of government. Labour and management have their rights and privileges but both must be equally subject to and obey the law, and workers or employers who violate the law will meet the force of the law. To do otherwise would be to invite anarchy and chaos.

The law does not contemplate violence unless violently assailed; the law is a mighty organ and must prevail and be upheld, because it involves individual liberties and the security and safety of the State.

There seems to be a grave misconception by most workers in this country concerning the meaning of strikes. Trade Unions have either been derelict in this respect, or have misled the workers, or at least those of them who are not capable of grasping and understanding things as well as they should; but ignorance is no excuse. For instance, a few months ago when the workers staged a strike at the Mano Iron Ore Mines, the officials of the Labour Bureau contacted them and asked why they had staged the strike without first referring their grievances to the Government if they and the employer could not agree. The strikers replied that they had not yet gone on strike; they had only put down their tools and refused to work but that they would strike on the 15th. Asked what they meant by this, they said that they would fight and destroy property. Then they put the following question to the representatives of the Labour Bureau: 'Isn't this what "strike" means in English: to hit, to strike, to fight?' Exactly the same statement was made by the strikers later, in the case of the strike on the Firestone Plantations.

Management and labour must co-operate for greater production and higher standards of living in the interest of both management and labour, and labour, like management, must receive fair and just compensation and other social benefits for their services.

It is regrettable that the Government was forced to pursue the course it did, forced by the deliberate, wanton and lawless attitude of some of the workers, inspired and influenced from within and without.

Mischief is afoot and the Government will not permit it to take what course it likes and will be prepared to cope with this new policy of certain unscrupulous, unconscionable and ruthless insurgents to create confusion, disturbance, insurrection and revolution.

I therefore recommend to the Legislature a law which they have enacted, which provides that any labour union that is found to be under the influence or direction of, or receives financial support or benefits from, any foreign or outside source, shall be declared illegal and shall not be permitted to function as a Union within the Republic of Liberia. I also recommend to the Legislature a law which they have enacted, to provide that Industrial Unions shall neither exercise themselves in the affairs of agricultural workers, nor represent them, neither shall Agricultural Unions exercise themselves in the affairs of industrial workers, nor represent them.

We extend regrets and sympathy to the families of the wounded, and of the one that was killed, but again I must repeat that the law does not contemplate violence unless violently assailed.

Let every citizen regard it a sacred trust to be watchful, patriotic and loyal to his own country, refusing to be persuaded by the mysticism of unrealistic ideologies that are illusionary and fantastic. Let every citizen, every man and woman be prepared to stand up and fight against any forces that seek by interference to subvert and overthrow by force, artifice or stealth our sacred heritage.

May God save the state, strengthen and prosper its people.

At the Salzgitter Corporation
West Germany, 8 September 1966

We have embarked upon a policy of industrialization, and we need mutual co-operation and assistance in order to accomplish this objective.

Introductory Note

In August 1966, President Tubman went to Switzerland on a much deserved health mission; but because of his consuming passion to push ahead Liberia's economic and industrial development, he nonetheless seized the opportunity to establish contact with certain business companies in West Germany, confident that such a move was in his nation's interest. One business house with whom contact was made was Salzgitter Corporation. This Corporation was invited to Liberia for the purpose of providing assistance and guidance in co-ordinating the nation's diversified industrial pursuits, and to plan effectively for greater industrial growth and expansion of the Liberian economy.

West Germany, 8 September 1966

I ASSURE you that it is a great pleasure and privilege for us to be here at your works at this time. Already we have been greatly impressed by what we have seen and by the explanations that have been made by your representative, with whom we drove here.

The planet on which we live has been made so small by scientific and technological investigations, research, inventions and advancement that all nations, all peoples are neighbours. There is no such a thing in this time and age as the seclusion or separation of any nation. We live in one world. Within twenty-four hours modern aeroplanes and other means of transportation can encircle the whole earth. This fact alone argues, more articulately than any words that I could use, the necessity for co-operation and understanding between nations and people.

Coming to the purpose and object of our being here upon your invitation, Liberia, while not as young as the recently liberated nations of Africa, is a developing country. Until this liberation movement started in Africa, Liberia was virtually so economically and politically strangulated, that she could not move forward, or advance faster than the colonial peoples in Africa who were under colonial administration at the time. But we in Liberia have had the experience of independence and sovereignty. Even though we have been unable to move forward and develop because of circumstances beyond our control, we have learned to possess our soul in patience, act rationally and exercise patience, soberness and good judgment. We have launched or embarked upon the policy of industrialization, and we need mutual co-operation and assistance to accomplish this. We have enormous natural resources that the world needs which are not being tapped.

Taking office as President, one of the first things that we did was to announce what we call an 'Open Door Policy'; a policy by which we sought to induce foreign investment in the country to explore and exploit our natural resources and, in the meantime, to teach Liberians to manage these things and, eventually, to take over.

Besides our knowledge of the unique ability of the Germans in business of every kind, we are familiar with the Germans in general because there was a time in Liberia when they conducted and controlled the commercial activities of the country. In those days they contributed greatly to the maintenance of the country's economy. I myself once worked for a German firm in Liberia. And so, when we were invited in 1956 by President Herst to make a State Visit to Germany, we came here and discussed business. We discussed German investment in Liberia, we discussed technical and economic assistance by the German Government for Liberia. We have received some technical and economic assistance from the German Government.

Now, the new proposal or proposition is that Salzgitter and Motor Columbus form a consortium not only to assist, invest and advise the development and industrialization of Liberia, but also to serve as promotors, consultants and advisors to the Liberian Government in its plan for industrial and economic development. Exactly what form and what extent this new proposal will have is what will have to be worked out by representatives of the parties concerned. But we would like to see this on a partnership basis, for the mutual benefit of all parties concerned. We would prefer this consortium not only to advise and attract others to invest in Liberia but to invest themselves. Perhaps Salzgitter themselves would open an iron ore mine and operate it in Liberia, investigating other deposits of iron ore, manganese and any other natural product.

We know that Salzgitter, Motor Columbus and this consortium have the know-how and the ability. We assure you and pledge you our word that our co-operation and participation with you will be such as will ensure a fair and square deal, so that no advantage will be taken. No such thing as nationalization, under any circumstances, will be your fate. That any investment in Liberia will be safe is evidenced and proven by this: that we have in Liberia already, besides the agricultural companies and corporations, a number of operating iron ore concessionaires. Today, Liberia is the third largest iron ore producer in the world. In these different concessions and businesses we have nationals of many countries, Americans, Swedish, a number of other nationals, who can testify. We cite them as evidence of the good faith of the Liberian Government and its sacred regard for agreements and conventions.

Finally, we would like this consortium to be not only interested in investing themselves, but also in inducing others to invest in various and varying business possibilities in the country. I thank you very much.

To the Liberian Businessmen's Conference

Monrovia, 11 January 1967

While we encourage and support foreign investments, it is also desirable that we encourage local business enterprises undertaken by Liberians, or in joint venture with foreign investors. It is only when Liberians engaged fully in business that the Liberian economy will be able to sustain and regenerate itself on a permanent basis.

Introductory Note

The plight of the Liberian businessman has always been an acute one, faced with competition from the foreign businessman, coupled with his lack of wide capital layout and technical knowledge. The Foreign businessman always appeared to have a better deal in Liberian business opportunities. Nothing could arouse the envy and jealousy of the Liberian businessman more than to see the foreign businessman getting away with everything. They have complained about what seems to them unfair competition. President Tubman in this major address to the first organized conference of Liberian businessmen gave the reasons underlying the plight of the Liberian businessman and dwelt at length on how the situation could be alleviated. He stated what should be the limits of the activities of the foreign businessman who engages in both wholesale and retail trade. Assistance was promised the Liberian businessman while at the same time the foreign businessman was assured that his business interests too would be protected.

Monrovia, 11 January 1967

CONFERENCES OF this nature have always been regarded with favour and in recent years, especially in this age of science and technology, when events are moving at a kaleidoscopic pace and changes occur within the twinkling of the proverbial eye, a conference such as this is most desirable and of the utmost importance. It brings together people of common interests, who realize that in addition to economic independence, political freedom becomes meaningful only if the people of a nation participate fully in its economic, commercial and business life. I therefore express approval of, and congratulations for, the initiative made manifest in the gathering of this Conference of Liberian Businessmen.

It was in recognition of this that, in our first Inaugural, twenty-three years ago, we postulated: 'Our commerce must be organized and developed. Our raw materials and resources require exploitation, advertisement and large scale exchange. The way is open to us to take our legitimate place and play an important part in the industrialization of West Africa on the basis of maximum development and exploitation of our agricultural resources.' It was also in the framework of the pronouncement of this policy that we enunciated the Open Door Policy whereby foreign investors and business-men of various kinds could invest and create business relationships with Liberians, and the Liberian Government, on the basis of mutuality. This has paid substantial dividends to the mutual interest of investors, the people and Government.

While we encourage and support foreign investments, it is also desirable that we encourage local business enterprises undertaken by Liberians them-selves or in joint venture with foreign investors. It is only when Liberians en-gage fully in business that the Liberian economy will be able to sustain and regenerate itself on a permanent basis. *Liberian capital must and should be ploughed into Liberian business undertakings in order to accelerate the growth of commerce within the Liberian context.* It is in this perspective that I invite all patriotic and devoted Liberians to renew their efforts and to invest in business on a larger and ever-increasing scale.

The Open Door Policy has succeeded over the years and there is increased income in both the public and private sectors of our economy. We will con-tinue to pursue these policies for greater benefits to the nation and its people.

The recent passing into law of the Investment Incentive Code by the National Legislature, together with the assistance of the Liberian Bank for Industrial Development and Investment and the Liberian Development Corporation, should make it practicable for Liberians to engage in various kinds of business with the same fiscal, financial and other facilities as foreign investors, while at the same time eliminating some of the bureaucracy which in the past has slowed the pace at which we attracted foreign investment.

In a developing economy there is generally a shortage of investment capital; therefore it is essential that we endeavour to attract and encourage foreign investment in an atmosphere of fairness, mutual confidence and opportunity. Nevertheless, while several avenues for the import of capital have been opened to the Government, we are determined to encourage Liberians to participate more fully in the economic wealth, development and growth of the nation. The Liberian Bank for Industrial Development and Investment has been instituted to provide long term financing for Liberian Businessmen on terms more favourable than those provided by Commercial Banks; the Liberian Development Corporation was established in 1961 to assist Liberians in studying and preparing projects for financing. In addition to providing technical assistance in the management and operation of business enterprises, several other facilities are provided by Government as an encouragement for Liberians desiring to enter business on competitive basis with foreign capital and know-how.

I regret having to state however, that very little benefits have accrued to the general public because of the operating policies of the agency and institution concerned. As a result, only a few have been privileged to use the facilities for capital formation, technical advice and fiscal exemptions that should have been available to all sections of the nation, and not merely to a particular class according to the intent and purposes for which these institu-tions were organized.

I have heard it repeatedly said in certain circles that only those who can present feasible proposals are privileged or entitled to receive the benefits of financing by the institutions provided by Government for this purpose. How can the average man present feasible proposals when he does not know how to do it? How can he do it when the experts specially trained by Government for this purpose group themselves together, formulate programmes that they know financial institutions will regard as feasible and form companies restricted to themselves, leaving the masses of the public without benefits from the Government's strivings? Measures must be immediately taken to ensure the full implementation of the objectives of these organizations. The experts, the economists, the financiers and other appropriate Government agencies must formulate programmes and projects that are feasible, and that will include ordinary people from all over the country and present them for consideration by the financial institutions. This is the Government's responsibility. And action will be taken against any expert, economist or banker not adhering to this principle.

The Government is the axle in a wheel around which the business circumference rotates in the making of our free enterprise economy, and we reaffirm our faith in this system of government that has been tested and tried through more than a century. But we must realize that the continuation and success of this type of economy depends on the degree to which the Liberian businessman is interested and able to participate in business.

In this connection, the Liberian businessman has a vital rôle to play in the development of the economy. It has been our hope that advantage would be taken of opportunities created by the presence of large investment projects for the establishment of ancillary industries by Liberians. The operations of the Firestone Plantations Company have created thousands of Liberian rubber planters. It is therefore expected that as a result of the mining operations more Liberian stores, services and other businesses will be established in these areas, encouraged and assisted by the concessionaires, just as Firestone assisted Liberians in becoming rubber planters by giving them technical advice, distributing stumps and the like. Equally so, it is expected that as a result of concessions to Lumber Companies more furniture and other factories will be established. It is also expected that more Liberians will participate in producing additional primary commodities for export, such as coffee, palm oil, and such products, on a small scale to begin with. It is further expected that more Liberians will produce larger quantities of rice, sugar cane, cattle and other livestock – all of which are vital to our own needs. This is the principal intention of Operation Production and the responsibility of the Liberian businessmen and people.

Recognition and credit should be given to the number of Liberians who in recent years have moved from the traditional investment in rubber, real estate and transportation to investments in fisheries, gases, paints, cosmetics, furniture, beverages, construction, architectural designing, cinemas, medical facilities, soaps, etcetera, and also those who have capital participation in the Iron Ore Mines, the Shoe Factory, the Explosives Company and Banking Institutions. The Government welcomes this progress and will give continuing encouragement and support to such ventures.

A special problem to industrialization in this country is the rather limited size of the Liberian market, but this can and must be surmounted by the ingenuity, practical analysis and business acumen of the Liberian businessman. It is therefore essential that pride be developed in the purchase and use of locally produced commodities, where their qualities and prices are competitive, and that markets outside of the country be found to purchase and patronize our products. This is where the Regional Grouping Policy and Free Trade Area would be useful.

I solicit and insist that all concessions, companies and individuals within the country, including Government Agencies, give priority patronage to locally manufactured products, particularly concessions using products which are now being produced, can be produced or are otherwise available here, giving preference in their purchasing to Liberian-produced products, particularly when they meet required standards. By this it is intended that all investors in Liberia, whether they be Liberians or foreigners, be given due patronage.

Further, it shall become a policy of the Government that in the awarding of contracts for construction of roads, buildings and so forth, or in the purchasing of supplies, priority will be given to those products obtainable in Liberia and of local manufacture.

Full implementation of the law prohibiting foreigners from engaging in public transportation by land will be vigorously enforced, as it is essential that this important service be wholly owned and controlled by Liberians as required by Statute.

Some ruthless foreign businessmen, of a particular nationality, diligently seek to oust Liberian small businesses by engaging in peddling, butchering, barbering, block-making, snuff-selling and other such businesses that require very little capital and create unfair business practices and competition to Liberians, in direct violation of and contrary to the spirit and intent of the Open Door Policy. Their own sense of common decency should tell them that they ought to leave these types of enterprises for the people of the country, whose responsibility it is to maintain and defend the country in which they operate, and who even extend to them protection under the law.

This can no longer be condoned, and immediate action must be taken to prevent this particular type of foreign businessmen from continuing their reckless and unconscionable tendencies.

On the other hand, it is obligatory for Liberian businessmen to maintain a high standard of integrity, honesty and respect for their commitments. The conduct of some Liberians in business does not comport with or measure up to respectable business standards. I refer specifically to the issuing of worthless cheques, defaulting in paying bills and in meeting Bank commitments; but even in these practices, the foreign businessmen of the nationality mentioned above are the greatest transgressors and sinners, and by their ignoble attitude toward their financial and business obligations damage to a great extent the business reputation of the nation by impersonation, and by fleeing the country with their obligations unpaid.

In describing this class of foreign businessmen, we refer to the following incidents:

In their dealings with people of their own nationality and Liberians they discriminate against Liberians; for instance, when the Commercial Bank's financial position was threatened and they sought a Company to lease the Rivoli Theatre, the Liberian Amusement Limited, a Liberian Company, indicated its interest; but the terms were so high and unreasonable that they had to withdraw. At the same time, an offer was made by the Commercial Bank to the Roxy Cinema, a Lebanese-owned business with terms entirely different and so much more lenient that their attorney was forced to call their attention to the disparity and advised them against taking this course. They were then advised to approach the Liberian Amusement Limited again and agreement was later reached for lease of the theatre. Now, it is reported that negotiations are being stealthily made by the Commercial Bank with a Lebanese Group from Freetown for purchase of the Rivoli without any reference to the present Liberian management, which has invested time and money to keep the Rivoli in operation.

They have committed crimes, and when unable to meet their obligations they have planted bombs in their shops and destroyed them for the benefit of collecting insurance; they have shot and wounded proprietors of businesses to get away with their loot; they have burned down stores to collect insurance; they have committed acts of great turpitude as instruments of business policy.

Such is the conduct of this particular group of people to whom the Government has shown great tolerance, even to the extent of indulgence; but they move from design to design and there is no limit to their wrongdoing.

We have reiterated these examples to indicate the need for you, the Liberian businessmen, to organize and formulate programmes to upgrade your performances, so that the Government will no longer have to tolerate those who come here with criminal intent because of the lack of Liberian business institutions.

This represents no change in policy, nor is it calculated to prevent foreigners from engaging in business and investments in the country, but it is intended to protect the people of this country and the country itself against exploitation by scheming immigrants, and I stress the point that this course of conduct refers to a special class of foreigners of a particular nationality who enter the country, and not to foreigners generally.

According to a recent report of the Bankers' Association the total amount of overdue obligations of all of the Liberian population in the entire country is $1,330,441 while the amount overdue by foreigners particularly by the same class and nationals in the country is $1,911,785 which, considering the number of foreigners of this particular class and the whole Liberian population presents an unfavourable contrast. This is why in our last Annual Message to the Legislature we recommend legislation to deal with these situations and to ensure greater security to Banks and financial institutions.

In this New Year, it is our hope that Liberian businessmen, firms and corporations will resolve to take advantage of the opportunities available to them in the country and that the Liberian Bank for Industrial Development and Investment and the Liberian Development Corporation will organize and formulate programmes for lending, with security safeguards, to Liberian businessmen, as contemplated when these two institutions were established.

It is pleasing to note the presence here at this conference of representatives from all over the country. This is the spirit that the Government desires to see pervading the nation. It represents a move away from sectionalism, parochialism and tribalism.

Finally, please accept, Mr. Chairman, and Members of the Liberian Businessmen's Conference, my unbounded gratitude for the honour done to me, your humble servant, by this testimonial of your affection and respect.

I express the high hope that your deliberations will see fruition in the rapid growth of local, commercial, industrial and other businesses throughout the country and not in any one particular section of the country, as a result of the Liberian initiative.

Speech to the Rubber Planters' Association of Liberia

Monrovia, 14 March 1967

This industry must be kept alive, it must be strengthened; for if it fails or becomes stagnant, it would mean almost the death of our economic position.

Introductory Note

For many years natural rubber was the strength of our economy. From 1926 to 1952 Liberia appeared to encourage a one-crop economy. With the start of the export of iron ore in 1952 however, our economy began to develop a promising outlook. But so great had our dependence on rubber become that the Firestone Rubber Plantations Company which bought the rubber of small Liberian planters and set the price for its purchase confronted the small planters with an alarming situation, brought about by an ever-increasing slump in the price of natural rubber. Correspondingly, there was no increase in the cost of manufacture of consumer rubber products. This then was the dilemma which faced the local planters in the decade of the 1960's. President Tubman's interest and concern for the future of the natural rubber industry and the plight of the small planters are expressed in this speech to the Rubber Planters' Association of Liberia.

Monrovia, 14 March 1967

I CONSIDER it a pleasure and an honour to have the privilege, in response to your invitation, to speak to this distinguished assembly of Liberian Rubber Planters on the occasion of the Second Annual Meeting of the Association, and to avail myself of this opportunity to share with you some of my views as a layman, and as one also involved in the planting and growing of rubber.

The Liberian Rubber Planters have organized themselves into an Association; a long overdue and remarkable step forward. It is an action which ensures progress and which will enable Liberian Planters to study, investigate, formulate and execute programmes and policies that may tend to the effective and beneficial interest of the rubber industry in Liberia.

There is so much that your Association should and must do in the interest of the rubber industry, which represents the oldest foreign investment in our country, and is one that has stretched out its tentacles and touched citizens all over this nation in every walk of life. It is one that affords an opportunity to the individual citizen, the individual family, and small as well as large companies of Liberians to enter into the planting and growing of rubber.

In any business there is nothing more important than organization, the proper and right kind of organization, and in this respect it appears to me, from what I have read, seen and heard of the administration and operation of your organization, that you have proceeded upon a sound, practical and rational basis. I congratulate you upon this course of action.

I have always given expression to the belief and feeling that capital and labour are interdependent and that one cannot function without the other. Because of this tendency there are abundant reasons why management and labour, although separate and distinct in outlook and operation, should be mutually interested in giving a fair deal to one another; management duly considering the labouring man's reward for his labour and the labouring man considering his responsibility to management by justifying and earning his wage. Neither should enter upon a policy of undue domination or attempt to over-ride the other.

In this connection, there is a difference in the operation of industry, commerce and other businesses in Liberia and in those of most other countries, or I should say, in the more developed and industrialized countries in the world. In Liberia, as in many developing countries, management is almost entirely on the side of, and controlled by, foreigners and foreign investments, while labour is composed entirely, or very nearly so, of Liberians. This is considerably different from management and labour practices in more developed countries, where both management and labour are comprised of people of the same nationality. Human nature generally preponderates, and in a country such as ours, where this difference between management and labour, as pointed out above, exists, the task of inter-relationship between management and labour is rendered more difficult, because one is invariably suspicious of the other. This creates a situation where it becomes necessary for Government to keep an ever-watchful and inquiring eye on the procedures and practices of both management and labour, to see that neither takes advantage of the other, nor is given privileges or considerations that will be prejudicial to the rightful interest of the other.

This has been the policy of this Administration; this has been the aim and objectives of all the laws enacted by the Legislature relating to management and labour, industries and business, and this will continue to be the Government's policy. The execution and prosecution of this policy will be pursued, now and hereafter, with greater vigilance, diligence and despatch.

I have elected to move somewhat away from the actual purpose of the remarks you expect me to make, and used this diversion as a means of expressing how strongly I feel about the necessity for understanding between management and labour.

As previously mentioned, you have marched forward in organizing the Liberian Rubber Planters' Association; you have administered it, and your progress and success have been and are commendable, and I feel that this achievement should spur you on to greater achievements in the interest of the rubber industry in Liberia in which so many Liberians have invested, some by small holdings and others by large ones. This industry, therefore, must be kept alive, it must be strengthened; for if it fails or becomes stagnant, it would mean almost the death-knell of our economic position. I say this because it is recognized that at least two hundred thousand Liberians are depending on the rubber industry for their livelihood, their day to day existence and the assurance of their future economic well-being.

The uniqueness of this situation is that a large group of citizens who themselves worked as labourers in mining and other industries and even as labourers on rubber plantations, have invested in the growing of rubber and in this respect have become managers and capitalists, which makes the rubber industry very unique in our economic setting.

Statistics show that since the mid-1950s the price of rubber has dropped by more than fifty per cent and appears still to be on a downward trend. However, Government economists tell us that the price decline will be of short duration. According to them, we may therefore expect some modest rise in prices before 1970. We hope they are right, and we live in hope even if we die in despair.

Among the reasons given to us by the economists for the fall in rubber prices are:

(1) The release of rubber from stock piles by the United States and British Governments.

(2) The political situation in Indonesia and the end of that country's confrontation with Malaysia.

They argue that these two factors are of short duration and their effect on the natural rubber market could not last very long.

Whatever the future of the price of rubber, we cannot avoid great concern about the plight of the primary producing countries in the face of the rising costs of finished products and the continued decline in the price of raw materials. This course is especially true for the natural rubber-producing countries, who have been severely affected as the following statistics show. In 1953 the average price of rubber on the Liberian market was 31·6 cents per pound. In 1956 the average price was 28·4 cents. In 1966 the average price was less than 16 cents and now in 1967 the price of rubber has declined to less than 13 cents per pound. At the same time the cost of the finished product, including the price of manufactured rubber, has increased. Between 1952 and 1961 the price of manufactured rubber goods increased by four per cent, while the price of primary products decreased by sixteen per cent.

Unless there is some reversal in the present trend, it might become necessary for rubber-producing countries to hold consultation among themselves as a means of protecting their economies. It seems to us and our experience has shown that we on our part can take certain measures to reduce costs and increase production.

When we took office in 1944 there were 184 private Liberian rubber farms comprising 12,000 acres and producing 778,000 pounds of rubber per annum. Today through joint efforts of Government and the Rubber Planters' Association, this number has increased to well over four thousand farms comprising 139,000 acres and producing over 32 million pounds of rubber per annum. This increase seems to represent your confidence in the future of rubber and your faith in the Government's free enterprise system. It therefore becomes imperative that we remain always vigilant and alert to the cost, quantity and quality of rubber produced in Liberia.

Now, if I may, I would like to make the following proposal or suggestion for your consideration: that a Rubber Institute be created or instituted on a co-operative basis with Government and the Rubber Planters' Association participating. This Institute would engage in:

(a) Research
(b) Management and Training
(c) Establishment and Organization of Co-operatives, and
(d) The processing and export of rubber by Liberians.

Research. In an industry such as rubber where, as I have said before, the producers have very little or no control over the price structure and labour costs, we have to engage in more research to improve the quality of planting materials, production methods, quality control and transport facilities. In this regard, the Firestone Plantations Company not only started the rubber industry in Liberia but has been helpful by continuously making available to the Liberian farmers the benefit of research in its laboratories. While Firestone is still willing to assist the Liberian farmer, we should be prepared to do something for ourselves by establishing additional research facilities, not to duplicate what is now being done but to supplement and more effectively disseminate research information to all rubber planters. On the part of Government, more support will be given, especially in the field of rubber technology and research.

Management. As in the case of research, proper management of farms is indispensable to reduced production costs, increased productivity and quality control. Most Liberian Planters are engaged in other day-to-day activities and their farms are therefore deprived of their personal super-vision. I understand that this question is now being considered by you and therefore shall not speak in detail on the subject except to make the following brief comment. In an effort to attract qualified, dedicated and effective management personnel, you could embark on a programme of training followed by a salary scale, including other fringe benefits, which would attract the best talents necessary to maintain this vital industry in our economy.

Many rubber farms are now being managed by foreigners, because of the lack of trained Liberians to protect investments and assure proper manage-ment. Although we appreciate and are indebted to these managers, this will not solve the problem until you have trained and made available a nucleus of Liberian farm managers who would be able and willing to fully devote their time and energy to operate and expand the rubber industry.

Co-operatives. I have been told that Mr. A. W. Lotz, General Manager of Firestone Plantations Company, has suggested to the Liberian Bank for Industrial Development that this bank should consider the financing of rubber processing facilities for Liberian farmers. I find this proposal of Mr. Lotz's appealing and suggest that the Association follow it up from the standpoint of the economic benefits to be derived therefrom by rubber producers, and by the bank itself. The Government would be willing to make available to your group the necessary expertise for a study of the feasibility of this proposal to be submitted to the Industrial Bank.

Along these lines, I would suggest further that the Rubber Planters' Association begin to give thought to forming co-operatives all over the country to assist especially the small farmers, so that production costs may be reduced and increase in income be derived from the sale of their products. In this connection, the rubber planters, by forming co-operatives, could buy their supplies in a wholesale market and eliminate the expense of the middleman and the purchase of heavy equipment for clearing, etcetera. By the same process of reasoning, they could sell directly to the users of rubber and eliminate the cost of a middleman handling their product.

Your Constitution provides that membership in the Association be limited to farmers with a minimum of one hundred acres of planted farm. This limitation, I am sure, is based on careful study and consideration, and is intended to make the Association more effective. However, I think that since a large number of Liberian rubber farms are less than one hundred acres, and the size of these holdings make their owners ineligible for membership, you might want to consider voluntarily sharing with them the privileges and benefits which belong to members of the Association.

If the suggestions that we have made appeal to you, Mr. President and Members of the Association, the Government would be willing to place at your disposal the facilities of the Department of Agriculture assisted by the Department of Planning and Economic Affairs to assist your Organization in implementing them.

In closing, I appeal to the President, Officers and Members of the Association to continue their efforts to promote greater interest in the rubber industry and to increase the economic benefits to the highest possible level, so that the future of investors in this industry may be assured.

EDUCATION

At the University of Liberia

Monrovia, 13 March 1961

To make the University a true beacon of learning.

Introductory Note

From the beginning of his first term as President of Liberia in 1944, William V. S. Tubman was preoccupied with ways and means of improving the quality of Liberian education. The institutions at home must be strengthened, in particular the University of Liberia. In 1961 the University of Liberia, formerly known as Liberia College (1861–1951) celebrated its centenary. The President in this testimonial address recounted the past efforts of the University and its administrators to keep the flame of learning burning bright. As it entered its second century, he exhorted them to achieve still nobler heights, and pledged his support, and that of the Liberian tax payer, for the realization of this objective.

Monrovia, 13 March 1961

YOU HAVE just celebrated a century of fruitful work in higher education in Liberia. During that span of time Liberia College has grown from a one-building institution to a University of four buildings; from a single Liberal Arts College to a University of five degree granting and four non-degree granting schools; from a teaching corps of ten to the present Faculty of ninety-three trained and professional workers; from an administrative body comprising three to one of eighteen; from a student body of twelve to the present enrolment of six hundred and fourteen. The men and women who have drunk deep of the Elysian stream have identified themselves by the leadership they have given to the functioning life of the nation and their contributions have become, not only valuable, but some of them imperishable. My hearty congratulations to the University authorities and to those who played a part in the programmes which, I understand, were thoroughly planned, efficiently executed and highly successful.

With a sense of satisfaction for the task which has been accomplished, we face the second century with a more comprehensive vision and a greater determination to make the University a true beacon of learning. Already the plans for the new campus where a real academic atmosphere would be experienced are under way, where the pursuit of learning would be more vigorously and conscientiously undertaken and where academic freedom would be encouraged. Proposals for strengthening and enlarging the University's offerings have been discussed at length and these will receive implementation in the near future. The decision to make the aim of the University more significant and dynamic in the life of the nation has received generous support from many quarters, and I believe that the

395

institution received very great impetus and inspiration from the centennial celebration, as reflected in the catalogue of achievements and the new perspectives which have been advanced for the future.

With this growing awareness of the rôle which the modern university should play in the life of the nation, we are encouraged that support will be generously given to the idea, and that everything will now be done to forge ahead in the direction which will make us more fully alive to the importance of higher education in our nation. I feel sure that the men, women, students and everyone taking a part in this programme will renew and redouble their efforts to make the University a true sanctuary of learning for this generation and future ones.

President, Faculty and Members of the Student Body, we meet today not only to welcome you here, but to pay recognition to the true significance of your coming. The sense of joy that the University feels in having you here and the stirring sense of pride that she feels in having so many of you for her sons and daughters has a deeper meaning than the mere happiness of association. What seems important, however, is what is it that has brought you here; what is it that you have put your faith in and that has led you to come and enlist for your precious years under the banner of the University of Liberia?

Perhaps you think you have come to get your pre-Med course, or pre-Engineering, how to get more social prestige, or even to become a scholar. While I grant that these are easily understandable motives, and the University can perhaps respond to them all, there is a deeper motive than a desire for physical satisfaction or success. For above and beyond all these is the cultivation of an attitude, an atmosphere, a way of life. It is a way of life based on the innate passion for the intelligent way of doing things; it is the intellectual way of life which declares that curiosity, the spirit of free inquiry, the passion to know, is as natural in a human being as the desire to breathe or to eat. The University of Liberia stands for a natural loyalty to truth, to patriotism, to work; to live a life at its fullest and best through the intellectual way.

I have every confidence that in this splendid business you will so take your part that this year will make a great and definite step in your individual growth, and make of this spot and of this institution the birthplace and matrix of the best production of any civilization – masterful, resourceful, intelligent men and women who are eternally and invincibly loyal to their highest natures.

The events of the first one hundred years are over and with them the successes and failures. This second century imposes on the authorities, student body and personnel of the University tremendous duties and new and challenging responsibilities. In 1947 when the nation celebrated her centenary, I experienced the weight of a greater burden than I had felt in 1944, when I first took the office of President of the nation. When the centenary was over, therefore, and the nation on the threshold of the second century, I concluded that it was imperative for us to move in a new direction by utilizing the human and natural resources at our command, by calling upon the patriotism, loyalty, and devotion of all to join the challenging task of making this nation one of which we and our posterity would be justly proud. While much remains to be done, thus far our highest hopes have not failed us.

So too with the University, which has a revised charter, greatly improved educational facilities, an invigorated programme, new personnel and new perspectives. It becomes indeed the professional obligation of all concerned to take a new look at the educational challenges of this second century and resolve thereby to make it one of the great intellectual achievements in the history of higher education in Liberia.

At the beginning of this second century, the increased responsibilities to which I have referred are also shared by Members of Trustees. One reason for the change in the Charter of the University is to enable Members of the Board to become an active force in the life of the University by engaging in the raising of funds, soliciting donations, contributing toward the physical and financial life of the institution, and doing everything to enhance the healthy growth, development and progress of the University. It is part of the responsibility of the Board Members constantly to make plans for the advancement of the University, and to see that the institution is administered in keeping with the terms of the Charter, as well as to be certain that members of the faculty and other functionaries are performing their duties faithfully, consistently and with professional integrity.

Similarly, I feel that the President and Faculty Members should find opportunities to do scholarly research, develop public relations, and engage in activities geared to augmenting the budgetary appropriations of the University: for, if the Government should continue to carry the entire financial burden there would be no difference between the new and the old Charter when Senators and Representatives were Members of the Board.

A century, indeed, spans the period between the Presidency of Liberia College under our revered Joseph J. Roberts and that of our present dynamic President Dr. Weeks. In an age which caters predominantly to the advancement of science and technology, it is of the utmost importance that this field should become an important adjunct of the University's offerings, so that our State Institution of Higher Learning may keep abreast of the developments in this area. I trust that the resources now provided by the personnel of UNESCO, CIA and other collaborating and co-operating agencies will contribute towards the intensification and enrichment of the science programme.

Culture as learning, science as investigation, and work as utility, each has an external life of its own and to perfect each of them for the performance of the special task will always be a highly desirable aim of the University. It was Tyndall in his unforgettable address made in 1874 who pointed out that it is not through science, nor through literature that human nature is made whole, but rather it is through a fusion of both. Thus it is that through an attempt to make a new fusion of both with work during the constructive years of our educational system can we catch the impulse of a new and dynamic culture.

You may congratulate yourselves upon the achievements of the University of Liberia. But there is unfinished work to be done. It is to this sense of an unfinished business that I commend your highest, best and dedicated efforts in the years ahead. In this effort, I call upon the University authorities, students and faculty members, parents and guardians, and all who have any vested interest in the education of youth to take a renewed interest in the University by respecting its philosophy, supporting its programme, and helping to prove that education indeed ennobles.

Address to the College of West Africa
Monrovia, 9 July 1961

Education has always been and will continue to be man's only real emancipator.

Introductory Note

The College of West Africa, a missionary pioneering effort of the Methodist Church for better educational standards in Liberia, was commended for its work in the further expansion of facilities for the improvement of the quality of education that it gave to the Liberian youth.

Monrovia, 9 July 1961

'YOU ARE the educator, I am the student; educate me, if you can!' is a challenge which many students are inclined to pose to administrators as well as professors. Whatever the rewarding considerations which engage the thinking of educators, sooner or later they come face to face with the reality of the impact of educational philosophies and goals on the attitudes, ideals, and impulses of the students who present themselves at the door of a school or college and say, 'educate me, if you can'.

Educators tell us that after formal education is completed a satisfying synthesis takes place only when young people are enabled to go out from schools and colleges with a coherent vision of their educational experiences, and, in the light of that vision, act as integrating forces both in their national and international societies. For professors and those who bear responsibility for molding the future of students, this synthesis means the emergence of the finished products, proud representatives of schools and colleges, so that whether as churchmen, administrators, lawyers, teachers, doctors, or engineers, these students will, above all, become outstanding citizens. And so through the ages one supreme issue has engaged the constant thinking of great educational reformers, this ideal forming the basis of their entire educational practice: to tangle the web of materialism and thereby liberate idealism through the mastery of life's deeper human relations.

We who have witnessed the work of the College of West Africa through these many years, can bear testimony to the vital place which the institution has filled in the life of the students who have passed through her doors and the dynamic rôles which these students have played and are playing in the nation. We have praised the soundness of her educational programme, and the professional preparedness and integrity of the workers, and admired the spiritual and intellectual quality of the leaders. The end results have amply justified our admiration.

And as we have come to witness the dedication of these buildings for the further promotion of the educational welfare of the youths of this nation, we do so with the firm conviction that education has always been, is, and will continue to be man's only real emancipator, and the greatest pre-occupation of any nation. Cognizance of its significant impact on our own national progress motivated the framers of the new nation to make it one of their primary considerations. From that time until the present, missionary activities and contributions have been consistently considerable, and the work of Christian education and evangelism has provided sturdy anchorages in our advance to true national stability. To all missionary enterprises within the confines of the Republic in general, and to the devoted Christian workers in the history of the College of West Africa in particular, the Government and people of Liberia express deep gratitude for a part which has been so well played in helping to popularize education as the heritage of a free people.

In paying tribute to Dr. Wickstrom recently, I referred to his uncompromising attitude to excellence in scholarship, and to the tradition of learning which he imparted to the students of this institution. If these legacies are held sacred, there is no doubt that they will be greatly honoured by future generations of students, and that the institution will attain heights of great eminence in the history of our educational programme. May the students of this institution of learning continue to grow intellectually strong in the long shadow of this rich tradition.

It has been well said that the scientific revolution of the nineteenth century gave a new framework to human thinking, understanding and conduct, and so created a century which has already become a wonderful chapter in the history of civilization. It was inevitable too, that this great period was to be followed by a period of application in which the wonders of science and invention were translated into practice and once again gave a new framework to man's thinking and conduct, to his material welfare and, through revolutionized conditions of human associations of free men at work in a world of industry, to a new philosophy of life and a new social conscience. Education for the scientific and space age has therefore become a necessary part of the curricula of the schools, for undoubtedly science is destined to give man unprecedented knowledge of and power over the universe. Will man channel these vast possibilities constructively? Herein lies the real challenge of our scientific era.

The buildings which have been dedicated today will be used this year, and for many years to come. It is our hope that they will become more useful, since they will continue to house the same ideas and ideals, the same goals for which they have today been dedicated and the same faith in education. It is our hope that the students who will live in the dormitory, and those who will study in the science building, will welcome the challenge and the opportunity which has today been made available to them. Knowing that whatever contributions this college makes to the progress of young women and men will come from their own valiant desire for achievement while they study here, it is our further hope that students' interests will merge successfully with those of the institution's toward desirable and acceptable goals.

It is, therefore, with a deep gratification that I congratulate the Board of Trustees, Faculty and all those who have been responsible for this achievement, another worthy accomplishment in the reinforcement of the goals of education for the benefit of the youth of this country. These buildings, we hope, will stand as true testimonials of the faith and magnanimity of those who see in the future of the youth of this country all the vast potentialities of power and the transforming influence which Christian education can confer. But these structures must be more than mere buildings; they must be symbols of a better and richer life for the people of this community and the new Liberia, in the active and creative uses which will be made of them. In this science building we trust that some of the future scientists of the nation will get their basic training.

Different institutions can perhaps show, according to the circumstances of their foundation and history, different reasons for their existence and for being what they are. But all of them, whatever their date of origin, and whatever their place, have come into being in response to certain social needs of their place and time. The educational institutions of this nation are no exception to this rule, and thus it is my hope that all those engaged in educational activities will join hands with the Government's continued efforts to provide greater and more up-to-date educational facilities for its citizens until the last vestige of illiteracy is obliterated from the nation. This is the task to which I challenge the College of West Africa and all other institutions of learning today.

May the future years of our educational programme be more meaningful and productive of the results which we so earnestly desire for our nation, and may those who carry the responsibilities for educating the youth of our land dedicate themselves anew to the ideals of a new day for all the peoples of Liberia, Africa and the world.

In closing, let me quote two stanzas of Caleb T. Winchester's hymn –

> Thou sovereign God, receive this gift
> Thy willing servants offer Thee;
> Accept the prayers that thousands lift,
> And let these halls Thy Temple be.
>
> And let those learn, who here shall meet,
> True wisdom is with reverence crowned,
> And science walks with humble feet
> To seek the God that faith had found.

Statement on the Goals of Liberian Education

Monrovia, 24 August 1962

Toward better standards in Liberian education.

Introductory Note

The Liberian system of education, like the process of education itself, periodically undergoes changes, and new policies are set forth to govern and guide these changes. Caught in midstream in the application of both the traditional method of teaching and the progressive method, there have been numerous debates on which method should take precedence in our schools. President Tubman made a re-examination of the educational policies of Liberia. While appreciating the rôle of modern education and its trends, he stressed the value and rôle of the traditional method for the achievement of better results in the education of the whole child. He found the latter method more effective.

Monrovia, 24 August 1962

ON THE one hundred and fifteenth anniversary of the raising and unfurling of the nation's flag, I consider it an appropriate time to address you, and in particular the parents and guardians, and the professors, teachers and students of the institute of learning of the nation, on the subject of education in Liberia.

Education is an essential and indispensable element in the life and progress of a nation. It is one of the safeguards of the liberties of a people, and the index finger pointing to the future prospect of the continued survival, progress and life of any nation. Within this context, I feel very strongly that an assessment of the educational system of the country is highly desirable and essential, since it will determine the basis of our national outlook, efficiency and preparedness, constitute our underlying philosophy and give a clearer revelation of the relative importance which we place upon education in the valued hierarchy of our society.

My confidence in education and a well organized school system as the basis and sheet-anchor of our democracy is derived from my awareness of the extraordinary need for its present and future service to the nation and its growth out of a comprehensive vision, a willing spirit and an intelligent co-operation by all concerned in its socially desired end-results.

The story of our educational advancement is one of sublime faith and daring perseverance in the face of imponderable odds. On the long road to nationhood and the resultant social progress and economic advance, both Government and foreign philanthropy and benevolent agencies, as well as foreign and local enterprises, have played important rôles in shaping the educational standards which today guide the nation. Born of an ardent passion and a rugged determination to establish schools for the training and education of their children, our Pioneer Fathers laid the foundation which was to popularize education as the priceless possession of a free people. For even with the meagre financial resources available at that time, they never ceased their constant concern for education, nor did they ever relinquish the hope that education would always be the bulwark of their political freedom.

More than this, they entertained the reassuring conviction that religious education would enable them to create a new society in an atmosphere different from the one in which their bodies had been incarcerated; although their souls and minds had been sustained amidst the trials and tribulations through which they had passed and were able to endure. For in the religious songs which had become the great heritage of the Negro, the spirituals brought them hope, consolation, courage and patience. They dreamed. They laboured. They waited. They confided in themselves and looked to God and to friendly peoples to help them find solutions for their problems. They profited from their experiences. They kept faith with those who had led the way to a fuller life, through a better educational process.

It is a tribute to our past leaders and people, their vision, their unselfishness, their sacrifices, that they struggled to give their children the better educational opportunities which had been denied themselves, for despite the fact that their schools were scanty, equipment almost non-existent, standards shockingly low, teachers few, inadequately prepared and poorly paid, the light of learning was kept burning in the schools of this nation even though with an uncertain and flickering glow at times.

Throughout the years there has been a continuing and consistent interest shown in, and more support given to, education, even when the finances of the nation were inadequate and salaries and allowances of officials and employees of Government were unpaid for as much as five and six months successively; but, as conditions progressively changed and resources and revenues increased, greater appropriations have been provided. Foreign contributions and support for the extension of education have increased with the result that there are now more improved and better facilities as well as a higher standard of teachers and administrative personnel in our schools. There is a more favourable atmosphere for learning and, what is most gratifying, men and women, boys and girls everywhere in the nation are responding enthusiastically to it, clamouring for the improved educational opportunities and taking advantage of the facilities at hand. We are happy about this, and proud of the awakening interest in, and support given to education.

But this imposes an even greater challenge to Government, to professors, teachers and educational institutions of every kind to cope with the nation-wide urge and demand of the young people for better facilities, greater opportunities and better standards of education.

Despite all this, there are, it seems to me, some vital missing links in our educational system. In the first place, I have a feeling that emphasis is being placed only on the mere academic type of education while a greater indifference is shown to the cultivation of the finer and more lasting disciplines of life – the moral, spiritual and aesthetic values.

I note with growing concern the lack of emphasis on the teaching of classics, music, drawing, painting and other works of art which nourish the mind, broaden the understanding, deepen the intellect and awaken appreciation for love and beauty from which the possessor finds joy and significance in human existence and achievement. While it may be that not all of these areas are being neglected *per se* their visible results in the lives of the young people of our nation are not eloquent enough to be functional and vitalizing forces. The challenge to achieve, the joy in creativity, the love of scholarship, the genuine pursuit of truth and the discovery of knowledge have become almost lost in the superficialities of the age, often under the misconstrued semantics of progressive education.

Consequently, education has become, in the view of many, so sugar-coated that it has been bereft of its challenge, mysterious enchantment and wonder of discovery.

Secondly, religious education as literature has been entirely eliminated from our schools.

Under the declaration of the religious rights of the citizen, the Constitution of Liberia provides that no sect of Christians shall claim exclusive privilege or preference over any other sect. If we construe this to mean that in a community which is predominantly Christian, the Bible, which is the sacred book of that sect, should not be permitted to be taught in the public schools, then it would be a deprivation of the constitutional rights of those Christians living in that community. Similarly, in a community where the population is for the most part Moslem, it could be a violation of religious freedom to prevent the Koran, which is the sacred book of that sect, from being taught.

I agree that in the public schools no religious dogmas, canons or rubrics of any particular denomination may be expounded, but I contend that the teaching of the Bible, the reading of the Koran or of any other sacred writing in our schools, colleges and universities is no violation of the provisions of the Constitution in respect of religious freedom.

Furthermore, it seems to me that objections to conducting devotional exercises and reading the Bible, the Koran or any other religious literature in schools, colleges or universities involve a question which is individual in character and could be raised only by the individual who conscientiously objects because of his disbelief in the Bible or any other religious literature. But a whole community of students who profess any religious belief should not be deprived of the right and privilege of their religious worship in our institutions of learning because of the objections of one or two persons with atheistic or agnostic attitudes.

The next question on which I desire to speak is corporal punishment in the elementary schools. This we consider to be important also, but there are those who are inclined to talk a lot about child psychology. To know the psychology of a child is rather like the utterance of the apostle Paul: 'O to know the love of God that passeth knowledge.' To know the psychology of a child passeth all knowledge; for it is my opinion that a child actually has no psychology. Psychology must be stimulated or instilled in the child by its parents, its teachers and those who are charged with the responsibility of nurturing the child in its immediate environment, in the home, and in its contacts with neighbours and friends. All of these influences tend to create and develop its outlook, its psychology, its character and its attitude.

In any case, I must admit that this is a specialized subject and may better be left to the experts; but from a layman's point of view, I do know that in the days when children were not left to be governed, trained and controlled by the psychologists but by the use of what Solomon, the wise man, calls in his proverbs 'the rod' and we in Liberia call the switch or whip, there were fewer juvenile delinquents, fewer wayward children and fewer truants in our land and in the world generally than we have today, when so much emphasis is placed on child psychology.

The wise man in his proverbs has declared: 'Spare the rod and spoil the child.' He said further: 'The rod is made for the back of the fool' and in Proverbs, Chapter 19, verse 18, he declared: 'Chasten thy son while there is hope and let not thy soul spare him for his crying.'

These are the admonitions of wisdom, handed down by that wise man, which were followed and practised since the incipiency of our nation until recent years. Then, having an apparent desire to imitate or emulate what is known as the modern educational practice of other countries, we abandoned this tried, tested and proven educational system, with the result that we are beginning to have on our hands unruly, criminally-minded and delinquent young people. The responsibility attaches to us who are responsible for elimination of the rod or switch from the elementary schools; to us parents who fail to co-operate with teachers in disciplining our children; to us who threaten physical combat with teachers who attempt, in the interest of the correct upbringing of the children, to admonish them rightly; to us parents who threaten legal action against teachers and professors who rebuke and chastise our children.

In consequence and in recognition of our responsibility in this respect, I appeal to all leaders of state, parents, guardians, prelates, clerics, professors, teachers, wards and the students themselves to co-operate with us in our efforts to stamp out rudeness, criminal tendencies and delinquency by supporting teachers and all those having to do with the training, upbringing and nurturing of children and youth of the nation in administering corporal punishment in the elementary schools, when necessary, and in rebuking and punishing students in the high schools when expedient as well as in imposing discipline by suspension or even expulsion when necessary in colleges and universities, in the interest of the maintenance of a higher standard of discipline and a moral course of conduct.

Let us support them in the way that my father did in a particular case of mine when I was growing up, if I may be permitted to narrate it here. It is an incident in my school life when my professor in music was teaching tonic sol-fa on the blackboard: I mischievously sang in falsetto and although he called my attention to this immediately, I repeated the falsettos and he jumped on me with a switch and whaled me properly, inflicting one lash on my head which brought the blood streaming down. I rushed out of school to my parents, as mad as I could be, and reported the incident, crying.

My mother became annoyed, as is more characteristic of mothers than of fathers, but my father said, 'You must have done something that caused the teacher to do this to you.' I said, 'I did nothing.' He said, 'Come, let us go up to the school.' We went and when we arrived there my father inquired of the teacher, 'You whipped this boy and cut his head; why did you do it?' The professor replied, 'I was teaching tonic sol-fa on the blackboard and Shad sang falsetto. When I called his attention to it he persisted and so I whipped him and mistakenly cut his head, which I did not intend to do. I meant to whip him severely for his misconduct but I didn't mean to wound him.' My father turned to me and said, 'Boy, I knew that you had done something wrong.' Turning to the professor, he said, 'Beat him again in my presence.' The professor ordered some of the strong boys in the school to take hold of me, put me on the back of one of them; whereupon he gave me another severe whipping in the presence of my father. Thereafter, my father took me home, cut the hair from around the wound and applied alcohol and plaster.

This was the kind of training and upbringing we of our generation and those before and after us had, until recently, when corporal punishment was outlawed and the knowledge of the psychology of children as a means of training and upbringing took its place.

The Government, parents, teachers and professors of educational institutions and all those who have to do with the training and nurturing of the young people of this country, have created and offered virtually nothing to occupy their minds outside the classrooms; and even when they are in the classrooms, there is hardly anything to keep them occupied except their academic subjects.

In days past, there were rhetorical exercises and social programmes in all of the schools. There were exercises when the students had the opportunity to appear on the stage and debate some topic of current interest. There were spelling matches which were commonly called 'spelling bees'. There were mental arithmetic drills and both vocal and instrumental music classes. There were spelling definers when the student spelt the word and gave its definition. There was competition in the correct pronunciation of words. Then there was a practice that after school hours when work was done, the older folks in the communities saw to it that from four to six o'clock in the afternoon the young people engaged in such games as leap-frog, baseball, quoit-pitching, 'chordor', wrestling and tug-of-war.

The children were so well disciplined that regularly in the evenings at different seasons of the year, all of the school bells rang at seven o'clock for those students not in boarding schools to assemble in their home for study and parents were responsible for seeing that this was done. Then another bell rang at nine o'clock for the children to cease study and retire to bed. Thus there was not much time left for the children to engage in degrading and demoralizing practices during their tender years.

It is therefore a sad commentary on the age that today lads and lasses (teenagers) are permitted to wander about at night, attend parties, bars and cafés and remain out until one and two o'clock in the morning without restraint, restriction or scoldings. It seems that we are afraid of our own children.

I appeal to all of us to co-operate in the interest of the church, of society, of our children and of the future of the nation, to advocate and resuscitate reforms not only along the lines or mentioned herein but by such other means and methods that any of us, each of us or all of us may envisage or perceive as salutary to the benefit of reforms.

The Government, on its part, has given serious attention to, and taken positive action in trying to retrieve its negligence toward the youth of the nation and is therefore inaugurating special schemes for the young people under special arrangements and provisions with the Israeli Government. Already a number of Liberians over the past three or four years have been sent to Israel for specialized training and are now back in the country with

Israeli experts who have come to assist us in inaugurating and executing this programme.

Here is a brief outline of what the programme envisages:

1. The Liberian National Youth Organization will be a part of the national educational framework. It will function in close co-ordination with the Department of Public Instruction and the Department of National Defence.
2. The Organization will educate the young people of Liberia to be ready, both morally and physically, to answer the calls of their country for its present and future needs.
3. The Organization will deal with youth – male and female – between the ages of fourteen and twenty, in two age groups: fourteen to sixteen, and seventeen to twenty.
4. Pre-military subjects will be introduced for the seventeen to twenty age group in addition to the normal subjects for young people with which the Organization will deal.

ORGANIZATIONAL STRUCTURE:

The structure of the Liberian National Youth Organization shall answer in a practical way the needs of the above-mentioned aims. There shall be an Executive Office consisting of the following functionaries: Leader of the Organization, Deputy Leader, Education and Youth Activities Officer, Organization and Administration Officer.

The Organization shall have a National Training Centre for courses and youth training and sectional units shall be established in the various areas (schools, clubs, etc.).

PROPOSED FRAMEWORK OF ACTIVITIES:

Activities in the organization will be carried out on a voluntary basis, boys and girls together (except for special activities) according to age groups, as follows:

(a) In the framework of existing youth organizations (sports clubs, community centres, youth clubs, boy scouts, girl guides, etc.) with whom there shall be close co-ordination and co-operation.
(b) In the framework of formal educational institutions (secondary schools, vocational and agricultural schools, evening classes, etc.).
(c) In the framework of proposed activities for as yet unorganized youth centres, youth clubs, etc. which are to be established.
(d) Two senior youth instructors' courses annually.
(e) Junior youth instructors' course during school vacation.
(f) Special group courses for specific needs (sea and air).

SUBJECTS FOR YOUTH ACTIVITIES:

(a) Camping
(b) Foot Drill
(c) First Aid
(d) Outdoor Games

(*e*) Recreational Subjects (folklore, singing, dancing, etc.)
(*f*) Handicrafts
(*g*) Physical activities
(*h*) 'Know Your Country and Your People'

The additional pre-military subjects for the seventeen to twenty age group will be as follows:

(*a*) Foot and Rifle Drill
(*b*) Use of weapons, stressing rifle and sportsmanship with small bore rifle
(*c*) Topography
(*d*) Fieldcraft and outdoor field life
(*e*) Physical fitness – obstacle course.

WAYS OF WORKING:

(*a*) Regular local activities once or twice a week (1–2 hours).
(*b*) One full day's activities once a month (Saturdays or Holidays).
(*c*) Intensive training in a national youth centre, 1–2 weeks a year during school vacations, for the fourteen to sixteen age group.
(*d*) Two weeks to one month of annual national service in development areas for the seventeen to twenty age group. This will be for the reclamation of the land, for road building, cultivation and other manual work of national importance.

All the above proposed ways of working will stress the bringing together of youth in Liberia from the various counties and provinces, for the strengthening of national unity.

It is expected and requested that all educational institutions and other organizations concerned with the nurturing and training of the young people of the country, as well as all parents and guardians, will co-operate to the fullest extent in making this programme a success.

I must here emphasize what I consider to be some of the vital needs of our society, and some of the things that our educational institutions can do in this advancing age of science and technology to achieve comparable results in a highly complex and competitive society. I believe that education should

1. make of pupils changed agents who are serviceable not only as great scholars but as outstanding citizens.
2. extend the horizons of the possessors, quicken their understanding and deepen their appreciation for the past and present history of our race and country and make them visualize more realistically their individual contribution and contemplate the rôle which the nation can and must play in contemporary civilization.
3. renew the will and steel the determination to make society better than it was yesterday, so that the noble ends of democracy may be more assuredly furthered.

It is toward the achievement of such objectives that we can look with optimism and determination, so that our institutions of learning will steer the way clearly in the critical days that are upon us and ahead of us and of all mankind.

Such, in brief, is the story of our educational progress over the years. Our programme is still expanding, being strengthened and improved from within and without and enriched insofar as the resources of the country permit. Consequently, the educational budget has continued to climb steadily but even now the resources available are negligible. We need more and more funds so as to enable more and more up-to-date schools to be opened and staffed by competent and qualified teachers; trained personnel to be employed; educational experts and foreign agencies to share their knowledge in the service of our nation; more school equipment to be bought; foreign and local scholarships to be given additional boost, and a better learning climate to be created.

To top all this, the State University must enlarge its programme, which may well evolutionize education in Liberia and give it new dimensions.

All in all, the fruits of one hundred and thirty-nine years of educational endeavours have been encouraging, if not satisfactory.

It appears to me to be a coincidence that just at this time, on the anniversary of our National Flag Day, the members of the Peace Corps from the United States are arriving in the country under the United States programme of assistance to developing countries, to assist us in this all-important national programme for education.

We express our gratitude to that Government, private corporations, concessionaires, business enterprises, foreign missions and foundations as well as individual foreign citizens for their contributions to our struggle for the education of the people of this nation.

The Department of Public Instruction is optimistic that in less than ten years, roughly all children of school age in Liberia will be in organized schools, with a modern elementary school in every district. This is indeed an ambitious programme, but the pace has been set and must be pursued with bold imagination and dedicated service.

Summing up, then, I have reviewed the story of our educational struggle and the importance which our forefathers attached to education; abridged the story of our progress and portrayed the opportunities and achievements of the present. I have spoken of the lack of emphasis on the moral, spiritual and aesthetic values in our schools, the absence of religious training, and the constitutional safeguards. I have stressed the need for corporal punishment in our elementary schools, and finally, I have called the attention of the old and young, boys and girls, to the enriched opportunities of the present. I urge you in the saying of the old Latin master, *Carpe diem* – seize the day.

Today, our budding university, our improved colleges, our enriched curricula in the high and elementary schools and other educational adjuncts stand as a testimony to the reinforcement of the ideas of our fathers in education and our own determination that it will continue to be the bulwark of our society – now and forever. The challenge is great. We cannot renege, nor must we compromise it in a single detail.

Speech delivered at Haile Selassie I University in Addis Ababa during the Conferment on President Tubman of an Honorary Doctor of Laws Degree

Addis Ababa, Ethiopia, 16 May 1963

The great university is one which constantly supplies the people it serves with a correct and enriched programme of guidance.

Introductory Note

Although President Tubman has received numerous honorary degrees from foreign universities, this was the first honorary degree bestowed upon him by an African University. In the acceptance of this singular gesture, the President stated his belief that one way to bring about African unity is through education. In this brief address, therefore, he seized the opportunity to initiate a scholarship exchange programme between Liberia and Ethiopia, in the furtherance of that belief.

Addis Ababa, Ethiopia, 16 May 1963

IN THE conferring upon me of the degree of Doctor of Law by this institution of learning, a great honour has been done my country and me, and I assure you that I am truly humbled by this preferment and grateful for the academic distinction.

Colleges and universities are established to help to identify and satisfy the deep human needs of the times. In their search for knowledge and the discovery of truth, academic freedom is their watchword. These institutions aim to realize, for men and women, life's richer possibilities and to help equip them to derive a true interpretation of these relations through the media of careers and professions. The great university, therefore, is the one which constantly supplies the people it serves with a correct and enriched programme of guidance, which seeks a way out of the difficulties through which humanity is trying to find a way, and which prepares its students to be representative citizens of the era in which they live. To the degree that a university succeeds in doing this, it rises above the *status quo*, and it falls away when it merely repeats, in mechanical fashion, traditional exercises entirely out of keeping with contemporary times. A university should thus seek to perpetually stimulate its students to the search for knowledge and to awaken in them a continuing intellectual curiosity.

The rôle which this University has played in the life of this Empire, is vital; the men and women who have received its training and guidance and passed through its doors are now the representatives of their country, making valuable contributions to their nation and people. What greater reward can an institution hope and work for? I congratulate the officials of this venerable seat of learning in the great task which they are doing to build up an enlightened citizenry, and to perpetuate the tradition of learning.

With the new awakening which has taken and is taking place in Africa and the world, with the African states now being brought constantly in contact with each other at the United Nations, through state visits, conferences and seminars, the peoples of this vast continent have for the first time begun, while facing the complexities of their problems, to realize the great opportunities in the challenge for peace and unity, in the creation of a strong partnership in economic, cultural, social, technological, educational and other related areas.

I know of no single effective approach than the exchange of teachers and students in our higher institutions of learning. It is in this way that the language barriers between the English, French and other different language speaking countries could be broken down in the emergence of a generation which will not only be bilingual, but which will be versed in the history and culture of all groups. It is my wish and hope that between Ethiopia and Liberia such a programme will be initiated, just as it has been tried successfully between Liberia and Guinea. I feel that this is a fertile field for fostering better understanding between the peoples of Africa and one which requires study and experimentation.

In acknowledging this great honour done to my country and me today, I bring you greetings and felicitations from the President, Board of Trustees and Faculty of the University of Liberia, our state institution, which, like this University, has steered the course of higher education in Liberia for over a century.

To the students of the University I wish to pose a simple question – what do you want here and what are you willing to pay for it? You may remember in your mythology, and in your Grimm's fairy tales, that when the hero's luck was so great that the kind fairies put themselves at his service, they always asked him what he wanted. He had at least to CHOOSE. And so I say to you, 'O wonderful youth, whoever you are, that have come to this fairy godmother of modern times; she will mean to you what you will, and what you will she will give you.' I challenge you therefore, to answer with a choice, and I call upon you to consider with all intentness and manly intelligence what your momentous choice is going to be, and once having made it, to put behind that choice every ounce of power you possess.

God bless you in the maximum development of your abilities for true and effective service to your God and country in the years ahead of you.

Speech delivered at Cuttington College during the Ceremony for Laying of the Cornerstone of the Bishop Harris Building

Suacoco, Liberia, 1 December 1963

May the Bishop Harris Building become a living symbol of the dynamic and moving quality of his great personality and his life, which has been an example of ideals of Christian love, stewardship and service.

Introductory Note

This was a testimonial address to the retiring Bishop, the Rt. Reverend Bravid W. Harris, who served for nineteen years as Bishop of the Protestant Episcopal Church in Liberia, on the completion of his ministry. The Bishop received the grateful appreciation of the Liberian people, through their President, for his immense contributions to Liberian education.

Suacoco, Liberia, 1 December 1963

THE CEREMONY in which we have come to participate today is the first step toward the implementation of a project conceived and intended as a memorial to the great and effective work in evangelism, education, agriculture and science of one of the most outstanding personalities of the ecclesia of our time.

This is a significant act, in recognition of nineteen years of unbroken service by the man who, with utter dedication, devoted his time, energy and life to his church's work in Liberia and who by the rich and strong quality of his spiritual leadership, his great intellectuality and his dynamism, has done so much to revitalize the Ministry of the Protestant Episcopal Church and to foster vigorously and successfully the concept of an expanding and growing church and ministry. That Right Reverend gentleman is none other than our revered Bishop Bravid W. Harris.

Bishop Harris arrived on the Missionary Field of Liberia when there was a virtual lull in the activities of the Protestant Episcopal Church and when Cuttington College and Divinity School, where the Episcopal Church's work had culminated in the creation of a strong and recognized educational centre, had been closed for seventeen years. The institution had been widely acclaimed for its strong curriculum, its high academic standards and its stern discipline. For many years it had given trained and capable men to the Ministry and national life of the nation, and the closing of the programme of religious and academic education in Maryland County was a nasty shock to the nation.

It was natural that the leaders and people of the country should be concerned about the re-opening of Cuttington College. To this end many conferences had already been held and proposals made to the American Church; but it was not until after the arrival of Bishop Harris in Liberia that plans for the re-opening of Cuttington took positive shape and he became the moving pivot, for when word finally came that Cuttington College would be re-opened, the suitability of the old site became a highly controversial issue. After repeated protests from Old Cuttingtonians, Marylanders, and people from all over the country, including some missionary groups, and the holding of several conferences, in a few of which I chanced to have participated, Bishop Harris won his argument that the new-old institution be re-located in the Central Province, in an area where, because of the greater availability of larger acreage of fertile farming land and other facilities, it would lend itself to expansion.

During those difficult and trying years which preceded the building of this campus and the development of the college community, only a man of Bishop Harris' great comprehension, depth of human understanding and compassion, courage, determination and sacrificial spirit could meet face on and master the adverse conditions, trials and disappointments which arose. Planning ceaselessly for the strengthening and expansion of his programme, working arduously at a mammoth building programme, travelling extensively at home and abroad, recruiting highly qualified personnel for the execution of this programme, opening new schools and improving old ones; such has been the busy schedule of this distinguished and illustrious leader.

In the years that have followed, the initial difficulties have been overcome and Cuttington College is today a blooming institution with greater possibilities for an expanded, strong and enriched programme, which proves that Bishop Harris and those who stood with him were right. The work which is being done here and the revitalization of the entire programme of the Liberian field reflect credit to the zeal, wisdom, courage and realism of Bishop Harris, a truly great and indomitable executive. From my point of view, one of the most outstanding characteristics of this eminent personality is his disinterestedness. Bishop Harris looks not for fame, vainglory or pomp, but is mainly concerned with the work to which he has been assigned and to which he has dedicated himself.

Believing that it would be in the interest of the Institution and would serve as an incentive to students coming here for training, as well as respond to the obvious national pride of the Liberian people, Bishop Harris began searching for a trained and competent man to assume the presidency of the College and did not relent until he had the present incumbent, Dr. Christian Baker, installed as President. I pay high compliment to the Bishop for this broad-minded action which fills us with pride, and feel confident that Dr. Baker will, in the future as in the past, with ever increasing momentum, lift higher and strengthen the standard of this College.

Bishop Harris has set a remarkable example of the dignity of labour which the people of Liberia must emulate, since this is aligned with Government's new programme of Operation Production which is being promulgated and insisted upon as national priority number one.

Today, the building to be erected and for which we are laying the cornerstone is only a very modest testimony and tribute to him who, through the programmes of development since his incumbency, has contributed greatly to the progress which we see not only here but throughout the nation. The force of his personality, the depth of his religious convictions and the genuineness of his love for the work have won for him the affection, admiration, response and respect of the Liberian people.

It is therefore an honour done me by the President and authorities of the College to have afforded me the opportunity of paying a modest tribute to Bishop Harris, whom I consider not only as a man who has fundamentally advanced the work of the Episcopal Church in Liberia but as one who has also contributed immensely to the advancement of education throughout the nation, and to his very faithful wife, better half and help-mate, Mrs. Harris, who has lived up to the letter and spirit of the appellation given by each to the other 'partner'.

May the Bishop Harris Building that will be erected on this spot become a living symbol of the dynamic and moving quality of his great personality and his life, which has been an example of the ideals of Christian love, stewardship and service.

It must be more than a building – it must stand for an ideal translated into an idea of service to God and humanity. As a cafeteria where many will meet daily and as a women's dormitory where social and graceful living will be combined, we hope that it may be a constant reminder and a living embodiment of a life of worth-while endeavour and positive accomplishment. This building must be an inspiration which will fire its users with those qualities with which we will always associate Bishop Harris.

Finally, I congratulate the leaders of the Protestant Episcopal Church in America for the continued support given to the operation and administration of the work of Christian education in Liberia for more than a century; I congratulate the Bishop of the District of Liberia for the spiritual and administrative leadership which he has provided; I highly commend the President and Faculty of Cuttington College and Divinity School for their contribution to the enriched programmes to which the youth of the nation are being exposed. I urge the young men and women of this institution to strive constantly and conscientiously to make this a true citadel of Christianity, so that, living and learning, they may go forth in their chosen fields of endeavour and activity as examples of the Christian education, which truly ennobles, enriches and strengthens the mind.

Speech delivered at the University of Liberia

Monrovia, 8 March 1965

The University of Liberia must become an outstanding and first rate institution of higher learning in the country and as good as any in Africa. The University of Liberia is our national pride. Let us support it.

Introductory Note

Again and again the President has personally led several drives to raise funds for the University of Liberia – an expression of his deep concern for the improvement of the nation's highest institution of learning. When assistance in this endeavour from a friendly country was withdrawn, undaunted, the President in this address pledged his support and contribution, and also that of the entire citizenry of Liberia, for the realization of the objectives of the University in the area of growth and expansion.

Monrovia, 8 March 1965

IT WAS the French political philosopher Montesquieu, who said that as the principle of an aristocracy is honour, and the principle of tyranny is fear, so the principle of a democracy is education. The democratic ideal, therefore, is universal education; for none of the great changes – the rise of experimental science, specialization and industrialization will make universal education irrelevant. On the contrary, these changes will make education more necessary and urgent.

Our present gathering here this morning is to assert our faith in education, and, at this formal opening of the 1965 academic year of the University of Liberia, to project some of the worthy objectives of the institution in an attempt to spur the faculty, students, the supporting agencies of this community and the nation in general to greater, more concerted and conscientious efforts on behalf of the University so that it may continue to function effectively and usefully in the political, social and intellectual life of the nation. I wish to draw attention to the necessity for an intensified adequate training and education of the mind and body of our youngsters in all our institutions of learning.

We speak of the unity of mind and body, the one intangible and the other tangible or physical. Time was when more social prestige was attached to the care of the mind than to the care of the body, and therefore teachers who gave intellectual instructions were usually indifferent to the questions of health and the signs by which the first appearance of any physical ailment could be detected. However, we have not entirely lost the Greek ideal that mind and body are inseparable; a theory and a practice which caught the

414

imagination of the Romans when they insisted and practised 'a sound mind in a sound body'.

The distinction between mind and body is therefore artificial and unreal, and physical care and mental activity are not to be completely separated. And even if in the adult there is a gulf between these two, the gulf has no metaphysical basis or necessity, for if we accept the proposition that mental activity is that which does not involve the use of arms or legs, and that physical activity is that which does, then mental activity is superior to the physical, because those who practise it exclusively need servants to do their physical labour. It follows therefore that the soul is nobler than the body, that matter is the evil principle, and so on. It is not my intention to enter into a philosophical discussion of the mind and body; I only want to show the unity of purpose which should exist between the two and to stress the adequate training which should be given for and in the interest of their dual development.

In spite of the fact that you and I live in the serenity of this land, the comfort of our homes and the stability of our Government, there are many conditions and problems in the world today that threaten our freedom and independence. To offset these dangers, universal education must be placed in the forefront of our foreign and domestic policy if our nation is to rise in the hierarchy of nations and come to exert its influence on the history of civilizations, in Africa and in the world. Truly, the rôle of the teacher in a free society has always been difficult and often dangerous, but that has not, nevertheless, made his rôle less important in the annals of education anywhere in ancient, medieval or modern history. Never was it more eloquently stated than on that far-off day when the great Athenian teacher made his final salute to his people and to his profession. 'It would be bad,' he said, 'If I, who stood fast in the ranks of Potidea and Amphipolis and Delium, where the officers you appointed over me told me to stand, and did not fall back in fear of death — it would indeed be bad if now through fear of death I should desert the post in which the gods have placed me... I love and respect you, men of Athens, but I love and respect the truth of the gods more... I go now to die and you to live; which of us has the better deal is known but to the gods.'

The issues are clear and they have been debated on strange battlegrounds: the issue of freedom of enquiry versus inculcation of fixed answers; the issue of the right of individuals to decide from among alternatives versus imposition on people of somebody's pet truth; the issue of freedom of education versus censorship of education.

But you and I live in a world today where many changes have taken place: where the pursuit of scientific investigation, discoveries, and achievements have been phenomenal, thereby changing man's outlook and opening up new horizons. Thus science has had a tremendous relationship to human progress, not in the production of things but in its readiness and its truth. There is no field of human endeavour to which science has not offered something — to social science, it offers a great body of facts concerning animal relationships, metabiosis, symbiosis, antibiosis, co-action and co-operation; to economics it offers much material for food, shelter, and clothing; to the political scientist, it offers its services in the promotion of the health and welfare of the people, and new weapons for protection; to the psychologist it offers an ever-growing understanding of the laws which govern animal

behaviour, physiological mechanisms and neural integration; science offers
to religion the knowledge of God's handiwork from the components of the
atomic nucleus to the most distant galaxy in the universe. Of mankind
science asks only freedom, freedom in which to pursue the truth, for he
believes from the depths of his heart that to find what is true in order to do
what is right is the summing-up of the total duty of man. The University of
Liberia and all other institutions of higher learning have this obligation —
the pursuit of scientific truth.

It is not my intention or desire to enter into a profound analysis of the
investigative nature of science or to express any certain opinion because I
know too little about it; but of this I am deeply convinced, that to all thinking persons science offers the thesis that the search for truth should not be
static but rather a dynamic process, ever evolving, ever growing, ever becoming, and that if mankind is to survive as a species he must relentlessly
pursue this truth. We believe that the pursuit of truth is one of the finest
and greatest challenges of any University. But more than this I am convinced that in spite of the great challenges of the scientific age, knowledge is
wisdom, and that it is the principal thing. But knowledge by itself creates a
void and a great deficiency, and therefore education founded solely on
knowledge is inadequate to equip man to live in the new world that he has
created by the scientific investigations and researches which have produced
amazing results.

Along with this scientific training, there should emerge patterns of thought
and behaviour which portray unity and community; it must be an education
which shall emphasize those aspects in which men are the same, rather than
those in which they are different, for the aim of education is wisdom and
each person in a democracy must have the chance to become as wise as he
can.

It was Rousseau who said, 'It matters little to me whether my pupil is
intended for the army, the church, or the law. Before his parents chose a
calling for him, nature called him to be a man. When he leaves me, he will
be neither a magistrate, a soldier, nor a priest; he will be a man.'

Among the proverbs of Solomon it is written, 'with all thy getting, get
understanding'; understanding to know what the ultimate effect of these
phenomenal scientific advances will bring to the human race and the earth
on which he lives; understanding that will make him realize the pre-
requisites of living in the new world that he has created; understanding that
shows him how to live in peace, safety and happiness.

The University of Liberia must become an outstanding, first-rate institution of higher learning in the country and as good as any in Africa. We must
see that it achieves this ideal. It must lead and take its accepted rôle in the
system of human values. It must exert leadership in the search for truth and
become identified with the triumph of the spirit of man over matter. The
University must seek truth relentlessly, dispassionately and fearlessly, and
become the means through and by which the portals of knowledge, understanding and wisdom will be opened wide and where all good learning will
flourish, abound and be transmitted to future generations. The University of
Liberia is our national pride; let us support it.

Our forefathers sought to build, maintain and enhance these concepts
and institutions of freedom; they were ambitious and desirous of supporting
them with a programme of free and universal education. Thus it is seen that

from the very beginning the relationship of universal education to the possibilities of men being free was recognized. You and I know that the basic decision was finally to make this a nation where each man was to count; where he would count in terms of his innate capacity, enhanced by how he could develop it, and pushed on by hard work and his commitments to himself, his fellow men and his nation. They made a wise decision in the direction of the concept that each man, each woman, and each child was to have a place in this nation. This decision has become one of the great controlling, guiding and motivating influences in the democratic way of life which we must continue to cherish and uphold.

And so if we are to be guided by these lofty principles, we should seek to make Liberia strong, not in men and machines, *per se*, but strong in trained intelligence, love of country, the understanding of its ideals and integrity, a sense of responsibility and devotion to concepts which can become a part of the thought and living pattern of every citizen.

But any training, any educational policy or system which ignores the spiritual is inadequate, dangerous and unsafe. We read in Holy Writ that Job in his distress and afflictions declared, 'there is a spirit in man and the inspiration of the Almighty giveth him understanding'. I advance the proposition that 'science should walk with humble feet to seek the God that faith has found'.

Let me also direct attention to the fact that civics should be given a special place in the curriculum of our schools, so that our young people may come to understand and appreciate the structure and place of their political institutions as they relate to their growth and development, and the part they can play in the life of the nation. Training in citizenship, no less than training for other professions, is today a science, the study of which is both necessary and indispensable to present day living. Because I attach great importance to this subject, I recommend its inclusion in the syllabus of our schools.

What are the specific goals of the University of Liberia? They are:

To provide a centre of higher education with high standards of competence and proficiency.

To provide well prepared personnel to meet the leadership and high-level manpower needs of Liberia, and, where practicable, other countries, particularly of Africa.

To undertake research activities appropriate to the needs of a developing and growing Republic.

To provide for the pursuit of academic excellence, the search for truth, the continuity of intellectual curiosity, the broadening and extension of man's cumulative knowledge and the transmission of the priceless values of our culture.

During the year under review the University of Liberia will seek specifically:

To relate its activities and programme more clearly and closely to the needs of the people and the country.

To formulate defensible short, intermediate and long-range plans for the development of the University.

To bring to the public, particularly the Alumni Association, a greater awareness of the programmes and activities of the University.

To improve the physical facilities available on the campus in Monrovia, with particular reference to facilities for students.

Towards these ends, it is my considered opinion that the academic growth of the University and its ability to contribute effectively and maximally to the trained manpower requirements for the economic and social development of the nation can never be entirely fulfilled if the institution remains at its present site. The question of its re-location in the near future must therefore be given serious and immediate consideration.

Four years ago our hopes were raised when the government of a friendly nation agreed, as part of its assistance to Liberia, to take part in the development of higher and professional education by financing plans for the physical development of a new University campus. Accordingly, blue prints were prepared, specifications and the model of the new University campus submitted and approved; 5,500 acres of private land were surveyed and acquired by Government as a part of their contribution and work commenced on the new site. Later the President of the University was informed that the Government entertained reservations about the timing of the development of the new University campus; the necessary Task Order was therefore not issued. Thus, work on the re-location of the University which was considered of great importance, has had to be stopped, to our great mortification.

Secondly, the University is in need of adequate funds to meet its present obligations, and, while the educational levy will assist substantially in this respect, there is need for more funds for operation and extension purposes.

We suggest and appeal to the members of the Board of Trustees, including the Visitor, to raise and contribute $100,000 in the current year, the President of the University, Faculty and Students $25,000, the Alumni Association $25,000, all social, political, fraternal and religious organizations in Montserrado County, foreign friends interested in education in Liberia including businessmen, concessionaires and those engaged in other activities $50,000, from officials, citizens, foreign businesses, and social and fraternal organizations in the County of Grand Bassa and the Territory of Rivercess, Sinoe County and the Territory of Sasstown, Maryland County and the Kru Coast Territory, Grand Cape Mount County, the Counties of Grand Gedeh, Nimba, Bong and Loffa $25,000, and thus play a part in preparing the future statesmen, scientists and other professionals of the country. Let us remember that there can be no sounder investment in democracy than that made in education. I call upon everyone to take a part in this crusade.

Finally, if the general goals and the specific aims of the University are to be achieved, the President has outlined the following needs:

1. The development and maintenance of a highly competent faculty.
2. The assembling of a highly motivated and qualified student body of increasing size.
3. Provision for appropriate physical facilities adequate to carry out its programme.
4. Assured financing at a level permitting the full utilization of the University's potential.
5. The establishment of a Commission on Higher Education similar in purpose to the Commission of Higher Education established in 1961.

These and sundry matters will receive the attention of the Board of Trustees and those responsible for the programme of extension and strengthening of the University.

To the members of the Board of Trustees, faculty, students old and new, and all personnel, I extend a hearty welcome and hope that the year will be one of harder work for you and joyous achievements in the knowledge of work well done.

We express thanks and appreciation to USAID for the construction of dormitories, etc., on the present campus, which I am sure will greatly enhance the overall programme of the University.

May you who are charged with the supreme responsibility of guiding the young people to grow steadily in their ability to understand the democratic aspiration and to contribute to its enrichment, accept the challenge of the teaching profession and stand firm in devotion to its main task – the development of free men in a free society.

Statement on Liberian Education

Monrovia, 3 July 1965

Never before have so many shown a keen interest in education and expressed the desire to learn.

Introductory Note

President Tubman appreciated the growing awareness of the significant rôle which education must play to build a new Liberian society, and the response of Liberian youth to seize every means offered by the Government and private institutions to become educated and responsible men and women.

Monrovia, 3 July 1965

DEEP WITHIN our democratic heritage is embedded our commitment to education and the necessity of making our schools the chief and most effective instrument of our political and social institutions, in order that the democratic ideal may not only be fully meaningful in the present, but that it will also become the spearhead of social and political reforms in the lives of succeeding generations. For never before has the absolute importance of education been more recognized than now.

Never before have so many shown a keen interest in education and expressed the desire to learn.

Never before have so many educational opportunities been provided, and never before has the education of men and women, boys and girls, the old and the young, been more urgent and necessary.

Never before has our faith in education as the foundation of all progress and the yeast of a free society been as reassuring as at the present day.

We remain committed to the task of educating the whole man and woman, boy and girl, as an individual to become effective and contributing citizens; and above all, of inculcating moral and spiritual values in the hearts and minds of the younger generations, without which all education is meaningless.

I am indeed happy that this special period has been set aside as Education Week, and I congratulate the sponsors for this laudable effort. It is befitting, during this week, that we focus our thoughts on the rôle of education in our scheme of national development, so that we may become increasingly aware of the tremendous responsibilities which we owe to ourselves and the nation, to take adequate advantage of the opportunities for mental, physical and spiritual development and growth.

I call upon all citizens of the nation, the young and old; I call upon all authorities of institutions of learning; I invite all Ministers of the Gospel and every institution charged with the care and nurture of the young and old, to participate in preparing suitable programmes for execution in connection with Education Week and join the co-ordinating agencies to make the week highly successful and productive of worthwhile results.

Statement to the National Teachers' Association

Gbarnga, Bong County, 26 March 1966

Your concern for moulding the minds and character of our young population and in strengthening our educational efforts is one in which both you and I share an equal interest, based upon a commitment that is unalterable.

Introductory Note

In recent years the teachers of Liberia have organized themselves into an effective body for better teaching and training of the youth of Liberia. They meet in annual conventions to review their work and renew their dedication to it. The President, in this brief statement, assured them that he was grateful to them for such a strong sense of dedication to duty, and that their performance fulfilled the most vital function in the new Liberia that he and all Liberians daily seek to build and preserve.

Gbarnga, Bong County, 26 March 1966

I CONGRATULATE you on the occasion of the Tenth Annual Convention of the National Teachers' Association of Liberia. In such a professional atmosphere you are creating an ideal opportunity for the exchange of views and the discussion of problems of general interest not only to each of you, but to all the people of the country who are interested in education. Your concern for moulding the delicate minds and characters of our young population and in strengthening our educational efforts is one in which both you and I share an equal interest, based upon a commitment that is unalterable.

I cannot over-emphasize the important position of the teacher in a democratic society and the tremendous responsibility that devolves upon him in the building of a nation. The teaching profession of which you are a part should give you pride and great satisfaction, although it is sacrificial, often under-rated and poorly compensated. What greater joy and reward can there be for you than to know that you are being entrusted with the tender care and development of the Leaders of State of tomorrow?

Liberia's most precious possession is her human resources, particularly the younger generation. The most valuable security that our nation can acquire is a strong, virile, well-trained and disciplined citizenry. It is to this end that the teacher's rôle is indispensable.

Your theme 'The Rôle of Teacher Organization in National Planning' is one from which the many facets of a teacher's responsibilities and scope of activities can be seen and determined; but it is not enough for teachers merely to discuss the meaning and purpose of educational planning. They need to go further and strive to overcome their weaknesses, improve their methods and techniques of teaching so that they may be able to achieve the greatest good from an improved programme of education to which they have dedicated their lives.

I am confident that you will continue to work diligently and tirelessly in raising the standard of education throughout the country and will remain loyal to the noble profession of your choice, and I congratulate you for your sacrifice of service to humanity, democracy, freedom and justice and wish you continued strength and success.

An Appeal to the Nation for a Fund Drive for the University of Liberia

Monrovia, 23 June 1966

Because of the demand and need for the strengthening of the University of Liberia, our highest institution of learning, I make this appeal and court your enthusiastic response.

Introductory Note

President Tubman often lent his name, person and influence to numerous fund raising drives for various community projects, but none perhaps was given more constant enthusiasm and support than the Fund Drive for the University of Liberia. Because of his dedication to that drive, the response by the people of Liberia to it was enthusiastic and spontaneous. In this appeal he devised a comprehensive plan and timetable for the raising of funds for the University.

Monrovia, 23 June 1966

I BRING you greetings and tell you that because of the emerging demand and need for the strengthening of the body fabric of the University of Liberia, our highest institution of learning, which is and must be concerned with the training and preparation of future statesmen, civic workers and professional men and women, to maintain, promote and accelerate the standard of our national equilibrium and growth, and

Because of our desire to awaken in the people of this nation a greater willingness and anxiety to engage in activities of self-help by making voluntary contributions to charity and worthy causes as a matter of national pride and patriotic obligation, and

Because the University of Liberia is in need of improved and extended facilities which would include additional classrooms to cope with increasing student enrolment, expanded office space, a modern auditorium and laboratories for teaching the sciences and other related subjects in order to meet the present challenge and advancements being made in the field of research, experimentation and invention, greater interest must be shown and sacrifices made by individual citizens, corporations, religious groups and educational entities as well as social and political organizations to raise its standard to that of a modern Institution of recognized higher learning;

Therefore, at the opening ceremony of the University of Liberia in 1965, in an address to the Board of Trustees, President, Faculty, Alumni Association and Student Body, we suggested that the University embark upon and expose itself to a vigorous drive to raise at least two hundred and fifty thousand ($250,000.00) dollars for its use at this time. The Board of Trustees, Faculty and Alumni Association of the University having approved the proposal, have started the venture for the benefit of the young people who are intensely yearning for higher education.

I, therefore, in this form and manner, appeal to all our citizens, foreign residents and friends, professional men and women, concessionaires, fraternal, political, religious, missionary and social institutions and societies throughout the length and breadth of the nation, to rise up and join us in this undertaking which we believe is a laudable cause and an investment that will yield greater dividends in the interest of the nation than any other investment that could be made.

Thus far, the Firestone Plantations Company has subscribed $50,000.00, Liberia Mining Company and LAMCO ten thousand dollars each, your humble servant and Mrs. Tubman ten thousand dollars. Let us now go on from one dollar to five, ten, fifteen, twenty-five, fifty, seventy-five, one hundred, one thousand, ten thousand and up to one hundred thousand dollars, in an effort to make this drive a big success.

Let every student throughout the country raise at least one dollar and hand it to his Principal to be paid into this fund. Let each High School, each Elementary and Kindergarten School make its contribution to this drive, because each student expects some day to enter the University of Liberia and to live in one of the dormitories that will be constructed. If you make this contribution now, as you one day move about in the hallways, sleep in the beds and enjoy the facilities of the University Campus, you will have the satisfaction that although you contributed as a High School, Elementary or Kindergarten Student, you are reaping some of the physical benefits that your own money has provided.

Let the Masonic Craft, the Order of Eastern Star, the United Brothers of Friendship, Sisters of Mysterious Ten, the Grand United Order of Odd Fellows, the Household of Ruth, the Porror, the Sande, the International Order of Good Templars, the Union Mechanics, the Gee Craw Society, all social clubs in every city, town and village and all others join in this great project, and last but not least, let the great True Whig Party that has conducted the affairs of the Nation and kept the torch of liberty burning within our borders, by the support which it has received from the people of this country, contribute at least one hundred and fifty thousand dollars and assist in raising not less than two hundred and fifty thousand dollars for this first drive.

I make this earnest appeal and court your enthusiastic response.

The drive will be formally opened on the 15th of July 1966 and terminate on the 16th of November 1966. Your donation should be made payable to the University of Liberia Fund Drive, through your humble servant or the President of the University of Liberia, not later than the 30th of October, 1966.

Statement to the National Teachers' Association

Monrovia, July 1966

Press forward to a sound and progressive educational system.

Introductory Note

The National Teachers' Association received an expression of appreciation for their work from a grateful President.

Monrovia, July 1966

THE INCENTIVE for your convoking the national body of teachers to observe what you call 'Education week' I consider as being one of the fundamental elements and developing processes in the building of a sound and progressive instrument that will serve the nation; principally because the motive is centred around and has to do with the moulding of the lives of our younger generation, whom we expect to succeed us in taking over the conduct and administration of the affairs of State. I therefore salute you with national pride, greet and congratulate you for the continuity of your endeavours in your search for improved methods and techniques of teaching.

We advance the theory that teachers, who have the all-important rôle of shaping the minds of young people, should be thoroughly moulded, lead an exemplary and well-balanced life and possess a professional approach and attitude toward education.

I am happy to associate myself with your organization which reflects a policy of seeking better ways, methods and techniques for advancing and upgrading our level of education to that comparable with systems now being used by the best institutions in our world, which is pregnant with unrest, agitation and instability. I also compliment the Teachers' Organization because it is making a tireless and unrelenting search for wholesome and commendable methods of creating a better society in which man may live at peace with his fellow man in a world void of acts of inhumanity. This would only be possible through meaningful ways and methods for raising the rate of literacy in our country and the world, which can be done by the professional planning of organizations such as yours.

Now, Mr. President, Officers and Members of the National Teachers' Association, with these ideas in mind and with whatever else may be on your agenda for discussion, I charge you to press forward with every spark of understanding at your command in making your contribution to the accurate planning of a sound and progressive educational system, and to exert every iota of energy you possess until that Herculean Monster — IGNORANCE — disappears from our society and is laid to rest.

HEALTH

Speech delivered to the Annual Convention of the Liberian Midwives' Council

Monrovia, December 1963

Yours then is a task to be proud of, for by your knowledge and skill you help to herald into the world each day a citizen, a newcomer endowed with God-given potentialities.

Introductory Note

When President Tubman spoke to the Liberian Midwives' Council, he responded to their request as to a most pleasing duty. The nation's health was a matter which ceaselessly claimed his attention and to which he contributed all the resources the Government could afford, with great emphasis on the provision of still better facilities. The rôle of the Midwives' Council of Liberia, therefore, did not go unnoticed by him, and he paid them tribute on this occasion.

Monrovia, December 1963

IT IS a happy privilege for me to extend a very warm welcome on behalf of the Government, the people of Liberia and myself, to the officers and members of this convention, and to congratulate you upon the organization of the Liberian Midwives' Council, which is dedicated to improving the practice of midwifery in Liberia.

'Knowledge is power', it has often been said; but knowledge is power only when it can be applied successfully to the solutions of human problems, and in the case of your particular profession, this knowledge should lead to a greater degree of enlightenment, and effectively eradicate some of the persistent ills of humanity. Because it is of the utmost importance that you bring to your work a sense of dedication in all you have to do, I wish to address you tonight on the subject: 'Your job and you'.

In various periods of history, the tide of opportunity comes from different directions; it is then that the wise person chooses to take advantage of an opportunity which, if ignored, may cause his venture to be lost, or, to put it more specifically, cause a human life to be lost. In considering, therefore the subject 'Your job and you' it is necessary to face the fact that even though you may possess the training, knowledge and skills, and have the right attitude toward your work and to people in general, one of the pre-requisites of your job is to have confidence in yourself. Confidence begets confidence, even as love begets love. The fear that you may not succeed with a certain delivery, that its complication is beyond your competence, or that your service will not be adequately compensated, are all bugbears which paralyse efficiency and create for you a psychological bloc which may always be a hindrance to you in your work. My first advice to you then, is to have confidence in yourself and even develop a little sophistication, so that others may have confidence in your ability and faith in your skill. To instil this confidence in yourself, I admonish you to keep constantly at your work by developing your competence and capabilities until you have so much to offer that your contribution will be obvious to all. Then you will advance rapidly along the road which leads to distinction, appreciation and success.

There is another factor which is of vital importance to 'Your job and you'. It is service: the performance and the contribution of your labour for the benefit and advantage of others, by means of supplying a general demand. Your willingness to serve efficiently and cheerfully when you are needed, your presence of mind in critical cases, the manner of your professional attitude and behaviour and, above all, a display of human compassion and understanding, will always contribute very significantly and with satisfying results towards enhancing the service you are professionally bound to render at all times. It is service first which should claim your attention; other concomitants such as reward, recognition and praise are aftermaths which should never be allowed to supersede the bigger and more important requirements of your profession. Have you been proud to serve your patients? Will it always be a delight to go on serving faithfully, efficiently and willingly the needs of the mothers of your communities? Let each of you look within herself and reflect seriously on the implications of the kind of service which society requires of you. Be proud to say that you tried to serve with fervour and zeal.

A third requirement of 'Your job and you' is to make your experience yield for you bigger dividends, capitalize on your experience and not take it for granted. There is a story of a man who once complained to his superior that he should have more consideration. 'After all,' he concluded, 'I have had fifteen years of experience.' 'Oh no,' said the superior, 'that is where you make your mistake, John. You have not had fifteen years of experience at all. You have only had one year's experience fifteen times.' The point here is that unless one's experience is broadened, enriched and utilized beneficially, it will be valueless. If you apply this to any human situation you will surely see that it fits admirably. It is growth which is important. In this day and age, see to it that you get out of the mental or professional rut and well into the ever broadening, demanding and challenging race of life. You must make your experience of great value to yourself and those you will be called upon to serve.

Try the experiment of doing a few things you are not specifically paid to do, especially if such services involve added skill or responsibility. Remember, if you are to earn more, you owe it to yourself and society to make yourself worth more. For I need not remind you that every employer who is worthy of his salt is ready to pay more money to the person who assumes increased responsibility. There is always room at the top you know, but it is reserved for those who have ability-plus.

We live in a scientific age, and practices which were once carried on under unfavourable conditions are fast yielding to the certain and progressive principles of science. Thus, while the practice of midwifery in Liberia has always gone on, its development on a scientific basis is gaining in importance and popularity and it is gratifying to know the practical good results which have already been reaped and are still being reaped. What this means to the maintenance of the steady rise in our population growth is easy to comprehend, since midwives are privileged to take part in and contribute to one of the greatest miracles of all times – birth.

Yours, then is a task to be proud of, for by your knowledge and skill you help to herald into the world each day a citizen, a newcomer endowed with all the God-given potentialities. Did any profession ever hold such a grave responsibility to society and mankind?

And as you come to the close of this convention, I commend you for the work you have thus far accomplished, and challenge you to the work which is yet to be done. If you rise to every occasion with confidence in yourselves, putting the idea of service first, and allowing your experience to be broadened and enriched, you will become useful members of the communities in which you are working; you will develop into indispensable members of the Midwives' Council of Liberia and, what is more, you will be valuable in the divine economy of God.

A team of British doctors is due to arrive in Monrovia about the 22nd of February 1964 to investigate the principal causes of mortality in both mothers and babies, and to make recommendations for the amelioration of the situation within the present and expected resources of Government.

According to their qualifications, a few of the matters to be enquired into by the members of the team are: (1) the organization of consultant obstetric and gynaecological services in hospitals and the provision of facilities for pre-natal and post-natal care in the maternity hospital, (2) the teaching of midwifery, standards of entry for midwifery instruction, length and content of course, refresher courses; traditional methods of midwifery, domiciliary midwifery, and (3) family customs relating to contraception, and the feeding of infants.

All of these doctors are high calibre specialists in their respective fields, and it is expected that they will be given your full co-operation and that you will benefit from their association.

I sincerely hope that you have had a very stimulating and rewarding session, that the decisions and plans made will lead to a greater enhancement and enrichment of midwifery in our nation, so that the council may become a positive factor for good throughout the country and a guiding influence in the lives of present and future generations of midwives.

An Address to the 1964 Graduating Class of the Tubman National Institute of Medical Arts

Monrovia, 6 February 1964

The nursing profession must be given increased encouragement, and it is the obligation of the Government, and its policy, to endeavour to raise this profession to a higher level of recognition and consideration.

Introductory Note

In this opening address President Tubman reminded the graduates of the seriousness and complete dedication which a career in nursing demands. He paid tribute to Liberian nurses who had rendered outstanding services in the past history of nursing in Liberia, and asked the graduates to emulate their dedication to duty. The President further revealed elaborate plans which were being undertaken to upgrade the nursing profession in Liberia and informed the graduates of the recognition which their profession received the world over in an ever increasing manner. He therefore pledged the Government's support for the strengthening of its nursing programme, with the objective of increasing the enrolment of those who would choose it as a career.

Monrovia, 6 February 1964

EVERY GRADUATION exercise connotes the end of a prescribed theoretical course of study on the one hand, and the beginning of a period of practical application of the knowledge which is supposed to have been gained on the other. By the same token, this graduation ceremony of those who have completed the course of study of the Tubman National Institute of Medical Arts, School of Nursing, is a public declaration that these young people are now ready, because of their professional preparedness, to step out and take their places in the service of humanity. And now that the hour has struck I know the hearts of many of them are filled with mixed emotions, because they are about to leave the sheltered walls of this institution.

Nursing as a profession ranks very high among the social services. In fact, nursing, teaching and secretarial careers are not only fields where many women have found gainful employment, but also are professions which have brought emotional satisfaction and social prestige to many.

In a survey made some time ago by the American Institute of Public Opinion, professional nursing ranked first among the choices made. This is a clear indication of the importance which is attached to the profession and certainly opens up many possibilities for women who want careers in nursing. In our own nation the need is so great that all nurses are being absorbed as rapidly as they complete their training, but there is still need for a great many more to staff the new hospitals, the Medical Centre, the Medical School in connection with the University of Liberia, clinics and dispensaries. Because of the national need the objective of the Government is to encourage and train as many nurses as possible.

The nursing profession has come a long way and passed through many important phases in our nation. In the country's growth and development the members of this profession have contributed in assisting to keep people well, for physically fit people are more capable of ensuring and promoting a rapid pace of development than people who are ill or otherwise physically handicapped. The nursing profession must be given increased encourage-ment, and it is the obligation of the Government, and its policy, to endeavour to raise this profession to a higher level of recognition and consideration.

What the future holds for the profession can be foreseen from the direc-tion in which medical science is moving. I would therefore like to ask you one or two simple questions emanating from a layman's point of view:

Have you, who are graduating this evening as members of this class, decided to follow nursing as a career, to work through late nights and at any time that your services are required, to attend upon the sick and helpless with a desire to alleviate pain and suffering, and thus fulfil your obligations as a nurse?

Do you wish to help all sick persons, regardless of inconveniences to yourselves, the status of the sick or their station in life, their race, colour or creed, and possible unco-operative attitudes and dispositions often found in sick patients?

Have you chosen the nursing profession because you love and believe in it and all that it represents both in the textbooks and the traditions of the profession?

Are you willing, and have you decided, to risk your own health and life in the service of the sick where there may be the possibility of your health being affected from contagious diseases, even after taking due precautions?

These are some of the questions I am sure are in the minds of those who wish to become good and true nurses, and if you can honestly answer 'Yes' to them, after conscientious reflection, then there can be no doubt that you will become a good nurse, and have, by your training, earned the right to be one.

A few years ago the care of the sick in the hospitals of our country was in a lamentable condition. But happily, in recent years with more hospitals and clinics being built throughout the nation, on the littoral and in the hinter-land, as well as with increased opportunities for advanced training for doctors and nurses, some of the unfavourable conditions have disappeared. Someone has observed: 'while society has taken generations to develop a profession, the present generation has seen two new professions – nursing and social work – become fully established, and their influence has spread far and near'.

Each of you, of this class of 1964, should go out determined to emulate and become as famous and outstanding as the founder and symbol of your profession, Florence Nightingale. Each of you should be prepared to go out and follow the example of Magdalene Cooper who, I was happy to observe at the Midwives' Convention on Monday evening, was given loud and extended applause when her name was called, and as she came to the platform received applause and acclaim even greater than that given to the President. This is an indication of the high place of recognition for contribution and services rendered the nursing profession by this eminent female nurse. Some of you may become Public Health nurses or even Red Cross workers like Mrs. Jeanette King who has given most outstanding services to the profession and was loath to leave the active practice of nursing, but who after marrying her second husband was unable to persuade him to permit her to continue the regular routine practice of her profession. However, because of her impelling opportunities for the profession, she found a way to engage in this service by promoting the Red Cross Society and building it up until it has reached its present status as a growing institution.

To achieve your goals as professional nurses, and to be of real service to the sick and well, may I offer some non-professional but practical advice:

1. Be a human being filled with the milk of human kindness, compassion, sympathy and understanding.
2. Strive to be *the* nurse, not just another nurse.
3. Strive for excellence at all times.
4. Dedicate yourselves in word and deed to the work which you have to do, or in the words of Holy Writ: 'Whatever your hands find to do, do it with all your might.'

It is of particular interest to mention at this time the National Medical Centre programme, the objectives of which are:

1. To increase the number of well-trained para-medical personnel for the health facilities in Liberia and
2. To provide, through the facilities of a 300-bed general teaching hospital, the best in modern medical diagnosis and treatment. The target which has been set is to produce at least ninety graduates annually by 1969 in the fields of nursing, midwifery, medical technology, sanitation and health education. In addition to providing facilities for care and treatment of three hundred hospital in-patients, an expanded well equipped out-patient department can provide medical care for two hundred to three hundred patients daily. The two-storey dormitory for the nurses and other para-medical personnel will house at least two hundred and fifteen students.

Growth and development in the social and economic sectors of every country depend upon human beings, their attitudes, abilities and will to achieve. Their capacity to achieve is measured not only in terms of their skills but in their health, strength and vitality, as well. The high incidence rates for many chronic debilitating diseases and infections are directly responsible for much absenteeism and lack of stamina and vitality, as well as the inability of so many of our people to perform their daily tasks and responsibilities adequately and consistently.

The solution to these ills is to make available adequate preventive and curative health services for every county, district and village in Liberia. With a total of only 107 physicians in government concession, missions and private practice in Liberia, an immediate National Medical Centre programme for expansion of health services throughout the country can best be accomplished at this time by rapidly increasing the quantity and quality of sub-professional and para-medical personnel, who can serve effectively under the guidance and supervision of our doctors.

The National Medical Centre programme, with its training institution and large general teaching hospital, is the first step in the improvement of nation-wide health services. This co-operative programme between the Liberian and United States Governments also includes provision for technical assistance in (1) up-grading and expanding the teaching of the training institution (TNIMA) and (2) in the administration and operation of the hospital for a period of from six to ten years. More extensive programmes of affiliation and field training in other Liberian hospitals and health facilities will be developed, and impetus will be given to a more rapid implementation of the already adopted Regional Hospital Plan.

The National Medical Centre will provide new, modern facilities for the present Liberian Government Hospital in Monrovia and the National Institute of Medical Arts, and it will be a great step toward the implementation of some of the goals of national progress and development.

I congratulate you graduates, who are tonight stepping out into the field of human endeavour to do the work for which you have been prepared and trained. There remain many unexplored areas in medical science. There is no telling what new vistas the future will open up for medicine, even in our nation, in the eradication of malaria, leprosy, elephantiasis, trypanosomiasis, smallpox and chicken-pox, the diminishing of infant mortality and in the general all-round development of health and sanitation. In all these endeavours you will be expected to play an important part in helping humanity to survive and live longer, useful and happy lives. If you act your part well, generations to come will remember you and humanity will honour the profession as one which is indispensable to our survival and happiness.

It may be useful that I repeat this evening what I mentioned at the Midwives' Convention two months ago, concerning the visit of a team of British medical doctors to investigate the principal causes of mortality in both mothers and babies, and to make recommendations for the amelioration of the situation.

According to their qualifications a few of the matters to be enquired into by the members of the team are: (1) the organization of consultant obstetric and gynaecological services in hospitals and provision of facilities for pre-natal and post-natal care in the maternity hospital, (2) the teaching of midwifery, standards of entry for midwifery instruction, length and content of course, refresher courses; traditional methods of midwifery, domiciliary midwifery and (3) family customs relating to contraception and the feeding of infants.

All of these doctors are high calibre specialists in their respective fields, and it is expected that they will be given your full co-operation and that you will benefit from being associated with them.

In closing, I would like to leave the words of a poem written by an anonymous author when he was leaving the hospital after a long spell of sickness:

> 'We often hear of wonderful gifts
> bestowed by people with purses,
> and though I can't be a giver of gifts
> I can write a line for the nurses.

'For now that I am going to leave
and won't get to leave them a token,
I shall say a few words which I have up my sleeve,
of things I haven't yet spoken.

'When some friends of mine become ill
I shall tell them of a very grand place
where they lessen one's pain with a cheery goodwill
and with charm and with ease and with grace.

'When they enter the room with light, winsome smiles
and faces as bright as the sun,
and they say as they smile in a sweet kindly way,
"And now, do you wish something done"?

'In such an atmosphere as this,
one cannot help but feel fine,
and any mother of one of these girls
can proudly say, "She is mine".

'And when I leave here, I shall take away a thought
which will always remain a sweet vision;
and I'll never forget the glad, hospital days
When I worried about my incision.'

World Health Organization Day Message
Monrovia, 7 April 1964

Let us gird our loins for the unflinching effort required for the healthy preservation of ourselves and of our surroundings.

Introductory Note

Liberia supports actively all universal programmes of the United Nations – the World Health Organization being one of them. Its theme for 1964, 'Man and his cities', was an appropriate one which caused every member nation to look at its cities in a way in which it had probably never done before. President Tubman further emphasized this theme in this message, as an effective measure for the promotion of environmental health, and as a crusading adventure which required the active participation of all Liberians.

Monrovia, 7 April 1964

TWENTY-TWO YEARS ago the World Health Organization, commonly known as WIIO, made its advent into the arena of international affairs, with a constitution focusing attention on the vital problems of the health of the peoples of the world.

In its constitution, the collective conscience of mankind has found increasing expression of international concern for the alleviation of the unhealthy conditions of humanity through the co-operative efforts of member states of the United Nations. By virtue of Liberia's status as a signatory member of the United Nations Charter and a foundation member of the World Health Organization, all Liberian citizens inherit a moral obligation to work for the prevention and spread of disease in their various communities and cities.

Liberia joins the other nations of the world in recognizing the important rôle of the World Health Organization in attempting to make the world a healthier place in which to live. When we keep our homes, our surroundings and our communities constantly clean, we will have made the first essential step in this direction.

In the demonstration of the purposes and objectives of this specialized agency of the United Nations, enormous benefits have been derived by the people of every coast, clime and country throughout the world. Diseases, epidemics and pandemics have been attacked and in some instances eradicated. In other instances, their incidence has been greatly reduced, and people have generally enjoyed better health, happiness and prosperity.

The war of the World Health Organization against disease has been extended to mental illness, sanitation, ignorance, personal hygiene and malnutrition, which are only a few of the menaces to good health, as well as

437

dangerous threats to the advancement of a nation and the increase of the human species. The discomforts which these maladies impose upon mankind are just as hazardous as war, and therefore require the concerted effort of every citizen and resident throughout the country to eradicate them from our environment.

The explosive growth of cities from a rural to an enticing urbanized environment, the negative and positive, impact of cities on man with resultant industrial civilization and its social problems, create the dilemma in which we find ourselves today and make it most appropriate to designate as the theme for the year 1966, 'Man and his cities'.

It is often alleged that the rural villages and towns are usually kept cleaner and more orderly, but that the communities which we call 'cities' tend to be characterized by undesirable conditions which violate the mores, customs, traditions and moral ethics of the tribal habitat. This seems to be true, because people in the cities seem to be pre-occupied with the greater problems and issues of life in a metropolis, which excessively tax their minds and time. It is to be noted that several complex factors are involved in such a theory and only systematic research and analysis may give us a clearer understanding of the two extremes.

As further evidence of its timely reminder of our moral obligation in promoting the tenets and objectives of the World Health Organization and the undaunted support required of every city dweller for the implementation of the campaign that has been charted by the National Public Health Service and its related agencies, let us sound the clarion in unison for cleaner and more sanitary communities. Let us gird our loins for the unflinching effort required for the healthy preservation of ourselves and of our surroundings, and undertake the functional utilization of the rudiments and principles of hygiene and sanitation which we have practised in the past.

Speech delivered at the Dedication of Phoebe Hospital

Suacoco, Liberia, 16 May 1965

> *We have no doubt that this hospital will come to wield a great influence in this part of our nation, and that there will be concentrated here a corps of dedicated Liberians and foreign workers, imbued with the traditions of the medical profession — service to God and humanity.*

Introductory Note

The erection of Phoebe Hospital, situated in the heart of Liberia in Bong County, symbolized a shining example of the world movement toward a spirit of ecumenity in the Christian religion. Undertaken by the Lutheran Mission, the project received the co-operation of the Episcopal and Methodist denominations. President Tubman congratulated these three Christian bodies, especially the Lutherans, who originally conceived the idea, for this fine and joint co-operative effort which he further appreciated as another major step forward in our nation's development programme to provide better health facilities for the people of Liberia.

Suacoco, Liberia, 16 May 1965

WITH THE dedication of the Phoebe Hospital today, another important contribution has been made towards strengthening one phase of our development programme, that of providing increased and better health facilities and thereby raising the life expectancy of the people. Another significant goal in the trinity of ideals of the missionary endeavour has also been realized.

This hospital, with its modern architecture and equipment, containing a school of nursing, and situated in these beautiful surroundings, is the quintessence of faith, broad planning and splendid co-operation. We who have come here to participate in and witness these ceremonies, share the joy and pride of the Missionary Board of the Lutheran Church, the missionaries of the Liberian field, and the many churchmen and women of the Lutheran and other denominations who had the faith and courage to join in this creative and constructive Christian venture.

A hospital at its best represents the fulfilment of the tremendous responsibilities which are placed upon it for the lessening of human suffering and the preservation of human health and life. The old saying, 'A sound mind in a sound body', has never been truer than it is today. In its efforts to reach out and co-ordinate the activities of the several dispensaries which the Lutheran Mission now sponsors, the Phoebe Hospital, in the future, may well become a medical centre in this part of the nation. In addition to this, the hospital is expected to strengthen and reinforce the techniques and skills of the nursing profession and open a new chapter in partnership which may serve as a useful pattern for other types of productive co-operation.

We have no doubt that this hospital will come to wield a great influence in this part of the nation and that there will be concentrated here a corps of dedicated Liberian and foreign workers imbued with the tradition of the medical profession – service to God and humanity.

The missionary in Africa or in Liberia, so far as that goes, is no longer a legendary figure. It was he who braved the hostile climate, the dangers of the wilds and the strange customs he encountered; it was he who confronted unfriendly peoples and overcame inconceivable barriers; it was he who made costly sacrifices to bring the good news as a balm for the mind, body and soul. The trials and tribulations he endured, the persecutions he suffered, the patience he exercised, the love he manifested and the deaths he died, together with his other traits, all helped to enlarge the missionary task and gave him a secure place in the minds and hearts of those whom missionaries continue to serve in the schools, churches and hospitals of our country.

Today we pay homage to the Lutheran Church in a particular manner, for being among the first religious groups in Liberia to engage in the establishment of a hospital which has continued, over the years, to make medical care one of the primary aspects of its programme, and from which has emerged this beautiful compound as a monument to the work of administering to sick and suffering humanity. We hail this achievement as a great accomplishment and express the gratitude and appreciation of the Government and people of Liberia to all those who have been responsible for the planning and execution of this worthy project.

We commend very highly the co-operative partnership involved in this undertaking whereby Episcopalians and Methodists have agreed to work together with the Lutheran Church. It is a partnership which has great possibilities for the enhancement of Christian and world brotherhood, which much has been discussed in recent years. Certainly, it holds great promise for a more comprehensive realization of social, political and cultural unity. If unity is possible on the political front, why can it not also be advance on the religious level?

Of great importance to the Government's programme in providing medical services to the people of the nation, is the fact that plans have already been virtually concluded for the construction of a medical centre which will serve as a nucleus for the medical courses at the University of Liberia, and lay the basis for a regular supply of medical students. In addition to this it is gratifying that the Roman Catholic Church has launched out on a similar programme, which will increase very substantially the facilities in the medical profession, bring in more doctors, and reach out to a larger segment of our population. Thus we shall have moved another step forward.

And so on this occasion we again express the appreciation of the Government and people of Liberia for the culmination of this dream, for the hard work which it has entailed and for the bigger plans still in the offing.

But, with the construction and dedication of this building, our tasks have just begun. There is necessity for improved hospitals and clinics in other parts of the country such as Sinoe, Bassa, Cape Mount, Maryland, Nimba, Loffa and Gedeh. The Government has built hospitals in all of these places, but they are not sufficient to meet the requirements of the people. There is need for more and yet more facilities to preserve the health of the people; there is still much to be done and we assure you of the Government's co-operation and support in the great and rewarding programme of education and evangelism.

May God bless the labours of your hands and raise up many helpers in this noble enterprise.

At the Laying of the Cornerstone of the John F. Kennedy Memorial Hospital

Sinkor, Monrovia, 2 August 1966

This edifice is not intended to be only a hospital where the sick, the maimed and the lamed are cared for. It is to be more than that. It is to be a place where Liberian hands, minds and intellects will be trained to take care of the sick; to give succour and assistance to the suffering and dying.

Introductory Note

The construction of the John F. Kennedy Memorial Hospital represents the greatest major effort of the Government of Liberia to provide every facility for the health of its people. It was conceived as a joint project of the Liberian and United States Governments. President Tubman emphasized in this address a major purpose and function of the hospital, that of diagnostic treatment. It is a function which he considered essential and paramount for the prolongation of the lives of the citizens of Liberia. The hospital was named in honour of the late President of the United States, John F. Kennedy who had shown great sympathy and active interest in Liberia's industrial programme during his years as President of his country. This was the manner in which Liberians chose to show their gratitude to his memory.

Sinkor, Monrovia, 2 August 1966

WE HAVE gathered here today to place a mark of identification upon this structure that is about to rise as a future medical centre. This is the beginning.

The general appellation given to what has happened here today is called the laying of a cornerstone, sometimes known as a 'foundation stone'. But the purpose of this act, whether it be to lay a cornerstone or a foundation stone, is that the edifice may be identified in the present and in the future.

I listened to a portion of the prayer of the Grand Chaplain and of the address of the Grand Master. They both prayed that this edifice may stand against hurricane, invasion of the enemy, the sword, earthquakes and all of these things; and that centuries from now, its identity may still be known. How? In only one manner: by the cornerstone or foundation stone which I call the 'Identification Stone.'

Today, we have identified this building by placing there a symbol with the inscription *John F. Kennedy Memorial Medical Centre*. There is a lot to be said in an act symbolizing a name. Some people say that names do not matter; I say, names matter. God, speaking to Moses when He had a great and almost impossible task for him to perform, addressed him in this fashion: 'Moses, I know thy name'.

And so this centre has and bears a name that was given by the Legislature a few years ago. We have come here today as a people to fulfil the directives of the Legislature and give this building the name of John F. Kennedy, late President of the United States of America, a great man, a courageous and fearless man, a man who had the courage of his convictions, who dared in his public life to go forward against social and political evils in his country which had abounded for more than a century. He attacked them head on. The reforms, both political and social, were great. They cost him his life. But though dead, he speaketh. His name is still heard in all the councils of the world – even his own most inveterate enemies, even the enemies of his country, acclaim John F. Kennedy a great man. And so today, we have called this structure that is to rise after a great man.

Greatness carries with it corresponding responsibilities. This edifice is not intended to be only a hospital where the sick, the maimed and the lamed are cared for. It is to be more than that. It is to be a place where Liberian hands, minds, and intellect will be trained to take care of the sick; to give succour and assistance to the suffering and the dying. But it stands for more than that. It is to contribute to the well and healthy, to keep them well and healthy by means of preventive medicine. These are only a few of the things expected of this centre which has been named in honour of that great world statesman. Not only was he a statesman; he was a very religious man, a Christian. And I know that he basks today in heaven's auroral day, thinking of things on earth he can never forget.

The funds for the construction of this edifice have been made available by loans from the United States Government on low interest and long payment terms.

Some of us think that people have an obligation to help one another. I do not believe that any man is compelled to help me to get what I need and want, especially when nobody helped him to get what he has achieved. He got it by the sweat of his brow and his own initiative. At least if we receive gifts and benefits, we should say 'thank you'. To do otherwise would be the embodiment of ingratitude, and ingratitude never pays.

I wish to extend to Dr. Barclay, the Director-General of the National Public Health Service, the thanks and appreciation of Government and to tell him what the people of Liberia expect from this diagnostic clinic.

In this connection, I am reminded of an incident which occurred some years ago. I once had the pleasure of accompanying President Edwin Barclay to the United States. He had been suffering from a foot ailment which a local physician had diagnosed as gout. But while we were in the United States, examination by physicians there revealed that the President had a broken bone in his foot. When questioned about who had made the first diagnosis, President Barclay disclosed the name of his physician and said that he too was in the United States. The doctors then called the physician to look at the X-ray of the President's foot to see if he actually had gout. The doctor went, saw the X-ray and then said, 'I made a mistake.'

We do not want this kind of mistake here again. That is why we have insisted on building a diagnostic clinic. To locate or find out what is wrong is more difficult than to treat an ailment, because available medical books only describe certain symptoms. The physician ought to learn more, in order to know more than what is written in the books so as to be able to diagnose a case. For when the correct diagnosis is made, the right treatment is given and the patient no longer suffers untold pain.

Our hopes are, therefore, that very shortly this building shall be finished to contribute to the health and life of the people of our country.

Address delivered by President Tubman during the Dedication of the St. Joseph Hospital and Medical College

Monrovia, 19 March 1967

We have the privilege of participating in the dedication and formal opening of the first Catholic Hospital and pre-medical college to be built in Liberia.

Introductory Note

Catholicism in Liberia took on new meaning when a teaching hospital was dedicated, thereby opening a new chapter in Liberian-Italian relationships. Having already made substantial contribution in the area of education the Catholic Church embarked upon providing excellent medical facilities for training and for the care of the sick. President Tubman recounted in this address the events which led to the establishment of our new relationship with Italy (the Vatican), and made an appeal for financial assistance from the Liberian people for the erection of cathedrals by the Catholic Church and the Protestant Episcopal Church in Liberia.

Monrovia, 19 March 1967

ON THIS occasion, which is to us exceedingly exhilarating, we have the privilege and honour of participating in the dedication and formal opening of the first Catholic Hospital and Pre-medical College to be built in Liberia. This gives the medical services of our country a new perspective. I find myself, however, moved by a somewhat sombre feeling, which persuades me to quote at this point the statement: 'The workman dies but his work remains.'

In 1956 we had the distinguished honour and pleasure of making State Visits to six European Capitals upon the invitation of their respective Sovereigns. Among these was a visit to the Holy See upon an invitation of His Holiness Pope Pius XII, who received us in audience, with an array of Swiss Guards and the great pomp, fascinating pageantry and captivating and overawing dignity that is known only to the Holy See.

After friendly discussions, His Holiness bestowed upon us his blessing, and mentioned that he had heard of our development programme and of the assistance and consideration given the Catholic Church by the Liberian Government. He also stated that he would like to assist with the development programme in such a manner as I would suggest, within the limits of his ability. I replied that we were greatly in need of a modern hospital and medical school. He promised to give consideration to my proposal and assured me that I would be hearing from him on the subject.

445

The machinery for the fulfilment of his promise was set in motion, plans were laid and arrangements for financing begun, but the Decree of the Grim Reaper ushered him from the ranks of mortals into the eternal portals and this project, insofar as it relates to the life work of His Holiness, became a broken column. This however, did not cause the Catholic Church to abandon the scheme.

This endeavour experienced numerous set-backs and difficulties and hence dragged along for some time. Locating a suitable site for the hospital was one of the difficulties that arose, the raising of funds was another, and several other problems beset it. The Italian Government came in and gave assistance as did also the Liberian Government. Professor Mario Dogliotti of sainted memory, that great humanist and lover of men, came in with might and main and made invaluable contributions toward its effectuation. He too is absent at this new moon of the dedication and his seat is vacant because he is dead, but his labours live on and his memory remains evergreen in the hearts of the Government and people of Liberia.

The successors of Pope Pius XII, Their Holinesses Pope John and Pope Paul respectively, and the Catholic Hierarchy continued from where Pope Pius left off and pushed the project forward to completion, and as a result we are here at this time to dedicate these buildings and grounds, together with the equipment, machinery and all contained therein to the service of God and for the benefit of the sick and suffering; and where possible to save them from death.

In brief, this hospital and its adjuncts, like all other hospitals, should be citadels waging war against the enemy of our commonality – Death. Sometimes its Captains, Lieutenants and Non-coms, the doctors, nurses and attendants, succeed in compelling him to retreat but at last he wins the battle and takes men away as his prey: but the battle goes on and those engaged in the medical army continue their fight against death in what I consider the most glorious warfare on earth.

The Medical College connected with St. Joseph Hospital is to me an exciting and eventful achievement. For the past fifteen years I have been exploring the possibility, and negotiating for the institution of a Medical College or Pre-medical School in Liberia. This was one of the requests made of the late Pope Pius XII which today has seen fruition; its doors will be open not only to Liberians but also to students from other African countries and elsewhere.

This important Medical College, which will give Liberians and people of other nationalities the opportunity of beginning their medical training here, cannot be over-estimated. It is a presentation from the University of Torino, Italy, with the assistance of the Italian Government, and forges another significant link in the chain of friendship that binds our two nations and people.

Unlike the mighty armies of great military powers, which are armed with weapons of destruction, and which induce fighting and battling on the side of death, engaging in mass destruction and the carrying away of human beings like a flood, the hospital and clinic stand as a formidable fortification in the fight between life and death. Therefore, the rôle of doctors in all fields of the profession, graduate, student and practical nurses, midwives, medical aides and hospital attendants is beyond compare, for they are rendering a service to humanity that is more noble and more grandiose than all the formidable military armies of the world. They fall within the category of those to whom Christ referred when He said:

'For I was an hungred, and ye gave me meat: I was thirsty, and ye gave me drink: I was a stranger, and ye took me in:

'Naked, and ye clothed me: I was sick, and ye visited me: I was in prison, and ye came unto me.

'Then shall the righteous answer him, saying, Lord, when saw we thee an hungred, and fed thee? or thirsty, and gave thee drink?

'When saw we thee a stranger, and took thee in? or naked, and clothed thee?

'Or when saw we thee sick, or in prison, and came unto thee?

'And the King shall answer and say unto them, Verily I say unto you, Inasmuch as ye have done it unto one of the least of these my brethren, ye have done it unto me.'

Thus, I appeal to the doctors, nurses and all who shall minister at the medical altars of this hospital, rendering service to the sick and helpless, to do so with all diligence, realizing that such a service involves humanity and that your sure reward is not necessarily dollars and cents, nor the hallelujahs of the crowd, but in the satisfaction that you have relieved pain, suffering and distress and oft-times prevented death.

We must not and cannot overlook the great contributions made by the late Bishop Collins and Archbishop Carroll, Ambassador Lawrence, our Diplomatic Representative to the Holy See, Mr. Motta, and numerous others who gave of their energy, time and talent toward the success of this project, and we appreciate their interest.

We recall the valuable contribution of Mrs. M. Eva McGill Hilton, the only individual Liberian to make a donation to this institution, giving the land upon which these buildings have been constructed, and we thank and congratulate her for this generous act. We are happy, we are proud, we are illumined by this addition to the medical facilities of our nation, through the benevolence and philanthropy of the Catholic Church, and are deeply grateful to the Brothers of St. John of God, a five hundred year old order, usually referred to in Europe as 'The Do Good Order', who completely financed the construction of the hospital. To all of them, from the smallest to the greatest, we extend our gratitude and feel certain that their reward is assured.

I will now digress a little from the dedication of the hospital and medical college to a subject not completely unrelated, irrelevant or inappropriate to mention on this occasion. The Divine Injunction clearly states: 'Freely ye have received, freely give.' We have hospitals, we have colleges, schools, a university, hotels, attractive homes, churches, chapels and a hydro-electric dam, but we do not have a single cathedral in the country.

The Protestant Episcopal Church, during its work in Liberia, erected and has maintained Cuttington College, as well as a number of high schools and elementary schools. Similarly, the Catholic Church has given us the College of Our Lady of Fatima, high schools, convents and elementary schools and now this unique gift of a hospital and Medical College.

The Protestant Episcopal Church has commenced construction of a cathedral to which most of us have liberally contributed, but there is need for further financial assistance by the entire Liberian public.

The Catholic Church is contemplating the erection of a cathedral and we should be delighted at the prospect of having two cathedrals with spires towering heavenward into the skies, overlooking the city in solemn silence and adoration to God.

I reiterate the keynote of this portion of my remarks, 'Freely ye have received, freely give.' Let us organize all churches, institutions, commercial, industrial, political and social organizations and raise at least two hundred thousand dollars to assist in the completion of the Protestant and the commencement of the Catholic cathedrals, remembering that all things come of the Lord and that whatever we give unto Him is His own. Freely have we received this hospital and Medical College, freely let us give toward the construction of a Catholic Cathedral and the completion of the Protestant Episcopal cathedral in Monrovia, our capital city. Thus, we will not only be on the receiving end of the line but will also place ourselves on the giving end. We shall organize this endeavour, and feel assured of your full co-operation.

Finally, we are happy to see and welcome our many foreign friends, particularly from Italy, representing groups and institutions that have been involved in financing this venture or connected with it in one way or another. We extend to them the thanks and appreciation of the Government and people of Liberia and pray God's blessings upon them, upon this hospital and Medical College, all who serve here and upon our respective nations and peoples.

RELIGIOUS AFFAIRS

On the Thirty-fifth Anniversary of the Establishment of the Liberian Mission of the Seventh Day Adventists

Monrovia, 27 January 1963

I suggest that in the days ahead Christians in Liberia move under the influence and guidance of the cross of Christ so that Christianity may become a winning religion in this land.

Introductory Note

William V. S. Tubman as President of Liberia became famous not only because of his buoyant spirit of ecumenity. Every religious denomination had a claim on his generosity and was accorded by him the attention it deserved in its spiritual and self-sustaining efforts. One might call him a democratic Christian, because the Constitution of Liberia provides for equal rights and protection to all religious bodies, but also because he himself, in his formative years, had known and had received no other training than that provided by missionaries, in his own case, Methodist missionaries. Missionary activities are inseparable from the historical, political, social, cultural and every other aspect of the life of the Liberian nation.

In this address President Tubman made mention of the success of the work of Christian missions undertaken by the Seventh Day Adventists in Liberia in evangelizing, teaching and preaching, and their exemplary life of Christian living.

Monrovia, 27 January 1963

TODAY MARKS the 35th anniversary of the establishment of the Liberian Mission of Seventh Day Adventists in Liberia. From a modest beginning and a small staff in 1927, this work has grown until its membership today numbers over 1,800. It may well be said that Paul has planted, Apollo has watered and the increase has come from the Lord.

In the years which have gone by, God's Messengers of goodwill have, under the guiding influence of The Holy Spirit, toiled to make known His will on earth and among the people of this country, and the ministries of evangelism, healing and teaching have been instrumental in adding followers to His Kingdom.

How proud the pastors, workers, laymen, schoolboys and girls must be of today's mark of achievement, because the missionary enterprise in Liberia is one of sacrificial and daring exploits of love and has been a great blessing to the people of the nation. In fact, the love of the Liberian people for religion, and their zeal and devotion, are reflected in their political and

451

social institutions. Thus it is, that trusting in the God of their Fathers, acknowledging His Omniscience, His Omnipotence and Omnipresence, we have continued to steer safely our ship of state, often through uncharted seas amidst rocks and shoals, always conscious of and dependent on His guiding Providence. If the work of missions has done any one thing for Liberia, it has brought the people of this nation to a constant awareness of the transforming power of the Grace of God. For, is it not true in Holy Writ that those who identify themselves with Jesus always bear a characteristic mark, as did the disciples who were constantly with their Master?

In the work of Evangelism, teaching and healing, the Seventh Day Adventists' Mission has made significant gains for the Kingdom of God, and although the observance of their Sabbath is on Saturday, which is indeed the seventh day of the week, other Christian denominations, I am sure, have no quarrel with them nor they with us. For while Saturday is the seventh day of the week which you observe as the Sabbath, the early Christians came to recognize the first day of the week as the day on which Christ, the Redeemer of the world, arose triumphant from the grave and over sin, hell and death, and thereby proved His divine Messiahship. What is important is the observance of one day in the week for the cessation of all regular activities for a period of rest and worship.

Over and over in the annals of our political history, the nation has paid glowing tribute to the work of missions in Liberia and in the world. Men and women in all walks of life owe a debt of gratitude to the zeal of missionaries, their evangelism and their art of healing. The Government's recognition of their invaluable contribution and assistance has taken the form of subsidies to encourage awareness of the critical period through which the world is passing and the glorification of materialism against the things of the spirit.

Liberia, as a nation which has always acknowledged Him, needs the work of missions, missionaries and workers. The dearth of workers in our missionary institutions, and the unwillingness of the young to join the ministry, are issues which face the churches in Liberia. The time has come when Christians must rise up with a singleness of purpose and a clearer vision of Christ crucified to the obligation of their calling.

On this 35th anniversary, I congratulate and salute the sixteen Evangelists, the twenty-one school teachers, the 650 students in the schools and the 1,800 members of the Seventh Day Adventists for the rôle they have played and are playing to add greater reality and lustre to the spiritual foundations of our people. May the years ahead give you increased wisdom, a firmer determination and courage to win more souls to the Master's vineyard, and may all Christendom continue to march manfully forward under His banner against sin, the world and the devil.

Liberia is now a changing nation. The changed and changing face of the country should remind all Christians of the greater job of nation building which remains to be done – the remaking of man, in Liberia, in Africa, and in the world. To achieve this to some degree, I suggest that there be a greater articulation between the home and the church, the parents, the teachers, the priests and people. I suggest that practical religion find a permanent place in the everyday life of everyone: I suggest that the family altar be re-established in the home, Bible reading encouraged among the young and church-going become part of the moral and religious obligation of Sundays;

I suggest that the family life be more intimate and the joy of living extolled! I suggest that we forge ahead in one great phalanx so that the over-reaching power of the Gospel may become a true force in Liberia and Africa! I suggest that in the days ahead Christians in Liberia move under the influence and guidance of the cross of Christ so that Christianity may become a winning religion in this land.

I trust that the events of today will sink very deeply into your hearts, so that you may have the satisfaction and pride of saying that you have served your country and God with fervour and zeal.

I cannot close this brief address without paying special tribute to those who have laboured in this missionary field and set the stage for the accomplishments of the present and future, I pay high compliments to the past and present corps of workers who have dedicated and are dedicating themselves to the service of humanity. Be assured that a crown of life and glory awaits you as you administer to the sick and suffering, as you clothe the naked and feed the hungry and as you lead others to the saving grace of our Lord and Saviour Jesus Christ.

I note with special interest and pleasure the presence here at the celebrations of Dr. and Mrs. Henri, they who were the first to put me in touch with the Seventh Day Adventists' Mission in Liberia. May God continue to give them and all of you the fuller outpouring of His Holy Spirit and richly bless you in your expanding work, and may He bring helpers to your call and open the hearts and pockets of your members and well-wishers, so that the programme of the Seventh Day Adventists may go forward more vigorously in the future.

Announcing the Retirement of the Rt. Reverend Bravid W. Harris of the Protestant Episcopal Missionary District of Liberia

Monrovia, 12 January 1964

His has been a life of dedication and true service for the spiritual enrichment and material advancement of the people of this nation, from the littoral to the remotest part of the interior.

Introductory Note

The Rt. Reverend Bravid Washington Harris was one of those immortals who walked the earth and who in life or death shall never cease to walk upon it. In 1964, in obedience to the rules of the Protestant Episcopal Church, Bishop Harris retired from active service in the Episcopal Missionary District of Liberia. President Tubman decided that such a transition in the life of a devoutly religious leader should not go unnoticed. He informed the people of Liberia of this transition, which was of significance not only in the life of Bishop Harris, but in the life of our nation.

Monrovia, 12 January 1964

IN THE retirement of Bishop Bravid W. Harris from the Missionary work of the Protestant Episcopal Church in Liberia I feel a deep sense of national and personal loss, for his activities touched not only the lives of the adherents and communicants of the Episcopal Church in Liberia, but of many other religious denominations and of every phase of worthwhile endeavour. His has been a life of dedication and true service for the spiritual enrichment and material advancement of the people of this nation, from the littoral to the remotest part of the interior.

I have always experienced great spiritual inspiration from his conduct of divine service, particularly his celebration and administration of the Holy Eucharist, and have been uplifted by the deep, stirring, rich and profound quality of his sermons.

Under the dynamic spiritual leadership of this great man of God, the work of the Missionary District of the Episcopal Church in Liberia has expanded and improved, and his emphasis on Christian education, evangelism, science and agriculture has played an important rôle in setting the pace for advancement in these fields of study.

Bishop Harris's counsel and advice during the early period of the present administration on education and planning for the nation was invaluable, and has been of great assistance to me.

454

As he retires from active service, he leaves in the hearts of the people of this country a void and a feeling of deep regrets; regrets springing from love and affection generated by approximately twenty years of selfless and fruit-ful service in the Episcopacy of the Episcopal Church in Liberia.

I am confident that the fruits of Bishop Harris's tenure of service in Liberia will ever remain a fitting memorial to him and that the programme of Christian education initiated by him will go on vigorously from genera-tion to generation.

Finally, although perhaps a little out of tune with the subject of this state-ment, I think of his successor and pray in the words of one of the verses of a hymn in the hymnology of the Episcopal Church:

> God of the prophets, bless the prophets' sons;
> Elijah's mantle o'er Elisha cast.

On the Retirement of Bishop Bravid W. Harris

Monrovia, 18 January 1964

Episcopalians in particular, and Liberians in general, regard the years which Bishop Harris spent here as the acme of his life's work.

Introductory Note

Having officially announced to the people of Liberia that Bishop Harris was soon to retire from active service in the Lord's vineyard, President Tubman further participated in a religious ceremony which marked the observance of the occasion. As a testimony to the breadth of the Christian faith and belief of Bishop Harris, this ceremony was an interdenominational event. The President once again paid tribute to the Bishop in these befitting words.

Monrovia, 18 January 1964

THE RIGHT REVEREND Bravid W. Harris retires today as Bishop of the Protestant Episcopal Missionary District of Liberia. This retirement will cast a long shadow over the Diocese that he leaves, as well as over missionary work in Liberia generally, for the spiritual leadership which he exerted has brought manifold blessings and great spiritual and temporal upliftment and expansion to the nation and its people. Episcopalians in particular, and Liberians in general, regard the years which Bishop Harris spent here as the acme of his life's work; they have been so rich, so full, so rewarding; they have been years of great activities, of growth and development, and of beneficial results derived from the faith and hard work of this servant of God in the interest of humanity, education and religion.

The Protestant Episcopal Church in Liberia has been fortunate to have had the benefit of Bishop Harris's vision, depth and breadth of understanding, humility of spirit, human compassion, deep interest in evangelism and yen for hard work, which have all combined to bring to reality the re-opening of numerous mission stations, collegiate, elementary and primary schools that had been closed, the opening of new ones and the erection of numerous church edifices, office and other permanent buildings, as well as plans for the erection of a cathedral. In addition to his building programme, the Bishop has promoted the idea of a self-supporting church as the sacred obligation of a free people in a land where religion and the founding of the nation were coeval. I feel confident that our country has been made richer because of the unselfish and sacrificial services this devout servant has so faithfully and fruitfully rendered in the Master's vineyard over the years, and his association with the people has had a tremendous impact on their thinking and attitude toward religion, education and evangelism.

The many accomplishments of Bishop Harris during his tenure of service here have not been brought about without difficulties, set-backs and disappointments which might have caused the faint-hearted to despair; but he was made of sterner stuff and remembered perhaps the Proverb which says: 'If thou faint in the day of adversity, thy strength is small.'

The persuasive charm of Bishop Harris and his ability to get things done have won for him the admiration and affection of those with whom he came in contact. It is therefore only natural that we have mixed feelings at this time, since so many have benefited from the inspiration, assistance and spiritual guidance which he has so fully and freely given.

This is for me a sad event also; the personal relationship that has existed between Bishop Harris and myself has been intimate and mutually beneficial, and our association has been meaningful and understandable. During the nineteen years of our association I have had every occasion for increased confidence, respect and affection for the Bishop, as our association and intimacy developed through the years. Another reason for my tender feelings that must be brought to mind at this time of Bishop Harris's retirement from active work in Liberia, is the fact that we are of the same age, or what we would call in our Liberian colloquialism, 'crowd of boys'.

The Divine decree handed down shortly after the Biblical account of the creation of man, 'it is not good for man to be alone, let us make a helpmate for him', was aptly applied and essentially true in the case of Mrs. Harris and her relationship to her husband, not only as a wife but as a helpmate and partner.

Mrs. Harris has stood shoulder to shoulder with her husband in the difficult tasks which followed as a natural sequence to the position he held in the Episcopacy of the Protestant Episcopal Church. She has been liberal in her assistance to the poor and needy, valiant in her stand in support of the progress of the work in which her husband was engaged and very often, like gravitation, which is unseen and unheard but is the most powerful force in nature, she served greatly in attracting him and keeping him fast-bound to the high calling to which he had given his life.

Our highest compliments go to her for the contributions which she has made during their stay in Liberia, and our sincere regrets that she also must leave the friends that have come to know and love her.

It is my privilege and honour, on behalf of the Government, people of Liberia and myself, to express our profound gratitude and grateful appreciation for the part which this great outstanding religious leader and Presbyter has played in hastening the coming of the Kingdom of God and His Christ in this part of His vineyard, providing so many opportunities for increased and better Christian education and training and in general, contributing to the enrichment of the family and public life of the people of the nation. These are things which we cannot forget; these are memorials which we shall always cherish.

The historic rôle which the Protestant Episcopal Mission of America has played in the religious, educational and social affairs of the country from the days of its incipiency, has been marked by contributions that enter into the very life of the nation in every aspect, not excluding the political, for a great number of the leading statesmen, educators, clerics, businessmen and lawyers received their training and preparation from the benevolence and philanthropy of the Board of Foreign Missions of the Protestant

Episcopal Church. The continuing contributions to the Missionary District of Liberia which have been made by the Board in the past and up to the present, deserve and demand our gratitude and support which we most freely give.

You may be assured, Bishop Harris, that the hearts of the people of Christian churches in Liberia will go with you and that our prayers will ascend to the throne of the Triune God, praying always that He will continue His guiding care and grant unto you peace, prosperity and contentment in your years of retirement from active service; that although retired, you will continue to give mankind the benefit of your forceful and dynamic spiritual influence and experience to guide them to fuller lives of rectitude and holiness in a world where East and West must meet, and where the Fatherhood of God and the Brotherhood of Man shall become a living reality.

On the Tenth Anniversary of the Establishment of Radio Station ELWA

Monrovia, 18 January 1964

Radio Village has now become a vital part of the nation's religious, educational, social and cultural programmes.

Introductory Note

In 1954 an American Christian and evangelical broadcasting network was established in Paynesville, Liberia with the evangelizing title of Eternal Love Winning Africa, ELWA. Many church-going Liberians looked upon this new approach to missionary activities and evangelism with alarm, and as no substitute for meeting people face to face and converting them to the Christian faith. The new radio network, after having its plans meticulously scrutinized by no less important a committee than one appointed by the National Legislature, overcame the initial difficulties. ELWA has become a vital and inspirational force in the daily lives of many Christians all over Africa. The President acknowledged with this tribute the success of Radio ELWA and its allied activities in preaching, healing and teaching, following the footsteps of the Lord Jesus Christ.

Monrovia, 18 January 1964

WE ASSOCIATE ourselves with the managers and staff of ELWA in Radio Village which represents the first religious broadcasting and teaching service in the nation, as they observe the tenth anniversary of their establishment. It has been a decade during which faith and hard work have overcome discouragements, trials, disappointments and handicaps and led to such rich and rewarding experiences, with visible results for this work of dedication and service. It has been a period in which the service has grown, expanded and improved to such an extent that Radio Village has now become a vital part of the nation's religious, educational, social and cultural programmes. To visit the area, hear about and see the developments taking place is to be wonderfully inspired by the realization of a vision.

How interesting it is that over and over in the history of mankind, the bitterly opposed ideas and projects of yesterday become, in the long run, great blessings to the cause of human advancement! Such was the beginning of this broadcasting station, for when the request was made ten years ago, the section which has now developed into Radio Village, was so completely isolated that very few persons could conceive of such a project succeeding. Besides being an isolated area, many of the surrounding inhabitants believed that the installation of modern instruments would bring ill fortune, disease and death. Arguments ensued among the pioneering staff, some of whom felt the project should be abandoned since the place was unsafe, and opposition to the idea grew from without and within.

The matter was further complicated when a formal application made for a grant of land in the area was opposed in the National Legislature on the basis that it involved too large an acreage of land for such a project. However, we suggested that a committee from the Legislature visit the area and determine the rationality and feasibility of the request. The Legislature sent a committee to the spot and after seeing the work that was begun, the committee was satisfied and recommended that the authorities of the new Radio Station should have the area of land asked for, and more if they desired it. And so from this controversial beginning the nucleus of Radio Village, of which we are all proud, was established in Congotown. Over the years, the religious, educational, social and cultural programmes have become popular, and they now touch every aspect of our national life.

Other difficulties arose and had to be overcome in those days: physical and psychological barriers had to be removed through religious education and training, doubts, suspicions and fears were replaced by faith, practical results, and a willingness to face the facts, test them, and utilize them for what they were worth. As some had pointed to the futility of such a scheme ten years ago, so did those who had conceived it and were convinced of its great value argue for its establishment, and today we can boast of the blessings and joys derived from a service known and styled as – Eternal Love Winning Africa! It is a recognized fact that religious and educational programmes, new broadcasts and a rich variety of public services have made ELWA's contributions to Liberia invaluable through the medium of radio.

On behalf of the Government, the people of Liberia and myself, we extend congratulations to ELWA for a decade of work and dedication in fostering this outstanding project. The managers of Radio Village may be assured of our continued co-operation and encouragement for the enhancement of the rich and permanent contributions which they are making to the nation's progress and development.

As you face the future, we wish for ELWA and all its members at Radio Village continued success, good health and happiness, and the expansion of its vitalizing rôle in our Republic throughout the years.

May God continue to multiply a thousandfold the offerings of your hearts and hands to His greater glory.

To the Methodist Annual Conference
Monrovia, 23 January 1964

Some forty-odd years ago, we were told to begin to think in terms of standing on our feet and assuming our own responsibilities for the support and administration of the work here in Liberia. While this has not been an easy decision to make, being a bold and daring forward movement, the changing condition of the times point to the fact that the situation will have to be faced at any cost.

Introductory Note

William V. S. Tubman will be remembered as one who was born to inherit great causes and whose life was dedicated to their advancement and fulfilment. What he accomplished in the field of emancipation and political equality, not to mention the industrial revolution he brought to his nation, he sought equally to effect in the area of religion. The work of the Methodist denomination in Liberia, which he generously supported, following the footsteps of our first President, Joseph Jenkins Roberts, who was also a member of that denomination, was given encouragement by him through his emphasis on self-reliance. With the nation making great strides in its development under his leadership, he thought it was also time to take advantage of a challenge which had been given to Liberian Methodists by their Parent Church in the United States, to assume the leadership and responsibility of a national Church.

Monrovia, 23 January 1964

THE CHURCHES in Liberia today face a new challenge; it is a challenge in which both the awareness and acceptance of the changed and changing concept of their rôle are of prime consideration and importance. To an increasing extent, the suggestion that responsibility should eventually be assumed by those who have for so many years been the spiritual and educational recipients of a Mother Organization, has been gaining acceptance. This view has in turn sparked off the generous giving that has recently characterized so many of the churches in the nation. For, if the vital message of Christianity and the coming of the Kingdom of God is to have any pertinence and thus become a living reality, the stage should be reached where, having benefited from the philanthropy and guidance of a Mother Church, autonomy would be the next step in any forward-looking programme. We of the Methodist connection in Liberia have therefore accepted the challenge of an autonomous Church with all its implications, and taking advantage of the present opportunities, utilizing the resources at our disposal and creating new ones, we shall face the future with faith, determination and fresh impetus to shoulder our Christian responsibilities in the light of the changed conditions and times in which we live.

In this connection I want, first of all, to compliment not only the members of the Methodist Church, but also those of other denominations, our foreign friends and all well-wishers who have substantially assisted the Methodist Church in drives aimed at raising funds for the expansion of education and evangelism. It is a source of encouragement that nearly all denominations have supported each other's efforts in these financial drives, with the result that everyone has benefited immensely.

Because of the many engagements and exacting obligations of individual churches which were also pre-occupied with building and other projects, the Advance Committee was not able during the past two years to accomplish as much as it did in previous years. Nevertheless, through personal donations, gifts and special arrangements, at least fifty thousand ($50,000.00) dollars have been realized and presented by the Advance Committee each year during this period, and I can assure you that with our expanding programme these efforts will be intensified in the years ahead.

Without a desire to appear selfish or sectarian, I consider it not inappropriate to mention what most people in Liberia may not know when they speak comparatively of the financial contributions of other denominations to education, evangelism and missionary work in Liberia. Some of these denominations are engaged in missionary operations principally in Liberia and a few other places outside of the United States, while the Methodist Board of Foreign Missions reaches out its tentacles of love, Christian benevolence and philanthropy to the four corners of the earth, on every continent and some of the isles of the sea. Hence the share that comes to us at the present time is what it is.

However, since Liberia was the first foreign field to which the Methodist Church of America sent a Missionary, Melville B. Cox of blessed and sacred memory. Frail and feeble in body but strong in spirit, he declared: 'though a thousand fall, let not Africa be given up!', and it is natural for the Liberian Church to feel that they should have better consideration. Nevertheless, after taking everything into account, I truthfully declare that we in Liberia have to be grateful for the establishment of churches, schools, hospitals and clinics, and for the guidance, support and direction which the Church in Liberia has received from the Mother Church in the United States for a century. The influence of Methodism in Liberia has been as pervasive and persuasive as it has been deep.

Some forty-odd years ago we were told to begin to think in terms of standing on our own feet and assuming our own responsibility for the support and administration of the work here in Liberia. While this has not been an easy decision to make, being a bold and daring forward movement, the changing conditions of the times point to the fact that the situation will have to be faced at any cost. We therefore must think in terms of an autonomous Church to be affiliated with the Mother Church in the United States.

We are petitioning the General Conference for a three year transition period for the effectuation of the autonomy of the Liberian Church, and requesting that a small Committee be set up, on which the Church in the United States and the Church in Liberia will be represented, to have general supervision of the work, and that Bishop Taylor, with Episcopal residence in the United States, should have Episcopal supervision of the Church in Liberia during this transition period. After two years, we will elect a Bishop who will be associated with Bishop Taylor for one year should the General Conference grant our request, and thereafter assume the responsibility of the Episcopacy of the Liberian Church.

The point I desire to impress upon you and drive home, is that this has not been the result or outcome of any inordinate ambition, nor is it an act of secession. Rather, our self-respect and denominational honour impel us to this decision, not ingratitude for the work which the Mother Church has done for the nation during these many years. But if Christianity is to spread, have a captivating appeal and bear abundant fruit, we, the people, must assume the major responsibility and thus extend the dimensions of the missionary purpose by assisting ourselves and the world in the great tasks of evangelism and education. If we succeed in these endeavours, and succeed we must, it will be a creditable and everlasting reflection on the foundation laid by the American Church in Liberia upon which we will build still further.

For the past eight years the spiritual leadership of the Methodist Church has been exercised by one whom we respect, revere and love. Bishop Prince Taylor combines the rare gift of humility with intellectual brilliance and practical wisdom. His leadership during these years has had a profound effect on Methodism in Liberia. His rôle has been that of revitalizing the Church's programme by giving it new impetus. Under his dynamic guidance the work has improved both in quality and quantity, and thus taken on a newer significance in the history of the Church. The deep interest he has manifested in the many facets of the programme, his concern that a high degree of excellence be attained and his personal and public appeals and encouragement to his membership to give voluntarily, have all resulted in many practical achievements – modern school edifices, churches and hospitals. School enrolments have increased, Church membership has increased, and a spiritual growth has been experienced. In general, a great revival has taken place in the varied activities of the Church.

Whether in administering the affairs of the Church or in dealing with the manifold tasks which were his, Bishop Taylor has exhibited at all times a nobility of soul and greatness of mind. All in all, his concern to inform and encourage membership to support the cause of education and evangelism, to be 'doers of the word and not hearers only' has been noteworthy. I feel sure that the image which Bishop Taylor has created of the Methodist Church in Liberia will never be forgotten. We pray for him God's continued blessings in the enrichment of his understanding, the renewing of his zeal and the dedication of his will to the great cause to which he has already devoted a considerable portion of his life.

As we prepare to enter a new era in the history of our Church, launching out into the deep, let us ask the blessings of the Almighty in this new venture so that we may realize fully the obligations involved, face the responsibilities, and having done so accept the challenge with faith and determination, moving forward not in our own strength, knowledge or ability but in the power, might and strength of God, through the propitiating atonement of His Son, Jesus Christ; for it is apparent that the next one hundred years will see many significant gains in Methodism in Liberia and the world, and whatever we do now will add to the sum total of the programmes of expansion and strength, so that coming generations may rise up and call us Blessed.

The new status of autonomy for the Methodist Church in Liberia that we have resolved to take, and have appealed to the General Conference to grant, as an affiliate of the American Church, imposes upon us tremendous responsibilities. It means that we must give sacrificially; it means that we must assume attitudes of regularity, punctuality and devotion to our religious and temporal duties and obligations in their every respect and aspect; that our giving must not be periodic or spasmodic because the Church must be maintained; there must be growth, materially and spiritually; there must be expansion; there must be the raising of the Christian lives of the people to higher standards. Ministers must be educated and given a sound theological background; they must be better supported; provisions for retirement benefits must be provided, and more schools must be built and adequately staffed.

This is no easy task, it is not a situation that can be lightly regarded, and, as evidence of our deep and abiding interest in this great cause, we suggest the creation of a foundation for education and evangelism in the new status the Church has taken on. I will personally donate fifteen thousand ($15,000.00) dollars annually for three years and ten thousand ($10,000.00) dollars annually for another seven years toward this foundation. We hope that other members of the Church, according to their abilities, will make similar contributions to this foundation as an indication of their support of the Independent Church, and their desire to forge ahead in the direction we have already taken, thus assuring the progress and success of the work we have set ourselves to do.

As mentioned before, the Advance Committee has been successful in raising fifty thousand ($50,000.00) dollars this year for the Conference and a detailed report of this amount and payment will be made by the Chairman of the Committee.

I pray that, inspired by the results of this Conference, we will go forward with greater determination and Christian zeal to work unitedly for the success, advancement and continuity of the Liberian Annual Conference of the Methodist Church in its new rôle as an independent and autonomous Church.

To the Annual Methodist Conference
Monrovia, 26 January 1964

Methodists throughout Liberia will always remember him with pride and gratitude, for it was he who first assisted us in our efforts to strive for an autonomous church.

Introductory Note

When Bishop Prince A. Taylor, Jun., was assigned to Liberia by the parent Methodist Church in the United States, he brought with him dynamism and vigour which the Methodist Church in Liberia needed most at that time. A new drive was launched for greater expansion of the Church's work and for a programme of a trained clergy. Under his leadership the Methodist Church began to prepare itself to become an autonomous body, and Bishop Taylor not only gave the idea guidance and encouragement, but supervised the transition of the Methodist Church in Liberia during this period of achieving autonomy. The President was grateful for the Bishop's contribution to this task which he also cherished.

Monrovia, 26 January 1964

EIGHT YEARS ago all Liberian Methodism was moved, and the hearts of Methodists thrilled beyond compare, at the announcement of the assignment to Liberia of a Bishop with Episcopal residence in Monrovia. This assignment had come in response to a Memorial and Petition sent to the Council of Bishops and General Conference by the Liberian Annual Conference and the Laity of the Methodist Church in Liberia after it had become known that Bishop Willis J. King, who had served faithfully as spiritual Head of the Methodist Episcopal Church in Liberia for several quadrenniums, was to retire.

In the Memorial and Petition that were sent from Liberia it was stated that the time was opportune for a revitalization and expansion of the Church's work here, because the nation was entering a new era of progress and development in which travel and communication media were being improved and the remotest parts of the country were being opened up and made available for increased evangelical and educational operations, while other aspects of the nation's development programme were receiving encouraging emphasis.

A century of missionary endeavours had brought great success through the earnest sacrifices and service of foreign missionaries, local ministers and teachers preaching the power and saving grace of the Lord Jesus Christ: but because we felt it necessary for the continued success and expansion of the work, we also requested that, if our Memorial and Petition were favourably considered, we would like some of the qualifications of the assignees to this field to be virility, physical energy and general experience in the Church's

465

polity, which would afford the ability to inaugurate and demonstrate the
new programme of development and expansion both spiritually and
materially. When we were informed that our petition had been favourably
considered, we were fortunate to have assigned to us a man who fitted
ideally into these categories, a man who was abundantly endowed, not only
with admirable physical qualities, but with qualities of spiritual leadership
and intellectual acumen which were to be greatly instrumental in revitalizing and expanding Christianity through Methodism in this country. This
man was Bishop Prince A. Taylor, Jun.

From the time of his arrival on this field to the present, he has succeeded
in making himself accepted, admired and loved, not only by the members of
his own communion, but by people of other religious connections throughout the nation. His rectitude of life, his high moral principles, his deep
Christian devotion and above all, his concern for the improvement and
expansion of Christianity and Methodism in Liberia are a great tribute to
the wonderful results which have accrued from his eight years of service and
dedicated leadership.

To gain first hand information, to know intimately what the problems
and needs of the Church were, and to acquire necessary background
material, the Bishop travelled through the country in order to formulate a
new and ambitious programme for the advancement and uplift of the cause
of Methodism and Christianity, to resolve some of the difficult issues and
problems, and to bring more depth, greater breadth and Christian reality to
his flock.

The appealing quality of his sermons, rich and profound in doctrine, were
full of practical wisdom and have inspired many and opened up for them
new spiritual horizons. In this respect I find myself one of those who have
been thus benefited and affected.

Besides the excellent performance of the duties of the high and sacred
office of Bishop, he has rendered valuable services to the State and the
people of Liberia by serving on the Board of Managers of the Booker
Washington Institute and other institutions of learning, and has been of
personal assistance to me in a consultative capacity on matters affecting our
national educational programme.

Even though Bishop Taylor is leaving the Liberian field, his work remains
as a living testimonial to the character of a great Christian worker and
organizer. Methodists throughout Liberia will always remember him with
pride and gratitude, for it was he who first assisted us in our efforts to strive
for an autonomous Church by inaugurating a training programme for
Ministers, creating a pension scheme, and setting up financial reserves for
the autonomous Church through the Advance Committee. His perseverance
and zeal have been an inspiration to us in our efforts to forge ahead with
this new idea for Methodism in Liberia, and I am sure that it is with pride
in what he has wrought that he leaves this Episcopal area.

It is our hope that the General Conference will grant our request that
Bishop Taylor be allowed to supervise the formative years of the autonomous Methodist Church, for with his experience, deep interest and guidance
we will face the future bravely and with great expectations.

Side by side with him has been Mrs. Taylor, a genial, devoted consort and
a beacon of inspiration to him in meeting and performing the tasks incumbent upon him; a modest yet strong and influential Christian character and

companion who has shared with her husband the successes, disappointments and other untoward circumstances common to all mortal beings. Without her constant support, encouragement and faith, many of the achievements which we now are privileged to attribute to the Bishop may have been difficult for him to achieve. But thanks to her own deep spiritual and Christian character, she has given her best to the furtherance of his work and has identified herself with movements which were extensions of his Christian ministry. She, too, has won the love and affection of the people of Liberia, and we see in her the quintessence of a true Christian companion and mother and an exemplary wife.

All over the country many modern and representative schools, churches and other edifices can be seen, true memorials of the years of dedicated service to God and this country. But surpassing all of these is the sense of self-reliance which has been impressed upon the membership of the Methodist Church in Liberia, with the consummation of which Bishop Taylor wholly identified himself, and towards which worked hard and conscientiously.

In the changes that we expect to take place in the Church, we cannot ignore the fact that foreign missionary boards and foreign missionaries have played an enormously important rôle in the formulation and shaping of the destiny of this nation, from the period of its founding until the early nineteen hundreds when the Government's efforts were turned in this direction. Before then there was no Department of Public Instruction or Education. The Government exercised no control over educational work in Liberia and was able to contribute to education only along the littoral; it was the Boards of Foreign Missions of different denominations that opened schools in many parts of Liberia and gave education and Christian training to the people of this country.

I am happy and proud that I can speak to you at this time as one of the products of the missionary effort of the Board of Foreign Missions of the Methodist Church, for I have never attended a public school in my life, only the Methodist Seminary, a mission school in Cape Palmas, and I feel completely indebted to and appreciative of the great and invaluable services of the Foreign Board of Missions of the Methodist Episcopal Church and other Foreign Mission Boards. I state with all the emphasis at my command that we need them now and will need them always. We Methodists never say 'forever and ever'; even at the end of our prayers we say 'forever', therefore I say we shall need them forever and they shall be welcome here always and forever. Any attempt to oust, underrate or uproot missionary work or missionaries from this country would mean virtually uprooting the stability and progress of the nation. Anyone who desires to test the veracity of this statement may give it a trial should they have the opportunity, but I hope this will never happen.

It is my great pleasure, on behalf of the members of the Methodist Church, the Government and people of Liberia, Mrs. Tubman and myself to pay you, Bishop and Mrs. Taylor, the Board of Foreign Missions, and the Methodist Church of the United States of America, this modest public tribute and homage, and to convey the thanks and appreciation of a grateful people.

At a time when great forces of nationalism are asserting themselves, and leaders and people of old and new nations are concerned about stability, progress and prosperity, you have, by your devoted and selfless services, succeeded in enriching and strengthening the spiritual foundations of many of God's children in a nation which has never ceased and will never cease to look up 'unto the hills from whence cometh their help' and to which they ever look for help and for strength.

We shall look forward to seeing you return periodically, not only during the three years of your supervisory status, should the General Conference grant our appeal, but even after that period; and after you have retired from the active work of the Church, you may be assured that the Liberian Church and people will ever welcome your presence in this country.

In the history of Liberian Methodism we have had two Bishop Taylors – one was William Taylor and the other our present Prince Taylor, both of whom have imprinted their names most outstandingly and indelibly in the hearts of the people of this country in such a manner that time cannot efface them.

This service and ceremony today, Bishop, is not to bid farewell or good-bye but merely to say 'au revoir'. It is not to apply the old Methodist dictum of parting of Christians at death, 'we will meet again on the sunny banks of deliverance', but that we shall meet again and again on the soil of Liberia, the United States and perhaps elsewhere.

May God go with you, bless you, continue you steadfast in the faith and keep a watchful eye over you 'while we are absent one from the other', and when the time comes for your retirement from active service in the Episcopacy of the Church, again in our old Methodist terminology and parlance, 'we pray that your latter days may be your best'.

To the 133rd Session of the Liberian Methodist Annual Conference

Careysburg, 4 February 1965

With nationalism at a high level, no more opportune time could have been chosen to grant us the privilege of supporting a Central Conference and choosing a Bishop of Liberian nationality.

Introductory Note

By 1965 the Methodist Church in Liberia was approaching a state of greater autonomy within the parent body in the United States. Therefore complete independence was not its ultimate objective. Liberian Methodists stood up to the challenge and it seemed that a new and dynamic spirit of nationalism was upon them. The stage was set for a great and positive step forward. President Tubman's own personal leadership gave guidance in this transition.

Careysburg, 4 February 1965

I EXTEND a very warm and fraternal welcome to Bishop Taylor and the officers and delegates to this Session of the Annual Conference. I hope that the lofty purposes of your gathering at this time will be abundantly fruitful; that peace and harmony will dwell in your midst to bless and enrich your discussions and plans and that the wisdom of the Almighty will guide you continually as you seek to understand His will and do His pleasure.

In a statement bidding 'au revoir' to Bishop and Mrs. Taylor a year ago, I said, 'We shall look forward to seeing you return periodically not only during the three years of your supervisory status, should the General Conference grant our appeal, but even after that period; and after you have retired from the active work of the Church, you may be assured that the Liberian Church and people will ever welcome your presence in this country.' That our request has been fulfilled sooner than we anticipated is attributed to the bond of brotherhood which has been established between us and the blessings which their lives of dedication and service have brought to the Methodist Church and work in Liberia.

For us, therefore, it is a unique pleasure that Bishop Taylor is presiding at this Conference. During his domicile in this area as Resident Bishop for approximately nine years, we became accustomed to his presence and benefited immeasurably from our association.

We admire the execution and performance of his function in carrying out the obligations and responsibilities of his sacred office, and welcome him at this time in a dual capacity. Bishop Taylor now stands in a twofold relationship to the Liberian Church and Methodism in general; he is presiding over the Annual Conference in a supervisory capacity, and as President of the Council of Bishops of the Methodist Church. Thus it is a deep source of satisfaction and pleasure to have with us one who has contributed so much toward the enrichment and extension of Methodism and Christianity and the deepening of the spiritual quality of Methodists in Liberia; one who has, by his life of service, demonstrated his love for his fellowmen.

It is generally known to all of us that during the sitting of the 132nd Session of the Liberia Annual Conference we sent a Memorial to the last Session of the General Conference requesting autonomy if under the laws and polity of the Church there was no possible means of granting the Liberian Conference Episcopal leadership.

The Memorial, having been approved by the Conference, was entrusted to the hands of the Rev. Urias B. Freeman and the Honourable James B. Dennis, ministerial and lay delegates to the last Session of the General Conference and Council of Bishops. After careful and prayerful consideration of the appeal of the Liberia Conference, we were offered the privilege of choosing to become autonomous and an affiliate of the General Conference of American Methodism, or of organizing a Central Conference and remaining with the Mother Church in the United States within the jurisdiction of the General Conference.

It is our belief and studied conviction that the Central Conference with Liberian Episcopal Supervision is the better path and the one we should choose. We have seen the reason for our choice; we know that the Liberian Church represents the oldest foreign missionary enterprise of the Board of Foreign Missions of the American Church, and for this reason we feel that we should create a three-fold bond of fraternity and identity that cannot be broken.

Under the dedicated leadership of Bishop Taylor, Methodism in Liberia has experienced a great spiritual renaissance. His broad vision, his Christian preparedness, his dedicated ministry and his love for humanity rendered the field fertile and brought forth a hundredfold for the extension of the Kingdom of Christ on earth. It is because of his selfless service and God-guided life that so much was achieved and that the work has now started out to conquer new fields and win more souls to Christ.

Perhaps some of us have wondered why Bishop Taylor should have led a movement that on the surface appeared to be an attempt to displace him. That the Bishop is a true servant of God endowed with humility of soul, looking to the ultimate good and redemption of the flock entrusted to his care; that he came to build, develop and produce a new generation of Church people deeply conscious of their sense of mission toward attaining true spiritual and material progress, are facts which have characterized Bishop Taylor's life and ministry. It was therefore not unusual that he should have encouraged and led us in the great forward step which we have taken.

We express our deep gratitude to the General Conference of the American Methodist Episcopal Church and the Board of Foreign Missions for their support and encouragement, since the establishment of the Church in Liberia up to the present, for with nationalism at a high level, no more opportune time could have been chosen to grant us the privilege of supporting a Central Conference and choosing a Bishop of Liberian nationality. Fired with this new resolution we entreat the Mother Church to act now in assisting to promote the vigorous growth and expansion of Methodism in

Liberia, at this period of our assumption of a new status and a new life for all Methodists; a life of endeavour in faith and action, a life of sacrifice and conquest.

One of the fundamental criticisms hurled against the Church today is that it has lost its central vision, its vital force to draw all men to Christ, and its incisive message. Divisions among sects, divisions in churches, dissension among God's children, the utter disregard for religion as the integrating force which binds man to man and to his Creator and the growing weakening of morals, seem to indicate that man is losing ground. But be that as it may, he must get hold of himself, come to the Source of his being and worship Him in spirit and in truth, with emphasis on unity rather than on dogmatism and creed. For religions may be many but God is one.

The growing desire of all Christendom to come together, and the progress which has been achieved in this direction, are gladdening signs that God's will shall ultimately be done on earth. We hear the clarion call: 'In order that they may all be one' as loudly and steadily today as when the Master uttered it almost two thousand years ago.

Scholars speak of sociological determinism or economic determinism, that vital force which is capable of binding the whole world into one common brotherhood of man and Fatherhood of God, and which will become the motivating factor, the guiding principle and the *sine qua non* of human existence. It is religion which must draw all men together, lead all men eventually to God, and make the Divine injunction: 'That they may all be one' not just an ideal or a prayer, but a reality. Its need should be desired and its presence felt in the spiritual and material affairs of men every day and in every way.

We have chosen the path of sacrificial labour, self-support and independence, which will bring new and bigger demands. If we do not permit our personal ambitions to assume significant proportions and if we do not allow personal considerations to enter to such an extent as to bring discord, confusion and strife, especially at the time of the election of the first Bishop for the Central Conference, we shall usher in a new era in which the healthy growth, development and unity of the Church will be given full play and great progress assured.

Let us all, therefore, resolve to support the new status we will assume; let us be God-guided in the election of our first Episcopal leader; let us spare no efforts to establish, in our human and spiritual relations, those factors which will be best conducive to the maintenance and survival of our new status and let us strive unceasingly to establish His Church so securely in Liberia that 'the gates of Hell shall not prevail against it'.

As Chairman of the Advance Committee, it is my happy privilege to report to the Bishop, Officers and members of this Annual Conference that the Committee has realized the sum of $50,000.00 for the work of the Church. Everyone has worked hard and given generously.

Realizing the tremendous responsibility implicit in the new status that the Liberian Church will assume by the creation of a Central Conference, our financial responsibilities will become greatly increased, our material and spiritual alertness must become more active and, in fine, we must realize that it is our responsibility and service to maintain and promote the work in Liberia. In the meantime, we expect and crave the continued interest, contribution and assistance of the Mother Church to a greater extent, especially in this transitional period when most of what we do will be virtually on an experimental basis.

With these stern realities before us, on behalf of the Advance Committee I submit a Financial Plan for the consideration of the Annual Conference which, if approved, will impose upon all District Superintendents, Pastors and Laymen alike, the responsibility of pushing the execution of the plan to the very gates with all of our might.

May the day soon come when the artificial curtain of divisions and dissensions between Roman Catholic and Protestant, Orthodox and Non-orthodox sects will be broken down and when all the followers of God will worship the King of Kings and Lord of Lords, and in one glad acclaim raise their voices together singing, 'HOLY, HOLY, HOLY, LORD GOD ALMIGHTY'.

May God bless the labours of our hands and accept the gifts of our hearts to His Honour and Glory.

On the Closing of the 133rd Session of the Liberian Methodist Annual Conference

Careysburg, Liberia, 7 February 1965

I am sure that Methodists all over our country are justly proud to be part of this new beginning and of a movement which may well revolutionize the history of Methodism in Liberia.

Introductory Note

The 133rd Session of the Liberian Methodist Conference was one of the most historic sessions of that body. The decision was finally taken, with the consent of the Parent Church in the United States, to assume autonomy, after years of preparation. The event, though it gave cause for jubilation, made Liberian Methodists cognizant of a newer type of responsibility – that of Christian responsibility for a self-supporting Church, and infused in them a spirit of independence. The precedent set by this transition saw a new day dawn for other Christian denominations to follow. The President was gratified to see how nobly Liberian Methodists faced this new challenge.

Careysburg, 7 February 1965

WE HAVE come to the end of the 133rd Session of the Liberian Annual Conference with new perspectives, a greater courage and a clearer recognition of the tremendous but challenging responsibilities which the Methodist Church in Liberia has now assumed. I extend congratulations to the members of this historic Conference for the farsightedness and wisdom they have shown in reaching a decision to organize a Central Conference entitling them to elect delegates to constitute the Central Conference. We regard this as a great and important step forward, full of great potentialities and promise for the effectiveness and pervasive influence of the work of the Church. I am sure that Methodists all over the country are justly proud to be part of this new beginning and of a movement which may well revolutionize the history of Methodism in Liberia.

We are all convinced that we have arrived at the crossroads in our Christian endeavour. We should go forward therefore from this Conference with abiding faith in the course we have taken, in unshakable conviction that our cause is just and with a rugged determination to play the part which the Master has assigned to us, in the hope that the years ahead will richly bless our efforts and contribute to the expansion of Christ's Kingdom on earth; not only in Liberia but everywhere, so that many more may come to know and worship Him as their Lord and Saviour.

It is a unique and extremely fortunate experience for us that Bishop Prince Taylor who has for the past eight years been resident Bishop of the Liberian area should have presided over the present session of the Annual Conference when this potent action was taken. This fact is the more remarkable because of the new status which the Bishop now enjoys in the Council of Bishops of the Methodist Church. It is to be remembered that an identical privilege came to him when, after his election to the Episcopacy, his first assignment was to the Liberian area. This signal honour which has been accorded him, and of which we are now the beneficiaries, took place at the last General Conference of the Methodist Church. Coming directly from the missionary field in Liberia, we are indeed happy and exceedingly pleased that Bishop Taylor, now President of the Council of Bishops of the Methodist Church in the United States of America, still has general supervision over the work here and will continue to have until a Liberian is elected by the Central Conference as Bishop.

While I do not believe in over-emphasizing or stressing the question of race, creed and class, I am sure that all the members of the Liberian Annual Conference and the Liberian people in general are grateful, happy and proud that a Bishop of the Liberian Annual Conference has been elected President of the Council of Bishops of our great Methodist Church. Certainly, this is an outstanding achievement and one which will bring greater recognition to the oldest of the foreign missionary-operated fields in American Methodism.

There are two significant factors associated with this new position which the Mother Church has taken. The first is the breaking-down of racial barriers in the Methodist Church, truly a marvellous first step, a realization which could not be imagined in the past. In the midst of the great controversy which faces all Christendom and men everywhere, when places of worship are segregated and when one man is not permitted to worship with another because of race, this new approach, this new action strikes at the core of the Christian Gospel in its insistent appeal for all to be one.

Secondly, this step points clearly to the progress which has been and will be made toward Christian brotherhood in a world where mankind sorely needs the unifying force of religion, so that all men can stand as equal partners in worshipping their Lord and Master. With grateful hearts we welcome and applaud this enlightened action of the Council of Bishops.

The Annual Conference just ended has decided to tender this reception to our honoured guest as a small token of their love, gratitude and appreciation for all that he has done for the strengthening and expansion of the Church's work in Liberia. By his lofty examples of Christian leadership and brotherhood Bishop Taylor has ingratiated himself into the hearts of Liberians and will long live in their hearts, thoughts and minds, because on every hand we shall continue to see, and to be benefited by, the fruits of his service. We pray, Bishop, that you may be blessed with health, long life, wealth and endowed with greater wisdom and courage to continue your usefulness to your fellowmen. Our prayers and good wishes go with you.

On behalf of the people of Liberia and of Methodists in Liberia, we ask you to convey to the Council of Bishops our profound gratitude for the signal honour which has been bestowed upon you, and through you on the people of Liberia, by your preferment. We associate ourselves with you and Mrs. Taylor in this elevation, and we also ask that you convey to her our deep sense of appreciation for the love and loyalty she manifested in the work here and the contributions she made toward enriching and extending the dimensions of our opportunities and possibilities. We assure you that even with the new status which the Liberian Church has taken by choosing to become a Central Conference which will give us the right and privilege to elect a Liberian as our Bishop, we shall rely upon the continued support and co-operation of the Mother Church, the missionaries now assigned here and the many others who we hope will be forthcoming to assist in this great and responsible task we have undertaken to perform.

May the bonds of Christian Fellowship between us become stronger and stronger in the years ahead and may we continue to be steadfast and true exemplars of the faith to which He has called us.

At a Dinner Honouring the Vice-President of Liberia, the Honourable William R. Tolbert, Jun., as President of the Baptist World Alliance

Monrovia, 14 July 1965

His preferment as President of the Baptist World Alliance comprising a membership of millions of all races ... the first of his race to be so elected, and what is more, the first Liberian, does great honour to all of us and fills us with pride.

Introductory Note

William R. Tolbert, Jun., exemplified the work of a great missionary and evangelist. The honour which he received upon his election as President of the World Baptist Alliance was a unique event, calling upon him to occupy such a spiritually rewarding position while serving simultaneously as Vice-President of the Republic of Liberia. President Tubman considered the event historic, and a singular honour bestowed upon Liberia. The occasion was given the recognition it deserved and he spoke of the sterling qualities of the Liberian so honoured.

Monrovia, 14 July 1965

MRS. TUBMAN and I are happy to extend a welcome to our guests who have come hither this evening to join us in doing honour to a public servant who has always been devoted to the highest ideals of service; a dedicated cleric who by his life, work and dynamic leadership has greatly contributed toward expanding, deepening and broadening the work of the Baptist Church in Liberia; a man whose family is a proud product of the ideal Christian-based home where love flourishes and where the nurture and training of their children on Christian principles is the consuming passion of both father and mother.

In recognition of the signal preferment which has come with his election as President of the Baptist World Alliance, Mrs. Tubman and I are very happy indeed to hold this banquet as a modest expression of admiration and appreciation to the members of the Congress of the Baptist World Alliance held in Miami, Florida, USA. We offer our congratulations to Dr. William R. Tolbert, Jun., and are proud of his outstanding services to God, the Church, State and humanity which has resulted in this outstanding recognition by the World Organization of the denomination of his birth and choice. I am sure that everyone here, as well as a host of citizens throughout the nation, associate themselves with us in welcoming and congratulating most heartily our guest of honour.

Clarity of vision, reliability, diligence, resourcefulness, determination and the rare ability to create and develop, out of virtually nothing, tangible and intangible edifices for the benefit of man and the glory of God, are some of the fine attributes which distinguished him long before this time and which have been the mainstay of his phenomenal rise in church and state. No man who regards himself as a trustee of the gifts with which his Maker has endowed him and who uses them in the service of his fellowmen, no man who strives ceaselessly and conscientiously to improve the *status quo* and bring to it new meaning and limitless opportunities for growth and expansion, no man who serves so efficiently and faithfully, can fail to win the gratitude and recognition of his countrymen and the plaudits of those he serves in a wider sphere.

Under his dedicated leadership as President of the Baptist Missionary and Educational Convention, we have witnessed tremendous strides in Liberian Baptistism; a new building programme has been launched and executed, the Christian education programme has been revitalized, enriched and strengthened; physical plants have been improved; living conditions and standards raised and in general the Church's work, whether along educational or evangelical lines, has experienced a great awakening. New spirit has been generated which holds a bright promise for future advancement in Christian Education and Evangelism.

The nation is proud of the results which have been achieved and grateful for the ministry of this servant of God and State, and I feel equally sure that the Baptist world is convinced of the correctness of their choice of Dr. Tolbert as Vice-President of the Congress of the World Baptist Alliance and President of the Baptist Missionary and Educational Convention. All of these accomplishments of our guest of honour convince me of the truth and sincerity of the Biblical reference 'Seest thou a man diligent in his business? He shall stand before kings and not before mean men.' It is self-evident that Dr. Tolbert richly deserves this commendation, and we are proud of him because of his accomplishments and prouder still because of the opportunity now afforded him for greater service.

My close relationship with Vice-President Tolbert in public life had its beginning in his election to the Legislature as a Representative from Montserrado County when I was elected to the Presidency on the same ballot. This contact was the beginning of my respect and admiration for him, so that later, when he became Vice-President of the nation, my assessment and opinion of him and of his greatness was confirmed and affirmed. It is a fitting tribute to him to say that throughout all these years, I have had no single occasion to become restless, restive, anxious, apprehensive or uncertain about his course of conduct. He has always been a man with a singleness of purpose, a deep conviction for justice and fair play and a man of guarded ambition.

Just as he has served the church with profound dedication and a high sense of moral responsibility to his duty conceived in the best tradition of his Master, the Christ, so has he served the state unselfishly and has sought constantly not his own interest but the welfare of the state and its people. His patriotism, his dependability, his keen perception, his lofty ideals and his unswerving devotion to duty have not been marred by successes; he continues to be humble and unaffected.

With a man of such sterling worth and qualities, not given to intrigues, subversion, treachery, bribery, nor to the sale of the interest of his country and the sacred trust committed to him for the proverbial mess of pottage or filthy lucre, any man, as President, would be content to think that in the event of his death, resignation or retirement, the man holding the position of Vice-President could be fit to take on the toga of the Presidency; and that the nation and its people, I emphasize its people, would be in safe and dependable hands.

His preferment as President of the Baptist World Alliance, comprising a membership of millions of all races and tongues, from all climes and coasts, the first one of his race to be so designated, and what is more, the first Liberian, does great honour to all of us and fills us with pride. I am certain that you join Mrs. Tubman and me in wishing for him a long life of greater usefulness and service at a higher political plateau, and continued effectiveness to universal Baptistism in the position he now holds.

To Mrs. Tolbert who has stood loyally, honourably and devotedly by him through the years of their marriage, shared his joys and sorrows, his successes and failures; and nurtured him in health and in sickness, we pay a tribute of congratulations and salutations *in absentia*. May their years together continue to be enriched and strengthened by mutual love, respect, loyalty, fidelity and devotion and all the attributes that make for a happy, unwavering and stable home.

It is a pleasure for Mrs. Tubman and myself to pay this tribute to Dr. and Mrs. Tolbert and we ask our guests to join us in drinking a toast to their health.

In Memory of the Rt. Reverend Bravid Washington Harris

Monrovia, 14 November 1965

Now at last he knows the full meaning of infinite love.

Introductory Note

Less than two years after his retirement as Bishop of the Protestant Episcopal Missionary District of Liberia, Bishop Bravid W. Harris departed this life as a result of an automobile accident. The void he created in the hearts of his Christian flock in Liberia and also in the hearts of Christians generally in Liberia upon his retirement was unsurpassed even by his death. His loss, first by retirement, and later by death, was deeply felt. His Liberian congregation and friends mourned his loss on both occasions, and almost in the same manner. The President of Liberia and the Bishop were intimate friends. Greatly moved by the news of the death of the Bishop, he gave this final tribute to a friend, a sacred and humble Christian who had enriched greatly the lives of all who came to know him, and who knew him as one who daily imitated the life of Jesus Christ, whose servant he became.

Monrovia, 14 November 1965

FOR NEARLY three score and ten years the beautiful soul of Bravid Washington Harris expressed itself under conditions of space and time, and then, just as the morning light was breaking upon his several years of life, following a serious attack of illness from which he had just recovered, he faded from the view of human eyes on October 22nd, 1965, and moved out into the limitless freedom of eternity. Now at last he knows the full meaning of infinite love and understands the unfathomable mystery of perfect power and inscrutable wisdom which, in the name of Jesus Christ, he had preached for more than forty years.

Bishop Harris was one of God's noblemen, possessed of that fine common sense, courage and love for men and justice which characterized the early Christians and their Master. He was always a true democrat and none of the many recognitions that came to him during his life of nearly seventy years succeeded in swerving him from his ideals of human equality and service to God and man. In the pulpit Bishop Harris was at his best. His whole career and the dominating purpose of his life were identified with the interest of his flock and his missionary district. He relied on Christ as His Saviour and friend and believed in the Kingdom of God and in the Church as the doorway to that Kingdom. Through his winning personality this noble man made genuine friends whom he grappled to his soul with hoops of steel.

At the time that I was first elected to and assumed the position I now occupy, Bishop Harris was also elected Bishop of the Protestant Episcopal Church of the Missionary District of Liberia. Upon receiving information of his election, although I had never met him, I cabled him a message of congratulations, assuring him of the Government's and my support and co-operation and that the doors of Liberia would always be wide open for him and his missionary enterprise, that had contributed so much to the people of the country in evangelism and education. Bishop Harris sent a very warm and fraternal reply and when he came out to the seat of the Missionary District in Monrovia I had the pleasure of meeting him for the first time during worship at Trinity Pro-Cathedral. It was then that I first heard him preach. I was deeply moved and touched by the forensic attraction, spiritual power and dogmatic syllogism of his sermon. His unpretentiousness and realism, evidenced by his insistence upon 'keeping your feet on the ground', formed the bulwark of his strength.

Bishop Harris, as the new Bishop of the Protestant Episcopal Church in Liberia, and Bishop King of the Methodist Church, co-operated to a large extent in assisting with the implementation of the educational policy of the new administration, particularly with reference to teacher training and vocational education. The re-opening of Cuttington College and Divinity School, which had prepared a larger number of men and women for useful service to Church and state than any other single institution in the country, was one of the principal projects undertaken for the training of ministers for the churches in Liberia regardless of denomination.

Being in the same age group, Bishop Harris and I spoke freely to each other on various subjects. Mrs. Tubman and I, while living at the old mansion, often went to the old Bishop's house on Sundays and other occasions for Mass.

At the celebration of my sixty-seventh birthday by the people of Sinoe County the Bishop was present. I went to worship at the Methodist Church on the birthday morning; they celebrated the Holy Eucharist but the individual cups in which the wine was served were so small that it could not wash the bread from the roof of my mouth. The following morning the Rector of St. Paul Episcopal Church invited us for Mass and we went; again, the priest held the communion cup so tightly that the wine did not even wet my tongue. Returning home after service I told the Bishop that I had communed at both the Methodist and Episcopal Churches since my arrival in Greenville but on neither occasion did I get enough wine to wash down the wafer from the roof of my mouth. He laughed in his usual deep voice and said, 'That's the way they are, that's the way they are these days; they like to hold everything to themselves. The law of the Church states that they shall deliver it into your hands, but they will not do it.'

The Divinity School at Cuttington was established under special arrangements between Bishop Harris, Bishop King and myself, and when I arrived at the General Convocation in Grand Bassa County two years ago and found that a decision had been made to close down the school because of the lack of students for theological training, I regretted this, not only because I was fully aware of the dire need for trained ministers, but also because one of the pet projects of Bishop Harris had been discontinued, at least temporarily, and I remembered his insistence on a trained clergy as inevitably essential to an effective Church. The leadership which the Bishop gave to the Church during his tenure was outstanding and singular. He rejected platitudes, superfluities and unnecessary formalities.

After the passing of the late Bishop Samuel David Ferguson there was a lull, if not a deterioration, in the work of the Protestant Episcopal Church in Liberia, but when Bishop Harris was assigned and made his advent here, the work took on new impetus and achieved new dimensions. Working hard and regularly with his own hands, he required each person to work fervently and to be productive. In his new programme he reopened most of the old stations that had been closed throughout the country and created new ones, thereby expanding the Church's work of evangelism and education. He gave personal attention to the remotest station as a matter of routine duty. His far-sightedness and comprehensive vision urged him not to be content with merely procuring support for the work of the Church during his own tenure of office but to seek avenues that would be revenue producing for the continuation of the work in the future.

No Church problem, however delicate, difficult, exacting or far-reaching in its issues, baffled him. He did whatever his hands found to do with all of his might, and at once. He was unruffled. Calmness, steadiness and positiveness characterized his service and his administrative work will withstand the test of time.

As a worker, he was silent, tireless and prodigious. He never asked others to do what he declined. He led the way in self-sacrifice. Rest and vacation were foreign to him. His work was constructive; he lives posthumously; his ministers and all those who worked or were associated with him in one way or the other had a love for him born of deference, reverence and esteem. Fawning and currying favour were foreign to him. He did not know how to be a sycophant. He attracted friends and bound them to him by his superb worthiness.

To the timid he was as a rock, as a highway for the weak and a covert for the clinging spirit. He had the strength of ten for his heart was pure.

He had a genuine sense of humour, a contagious buoyancy of heart, an infectious laugh and a resounding basso profundo voice that I delighted to hear. When the choir and clergy were marching in procession into and out of service, he usually sang while he marched in procession in a bass that was peculiarly his own. He held that the social life of the Church could be channelled so as to promote Christianity. He never complained; never explained. I have known him to suffer in silence adverse criticisms, making no remarks lest he cause pain to others by explanation. His forceful personality was never neutral in any assembly. His position was made known, not obtrusively but unmistakably. His convictions were clear, and he cleaved to them with full purpose of heart. He could not be stampeded into changing his opinion. His disinterestedness for personal gain attracted others to his conclusion. He was no radical. He did not flare up at a tangent. In the intensest debate he was calm and polite — nothing disturbed him. He merited the position of constructive ecclesiastical statesman. If Diogenes had lived in our time and cast his lantern on Bishop Harris he could have said, 'verily, I have found a man'.

As a preacher, Bishop Harris was instructive, uplifting and heartening. He lived the evangel. His proclamation of it was without reservation. He believed his love and spoke the answer to Chalmer's prayer 'Let me not fall from earnestness', which was evidenced in all his pulpit ministry. He never indulged in verbal pyrotechnics. He never cheapened religion. The verities of the Holy Faith he preached as Apelles painted for eternity. He was a conserver of the faith once delivered to the saints, yet hospitable to progress.

Bishop Harris's life was enriched by his marriage to Miss F. Mae Adams, whom his heart safely trusted. She helped to make him known in the gates and did him good all the days of his life.

I shall ever remember the elaborate and well-planned retirement service tendered him and Mrs. Harris upon his retirement, and how the whole nation, regardless of dogma, creed or station, packed into this same building almost two years ago to do him honour, to sing his praise, to laud his work, to express appreciation for his service to the people of this land, when he appeared accompanied by Mrs. Harris, seemingly in good health and with his usual buoyancy.

But alas, today we gather here in this same place to hold a memorial service, to sing a requiem, to deliver a memorial address and a panegyric which suggests that Bishop Bravid Washington Harris is dead; that he lives, moves and has his being no more among the living but that his remains lie lifeless in the honoured Arlington cemetery, Washington, D.C. where men of valour, patriotism and honour are given a place. They sleep together, those who have done great deeds for their country, for freedom, for liberty, in the city of the dead.

We cannot but bemoan and regret the tragic and sudden nature of his death, but let us not mourn that his departure was so sudden, nor fill our imagination with horror at its method. When the Church and good men pray for deliverance from sudden death, it is only that they may not be plunged without preparation into the presence of the judge. Men long elude and evade sorrow, but when suddenly overtaken seem enchanted to make the glide to the utmost. When one is ready to depart, suddenness is a blessing. It is a painful sight to see a tree overthrown by a tornado, wrenched from its foundation and broken down like a reed; but it is yet more painful to see a vast and venerable tree clinging with vain strength, when age and infirmity have marked it for destruction. The slow process of decay is a humiliating and painful spectacle; but it seems good and grand for one to go from duty done with pulse high, with strength full and nerves high, terminating a noble life in a fitting manner. In the scriptures we read: 'Let your loins be girded about. Blessed are those servants whom the Lord when He cometh shall find watching.' Not only those who die in a stupor are blessed but they who go with all their powers about them, as wide awake as to a wedding. Bishop Harris died watching, he died with his armour on, he died in the midst of hours of labour en route to Virginia on a fund-raising mission for the Church. No fever dried his blood, no slow waste consumed him. All at once, in full strength and manhood, with his girdle tight about him, he departed this life and walks with his God.

Mrs. Harris, the partner of his life, was with him in the tragic accident that brought death to him and serious physical bodily injuries to her; almost like Saul and Jonathan, they were loving and pleasing in their lives and in death they were not divided.

On the Special Week of Prayer and Fasting

Monrovia, 21 February 1966

Life, even religious life, is warfare.

Introductory Note

In February 1966, the Protestant Episcopal Church in Liberia lost one of its stalwart priests through death. A devoutly religious and saintly man, the Reverend J. D. K. Baker never ceased to speak out or to warn the Liberian nation and its leaders of man's vital need and dependence upon his Creator. A few moments before he died he sent a message to President Tubman requesting that Liberia observe a Special Week of Prayer and Fasting. The President obeyed the dying wishes of this man of God.

Monrovia, 21 February 1966

FROM ANCIENT times devout men under the influence and power of God and inspired by that power, dreamed dreams, saw visions and prophesied in the name of God. This Special Week of Prayer and Fasting authorized by the Legislature emanates from the dying request of one of Liberia's outstanding clerics and religious leaders, honoured, respected and revered by adherents of all denominations and sects, who in a message sent to the Government by one of our prelates suggested that a Week of Prayer be ordained and declared; prayer for the peace, security and safety of the Liberian State and for the peace and brotherhood of mankind throughout the world.

Even in the criminal and civil law the testimony of dying men is accepted as evidence of very high calibre. We therefore regard with great significance the call of the late Father James D. K. Baker, communicated to the Chief Executive about four hours before his passing, which has resulted in our gathering here at this time to pray together fervently, earnestly and incessantly for peace, for brotherhood and for the safety and security of our Government and people as well as for all mankind.

What is prayer? I like the definition given in the lines of the hymn-writer James Montgomery, written in 1818 in his hymn:

> Prayer is the soul's sincere desire,
> Unutter'd or expressed,
> The motion of a hidden fire
> That trembles in the breast.
>
> Prayer is the burden of a sigh,
> The falling of a tear,
> The upward glancing of an eye
> When none but God is near.

Prayer is the simplest form of speech
That infant lips can try;
Prayer the sublimest strains that reach
The Majesty on high.

Prayer is the Christian's vital breath,
The Christian's native air,
His watchword at the gates of death:
He enters Heav'n with prayer.

O thou by whom we come to God,
The Life, the Truth, the Way,
The Path of Prayer Thyself has trod:
Lord, teach us how to pray.

The services of this week are not the outcome of fear, fright or the result of the quickening of timorous hearts and souls. Nor are they the outburst of excited emotions of alarm, for we fear nothing but God in Heaven and sin on earth. God being with us, who can be against us?

Life, even religious life, is warfare, therefore surely we must fight if we would reign. So these services are an earnest desire to convince ourselves of our sins, transgressions and wickedness; to repent of them and to seek forgiveness and blessings.

May these services create within us new hearts and uplifted spirits and may the Holy Ghost breathe its Spirit of comfort and peace upon us — that peace which the world cannot give — the peace that comes only of God.

A Closing Statement on the Observance of the National Week of Prayer and Fasting

Monrovia, 28 February 1966

Our forefathers believed that with the strong arm of the Almighty supporting their efforts there could be no imponderables to defeat them.

Introductory Note

Liberia annually observes a week of prayer. On special occasions there can also be a call to prayer if a request is made by an outstanding theologian. Such events are not inconsistent with the life of our nation. Liberia was founded by Christian men and women, and materialism has not, as in many parts of the world, shaken their faith and dependence upon the Creator of our world. Christianity, one might say, remains one of the intangibles of the Liberian way of life. The President reminds his people of their great religious heritage and responsibilities.

Monrovia, 28 February 1966

THE FOUNDERS of our country established it not upon economic wealth, or military might and power, but upon a deep and well-founded belief and trust in God through prayer. Inspired by strong religious and spiritual convictions and determination, they believed that with the strong arm of the Almighty supporting their efforts there could be no imponderables to defeat them and that with Him all things were possible. In this spirit and with this conviction they laid the foundations of this democratic society – a nation conceived and founded upon the principles of democracy, freedom and justice.

The facts of history unquestionably reveal their indomitable knowledge, their unquenchable thirst for liberty and their unconquerable will to maintain and sustain for themselves and posterity a home where the enjoyment and exercise of the rights, benefits and privileges of free men could be the satisfaction and glory of a land of liberty by God's command.

The test of their loyalty and faithfulness to the principles for which they stood, is made positively evident by their survival through a period of history when colonial expansionist movements were the order of the day. They stood alone amidst and against it when none but men and women of their rare and steel-clad calibre could have survived.

Following in the wake of these great and venerable sires of this nation, we must always find solace through a free and easy approach to the Throne of Grace which is a calm and sure retreat around one common mercy seat.

SOCIAL AFFAIRS

At the Acceptance of the Tubman Centre of African Culture

Robertsport, Grand Cape Mount County, Liberia, 29 November 1964

I accept with great gratitude this symbol of African culture which you have erected and named after me in honour of my sixty-ninth birthday anniversary.

Introductory Note

The annual observance of President Tubman's birthday on 29 November was an occasion for jubiliation and numerous festivities. Although he never gave official consent to declaring the day a national holiday, the people of Liberia, encouraged by the National Legislature, observed the day as a public holiday. The occasion was also one when there were demonstrations of self-help projects undertaken by the various counties, each celebration becoming more elaborate than the last. In 1964 Grand Cape Mount County presented to President Tubman a National Centre of African Culture which was meant to immortalize him for ever. President Tubman gratefully acknowledged the gift of the people of that county, and promised them Government assistance in their local programme of development.

Robertsport, Liberia, 29 November 1964

THE PHYSICAL transformations which have taken place in the City of Robertsport since we were here last to propagate Operation Production, the crowds that are here to witness this occasion and the great enthusiasm and merriment seen everywhere, are very impressive, and convince me of the careful planning, the hard work and the tremendous sacrifices of the citizens and residents of Grand Cape Mount County in preparation for the observance of this occasion. The booklet, 'Grand Cape Mount County', written by Dr. Abeodu B. Jones of the Department of State, Division of African and Asian Affairs, and the pamphlet, 'A Look at Cape Mount', put out by Mr. Willie Givens of the Liberian Information Service, are literary achievements which will be among the first contributions to this Centre for African Culture. We hope that they will be an incentive to other budding authors and an inspiration to all those who read them.

When we look at the streets of the city, when we consider the refurbished buildings and new homes and when we behold the Tubman Centre for African Culture standing so majestically on this hill, a region formerly all bush but now well laid out and landscaped, we are convinced that with vision, initiative, hard work, know-how and co-operation, great things can be accomplished on the local front. I believe that all of us can learn a valuable lesson from this; to roll up our sleeves, and go to work to see what further accomplishments we can effect for our counties, people and country.

As far back as I can remember, Robertsport has always been commended for its picturesque mountain and hills, the delightfully sparkling and cool water from the 'waa', the plentiful fish and the high educational standards of the schools. I must admit, however, that when one thinks of the access to the city by sea and the hazards to be encountered, especially in the days when surf boat travel was the quickest means of transportation, a certain degree of disenchantment is bound to set in.

But it is to be remembered that despite the travel hazards, for many years the history of Cape Mount owed its existence mainly to three social agencies – the church, the school and the hospital; these three have been great moulding influences throughout the years and I am proud and grateful for the educational and spiritual work which has been carried on in this part of our country, and the monument that has been erected to the glory of God, and for the benefit of mankind.

There was a time when people suffering from ailments of various kinds made their way from all over Liberia, including the capital, Monrovia, to Robertsport in search of medical service, and students from all over the country flocked to Robertsport in search of education and crowded the halls, domitories and walls of Saint John and Bethany in quest of what was thought to be the soundest education in the country. This was principally due to the contribution of the Boards of Foreign Missions of the Protestant Episcopal Church.

Now, in conjunction with the expanding educational programme in which the Government is involved, because we are more than ever convinced that education is the right of a free people and the open sesame to progress and development, we must continue to strive to maintain our partnership in the society of the free. During the coming years every effort must be exerted by Government and Mission agencies to intensify and co-ordinate our programmes so that the church, the school and the hospital, along with other social institutions, may be instrumental in accelerating the pace of progress and development in this community and thus make Cape Mount one of the strongest and most influential counties in the Republic; for not only has the educational standard of the county been high and comparable with any other in the country, but it continues to remain so.

In all conscience, I must confess that the counties of Grand Cape Mount and Maryland appear to have received less economic attention and consideration in the development programme than any of the other counties. This has been due to the limited resources at our disposal and our policy of distributing those resources in order of seniority of the counties, but that is not the sole or only cause for this apparent discrimination. It is further due to the fact that deposits of natural resources thus far discovered in Grand Cape Mount and Maryland Counties have been found to be of a lesser degree, variety and concentration than those discovered in other counties. Notwithstanding, if other nations can transform deserts into flourishing agricultural lands, Cape Mount and Maryland, the two extreme points of the Republic, must now be given priority consideration, together with the new counties that have just been created. In order to accelerate business, the need for a small port construction in the City of Robertsport is apparent and will be given due consideration.

Touching on the question of the construction of a road to link Monrovia with Robertsport, the project has in the past been considered a major engineering feat. But now, with the work which was undertaken and accomplished for this celebration, it is clear that this argument has lost its validity. This matter must and will be given immediate attention by the Government.

This Centre for African Culture, the crowning gift of all your planning, work and sacrifice, is a great tribute to the vision and fine sense of values of the people of this county, because it is a gift which, while it bears my name, will be greatly instrumental in extending the national image of the county and country. I hope that the present generation of young Cape Mountainians will see in it the vast possibilities which the Centre offers and symbolizes, as a potential storehouse of African history, art and literature; that future generations will regard it as an acheivement which indicated a new beginning in everything which makes for county pride, initiative and development. Standing on this magnificent hill, the Centre will always be an inspiration to those who will come here and be a constant reminder to the people of this county and the Republic of the unfinished work to be done even after the physical structure for the building is completed. The Centre must always be a place where with each visit interest will be deepened and a rewarding experience gained.

I thank the county leaders, for extending me the invitation to spend my 69th natal anniversary in Robertsport. I commend their vision, initiative and determination, in spite of the many discouraging features which they may have encountered, to make this occasion successful. I pay special tribute to the General Chairman and his associates for the specific assignments they have all performed. There are many indications that the various Chairmen of Committees and Committee Members performed their tasks well so that there appears to have been a perfect co-ordination of activities. I compliment the citizens who co-operated so splendidly by sharing responsibilities which contributed to the success of the events for this occasion. In fact, to everyone who has had anything to do with the observance, I extend, on behalf of the Government, Mrs. Tubman and myself, our grateful thanks and appreciation.

That you have devoted a section of this programme to an Operation Production Fair does great credit not only to your continued interest, but also to your quickness to comprehend and translate into action a programme which holds so much for the future prosperity of our nation, whereby the agricultural resources of the nation can be bountifully and usefully tapped to serve national and world markets. I trust that this fair will continue to be held and that the inspiration derived from it will spread to other parts of the county and country. I commend you very highly for the forward step you have taken in opening this Operation Production Fair at this time.

I accept with great gratitude this symbol of African culture which you have erected and named after me in honour of my 69th birthday anniversary; I am deeply appreciative of everything you have said about me and of every demonstration you have put on to make this occasion a grand and memorable one. This gift is more than I can ever repay in expression or kind. I can only say thank you from the deepest recesses of my heart, and as long as I live this act of yours will ensure an important place in my heart for you, the citizens and residents of Grand Cape Mount.

God bless you and give you helpers to enable you to carry this noble structure to a successful completion. I am sure that the Legislature will give consideration to this grand and potent effort by providing it with an annual subsidy. May this Centre expand and grow until it becomes a place of attraction not only for Liberia but also for Africa, as well as for people and institutions in other parts of the world.

Remarks made at the Celebrations of his Seventy-first Birthday Anniversary

Sanniquellie, Nimba County, 29 November 1966

It is gratifying to see the trend which these birthday celebrations have taken — the form of self-help by which the social conditions, cultural heritage and economic opportunities of the various counties are being improved.

Introductory Note

The celebration of the birthday of President Tubman assumed a national character little more than a decade after his becoming President of Liberia. The people of Liberia soon realized that it was not a sufficient demonstration of their affection and esteem for him as President to present him with mere personal gifts. Every county soon seized the occasion of his birthday to embark upon one or several self-help projects, each county by turn competing to excel the activities of the last birthday anniversary. President Tubman thanked the people of Nimba County for the observance of his birthday. Being further in the reflective mood which birthdays tend to induce, he expressed a few profound sentiments on his long tenure, both in terms of his earthly existence and as President of Liberia. Would the people of Liberia consider his own feelings on this matter and permit him to retire to private life? It seemed unlikely that they would permit his retirement, notwithstanding his personal feelings on the matter.

Sanniquellie, Nimba County, 29 November 1966

ONCE AGAIN I have reason to be filled with a deep sense of gratitude to my fellow countrymen and friends, particularly to the people of Nimba County who have undertaken these elaborate celebrations of my seventy-first birthday anniversary.

We are particularly grateful for the many kind things that have been said about us and our contributions to the national, industrial, educational and economic development of our country, but I assure you that this could never have been possible without the full support and co-operation of each and every one of you. Today, it is gratifying to see the trend which these celebrations have taken — the form of self-help by which the social conditions, cultural heritage and economic opportunities of the various counties are being improved. This trend indicates an intention on the part of the people of this country to participate on a voluntary basis in the development of their respective communities.

Since we first took office in 1944, there has been a change in the method of celebrating November 29th. Originally, friends would drop by from early

493

morning until late at night with a bottle of champagne, or just a card to extend birthday greetings. Later, in 1957, Vice-President and Mrs. Tolbert sought our consent to entertain us at a picnic at their Bensonville home. This kind gesture of the Tolberts seemed to have sparked off a chain reaction which spread to the various counties, and we have been the recipient of the consideration of the citizens and residents of the counties of Grand Bassa, Maryland, Sinoe, Lofa (then Western Province), Grand Cape Mount and Montserrado. The presentations made on these occasions were originally of a personal nature, but the trend changed in 1963 from durable personal gifts to those of an impersonal, cultural and monumental value designed by the givers to stand as a shining example of their expressions of values for the future.

Today, we are privileged to observe the first celebration, after three score years and ten, in the first of the recently constituted new counties – Nimba. This young but progressive County of Nimba, with its natural wealth and energetic human resources, has added to the significant and valued gifts of an educational and cultural nature another set of gifts of fundamental importance, namely: the Administration Building and Annex at Sanniquellie which they named Tubman, the Guest Lodge at the St. John River Bridge, which they also named Tubman, the Paramount Chief Toweh Clinic at Tappita, the Park, which they have also named Tubman, the Nimba County Silver Band, a county electric organ and the construction of the main Administration Building and Clinic, to be completed later. Of particular importance and significance is the gift by the foreign employees of LAMCO of a school built by them which they have called the Open Door Elementary School to serve the children of Nimba County as a token of their good wishes and felicitations on the occasion of this birthday. The Lebanese Community here has also contributed a Silver Band as an expression of their appreciation for the protection accorded to them by Government. The Government, the people of Liberia and I myself deeply appreciate this gesture of co-operation and thoughtfulness on the part of our friends and I thank them in this public manner for their contribution toward the educational development of the youth of Nimba County.

For all of these civic projects we salute and congratulate Superintendent Farngalo, the citizens and residents of this county and all others who contributed to them, and we hope that they will remain a perpetual testimony to your thoughtfulness and an inspiration to the young people of this young county.

Apart from this new attempt to rebuild our social system, which we hope will provide a source of reflective thinking for future generations, the spirit of self-help, genuinely generated from within and among the people themselves, has carried along with it marked evidences of economic progress. We hope that as this new trend becomes deeply rooted in the thoughts and actions of the people it will culminate in the formation of co-operative businesses throughout the country and further economic development and progress. If this is accomplished November 29th will have taken on a new meaning in fostering greater economic progress and co-operation.

We cannot now accept or take credit for this new trend, but we have undaunted faith in the ability of the Liberian people to do for themselves those things they most value, and we hope that hereafter, regardless of social, political or philosophical outlook, and while we recognize the values and practices of other people and nations as symbols of their different concepts, we will earnestly seek to encourage every citizen of this country to respect first and foremost those things that are basically Liberian.

The celebration of this birthday by the Superintendent, his Official Council and the people of Nimba occurs during the throes of a general election for the election of a President, a Vice-President, Members of the House of Representatives and one-half of the Senate. The people of Nimba seem to realize this, for they have presented a resolution reaffirming their previous resolution that we accept a sixth term of office. These must therefore be active and anxious days for all the politicians of our country.

The people of our nation, from every county and territory, began three months after the last Inauguration to bring in Resolutions and Manifestoes requesting me to succeed myself for a sixth term of office and have made similar requests of the Vice-President.

For three and a half years I made no reply, nor indicated whether I would or would not accede to their request and call. In my last Inaugural Address I expressed the hope that it would be the last Inauguration for me. The people of Liberia have been tolerant, kind, considerate and even indulgent towards me; they have given me more honours and privileges and consideration than any other citizen has received since the founding of our nation, and there is no price that I could pay to compensate them for such extraordinary, unparalleled and unprecedented affection and support.

Some of the policies which we enunciated and have been trying to demonstrate during these years were revolutionary and met with turbulent and vicious opposition from some quarters, but the body and mass of the people of the Country, together with the Legislature and leaders of thought, were so greatly in favour of these policies that the small group of opponents could hardly be seen or felt. I refer in particular to the Unification and Open Door Policies.

A period of twenty-two years is a generation, it is almost a quarter of a century and it is extraordinary that a single citizen should have had the preference and consideration of his fellow citizens to control the administration of the affairs of Government as its representative citizen for this duration; and more than this, that they should request and demand that he continue in office for a further period of time. There are many aspects to this question, one of which is the principle of Democracy; another is the right of all citizens to enjoy the responsibilities and privileges of attaining the highest office in the gift of the people.

There is also the matter of the physical and mental strain that I have carried for the past twenty-two years; entering World War II as a belligerent, participating in the peace negotiations, being involved in the revolutionary onslaught prevailing in most countries since World War II, the emergence to independence of African States and the political changes taking place in Africa as well as the advancement of science and technology — all of which imposed on the President the responsibility of shaping and directing the course that Government should and ought to take in this new epochal era.

I am so indebted to the people of our land that I could not, under any circumstances, make my answer to them a definite NO, but I think it is due to them, to you and to me that I make mention of these responsibilities and burdens, and tell them that if they would relieve me of these responsibilities by nominating another as my successor I should be happy. I mention this so as to give you an opportunity to think it over from my point of view; and perhaps at the Unification Council in Bassa next month we could meet and agree to suggest someone as my successor, whatever course we see fit, as members of the True Whig Party.

The census has been published and whilst it has not been approved by the Legislature it is obvious that the new counties are entitled to additional representation in the House of Representatives. In the meantime, I shall recommend to the Legislature in my Annual Message that each of the new counties be allocated two additional seats in the House of Representatives, effective as of the forthcoming quadrennial elections.

Lastly, I would like to pay special tribute to Superintendent Farngalo and the people of Nimba County for the lavish and extraordinary entertainment they have accorded us and our guests for the past few days. We sincerely appreciate their consideration of our every wish and say to them a fond Thank you.

To the President and the Members of the Board of Directors of LAMCO and the General Manager, staff and employees of this company I again wish to express my gratitude, as well as that of the people of this country, for the co-operation afforded Superintendent Farngalo and his associates during the preparations for these celebrations and for your assistance in providing housing and entertainment for a large number of the guests. This type of co-operation between foreign concessions and local administration is praise-worthy, and we hope that the friendly relationship now existing will continue to grow in the years ahead.

Special thanks are due to our friend, brother and colleague, His Excellency Felix Houphouet Boigny, President of the Ivory Coast, who has designated His Excellency M. Coulibary, President of the Economic and Social Council of the Ivory Coast and Treasurer of the Party as his personal Representative at these celebrations, and I extend to Mr. Coulibary and his eleven-man delegation a sincere and fraternal welcome. We trust that their stay with us will be pleasant and indicative of our deep feeling for their illustrious and eminent President, and my personal friend, and the people of the Ivory Coast.

We also extend a hearty welcome to our many foreign friends, who have come all the way from across the Atlantic to join with us in the celebration of our 71st Anniversary, and we thank them for this warm manifestation of their feelings for us.

I have just learned that yesterday, the 28th of November was the birthday of Mrs. Farngalo, wife of the Superintendent, and on behalf of Mrs. Tubman and myself I extend to her our felicitations and would like to present her with this small token of our good wishes.

May God bless the people of Nimba County and prosper the state.

AFRICAN AFFAIRS

At the First Independence Celebration of the Republic of Guinea

Monrovia, 2 October 1959

Our relationship with Guinea goes beyond mere abstractions.

Introductory Note

When the Republic of Guinea celebrated its first independence anniversary, President Tubman paid tribute to President Seku Touré's heroism when he voted 'NO' to France's proposal to have Guinea remain a member of the French Community. Liberia, President Tubman noted, could well appreciate the lonely position of the Republic of Guinea at that time when the Government of Charles de Gaulle, in retaliation, undertook certain austere measures to reduce Guinea to abject poverty. He therefore assured President Touré and his people of the moral support and strength which Guinea could draw upon in such adverse circumstances from the other African states, and that Liberia would give it all the encouragement it needed and strengthen further the bonds of friendship which Liberia, in many practical ways, had always shown to Guinea.

Monrovia, 2 October 1959

COMPARED WITH past centuries, our twentieth century involves urgent problems in living, in self-help, self-determination and national consciousness which every thinking man must recognize. The once inert, subjected peoples of Africa are fast acquiring Western methods of education, commerce, industry and even war; and are restive in their demand for a just share in the prerequisites of a refined and cultured life, long denied them by the cruel principle of might makes right.

In this new outlook, they have turned to the provisions of the Liberian Constitution, Thomas Jefferson and the American Declaration of Independence to assuage their grief in the knowledge that 'all men are created equal, that they are endowed by their Creator with certain inalienable rights such as life, liberty and the pursuit of happiness'; and by these eternal principles have proceeded to acquire the fundamental rights to choose their own governors and to frame a government for themselves. They are determined to revise their points of view and the shibboleths on which they are based.

Since we are striving for peace, and the peace of the whole world, it will not be amiss to call attention to this simple fact of history: that expansion and peace are incompatible principles.

The doctrine of territorial expansion as a political policy had its genesis in greed and in warlike pretensions; it has invariably generated friction among nations and thereby jeopardized the peace of the world. We therefore appeal

499

to all men and nations to lend their efforts to the attainment of freedom and independence for all peoples, in the fervent hope that our labours at the United Nations may not have been undertaken in vain. Let us strive to make the idea implicit in the brotherhood of man significant and meaningful to the extent that men may be induced to convert their swords into plowshares and spears into pruning hooks.

In passing, may I observe that there is enough living space in the world for the entire population and sufficient material potentialities for all nations to share equally. The emancipation of Africa should then be conceded as a valuable contribution to world peace and to the assurance of abundant life for all mankind.

One year ago the world awoke to find that a new nation was born. The Government and people of Liberia were jubilant at the thought that the ninth state had been added to the constellation of African nations. By signs, symbols and diplomatic missions, and by concrete undertakings the people of Liberia demonstrated their goodwill for the new Republic of Guinea, and welcomed to this capital the courageous, bold and brilliant leader and distinguished President, Sekou Touré.

At that time many thought that circumstances would force a reversal of this decision and a return to the *status quo*.

We of Liberia did not share that view, for we had learned the hard way, and from bitter experience, that it is more honourable to be poor in freedom and political independence than to possess all the wealth of the world in servile fearfulness and political domination.

Out of the crucible of time has emerged this new nation, the Republic of Guinea, whose first anniversary of political independence we are gathered here to celebrate.

President Sekou Touré and the people of Guinea when they voted 'no', evinced that rare genius and attribute of making correct decisions spoken of by Napoleon Bonaparte, one of the greatest Frenchmen who ever lived, when he declared, 'The rarest attribute among generals is two o'clock in the morning courage, that courage which, amidst the most unforeseen events, leaves full freedom of judgment and promptness of decision; nothing, nothing is so difficult as to decide.'

That we have come to join you, Mr. Ambassador, to share the joys of this day is an index of the high esteem, admiration and neighbourliness the Government and people of Liberia have for the President, Government and people of Guinea. As an earnest indication of our friendship we have sent as our personal representatives to your celebrations in Guinea, the Honourable C. L. Simpson, former Vice-President, and the Honourable J. W. Garber, Attorney-General of Liberia, bearing felicitations to the President and people of Guinea. As a further gesture of our close ties with the Government and people of Guinea, we have proclaimed this first anniversary of your independence a national holiday in Liberia.

In the twelve months of independence President Touré has improved the economy of his country, planned for a wider diffusion of education and technical training, and assured the women of Guinea equality with men in public life. These are landmarks of greatness and statesmanship, on which I congratulate him.

Our relationship with Guinea goes beyond mere abstractions, as you may see from the large population of Guineans in Liberia, and we express the hope that no unforeseen event will loose the ties that bind our two peoples together in peace and tranquillity.

As evidence of the solidarity of our two peoples, we may cite the emergence at the Sanniquellie Conference between the leaders of Liberia, Ghana and Guinea of the proposal for the Community of Independent African States as a pattern of our unity. It is our hope that through this Community the present arrangements which make some Africans French subjects, some British subjects, some Portuguese and Spanish will be relegated to the limbo of forgotten adventures. Through this Community we hope to ensure to non-independent peoples a hearing in the chancelleries of the Western world; and for ourselves a form of independence comparable to and ranking with other nations of mankind. Our struggle is for the total liberation of Africa. Let eternal vigilance, as the price of liberty, be our watchword!

Your Excellency, please convey to your illustrious President and my distinguished friend, Sekou Touré, expressions of our heartfelt greetings on this your First Natal Day, and assurances of our continued fervent wishes for abundant success during these festivities, emphasizing the fact that the Government and people of Liberia are morally and practically with him in his determination to secure for his people the blessings of life, liberty and happiness. We sincerely pray that God may endow him with long life, prosperity and internal solidarity and peace.

Broadcast to the Nation on Africa Freedom Day

Monrovia, 13 April 1961

Africa Freedom Day should remind and inspire us to renew our struggle for the total liberation of all Africa.... we forge ahead knowing that our cause is just.

Introductory Note

On April 15, 1958, ten independent African states met in Accra, Ghana to deliberate on the future of Africa. Too many African states were still not free. The world took note of this coming together of different African states to work out some concerted action. They created a moral force whose impact was so great that the colonial powers saw a day of reckoning. That nearly ten more African states became independent two years later can be attributed to the new African voice of freedom, which vibrated throughout the world and helped to pave the way for Africa's freedom. To commemorate the occasion, the fifteenth of April of each year was agreed upon by that first meeting to be observed annually as Africa Freedom Day with proper ceremony. President Tubman spoke about the new Africa in the making of new world order.

Monrovia, 13 April 1961

AFRICAN FREEDOM YEAR has undoubtedly had a great impact not only on the Continent of Africa and its peoples, but on the whole world. It is therefore, highly significant that its observance this year is to be followed shortly by an important Conference of African States on May 8th.

It is too early to predict with any degree of certainty what the outcome of this Conference will be, but certainly one may hope that a greater measure of understanding and a more positive attitude for co-operation and collaboration towards mutual ends will emerge. Africa Freedom Day should remind and inspire us to renew our struggle for the total liberation of all Africa. We cannot now fail those who are still the victims of oppression and of sundry ways of life incompatible with the dignity and humanity of the human being.

The passionate urge for liberty and freedom and the desire for peace among mankind are ideals with which men have toyed throughout the ages. And as we see what may fittingly be regarded as the end of an era in the history of the African Continent, a period which has brought mixed blessings, we have reached another era in which the ideal of self-determination for millions of people can be assured and the opportunity of planning and working for a better future envisaged and given free scope.

We approach the observance of Africa Freedom Day this year in the hope that the leaders of Africa will continue to consolidate their efforts in guiding and giving the unselfish leadership to their nations, and that these peoples will work unceasingly for the cause of liberty and freedom and devote themselves unswervingly to the ideals which have inspired nationalism all over Africa and the world. We approach this Freedom Day forgetful of the bitter past and resolved to look to the splendid and challenging opportunities of the future for Africa and the world in general.

Despite the pleasing transformations which have already taken place, there is yet much to be accomplished before absolute independence is achieved. But the stage has been set and the point of no return has long been passed. We forge ahead, therefore, knowing that our cause is just and believing that our struggle follows the historic trend of nations great and small.

May the events of the present and past years invigorate, inspire and fill us with faith in the ultimate triumph of the cause of truth and justice, so that even in an area where some ideological and political theories still constitute a deplorable anachronism, we may yet hope that a change of heart and attitude will eventually come about.

Let us hope and pray that African leaders will continue to work fervently for a greater degree of understanding, goodwill and peace among themselves in the economic, educational, spiritual and political sense. In this spirit let us look forward with hope for a new Africa and for a better day for all its peoples.

Welcome Address to the Heads of State and Governments and Delegates to the Conference of African Heads of State

Monrovia, 8 May 1961

In our long struggle for respect for the sovereignty and independence of all states, and for the total liberation of the peoples of the continent of Africa, we have come to believe that unity, understanding and tolerance are the principal means of achieving and perpetuating our objectives . . . We are striving for cohesion, for a changed social political order, for independent states to retain their own way of life.

Introductory Note

In 1961 the Congo crisis threatened to unbalance political stability in Africa and to encourage regional alignments of independent African States. President Tubman, seeing the potential dangers to African unity which all Africans have set their hearts upon as the ultimate goal for continental advancement, sponsored a meeting of independent African States in Monrovia to find a way out of the alarming situation confronting Africa. It was a major step which led to the formation of the Organization of African Unity in 1963.

Monrovia, 8 May 1961

IT IS with a sense of deep humility and profound personal and public pleasure that I welcome, on behalf of the Government and people of Liberia, our brothers and friends from the other sections of Mother Africa. I welcome you with the sincerity and warmth of a brother and member of the African family.

Although faced with varying political vicissitudes, the sponsors of this conference have never been unmindful of their responsibilities, as individuals and as a group, for the total liberation of their continent from the debasing state of national dependence and serfdom to the exhilarating status of political independence and equality. In an earnest endeavour, therefore, to resolve some of the disturbing issues of our times, we thought it expedient to request a congress of this kind, to which all Heads of African States were invited. Your presence here today is indicative of the common interest we hold in the purpose of our gathering. How generously and enthusiastically you have responded to this invitation.

We live in a period of conferences. But this conference, we hope, will be labelled the Stocktaking Conference of 1961. We do not want our endeavours to be construed in the light of personal rivalries or ambition for recognition or leadership. We have no desire to seek fame for ourselves, nor is this conference intended to undermine the conclusions of previous conferences; nor will we fail to endorse and support such decisions of other conferences which we know to be in the best interests of Africa and the world. Rather, all that we seek to achieve is to bring all African leaders to reason together towards determining a consensus in the interest of peace and better understanding, and to endeavour to provide a climate in which large as well as small states will participate as equal partners in building a new Africa and a new world order.

In our long struggle for respect for the sovereignty and independence of all states, and for the total liberation of the peoples of the Continent, we have come to believe that unity, understanding and tolerance are the principal means of achieving and perpetuating our objectives. Unity, therefore, should be the watch-word of this conference.

Within this frame of reference, we can seek to utilize our potentialities, our combined forces, our best talents and our opportunities to more useful and practical advantages; we can employ the knowledge of our common racial background, the history of our common struggles and the fact of the identity of our aspirations and struggles to work towards a better and securer future for the present and future generations; we can stand on the ideals and ideas which now find unanimity among us as a prelude to seeking possible solutions to those in which we differ and resolving those problems which plague us and mankind; we can come together, we can deliberate, we can reason together, we can plan and work together and thus engender mutual understanding and establish lasting friendships. In all these endeavours, nothing must be permitted to stand in the way of our attaining these objectives.

For these and other reasons, the sponsors of this conference realize that as in military operations, after a major success in battle is achieved, good strategy dictates the necessity for the coming together of the generals and other arms of the various services for conferences and discussions on the causes of the success; to consider the mistakes that were made, to find solutions to the problems involved and to lay the foundation and plans from which to proceed and to follow, to consolidate their position so as to enable them to continue their struggles with confidence and certainty for complete victory; so this also obtains in all well organized civic affairs.

We have assembled here today, as representatives of African States, to consider the successes that have been ours over the last five years, to discuss some of the pressing problems that confront us, to seek solutions to these problems and to prepare for pushing forward toward the cause we represent, the cause of African freedom, to the goal of engendering a better understanding among ourselves and the nations of the earth, to pose suggestions for easing world tension and to formulate plans aimed at reconciling and bridging as fast as possible the gap between conflicting international ideologies which have created tensions and persist in dividing the world into opposing and apparently irreconcilable political blocs.

Just as the interdependence of nations has never been more apparent than at present, so too the fear of annihilation has never been more ominous than today. We sincerely believe that African States should have a mission of new dimensions to the old world, otherwise our struggle for liberation in an atomic age will be more difficult. We should be the harbingers and proponents of a changed world order. And to do this effectively we need to shoulder our task without personal ambition but solely in the interest of the greatest good to the greatest number. In this light we must voice our concern that should a nuclear war occur it would virtually destroy mankind, and those nations which recently won their freedom and independence would be affected beyond measure, for their independence would have been emphemeral.

It should be crystal clear to every leader that Africans cannot live in isolation if they expect to allay suspicion, fear and tension. The idea of *primus inter pares*, first among equals, is destructive to African unity and peace. Tolerance, good faith, honour, good neighbourliness, justice, equality and mutual respect are the most vital constituents of unity and solidarity.

The sense of oneness should be deeply rooted in the breast of every African. But the toils of circumstances and ambition can make it difficult for us to fit ourselves into the picture of a unified Africa, the foundation for which we hope will be laid before this conference closes.

Recent trends in human affairs reveal an insatiable tendency to short cuts in the achievement of social progress. In the process men lose their poise and self-control and become enmeshed in enmity, rancour and revenge, and in the conflict and confusion which have characterized the state of human affairs in the world.

It is our heart's most fervent wish that the states of Africa, individually and collectively, will set a new pattern of social and political behaviour and thus work out a changed social reconstruction. Whether this pattern takes the form of democracy, socialism, communism or African nationalism should be determined by the voluntary choice of the people affected. Whatever may be its form, it should ever be dedicated to the peace and prosperity of all peoples in all lands.

Africa, once considered the cradle of world civilization, can by our combined efforts again become the pivot of a changed social-political order directed to world peace, in which faith in moral and spiritual forces would supersede the fear of even atom bombs.

Up to the present, the greatness of states has been based on military power and possessions rather than on justice and morality, and hence their conceptions of right and wrong have been governed generally by expediency. The world has, as a consequence, been in perpetual turmoil of wars and rumours of wars. If this mistaken conception is adopted by African States as a policy it is bound to rupture good relationships and the mutual co-operation we so ardently seek.

According to some recent writers who have given much thought to world politics, we learn that a nation's greatness lies neither in the abundance of its possessions nor in the strength of its arms. In this connection, Straus Houpe writes: 'A people finds greatness in its response to the historical challenge – by how it manages to harness its strivings to the aspirations of the age. Thus to be great is to fulfil a promise that surpasses the national interest.' The greatness of the new Africa should be demonstrated in the creative use of the forces at our disposal in solving the great problems of our time and of ensuring a new order out of the present disorder.

We have met as representatives of free, sovereign and independent States to design policies to secure the perpetuity of our national existence, friendship and amity among ourselves and all peoples. May our deliberations be richly blessed and so yield abundant harvests in the years ahead.

It is unfortunate that while we are enjoying the benefits of freedom our brothers in Angola, Mozambique, Algeria, South Africa and other parts of this great continent are still smarting under the heel of oppression and tyranny; their fight for freedom is our fight. They must know in unmistakable terms that we stand behind them and will not desert them by the plans we evolve for their assistance.

Our deliberations at this conference will be a mere rhetorical exercise if we do not seek to formulate principles of conduct which will be realistic, rational and an effective contribution to the eradication of the last vestige of domination and social inequality in Africa and the world.

There is not a man present who is undisturbed by recent events in the Congo and Angola and the dread and despair those events arouse in all men of goodwill. After mature reflection upon the gravity of those events and their consequences, and convinced that their possible solution is not within the competence of any one nation, or of a few Heads of State or Governments, a conference of *all* Heads of State was considered the most competent authority in the present circumstances.

I come now to the question of leadership of Africa. On this issue I repeat what I said in an Independence Day Message delivered on July 26, 1958, when there were fewer independent African States. 'In this connection I have observed that there seem to be three schools of thought on this subject. There are those who feel that Liberia should assume leadership based on the fact that she is the oldest African Republic and is riper in political experience; but it will require more than age and political experience to assume leadership of Africa. There are others who hold that Ghana should assume that rôle because she is physically more developed and embraces larger territories. It will require more than development and larger territory to assume leadership of Africa. And there are yet those who opine that Egypt with its rich traditions dating back to the remotest antiquity, should do so. It will require more than rich traditions of antiquity. It will require, in my opinion, the aggregate of all three of these and more besides. It will require the aggregate of the best that is in all, compounded in such a manner as to represent the divisibility of Africa indivisible.'

Excellencies, on the long road of human evolution from international disorder and confusion to systems of global institutional co-operation, the United Nations, we believe, offers the best hope and the means whereby we can strengthen the ties that bind nations and preserve those things which are necessary for peaceful progress among mankind.

The turbulent speed of events which have transformed the political status of our continent, imposes upon us the responsibility of setting up a new guide-post toward an international society, buttressed by wisdom and knowledge adequate to overcome the failures, pitfalls and fumblings that brought the world to the rim of the abyss.

In the fifteen years of its existence, which is indeed a relatively short period in the life of a nation, the United Nations has brought together ninety-nine independent states to deliberate as equals in a meaningful partnership to implement and enforce decisions where necessary, and by so doing has averted wars.

By the adherence to the principle of self-determination and the fundamental principle of human rights it has accelerated the liberation of many countries in Asia, Africa and Europe from colonial status. While we do not underwrite every item of its activities in the fifteen years of its existence,

we feel that it is entitled to our support and the affirmation of its fundamental tenets. Everything must be done to ensure its continuity, and nothing
must be done by any state or group of states to undermine its great objectives.

Some of the leading considerations this conference should discuss revolve
around such issues as:

1. Contributions of the African States to world peace.
2. Threats to peace and stability in Africa.
3. Promotion of better understanding, unity and co-operation among
   African States.
4. Development of a permanent machinery to provide consultation among
   the African States.
5. Formulation of a general policy attitude toward peoples striving for
   independence.
6. The situation in the Congo.
7. Working out general principles for the settlement of frontier and
   border disputes which may arise from the emergence of independent
   states.

The unsettled state of affairs in the Republic of the Congo is a matter of
grave concern to all African nationalists. The presence of the soldiers of
many of the African States as well as other nations in that country in an
endeavour to assist in preserving peace and keeping the country from being
torn by civil war, is an eloquent testimony that we cherish freedom and
independence and are determined to fight for it if needs be. And so we hope
that eventually conditions in the Congo will return to normal, so that its
peoples may enjoy the blessings of liberty and freedom in common with the
rest of mankind. This situation should be one of the items of our deliberation.

We are striving for cohesion, for a changed social political order, for
individual states to retain their own way of life, united by mutual exchange
of peoples, goods and ideas in the common defence of our heritage, and for a
just and lasting peace.

Excellencies, this conference will, I doubt not, concern itself with all
declarations and resolutions of previous conferences relating to this
continent. The decisions of previous conferences of African States, including
the Casablanca Conference, should be studied, and such aspects which
require more time and perhaps conscientious study referred to a subsequent
conference.

This suggestion reminds me of an incident recorded in the sacred history
of the Christians where it is reported that on one occasion the disciples of
Christ reported to Him that they saw one casting out devils in His Name
who was not one of his followers. Christ replied, 'Forbid him not; for there
is no man which shall do a miracle in my name, that can lightly speak evil
of me. For he that is not against us is on our side.' Thus although previous
conferences have convened at different times, the general aims have not been
entirely contradictory, nor are they completely inimical to the basic objectives we are now trying to pursue.

Excellencies, we should be guided by history and manifest justice so that
we do not repeat the mistakes that laid the foundation for the intervention
of great European states in the affairs of other states. What we should do is

to strive to strengthen the independence of all states regardless of their alignments into communities or commonwealths, for no one can say with any degree of truth: 'I am holier than thou.' We must remember that nations grow from lower to higher forms of association.

History has clearly demonstrated that political union, as opposed to political domination, can be more rapidly achieved where there is a community of economic interest, cultural cross-fertilization as well as free social intercourse and association.

It would probably be unreasonable to expect that we can, at this Conference, work out a complete pattern of mutual action in this respect. However, we trust that agreement can be reached on the guiding principles which would enable technical experts representing us to establish proposals for economic co-operation and collaboration as well as the establishment of common identities toward which we may strive in the immediate future. In this way, we believe, steps can be taken now to reach goals which will enable each member country to make a distinctive contribution to lasting, natural unity in Africa.

Again, Excellencies, I welcome you and may our deliberations lead to a consensus of values and methods that will constitute the social, economic, cultural, political and moral foundation of a changed world.

On the Occasion of the First Anniversary of the Independence of the Federation of Nigeria

Monrovia, 12 September 1961

Without doubt the independence of the Federation of Nigeria added a new significance to the history of nationalism in Africa.

Introductory Note

The independence of the Federal Republic of Nigeria was a high-water mark in the struggle of Africa for self-determination. It was the largest African nation to overthrow the yoke of European colonialism. The impact of the occasion was far reaching, and added greater momentum to the drive for African independence. President Tubman noted with pride the new ray of hope which the independence of the Federal Republic of Nigeria created in the breast of freedom-loving people in Africa and in the world. The old world order was fast crumbling away.

Monrovia, 12 September 1961

ON OCTOBER 1, 1960, the Federation of Nigeria attained its independence and became the largest, most populous and richest country of the West African states to do so. That even brought unbounded enthusiasm and great rejoicing to the nation's 36,000,000 inhabitants, to the free peoples of Africa, to those who were still bidding for their independence, and to the peoples of the entire world. It was an occasion of great jubilation and the cause for a new upsurge of hope to those who are still in oppression and denied the right of self-determination. Without doubt, the independence of the Federation of Nigeria added a new significance to the history of nationalism in Africa.

From that date up until the present, ideological differences have not been permitted to deter the leaders from combining their forces with those of other peace-loving countries in the fight for the total liberation of Africa. Simultaneously they have busied themselves with the more important problems of making Nigeria internally strong by trying to create a sense of common identity and working toward a more productive economy. At national and international conferences these leaders have proved themselves men of action, stated their national aspirations and goals to the world, and expressed in no uncertain terms their dedication to work unswervingly for the success of the Federation of Nigeria.

Already statesmen of the stature of Dr. Nnamdi Atikiwe, Sir Alhaji Abubakar Tafawa Balewa and others have made the history of the Federation remarkable by their superb and statesmanlike performances. I foresee nothing but a brilliant future of progress and prosperity for the nation.

It was my privilege last year to pay a State Visit to this great country upon the invitation of Her Majesty, Queen Elizabeth II. That visit will always be a vivid reminder of the identity of the histories of our two nations, of the aspirations we hold in common, and of the strong links of friendship which can be forged between the two countries. I came away greatly impressed, utterly convinced and highly hopeful for the future of our continent and with the makings of a new design for the possibility of unity in my imagination. Since then the Federal Prime Minister's presence in Liberia and my own contacts with the Governor-General and other men of eminence in Nigeria have added new dimensions to my hope.

On the occasion of the first independence anniversary, I am happy to send hearty felicitations on behalf of the Government, people of Liberia and myself. May the years ahead bring our peoples and nations closer together into firmer bonds of friendship, and may the Federation of Nigeria grow stronger and stronger.

Speech delivered upon his Return to Monrovia from the Lagos Conference and State Visits to the Federation of the Cameroun and the Republic of Gabon

Monrovia, 16 February 1962

A new day in international relations has arrived and men of all climes are seeing in it the pathway to true human brotherhood, peace and goodwill among the nations of the earth.

Introductory Note

In January 1962 President Tubman attended the Lagos Conference at which twenty-one African Heads of State were also present. This conference was a follow-up to a previous conference which was convened in Monrovia in May 1961. The African independent states were then discovering means of common understanding of problems created by the transition to independence from colonial rule. The Congo crisis had divided them into two blocs which became known as the Casablanca Group and the Monrovia Group. The Lagos Conference was intended to bring both groups together to arrive at a common understanding to their mutual problems. The Lagos Conference further paved the way for the historic Addis Ababa Conference in May, 1963 which saw the birth of the Organization of African Unity. Out of this conference came further preparatory work for a Charter of African Unity on which the new Organization of African Unity Charter was based; a permanent secretariat and the setting up of various committees to undertake common tasks with the co-operation of all member states of the Organization. Liberia played a rôle in all of these matters. The period evinced a high degree of optimism and President Tubman echoed in this speech, as he did in several other speeches, a new spirit of internationalism heightened by State Visits as a result of invitations extended to him to visit two West African States at the termination of the Lagos Conference.

Monrovia, 16 February 1962

ONCE AGAIN I have returned from participating in a historic meeting of our continent combined with making State Visits to African States. Once again your sense of patriotism and loyalty and your devotion to and affection for us have moved you to give such a warm and enthusiastic reception on our behalf.

I am deeply touched, as I have been on other occasions, and greatly moved by all the sentiments expressed and the cordial welcome which you have accorded us. God helps us all to reap the fruits of our love of country and our sacrifices and to dispense our obligations in our various capacities by accepting with heroism the concomitant responsibilities, which we must all shoulder to ensure the maintenance and perpetuity of our proud heritage, the Republic of Liberia, and to work unceasingly for her welfare. And so I wish to assure you that I am indeed happy to be back home that we may join our forces in the national task which lies before us.

The Lagos Conference of the Heads of African and Malagasy States convened on a note of high optimism, was conducted in an atmosphere of harmonious deliberation and ended with deep satisfaction in the results achieved. It was a meeting which brought together leaders of twenty-one states, the single largest conference ever to be convoked in Africa. The theme, 'Let us build a new Africa' contained in the opening address by the Governor-General of the Federation of Nigeria was so well received that it pervaded the entire course of the meeting. Our hope for achieving this great objective hinges upon our belief in and support of the Charter which is the embodiment of the Monrovia and Lagos Conferences, and our decision to set up a Permanent Secretariat which would be the instrument by which our greater objectives would be achieved.

Basically, we have always been opposed to the formation of blocs and groups; we remain committed to this proportion. When the group of states known later as the 'Casablanca Bloc' decided to meet with a limited number of African states to discuss the Congo crisis, I was invited to attend that conference. Two considerations, however, stood in the way of my accepting the invitation.

Firstly, only a limited number of African states had been invited. Because of this I felt that the conference would have the tendency to divide the African states into blocs and since the question centred on the Congo it seemed to me that at least those states with troops in the Congo under the aegis of the United Nations Command should have been invited.

Secondly, the fact that it was near the end of the year and I was busy with the national budget for presentation to the Legislature, which was then in session, made my attendance at that time impracticable.

As you know only too well, the Monrovia Conference came into being at the request of a number of states, including English- and French-speaking nations, that desired to tackle in a realistic manner some of the vexing problems which independence posed for the twenty-eight African nations. In a larger context its objective was to invite every African Head of State and Government to view and discuss in a frank and friendly manner some of these thorny problems with the ultimate objective of paving the way for a much needed unity in things economic, cultural, technical, educational, scientific and social which, in the world of 'divide and rule' had hitherto been impossible.

When therefore, I convened the conference in May of last year, three representatives of the Casablanca Group — Ghana, Guinea and Mali were asked to be co-sponsors. Also invited were the French-speaking nations of the Ivory Coast, Cameroun, and Togoland, and the English-speaking states, Nigeria and Liberia. Here, conceivably, was an attempt to get a representative cross-section of the continent which would constitute the beginning of a genuine union. Of the states invited all accepted, with the exception of Ghana, whose President felt that the Casablanca Group had

covered all the grounds which the present conference, the Monrovia Conference, was seeking to explore. Thus it was that when the Monrovia
Conference was convoked in May of last year the Casablanca Group failed
to attend.

What the Monrovia Conference accomplished substantially is well known
to you – a decision for a corps of experts from participating nations to meet in
Dakar to draw up a blueprint based on economic, educational, technical,
cultural co-operation and collaboration to be presented to the next meeting
in Lagos in mid-January. The proposals were presented at the recent meeting and received unanimous approval. With the stage now well set, it remains for the proposals to get the necessary implementation so as to start
the machinery in motion in the direction of our desired objectives. As far as
I know, all the member nations of this conference have pledged their moral
and financial support to advance these ends.

When it comes to the question of the attendance of Foreign Ministers to
deliberate with Heads of State and Government at a conference, it is my
considered opinion that such a step is mistaken and indeed obscures the
spirit which the conference is seeking to achieve. Only when a Chief of State
is ill and unable to attend would I consent for a representative lower than a
Prime Minister to sit and debate with me or other Chiefs of State and
Government, within certain limitations, in a conference of Heads of State
and Government. It is clear that the Casablanca Group did not intend to
attend the Lagos Conference because of considerations which it is not within
my province to explore at this time.

Unfortunately, however, their non-attendance was blamed on the failure
of the Lagos Conference to invite the Algerian National Government,
although neither the Chiefs of State nor Government indicated their desire
to attend, merely suggesting that they would be represented by their Foreign
Ministers, a step which we considered irregular and one which was entirely
repugnant to the participants of the Lagos Conference. If agreement had
been reached for the Foreign Ministers to attend and debate issues with the
Heads of State and Government, I would not have attended the conference,
because at the Accra Conference I was the only Chief of State to attend
when the others failed and refused to be present. I did not intend to subject
myself again to any such humiliation.

Despite all this, the Lagos Conference, I am pleased to say, went on record
as accomplishing a major feat in the history of the Continent by bringing
together twenty-one Heads of State and Government, formulating a Charter
for African Unity, presenting proposals for the setting up of a Permanent
Secretariat and accepting the proposals of the Dakar Meeting of experts for
economic, educational, technical and cultural enterprises. By unanimous
decision the next meeting is scheduled to be held in Addis Ababa, Ethiopia.

Upon invitations received from two Heads of African states, we made the
following State Visits after the Lagos Conference:

To the Federal Republic of the Cameroun from February 1 to 5. This
visit entailed flying from Lagos to Yaounde, capital of the Cameroun, a
flight of three hours. At Yaounde we were met by His Excellency, President
Ahmadu Ahidjo, officials of government, members of the Diplomatic Corps,
the Liberian Ambassador and Mrs. Marshall and his staff, and dancing,
clapping, singing and cheering citizens of all ranks. Military honours and
every courtesy were given us. The enthusiastic welcome, the gracious hospi-

tality and the general friendliness of the people of the Cameroun made our stay here memorable.

From Yaounde we flew to Buea, a distance of about one hour's flying time, then back to Yaounde the same day. The following morning we left Yaounde for Garoua again by air where the gallant display of 1,000 horses and their proud and skilful riders were reminiscent of the days of chivalry. The colourful ceremony of horses and their riders was a glorious and moving spectacle, and reminded one of the traditions which embellish all ancient civilizations. Here President Ahidjo took formal leave of me after the signing of a Joint Communiqué between us. The following morning we flew to Douala, economic capital of the Cameroun Republic, two hours and fifteen minutes distant, where we were met by the Prefect of Douala and other high-ranking officials. Here every formal courtesy was paid to us and to members of my party.

For President Ahidjo I have great respect. Although he is the youngest of all the African Heads of State, he possesses great wisdom and keen perception and has a comprehensive grasp of the problems which confront the peoples of Africa. I have been with him at work at several conferences and have the utmost respect for his ability. We came away with our respect and admiration deepened, and with great faith in the future progress of the Cameroun.

Next, we visited the Republic of Gabon, from February 5 to 8.

We flew from Douala to Libreville, Capital of the Republic of Gabon, where we spent three nights. Our reception was no less warm and enthusiastic and exceedingly friendly. President Leon Mba, the Government and people of the Republic of Gabon did everything to make our stay pleasurable, rewarding and happy and we came away with a very warm spot in our hearts for the Gabonese, who seem to have handled very successfully the question of racial integration. For in Gabon whites and blacks live as one. There are no social barriers and hence after independence was achieved, there was no difficulty about the social transition. What we saw impressed us very much. President Leon Mba is greatly loved and respected by his people for the part he played in their independence. Under his leadership the proud Gabonese are bound to make progressive strides in things economic, educational, technical and other aspects of a strong and progressive government. One indication of this rapid advancement is the fact that eighty per cent of the children of school-going age are already in school, and every effort is being made to increase the number so that in a very short time the literacy rate should be high in that nation.

Our visit to the Republic of Gabon came to an end on the eighth of February when President Leon Mba and a large crowd of officials and citizens escorted us to the wharf in Libreville where, after military honours, the President took his formal leave. A delegation of Gabonese officials led by the Foreign Minister accompanied us on board and there they took their formal leave. The ship then weighed anchor at twelve-forty-five for Douala, the next port of call.

On the 8th February we docked at Douala, the economic capital of the Federal Republic of the Cameroun, where the Prefect of the City, Camerounian officials and the Liberian Ambassador boarded the ship to pay their official courtesies.

Leaving Douala on the afternoon of the 9th we arrived in Apapa, Lagos, on the 11th instant. Here a delegation comprising the Nigerian Federal Minister of Labour, the A.D.C. and the Press Secretary to the Governor-General and the Liberian Ambassador came aboard and the Press Secretary handed me a letter from the Governor-General of the Federation of Nigeria in which he welcomed us to the shores of their city and regretted his inability to be present in person. Just before the ship left crowds lined the dock and waved and shouted as the ship slowly steamed out of port.

Our next port of call was Lomé, a beautiful city of over 72,000 inhabitants. Although the landing was difficult and involved the mammie-chair, President Sylvanus Olympio, the Liberian Ambassador and other local officials came aboard the ship and invited me to visit the city. Enthusiastic and cheering crowds greeted us wherever we went. The six-hour visit was filled with sight-seeing, receptions and an interview between President Olympio and me. I came away very much impressed with the sincerity, patriotism and dedication of the President to the cause of freedom for his people and all Africa, and by the friendliness of the Togolese.

Arriving next at Abidjan, where the ship stopped for a day and half, we received a very warm and enthusiastic reception in spite of the fact that President Houphouet-Boigny was away. The Vice-President Tboi Denise and other officials of the Government accorded us every courtesy including a state dinner, an address to the members of the CCTA and visits to a laboratory and a museum. The stop-over was spent most delightfully. When we arrived at Sassandra yesterday a group of Liberians who are residents in that city boarded the ship with the Liberian flag flying high and presented us with an address of welcome. In my reply of appreciation to them I reminded them of their obligation to be peaceful and law-abiding citizens in Sassandra so as to reflect credit upon their country as well as upon themselves, and finally told them of the many economic opportunities now in Liberia should they choose to return home.

I must mention Commandant Paul of the *S.S. General Leclerc*, his crew and the passengers in general who were very accommodating and did everything to make the voyage pleasant and enjoyable. It seemed as if everyone was anxious to make travelling conditions as pleasurable and enjoyable for us as possible. To all of them we owe a debt of gratitude, and, as an expression of my thanks for the safe voyage, I decorated the Commandant and his leading officers and awarded six gold and six bronze medals to the stewards and other helpers. It was also my pleasure to decorate some of the members of my suite for their contributions to the success of the two State Visits.

Truly, our world has shrunk, and just as science has disintegrated the barriers of space and time, so man by his inter-personal relationships must break down the hurdles to friendship, understanding, co-operation and collaboration among nations and peoples. A new day in international relations has arrived and men of all climes are seeing in it the pathway to true human brotherhood, peace and goodwill among the nations of the earth.

May Liberians everywhere continue to open wide the doors of their homes and their hearts to those who visit our shores so that they may help to hasten the reality of this human brotherhood.

Again, I thank you from the bottom of my heart for this spontaneous and enthusiastic welcome and assure you that it is good to be back home again, 'for there is no place like home'.

Broadcast to the Nation on the Eve of his Departure to the Addis Ababa Conference of the Organization of African Unity

Monrovia, 11 May 1963

Early in our evolution as a nation, the architects of our political superstruction imposed upon us the responsibility of a mission in Africa. Despite conflicting interests and the dubious vicissitudes of existence we have been able to implement that mandate to the utmost of our ability and resources; and, in our particular circumstances, in a manner unprecedented in the history of nations.

Introductory Note

The summit conference of the Organization of African Unity, about to be convened in May, 1963, was preceded by a crying need for unity. Various blocs of African states had begun to experiment in the type of unity best suited for Africa and no general agreement could be reached. At Addis Ababa there was great expectation which every African state believed would finally provide common ground for understanding and strengthening bonds of co-operation. Above all they sought an end to the growing regional competition and power struggle which tended to sow seeds as divisive as those planted by European colonizers. President Tubman pleaded that it was time that the old divisions created by the colonizers and those that were being perpetuated in novel forms by the new nations of Africa be done away with, and that unity in Africa should transcend those disruptive tendencies which were already showing signs of being harmful to Africa's future and growth.

Monrovia, 11 May 1963

WITHIN a few days I expect to leave the country for a State Visit to Ethiopia; later to attend the Conference of Heads of African and Malagasy States and Governments at the same place and thence go to Europe on a State Visit to Yugoslavia.

Before embarking upon what is now recognized as the most important and stupendous mission in the history of Africa, I avail myself of this opportunity to intimate to you some of my views on the conference and a few of the issues that I think are likely to arise and be discussed.

Very early in our evolution as a nation, the architects of our political superstructure imposed upon us the responsibility of a mission in Africa. Despite conflicting interests and the dubious vicissitudes of existence we have been able to implement that mandate to the utmost of our ability and resources; and, in our particular circumstances, in a manner unprecedented in the history of nations.

Actuated by the desire to preserve the peace of Africa, to ensure its unity in confident collaboration, and to promote the welfare of its peoples, free of the convulsions to which our age appears to be heir, we go to the conference with joy and satisfaction in the fact that we leave behind us a people united in heart, purpose, and high resolve to protect, maintain and foster anew the prestige, honour, liberty and equality which characterize the Liberian way of life.

The march of Africa from colonial status to autonomous statehood in the past decade is an unparalleled phenomenon in history. Since 1951 many countries in Africa have achieved political independence. No one state standing alone will be able to solve the problems facing humanity and itself. Unity is therefore necessary; but the crucial question is one of design for the future – the creation of a community in which free men may live in peace under their own laws.

Liberian policy is committed to the concept of a free enterprise system, democracy, and a pragmatic search for solutions to problems of multinational existence. Conditioned by hard experience, we should contribute a consensus of values which will incorporate the tenets of nations different in ethical and historical formation. It is a difficult adventure, but not outside the range of our collective experiences to resolve. We envisage a synthesis composed of individual states, retaining their own way of life, but united by mutual exchanges of peoples, goods and ideas, by pacts of non-aggression, non-interference in the internal affairs of other states, and of perpetual peace. In the past, African States have taken counsel together; at Addis Ababa we should begin to act together.

We of Africa are faced with a race between chaos and order, illiteracy and education, poverty and prosperity, which implies the changing of our ideas of nationalism and abstract ideological remedies, if our hard-won freedom is to contribute meaningfully to the peace, welfare and progress of all Africa. The struggle for ascendancy, which characterized the Western European state system and the civilization which gave it birth, with its ephemeral and short-lived patterns of political unification and fragmentation of power within well defined periods of feudalism, of absolute kings based on power and prestige diplomacy, and of aristocratic absolutism, should, we hope, never find a counterpart in Africa or in any formula of unity approved or adopted by us.

One of the worst alternatives to African unity is African anarchy. It can be engendered by armed and militant nationalism of 'my country right or wrong', by the pride of power, by the penchant for prestige, the lust for conquest, the thirst for glory and the quest for fame. It can also be engendered by journalistic irresponsibility which may set Africans against one another with consequent hatred, possible bloodshed and destruction, social unrest, collapse of governments, retardation of progress and incalculable human suffering and misery.

To say that the salvation of Africa lies in unity is to suggest that divergent interests be reconciled; that common values and African welfare be substituted for exclusive and competitive self-seeking.

Some of us may be pessimistic of the outcome of the ensuing conference because of the seeming division of African states into groups resulting in a divergence of ideas, but we do not share this view. There is a professed desire and anxiety of leaders of all groups for unity in Africa; and we are persuaded that all Heads of States and Governments will go to this conference with open minds, willing to advance, discuss, adopt and accept the most objective and realistic propositions offered from any source based upon free discussions and common agreement. This shall be the guiding rule concerning the Liberian representation at the ensuing conference, and indeed all international conferences.

Difficulties will arise in many areas, but I feel certain that sober reasoning and judicious objectivity can overcome them when they appear. The principle of give-and-take, of negotiation and compromise, which has governed our action in the past will continue at Addis Ababa with new meaning.

The question in some circles as to the form African unity might take is causing concern. Some have asked whether it is to be on a global, continental, ethnical or geographical basis. Any of these possibilities poses serious problems which may aggravate a tendency to regionalism, revive boundary disputes, and intensify minority tension which could undermine continental peace and solidarity, and engender the spirit of rivalry in every aspect of national life.

Viewed historically, political unions and/or world parliaments have offered no permanent solution to international problems of unity. They have never allayed suspicions, fears, subversions and distortions aimed at the destruction of smaller states by more powerful ones. At this stage of our evolution, types of unity should be carefully thought out in the light of precedents. Unity on a functional basis and a geographical approach seems the most realistic and achievable solution, if effectively insulated against wanton ambition, centralism and subversion.

Unity, if not integration, becomes more imperative when it is realized that there are twenty-two African colonies and territories not yet free, some of whom are groaning under the degrading load of oppression and servitude, and are at this time looking to Addis Ababa for their emancipation. What is taking place in these territories today, the brutal and inhuman treatment meted out to black men in those areas because of their colour, is an insult not only to the dignity of humanity but particularly to all African States, as well as to the nations of every continent of the earth that regard the natural right to freedom as inherent in all men.

To promote unity on a cultural, economic and scientific basis, it would appear essential that an accelerated programme of cultural, scientific and economic exchange between African States be initiated.

Such a programme, if well planned and carefully pursued, would not only cultivate stronger ties of friendship and unity among Africans, but would also lay the foundation for developing closer understanding as the basis for new forms of unity.

As Africans we must realize that we face grim challenges. Africa is not a world unto itself but an integral part of our one world. It is our responsibility to fashion and build a New Africa in which all races of men may live and work together in the great task of reconstruction. The problems are many. The situation is urgent. We cannot but heed the call.

I have no doubt that as we enter upon the business of the conference we shall do so objectively as Africans, and not as members of any particular group – be it Casablanca, Monrovia, French Community or any other. If we do this we shall then raise ourselves above the level of group complex, regional and such other elemental tendencies that might subject us to contracted thinking and selfish actions.

We from Liberia are going to this conference with open minds and hearts permeated and imbued with an impelling urge and burning anxiety for understanding, friendship and concord on the basis of mutual respect and regard for every state and community. We shall place special emphasis on the African situation because of its present peculiar nature which, although greatly improved by the assistance of other continental friendly powers and by our own endeavours, has still not fully emerged from the state of degradation to which it has been subjected for centuries.

At this conference many matters of grave importance are expected to be considered and discussed, chief among which will be the determination of the type of unity the African States might adopt. This is no easy task. It is not a question that can be determined at a single conference. It will require careful analysis of the many proposals that have been made. A union of this type requires serious study and may take years before its full implementation is realized. More important, perhaps, would seem to be a method whereby the cultural, scientific, economic and educational facilities available to all Africans might be examined, combined, improved and expanded.

There have been a number of proposals submitted, many agreements reached and charters approved between different African States, suggesting various forms of unity and unions. I refer to the Ghana-Guinea Conference, where the organization of a United States of Africa was suggested; the Guinea-Mali Conference and Charter; the Ghana-Guinea-Liberia Conference at Sanniquellie which suggested a Community of African States; the Casablanca Group Charter; the Monrovia Group Charter; the French Community Accords; the Resolutions adopted at the Lagos Conference in respect of economic and financial co-operation, health, labour and social welfare, transportation and telecommunication, education, and press and information services, as well as President Nkrumah's proposal for a continental parliament, etc. These and any other proposals, agreements and arrangements that have been or may be made by African States should be correlated, examined and studied by a Commission specially set up for this purpose.

The Commission could then cull from all or such of them as may be deserving, and formulate recommendations for what might seem most feasible and adaptable to the actual form of unity which the African nations and their people should establish.

There will be disagreements and divergence of views on this subject but I take confidence and assurance from our profession of a deep-rooted desire for unity, that all of us attendant at this conference will have but one singleness of purpose – the creation of a strong and free Africa, united by its own effort and desire.

It is in this spirit, fellow citizens, that I go forth to the ensuing conference of African and Malagasy Heads of States and Governments, strong in the hope that I carry with me your solid support and fervent prayers for its peace, concord and overwhelming success.

Speech at a State Banquet given in His and Mrs. Tubman's Honour by Emperor Haile Selassie I of Ethiopia

Addis Ababa, Ethiopia, 15 May 1963

Our two countries have successfully collaborated with implicit confidence, and subscribed to identical principles of political behaviour.

Introductory Note

In this speech President Tubman again reaffirmed his belief in the necessity for African co-operation and the contribution which African unity could make toward world peace. He reminded the people of Ethiopia of their heroic rôle in African and world history, and of what was still unfinished business in our common engagement for the liberation of Africa and for unity among all its people.

Addis Ababa, Ethiopia, 15 May 1963

TWO YEARS ago, a great honour was conferred upon us by the gracious invitation which Your Majesty extended to us to witness the 31st anniversary of your accession. For an Emperor who has always believed that the genuine test of any administration or reign should be the benefits derived therefrom for the welfare of the people, the occasion would have indeed been one of unique significance. But the unfortunate illness of Her Imperial Majesty, and her subsequent greatly lamented death and passing from time to eternity, deferred the elaborate preparations.

Having read much and heard a great deal about this ancient Empire, having met many of your officials both in Africa and abroad, having met Your Majesty at the Conference of the Heads of African and Malagasy States and having, above all, had the distinguished pleasure and honour of receiving Your Majesty in Liberia in 1960, it is highly gratifying that we should be visiting a land so pregnant with history and to be beneficiaries of the generosity and unbounded hospitality of Your Majesty and the Ethiopian people. On behalf of the members of my party, Mrs. Tubman and myself, I express our great delight and profound appreciation at being in your great country at Your Majesty's invitation.

The growing relationship between our two countries, the many grounds of unanimity between us, our common concern for African unity and solidarity and the past struggles in which our two countries have engaged for the maintenance of our sovereignties have made our kinship over the years more and more meaningful. Your Majesty's passion for freedom and your constant concern for the walfare of your people are ideals which have characterized your history. I feel confident that the years will significantly

521

enhance a growing comprehensive understanding of our peculiar problems and bring us closer into a creative partnership for the greater good of our countries and peoples.

Thus far, the exchanges between our governments have been conducted in an atmosphere of harmony, peace and fraternity and they hold great promise in making our economic, social and cultural relationships even more significant. It is my firm belief that Your Imperial Majesty's visit to Liberia in December, 1960, your country's participation in the Monrovia Conference and now my own visit to Ethiopia at this time, will consolidate our ties of friendship and greatly enhance the basis of our mutual understanding and co-operation.

I now pay tribute to a great patriot and statesman, a humanitarian, a man of intelligence, broad interest, warm sympathies, high integrity, a scholar and a dedicated leader of his people; His Imperial Majesty Emperor Hailé Selassié I. Your Majesty's reign has been distinguished by the first written Constitution in the history of the country, in which you delegated weighty governmental responsibilities to your people; your farsightedness resulted in the creation of a Chamber of Deputies. Thus you have wrought great political, social, economic and educational reforms, and established and seen the completion of numerous development projects. Your determination to ameliorate the conditions of the poor and lowly became your personal responsibility, and your personal contributions to the victims of World War II, and the provisions you made for scholarship opportunities for students, have all added to your great stature as a renowned and beloved leader of your people and the world.

The qualities of true leadership which have characterized your reign have been utilized in the service of your country through these long years and your genius for statesmanship and diplomacy will dub you as one of the greatest world leaders of our times.

The rich heritage of achievements and the centuries of independence of Ethiopia verily stand as a great support and shining example of the valour and determination of a brave people to the rest of Africa. History reveals that your people are the inheritors of a long and rich tradition which has come down to them as the fruits of the unswerving devotion, discipline and sacrifice of their forefathers in defence of their fatherland.

Our two countries have successfully collaborated and subscribed with implicit confidence to identical principles of political behaviour. We believe that freedom must be the inheritance of all peoples; we advocate self-restraint in our dealings with other nations; we believe in the United Nations as the greatest bastion of human liberties; we believe that all problems of international relations should be settled by a process of peaceful negotiation and agreement, and finally, we advocate abstention by all nations from the use of force and interference in the internal affairs of other states.

It is my fervent hope that we, the leaders of Africa, will view these issues in their right perspective and so combine our efforts toward their realization.

Concerned as we are with the trend of world events, we are happy that on the continent of Africa practical ways may be found to foster understanding, and thus to lay the basis for future co-operation and collaboration in technical, social, economic, educational and cultural fields of endeavours.

Inter-state visits, contacts at international conferences and seminars, the exchange of delegations, all these are helping to broaden the base of our understanding of each other and, I dare say, preparing the way for unity and the fulfilment of our obligations to each other as brothers of this vast, historic and fascinating continent.

Speech at a State Dinner in Honour of Emperor Haile Selassie I during President and Mrs. Tubman's State Visit to Ethiopia

Ghion Hotel, Addis Ababa, Ethiopia, 18 May 1963

In an age so sensitive to nationalism, the people of Africa will ever remember with pride Ethiopia's gallant struggle for sovereignty.

Introductory Note

Liberia and Ethiopia, besides being Africa's oldest continuously independent nations, have also in common a record of having won moral victories in the defence of the integrity of their homelands, and in representing stability in Africa. Their leaders too were engaged in a common struggle for a redefinition of national values for their respective peoples, though not without opposition. It was therefore necessary to forge links of contact, friendship and co-operation between their two governments, and to gain inspiration and courage to pursue the humanitarian policies they had set for attainment. When in 1963 President Tubman was able to repay a visit to Ethiopia, the Emperor having first visited him in 1960, he took the opportunity to strengthen these links and to discuss the problems which confronted the African Freedom Movement on the eve of the birth of the Organization of African Unity.

Ghion Hotel, Addis Ababa, Ethiopia, 18 May 1963

AFTER NEARLY a year and a half in anticipation of this happy visit, we set foot on Ethiopian soil a few days ago. The beautiful scenery which surrounds us, the warm, orderly and enthusiastic receptions we have received everywhere, and, above all, the feeling of kinship we have experienced, have all contributed to the realization that we are really not strangers but brother Africans.

Already we are convinced that this visit will bring us closer together to the unity we have been talking about and planning for.

From the Government and people of Liberia, I bring to Your Majesty and the people of Ethiopia hearty greetings and fraternal felicitations. We recall the great pleasure which your 1960 visit afforded us, an occasion which the people of Liberia will always remember with joy and gratitude.

A week from now one of the most significant, fascinating and historic conferences the people of Africa have ever witnessed will take place in Addis Ababa. The presence of thirty-two Heads of African and Malagasy States alone could create a wonderful feeling of oneness and with it a splendid opportunity for African unity and solidarity. We hope that out of it will evolve a greater degree of understanding among African nations and peoples, as a precursor to paving the way to closer co-operation and collaboration, and as positive contributions to peace and unity in a divided world.

At least, we opine that all the African leaders who will be attending the conference will be doing so from their innate love of Africa and Africans and their common concern for the next steps to be taken, now that a new kind of nationalism has exerted itself on the continent and many nations have already won their independence.

It does not require a great stretch of the imagination to understand what the rôle of Ethiopia has been in the African Freedom Movement. Yours is the oldest African nation which was a member of the League of Nations; at the establishment of the United Nations only two African States were represented – Ethiopia and Liberia. Today, in a little less than two decades, thirty-two African nations by their vote hold the balance of power. In all these deliberations wherever the fate of Africa was concerned, in the moral and financial support given to the cause of liberation and in heated and passionate debates for freedom and independence, the voice of Ethiopia has not been silent. What a unique setting, therefore, for a major African Conference to be meeting here where the tradition of freedom and liberty has always been greatly cherished.

In an age so sensitive to nationalism, the people of Africa will ever remember with pride Ethiopia's gallant struggle for sovereignty. Your Majesty's great sacrifices in the interest of your people and nation, the prosperity which has characterized your reign, and your people's dedication and devotion to you make you a great leader of Africa and an outstanding world statesman.

The work of liberation is not yet completed. There are millions in Africa whose bid for the right of self-determination, while arousing world interest and sympathy, has met with opposition from those directly concerned. It is for these people that every available support should be given, to the end that they too may enjoy the blessings of liberty and freedom to which all men are entitled. We must continue our support for them until the fight is won.

The unfinished business which lies before us is the determination to resolve all differences which now keep Africa divided; language barriers, different cultural backgrounds, training opportunities and other causes notwithstanding. I have faith in the course of the history of nations and I believe with all my heart in the great national ideals which now permeate African leaders and peoples. However, I am not a radical who expects that all this will be accomplished in a short time. At best, we can lay a realistic foundation and continue the great work optimistically so that our successors may take up where we shall have left off.

To the Addis Ababa Conference of African Heads of State and Governments

Addis Ababa, Ethiopia, 25 May 1963

> *May we be able to come near to the heart of the basic questions so necessary to our survival in a divided world, so that we may go away strong in the conviction that unity is not only desirable but feasible.... Never before has unity of action been more desirable and urgent; never before have independent nations faced such a challenging and splendid opportunity for concerted action.*

Introductory Note

In May 1963 thirty-two Heads of State and Government met in Addis Ababa to resolve their differences, which had become acute as a result of their disagreement about the Congo crisis. The result of that meeting was the creation of the Organization of African Unity. It was a splendid opportunity for the meeting of minds. Africans had the opportunity of discovering one another, having been separated from one another through a rigid colonial régime which lasted for nearly a hundred years. President Tubman addressed this meeting and pleaded for a common and united approach to the problems of the new Africa.

Addis Ababa, Ethiopia, 25 May 1963

THE ADDIS ABABA Conference, to which African leaders and governments have looked forward and on which world attention has been focused, has today brought together thirty-two Heads of African States and Governments in this historic city of Addis Ababa, in this beautiful setting, to discuss and find practical solutions to some of the questions that may arise from the agenda prepared by the Foreign Ministers.

The magnitude and importance of this gathering, the efficiency with which preparations have been carried out and the personal attention which has been given by His Majesty and the Ethiopian Government deserve great commendation.

We extend to His Imperial Majesty and the Government and people of Ethiopia our grateful thanks and sincere appreciation for the magnificent and elaborate preparations which have been made for the Conference and for the gracious courtesies extended and the unbounded hospitality given to us since our arrival here. May we, in this seat of the oldest independent African kingdom, be able to come near to the heart of the basic questions, so necessary to our survival in a divided world, so that we may go away strong in the conviction that unity is not only desirable but feasible.

What will come out of the Addis Ababa Conference has been in the minds of Africans and on the lips of the peoples of the world, and since the opening of the Foreign Ministers' meeting, a listening world has tuned in to Addis Ababa.

His Imperial Majesty, in his speech, referred in a very forthright manner and positive terms to the need for African unity, and presented the aims of the Conference to this body. How unity can be achieved and what steps can be taken towards its practical implementation, so that it may bring us into a creative partnership in which we can live and work in peace for our mutual benefits and thereby make Africa strong in the economic, educational, cultural and technical phases of development, are issues to which much thought has already been given. Various proposals have been made and plans of procedure advanced. Now we are afforded an opportunity to create a synthesis of the whole for study and discussion, so that a useful, effective and acceptable plan of procedure may be devised.

Never before has unity of action been more desirable and urgent; never before have independent nations faced such a challenging and splendid opportunity for concerted action; never before have our problems been graver and our needs more crucial.

The Liberian delegation, while having its own views, some of which will come up during the course of the Conference, has come with an open not a closed mind; a mind susceptible to reason and good judgment about the views of other states and groups. We subscribe to the principle of compromise, of give and take. I believe that all who have assembled here today have come with the same attitude.

I crave your permission to refer to a practice sometimes indulged in by delegations at conferences such as this: walking out of committee or general assemblies during debates when the trend is contrary to their delegation's views. It appears to me that such actions are harmful to the success of a conference.

If a decision taken is against the view or interest of the delegation, the delegation might ask for its protest to the decision to be noted for the benefit of the record and future generations, for there may be other matters which may arise where the interest of the delegation may be affected or when the advice, counsel and assistance of the delegation may be necessary and helpful. We lose the benefit of their advice, counsel and assistance if the delegation has walked out.

We earnestly hope that at such an historic and significant Conference, the general and not the personal or purely national interest will influence our thinking and action, and thereby enable us to participate dispassionately and selflessly in debates designed to achieve the greatest good for Africa, as pointed out by His Majesty. It is towards this end that we have assembled here; it is for this purpose that we have worked, planned and prepared for the Conference. Certainly this is not a conference to end all conferences, but it is one to which African leaders imbued with an avid desire for unity have come to find a way.

To His Majesty and the Government and people of Ethiopia we again pay high compliments for this great occasion in the annals of our continent.

In the great task to which we have set ourselves at this crucial moment in our continent's history, let us think like men of action and act like men of thought.

To the Nation on his return from the State Visits to Ethiopia, Yugoslavia and Austria

Monrovia, 13 July 1963

> *One common purpose unites us. One common task awaits us. If ever there was a time when the spirit of true patriotism and unity have required re-assertion that time is now.*

Introductory Note

When President Tubman delivered this address to the people of Liberia, he had just been recently re-elected President of Liberia for a fifth term of office for four years. Immediately thereafter he undertook several visits upon invitations extended to him. One of these visits took him to the first Organization of African Unity Summit Meeting in Addis Ababa, Ethiopia, following an official visit prior to the convening of the Summit Conference. When he returned home he was in an excellent position to take a look at the new Africa that was emerging, at his years as President of Liberia, at himself personally, and, what was most dear to him, at the progress Liberia had thus far achieved, and what was ahead. The nation now accepted the fact that a period of austerity was upon it. With the realization of this sudden turn of good fortune (and indeed there had been an abundance of it) the President appealed to every citizen and resident to accept the bad times as well as the good times which are concomitant features of the growth of any economy. Operation Production, he again emphasized, was capable of easing some of the sterner measures of the austerity period. Gradually, Operation Production took on the appearance of becoming as meaningful and vibrant as the Open Door and National and Integration Policies. The President gave serious thoughts to its execution, as he had done for the Open Door and Unification Policies. This address was one of his most comprehensive messages, a mid-year examination one might say, of the state of the Liberian nation. As usual he did not fail to commend those who had ably managed the affairs of Government while he was away.

Monorovia, 13 July 1963

FOLLOWING IMMEDIATELY upon the General Elections in May last, preceded by the National and County Convention and the National Unification Council, on the day after the mammoth demonstration by the officers and partisans of the True Whig Party when we were officially notified of our election for a fifth term, we embarked on an Ethiopian jet airliner for Addis Ababa. This was the beginning of a journey to fulfil an engagement of a State Visit, participate in the African Summit Conference, and thence

529

proceed to Switzerland for a medical check-up before our next official engagements, which included two State Visits – one to the Socialist Federal Republic of Yugoslavia and the other to the Federal Republic of Austria.

Today we have returned and our souls have been refreshed by the solemn service of thanksgiving to Almighty God for His Guiding Providence over us during our travels abroad by air, rail, highway and ocean, and our hearts are gladdened by the enthusiastic welcome which you have extended us on our safe return home.

Leaving Robertsfield on the night of May 14th, we arrived in Addis Ababa on the morning of the 15th and were received into that city 'that is set upon a hill and cannot be hid', in the most grandiose manner with all its ancient pomp and ceremony. The lavish receptions, the genuine manifestations of friendliness and the unbounded hospitality accorded us, made our five-day State Visit there most delightful, interesting and fascinating. We saw great developments taking place under the stimulus of Ethiopia's second Five-year Internal Development Programme. We encountered a noble, hardworking, productive and ingenious people. Above all, we were greatly impressed by the effervescence of the new nationalism which we felt everywhere we went in that country.

While the visit deepened our respect and admiration for his Imperial Majesty, Hailé Selassié I, and broadened our understanding of His Majesty's government's policies, it also provided a fitting prelude to the Addis Ababa Conference of African States – a conference which will certainly play a significant rôle in the annals of African and world history.

The political history of Africa in the latter part of the twentieth century provides a fascinating field for analysis. The picture presents the continent in a state of flux and its transition from the status of dependence and servitude to one of independence and sovereignty. While the foes of nationalistic movements have been and are still baffled by this swiftly moving and dramatic situation, the Africans themselves and their friends are pushing forward their claims for freedom and independence with the resultant gains of emergent nations, thereby changing the political map of this continent.

Africans, by dint of perseverance and tremendous sacrifices, have regarded these changes as part of the historic process, and, early cognizant of the attendant responsibilities of the new situation, have endeavoured to create a unity out of diversity. Thus all the conferences which preceded the Addis Ababa Conference were efforts designed to bring together peoples long separated by the most exploiting forms of colonialism. The Addis Summit was a unique success and one which politically, socially and economically will have far-reaching effects on the continent and its more than two hundred and fifty million peoples.

While the Conference lasted, world interest was focused on Addis Ababa and the Africans themselves and their friends could congratulate themselves as the climax was reached, when each Head of State approached the dais in Africa Hall and signed, with pride and dignity, the Charter of Unity of African States, dedicated to peace and unity among the nations of the world. Now we are further dedicated to work towards its implementation, knowing that the experiences we have severally gained in the past in the struggle for freedom and independence, and its maintenance, have taught us the wisdom of uniting our forces toward one common and glorified end. Whatever else might have been the outcome of that great and unique

conference – and I believe there were many, perceptible as well as impercep-
tible – we did achieve the major first step by our consensus to meet together
as equals in an attempt to clarify our common problems and endeavour to
effect conciliation on issues which have divided us. The Charter which
emerged at the end of the Conference was the embodiment of our ideals and
our practical endeavour for peace and unity among ourselves. It represented
our determination to press for the total liberation of Africa. It contained our
objective to strive for the total development of the Continent and it expressed our desire to work for the attainment of peace with all mankind.
We came away greatly inspired by what we had heard, seen and accomplished.

Great credit is due to the Foreign Ministers of the African States who
met in advance to prepare the agenda for the Conference and were later
charged with the responsibility of presenting a draft Charter embodying the
ideals of African unity and solidarity. Their brilliant performance reflected
credit on everyone who participated in that historic meeting. I pay tribute
to the special contribution of our conscientious and hard-working Secretary
of State, J. Rudolph Grimes. The Government and people of Liberia,
including your humble servant, are proud of his performance and the members of his delegation, which included the Honourable Ernest Eastman, for
the part each rendered toward the overall success.

As I have been accustomed to do in the past, and aware of the increasing
and onerous responsibilities of the Presidency, and particularly conscious of
the physical toll which the past nineteen years have taken upon me, I underwent a very thorough medical check-up in Zürich which took a little more
than two weeks. In the end, the specialists decided that my general physical
condition was excellent, but that I had been overworked and therefore
needed rest rather than any prescribed medication. This means that there
must be a change in the routine of business which I handle personally. It
applies especially and particularly to personal and private interviews, which
will hereafter be handled by the Administrative Assistants.

At the end of the check-up, a new development took place which necessitated a change in our European itinerary and a change of plans. His
Excellency President Adolf Scharf of the Federal Austrian Government,
sent a special Envoy to us in Zürich and a friendly invitation through our
Embassy in London, which we accepted, inviting us to make a State Visit to
Austria. Detailed arrangements had therefore to be made quickly, including
the assignment of an Ambassador *ad hoc* to Austria, and drawing up a
programme which could be compressed into three days. And so, from one
phase to another, and from day to day, the rest which I so much needed and
expected to get in Switzerland as prescribed for me, did not materialize.

As on other occasions when we visited Switzerland in a non-official
capacity, the President of the Federal Council of Switzerland and officials
of the local Government extended us befitting courtesies. A luncheon invitation with the President and the Federal Council in Berne, luncheon and
dinner engagements as well as visits to other parts of Switzerland, rounded
out our social activities.

On the afternoon of June 22, we bade adieu to the friendly and hospitable
people of Zürich and boarded a special train for Belgrade, Yugoslavia, in
response to an invitation extended us, more than two years ago, by His
Excellency President Tito of the Socialist Federal Republic of Yugoslavia.

Belgrade, where we arrived on the morning of the 23rd of June, was in a gala and festive mood to welcome us. The moving spectacle of gaily decorated streets with flags and buntings hanging from windows or else from the tops of roofs, the tremendous crowds, the cheering, shouting and clapping of hands by enthusiastic men, women and children touched us greatly. For two days we stayed in Belgrade, delighting in the friendship and hospitality of the people of Yugoslavia and enjoying the delectable dishes of Yugoslav cuisine. Wherever we went, to Zagreb, capital of the Republic of Crotia, to Brioni, the beautiful seaside city on the Adriatic, or to the island summer home of President Tito, there were crowds of friendly people, flags, streamers and banners expressing sentiments of friendship and the desire for close co-operation between our two countries.

The friendliness of His Excellency President Tito, the charm and affability of Mrs. Broz his wife, and the friendliness of the people in general were remarkable and made our five-day stay very pleasurable and unforgettable. It was a visit which broadened our horizon in our glimpse of another form of government, enabling us to see at first hand the way of life of a people with whom we had had very scant acquaintance. We came away admiring and respecting the Government and people of Yugoslavia and greatly impressed by the material progress achieved and the happiness which radiated from the faces of the people we saw as we went from city to city.

On Thursday, June 27, the final day of our visit, President Tito and I affixed our signatures to the Official Communiqué which has already been published, setting forth some of our basic convictions and enunciating certain principles upon which our two Governments have agreed to work co-operatively for world peace.

After the farewell luncheon, followed by the ceremonial farewell at the Pula Railway Station, we entrained and departed for Vienna on the third and final stage of our European State Visits.

The invitation extended by President Adolf Scharf was interesting from an historical point of view, for in spite of the fact that no diplomatic exchanges had yet been made between our two Governments, there has existed a Trade and Friendship Treaty between Austria and Liberia for almost a century. But more than this, Vienna had become to the whole world a symbol of music, an interest which nationals of our country share and a city to which many have gone in the past.

Accordingly, we arrived on the afternoon of the 28th, immediately after our Yugoslav visit, in the city of charm, hard work and tireless endeavour and were met and received at the Vienna Sudbahnhof Station by the President and high officials of the Austrian Government with befitting ceremonies. Our three-day stay in Austria included official receptions, sightseeing to historic and modern places, a visit to one of Europe's largest and most modernized steel plants and a hydro-electric plant, the signing of the commercial treaty between our two countries and the agreement to exchange diplomatic representation at Ambassadorial level.

Because our itinerary was to end in Upper Austria, we took official leave of His Excellency President Scharf on Sunday afternoon, June 30, and boarded the special train which took us to Linz, where having been the overnight guests of the Governor of that Province, we said good-bye to the people of Linz and the Government and people of Austria and departed by special train at ten o'clock on the night of July 1st for Bordeaux where we boarded the French ship *M.S. Foucauld* on the 3rd of July.

The privilege of visiting a country which is the virtual crossroads of Europe, the hospitality which was accorded us, and the new link which has thus been forged, fully justifies our visit to Austria.

The Honourable Stephen A. Tolbert, Secretary of Agriculture and Commerce, who travelled with us as a member of our party, was always ready and willing to respond efficiently to assignments accorded him, and worked hard and faithfully in the negotiations both in Yugoslavia and Austria, particularly in the negotiations of the Treaty Agreement between the Governments of Austria and Liberia and the Communiqués which were executed.

The Honourable Wilmot A. David, Under Secretary of State, also served admirably with Secretary Tolbert.

The ten-day voyage on the French vessel *M.S. Foucauld* was delightful. We were blessed with good weather and a calm sea the whole way. The Commandant and crew accorded us every courtesy and took great care of our wants and needs. We are thankful to the ship's company and to everyone for the part they played in making the voyage as pleasant as possible for us.

In these days of unrest and world turmoil, it is a credit to any government to maintain its stability by the continued orderly process of government operations. Let us continue to do so. That the public servants of any nation can become sensitive to this obligation and thereby function effectively in any circumstance, reflects honour to them and their government.

During our absence from the country we had the satisfaction to know that the members of the Cabinet headed by the Secretary of State, were true to their sense of duty and loyalty and that each Cabinet Minister made his willing contribution to the smooth operation of the Government machinery. I congratulate you. I congratulate every official, from the highest to the lowest, for your loyalty; and I congratulate the citizenry of the nation in general. In particular, I commend the Vice-President for the special assistance he rendered and the able manner in which he represented us at the Coronation of Pope Paul VI.

To the members of the Ministers' Association we are indebted for their continued solicitude of us. Your prayers, the prayers of the people of the nation, the service of thanksgiving on our behalf, and the good wishes of every citizen have all contributed, in a great measure, to one common end — keeping our nation united and its people secure and happy. May we always repose implicit confidence in the spiritual foundations of this nation, knowing that He Who keepeth us neither slumbereth nor sleepeth.

One common purpose unites us. One common task awaits us. One common concerted endeavour beckons us. If ever there was a time when the spirit of true patriotism and unity have required reassertion, when the love of country has demanded concrete expression, when the ideals of service have needed constant and even greater emphasis in our institutions of learning, and when our continued progress, prosperity and security have hinged more on deeds than on words, that time, I am persuaded, is now.

I call upon the citizens of this land, I call upon our friends, upon the old and young, upon everyone, to look constantly within yourselves in order to

determine what rôle *you* have been called upon to play in the implementation of the ideals for which this nation was founded and for which it stands.
Liberia needs your constant awareness of the ideals of service, your selfless
service, your love and patriotic devotion.

THE AUSTERITY PROGRAMME

As an outgrowth of the economic and financial crisis which we face, precipitated principally by the fall in the price of rubber and the failure of
some of the mining enterprises to come into production at the time anticipated, I directed the Secretary of the Treasury to proceed to the United
States and Monetary Fund with a view to assisting in this crisis. Accordingly,
he proceeded to the United States and after talks with the Directors of the
Fund and other related international financial agencies, obtained agreement
for a plan prepared by the Fund which the Government accepted and
directed the Secretary of the Treasury to see implemented.

Secretary Sherman has been kept busy conducting negotiations with the
Monetary Fund for setting up a stand-by arrangement which has been
concluded, and arranging with creditors for resetting the Government's
obligations with them. Generally, most of these creditors have been co-
operative and sympathetic, and they may rest assured that the Government,
on its part, will do everything humanly possible to meet its obligations as it
has done religiously in the past. It is our hope that conditions will improve
sooner than anticipated, so that even before maturity of the resetting dates,
the Government may be able to pay off these obligations.

Meanwhile the plan means for us Liberians the tightening of our belts.
It means deprivation; it means sacrifices. It means patriotic contributions by
every citizen, high and low, rich and poor. It means making such sacrifices
as are made by people all over the world in their times of austerity. Let us
not forget that sometimes austerity can become a blessing in disguise, to
teach many lessons to a wise and understanding people.

Under the Open Door Policy many foreign concessions have come into
the country and created a boost to our economy as well as provided more
job opportunities than ever before. The nation has experienced a great
economic upsurge from which everyone has benefited and there has been a
corresponding improvement in the standard of living. In fact, every phase
of our national life and of our private life has been touched and improved
one way or the other, and there is certainly a tremendous lot for which we
have to be thankful as a nation.

In this present situation of austerity, therefore, there is no doubt that
everyone should be willing, if or when called upon, to make sacrifices and
contributions. Hence I appeal to the citizens of the nation. I appeal to those
on the littoral and in the interior. I appeal to every Government official, the
members of the Legislature, the Executive and the Judiciary.

I appeal to lawyers and other professional men, who because of the nature
of their professions are compensated a thousand-fold in private practice,
now more than ever before, to the extent that the Government sometimes
finds it difficult to procure qualified legal personnel to fill its positions,
although the Government encourages them.

I appeal to the clergy and the laity who have also enjoyed the benefits
of the golden era of prosperity during which new church edifices, schools,

hospitals and other structures have been built, and salaries and subsidies appreciably increased.

I appeal to merchants, businessmen, farmers, craftsmen, fishermen and all artisans gainfully engaged to make some contribution. I appeal to students, stevedores, foreign friends and everyone who has enjoyed the benefits of the days of affluence, under the protection of a friendly government and people, to co-operate in the plan that may be recommended.

I am sure that, as you have enjoyed the benefits of prosperity, you will be willing to take a share in the austerity demands, and will be as joyful now as then; for it is written in the good old book: 'Shall we expect all good of God and no evil?' The evil days will soon be over and the *status quo* restored if together we join in the fight for national, financial and economic victory.

This by no means implies that there will be any requests for gifts or grants; or the giving of something for nothing; that will never happen.

Secretary of the Treasury Sherman deserves great praise for his patience, perseverance and ability in handling these negotiations, and I express my thanks and appreciation for his untiring efforts and the fruitful results which have been achieved. Mr. George Blowers has been of great assistance to the Secretary in these negotiations, for which we are grateful.

I have lauded the new Five-year Plan of the Ethiopian Government. I have praised the agricultural programme, animal husbandry and the industrialization of the Federal Republic of Austria. All of these, I am sure, are of interest to all of us. Let us now turn to domestic affairs.

THE ROAD BEHIND US

When we took office in 1944 we advanced the Unification and the Open Door Policies as the basis of the several reforms for the development programmes we had in mind for the country at the time. We emphasized the development of infrastructural projects throughout the country. These have included the construction of roads, city streets, public buildings, schools, hospitals, clinics, power and light stations, water and sewage facilities, forest conservation, land reclamation, radio and telephone systems, public information programmes, and others.

These policies were designed to make life happier and raise the standard of living of the people; but there was another reason also, and that was to make it more convenient and pleasant for private enterprise, particularly in the sphere of economic activity, to emerge, expand and produce greater quantities and a better quality of economic goods and services. For this purpose, the National Production Council was established. Much progress has been made by the Unification and Open Door Policies, but now we must advance in new directions and expand and deploy our programmes so as to exploit our agricultural and natural potentialities to their fullest extent.

THE ROAD AHEAD

An enlightened and progressive government, functioning within the bounds of a free enterprise system, seeks primarily to undertake the development of infrastructural facilities needed by the people of the country. It is expected, and imperative, that the people apart from enjoying these facilities, should take the maximum advantage of them in the successful and profitable creation and operation of private and productive enterprises.

However, if private initiative is not immediately provoked or inspired, or if it is not being ignited quickly enough, or if it is not being accelerated, the Government, in the interest of the people, (which, after all, is the purpose of any government), and with a view to increasing national production, national income, strengthening national stability, and honouring its financial obligations and commitments, must then employ certain catalytic agents to spark private initiative into action and get it off the ground.

Quite often, in developing countries like ours, even with the infrastructural installations and with an abundance of initiative, private enterprise is still slow in developing. In many cases this is because of the lack of long-term or short-term capital, technical know-how, experience, legal protection, co-ordination of agricultural or industrial activities, or clear economic programmes of government.

Furthermore, the Agricultural Credit Corporation must be made effective and be efficiently operated, and the proposed industrial Development Bank must also be soundly established and properly managed with all necessary legal safeguards and securities, in order to provide for the financing that may be needed, and which is not otherwise available to farmers and industrial enterprisers in the country.

Additional and more effective research must be undertaken, and careful experimentation conducted throughout the country on a wider scale, from which more people can benefit. This research and these experiments must seek to improve local practices and methods, particularly as regards the production of agricultural projects. They must also seek to introduce new projects that can be economically produced in the country. Clearly, research and experimentation are indispensable to any developing country which wants to continue to develop. I have emphasized and spoken of this on many previous occasions.

A programme for increasing gross national production must be formulated and made a part of the programme for the next administration and this is intended to serve as notice to those charged with the responsibility of stimulating and conducting the productive capacities of the nation within the framework of our private enterprise system, together with the planning and directing of the productive capacity of the nation. There must be carefully studied and prepared projects that will fit into such programmes, and suggestions for the means of implementing such projects successfully. New projects must be prepared and undertaken when others have been completed or co-ordinated. The necessary and relevant tests, research and experiments must constantly be carried on to ensure the best results.

The overriding emergency, the inescapable fact of the matter and, in our own case, the urgency we face, lie in this elementary economic axiom. It is impossible for any country to develop or for any developed country to maintain its standing if it fails to produce economic goods and services. Economic production is indispensable to economic development.

Our greatest attention and emphasis must be given to increasing our agricultural production. This policy is valid and economically sound, since we are basically an agricultural country whose potentialities and resources in this area of economic activity have scarcely been scratched. With present-day agricultural know-how, methods, production records, modern facilities, machinery and equipment available all over the world, there is need for a revolutionary new idea and a comprehensive agricultural development programme which is supported by facts and figures resulting from scientific research and experiments performed either at home or abroad, but which also has been accurately tested and verified at home—a programme that would change our outmoded methods of farming by introducing more practical and more economical modern methods, and would increase agricultural production abundantly in other areas similar to that which has been started by the Department of Agriculture and Commerce in rice production.

A programme such as this must also seek to reduce the need to import certain agricultural products, such as rice, meats, fish, poultry products, vegetable oils, sugar, coffee, vegetables and many other products which could easily be produced in our own country. This same programme must also envisage the exportation of agricultural products; the canning of fruits, vegetables, fish, etc.; the packing, drying and otherwise preserving and refining of locally produced agricultural goods. With such a well-formulated programme, capital for its implementation would, I believe, easily be found. This too is a part of the programme for the next administration being suggested by those who are formulating the plan.

Although priority should be given to the most progressive and enlightened development and utilization of our agricultural resources and possibilities, the time has come in our national development when industrialization is imperative for quite a number of reasons, and it would be to our severe disadvantage and grave economic loss not to undertake particular industrial operations, at least on a limited basis to begin with.

In the first place, we are at present only producers of primary products, except for the beer factory, and maybe one or two other very minor industries. What is happening in the world market today is that the prices of primary products, including rubber, iron ore, coffee, palm kernels, etc., such as we produce locally, are constantly falling, while the prices of the manufactured goods made out of the very same primary products we produce, are always rising. We, therefore, and all other developing countries like us, suffer from a continuous drain on our foreign exchange and national income.

In the second place, it is no secret that we could make cement, rubber tyres and other rubber goods, pig iron and steel, paper and other wood products, soap, as economically, profitably and of equal quality, as any other part of the world.

Thirdly, if we, and other countries who now produce only primary products, were to commence using such products, or a portion of them, for local manufacturing, and if such manufacturing were conducted on an economically sound and feasible basis, the world market prices for these primary products would rise, because the developing countries would be producing manufactured goods of equal quality at lower costs. Thus, in order to compete, the manufacturers in the highly industrialized countries would be obliged to reduce the prices of their goods on the world market. These synopses are designed to form the basis of a new Five-year Development Programme for Liberia.

Finally, we have seen and experienced much. We have participated in varying political, social and cultural activities, and we have benefited from the interest, sympathy and understanding of many friendly governments and nations.

In our national history, the path behind us has been strewn with varied and trying vicissitudes. But in each case we have emerged victorious from one crisis after another. We shall do so again and again and again.

The path before us is full of many opportunities and challenges which will task our ingenuity, determination and ability to the utmost and demand all our patriotic devotion. And while we cannot discern with absolute certainty the nature of the road ahead of us, if we keep our vision clear and apply our best endeavours to our national task with realism and dedication, there is no doubt that we shall meet the future confidently and successfully. To the effectuation of these supreme tasks, I have called upon and appealed to all the people of this nation.

God save the state and bless the united work of our heads, hearts, hands, minds, bodies and souls.

Speech delivered during an Official Dinner held in his Honour

Tunis, Tunisia, 1 October 1963

> *At Addis Ababa we sowed the seed of African unity in the hearts, minds and souls of men.... The endurance peculiar to our race made annihilation and extermination impossible.... We Africans must set an ideal example of stability, patriotism and social and political justice to the world, and send forth a great beacon of universal friendliness that will attract nations of every continent on the face of the earth.*

Introductory Note

In 1963 President Tubman visited Tunisia upon the invitation of President Habib Bourguiba. He was pleased to make this visit and reflected deeply on the new feeling of brotherhood and friendship engendered by the Organization of African Unity, during a state dinner held in his honour by his host. He lauded the Tunisian President for his rôle in the fight for African liberation and as a symbol of moderation.

Tunis, Tunisia, 1 October 1963

IT IS our great pleasure to be visiting Your Excellency, Mrs. Bourguiba and the people of Tunisia on this especially interesting and unique occasion. This visit is overdue by a couple of years, but the fates seem to have ordained that the present time should be the most appropriate.

Your Excellency and I had the pleasure of meeting and becoming personally acquainted with one another at the Addis Ababa Conferences, although we had before then had contacts by correspondence and through the exchange of our plenipotentiaries. The warmth, affection and feeling of oneness that characterized and permeated the Addis Conference still pervades all the African States and their leaders, and my visit to you, Mr. President, at this time will, I believe, generate greater mutual affection, fraternity and respect.

More than that, this visit following so closely on the Addis Ababa Conference, where the Heads of thirty-two African States met and sat around the conference table, gives lustre to our presence here and indicates stronger ties of friendship and brotherhood.

At Addis we sowed the seed for African unity, not in the earth but in the hearts, minds and souls of men. The process of germination is already taking place by the normal method of growth – heat in this case is the warmth of heart, light is the ability to see the fundamental necessity for unity and the third prerequisite – the presence of air and water – represents our hearts, minds and souls which breathe the breath of freedom, love, brotherhood and fraternity. This seedling must be nurtured with great care to see that nothing

539

happens to thwart, impede or retard its growth; this plant must grow with and through the years until it becomes a great and impregnable African forest under whose boughs and branches, spreading from north to south and from east to west, all can meet, embrace one another and find peaceful habitation, prosperity, happiness, freedom and liberty and a continental community of ideas and ideals, and where each will exercise himself in his internal affairs without interference, molestation, let or hindrance by others. It must be a place for all to work together for the great cause for which the Charter of African Unity was conceived and formulated. In the maturing of these hopes Your Excellency played an important rôle and became one of its most prominent supporters.

Like other parts of Africa, your country has not been without its sorrows, its woes and its sufferings. The intrepidity and endurance peculiar to our race made annihilation and extermination impossible and survival, which is inextricably implicit in every bone, sinew and nerve of the African race, possible. We have all known, experienced and endured sufferings, oppressions, humiliations, assaults and insults. We must remember that some of them served as incentives to keep alive in us that burning flame of determination to keep freedom, liberty and justice in our bosoms. We Africans must set an ideal example of stability, patriotism, social and political justice to the world and send forth a great beacon of universal friendliness that will attract nations of every continent on the face of the earth and cause them to exclaim, 'See how those Africans love'.

This is a great ideal that we have attempted to set for ourselves, and it can be achieved by realistic thinking, careful planning and concerted action.

In the struggle for African emancipation and the restoration to the African of the respect and dignity of man, you, Mr. President, have been one of the foremost personalities acting in the scene of evolutionary and revolutionary change, and under your leadership the staunch and indomitable people of Tunisia have thrown off the shackles of colonialism and become a free, sovereign and independent people. Under your leadership great progress and advancement have taken place and the honour and integrity of the people of Tunisia and the Tunisian territory have been restored and preserved.

The most outstanding quality in this development is your recognized ability to think clearly, make correct and just decisions and take sober action. We both seem to believe in not brooding over the past or remembering the painful and gruelling experiences of the years gone by, but in forgetting the past and reaching forth to the future with all of the resources, ability, power and strength at our command, for the benefit of the development of our respective nations, universal brotherhood and peace as well as for better understanding between all peoples of the earth.

Tunisia, once the seat of an admirable African culture and a political system, can never be forgotten in history. Here in your country are the ruins of the old Carthaginian Empire whence the great African hero, statesman and soldier Hannibal went forth on his march across the Alps with elephants. Although this was a great military achievement it is of the past; you are now building a new nation founded on the principles of democracy, equality, justice and equal opportunities and privileges for all. This type of society will survive through the centuries, for it is one that strengthens the spirit of the people and renders them indestructible.

We have been greatly impressed since our arrival by the beautiful scenery of Tunisia, by its healthy climate and lovely foliage, by the magnificent terrain of your country and the hospitality, warmth and genuineness of your friendship which we shall endeavour to bind to us with 'hoops of steel'.

On his return from a State Visit to the Republic of Tunisia

Monrovia, 14 October 1963

If we fail to engage in this undertaking of national priority, it will give proof that we are not patriotic, not interested, not anxious to see our country advance.

Introductory Note

President Tubman visited Tunisia in response to an invitation extended to him by President Habib Bourguiba of Tunisia. This was the President's first visit to a north African and Arab state. His sense of history was stimulated by what he had read in history as a schoolboy. But now he was especially pleased with the economic production of Tunisia. Upon his return home he immediately launched Operation Production as the nation's number one priority programme. He had, however, previously called for such a programme under a National Production Council Authority. But he was greatly impressed with the mode of production in Tunisia and unceasingly appealed to Liberians to accelerate their own programme of self-help. Operation Production became an added force to his National Unification and Open Door Policies for national growth, economically, culturally and politically. He took great pains to have the new programme of Operation Production nurtured in the hearts of his people and was heartened by the general response he received from them. This speech upon his return home from Tunisia was one of several major policy statements on this new drive for greater national production in every sphere.

Monrovia, 14 October 1963

IN THIS transitional period anong nations, new methods of procedure and approach are unfolding. It has become an international practice to make personal contacts by exchange of visits of Heads of States or Governments, in order to promote better understanding and comity among nations and peoples, and in an effort to become acquainted with one another, and establish the basis of friendship, co-operation and mutual respect. It was in pursuance of this practice that, on the invitation of President Habib Bourguiba of the Republic of Tunisia, we left Liberia by ship on the 17th of September for a State Visit to Tunisia, spent the night of the 28th in Marseilles, boarded the *President Cazelet* on the morning of the 29th and arrived in the enchanting city of Tunis on the morning of the 30th of September.

The lovely panoramic view that came in sight as we steamed slowly into port escorted by two Tunisian naval vessels, the stalwart Tunisian Royal guards resplendent in their red and white tunics, the smartly dressed soldiers, the members of the Government and Diplomatic Corps and the thousands of spectators who lined the landing stage made a moving spectacle. The landing and reception ceremonies were complete and dignified in every detail – the welcome salute of the cannons, the gaily decorated buildings and streets with photographs of President and Mrs. Bourguiba, and Mrs. Tubman and myself posted everywhere, the tens of thousands who turned out to greet us singing, shouting, and clapping hands, the hundreds of school children who lined the streets holding photographs of President and Mrs. Bourguiba, and Mrs. Tubman and myself, the welcome music of bands at various stations along the route of travel, the beautiful sky and the brilliant sunshine all added to the enthusiastic, warm and happy lustre of the welcome which was accorded to us that morning. President and Mrs. Bourguiba, the Government and people of Tunisia and foreign residents welcomed us to this ancient, fascinating and historic city with true fraternity and gaiety. It was an unforgettable welcome to a city of enchantment and history by a people who evinced every indication of their genuine friendliness and gracious hospitality.

That night at the magnificent Presidential Palace at Carthage, President and Mrs. Bourguiba gave a State Banquet in our honour and in the after-dinner speeches we spoke of the affinity among African nations, the rôle of the historic Addis Summit Conference and the bright future for the continent as an outgrowth of the determination of its leaders to unite and consolidate their efforts for the creation of a new Africa. President Bourguiba made special mention of Mrs. Tubman's absence and expressed his and Mrs. Bourguiba's regrets for her inability to be present.

In view of the absence of Mrs. Tubman, Mrs. Padmore, wife of our Ambassador *ad hoc* to Tunisia, was requested to act as hostess at official functions, which she kindly consented to do.

Aware of the significant strides which have already been made among African nations in the development of greater understanding and mutual respect for each other, in the increased emphasis on the equality of all states and non-interference in the internal affairs of other states, the events of the first day deepened our appreciation for the Government and people of Tunisia and confirmed our conviction that a better day is in the offing for Africa, where 200,000,000 people are already politically independent.

For three days after the 30th, we were accorded the most lavish receptions and courtesies and saw at first hand many evidences of the indestructible qualities of the Tunisian people, a fact which I had mentioned in my after-dinner speech.

The itinerary included visits to places of historic and significant interest: the S.T.I.L. factory where butter was being processed and packaged and where local beverages of orange, chocolate and other flavours were made; the valley of Medjardeh where an extensive and highly successful co-operative in agricultural experiment is taking place, where vegetables of all kinds are being produced and where wine and citrus fruits are being bottled and canned; the Bardu Museum where we saw some of the most precious collections of Tunisian antiquity, rich in remnants of Roman and Punic civilizations as well as in objects of modern art; the ruins of Carthage where we recalled famous passages from Roman history – 'Carthage must be destroyed', 'Carthage, I read thy fate'; the artistic centre of Denden where we were fascinated by the intricate designs of the weavers, entranced by the skill of the wood carvers and the artistry of the metal workers and those who wrought in ceramics; enraptured by the Souks, an endless maze of streets where thousands of Tunisian master craftsmen wait to display their wares and where one has the sensation of living in another world, a lively, colourful and perfumed labyrinth of fruits, wool, shoes and goldsmiths.

Every place we visited, everything we saw, had a background of cultural and political history, rich civilizations from which the nation has gathered a wealth of historical remains. Thus our four-day visit was not only pleasurable, but greatly revealing, enlightening and rewarding. While it helped to strengthen our relations with another African state, it also brought us face to face with a great civilization, a noble people with the indomitable qualities necessary for the survival and development of any nation and people. It taught us the wisdom, and indeed the strength, implicit in increased emphasis on our agricultural programme, so closely tied up with an abundance of production, of the necessity for the establishment of co-operatives in agricultural products and small industries in arts and crafts – particularly in metal and leather work, woodcarving, weaving and ceramics.

With a view to encouraging, stimulating and realizing some of these projects which attracted us, a policy is to be established whereby the Development Corporation and the Credit Corporation will provide some of the financing for such small industries. This must be a part of the Five-year Plan of Development to which reference has already been made and upon which this nation must embark speedily, conscientiously and realistically.

It is gratifying to remark that the political discussions between President Bourguiba and myself were held in an atmosphere of complete friendship, agreement and understanding. During the course of these discussions, a Cultural Agreement was signed between the two Governments by His Excellency Taieb Sahhani, Secretary-General for the Ministry of Foreign Affairs for the Government of Tunisia and His Excellency George A. Padmore, Ambassador *ad hoc* to Tunisia as Plenipotentiary of the Liberian Government. This agreement provides for exchanges which should greatly contribute to the acceleration of our Cultural Centre progress to be inaugurated in the near future, and which we hope will play an important rôle in enriching the cultural life and progress of the nation.

And so, having seen all that our four days could encompass, having partaken of the delicacies of Tunisian cuisine, and having enjoyed the hospitality and friendliness of our African brothers in that part of North Africa, on the morning of October the 3rd, after befitting and touching departure ceremonies, we boarded the ship *Wille D'Oran* for Marseilles where upon arrival the following morning, we immediately boarded the *General Mangin* which brought us home today, to you our fellow citizens and friends.

We acknowledge with deep gratitude the many courtesies which were accorded to us by the Heads of States and Governments of Senegal, Morocco, Algeria, the Italian port of Genoa, the French port of Marseilles, the Spanish port of Palma and the Republic of Guinea. To the officials of steamship lines and the ships' officers and crew who helped to make our voyage comfortable, we express thanks and appreciation.

HOME AGAIN

Addressing the people of the nation upon my return from Europe in July last and again in my acknowledgement speech to the Honourable House of

Representatives when informed of our re-election for another term of office, we stated that an expanded and aggressive agricultural programme and increased production would be the keynote and motto of the Five-year Development Plan of the new administration. Now again I am elaborating with greater emphasis additional outlines and basis for this programme. I declare, proclaim and announce our National Priority Number One Programme to be increased production. We must use all our human and natural resources to increase the productive capacity of the nation; in other words, all our human and natural resources must be correlated and utilized to develop our productive capacity, which in turn will be used to develop our human and natural resources. Because this will form an attractive circle of reciprocity between the development of our human and natural resources and the productive capacity of the nation, I feel that it is the primary and most certain road to prosperity.

At this time, therefore, I am appealing to the entire population of the country – Liberians as well as foreign residents – to resolve that production shall be National Priority Number One, using as our slogan 'Operation Production' of the new Five-year Development Plan.

We of this country must realize, know and understand that we must produce or perish, that we must produce to survive; that increased production is analogous to prosperity, progress, development, happiness, self-sufficiency, patriotism, national pride and even godliness.

Toward this end, in collaboration with the Departments of the Interior, Education, Agriculture and Commerce, the Liberian Information Service will be required to arrange a comprehensive programme of the 'National Priority Number One Operation Production Policy,' for publication and execution throughout the country to stir the nation to a new consciousness of obligation in respect of production in ever-increasing measure. For the effective execution of this programme, daily appeals must be made to the people by officials of Government at all levels, paramount chiefs, Government employees as well as people not in Government employ, all University, College, high and elementary school authorities and students, foreign residents, and all communication media throughout the country. I ask all bishops, priests and church officers to emphasize to their church members the importance of the Divine Injunction, 'By the sweat of thy brow shalt thou eat bread'. We expect all legislators, judges and other judicial officers to join in sponsoring this programme, since it is a veritable national programme that is essential to boost our economy, and is non-political.

In the appeals that are to be made, we are to persuade all of the people, young and old, that we have to use all of our potentialities and capacities to increase production; that our major defence against aggression is Priority Number One Operation Production; that our weapon against starvation, depression, oppression, poverty and sickness is Priority Number One Operation Production; that our self-respect and prestige among the nations of the earth lie in Priority Number One Operation Production; that the perpetuation of our sovereignty, independence and national autonomy depends on Priority Number One Operation Production. There is absolutely no doubt that if the people of this nation, by concerted action, undertake and pursue Operation Production as our National Priority Number One, we shall, in a relatively short period, reach a level of development equal to that of countries of comparable size.

REASONS FOR INCREASING NATIONAL PRODUCTION

The following are some of the rather obvious reasons which make it important and urgent that we seek to increase our gross national production:

1. An increase in gross national production would mean economic growth
   and service for the people of the country to enjoy goods which they
   need to live and to make life pleasant.
2. Increasing gross national production would mean more income for the
   people who wish to buy the goods and services produced in the country
   as well as those imported from abroad.
3. Increasing gross national production would mean revenue for Government with which to meet obligations and continue to instal more and
   better infrastructural facilities needed in the country, such as hydro-
   electric plants, dams, roads, highways, bridges, public buildings,
   schools, office buildings, sewer and water system, telecommunications,
   ports, hospitals and other national and social services.
4. It is well known that our mining operations constitute a primary source
   of income for many people, are one of the most important sources of
   Government revenue and represent substantial economic improvement
   for many Liberians who have invested in one or more of these companies. But mining operations *per se* represent a source of exhaustible
   income and sound economy would dictate that a substantial portion of
   the earnings from them be invested in non-exhaustible income-bearing
   enterprises in order to secure the future of the beneficiary, in this case,
   the nation. It is therefore important to increase our gross national
   production by investing a portion of the revenues from the sales of
   these exhaustible sources in enterprises the income from which could
   be considered perpetual or inexhaustible.
5. It is urgent that we increase our national production in order that we
   might measure up to other African states, some of which have experienced a rapid rate of progress by constantly stepping up their gross
   national production. African countries should develop in such a way
   that their economy would complement each other; each country
   should produce those products best suited to it and respectively undertake complementary industries rather than compete in industrial or
   other activities. On this basis we should trade with each other, increasing our national productivity in order to make our contribution to the
   African Common Market and to secure our share.

MEANS OF INCREASING NATIONAL PRODUCTION

As mentioned in my previous address, various Governments, depending on
the economic philosophy to which they subscribe, adopt various methods of
increasing production. The Liberian people are accustomed to the system of
private enterprise and our policy has encouraged the perpetuation of this
system.

In this nuclear age we in Liberia have to begin on a level that will ascend
immediately to modern day scientific standards, irrespective of the fact that
for nearly a hundred years we were kept in the proverbial national strait-
jacket barely able to breathe, unable to exercise ourselves beyond the point
of mere existence and survival imposed by forces that were too powerful for

us, and confronted with circumstances totally beyond our control; circumstances and conditions which made our existence and survival one of the
great feats of all time, if not a miracle. But notwithstanding all this, we
must now be prepared to develop at a much faster pace and commence at a
more difficult level. This is why the Government, through subscribing to the
private enterprise system as an economic way of life, believes that it has
played a rather practical rôle by providing or creating a programme that
would induce private initiatives and has given it a backing in our developing
situation.

This administration took that course through our Open Door Policy, our
infrastructural programme, our philosophies for a stable government and
our insistence and determination in maintaining our political, economic and
spiritual ways of life.

In this great national drive no one can be exempt; those engaged in agricultural industry, whether it be rubber, coffee, cocoa, palm oil or any other
agricultural product, must see that production is doubled next year and
those growing citrus fruits and vegetables of every kind must also see that
production is doubled in 1964. Every person, from the age of fourteen to
seventy-five, must produce something from the ground. We have a vast
quantity of fertile land, in many areas virgin, and one needs only to scratch
the surface, plant seeds and watch them grow. In most parts of the country,
because of the heavy rainfall, irrigation is not necessary. Why then should
our production not be stepped up and increased a thousandfold greater than
it is at present? If we fail to engage in this national priority undertaking it
will give proof that we are not patriotic, not interested; that we are sluggards
in the development of our country, not anxious to see it advance with an
abundance of agricultural products available to meet our needs at home and
with sufficient surplus to sell to the markets of the world. I bring to your
attention and consideration one of the proverbs of Solomon where he said:
'Go to the ant, thou sluggard: consider her ways and be wise: which having
no guide, overseer, or ruler, provideth her meat in the summer, and gathereth
her food in the harvest. How long wilt thou sleep, O sluggard? When wilt
thou arise out of thy sleep? Yet a little sleep, a little slumber, a little folding
of the hands to sleep: So shall thy poverty come as one that travelleth, and
thy want as an armed man.'

RICE PRODUCTION

The fact that rice is our principal article of food makes it imperative that
every effort be made and every device utilized to increase this product next
year by at least three hundred per cent. In my address delivered upon my
return from Europe in July this year, to which I have already referred, I
stated as a matter of policy that our principal farming methods should be
organized and modernized. But while we are organizing and preparing for
modernization of the new agricultural programme, the old methods must be
vigorously pursued and continued; each county, territory, province and district must produce next year at least treble the quantity of rice produced in
1963, and an agricultural prize will be given to the area producing the
largest quantity and best quality of rice. Because the need is imperative,
producers have the promise that the price of home-produced rice will be
increased.

I realize that the question of labour is becoming a serious problem. This is not altogether because there are insufficient people in the country to take care of and operate concessions, mining enterprises and individual agricultural projects, but because a large number of people have been habituated to living without working. The majority of such people migrate to concession areas, such as Harbel, Bomi Hills, Nimba and elsewhere, and live on the earnings of their relatives and friends. In these areas it is reckoned that there is a greater number of people unemployed, unengaged and doing no kind of work than there are actual labourers, and who claim that under certain international conventions no men shall be compelled to work.

The safety of the state is the supreme law, and I consider the economic safety of the state as greatly threatened by people who will not work to produce, thereby creating a slump and downward trend in production which endangers the prosperity of the country and causes starvation, hunger, malnutrition, disease and death, as when the nation is threatened by rebellion, invasion or civil strife. Under the authority of the Act of Legislature we shall promulgate an Executive Order to deal with and control vagrants and compel them to work.

Management and labour are interdependent entities, for the welfare of the one is bound up with the welfare of the other. But labour must produce more in order to help stabilize the economy of the nation. A case in point is that at the time when the price of rubber was high, labour demanded an increase in the minimum wage which was granted. Now that the price of rubber and other commodities has fallen and the nation is going through an austerity period, it is inconsistent to make further demands during this crisis, especially if the output of work by labour has not been increased and when the new Minimum Wage Act has increased the compensation for labour. When the quality of work improves and labour assumes added responsibilities it can rightly demand increased wages and it is the obligation of representatives of labour to educate workmen to this fact. It is only by and through increased production that the economic equation will be balanced and I feel that labour and its leaders should be more objective in their demands.

We also call upon the Chamber of Commerce, the Labour Unions and Congresses to join us and support Government in this national production drive. Because the Minimum Wage Act has increased the minimum wage for labour, labour should correspondingly assist in increasing national production. For if previously the output, or production, or the task of labour was less, now with the increase in wages and better facilities, such as schools, hospitals, clinics, for the labouring class, production should also be increased to enable overhead expenditure to be covered and a reasonable margin of profit left. For it is an economic truism that when production is increased labour can proportionately claim better facilities and wages. This is the principle upon which businesses operate and when they fail, the economy of the country collapses.

The above approaches are mainly intermediary or temporary steps which are being advanced in an effort to effectuate the immediate increase of production. I appeal to, adjure and call upon everyone to join in this great programme of Priority Number One Operation Production; let those who are now producing something produce more; those who are producing nothing produce something; let something be planted in the grounds of the various schools, hospitals, clinics, private homes and public buildings. Let the whole nation try with might and main successfully to promote this programme that will form the basis for our economic development and stability.

At the ensuing session of the Legislature I shall recommend the institution of the kind of machinery that I think will be necessary effectively to implement the Priority Number One Operation Production. In this connection it seems to me that the Department of Commerce, authorized by an Act of Legislature during its 1962 session, should be redenominated 'The Department of National Production and Commerce.'

Again I make reference to the necessity for entering upon a programme of industrialization. But this means that there must be a greater and better quantity and quality of agricultural products to justify the setting up of a cannery, for instance; there must be greater production of fish, vegetables, citrus, to feed these industries, otherwise it would be like putting the cart before the horse.

With the enormous quantity of iron ore available steel mills and other industries on a large scale would be practicable, and we should encourage such investments.

THE AUSTERITY PROGRAMME

Reports received from Secretary of the Treasury Charles Sherman indicate that resetting arrangements for the payment of Government's obligations under the Development Programme, which became necessary because of a sharp fall in the price of rubber, failure of certain mining projects to come into production on schedule and other factors beyond the Government's control, have been virtually concluded successfully, and that prospects for the Liberian Development Bank appear to be excellent. These negotiations were intricate and difficult and great credit is due to the Secretary of the Treasury and those who assisted him; they were: The Honourable J. Rudolph Grimes, Secretary of State, Mr. George Blowers, Mr. Romeo Horton, Assistant Economic Adviser to the President and Mr. Estrade Bernard, Counsellor to the Treasury Department.

It is also pleasing to note that our administration of the Austerity Budget under the Stand-by Arrangement with the Monetary Fund has been complimented by representatives of the Fund.

This means, however, that a stricter observance and implementation of the Austerity Programme must be insisted upon and executed. It also means that the tightening of the belt mentioned in my address to the nation on the Austerity Programme must be adhered to with greater and stricter enforcement.

REVISION OF THE PL-480 PROGRAMME

1. The PL-480 arrangements should be revised by negotiations.

2. One of the important changes in the operation of the programme should be that the selection and preparation of projects be undertaken and financing the PL-480 should be undertaken jointly by the Secretary of Agriculture, the Secretary of the Treasury and the Director of National

Planning Agency, subject always and in each case to the approval of the President.

3. The determination of the amount to be appropriated must be by the same three officials of Government with the approval of the President.

4. The direction and execution of projects financed with PL-480 funds should be the duty of the Secretary of Agriculture and Commerce.

ACTIVITIES OF THE LIBERIAN AGRICULTURE SERVICE (LAS) IN CONNECTION WITH PL-480

1. The policies and practices of LAS shall be carefully reviewed and re-defined in order to discontinue all monopolistic tendencies which might stifle or impede free and orderly conduct of private enterprise in the country.

2. The management of LAS should be reconstituted to provide the Government (which is the major share holder) with adequate security on its shares so as to ensure the best service for the community.

THE UNIFICATION AND INTEGRATION POLICY

I am absolutely convinced that this policy has been of greater significance in the life of the nation than any other single policy; it has saved the Government and the people of the country millions and millions of dollars which would have otherwise been expanded in financing military operations in internecine war, tribal uprisings and rebellions that might have resulted in bloodshed and the loss of life of the flower of the nation. On the contrary, the people of the country, of every class, group, element, tribe and clan have enjoyed the benefit of education and better living conditions without dis-crimination. It is apparent that unification and integration have taken the place of the old customs, internal strife, mistrust and suspicions, and on November 29 of this year I shall sign for promulgation a proclamation ordering special elections for the purpose of electing Senators and Repre-sentatives for the four new counties created by the Legislature. Following this, I shall on July 26 of next year sign for promulgation another proclama-tion declaring the four new counties duly and legally constituted.

I shall consider this Act, when consummated, an achievement of one of the boldest, most realistic and far-reaching approaches of the administra-tion's social and political programmes of reform. It will again fall to my lot, with the co-operation of the Legislature and the support of the people in the exercise of my leadership, to be the instrument whereby the dimensions of our political structure will have greater breadth, depth and reality. The people of the entire nation will face the future with a new courage, faith and optimism, believing that our Republic is truly destined to have a new birth of freedom and liberty. I feel modestly proud and happy about the realiza-tion of such ideals, especially since it nearly cost me my life by assassination.

THE OPEN DOOR POLICY

On the question of the Open Door Policy we stand today where we stood twenty years ago when the Open Door Policy was first announced. We shall continue to persevere with this Policy because the benefits that have accrued have amply justified it. We firmly believe in the free enterprise system of government as against government controls and nationalization.

SPECIAL HONOURABLE MENTION

It appears to me propitious and encouraging to make special honourable mention of some of our young specialists and technicians who have pursued specialized courses abroad under the scholarship programme and are now engaged in the services of the nation. My awareness of the ability, efficiency, effectiveness and, above all, the integrity of some of our young men in conducting negotiations on behalf of their country was voluntarily confirmed by several foreign investors with interests in Liberia. A foreign industrialist whom I consider a very tough businessman, speaking of Mr. James Weeks, Director of the National Planning Agency, said, 'I do not like him, but I must respect him, for in him you have not only a capable and efficient person who is an expert in his field and unyielding when he thinks he is right, but one who is patriotic, loves his country and is a man of unquestionable integrity.' Others of our young specialists to whom foreign industrialists have made similar high complimentary references concerning their ability and the quality of efficiency displayed by them in negotiations on behalf of the Government, are Mr. Arthur Massaquoi, Director of the Bureau of Telecommunications and Chairman of the Monrovia Power Authority; Mr. Lafayette Morgan, Under Secretary of the Treasury for Fiscal Affairs, who, some feel, is endangering his health by carrying too heavy a burden and therefore needs assistance; Mr. Clarence Simpson, Jun., Counsellor of the Department of Public Works and Utilities, who has also served several departments; and Mr. David Neal, Deputy Director of the Bureau of Statistics. To their credit and their nation's pride they have kept a clean record and maintained their integrity without impairing their own personal dignity and character or selling their country for a mess of potage. Their examples inspire hope and confidence for the future of our nation.

The pleasantness of our visit to Tunisia, our stay there and the voyage back to Monrovia was greatly enhanced by the kindness of the members of the party, all of whom were co-operative, responsive and solicitous for the success of the visit.

Each time that I have gone away and returned, my faith in the orderly processes of our system of democracy has been renewed and my admiration deepened. To those at home therefore, who have kept the machinery of government running so efficiently and smoothly, I commend your loyalty and patriotism; you have seen well to your charges. I congratulate the members of the Cabinet under the direction of the Secretary of State, the Honourable J. Rudolph Grimes and the Acting Secretary of State, the Honourable Wilmot A. David and the Cabinet supported by the Vice-President, the Speaker and other members of the Government as well as the citizenry in general for having conducted the affairs of Government as well as I could have done had I been present physically.

Finally, we are ever mindful of the continued prayers and solicitude of the Christian, Moslem and other religious groups on our behalf, when we are at home and when we are away. The knowledge that you are ever with us in spirit, whether present or absent, always gives us great inspiration and fortitude to face our tasks. In the years ahead I know that your intercessions will form a great bulwark in our national undertakings and accomplishments. May He Who is able to keep us all from falling, keep you perpetually in His grace so that your work will be instrumental in bringing all the people of this land to the recognition of the inscrutable wisdom and perfect power of God.

As in the past, let us fervently pray for His continued guidance and protection; 'for unless the Lord keepeth the city, the watchmen waketh but in vain,' and 'Paul may scatter, Apollos may water but the increase must come from God.'

God save the state and abundantly increase and bless the labours of our hands.

Broadcast to the Nation on the Eve of his East African Visits

Monrovia, April 1964

I ask every Government official, every boy and girl in whatever category they may be engaged, for loyalty and dedication to the state so that peace may prevail at home and the nation's march toward a better day be accelerated.

Introductory Note

The Organization of African Unity revived a new spirit of brotherhood among African states. Although President Tubman had visited several African states before the birth of that Organization in 1963 and in the days of European colonialism, his interest in visiting more African states now under the leadership of Africans was great. These visits were mutual and many leaders have also visited Liberia. In April 1964 he sailed to East Africa on a return visit to the Malagasy Republic, and accepted invitations to visit Tanzania and Kenya. He welcomed the opportunity to visit these countries. Because the trip was to be an extended one, he requested every citizen to maintain peace at home until his return. He further spoke of the lessons of self-discipline which a period of austerity had brought upon the nation, and the virtues of self-help incentives.

Monrovia, April 1964

ON SATURDAY the 25th instant, I shall embark on one of the most extended trips which I have undertaken since my incumbency as President of this nation. Because Malagasy is such a vast territory, the fourth largest island in the world, it could be considered a continent; in fact, when I was studying geography in school some maintained that it is a continent. I am therefore delighted and fascinated with the prospect of this visit, which will embrace Tanzania and Kenya, as I have been invited by President Julius Nyrere and Prime Minister Jomo Kenyatta to make State Visits to those nations. The details of these will be made known to you through radio broadcasts and other media of communication.

There are two facts which impress me about the Republic of Malagasy. The first is that although this island is situated in the Indian Ocean and is geographically close to Africa, its people are the outcome of ancient intermingling of successive immigrants including Africans and Arabs. Secondly, President Philibert Tsiranana who visited us in 1960 has closely identified himself and his government with the great revolutionary and evolutionary freedom and liberation movements throughout Africa. We are very happy about this association.

On the eve of this extended journey, I wish to speak on certain matters of public concern.

First, austerity is now a byword in the nation since everyone has felt the pinch of the programme as a result of the economic disciplines which we enjoined upon ourselves to tide us over the crisis. So successful have some of these precautionary measures been that we are encouraged to continue to adhere to some of them even after the sailing becomes smooth and safe. At the same time I express my satisfaction about the manner in which the austerity budget and other measures have been planned and executed. Certainly, we will all benefit from the discipline of self-denial which we are experiencing in this crisis and I feel sure that we shall continue to pursue some of its useful directions in the future.

Let us be clear, however, that the austerity we face and are encountering is an outgrowth, for the most part, of the general developments and the tremendous pace of progress which the nation has experienced, specifically the construction of roads, administration buildings, public edifices, hospitals, clinics, the Executive Mansion, the Law Court Buildings, the Tele-communications Building and the undertaking of other enterprises which could only be done through prefinancing. While we are thoroughly convinced that prefinancing is generally expensive, we had no alternative but to resort to it in view of the pressing demands for improvements all over the country, particularly for essential activities. Nor should we forget the failure of certain mining concessions to come into production at the time they anticipated and the fall in the price of our principal economic commodity, rubber, by more than fifty per cent. In spite of all these conditions, we are optimistic that we shall weather the storm successfully, and with the launching out on another programme so vitally needed to boost the economy of the country, Operation Production, I feel sure that better days are in the offing.

A MATTER OF CONCERN

The Liberian people have felt for quite some time now that they are not receiving the just consideration to which they are entitled in various fields, particularly in economic and social activities. It is generally charged that foreigners are given preferential treatment. I submit that as guests of our nation and as nationals who have come to help in extending the image of their country and, to some extent, helping in the development of our nation, we are obliged to extend to them the protection and the hospitality usually accorded to guests. Personally I believe in being liberal, yet there is a point to which liberalism can become injurious. In the past the trials, difficulties, injustices, tribulations and humiliations which the people of this nation suffered were borne by them alone. Only they were responsible and blamed for the conditions which existed, and if Liberians were incapable of self-rule, then it was in their best interest to give up their autonomy and be ruled by foreign powers, which had already established themselves in Africa as victors, or at the invitation of those who needed protection. But during those difficult and bitter years we defended and maintained our sovereignty and gradually established peace, law, order and unity. Today this state, as always, still provides protection and justice under the law for all her citizens and foreigners as well.

I fear, however, that there is a tendency on the part of some of these same foreigners to forget or ignore our past struggles, to underrate and even malign the ability and capability of the Liberians, to become remiss in their obligations to their host government, and worst of all, to be unimpressed by the direction in which the nation is moving. To all such persons who take this attitude and who behave correspondingly, I say that the fundamental difference between one people and another is only a matter of training and opportunity.

From the earliest period of our national history until the nation maintained its independence over a century ago, we were harassed by the iron-clad and ruthless onslaught of colonialism, heckled by racial prejudice and accused of the lack of ability for self-government. Our failures, not our ideals, became the yardstick by which we were judged. After so many years, our attempts at democratic government, the benefit of education and contacts with culture and civilization and the influence of the Christian gospel have provided impetus for a greater degree of progress and stability within our borders. Let the critics steeped in their preconceived notions continue their criticisms. We continue in the pursuit of the ideals which we have always cherished in keeping with the opportunities and assistance given to us for development and advancement.

Take a case in point. The San Francisco team here in Monrovia is charged with the responsibility of setting up the Monrovia consolidated school system. This team is providing education, training and work experience for the personnel that will be used in the school system, and at the same time selecting some of the workers as counterparts for on-the-job training experiences. There has been no problem in finding men and women who are capable of serving, for many have already been trained and prepared to take positions of responsibility and trust in the future when the team honourably relinquishes its assignment. If Liberians are to be truly helped, it is my feeling that adequate education and training should be provided them, and then the conferring of the responsibilities best suited to their training and experience.

I quote in this connection from my last inaugural address:

'The end of government being to evolve a better standard of living and to ensure the happiness, peace and security of the people in whatever political or economic system obtains in a nation, the socialist governments, reserving for themselves the factors of production, provide all training and other facilities for the people and assume the dual responsibility of government and management to labour. To attain this end in a free enterprise system such as ours, where the overwhelming portion of the ownership of the factors of production is in private hands, it is the obligation of private enterprise and business to assume this responsibility and the Government will require management to provide the facilities implied with such ownership to supplement and complement those provided by Government.'

In all employment situations, the laws of the country must be observed and administered accordingly. I am therefore directing and authorizing the rigorous enforcement of this directive.

All foreign concessionaires, businessmen, and industrialists, should realize and understand that it is exactly this same kind of reasoning and attitude which caused the peoples in Asia and Africa to take strong measures to assert their inherent rights, and to challenge the privilege of nationals of other countries resident in their states to benefit more economically and socially at the expense of the citizens themselves.

We shall no longer tolerate the slur and indictment that Liberians are incompetent. If Liberians are given the opportunity for training and then provided the responsibilities to correspond with their training and experience, I feel sure that the efficiency graph will rise. The men are here with their God-given capacities; and if you really desire to use them you can find, train and give them corresponding responsibilities.

As on other occasions when I was absent from the country, I ask every Government official, every boy or girl, in whatever category he or she may be engaged, for loyalty and dedication to the State so that peace may prevail at home and the nation's march towards a better day be accelerated. The full co-operation of everyone with the Cabinet headed by the Secretary of State and assisted by the Vice-President and the Speaker of the House of Representatives will be expected at all times.

Good night, and God bless you all.

To the National Assembly of the Malagasy Republic during his State Visit

Tananarive, Malagasy Republic, 31 May 1964

Let us work together in the spirit of true brotherhood so that the laws of our respective nations may lend themselves to the consolidation and implementation of the Charter of African Unity and as a machinery for realistic and effective co-operation among member states.

Travelling from one country to another has become not only an exploratory or goodwill mission but one in which one becomes identified with this new spirit and enters consciously into the new brotherhood which is spreading as rapidly as the ripples of a wave.

Introductory Note

In 1964 President Tubman paid a return visit to the President of the Malagasy Republic who had visited Liberia in 1960. The President congratulated the law-making body of the Malagasy Republic and further seized the opportunity to reflect on the one year of progress of the Organization of African Unity. Africans, he felt, had in their hands a powerful instrument for the peace of the world and for the advancement of the continent of Africa through co-operation. His visit was further evidence of the influence of brotherhood among Africans.

Tananarive, Malagasy Republic, 31 May 1964

THE OPPORTUNITY of meeting and addressing the members of this distinguished law-making body, is for me not only a great pleasure, but an unique experience. I bring you, first of all greetings and felicitations from the members of our own National Legislature, one of whom, the Honourable John Gray, is present with me on this State Visit. Yours is a noble task and I congratulate each one of you for having won the confidence of your constituents by your election to the lofty offices you hold. May the associations you will form here and the work you will accomplish be instrumental in bringing to the people of this Republic a great measure of the blessings of liberty and freedom which your nation has won and which you are now entitled to enjoy as 'a free and independent state, aware of its responsibilities, of its vitality and its potentialities.'

Just a little over a year ago, the Charter of the Organization of African Unity was signed at that historic meeting in Addis Ababa as a continental experiment in planning new approaches to the safeguard of our hard-won independence, and assuring the steady progress and development of member states comprising the organization. It is yet too early for the verdict of history; but even though the various commissions required by the Charter have not yet been set up, there were significant gains in the current year, and all member states share a great optimism that the organization will continue with ever increasing momentum in its efforts to keep the peace and to ensure the progress of the continent, and that it will come to have an impact on the history of mankind. We have cause to be proud of the challenge which faced us, the experiences we gained and the successes we achieved.

But we labour under no illusions about the many grave and important issues which may lie ahead, being confident that the will to unite and work for the ultimate redemption of the African continent and world peace are no longer debatable issues. The implementation of this great ideal may take years to reach fruition, but we are pleased and proud that the fight has been begun in a spirit which we are convinced will never die.

Because the basis of the establishment of the OAU is derived from our belief in the fundamental laws of democracy which guarantees to all men freedom to choose that form of government which best suits their aspirations and desires, and promises them the enjoyment of life, liberty and the pursuit of happiness, we know thereby that we have erected a superstructure upon which future generations will build, in keeping with the needs of their own times. Let us therefore work together in the spirit of true brotherhood, so that the laws of our respective nations may lend themselves to the consolidation and implementation of the Charter of African Unity as a machinery for realistic and effective co-operation among member states.

I am utterly convinced that we in Africa cannot escape involvement in the burning issues of world-nationalistic movements, the cry of independence for all men, the increasing rôle of the emergent nations in the balance of world power, unity and solidarity among African states and their correlation to world peace, economic progress, political stability, the growing importance of international relations and the insistent problem of world peace. We may add to these issues the breaking down of geographical and social barriers between nations. The fact that President Tsiranana visited Liberia in 1960, and that we met again at the Monrovia, Lagos, and Addis Ababa Conferences; the fact that the next meeting of the Organization of African States is to be held in Cairo, and the fact that I am here paying this State Visit, give force to the overcoming of barriers of communication among nations of the world and Africa, and in the near future, when telecommunication systems are installed, our continent will be one big listening gallery. Let me say that the possibilities envisaged in transportation and communications media are so important, that every state of this great continent will want to co-operate in some measure, to make possible such beneficial results and thus give acceleration to peace and progress in emergent Africa.

We approach these issues not in an attitude of an overwhelming sense of urgency, but in a sober, rational and broadened understanding of the process of evolution and the cultural curve of progress, as peoples and nations grow and develop into greater national consciousness, moulded by education, tutored by successive stages of experience and reinforced by the will to progress and advancement.

But whatever we undertake to do, whatever may be the discrepancies between what we set out to accomplish and what we actually achieve, we must never abandon our belief in the absolute rule of law. Is it not to be regretted, that in an age when man has discovered and learned so much more than ever before about our planet earth, the lessons of history constantly remind us of the fate of nations that relinquished the rule of law and resorted to violence and other expediencies? Anarchy, chaos and bloodshed are the result. Should we in Africa, having fought for and achieved our independence, resort to devious machinations to destroy that priceless possession? Nay, rather, let us become responsive to the lessons of history, to the needs of our times and to the enjoyment and maintenance of our valued heritage, those attributes for which men in all ages have valiantly fought — love, liberty, beauty, justice and truth. In the astounding scientific and cultural discoveries of the age, let mankind rise above the low level of man the brute to the supreme level of man the potential, and so let the day of human brotherhood dawn upon us.

Thanks to the great wave of nationalism which the world has experienced and which has sparked off the liberation of the greater portion of the African continent, President Tsiranana's visit to Liberia and my own visit at this time are very timely and appropriate. For since Africa Freedom Year, great developments have taken place in science and technology and in human relations, while contacts among the peoples of Africa on their own shores, and at the United Nations and other representative world bodies, have brought us closer than ever before. Is it not understandable that our problems in their exaggerated and unexamined forms have diminished at closer perspective and analysis?

Experience has taught us that if we determine to keep these avenues open while at the same time endeavouring to open up new ones we shall succeed in keeping our relationships active, vigorous and strong in the conscious pursuit of the ideals we have set for ourselves and coming generations. In particular, I entertain the hope that it will be possible for our two governments, which share the same political ideology, to explore certain areas in our economic, educational, cultural and trade and commercial programmes. We expect to discuss co-operation media in these and other related subjects.

As the oldest Republic on the continent of Africa, the history of Liberia has been punctuated with bitter, humiliating and frustrating experiences. While the road to nationhood may not have been long in the making, the question of our survival has literally preoccupied all our time, all our energy, all our ingenuity, and at times, all our meagre resources. Confronted with bitter criticisms, subjected to humiliating conditions, threatened with extermination and intimidated, we nevertheless faltered not, nor surrendered, maintaining 'the guard dies; he does not surrender'.

Liberia's concern, in common with the rest of Independent Africa, for peoples which have not achieved the right of self-determination, remains an hourly reminder of the obligations we owe to ourselves and those of our brethren who are not yet free to determine their own way of life. We shall continue to lend them support, to assure them that their struggle is our struggle and that we are one with them in their noble fight for freedom. To this end we shall continue to appeal to the consciences of those who now deny self-rule to millions of the world's inhabitants; we shall present our cause to the United Nations; we shall appeal to reason, fair play and justice; we shall pray for a change of heart and attitude to come. We are convinced that liberation for all of Africa is bound to come, and that our continent will have peace only when ruler and ruled live together as equal partners in political, social and economic settings.

I cannot help mentioning the great optimism which has been raised in me as I travelled from Monrovia to Marseilles, from Libreville to Monrovia, and now from Marseilles to Malagasy on this present visit. At all of these ports where it was our privilege to disembark while in transit, far beyond the official courtesies which were tendered us, I discerned a new spirit of genuine friendship and experienced a sense of belonging, indeed a kinship with all African peoples. Travelling from one country to another has become not only an exploratory or goodwill mission but one in which one becomes identified with this new spirit and enters consciously into the new brother-hood which is spreading so rapidly like the ripples of a wave.

Having now been in your beautiful island nation for a number of days, seen some of your progressive and flourishing cities, met the people of the various ethnic groups living and working together in peace and harmony, and enjoying the labours of their hands, viewed some of your industries and noted the great agricultural productions and the strides which have been made since independence, I salute the leaders for the part they are playing in keeping the peace, and keeping their people united and happy, thus help-ing to develop the nation and bring peace and prosperity to all. We are indeed proud of this opportunity to visit you and see at first hand the things which we have read about this nation, and to renew our relationship with your leaders and to make new friends. Now I assure you that we shall be happy to associate ourselves with you along lines which will be beneficial to our respective countries and peoples.

May this august law-making body of the National Assembly of the Republic of Malagasy continue to be a vital force and influence for good in the life of the nation, so that your deliberations will always be characterized by peace, harmony and concord and the laws which you enact will redound to the greater glory of your God, country and people. May generations of your fellowmen honour you for the work you have done in the preservation and consolidation, the safety and perpetuity of your nation.

At a Dinner held in His Honour by the President of Tanzania, and Mrs. Julius Nyerere

Dar-es-Salaam, Tanzania, 2 June 1964

Future African historians will refer to the latter half of the twentieth century as one in which bold political ventures were undertaken by the African peoples in the assertion of their inherent right to become free men and independent states.

One common cause activitates all the suppressed and oppressed peoples of Africa and of the world — the desire to achieve freedom and independence, so that where they have been dispossessed, divided and reduced to minority states, they may become restored to their rightful heritage.

Introductory Note

President Tubman became more and more motivated by the new spirit of African brotherhood, especially since the meeting of the Organization of African Unity in 1963. He made annual State Visits to other African states. In his numerous speeches to these new states, he often told of Liberia's own struggle for independence and survival, and was happy that Africans were now afforded the opportunity to know one another better and to share a feeling of oneness and kinship.

Dar-es-Salaam, Tanzania, 2 June 1964

THE GRADUAL disintegration of political, geographical and social barriers in the world of today has given great stimulus to increased international contacts among leaders in recent years. It is in this atmosphere that Mrs. Tubman and I find it a pleasure to be visiting the Republic of Tanzania at this time, as guests of His Excellency President Nyerere and Mrs. Nyerere. The anticipation with which we looked forward to this visit has already been amply compensated by the ebullient manifestations of welcome and the many courtesies which have been shown to us since our arrival on these shores. I acknowledge with appreciation the warm receptions, the gracious hospitality and the friendliness which have been extended to us and which have all contributed in many ways to make our stay thus far enjoyable and rewarding. Nothing has been lacking to make us feel welcome and at home among brothers and friends.

Future African historians will refer to the latter half of the twentieth century as one in which bold political ventures were undertaken by the African peoples in the assertion of their inherent right to become free men and independent states.

561

We, like you, have always valued liberty and freedom as prized possessions. It is one of the interesting observations in the history of our nation
that while we were hemmed in on all sides by formidable forces, it was
hardly conceivable that any experiment in democratic government could
succeed on the shores of Africa at that time; but nevertheless the experiment went on successfully, though at a retarded pace, and, thanks to the
indomitable courage of the Founding Fathers and the sympathy and support
given by friendly nations, the pioneers and succeeding administrations were
able to endure the many political, financial, and social crises in the pathway to nationhood and its maintenance. Today, while the ultimate in the
democratic process has not yet been achieved, we are happy that the
course has been set and that our objectives are now more definite than ever
before.

The great forward steps which you and your virile nation took in the
formation of the Republic of Tanganyika and Zanzibar has won the
admiration of many nations and peoples not only of Africa but the world.
Your nation's unwavering support of the principles for which free men in
all ages have lived; the high statesmanship evinced and the dedication to
the cause of African solidarity and unity displayed by Your Excellency and
the leaders of this nation have equally won the respect of the peoples of the
world; for no one has listened to the dynamic voice of President Nyerere
without the conviction that here is a capable, conscientious, scholarly and
erudite statesman of high calibre whose bold assertions and sincerity have
singled him out as a true leader, not only of the Republic of Tanganyika and
Zanzibar, but of Africa, and as a true fighter for the cause of African freedom and redemption. I heard him at the Summit Conference in Addis
Ababa; I read the account of his speech before the United Nations, and in
every instance my respect and admiration of this great statesman has
deepened. I hail and salute this great leader for all that he has already
accomplished in conjunction with the other leaders of the newly-formed
United Republic of Tanganyika and Zanzibar for their country's cause, for
their selfless leadership and for the dedication with which they serve the
political and social welfare of their people and country. With such leaders,
I feel sure that the Republic of Tanganyika and Zanzibar is bound to go
forward and the cause of African liberation assured. Thus, despite the problems experienced by the people of this new Republic as in the formative
periods of all nations, I am confident that the course has been set and I am
equally convinced that they will be correctly led and guided to approach
the future with hope, confidence and the reality of their duties and responsibilities.

One common cause activates all the suppressed and oppressed peoples of
Africa and the world – the desire to achieve freedom and independence, so
that where they have been dispossessed, divided and reduced to minority
status, they may become restored to their rightful heritage and unified into
a dignified human community.

The peoples of Africa stand for one common purpose – to see the liberation of those now under the sphere of foreign influences and domination, so
that they too may be able to determine the form of government best suited
to the fruition of their ideals and aspirations.

We in Africa fight for and demand one common goal – through the
organization of our effective and strong union – to join hands and march

together in the advancement of a continent which we are sure will again have an impact on the history of civilization.

To the maturing of these ideals we have dedicated ourselves in the Charter of the OAU, and we call upon all those whose consciences have been pricked by the indignities and lack of opportunities for progress and advancement suffered by the oppressed peoples of the world, to renew their solemn obligations for the reign of love, justice and equality to be established in the world.

With the growing concept of fundamental freedoms for all mankind, I am happy that the decision that the African people's desire for peace and unity has been reached, and that we have come to discover that our problems are more similar than dissimilar. In this framework we can now work with greater objectivity, and it is a source of joy to know that Africans are now bending their efforts to this new task of planning and working for the common welfare of all and in the interest of world peace.

In these endeavours may the continuing image of the United Nations be ever with us so that our participation in and support of that shrine of hope, coupled with our determination to see the Charter of the Organization of African Unity fully implemented, will bring enduring benefits to us and all mankind.

In the hope that this visit will bring our two countries and peoples together in a more active relationship and that new avenues for mutual friendship and co-operation will be found between us, I raise my glass, Ladies and Gentlemen, and ask you to join Mrs. Tubman and myself in drinking a toast to the health, happiness and personal well-being of President and Mrs. Nyerere, and to the solidarity and prosperity of the government and people of the Republic of Tanganyika and Zanzibar.

To the Second Summit Meeting of the Organization of African Unity

Cairo, United Arab Republic, 10 July 1964

Let us adopt a programme under which, by African example and initiative, a new meaning will be given to the United Nations and its existing organizations, and under which new avenues toward genuine peace will be opened to Africa and to the world.

Introductory Note

When the Second Summit of Heads of States and Governments met in Cairo, United Arab Republic, great was the optimism displayed for the future success of the Organization of African Unity. President Tubman in this speech presented a blueprint for African co-operation which he considered essential for African unity. Emphasis was laid on economic and cultural co-operation.

Cairo, United Arab Republic, 10 July 1964

WE HAVE gathered here today, in the capital of this ancient and historic country, for the Second Summit Meeting of the Heads of African States and Governments. In a spirit of brotherhood and co-operative endeavour we have come to re-assert our faith in the eternal principles of justice, freedom and equality and to pledge once again our faith in that unity of purpose which must and should be the sole determinant of our thought, action and concerted effort for the supreme welfare of our vast continent.

Without doubt what we wish to emphasize is a restatement of our determination, such as we expressed at that first historic summit in Addis Ababa and such as all lovers of freedom adhere to. There are certain rights of liberty and life inalienable for men everywhere, and whenever the vital growth of these rights is menaced, we will not hesitate to defend them with all the resources at our command.

We are happy that following in the wake of the great success achieved in fashioning the instrument of the Charter of African Unity, to which we subscribed over a year ago, we have again met to consider implementation of the ideals which will make that great instrument a pragmatic tool for the ultimate liberation of Africa. In so doing, we must by word and deed make this continent a lighted pathway to the world's fervent pursuit of peace, justice and equality for all mankind.

Egypt, the seat of this conference session, with its great wealth of recorded history, its distinctive civilization, the glories of its dynasties, its arts, architecture and literature, has made a significant impact on the history of world civilization. It is a happy augury, therefore, that this Second Summit should take place in a setting so pregnant with the sense of history and from which we can take more comprehensive bearings for the greater tasks that lie ahead.

Since the new régime in this great nation, numerous changes and developments have taken place under its valiant and patriotic President, whose inspiring leadership has brought his country a new outlook and lifted her to greater heights of progress and international renown. It was my joy and pleasure to travel twice recently through the Suez Canal and to see on our northward passage the tremendously impressive heavy traffic of ships through the canal and the gigantic construction projects which are being carried on to improve the services of the bridge between the Mediterranean and the Red Sea. We are grateful therefore to the President, the Government and people of the United Arab Republic, for serving as hosts to this conference and for affording us the facilities to expedite our mission to this Second Summit Conference.

The emergence of so great a number of African States to nationhood has reinforced our ideals of African unity, laid the basis for optimism and perforce given it great encouragement. Thus, the stimulus for this wave of nationalism must continue until self-determination for the peoples of this vast continent is assured; until the dignity of all men is recognized and respected; until all men stand on a pedestal as equal participating partners in the comity of nations. Until that time comes the states which are now independent must persevere in their efforts for the abrogation and elimination of every vestige of discrimination, racial superiority and apartheid in every form.

We pay tribute to nations that have already granted independence to those over whom they ruled; more than this, the fact that ruler and ruled now live together in the enjoyment of their political rights, life, liberty and the pursuit of happiness, gives cogency to the argument that we can all live together on the basis of equal and participating partnership and thus achieve social, political, economic and cultural goals.

No one can ignore the gains that have been made during the year that has elapsed since the charter of African Unity was signed, though the machinery of the Charter has not been set up in its entirety. During that period issues of the gravest nature arose with which it was impossible to grapple, because some of the important phases of the charter had not yet been fully implemented. In the absence of the proper machinery of enforcement, it is to the credit of member states of the organization, and a great reflection on their zeal, fidelity and determination to live in peace and develop their countries, that initiatives were taken to bring about arbitration, mediation and conciliation, without which serious crises might have erupted. But while our success in handling these unexpected developments has been gratifying, we must not forget that time is of the essence in our undertaking. It appears to me that it is essential that the fulfilment of the provisions of the charter be completed as far as practicable at this session. In the name of those valiant ones who have given their lives for the ideals of freedom, on behalf of those still fighting to be free, let us bear in our heart and hands the eternal torch and carry the complete liberation of our continent to a new and greater victory.

I should like to invite your attention, my honourable colleagues, to a situation that exists in the world today, about which, in the opinion of the Liberian Government, we as African Heads of States can do something.

On many occasions, we have individually and collectively reaffirmed our faith and determination in the United Nations as an important instrument for the promotion of the economic and social advancement of all peoples. To indicate this faith and belief, we extended an invitation to the Secretary-General of the United Nations to visit this session of our conference. We are happy to have him here and we feel honoured that he accepted our invitation in spite of his varied and exhaustive engagements.

One needs only to take a cursory look to see for oneself what the United Nations is doing for Africa. The Trusteeship System of the United Nations has engineered and steered many African States to full independence, and its special committee on colonialism continues to exert pressure on states with colonial possessions to grant independence to those colonies. Even the lot of those still under colonial domination has improved, because of action taken by the United Nations.

The geography of Africa has often afforded to our continent both protection and obstacles to progress. It protected us from being carved up as completely as may originally have been contemplated, but it has also presented us with immense development problems in health, education, transportation and many other areas. For example, improvement of transportation is difficult and expensive both singly and collectively. One glance at a map of the continent shows that there are no deep bays, or gulfs, or river systems penetrating into the solid continental mass.

This situation in recent years has led to economic as well as political problems in independent Africa. With the end of colonial rule and our resolve to unite, the persistent lack of contact and co-operation with neighbouring African States, because of natural and artificial barriers, has accentuated the need for fullest co-operation in all endeavours.

The situation which the development of transportation and economic co-operation between coastal and land-locked countries presents clearly demonstrates the need for co-operation along these lines.

The Liberian Government believes that there should be co-ordination of transportation networks between coastal and land-locked countries to facilitate the movement of people and the exportation of goods. Roads should also be constructed as feeders to railroads and a system of cross continental highways should be constructed with direct and accessible road links with each country. Africa has many short lengths of railroad networks which could be extended to connect with those from adjacent countries.

The Liberian Government therefore proposes that each member state bordering the sea, pledge and enter agreements that would permit the transport of goods and services through its ports and other transportation networks to sister African States that may be land-locked, on such terms, provisions and conditions as may be mutually agreed upon.

It has been the pretension of men and nations from time immemorial to seek ways and means to avoid and avert war, although without much success until now. The Organization of African Unity should therefore give consideration to and place emphasis on our abhorrence of war, and utilize its good offices toward the prevention of war by preparing and formulating plans aimed at bridging the gaps between all varying ideologies and systems of governments so as to prevent a threat to peace and the possibility of war.

In this context, therefore, it can scarcely be out of order to propose that Africa and, more specifically, the Organization of African Unity adopt a programme aimed at a persistent, determined, consistent and continuing effort at achieving a true and lasting peace. Let us at this conference take the first steps down the road to peace! Let us adopt a programme under which, by African example and African initiative, a new meaning will be given to the United Nations and its existing organizations devised to eliminate the possibilities of strife and conflict; and under which new avenues toward the elimination of war and the institution of genuine peace will be opened to Africa and to the world.

Liberia would, in this context, wish to propose the following immediate steps as a beginning – but only a beginning – of the bold, unequivocal effort which our continent and our peoples should make to achieve peace in the world.

First and foremost let us now make those decisions and take those actions necessary to maintain the great momentum achieved at Addis Ababa. Let us complete the work begun there; let us spare no effort to make the Organization of African Unity the objective, constructive and dynamic institution betokened by the charter. The road toward African unity has already been chosen. The instrument for African co-operation has already been fashioned – but incomplete though it still is, it already has great accomplishments which prove that it is effective and capable of even greater things.

The promise, the vitality, the significance of this organization cannot be allowed to waste away through meandering manoeuvres for advantage or prestige. Liberia urges that this conference give proof of our total commitment to meaningful African unity, to real African co-operation and to genuine African peace by completing here and now the organizational tasks necessary to the future effectiveness and progress of the Organization of African Unity under the provisions of the charter. Specifically, we propose that this conference provide this organization with a permanent headquarters, with a permanent Secretary-General and with a permanent staff.

Let Africa set the example for peaceful co-operation and for a steady, continuing progress toward real unity by proving that this organization will not founder on the shoals of organizational bickering which has undermined or killed so many noble efforts in the past. We have a creative, useful, effective instrument in the charter; let us complete and perfect it – here and now!

As a second African example for the world, let this conference adopt and let the Heads of State undertake to obtain before January 1, 1965, the necessary ratification of the protocol of mediation, conciliation and arbitration which has been submitted to us.

The commitment in article XIX of the charter of this commission of mediation, conciliation and arbitration is complete and unequivocal. It could become one of the most significant and promising steps taken toward the maintenance of peace in Africa. Prompt and unqualified adoption of this protocol would constitute a major example of Africa's determination to lead the way toward lasting peace.

As a third African example to the world, we propose for adoption by this conference and for subsequent ratification by member states, a resolution stating in clear and unqualified language that no African nation will commit any act of aggression – be it military, political or psychological – against any other African nation.

May the spirit of fraternity and friendship prevail among us at this conference, so that our deliberations will be conducted in a climate of mutual understanding and sympathetic goodwill, thereby yielding fruitful results which will richly redound to the welfare of our continent; may the unity for which we now strive bring us indomitable courage, unswerving devotion to our cause and mellow wisdom which will bring to a glorious fulfilment the noblest and most historic adventure of our century.

To the Nation on his return from State Visits to the Republic of Malagasy and Tanzania

Monrovia, 13 July 1964

> *Operation Production must be vigorously enforced and pursued, for we may already be a century late in the prosecution of a programme so indispensable to the life of the nation.*

Introductory Note

For President Tubman numerous State Visits became the order of the day; it seemed that his stature as Africa's grand old statesman never ceased to grow. When he returned home he brought back with him many lessons learned abroad from his encounter with new experiences. The good that he saw in these experiences he tried to relate to Liberia's own needs. His attention was further focused on progress made at home through self-help programmes. His addresses upon his return home were always most informative.

He reported that Liberia had embarked upon becoming once again the maritime nation she had been over a century before, and would now possess a National Shipping Line. He gave more attention to the virtues of Operation Production, and noted further that some agreement seemed to have been reached between the sellers and buyers of primary products in a recent conference, which could mean a good future for Operation Production. What he had seen in Malagasy and Tanzania gave him more courage to press on for the execution of this new national formula for growth and development.

Monrovia, 13 July 1964

AFTER MORE than eighteen thousand miles covered in travel by sea, air and rail, starting from the bulge of the African continent on the West Atlantic, to North Africa on the Mediterranean, Marseilles in Europe, Port Said on the Suez Canal, the Gulf of Suez and the Red Sea, to the Gulf of Aden, the Indian Ocean and on to the Island Continent of Madagascar, and returning thence by air flight from Tananarive, Madagascar, to Dar-es-Salaam, Tanganyika; back to Marseilles by sea, by rail to Zürich, Switzerland, again by rail from there to Bordeaux, and finally by ship to Liberia, I am exceedingly happy to be able to exclaim, 'home again' and thank God for His merciful care, protection and guidance of us throughout our travels.

In twenty-one days we visited the Republic of Malagasy and the United Republic of Tanganyika and Zanzibar and Zürich in Switzerland; we were extended much courtesy while in transit, and in many places lavish state and official gestures were accorded us, as we travelled from Monrovia to Marseilles and back again.

In all, we saw close to four million people, were deeply impressed by the cultural music, songs and dances of Malagasy and roused by the stirring Tanganyika Party Song in Dar-es-Salaam; we saw, with great interest, the countless fields of cultivated rice planted both in mountainous and swamp areas, saw great varieties of food products, noted the thriving local industries, particularly the work of indigenous artists and craftsmen, and admired the creative genius of the peoples of Malagasy and Tanganyika. The details of these visits have already been relayed to you by the Liberian Information Service. We can only add that the enthusiasm and spirit shown, the many kindnesses extended to us and the friendships which we formed deepened our appreciation and increased our understanding of the peoples of the host governments. Relationships between these sister states and our own have been greatly strengthened.

The Republic of Malagasy and the United Republic of Tanganyika and Zanzibar are states where people of different ethnic groups have lived together for centuries, achieved cultural unity, speak two common languages – Malagache and Swahili – and work with great dedication and determination to make their nations havens of peace, plenty and progress. The passion for hard work, the creativity in arts and crafts and the love of music contribute toward making these people great and noble.

Under the dynamic, courageous and distinguished leadership of their beloved Presidents, the two nations have a great future, for Presidents Tsiranana and Nyerere are not only greatly loved for what they are as men but for what they have done and are doing for their nations and peoples by their patriotism, sound and approved policies of development, the charm of their personalities and the warmth of their human compassion.

In East Africa they speak one principal language, Swahili, and in Madagascar, Malagache.

Madagascar has an ancient civilization which has been preserved even until today. In the Palace of the Queen we saw the gorgeous crowns, robes and other paraphenalia of the court that were used by the early monarchs and rulers before the French occupation. In the period of the reign of the Kings and Queens of this great Island-Nation, Ambassadors were sent to England and one group of them was received by Queen Elizabeth the First.

Because of circumstances beyond our control, we regret that we were unable to fulfil our itinerary by visiting Kenya and Uganda. After our arrival in Dar-es-Salaam we found that the visit to Kenya of His Imperial Majesty, Emperor Haile Selassie the First, and ours followed closely on one another, and because it was obvious that this would create an inconvenience to the Kenyan Government, some change of plan became necessary. Accordingly, readjustments were suggested; but as we were travelling by ship and the date for our departure had already been set we found it impracticable to accommodate the situation and therefore suggested a postponement. After the exchange of telegrams and emissaries specially sent to discuss the question, the Kenya Government acquiesced in our position. Following this, His Excellency the Minister of State of Kenya was sent to meet us at Mombasa and expressed his government's regrets that the visit had to be postponed, adding that he hoped the visit would be made in the near future.

When one travels today and encounters friendly, smiling, singing and hospitable peoples, the one family of man concept is brought forcibly to mind and with it a real feeling of human kinship. Thus at a time when so much is to be gained by contacts which form the basis of mutual understanding and lead to improved relations, visits of the kind we have just made have acquired added and new significance; no longer regarded merely as goodwill or official missions, they have become a medium of identification with and participation in the new spirit of unity and brotherhood which is rapidly drawing the peoples of this vast continent together. It is a hopeful sign that the circle of those who are trying to know and understand each other is becoming wider and wider.

There was another important aspect to these visits which have ended today. You will recall that in my outline of policy in the first Inaugural Address, I called attention to our approximately three hundred and fifty-mile coastline along the South Atlantic and said that we must have ships of our own to ply within our territorial and international waters. I also stated that the founders of our country anticipated a fleet of ships, both mercantile and naval, when they provided in the Constitution for a Secretary of War and Navy. In pursuance of this policy we recommended to the Legislature the repeal of the Act forbidding the flying of the Liberian flag on foreign vessels, and the Legislature endorsed and passed the relevant Act. As a result of this the Liberian merchant marine fleet is today the second largest in the world and substantial financial benefits have come to the country as revenues accruing therefrom; but since we considered this insufficient we have carried on negotiations over the years to enable ships not only to fly the Liberian flag but to be of Liberian ownership. These arrangements were concluded and Mrs. Tubman preceded me to Holland to christen the first Liberian-owned ship, and later joined me in Marseilles, after spending eight days in Zürich, Switzerland, awaiting my arrival. The second ship was subsequently launched and christened by Mrs. Victoria Tolbert in Cork, Ireland. Within less than a year, therefore, we expect to have at least two Liberian-owned ships of thirty-one thousand tons each, plying the seven seas and other navigable waters.

It was particularly heart-warming, as we travelled through the Suez Canal and the Gulfs of Suez and Aden, especially in Port Said, to see numerous ships, both large and small, flying the Liberian flag. Needless to say, I attach great importance to these events, because they represent a beginning of another important landmark in the nation's economic development and prestige and are the fulfilment of another of the policies we enunciated to the nation in 1944.

Great economic and social ends are effected by those who work hard to usher in an era of abundant production; this is where Operation Production must acquire a new significance for the people of this nation, so that, in short, it may become in practice the *sine qua non* of our very existence, preservation and creativity.

There is an indestructible quality in nations which, while preserving the old in indigenous arts, crafts, songs and artefacts, also strive to create new ones. The indestructibility of the culture of this nation will depend largely on the preservation of those forms which are indigenous to us and those which we create. Our institutions of learning and cultural centres wherever these arts and crafts now exist should begin not merely to collect and preserve them as such, but also to create new forms, so that this aspect may become a vital contribution to our educational, cultural and social evolution.

It is imperative to teach and thus preserve our arts, crafts and everything that is old in our culture and to create new ones. To achieve these ends, the Departments of Internal Affairs and Education, the Liberian Information Service, our University, colleges and schools must take the initiative in this new programme. A very good beginning has been made at Booker Washington Institute in Kakata, the Fundamental Education Centre at Klay and the Cultural Centre in Paynesville, under the auspices of the Liberian Information Service. These efforts must be increased, intensified and co-ordinated.

In a similar manner the question of sports and the athletic programme of the nation needs to be reviewed and reactivated, since the popularity of foreign games and sports has caused the complete disappearance of local ones. The Liberian baseball, pitching quoits, rope pulling and jumping, the bley, chudder, leap-frog, ann cansy, rocker-rocker, sally cunnie and other such sports that are entirely Liberian, the different kinds of wrestling, for instance, the Bassa, Cape Palmas and Sinoe wrestling styles are unknown in today's sports and entertainment. In this period of reactivation, more encouragement should be given to the teaching and popularization of these in the schools as well as their inclusion in the programme of the National Sports Commission.

OPERATION PRODUCTION

In the 1956 Inaugural Address we recommended the creation of a National Production Council which was charged with the responsibility of planning and executing a programme for increasing the agricultural and commercial output of the nation, thereby serving as an important support to our economy.

Under the aegis of the National Production Council, progress has been made in exposing the people to the benefits to be derived from the constant stimulation and encouragement of the Council's programme of national production. This much has been accomplished: the citrus cannery at Kakata, the coffee mill at Voinjama, the project at Kpain where a whole community has been set up and assisted by instruction in agriculture, each family working on a twenty-five acre block of land, where, at a ceremony specially arranged by the Secretary of the Treasury and the Executive Secretary of the National Production Council a year ago, I personally handed individual title deeds to members of the community so that they might utilize the land for the purpose of greater production. The oil palm nursery in Grand Bassa, the agricultural extension programme introduced in the counties, the distribution of seeds and plants, the assignment of agricultural aides and so forth; all these were inaugurated and promoted by the National Production Council under the direction of the Joint Commission with the Secretary of the Treasury as Chairman. From this beginning we must now enlarge our operations, lengthen the cords and strengthen the stakes and under the new slogan, Priority Number One Operation Production, tap all the potentialities of our land on a nation-wide scale.

Having personally undertaken to go from county to county and from province to province propagating Operation Production with a view to arousing genuine interest in the programme, I have been gratified by the national response and enthusiasm. But this will not suffice; the implementation of the programme must realistically begin on a nation-wide basis so that early results will be realized and reports made of our gains.

Already several Liberians have been sent away for training and observation periods who are expected, upon their return, to carry on the great tasks in connection with Operation Production. I realize that it will take time for us to reach the place we envisage, but we must forge ahead as quickly and effectively as possible, so that even while the technical programmes are being worked out and the needed know-how for modernization acquired, we can continue to use the old farming methods to stimulate interest and help increase production.

I return from this itinerary more than ever resolved that Operation Production must be vigorously enforced and pursued for we may already be a century late in the prosecution of a programme so indispensable to the life of the nation. And if ever there was any doubt in my mind about the benefits to be derived, I was completely reassured with the abundance of agricultural productions which we saw in Malagasy and the United Republic of Tanganyika and Zanzibar. The nation that has enough to feed its population is already a long way up the ladder of progress and development.

THE INTERNATIONAL SITUATION

After the protracted session of the Geneva Trade Conference, it is pleasing to note that the industrialized nations, together with the developing countries of primary producing goods, have reached agreement for setting up a kind of machinery to consider, to some extent, the imbalance in benefits derived between producers of primary products and finished goods. This is an important first step, and we hope that further advances will be made, so that fairer and juster benefits may accrue to all concerned.

A new gleam of hope seems to appear on the horizon and mankind looks with anxiety to the continuing efforts of the Great Powers for better understanding, reasonable adjustments and the exercise of sound judgment in dealing with ideological differences which may tend to lessen international tension. Some on each side have called it capitulation. I think of it as the exercise of common sense and a profound realization of the folly and futility of engaging in a global nuclear holocaust that is predatory in nature and suicidal in character. If it is capitulation, it is a kind that will tend to the interest of mankind, and if pursued in good faith may usher in the reign of peace on earth.

While en route to Zürich, it was my pleasure, at the invitation of the President and Officers of the ILO Conference being held in Geneva, to have alighted there to make a brief extemporaneous address; the text of my remarks appeared in the Journal of the Conference which most of you may have read.

Liberia is a free enterprise and democratic state and has been such, not only since our independence in 1847, but also from the founding of this state in 1822. This system of government, the only one known to us, preserved us through the commonwealth period into independence at a time when the onslaught of colonialism in Africa and the great expansionist movement were approaching their peak. I have no doubt that the people of this nation will never subscribe to, nor support any change in our present free enterprise democratic system, nor do I believe that there is any Liberian who would advocate a change of our century-old, tested, tried and approved system of government for a mirage of the desert.

We record our thanks to the members of the Cabinet under the leadership of the Secretary of State who was charged by our letters patent to conduct the affairs of State during our absence from the country. Special mention should be made of the Honourable Ernest Eastman, Under Secretary of State, who for the greater duration of our absence served as Acting Secretary of State, and who in the discharge of his duties reflected the same principles evidenced by his immediate Chief, Secretary of State, His Excellency J. Rudolph Grimes. To all officials in the three branches of Government, I give thanks for your loyalty and patriotism in carrying out your several responsibilities; to the Ministers' Association and the Liberian Clergy, we attribute our personal safety and the success of our visits largely to the prayers which you offered at the Throne of Grace on our behalf and particularly to Bishop Dillard Brown who requested the clergy of his denomination to offer special prayers for our safe travel to and fro and for the success of our mission and I thank the general citizenry, our foreign friends and residents most sincerely for your splendid co-operation.

Despite the fact that our absence from home this time has been of long duration (and never before have the Vice-President, the Speaker of the House of Representatives, the Secretary of State, the Chief Justice, Cabinet Ministers and other leaders of the country been absent at the same time), nevertheless, the Government was carried on smoothly and efficiently. This course of conduct gives testimony to the sense of responsibility, understanding, patriotism and love of freedom of the people of this nation. I beseech you to let us keep it so, not only for the present but also throughout the future, for by this manner of national demeanour we evidence maturity, good sense and a demonstration of a real spirit of loyalty to our country and its democratic principles.

Together let us continue to build a stronger and better nation now and in the years ahead, knowing that the success of the future will depend greatly upon the strong foundations we lay at the present time, so that coming generations may build a yet nobler superstructure thereon and that they will rise up and call us blessed.

On the Occasion of a Dinner in Honour of President and Mrs. Nicholas Grunitsky during their Visit to Liberia

Monrovia 25 July 1964

I observe that the frequency of contacts among Africans has been instrumental in breaking down some barriers and has led to the generating of better understanding and goodwill.

Introductory Note

Every visit between African leaders afforded an opportunity to discuss and review common problems in their search for unity, and in the struggle for the total liberation of Africa. It was always therefore a matter of inspiration for President Tubman to welcome African Heads of State to Liberia as often as possible. Here he discussed with President Grunitzky steps of co-operation and understanding leading to African unity.

Monrovia, 25 July 1964

IT IS an honour and a pleasure to all of us that your Excellency should be visiting us on the eve of our One Hundred and Seventeenth Independence Anniversary. We extend to you and the members of your party a very warm welcome and hope that you will share our joy with us at this time, when a new chapter is opening in the political and social history of our nation, as four new counties are legally added to the former five to expand the political and administrative structure of our country.

This second meeting with you, Mr. President, follows closely upon the first, when at the recent Summit Conference in Cairo Your Excellency's calm poise, dignified personality and comprehensive grasp of the African and international situations and the larger tasks which confront African leaders, made a favourable impression on our minds. Having participated in the Cairo Conference you have identified yourself with the purpose and noble work of that organization.

The growing number of African States creates a new challenge to our efforts to achieve unity, peace and concord on the African continent. But we must face this challenge together with courage and optimism, knowing that the basis of our hope and the nature of the task to which we have set ourselves are not irreconcilable or unattainable. We must face this challenge individually convinced that the human and material resources of our nations are still to be tapped and utilized; we must face the challenge collectively cognizant that the work we do now for African liberation will contribute to the enlargement of the image of the democratic concept and the conviction that we cannot evade our responsibility to the rest of the

575

world; together and hand in hand, we must face the challenge because millions of Africans are waiting to benefit by the results of our voices and concerted purposeful action, from which we may soon experience a transition in the realm of international politics and world diplomacy.

It is in this connection that I observe that the frequency of contacts among Africans, whether Heads of States or Governments, officials or citizens, have been instrumental in breaking down some barriers and have led to the generating of better understanding and goodwill among nations and peoples. May we continue to use these contacts as effective media in fostering good human relations, thereby winning more and more friends who are bound to live and work together as partners in a common cause.

We are aware of the circumstances that brought your Excellency to power as President of the Togolese Republic, as well as your strenuous efforts to bring reconciliation and national unity to the Togolese Government and people. We trust that your efforts will be successful and that the Togolese people will recognize that the safety and security of the state is the highest law, and that every citizen owes it to his country and its legally constituted government to be loyal and patriotic, and, forgetting the things that are past, to work for the future in the interest of national unity and solidarity.

We entertain the hope, Mr. President, that during your stay here our respect and affection for you and the people of Togo will be reflected in your talks with officials and citizens and that you will feel the warmth and genuineness of the friendship of the Liberian people.

It is worth mentioning that our contacts with Togo date from colonial times when large numbers of Togolese immigrated to Liberia and in due course became naturalized citizens. Their contributions to the social, cultural and economic life of the nation have been very valuable indeed. They have been law-abiding citizens who have identified themselves fully with the ideals of African brotherhood and unity. So you see, Mr. President, that long before we began to talk about unity on a continental scale, strong links of friendship had already been established between our two countries.

It is obvious, therefore, that this visit will strengthen the cordial bonds which have existed between our two nations and peoples, that we shall seek new avenues to enrich our cultural and social understanding and significantly develop our trade and commercial relations with your nation and its people, and that eventually the Republic of Togo will join other West African States in the proposed establishment of a free trade zone area.

Once again, Mr. President, in the name of true brotherhood and in the name of the larger unity we seek for all Africa, we welcome you.

For the success of the great task which has devolved upon him, I ask you, ladies and gentlemen, to raise your glasses and drink with Mrs. Tubman and myself to the health and happiness of President Grunitzky and Mrs. Grunitzky and to the peace and solidarity of the Government and people of Togo.

To the Nation on his return from the Cairo Non-aligned Conference

Monrovia, 30 October 1964

The urgency of universal crises with which all men are confronted and the utter destructiveness of the new instruments of warfare call for constructive thinking and action. We therefore have a responsibility to plead for sanity, to raise our courage to new heights and our minds to nobler thoughts, in order that human brotherhood and peace may be achieved.

Introductory Note

Because so much of the world's energy, time and ability were expended in either perpetuating the arms race or discouraging it, the non-aligned nations of the world saw an opportunity to act as a powerful moral force for intervention. Representing as they did most of the newly independent and developing nations, they had vital interests to protect. They appeared to be a third force whose sole objective was to persuade the powerful nations of the world to heed their counsel of universal peace and brotherhood. President Tubman appreciated the existence of this third force, one of several operating in the cause of peace.

His new programmes – Operation Production and an education tax levy, were also taking root among his people, which pleased him greatly. He further made mention of stability at home and the political maturity of the people of Liberia which had often been tested during his visits abroad, a few of which, such as the present one under review, had been prolonged without preventing the smooth operation of the Government of Liberia.

Monrovia, 30 October 1964

OUR TRAVELS this year in the interest of cementing and strengthening existing ties of friendship and creating new ones, as well as for the purpose of attending conferences affecting matters of national, international, continental and intercontinental concern, have been made principally within Africa, our own continent, and have necessitated our covering a larger mileage than ever before in any one year since our first incumbency.

The missions have taken us to nations and areas impregnated with history, ancient arts, civilizations and cultures which, although relatively forgotten, hold even now some of the great wonders of the world. I refer to the great African dynasties, the pyramids, the Sphinx, the mummies and other such amazing achievements of Egypt and other African countries.

In Egypt stand the pyramids in resplendent artistic splendour, having stood several thousand years and destined, apparently, to stand many more. Men are still baffled by the skill with which such enormous stones, to such

577

precise measurements, could be transported and placed in such geometric forms; or by the Sphinx with its ageless grandeur and awesome pose, attracting men from all around the world to its wondrous stare; or by the mummies of kings and other great rulers, whose mortal remains have been mysteriously preserved after four, five and even six millenia, with their nails still on their toes and the hair on their heads.

THE NON-ALIGNED CONFERENCE

The Conference of Non-aligned States from which we have returned today was numerically the largest assembly of Chiefs of State and Heads of Government known to have met at any one time in any one place in history. It was composed of representatives of states and governments from the four corners of the world and from all over the globe. Men with various ideologies, outlooks, religions, cultures, propensities, social and political orders and systems of government were there.

The Conference of Heads of State and Government was preceded by a meeting of Foreign Ministers who prepared the agenda. Secretary of State Grimes led the Liberian delegation which consisted of the Secretary of Commerce and Industry, the Honourable Romeo Horton and other Government officials. During the Conference, when it became impracticable for the Secretary of State to attend the other sessions of the Political Committee and the Foreign Ministers, Under Secretary of State Eastman led the delegation. It was this corps of workers who did the spade work and bore the burden of the day.

The Conference recognized the importance of disarmament as one of the serious problems harassing the world, and stressed the necessity of reaching both immediate and practical solutions intended to save mankind from the horrible feeling of insecurity and the dangers of war. It called upon the great powers of the world to reflect seriously upon the continuing arms race and the development of weapons of mass destruction, and to initiate new and urgent efforts toward achieving general and complete disarmament under strict and effective international control.

The Conference also recorded its conviction that a meeting to discuss disarmament under the auspices of the United Nations would provide powerful support to the efforts which are being made to set in motion the process of disarmament.

The declaration of the denuclearization of the continent of Africa by the African States at the OAU Summit in July last was affirmed by the Conference.

There were other decisions of the Conference which I believe will make an effective contribution to the peace and stability of Africa.

All of the participating states pledged material support to the fullest extent of their abilities to territories still under colonial rule and domination.

There was also unanimous opposition to a unilateral and illegal declaration of independence secured by a limited referendum of African chiefs and headmen by the present minority Government in Southern Rhodesia. It is my firm conviction that consultation with tribal chiefs holding office and exercising authority under the power and control of the Government of Southern Rhodesia could not reflect the opinion of the majority of the people of that country.

It is our belief that the decision of the Conference regarding South Africa, if implemented by all the participating states, will give substantial assistance to the erasing of the ugly policy of apartheid from the African continent.

The resolution on economic development and co-operation, conceived within the context of the United Nations Conference on Trade and Development, and the target of economic growth set out by the United Nations for the development decade will usher in an era of closer and fairer economic relations among the developed and developing states.

It may be useful to record the following definition of non-alignment, formulated by the Conference.

'Non-alignment can never or should never be viewed as a refusal to choose between good and evil, moral or immoral, to take sides with blocs or to remain neutral in a dynamic world. Rather, the political actions of states ought to make it possible for them to enter various agreements – commercial, economic, technical and other national and international activities – with other nations without affecting their independence of thought and action.

'The non-aligned nations are concerned with justice, freedom, independence and human well-being. Equally so, they are concerned about the ending of colonial rule and imperialism everywhere in the world where these forms have received their death knell and where the force and significance of nationalism have turned the conscience of the peoples of the world from unreality to reality and directed attention to the crossroads of a new human endeavour.

'Non-alignment should become a vital, moral and spiritual force, a helpful influence between the contending forces of peace and war, hate and love, broken human relationships and sacred treaties and obligations. Non-alignment should be made a great and formidable international causeway over which nations can find the path to conciliation, reconciliation and the adjustment of differences between nations and evolve an era of universal peace founded on justice, equality and equity.'

THREE MOMENTOUS EVENTS

On the 16th day of October of this year, three eventful and momentous occurrences took place within the space of twenty-four hours: Three great nations made certain decisions and undertook certain actions that may have great international repercussions. We hope that these decisions will uplift and strengthen our faltering world and accelerate our quest for peace and security.

The first decision was made by the electorate of Great Britain by their election of the Right Honourable Harold Wilson as Prime Minister. Mr. Wilson is known as a man of keen intelligence, perception and marked imagination. The world may well be enriched by him and we hope that he will be able to offer constructive alternatives to the fragile peace in the world and assist the African territories in their struggle for self-determination and independence. This is apparent in his pronouncement against the unilateral declaration of independence by Southern Rhodesia.

The next incident of the 16th day of October was an announcement by the TASS News Agency of the USSR that the Communist Party Central Committee had considered the request of Mr. Krushchev to be relieved of his duties as the First Secretary of the Central Committee, Member of the Presidium of the Central Committee and Chairman of the Council of Ministers of the Soviet Union, in view of his advanced age and deteriorating health. Mr. Alexei Kosygin was appointed to the post of Prime Minister and Mr. Leonid Brezhnev as Secretary of the Party. These changes, which arouse both interest and concern throughout the world, are internal affairs of the USSR and within their competence.

It is a source of some satisfaction that the new Soviet officials announced their intention to continue to work to pursue the policy of peaceful co-existence and world peace.

Mr. Krushchev, during the tenure of his leadership of the Soviet Nation, made substantial contributions toward peace and it had seemed that the prospects for peace had never been brighter than they were recently. We believe Mr. Krushchev realized, as we do, that nuclear war could mean national and international suicide and probably the destruction of the human race.

The news that the People's Republic of China had detonated its first atomic bomb came less than twenty-four hours after the announcement of Mr. Krushchev's desire to be relieved of his government and party posts.

This new development could add immense uncertainties to the peace and security of the world, or conversely to greater assurances of peace and security in the world.

It is a strange achievement which should make all states examine their policies afresh and ask themselves, 'How can the nuclear race be checked?'

Although we have spent more than four months (about one-third of the year) away from the country, the operation and administration of Government have proceeded normally just as though we were at home. This is conclusive evidence of maturity and stability.

I pay special tribute to my fellow citizens for their usual demonstration of the patriotism and loyalty which makes for stability of government and progress of our people. I express appreciation to the Cabinet under the direction of the Secretary of State for the conduct of the Government during our absence, the Vice-President, the Speaker and other officials for their dedicated and sustained co-operation.

OPERATION PRODUCTION

Preliminary reports indicate that progress has been made in the prosecution of Operation Production; we expect complete reports from those charged with the responsibility of promoting and developing this new programme. It should be understood, however, that it takes time to get such an enormous programme organized and off the ground and it is better to ensure a solid foundation when launching a programme of this magnitude than to move in haste. We are determined that this programme shall grow yearly and be expanded as organization and administration become better and more efficient with experience gained over the years.

Increased production by hard and sustained work, so that our exports may exceed our imports progressively and abundantly, is the main purpose and goal of Operation Production, and we shall make brief personal inspection tours throughout the country to assess and boost the execution of Operation Production.

EDUCATIONAL LEVY

As regards the levy for education, I congratulate the Revenue and Tax Divisions of the Treasury Department for the efficient manner in which they have presented this programme; but they have made one error in their misstatement that the payment of the levy should not begin until the 15th of December. As I understand it, the 15th of December is the final date in each year when the first half or the whole of the levy should be paid or collected, and if the Treasury and Revenue officials agree with me, they should make this correction.

It is proposed at this time that the period beginning on November 9 and continuing until December 15 be denominated 'Educational Levy Rally Period' and within this period all the people should endeavour to pay their annual levy of ten dollars, or at least fifty per cent of it; that those who are able to contribute more than ten dollars and are sincerely interested in the education of the youth and people of the country should not restrict themselves to ten dollars. Let us join hands and heart with might and main to expand education in our country to the greatest extent, including the Literacy Campaign which has been badly neglected in recent years, much to my regret.

Fellow citizens, this world is in a state of upheaval, caught in the throes of dangerous political and social crisis, a conflict of ideas transcending national frontiers. Human conduct and beliefs seem to be undergoing transformations more disturbing than at any other time in history. Our normal life seems to be affected by the disintegration of vital principles, customs and beliefs. The rate, complexity and variety of change in our time are without precedent. We seem to flounder in a sea of doubt; in the midst of unprecedented knowledge and power, humanity seems uncertain of its purposes, its values and it goals.

The urgency of this universal crisis with which all men are confronted and the utter destructiveness of the new instruments of warfare call for constructive thinking and action.

We have a responsibility to plead for sanity, to raise our courage to new heights and our minds to nobler thinking in order that human brotherhood and peace may be achieved.

Like the United Nations and its specialized agencies, social, political, religious and industrial organizations have in one way or the other organized themselves and made pronouncements against war and in favour of peace.

I firmly believe that those whose task it is to inform and to convey to the citizens of the nations of the world through the Press and other media of communication the daily happenings and events should understand that they are morally committed to disciplining their pens to clarity and truth; that they should be assiduously devoted to peace and ought therefore to serve with competence and courage.

A writer many years ago wrote:

> 'Of all the rule of men on earth so truly great,
> The pen is mightier than the sword.'

The Press is one of the most powerful forces extant today in the society of men and nations; those who serve in this profession should organize themselves on a national and international level and launch a crusade for peace.

They could unleash a force of immense influence for good and reshape international public opinion around the globe. Today more than ever before, we need men of imagination, prudence and vision.

Finally, fellow citizens, with unbounded reverence and grateful thanks to God for His guidance and protecting care of us during our absence from you, we give Him praise with glory and majesty as the great and only true and living God of our fathers and mothers. May we now and always forever hereafter hold, keep and recognize Him as our own God under the abiding influence of the Holy Spirit, the great source of perfect power and inscrutable wisdom.

Speech at Dinner in Honour of the Secretary-General of the Organization of African Unity

Monrovia, 8 February 1965

We need the kind of unity in Africa that is selfless.

Introductory Note

In Africa's quest for unity, Diallo Telli of the Republic of Guinea was the first African elected and given the responsibility for executing the programmes of co-operation toward this unity by the Organization of African Unity. His presence at the inauguration of the Free Trade Area plan for Africa in 1965 by the Liberian Government was welcomed by President Tubman who praised the leadership of this first civil servant of Africa.

Monrovia, 8 February 1965

FOR US in Liberia, it is an honour and a distinguished pleasure to have visiting our country for the first time the Secretary-General of the Organization of African Unity. We extend a warm welcome to him and assure him now as we have done before of our fullest co-operation and support in the discharge of his most difficult and onerous duties. When I think of how difficult Chiefs of States and governments find the administration of a single country, how much more must a man bear on whose shoulders depends the responsibility of guiding the organization of a whole continent.

Mr. Diallo Telli has been known to us since 1958, when Guinea was passing through the transitional period from colonialism to independence. He was among the first officials to come to Liberia on a diplomatic mission in the interest of his country, and here we learned to respect him, his good judgment, and his integrity. We had the pleasure of supporting him for election in Cairo last year as Secretary-General of the Organization of African Unity. Since that time he has discharged the duties of that office with great efficiency and effectiveness and there have been, as far as we know, no complaints against his administration; no one has charged him with partiality, indifference, inertia, or anything of that sort. He has always been active and wherever his services have been needed, he has always been found immediately on the spot.

The Secretary-General has come to Liberia upon our invitation to witness the opening of a conference which we hope will lay the basis for African co-operation and industrialization. We may talk unity; we may talk industrialization; we may talk co-operation; but words, words alone cannot bring anything into being; words are intangible. Once only in recorded history,

583

so far as I know, did words produce deeds. According to the Christian Bible, 'God said: Let there be light; and there was light.' Everything else has to be words which are intangible that spring from the mind; and then action, for action is that which translates the intangible into the tangible, and from the tangible we benefit.

We want African unity. We must have unity in Africa. But, to be realistic, we can have unity in Africa, Asia, Europe, the Americas, in Madagascar and in all the islands of the seas only if we act upon the principles that will produce unity.

It is just like a logical proposition; you must build up your premise, your premise must be correct and then your deductions must correspond to the premise that you lay down. You cannot lay down a false premise and then make a correct deduction. Or, if I may go a little further, it is said that you cannot enunciate a geometrical proposition and then build up a false premise in your demonstration, and get the Q.E.D. or Q.E.F. You cannot do it.

As a result, I think that this is a very important conference – not only this conference, but any conference that has to do with co-operation – regional, sub-regional or continental. Such a conference must be undertaken with broad and open minds. We cannot be narrow in our views and in our thinking and then expect to reap great benefits.

If I were angry with a man, says Justice Simpson, and wanted to fight him, and I opened my fingers and struck him with outstretched fingers, I would hurt my fingers. But if I doubled up my fist, folding my fingers together, and then hit him, I would hurt him and not my fingers.

Accordingly, we need the kind of unity in Africa that is almost selfless, at least unselfish. So that when we double up our fists in order to hit, we will be felt – our hitting will be effective. But if we open our fingers and fight, we would do ourselves more injury than we do our opponent.

We in Liberia have contributed, to the fullest extent of our abilities, to the liberation movements in Africa, from the beginning until today. We have not done much talking about it, but everyone who was associated with us in those troubled days can testify to the fact. In return we have asked for little or nothing. Let us take the Development Bank; it started from Liberia. We wrote to all the Chiefs of State and sent out our emissaries to talk about the Development Bank. When the time came for choosing the seat of the Development Bank, or the manager of the Development Bank, we asked for nothing.

Now, Liberia is known as the oldest and most developed country in the production of iron ore: bigger quantities, higher grades, and more production. We need steel, we need iron ore, we are shipping our iron ore out of Africa to foreign countries. Sierra Leone is shipping all of her iron ore out of Africa to foreign countries. Gabon, Nigeria and Ghana are doing the same thing. Is it not better, reasonable, and in the spirit of common sense that we get together and agree to combine our efforts so that all of us might benefit – Guinea, Ghana, Mali, Sierra Leone, Mauritania, Nigeria, and all the regions of West Africa? The benefits derived will be ours. But if we are contracted and narrow in our views and in our outlooks, nobody will benefit. We will only hurt our own hands and fingers and we shall find ourselves in a worse predicament.

Real, true independence must begin, must be rooted and grounded in economic independence. We talk about the inbalance in trade and other things. Raw products in Africa are sent away to foreign countries to be sold at negligible prices; when the articles are processed the refined products are then sold back to us at a hundred and even a thousand per cent increase. Then we complain about that. Our complaints are well founded in my opinion. However, we must seek an opportunity to establish ourselves.

In Europe there is the European Common Market. The members have differences of opinion among themselves and they talk about political unity, too. But they are preceding political unity with economic unity, because if one has nothing, one is not respected.

Now, I think we ought to be realistic and get together, not only in the iron and steel industry, but also in other programmes for regional co-operation. We must remember that the end – the goal we set for ourselves is much greater than our individual nationalism. Not only Africa but the world, all the nations of the world, need to lift themselves out of so much individual nationalism.

Dr. Aggrey (whom I knew personally as a friend), making a speech, said: 'Gentlemen, you talk about race, but we must forget our racial prejudices. Take for example the piano; you can play all of its white keys but you would get no harmony; or you can ignore the white keys and play only the black keys; you would still get no harmony. To get harmony, you must play the white and the black keys together.'

And that is exactly the situation we face. Our friend, our brother, His Excellency, Mr. Diallo Telli, has won for himself the respect of all of the nations not only of Africa but also of the world, even the United Nations. It is our great pleasure to have him with us upon his first visit here this evening.

We have invited you to come and join us; let us break bread together and drink wine together – although as a Moslem he does not drink wine – and exchange courtesies so that we may all feel that we are moving forward as one people not only as Africans, but also as Asians, Europeans, Americans, and all of the nations of the world.

Speech delivered to the People of Togo on a State Visit

Lome, Togo, October 1965

The search for unity and brotherhood is made more difficult by ideologies which tend to rend us apart.

Introductory Note

In 1965 President Tubman visited the Republic of Togo. He was particularly pleased to visit that country because of the ties of friendship and brotherhood which both countries shared. Togo's large immigrant community in Liberia had become completely integrated, and had developed over the years a new national consciousness towards the country of their adoption. President Tubman made mention of the loyalty and patriotism of Liberians of Togolese origin, and lauded the heroic rôle of President Grunitzky in the building of the new Republic of Togo.

Lome, Togo, October 1965

COMING TO Togo is really like coming to a second home. The people of Togo are no strangers to Liberians, for during the colonial period, when Togo was under German Colonial Administration, a number of Togolese subjects, among whom I name the Attiogbes, the Bruces, the Itokas, the Ajavons, the Gadegbekus and numerous others, emigrated to Liberia, were naturalized and became prominent and useful citizens, making a great contribution to the country of their adoption, and demonstrating the ability and the calibre of the Togolese people. Some of them still survive and their children, under Government sponsorship, have become doctors, nurses, engineers, electricians and plumbers. Therefore, Mr. President, we feel a close identity with the Togolese people.

You have uttered warm words of fraternal welcome to us and have said kind and flattering things about us and about our efforts to improve the lot of the Liberian people and to promote true African unity and brotherhood. You know, Mr. President, that this search for unity and brotherhood is made difficult by ideologies which tend to rend us apart. In these times it is gratifying to know that the African continent possesses its share of leaders whose prudence, realism, ability, patriotism and statesmanship are unquestioned. That you are one of such leaders is evinced by the able manner in which you have guided your country since attaining power.

I have no doubt that our stay with you will further strengthen the ties of true brotherhood which bind our two countries and people, and that our discussions during this visit will have concurrent effect in other parts of Africa, in the interest of African unity.

We thank you for the welcome you have given us and salute you, Mr. President, and pray that your efforts will redound in progress and prosperity for the people of Togo and thereby the peoples of Africa.

Long live Togo-Liberian friendship! Long live Africa!!

To the Accra Organization of African Unity Summit Meeting

Accra, Ghana, October 1965

The Organization of African Unity itself, by name alone, cannot establish unity.

Introductory Note

By 1965 the Organization of African Unity appeared to be losing some of its optimism, aggravated by border disputes, subversion, and allegations of subversion. Disillusionment and distrust began to have unwholesome effects on a few member states, some of whom did not want to sit at the Conference table with their alleged enemies. A proposal for a Union Government of Africa had come to be considered controversial and untimely, and a debatable matter. President Tubman, while committed to the ideal of African unity, saw the need for open-mindedness in all discussions, and the exercise of moderation in the hasty pursuit of certain ambitious objectives. His was a voice of moderation which often tended to guide the nations of Africa along a peaceful and noble path to continental progress and unity.

Accra, Ghana, October 1965

I MUST first of all take this opportunity to convey to His Excellency the President, the Government and people of Ghana our profound and unbounded gratitude, thanks and congratulations for the manner in which we have been received and entertained, and for these massive and beautiful buildings they have constructed for this conference. These speak more articulately than words of the greatness of the heart and mind of a people.

I deeply regret that I have to ask permission to leave the conference tomorrow morning because of a very important engagement on Monday morning. Before I leave, however, I shall endeavour to be very brief in what I have to say.

I have listened with great and intense interest to the speeches made this morning and this afternoon. I had intended to speak in detail on the matters of subversion, refugees, and union government. But I shall have very little to say after what President Ahmadu Ahidjo has said, after the suggestion made by President Sekou Touré that we forget the past and start anew, and the resolution or suggestion brought out by my friend President Modibo Keita. I think these suggestions are helpful but we would have accomplished a great deal more if we had rededicated ourselves to the principles of the (OAU) Charter. I know that the Charter exists, and that it speaks out against subversion; and in ordinary circumstances the existence of that provision of the Charter should be enough to inspire one's confidence, since, as has been pointed out, if we do not adhere to the Charter how will we adhere to our resolutions? That seems to me a fairly reasonable argument.

I see no harm in rededicating and recommitting ourselves if we find that we have strayed away from the Charter, and agree to renew our commitments and our pledges to it. I remember distinctly how impressive it was in Addis Ababa at that early hour of the morning when each Chief of State, in alphabetical order, marched to the rostrum and attached his signature to that Charter. Let us not stray from it, let us not treat it as a scrap of paper.

Now, briefly, on the issue of refugees: I do not see how we can say that no country should receive refugees. Any man who is in danger of life, limb or privilege, and seeks asylum in another country, is generally and universally permitted to do so under international law. But nowadays in cases of political offences, nations generally make treaties between themselves for extradition of prisoners.

The honourable gentleman from Uganda has said that there should be no refugees. Well, I have been President of Liberia for twenty-one years now. Suppose the people got tired of me and said 'You must get out of here', and wanted to kill me. If I wanted to go to Guinea, Sierra Leone, Senegal, or Ghana or anywhere else, should those countries refuse to take me? They should take me, but then they should impose restrictions on me so that I should not carry out subversive actions in their territory, and that I should have nothing to do with politics. It is the responsibility of the country receiving refugees to see that they do not carry out political activities or political propaganda against their own country. A good example of that occurred when ex-President Peron of Argentina left Spain and tried to attack his own country. You know what happened. I must agree with my friend from Senegal, that we cannot say 'no refugees'. We should accept refugees in our countries; but we should not permit them to carry out subversion or other acts of disloyalty or injury, neither against their home country nor any other country. Those are the principles upon which refugees are admitted into a country.

Now when it comes to the other kind of refugees, freedom-fighters, they stand in a different category altogether. Any African state would accept and assist them. In my opinion, their activities cannot be considered as acts of subversion.

There are two things that I have been considering. Firstly, it is of immense importance that we set up and institute the commissions on arbitration, conciliation and mediation, provided for in the Charter of the OAU. These commissions, if instituted, could attend to these matters, when they arise. Secondly, it has been my experience, in any organization, in any institution, in any government, if a member of that institution or government utters a complaint, it should be heard. If the complaints are not attended to and the grievances continue, then, in the case of an individual government, people would begin to form groups, to plan, and to seek an opportunity to destroy and overthrow the government. If, therefore, any member state of the Organization of African Unity utters a complaint against another member state, it is of vital importance. I think that, in the first instance, they should try to get together bilaterally. If they cannot do so, then they should call in other members. But if that too should fail, let the commissions be instituted. I do not understand why these commissions have not been instituted. This is the third year since the Charter came into existence, yet we have not instituted these commissions. I think we should institute them at this very session of the Organization of African Unity.

Now, just a few words on my friend Kwame's hobby: the continental Government. I have no objection to an African Government *per se*. But with the kind of confusion we have here among ourselves right now (and you have heard what has been said about the organization of one Government), what will happen? One Government!

So far as we in Liberia are concerned, our Constitution has not authorized the surrendering of any part of our sovereignty to a continental Government nor to any other authority. The Ghana Constitution, according to my friend President Nkrumah, has authorized that. Now, before the Liberian delegation can say that we subscribe to the setting-up of such a Commission, with a President and four or five Vice-Presidents, as a preparatory or basis for the Union Government, we will first have to amend our Constitution so that it authorizes this surrender. But I must confess to you that unless we co-operate more effectively than we do now, I will never recommend that to my Government nor to the Legislature.

Now, I think that we need to get together here; get ourselves organized as friends and brethren so that when I meet you and put my hand in your hand, slap you on the back, and kiss you on the cheek, every action that I do is from the heart and asserts what my heart says. If I do not agree with you I will tell you straight, 'I do not agree.' And because we differ, we need not fall out. We must differ, but, no matter what, we need not be enemies. Friendship does not consist only of 'Yes', so that whenever there is a 'No', the friendship is terminated. That is why I have always held that a professional soldier can never be a president or a politician, nor a statesman. As a military commander he says 'Go' and men go; he says 'Come!' and men come. In politics and statescraft, he says 'Go' and the fellow says 'No! I do not agree with you. Why should I go?' Therefore, professional soldiers cannot manage state matters. They get apoplexy, they get strokes, and all sorts of things.

And now, my dear brethren, gentlemen and colleagues, let us forget the past, as President Sekou Touré has said. Whatever I may have done to you, whatever you may have done to me, let us forget and start anew. Let us turn over another page. Let us clasp hands together as brothers, and let us unite in trying to establish African unity. The Organization of African Unity itself, by name alone, cannot establish unity. Union Government of Africa established by name alone cannot establish or create African unity. I am fearful of the Union Government because it is so large and global, immense and continental. When I think of the small federations that we have had in Africa, which have not succeeded but have fallen to pieces, I ask, why do we now call for a continental Government? Must there be one Government for this whole continent!

In my own country – a small country – we have twenty-eight different tribes and twenty-eight different dialects. I can hardly keep them together. We have had war upon war. Since becoming President, I have been trying to hold all the tribes together so that we have had no internecine or tribal conflict. That is in one little country. I do not know how many tribes there are in Ghana, Guinea, Libya, Mali and in all our different countries. To put all of these people together, as the Tanzanian President Nyerere has said 'three hundred and some millions' – to put all of them under one Government — I think at least that that is a tremendous risk! Once we agree to organize this Government, once we subscribe to surrender our individual sovereignty to this one Government, we will not be able to get out of it except at the point of a gun. And this whole continent will be in confusion. It will be an inferno. That is what I am afraid of.

I realize that in unity there is strength. I realize that our primary products are not well paid for, that we don't get what is due us for those things. I realize all that. But it is far better that, let us say, Ghana and Guinea, the Ivory Coast, Liberia and Sierra Leone form a federation including Mali. Let us see how that will work. And then another four or five countries form another federation. Now when we see how all of these federations work, and if their work is all right, then we can join both of them together and gradually expand. But I am afraid to organize this whole continent. As I said, I do not object *per se*, but I am afraid that for President Nkrumah, President Touré, President Tubman and Presidents from everywhere else to join together in this Union Government, will get this whole continent into trouble. That is what I want to say, and I thank you again.

I am sorry that I must leave. But I will vote for the resolution suggested by President Modibo Keita. I think we should all join together to get it passed.

Now I know that the absence of several of our very prominent member states from this conference stems from the complaints they uttered. I understood that the battle had been settled. I did all I could to try to assist in getting all of them here but they did not come. We cannot afford to have one African State out of this fold. The story is told of a man who had a hundred sheep and one sheep was missing; he left all of the ninety-nine and went to look for that one sheep. Let us go and look for those people who are not here and bring them into the fold so we can have African unity.

Statement on the Rhodesian Situation
Monrovia, 18 December 1965

We African states do not agree with the method and manner in which Britain is handling the Rhodesian Affair.

Introductory Note

The quotation above sums up the feelings of every African state about the Rhodesian crisis. President Tubman, however, in this statement unequivocally voiced his objections to the form taken by African protests, advocating either the use of force, or the severence of diplomatic relations. The Liberian position is stated forthrightly below.

Monrovia, 18 December 1965

ADVERTING TO the Rhodesian situation and the resolution adopted by the Council of Foreign Ministers requiring all African States to sever diplomatic relations with the British Government unless she crushed the Ian Smith rebellion by the fifteenth December, the Liberian Government's views are that the Council of Ministers who met in Addis Ababa exceeded the scope of their authority. No Council of Ministers on the Liberian political level could direct a breach of diplomatic relations between Liberia and any foreign government. This can be done only by the President of Liberia, generally in consultation with the Cabinet and the Legislature. Therefore I consider the act of the Foreign Ministers *ultra vires* (beyond one's power) and void *ab initio* (wrong in the beginning). The Council of Ministers adopted a resolution directing all African States to sever diplomatic relations with Britain if she had not crushed the Ian Smith Rhodesian rebellion by the 15th of December, which allowed less than a fortnight for Britain to declare and win a civil war. This procedure, and the conditions imposed by the resolution, I consider to be harsh, unreasonable and impracticable.

If Britain, or any other nation or group of nations, was disposed to intervene by force in Rhodesia, it would require more than a fortnight to organize and prepare for the strategy and logistics of the campaign; yet the resolution demands that Britain should accomplish all of this within less than a fortnight. I cannot in conscience support such an ultimatum.

I have followed this matter very closely and with great concern because I consider it a very serious and grave one in which the honour, dignity and personality of Africans and all members of our race are involved, but I wonder why we should be so severe with Britain when she has neither condoned nor supported Ian Smith's vicious régime, but has rather declared it a rebellion against the British Crown. Moreover, Britain has said that she will restore a legal government in Rhodesia and is opposed to minority rule. She has taken several actions which she thinks will ensure this but has declared that she will not resort to military force or measures to put down the rebellion, and feels that the measures taken and intended to be taken will retrieve the situation. We African States do not agree with the method and manner in which Britain is handling the affair. We feel she should take a sterner course and on this point there is a difference between Britain and us, but since it is a British responsibility to put down the rebellion, and since they have charted the course which they will take, a sufficient period of time to try their method out should be allowed to elapse, and to observe its success or failure. Without doing this, and in the face of Britain's humiliation by Ian Smith's régime we pay no compliments to Britain for not upholding and supporting the rebellious régime in Rhodesia, but condemn her and desire to sever diplomatic relations.

In the Liberian Government's view, the severance of diplomatic relations with another State is a very grave matter, and is only one step short of a declaration of war. I cannot bring myself therefore to join in or support such an attitude not only towards Britain but towards any other nation in similar circumstances. It seems to me that it would be preferable to have the rebellion of Ian Smith crushed by other means than the firing of guns and shedding of blood if this is possible, and that force and war should be utilized as a last resort, because more Africans in Rhodesia may be victims of wounds and death than members of the Ian Smith minority supporters.

Finally, the position of the Liberian Government is that the measures taken by Britain to quell and bring an end to the rebellion and restore order in Rhodesia are entitled to a fair trial since the aims and objectives of both the British Government and the African Governments are to put an end to the rebellion, though differing as to manner and means to be adopted. The situation justly and equitably viewed does not convince the Liberian Government as justifying the severance of diplomatic relations with Britain. If it were a question of severing diplomatic relations with Rhodesia (if she were an independent state), we would do so immediately, just as we did with South Africa, but if Britain agrees with us and we with Britain that the Ian Smith Government is an illegal rebellion, why then should we sever diplomatic relations with her?

Speech at Banquet in His Honour by the President of Dahomey, His Excellency Christopher Soglo

Cotonou, Dahomey, 29 April 1966

We are impressed with the cultural richness and traditional African patterns which the history of your country depicts.

Introductory Note

President Tubman's visit to Dahomey afforded him another opportunity to review the African scene, and African Unity, as on the occasion of visits to other African states. Its prospects and achievements were central in his talks with the President of Dahomey. He was filled with admiration at what he saw in Dahomey, one of the ancient and reputable centres of African civilization and history.

Cotonou, Dahomey, 29 April 1966

WE WANT you, Mr. President, to know how deeply grateful we are to the Government and people of this most friendly country and to your good self for extending us this gracious invitation and according us such fraternal welcome and stately honours.

Your inviting us here at this time forges another link in the historical chain that binds our two countries. Mrs. Tubman, the members of my party and I are particularly grateful and exceedingly proud to be here because, as Africans, it brings us closer together than ever before. In the past we heard of, read about and entered discussions on the activities of your great country; but now we are eye-witnesses to this progressive nation in action.

There has been a great wind of change in almost every direction in the world around us, especially on our continent. We are witnesses to unparalleled scientific discoveries in the nuclear and thermonuclear fields as well as in man's journey to the stars. Moreover, there has been a fundamental change in the political and economic concept of man's relation to his fellow man. These changes have helped to liberate Africa from the shackles of imperialism and have assisted the African in his dauntless struggle for freedom and independence. Today there are thirty-five African nations whose independence has been won within a period of less than a decade. The moral, spiritual and other implications of these developments cannot easily or readily be fully understood, nor all the problems easily solved. It therefore behoves us as nations to exercise patience and calm judgment, and make careful and practical plans, in order that our plans and actions may harmonize with those of other nations and international bodies of which we are a part.

594

We are impressed with the cultural richness and traditional African patterns which the history of your beloved country depicts. Furthermore, Dahomey's history and achievements, Mr. President, including her rich heritage, inspire all men of goodwill. For it is only when man understands and appreciates the historical path of the human family that he can fully enjoy an imperishable friendship deeply rooted in African civilization and tradition.

Mr. President, we would be betraying the trust of those tried and true Africans were no mention made of our position as regards the savage, monstrous ideology of apartheid practised in South Africa, South-West Africa, Portuguese Guinea, Angola and Mozambique and now gaining ground in the illegal Government of Southern Rhodesia.

Mr. President, unfortunately there are still areas on our continent whose struggle for self-determination and independence must be continued. Our Government, like yours, is committed to continue the struggle until the monstrous ideology of apartheid practised in South Africa and South West Africa is banished from this continent; we are also committed to securing the right of self-determination for our brothers of South Africa, South West Africa, Portuguese Guinea, Angola and Mozambique. And we are finally committed to ensure that our brothers who represent the majority in Rhodesia should exercise all their rights as free men, and should participate in that form of government which they, in the exercise of these rights, may choose. It is our Herculean task to rid our continent of this evil and we must use the sword of Damocles against these myriad-head dragons, and combine our efforts until they are destroyed, and the remaining sons of Africa's soil are unlocked from the shackles of fear, want and disease.

Finally, we take pleasure in acknowledging this unique opportunity for us to eat the corn of your hillside, drink the milk and honey of your native land, exchange views on common problems of equal concern to the brotherhood of mankind, our common continent and respective countries, and plan for greater future peace, justice, prosperity and the general advancement of the human race.

Long live Dahomey-Liberian relationship! Long live African Unity! Long live the United Nations!

FOREIGN AFFAIRS

Speech at Dinner in Honour of the Diplomatic Corps

Monrovia, 2 March 1960

Independence in Africa will be meaningless unless it sets a new pattern of human intercourse, decency, and solidarity.

Introductory Note

In 1960 the course of African history was radically altered. The ideals of the American and French Revolutions, with their emphasis on the inalienable rights of man, liberty, equality and fraternity, and, in some states, the socialist ideals of the Russian revolution, made an impact on the Freedom Movement of the non-western world in the years following the Second World War.

In this speech President Tubman reviewed the amicable relationship between Liberia and those nations represented in our capital city, Monrovia, the significance of the Freedom Movement for Africa and the world, the industrial needs of the new African states, and the importance of charting a new course of friendship and unity among African states and in Africa's new relationship with the international world.

Monrovia, 2 March 1960

IT IS a great privilege for Mrs. Tubman and myself, Gentlemen of the Diplomatic Corps, to share this evening with you on a social plane. We feel that this is indeed a unique privilege because it comes just a few weeks after our Inauguration and at a time when we most need the counsel, tolerance, understanding and goodwill of all nations and peoples of the world.

Looking back upon the relationship between this Government and Members of the Diplomatic Corps represented near this capital, I am encouraged to recall that our collective associations in the past years have been very exhilarating, peaceful and amiable. Although the issues with which we have had to deal have been disturbing at times, we have all maintained our equilibrium, retained our sense of interdependence in an atmosphere capable of assisting and sustaining each other, and have thus worked together without diplomatic incidents.

At this point, let me pause to pay tribute to each of you for your part in enhancing this condition of amity as well as the rôle you have played in our development programme. Some of you have done it through scholarships to Liberian youth to study in your home countries; some through loans, trade and public facilities. In short, everyone has contributed something to the sum total of our material progress. I ask you further to convey to your respective illustrious Sovereigns and Chiefs of States the gratitude and appreciation of myself, the Government and people of Liberia for the honour paid us in sending special representatives to our Inauguration ceremonies in January last.

This gesture must be recorded as a recognition of a one-world trend and a subscription to the principle of world-brotherhood amongst nations of the earth, great and small. We have tried to learn and to apply both of these lessons in our dealings with you at all times; and we know we are correct because our concept of right and wrong and of justice is planted in the soil of democracy and the rule of law as the indispensable condition for universal peace and internal tranquillity. By this gesture the sixty-eight nations that were represented at the Inauguration have laid down the basic principle of respect for the sovereignty of all nations, great and small.

In this shrinking and changing world of today no country is remote or isolated. The business of one is the business of all. A mistake at the North Pole may have its repercussions as far away as the South Pole. The way of life of the great powers of the world is on trial and smaller nations are standing at the cross-roads. They are at the cross-roads because they 'believe in the ultimate decency of things'.

Within the African immensity of eleven thousand four hundred and forty-five square miles, live two hundred million people of diverse tongues and cultural traits and traditions. While Africa was a no-man's-land, or Dark Continent, and a hunting ground for national power and prestige, Africans as a people played a passive rôle in world affairs. Their fate was determined and settled without reference to their own reactions. In fact, they had no rights which the world felt bound to respect. Then came World War I with its mandate system; and World War II with its Atlantic Charter and other political slogans which laid the foundation for the emergence of Africans, under leaderships of the people's own choosing, to the extent that it became imperative to concede the right of self-determination and independence to subjected peoples everywhere.

Since the formation of the United Nations Organization in which Liberia, the only independent state in West Africa at that time, was a foundation member, there has awakened a sense of national consciousness amongst the subjected peoples throughout Africa. Within a decade the movement spread to encompass all Africans pressing their claim for nationhood and independence. With Nigeria, Togoland, the Congo, Mali and Madagascar joining the ranks in 1960, we may safely predict the virtual independence of all Africa within the next ten years. Regardless of our feelings about it, national consciousness and independence is a fact and nothing can arrest its progress but the Will of God; and I believe that it is the Will of God that princes come out of Egypt, that Ethiopia stretch forth her hand unto God and that Africa shall be free forever.

Conceding that political independence for all Africa is a fact; that nations must adjust themselves to the new situation; that Africa is large enough to absorb the investments and technical skills of industrious nations; and that all have more to gain in material and moral returns from an independent Africa, it becomes the duty of all free nations of goodwill to strive to promote, in these new African states, the prerequisites of modern civilization along the lines of knowledge, science, technology, food production, transportation and mass education.

It is not enough to emerge as an independent state. Nations are judged by their contributions to the amelioration of human sufferings and disabilities, as well as by their contributions to the great march of progress that uplifts men and nations. Otherwise, we shall be only exchanging one set of masters for another, which is not the intention of the nationalist movement to which Liberia has given conspicuous support.

Independence in Africa will be meaningless unless it sets a new pattern of human intercourse, decency and solidarity. Therefore, we are and we must be devoted and committed to trying to develop a pattern of nationalism unlike that which has engendered so much strife, confusion and conflict amongst the people and nations of the world. It should be a nationalism devoid of individualism and selfishness – one imbued with an over-abundance of universal understanding, equality of enterprise, co-operation, association, tolerance and mutual respect.

Unity of this sort among independent African states is indispensable to growth and progress. In fact it is the woof and warp of our very existence and estate and should be pursued in a climate conducive to the sovereignty, independence and well-being of all contracting parties.

African unity should chart a course independent of all pre-existing patterns. It should steer away from motives that lead to *entente cordiale*, the balance of power concept, the Holy Alliance or the Pragmatic Sanction of Charles the Sixth of Austria and the 'I am the State' doctrine of Louis the Fourteenth. All ambition to dominate other states, and the propensities of cliques and intrigues to undermine the sovereignty of other states, should be discouraged with vigour. Otherwise we ourselves shall be guilty of imposing, or at least, aiding and abetting the imposition of another kind of neo-colonialism. Every independent African state, small or large, should be left free to choose its own way of life without external interference.

Although we may not like the manner in which African leaders may attempt to solve their local problems, it is not within our right to seek to impose our will or our conditions upon them. Our prime interest should be in seeing that the Government is in the hands of Africans and we should show a willingness to assist in offering advice when we feel that they are going off base, leaving it to them to accept or reject. It would be a travesty of the principles of African justice for any leader of any one African state to take sides in a factional dispute within another state. All African leaders should work in association, friendship and as equal partners in the great struggle for African emancipation, and not seek to apportion credit for what has been achieved. African nationalism has been going on for a long time now. In West Africa in particular we recall with pride the exploits of the National Congress of British West Africa. Who would forget the part played in this movement by men like Boncul Bright, Herbert McCaulley, Casely Hayford, Woods and others of blessed memory? They played their part and left the scene and we today are cashing in on their exploits.

I must draw attention to a new tendency among some nations since World War II, to violate the extra-territorial sanctity of Embassies and Legations by delegations of citizens entering Embassy and Legation premises to tender notes of protest. Governments communicate with Governments through diplomatic channels. Under our frame of Government the people have a right to meet in an orderly and peaceable manner, consult upon the public good and instruct their representatives and to petition the Government, or any public functionaries for the redress of grievances. They have a right to direct the representatives of their Government to file and make protests against anything that they feel to be against their interest or against the interest of humanity. But the people have no right, even in an orderly and peaceable manner, to trespass upon the premises of a foreign Embassy or Legation for any purpose whatever. All dissatisfactions, complaints or protests should be made to their own Government; and they should ask their Government to file protests. Therefore no such procedure will be tolerated in Liberia because it is wrong, dangerous and unlawful.

Mr. Doyen, Gentlemen of the Diplomatic Corps, Mrs. Tubman and I again express our pleasure and happiness in having you with us this evening. We feel that upon you rest the burdens of the day as representatives of your respective states in this country. Upon you devolves the responsibility of impressing upon the minds of men the world over and at your respective posts, the living fact that it is as impossible for nations as it is for individuals to live in isolation; that all nations are interdependent and should willingly share each other's joys, sorrows and burdens.

To the Sixteenth Session of the United Nations General Assembly

New York, U.S.A., 23 October 1961

It is not practicable to define, seek, or even determine the secrets and sincerity of men's minds, but we can arrive at certain conclusions in some matters from what men say and do.

Introductory Note

When President Tubman addressed the Sixteenth Session of the United Nations General Assembly in 1961, the world was gripped by the fear of the imminence of a third world holocaust. Man, for the first time in the history of warfare, possessed the deadliest weapons to exterminate all forms of life on this planet; and, besides that, the competition to invent ever more deadly ones was mounting year by year. Even the United Nations, man's hope for universal peace, could do little to dissuade the most powerful nations of the world, namely, the United States of America and the Union of the Soviet Socialist Republics, from manufacturing weapons. Other nations watched them and a few ventured to join in the competition. The United Nations stood in need of a restatement of its reasons for existence, and a revision of its charter. Its membership had grown, due to the admission, as full members, of many new independent states of Africa and Asia. President Tubman called for a new interpretation of the principles upon which the United Nations was founded and rededication to such principles.

New York, U.S.A., 23 October 1961

SEVEN YEARS ago I had the great honour of addressing this Assembly. Again today I deem it a distinct and esteemed privilege to address this Sixteenth General Assembly of the United Nations, presided over by Mr. Mongi Slim, the first African to be accorded that honour. I have the greatest respect and admiration for Mr. Slim because of his demonstrated abilities and his broad vision concerning the whole range of problems facing the international community.

It is indeed exhilarating to note that in 1954, when I appeared before this Assembly, there were only three African states represented here out of a total membership of sixty nations, whereas today there are twenty-six African states out of a membership of 101. This fact stands for us as the most striking and dramatic symbol of the changes which have taken place in this short space of time, which have resulted in the liberation of so many millions of our people, who are not only free to pursue their own national destiny, but who are also able to participate in the process of making the independence of all nations secure. And, perhaps the most significant aspect

603

of this development is that it is the United Nations which has contributed so greatly to facilitating the peaceful accomplishment of this result – a result in which we can all jointly take pride.

The delegates accredited to the General Assembly have, from time to time, witnessed many familiar sights within these walls and listened to many eloquent speeches on peace; but the vision which perhaps stands out clearly in your minds today is that of that great apostle of peace, optimism and dedication, the late Secretary-General Dag Hammarskjold, to whom the end came before his last mission of peace, Assignment Congo, was accomplished.

Henceforth, the ideals of this great organization and the work to which that international servant devoted his life should take on a newer perspective and have a greater impact on man's mind and actions.

The discordant and critical situation in the world today, according to my analysis, can be attributed to effects which emanate from deep underlying causes. I do not claim to be able to identify all the causes that have given rise to the effects which manifest themselves in the present terrible and dangerous world situation, which has developed among nations and peoples to the extent that it is reflecting itself in the United Nations in such proportions that this highest hope of mankind seems to be rendered almost helpless.

But may I, at this point, revert to the founding of the United Nations Organization in 1945. At that time, the nations which created and instituted this organization were those that had just emerged as victors and brothers in arms from the greatest and most destructive world conflict in the history of men.

They were the signatories to the present Charter of the United Nations. They were brothers and friends, men dedicated to the ideals of peace in a world freed from the shadows of war – men who believed in the establishment of the four fundamental freedoms. They strove throughout to establish relations of confident collaboration between states and thereby save succeeding generations from the ravages of war and its aftermaths and repercussions. This is the fulfilment of an honourable commitment by their solemn pledge as signatories to the Charter which is the organic and fundamental law of the United Nations.

Unfortunately, we have not permitted these good intentions to continue in their proper course. By the selfishness of states and statesmen we have segmented this institution into blocs of vested interests instead of maintaining it as a United Nations. In my opinion, our major point of concentration should be in the direction of a review of the fundamentals of the United Nations Charter in relation to our attitude toward it, and with a view to enforcing stricter adherence to the great obligations which all members undertook by subscribing to the Charter.

It is not practicable to define, seek out or even determine the secrets and sincerity of men's minds, but we can arrive at certain conclusions in some matters from what men say and do. Basically and primarily however, the world formed the impression that the great objective of the formation of the United Nations was to establish a forum where differences, disputes and disagreements among nations would be brought, and where participating member states would seek a formula for settlement around the conference table, without resort to violence and war.

Thus far, this world organization has succeeded in preventing another global war, localized conflicts and averted or at least minimized threats to peace. Thus it has ameliorated events in some trouble spots. It is obvious that the results achieved thus far by the United Nations have fully justified its existence; its impact on the political behaviour of states has been of some significance and without parallel.

But just as hope and confidence in this organization have been established, and men's aspirations raised to a higher and more secure plane of existence, in like manner a great *impasse* seems to have developed. It now appears that the very existence of the United Nations' further usefulness and effectiveness seems to be swinging in the balance. With this observation all mankind appears to stand on the threshold of universal disruption.

Earlier, we referred to the possible or probable causes of this situation, the deterioration in the relationship of nation with nation and the breach among the great powers which lead the world in science, politics, economics, technology and military might. One of the causes of this situation, in our opinion, is that decisions taken in this great parliament of the world are based more or less on national interest rather than on the merits of the particular issue or problem brought before it. I realize fully that this is not a juridical institution, but even in politics, the principles of right, fairness and justice in most matters affecting the welfare, integrity and privileges of nations and peoples are approached, discussed and decided on the basis of accepted rules of conduct and not merely upon self-interest and expediency.

As another cause, we opine that discussions and debates are conducted, and very often decisions are made, in the heat of passion and excitement, where all the niceties of diplomacy and the suavity of expressions by member states are totally disregarded. On occasion harsh and even profane and vicious language is employed in this uppermost echelon of highly civilized and cultured nations and peoples. Such practices indulged in from day to day, month to month, year to year, session after session, have bred envy, hate and prejudice which have become so deep-seated as to render friendly intercourse, understanding, reconciliation and compromise at any point difficult if not impossible. And because most of us have indulged too long in this unrewarding approach, we find ourselves now faced with a situation that must be overcome and for which a solution must speedily be found if the United Nations and the human race are to survive and be saved from a great catastrophe.

In his hands man holds the instruments of death and mass destruction. By means of technological progress, he has created a new earth in which he has the alternative of building either a happy, peaceful and fraternal society where men of all races can live a mutually beneficial, intelligent and creative life, or a society in which no one can be safe. And because he has created a new earth, he needs also to create a new spirit, a new outlook, new attitudes, new perspectives and new approaches to be able to live in this new world of his creation.

It took the belligerent powers six years to end the last global struggle and it has taken those very nations, and others joining them since, fifteen years of futile efforts at peace, crying, 'Peace! Peace!' and yet there is no peace. We cannot go on this way. An eruption is inevitable unless a new formula is discovered or designed.

There are many trouble spots in the world today. When these trouble areas occur among the smaller and less developed nations, the United

Nations provides its services in restoring peace and order. This has been the pattern of the organization since its birth. However, the Berlin crisis, in which the great powers are involved, not only presents a dangerous front to those concerned alone, but further constitutes a serious threat to the survival of the entire human race. Although the United Nations stands ready to combine its efforts with any nation or group of nations to avert a tragedy, it has not been called upon to do so.

This therefore, is undoubtedly a problem and issue which, unless immediately resolved, will not only affect those directly concerned, but all the nations and peoples of the earth. In the circumstances, this world organization cannot afford to permit such a state of indifference to jeopardize the earth and its people.

I come now to another of the disturbing and provocative issues of the day — disarmament. On this question, it is true that many views have been expressed by member states and different propositions advanced, but no satisfactory conclusions have as yet emerged to warrant the setting up of machinery to serve as an enforcement agency.

Believing that peace is not the sole concern of the great powers, but that of small nations or states, including the emerging African nations who also have a stake in it, the United Nations should review all precedents and submit a plan, either by resolutions or by some other instruments, tending toward the goal of total and complete disarmament.

Adverting now to the question of nuclear and thermo-nuclear tests, we have always been consistent in advocating their complete ban. We shall not relinquish our present position, no matter what reasons may be advanced for the continuation of tests. We have heard and read of the disastrous effects that radioactive fallout from nuclear tests can have on the peoples of the earth, and no one can say to what extent such effects could endanger the lives of the peoples of the world.

We are all agreed that all nuclear devices should be devoted to peaceful purposes; we stand foursquare by this commitment and will continue to denounce such tests as being diametrically opposed to peaceful intentions and pursuits.

I am dismayed at the resumption of nuclear tests after a voluntary moratorium of almost three years which we had welcomed most heartily as an encouraging first step along the road to disarmament. We had fervently hoped that this voluntary moratorium would mark the beginning of an epoch in which we would see the great powers shoulder more and more of that primary responsibility for keeping the peace which they undertook to do at the formation of this organization. We dared to hope that the moratorium would soon be followed by a formal treaty ending all nuclear tests in the stratosphere, in the atmosphere, under the earth and in the laboratories, and that this treaty would be accompanied by serious negotiations for a disarmed world — a world in which the awesome powers of the atom were employed for the enrichment of mankind rather than for its potential destruction. I take this opportunity to implore and call upon the great powers to reverse this most unfortunate trend by quickly and effectively banning all nuclear tests and by resuming at the earliest possible opportunity all efforts directed at world disarmament.

Another significant cause or source of conflict is the tendency of some nations to seduce and coerce other nations to subscribe to and adopt their system of government. This is a travesty of freedom, fair play and justice. One of the chief components of world peace is that all nations, small or large, should be left free to choose their own way of life. Whether that way be communism, socialism or democracy, there are good and evil features in all political systems. In any event, the choosing of a way of life should be without external intrigues, propaganda, infiltration or subversion and should be based exclusively on each nation's best judgment as to the kind of society that will best serve the true needs and interests of its peoples.

The tendency to superimpose alien ways of life has engendered the cold war which is being fiercely waged through all imaginable channels. I have an uneasy feeling that if this tendency persists, the cold war will, as surely as night follows day, eventually flare up into an unquenchable hot war which will involve all mankind.

Anyone who has followed with discrimination the activities of the United Nations since its inception will not fail to be impressed with the fact that it is the greatest bastion of human liberties in our time. Notwithstanding its obvious shortcomings and imperfections, it has striven assiduously and consistently for the emancipation of subjected peoples and for the maintenance of the territorial integrity of states. But for its institution and its principles of self-determination and fundamental human rights for all peoples, I dare say that the vast majority of mankind would have found it difficult, if not impossible, to exercise the right to independence and sovereign existence.

The United Nations is designed to ensure world peace; to serve as the clearing house for all international agencies. It is the centre where governments can maintain permanent liaison and thus by personal contact, resolve many problems that may arise. It must be made to endure through endless years. Its advocacy of self-determination, freedom and independence for all subjected peoples in Africa and in the world is not an empty dream; it is a categorical principle of social conduct whose momentum cannot be arrested by bombs and bullets.

Let me therefore, in all earnestness, implore you to support the principles for which this organization stands and to contribute generously and unreservedly to the furtherance of its work both morally and financially.

World attention and public opinion have, since recent trends toward independence in Africa, focused on such places as Angola, Algeria, South West Africa, Mozambique and other areas in Africa and of the world where the right of self-determination has not yet been achieved. While it is evident that the connotation is still confused in some parts of the world, self-determination is basically the right of any group of people to shape their own future, ensure their own cultural and spiritual heritage, be responsible for their own social order, enhance their own material progress, create their own system of values and, in the end, make their own distinct contribution to the civilization of mankind with the assistance of altruistic friendly states. To the degree that this inherent right is denied those who have risen in armed or peaceful rebellion, to that extent do we have trouble spots in the world today and in areas where, during the past half century, this age-long aspiration has manifested itself on a mass scale.

It is therefore my conviction that the United Nations resolution touching independence for all peoples from colonial yoke must be implemented to avoid discontent, disorder and rebellion. Regardless of alliance, members of the organization who voted for that resolution should be enthusiastic about its implementation. The principle of national self-determination must never be repudiated. No government should abandon a principle once espoused. This is an unwritten moral code.

I make bold to say that all Africans are united on certain fundamentals – namely: (1) the total and complete emancipation of not only the African continent from alien rule and domination but of the entire world and (2) the right to lead their own way of life without subversive interference from any source.

The world in which we live is large enough to accommodate all circumstances of men but it must be attained not on the archaic and obsolete principle of master and servant but on the basis of equality in a creative partnership.

I feel that it is of the utmost importance that a Secretary-General be elected at the earliest possible date to avoid the onset of the creeping paralysis which threatens the life of the organization. Moreover, I believe that it is imperative that the new Secretary-General be endowed with all of the powers, both specific and implied, which have been granted to him by the Charter. Only in this way will the United Nations be restored to operational efficiency. Only in this way will it be able to pursue the cherished goals set forth in the Preamble of that Charter and to exercise in full amplitude the dynamic rôle which the late Secretary-General envisaged for the organization.

Man's hope for survival primarily resides, it is true, in his ideal of world brotherhood, but ultimately it must be through the instrumentality of sober logic, calm reasoning and objective realism that these influences will become civilizing factors, not merely the footnotes of history. It is within the competence of participating nations to translate without delay into living realities, the principles which underlie our quest for peace, security and human happiness and the reason for the existence of this world organization.

Whether we shall live in constant fear, intimidation and panic, or whether we shall incessantly dream of world brotherhood and thereby work toward its realization, is a question to decide our fate.

Whether we shall destroy our cherished possessions and the things for which we have long laboured, or whether we shall refrain from the mistakes of other generations which twice in our lifetime have brought untold sufferings to mankind, is yet another question to decide our fate.

Whether we shall make existence for future generations intolerable, full of misery, anxiety and unhappiness, or whether we shall prepare the way for existence in a better world society, is still another question upon which hangs our fate.

These are some of the crucial issues of our times. In your hands, members of this world organization, lie tremendous responsibilities and great decisions. Guided by your calm deliberations, your sober actions, your unselfish motives, your nobility of thought and implementation of actions, your man's creative capabilities and genius may yet be channelled anew toward the building of a world endowed to him by his beneficent Creator.

We can and we must choose the better way. It is within our competence to do so.

This I believe! The new spirit to which I have already addressed myself lies in the discovery of a new meaning to man's existence and the creation of new horizons to human brotherhood and universal peace and goodwill.

I believe that in spite of the disappointing aspects of the situations which have mushroomed and given cause for grave concern in the hearts of men, the way to peaceful negotiation and compromise will always provide the most logical answer to the crucial issues of our times.

I believe profoundly that the powerful nations of the world will not fail the hopes of humanity by their unwillingness to support absolutely the fundamental tenets of mankind as embodied in the Charter of the United Nations, nor will they resort to unilateral or bilateral action for solutions which do not accord with those fundamental tenets prescribed in the Charter of this Organization.

It is only in such an atmosphere of faith and dedication that the ideals to which we have subscribed by our membership in this world body can mankind face the future fearlessly and bravely and work reassuringly so that eventually right might triumph over might, justice overshadow oppression, reason replace irrationality, the blessings of liberty obliterate the tyranny of domination, and human welfare transcend race-centredness. These are the ideals to which we have dedicated ourselves and we stand to them committed in the critical days which face us.

May the deliberations of the delegates to this session of the General Assembly redound to the greater glory of God and be instrumental in bringing peace and freedom to all mankind.

To the Nation on his return from a State Visit to the United States of America

Monrovia, 13 November 1961

> *Our times need men of clear vision, broad understanding, love of country, unselfishness, and devotion to duty who will lead the nation in her upward path to progress and solidarity. Our own contribution to world peace must stem from our ability to keep the peace at home.*

Introductory Note

Perhaps not since the benevolent interest shown to Liberia by the Virginian Presidents, Thomas Jefferson and James Monroe, and later Abraham Lincoln of Illinois and Franklin D. Roosevelt of New York State, has a kindlier approach to understanding the problems of Liberia been manifested than that which was given by John F. Kennedy, thirty-fifth President of the United States (1960–1963). President Tubman had in previous years made visits to the United States as President of Liberia, but he returned from this visit to that country in 1961 with a new sense and appreciation of the historic ties which exist between Liberia and the United States. Although there are some individuals who would not care to admit that such ties even exist, this visit of President Tubman tended to remove those doubts. President Kennedy gave a sympathetic ear to the views he received from President Tubman. One result of that visit in concrete form was the erection of a hydro-electric plant in Liberia. President Tubman expressed satisfaction with his visit, and further observed certain changes in the international scene towards the achievement of better understanding among the nations of the world.

Monrovia, 13 November 1961

IT IS exceedingly thrilling to return home and to be the object of so enthusiastic a reception and such touching expressions of welcome as have been ours by your spontaneous generosity. Let me say how very grateful we are for all these indications of your solicitude, affection and loyalty. On our part these spontaneous gestures from time to time have made us humble and truly grateful, so that we have pledged again and again our unceasing devotion to the country's cause and dedicated ourselves to carrying out the attendant responsibilities of our office. After seventeen years in the service of the nation as President we remain committed to serving the best interests of you, our constituents, and safeguarding in every way the safety and perpetuity of our common country.

By leave of absence granted us by the Legislature and upon invitations of President Kennedy of the United States and His Imperial Majesty Emperor

Haile Selassie I of Ethiopia we embarked on October 6 on a Farrell Lines' ship, the *African Crescent*, at the free port of Monrovia. From that date until today when we disembarked from the *MS General Mangin* thirty-nine days have elapsed. This period involved travelling by ship, rail, car, plane and helicopter, embraced a total of twenty-six days on the ocean, eight days in the United States and five days in Europe, included speechmaking and appearances before Press Conferences, television and a University audience, attendance at diplomatic and social receptions, diplomatic talks, business and friendly interviews; it also included stop-overs at Paris, Zürich, Barcelona, Casablanca, Dakar and Conakry where heads of Governments and local officials accorded us every official courtesy. Despite the rough weather and turbulent seas sometimes encountered and the long train journeys, the trip, which as you can well appreciate was strenuous, was nevertheless packed with fascinating and greatly enriching experiences. We expect that the results will be equally rewarding and satisfying.

The twenty-six days spent on the *US African Crescent* from Monrovia to New York, the *SS United States* from New York to Le Havre and on the *MS General Mangin* from Marseilles to Monrovia were for the most part restful and completely delightful. We received every courtesy and everything was done to make us comfortable. Even if we had travelled on a Liberian ship or the Presidential yacht we could not have received better attention. What was true of the ships was also true of the trains on which we travelled.

Through the media of the radio and press dispatches, and perhaps by letters, you have been apprised of the important activities of my official visit in the United States. That tour afforded me the opportunity of coming into contact with a great and outstanding American citizen and President, one whom I consider to be genuinely interested in extending the dimensions of democracy and whose policies have already made a great impact on the minds of statesmen and world leaders everywhere. After my talks with President Kennedy, State Department officials, businessmen, heads of educational institutions and men in private walks of life, I have come away more than ever convinced of the vital need for a more realistic strengthening of American-Liberian relations. However, the ultimate solution does not lie in this realization alone; the true solution must come from our own willingness and determination to make any partnership productive and meaningful, so that the results will engender a greater degree of mutual admiration, respect and benefit.

In talks to business groups and the Press, I made clear our desire for launching into industrial enterprises which will help to stabilize and accelerate the economy of the country and thus be instrumental in helping its manpower to advance simultaneously with the technological progress which we are experiencing at the present time, and which must rapidly increase with time. I am optimistic that steps along this direction will be taken in the immediate future. A fuller report on this official visit to President Kennedy and other officials of the United States Government will be made to the Legislature.

Of little political significance, perhaps, was my address at the United Nations on October 23rd before representatives of 102 member states. Our hope that that world organization will embellish the pages of world history in its fight for peace continues the same and our belief in and support of its fundamental tenets remain unchanged. It was my great pleasure to meet

many distinguished leaders and statesmen, both on this and other occasions.
My meeting and addressing a session of the Asian-African group was particularly stimulating and inspiring. There at the Headquarters of the United
Nations I felt as one with representatives of member states who assemble
every year to deliberate, plan and endeavour to solve the great problems of
world peace and human survival in a setting inhabited by ideologies which
vie for supremacy.

Having accomplished our mission in that centre of world democracy, we
set sail on the SS *United States* whose officers and crew showed us every
courtesy, and thus made the five-day crossing memorable and pleasurable.
We arrived at Le Havre and met Mrs. Tubman along with Ambassadors
Lawrence, Brewer, Graham, Wiles, Consul-General Hofer and French
officials who had come to welcome us. The formal greetings over, we
departed immediately for Paris in anticipation of our flight the following
day to Ethiopia via Khartoum.

The sudden critical illness of Her Imperial Majesty Queen Mennen of
Ethiopia caused Emperor Haile Selassie to send a message informing us of
this new development and asking for a postponement of the visit. Naturally,
I expressed great concern over this turn of events and in a return message
assured His Imperial Majesty of our profound regret as well as the sympathy
of the Government and people of Liberia. Such sudden and unexpected
tidings meant a complete change in our plans and itinerary, required quick
decision and new planning and because of this new development and with
Mrs. Tubman's health check-up in prospect I decided to go to Zürich to have
this accomplished while Ambassador Lawrence made arrangements for our
return home by ship.

On the day that we left Zürich for Marseilles to embark on the *MS General
Mangin*, the Executive Secretary, the Honourable Walter Moore, left for
Ethiopia with a special written message, the presents which I was to have
presented to His Imperial Majesty and a Memorial from the Legislature
upon the thirty-first anniversary of the Emperor's accession to the Throne
of Ethiopia. I commended highly the foresight, wisdom and magnanimity of
the Honourable Members of the Legislature and feel that this act will be
instrumental in forging another vital link in our growing relationship and
friendship with this sister Empire. Mr. Moore's mission was highly successful. He was received by His Majesty the same day of his arrival in Ethiopia,
so that he was able to return to Monrovia on Monday, the 6th of November.

I come now to world conditions and the growing tensions in international
affairs. You are not unaware of the incidents of recent weeks which have
given cause for grave concern in all areas of human activity. One can only
hope that world leaders and statesmen will resort to peaceful negotiations
as the only way to man's ultimate freedom and happiness, and not have
recourse to war and its aftermaths – human destruction and misery. And so
it is my hope that the one hundred and two member nations of the greatest
bastion of human liberties will effectuate in the end a pragmatic relationship
among nations, so that peace can become a reality, not merely an ideal.

Our own contributions to this great task impose on us certain duties.
Firstly, there should be no complacency, we need to be eternally vigilant,
a characteristic always epitomized as the price of liberty; secondly, we
should cherish the things we have always held dear, defend them and if
necessary die for them.

But these objectives can only be achieved by placing nationalism above personal considerations, the welfare of the state above individual interest, and loyalty, devotion and love of country in place of sedition, treason, sabotage, disloyalty and subversive activities. Our times need men of clear vision, broad understanding, love of country, unselfishness and devotion to duty, who will thus help the nation in her upward path to progress and solidarity. Our contributions to world peace must stem from our ability to keep the peace at home. This is the call which I sound today to citizens everywhere – men and women, old and young – on whom the Liberia of today and tomorrow depends. The correct approach to our national problems and our ability and willingness to stand for the principles of a Government for the people, of the people and by the people will be the real test of our patriotism.

And now I extend my profound gratitude to the members of the Cabinet who, led by the Secretary of State, carried on the functions of Government during our stay abroad. I was constantly kept in communication with the trends of events and I am very happy indeed that but for traffic fatalities and some deaths which we deeply mourn all has been quiet and peaceful on the home front. I appreciate the loyalty and co-operation of everyone who contributed to this state of affairs.

I thank you with all my heart and again express my joy and happiness on our return to our native land where I once more call upon you to join hands and with one heart march bravely and confidently forward to the frontier of a new Liberia.

Speech in Honour of Her Majesty, Queen Elizabeth II of the United Kingdom

Monrovia, 23 November 1961

*Future generations of Liberians will always remember with grati-
tude these significant acts of recognition, consideration, courtesy and
sympathy shown to us, and the support which Your Majesty's nation
accorded to ours.*

Introductory Note

The decade of the 1960's revived the recognition of Anglo-Liberian friendship. The occasion of the Queen's visit was significant because it was the
first visit of a British Monarch to Liberia, and it led to the renewal of
more exchanges of official visits. It was an historic occasion, and President
Tubman did not let this opportunity pass without giving expression to his
delight at the Queen's presence in Liberia.

Monrovia, 23 November 1961

THREE REMARKABLE incidents will always illumine the political and social
annals of our country; they are, first, the recognition of Liberia's independence by Queen Victoria of Great Britain in 1848, which was the first
official recognition to be extended our nation. The second is the gracious
welcome extended to our first President, J. J. Roberts, again by Queen
Victoria, illustrious Monarch of England, aboard Her Majesty's frigate,
when she gave him full official honours and negotiated, concluded and
signed a Treaty of Amity and Commerce with the new nation. Later,
President Roberts was invited to join the British delegation to the Peace
Conference in Brussels where he was accorded the honour of addressing that
imposing array of over two hundred world leaders. The third is the present
visit of Your Majesty and His Royal Highness the Duke of Edinburgh, a
visit to which we attach the greatest significance. Let me assure Your
Majesty of our profound appreciation for this high consideration. Although
your stay is a relatively brief one (and we wish it could be longer), we are
nevertheless overwhelmed by the great honour and pleasure which the visit
has given the Government and people of Liberia. We open the doors of our
hearts and of our entire country to you, and we hope that your brief stay
with us will be thoroughly enjoyable.

Future generations of Liberians will always remember with gratitude
these outstanding and significant acts of recognition, consideration, courtesy and sympathy shown to us, and the support which Your Majesty's
nation accorded to ours. Nor will serious students of Liberian history fail to
perceive in these incidents the basis of the real understanding and interpretation of our political and social history in the struggle for survival.

It is a circumstance of happy augury that Your Majesty's visit to West Africa has coincided with the near realization of the burning cause of nationalism which has taken place in Africa and brought in its wake the blessings of liberty and freedom to millions of the continent's teeming population. What a proud privilege it must be to you personally, and what a great historic opportunity, that Your Majesty's Government has played such a significant rôle in the fulfilment of the British principle of granting self-determination to Africans by the process of constitutional reform! It is because we have been encouraged by the political events of recent years that we have hopes for the eventual liberation of all Africa.

Thus we shall continue to present the cause of Africa before that great body of human liberties, the United Nations; we shall argue and plead with world leaders; we shall appeal to popular sentiments; we shall depend upon the support of the nations that have supported our cause in the past, and to others who may join this force in the present and future, to help in the attainment of the blessings of liberty and the right to lead the life to which the new nationalism entitles all men.

When I visited the Federation of Nigeria last year at the gracious invitation of Your Majesty, I was greatly impressed by the great respect, admiration and affection with which my fellow Africans regard and speak of Your Majesty. I was the grateful recipient of the warmth, hospitality and friendliness of the Nigerian people and I was greatly struck with the degree of material progress which the nation had made under British administration and, since Federation, under the Nigerian and British collaboration and guidance. This visit and another, which I had the privilege of making to Sierra Leone, brought me in contact with two outstanding Prime Ministers, Sir Alhaji Tefawa Balewa and Sir Milton Margai, two dynamic and dedicated African leaders. A subsequent meeting of the Heads of African and Malagasy States in Monrovia this year has deepened our regard for one another and given new perspectives and fresh impetus to our desire to bring understanding and peace to our continent, and by common consent to cast in our lot with all peace-loving and democratic nations of the world in the pursuit of the eternal principles of justice, truth and human dignity for all mankind.

Well do we look to those who have always understood our deepest longings, interpreted our emotions rightly and lent support and encouragement to work with us for the total independence and freedom of people in every part of the world, so that the scourges of oppression, ignorance, poverty and disease may be obliterated forever and man be permitted to walk the earth with a newer sense of human worth and dignity.

The Government, the people of Liberia, Mrs. Tubman and I, are particularly proud of the honour you have done us by the pleasure of this visit. Since Your Majesty ascended the throne, Liberians have followed with great interest the fortunes of your nation in this era of strain and stress.

Our long and close association in the diplomatic field and the fact that at present over one hundred Liberians are receiving academic and specialized training in elementary and high schools, colleges and universities in the United Kingdom and other places in the British Commonwealth of nations, place us under a debt of gratitude.

We have always been great admirers of your country, your people and your historic institutions. Thus we hope that these common interests will be increased over the years and that our two countries will continue to explore other ways of increasing and strengthening the ties which have characterized Anglo-Liberian relations.

We wish Your Majesty a continuation of the wisdom and great understanding with which the Almighty has so bountifully endowed you in the tremendous responsibility which you carry as Sovereign of a great Empire. May Your Majesty's tours in Africa be greatly rewarding and may they bring untold blessings to our continent and the British Commonwealth of nations.

An Address to the Diplomatic Corps and Officials of Government

Monrovia, 23 April 1962

As members of the human race, we have a common obligation to one another — it is the preservation of the world in which we live for the use and enjoyment of generations to come and a respect for life which we neither can create nor have the right to destroy.

Introductory Note

The early years of the nineteen-sixties brought hope to mankind as the beginning of the end of universal conflicts and tensions, and a lessening of those conflicts and tensions. This optimism was to a large extent inspired by the election in 1960 as the thirty-fifth President of the United States of John F. Kennedy, who became a symbol of hope and peace to the world. His years at President of his country were occupied to a large degree by easing tensions the world over wherever he could. Much of his concern in this pre-occupation was directed toward the Western nations whose arms race threatened the peace of the world. President Tubman shared the optimism of the early years of the nineteen-sixties. In this special address the Diplomatic Corps heard his views on the international situation for communication to their respective governments. Like President Kennedy, he feared a worsening of the international situation through threats of an impending nuclear war.

Monrovia, 23 April 1962

WE HAVE gathered here tonight just after the observance of one of the greatest events in history — the Resurrection of the Prince of Peace. Currently associated with that event is the perpetual and universal quest of that great bastion of human liberty, peace, in which all our concerted efforts are engaged, and which, almost two thousand years ago, the angels heralded to all men of goodwill. Of interest and perhaps of great pertinence to us at this time is the work of the Geneva Conference on Disarmament in the interest of human security and peace. We see gathered this array of diplomats from many parts of the world who are accredited to our capital, where we hope there are no bombs to disturb our friendliness and molest our mutual intercourse, and where for the time being our thoughts centre on the ties which bind us to our several countries and to one another. We have supped together as men and women who have a common purpose and a common task.

The exchange of diplomatic representation between nations has become the *sine qua non* of an orderly and accepted form of government. What these representatives say and do, how they circulate among the people, and the quality of the leadership they exert have important effects on the relationships between their respective governments and the governments of the host countries. With the growing ramifications of governmental functions, the rôle of the diplomat has been raised to a new status, and the men who are charged with the responsibility of presenting the true image of their nations abroad play a vital part indeed in interpreting their country's foreign policy, examining and weighing the facts as they are, and analysing them to get a balanced perspective. We can understand that this is no easy task and that those who have risen above the mundane existence of diplomacy and have left a brilliant reputation, are those who have brought depth of knowledge, keenness of perception, skill in human engineering and dedication to their tasks.

It is generally conceded that these diplomatic exchanges tend to foster the reciprocity of friendship and goodwill among nations. Unfortunately these motives are not always uppermost, and there are instances where the genuine purpose of the exchange has been travestied by the use of such opportunities to carry on subversive activities among the people of the host country. It is inevitable that such actions should develop into unpleasant situations. Fortunately, this constitutes the exception, not the normal state of affairs.

From the history of our diplomatic records, it is indeed a great pleasure and a source of deep satisfaction and pride to me that since the incumbency of this administration, the nationals represented near this capital and accredited to us by their respective governments have lived and worked within their frame of reference, fostered such relationships which have brought our nations a great degree of understanding and engendered a friendly and harmonious relationship. The intercourse between us has been most cordial and our deliberations and work together have been carried on in an atmosphere of cordiality and genuine friendliness. This is fortunately a happy state and is in marked contrast to situations where the seeds of subversion have been sown by some members of foreign missions, with the intent covertly or overtly to interfere in the internal affairs of others, create trouble, and cause dissension, all of which could well lead to sedition and revolution. That this happy state has existed and still exists here, I attribute to the high calibre of the men accredited to us near this capital, their appreciation and respect for the struggles of free men everywhere, their own adherence to the principles of fundamental human freedoms, their allegiance to the precepts of democracy which seeks equality of opportunities for all men, and lastly, their own deep understanding of the basic problems of the peoples of the world in general and Africa in particular. I am proud at this time to salute the Doyen and Members of the Diplomatic Corps accredited to us near this capital for this splendid record of achievement in the history of our nation.

Is it not true that mankind perpetually lives in a state of faith and despair, love and hate, safety and danger, war and peace? Most trends activated by chauvinistic tendencies, power complexes, and ethnocentricism forever create issues which, like the sword of Damocles, hang ominously over the head of mankind and thus threaten our safety and happiness? There are tensions, world unrest and insecurities of such proportions that, like Mark

Anthony, one is inclined to wonder whether 'judgment has fled to brutish beasts and men have lost their reason'.

But despite these ominous, ignominious and ignoble events, and despite the persistent battle for the minds of man, leaders of nations and government see in the birth of genuine understanding among nations today a great and positive accomplishment toward world peace. The present Geneva Disarmament Conference is a case in point, where it is generally conceded that, unless there is control of the manufacturing and possession of weapons of destruction, notably nuclear arms, mankind faces a dismal future, since war can be the only alternative. One can only hope that the great powers now involved in this Conference will reason objectively and work creatively on the issues involved and arrive at conclusions which will free mankind from the shadows of war and human suffering.

The Government and people of Liberia are profoundly concerned for the success of this Conference because the increasing dangers and threats in the nuclear arms race are so apparent that they will inevitably lead to world destruction. Cognizant of these facts, how can any rational individual or nation remain indifferent to what is taking place at Geneva or in other areas of the world where work is being done in the interest of peace?

But whether this conference succeeds or fails, it is my earnest conviction that it is absolutely essential that the United Nations should engage itself in a day-to-day programme of making an international survey of all trouble spots, whether in the East, West, North, or South and set itself to work out practical solutions either by means of a committee of the whole or by special commissions. For it is not enough that the trouble areas be discovered when they become apparent, it is also necessary that the causes be anticipated, diagnosed, and probable solutions found to be applicable when and if dissensions erupt. It is my further observation that even when a treaty on nuclear tests is agreed upon and disarmament arrangements effected, so that the risk of a nuclear war or wars be abolished or minimized, we must recall that there were global wars that afflicted men and nations before nuclear weapons such as bombs, missiles and other mass destructive instruments came into existence. It is clear, therefore, that a nuclear war might not necessarily put an end to the kind of war that we have hithertofore experienced, which inflicted untold sorrow upon mankind before the era of the atom bomb and nuclear missile.

The continents of the world no longer provide effective barriers among nations. As members of the human race we have a common obligation to one another — it is the preservation of the world in which we live for the use and enjoyment of generations to come and a respect for life which we can neither create nor have the right to destroy. The great council halls of the world attest the desire of man to usher in an era of peace on earth; we must continue in this great effort and thus save civilization from the ravages of barbarism or a worse catastrophe. Let it be said of our day and time that the leaders and heads of Governments and states of the Diplomatic Corps represented near the capital, were highly sensitive to the great moral law of nations, were mindful of the lessons of history, and that we did our duty in the best interests of our fellow men.

To all who desire our friendship the Government and people of Liberia have continually held out the right hand of fellowship; our attitude remains unchanged in this regard, and to those who continue to work with us in the closest and most friendly relationship we express our warm regards, friendly esteem and genuine appreciation for all their efforts on our behalf. May the future bring us into closer and stronger relationship so that our respective countries may be the beneficiaries of our vision, wisdom and work in this important area of human relationship.

Speech on the Occasion of a Dinner in Honour of President and Mrs. Tubman by the Israeli President and Mrs. Ishak Ben Zvi

Tel-Aviv, Israel, 15 June 1962

Israel's policy of peace and co-operation with all nations is gaining greater understanding and deeper appreciation among developing nations.

Introductory Note

Israel's policy of assistance to developing nations became an attraction for many African states, not only because such assistance was available, but also because Israel was even more appealing by virtue of being a new nation which had developed industrially in a short time, and was willing to share this experience with new nations. President Tubman, however, devoted some thought to the need for peace between Israel and her neighbours, and expressed his own delight at being able to visit the land of antiquity and religious fame.

Tel-Aviv, Israel, 15 June 1962

AFTER TRAVELLING for almost three weeks by sea and rail, we have reached this beautiful and historic country, so pregnant with mystery and so rich in religious traditions; a land of great transformations which is inhabited by a people of indomitable courage, business acumen and great religious zeal. When we arrived in the capital today, a sense of history permeated our entire being; we thought of the great kings, prophets and priests, of the law-givers, the renowned statesmen and the great Jewish writers who have played such prominent rôles in the history of their race and of the world. We thought too of the great throngs of people who, during the centuries, have visited this and other historic places in the Middle and Near East to worship at religious shrines. Then we recalled the story of the fierce determination of a people to build a new Jewish community in the midst of world turmoil and international bitterness.

Our joy to be in the State of Israel at this time, and what we have seen since our arrival, have deepened our admiration for Your Excellency's young Government and people. It will be a great privilege to see something of these historic places and to view with absorbed interest a land whence have emanated three great world religions. I feel sure that this visit will always remain an unforgettable experience for all of us, and I am grateful for the gracious invitation which you, Mr. President, have extended to us to visit your young, virile and progressive state.

Mankind stands today on the threshold of a great and challenging era in the history of the human race, and therefore no one can rightly be oblivious to the impact of the massive scientific inventions and discoveries, material achievements and gigantic struggles for the mind of man which have been accentuated by the presence of varying ideological theories. A great desire for peace is being acclaimed by the peoples of the world; but the achievement of this ideal is slow, because of the lack of a correct knowledge of the efficacy of the concept, and also because of the hesitancy of world leaders boldly to implement what they believe and know to be the principles that underlie universal peace.

Commenting on the international situation today, it is generally conceded that mankind has to discover a solution for world peace lest the alternative, war, will eventuate in a disruptive and costly holocaust. Sober reasoning seems to dictate that a broad and general policy should be enunciated by the United Nations for a complete and total survey of world conditions wherever they exist, and then by study and analysis endeavour to evolve a practical formula to resolve or alleviate these unfavourable conditions.

Because one of the objectives of the United Nations is to reduce tensions engendered by inveterate antipathies and to ensure a fairly wide distribution of science and technology, I believe that this world organization should not wait until a crisis has reached its climax before it acts. Rather it should concern itself with general conditions in the world as a preliminary, with a view to averting bloodshed and war. To wait for individual cases to erupt before concerted action is contemplated may be too late.

It is because of this conviction that I venture to suggest that under the aegis of the United Nations, perhaps the Afro-Asian members by virtue of their relationship with all international organizations, should work out a formula for a permanent peace between the State of Israel and her neighbours, who need the complete co-operation and mutual co-operation and mutual understanding of each other to live together in peace, amity, human progress and happiness.

Liberty and freedom: these are noble ideals which free men have always cherished, fought and died for, knowing that when men are deprived of them under any form of government, human dignity, human aspiration and self-determination become meaningless semantics. And so today those who cherish these ideals are engaged in an open rivalry with the forces that oppose them. The contest sometimes takes the form of civil disturbance, sometimes assumes the form of recrimination and scathing diatribes, and sometimes erupts into the violence of war. But the tragedy of the contest lies in the fact that the adherents of democracy have to defend and support a prevailing system of government, while the followers of an opposite system offer a change, something different and perhaps more exciting, with tempting promises of a greater share in the wealth and resources of the land or its peoples. It is a kind of hope which in a predominantly materialistic age cannot but have its corresponding enchantments.

It is highly significant that the State of Israel has, within a relatively short time, established diplomatic relations with twenty African states, and that she has ties with eighty-four of the one hundred and three member states of the United Nations Organization. It is interesting, too, that during the past year alone there came from the African Continent to Israel three Presidents, two Prime Ministers, eight other officials and a host of students.

Thus Israel's policy of peace and co-operation with all nations is gaining greater understanding and deeper appreciation among developing countries.

The impact of these delegations to Israel to study the nation's new social patterns, their scientific progress and labour movement and to benefit from scholarships provided by the Government, has been instrumental in strengthening the bonds of understanding and friendship between the participating states of Africa. Certainly these nations cannot but regard Israel as their friend since she continues to extend the hand of friendship and indicate her willingness to share her technical knowledge and experience with other nations. We hope that the years ahead will intensify the co-operation and collaboration between the people of this nation and Africa, as well as the rest of the world.

We are happy that, after a century, our strivings for national identification have not been in vain, thanks to our sympathizers and friends who extended and continue to extend to us the hand of friendship, to encourage and assist us in our nation-building.

The bravery of our people in the face of overwhelming odds, their patient courage, their deep and abiding faith in the ultimate triumph of goodness and the achievement of the true destiny of the people of Israel will forever emblazon the pages of sacred and secular history. The people and Government of Liberia are proud and privileged to associate themselves with the Government and people of Israel. Already on the diplomatic level and in business enterprises, Liberians and Israelis are blending their talents in useful and collaborative endeavours. We cannot but hope that these joint ventures will continue to enrich our relationships and be of mutual benefit to our nations and peoples.

Mr. President, you are the representative of the great political and religious ideals for which your country and your people stand, and which they have fought to preserve and transmit. Your own great sense of dedication, your undeviating purpose in the cause of freedom and independence, your depth of erudition, your love of country and your fellow men and your progressive policies for the nation have twice led to your election by your constituents. Because of your many achievements, you have identified yourself with the great leaders of the world.

Mr. President, let me assure you that in coming to Israel, meeting some of your hospitable people and visiting some of the great places of historic interest, Mrs. Tubman and I, and the members of my party, have been filled with inexpressible joy and that we shall take back with us a truly memorable impression of this visit. For, like the pious Moslem who is obliged to make a pilgrimage at least once in his lifetime, we feel that this visit is a fulfilment of our religious hope. May the years ahead bind our two peoples spiritually, morally and educationally and may the political ties which now exist between us continue to be stronger and richer as the years advance.

To the Nation on his return from State Visits to the Republic of Israel and the United Kingdom

Monrovia, 31 July 1962

We must offer our friendship and goodwill to the nations of the world.

Introductory Note

President Tubman's visits to the Republic of Israel and to the United Kingdom opened new horizons in internationalism for Liberia. Not since the visit of Liberia's first President, Joseph Jenkins Roberts, in 1848, had a Liberian President visited the United Kingdom on a State Visit. The Republic of Israel had a real fascination and attraction for many African states as a fast growing nation, and displayed a romantic industrial growth which appealed to them. These visits by President Tubman strengthened bonds of friendship between Liberia and these countries, and opened new vistas for international co-operation between them. President Tubman was pleased to make these visits and was grateful for the hospitality he received.

Monrovia, 31 July 1962

FROM JUNE 2 to the morning of this day, we have been separated from each other by thousands of leagues of the waters of the Atlantic Ocean, the Adriatic, Mediterranean and Irish Seas and the English Channel, and also by thousands of leagues of land on the continents of Asia, Europe and Africa. During the entire period that we travelled by ship, train and car, with the risks and hazards common to such modes of transport, we were united with you in heart and spirit. The great God in whom, like our fathers and mothers, we trust and believe has preserved our lives and spared us to re-unite under the circumstances and conditions in which we meet today, and which gladden the heart, inspire the mind and console the being. To Him we give thanks and adoration for His great mercies bountifully bestowed upon us, His unworthy and wretched creatures.

This great demonstration of welcome which you have accorded us today, and the general enthusiasm and rejoicing which you have portrayed cannot but touch us deeply. We are glad to be back home, and happier still to identify ourselves with you, and to engage again in the common task which we owe to our country and its people. We are aware that your constant good wishes and prayers attended us all along, and we here express our profound gratitude to all those who through telegrams, letters or in thought expressed or entertained solicitude for our welfare and the success of our visits.

But more than this, we are pleased to know that those who were charged with specific duties appear to have executed their responsibilities in the realization that the proper functioning of any government machinery is contingent upon the faithful performance of duty by each individual unit comprising the political structure. We are happy that a state of peace and harmony has, as usual, prevailed at home and that all seems well; thanks to your sense of responsibility, your loyalty and devotion.

Leaving here on the 2nd of June, after a pleasant and uneventful voyage, we arrived in Marseilles on the afternoon of the 12th of June, 1962. Here representatives of the French Government, Ambassadors Lawrence, Cooper and Graham and other officials were at hand to greet us. We left immediately thereafter by special train for Venice, that enchanting and fascinating city, where we spent two days. Although this was an unofficial stop-over, the Prefect of the Jurisdiction, the Mayor of the City, government officials and citizens accorded us a very warm welcome and made our stay very pleasurable. After spending two days here we travelled on to Tel-Aviv, Caeserea, Nazareth, Capernaum and Tiberias. In these cities we visited Mount Zion, King David's Tomb, the Hebrew University, the Medical School, Weizmann Science Institute, the Sea of Galilee, the childhood places of Jesus and the River Jordan. We were awed by the religious significance of these historic places and permeated by the sense of history.

In Haifa, on our return journey from Tiberias, at an impressive and imposing ceremony on Mount Carmel, a street in a new housing section of the City was named for Liberia, the cornerstone of which we had the great pleasure of laying while Mrs. Tubman unveiled the plaque.

During our State Visit to Israel we heard from the lips of all classes of citizens in the country expressions of an avowed interest in and anxiety for peace with their neighbours. We were struck by their yearning for peace throughout the world and we believe the Israelis to be genuinely sincere, in this age when all nations *profess* to be ardently desirous for peace and declare their aversion to war. It would be a great and happy event for restoring peace, goodwill and understanding in the Middle East if all parties concerned would come together around the conference table to seek a just and equitable settlement of all differences. This question should be of supreme interest to the United Nations in existing circumstances.

We speak truth when we say that the official receptions, the wild bursts of enthusiasm everywhere and the indications of genuine friendliness shown to us in Israel made an indelible impression upon us, while the great material progress made in the relatively short period since the State of Israel was born left us astonished.

At Haifa, on July 1st, we took leave of President and Mrs. Ben-Zvi and the government authorities in Israel, boarded the ship and amidst tumultuous applause, waves and shouts of goodwill, we bade adieu to the friendly people of Israel. Thus ended a most inspiring and rewarding visit to a land rich in history and antiquities, where the most mysterious and astounding miracles of all times were performed by law-givers, prophets, kings and Jesus Christ, the Son of God; a land where the present rate of development, the conversion of desert and droughty areas into fertile land and the drilling of sand to get springs and wells of flowing water are almost as mysterious as the miracles that abounded in the land of Israel in days gone by.

We are happy to affirm, as you already know, that His Excellency

President and Mrs. Ben-Zvi of the friendly State of Israel will be visiting our country in nine days' time. We are sure that we will extend to them, in our own way, a similar welcome with hand, heart and spirit, and give them our friendship so that they may return home with kindred feelings.

Having arrived in Zürich from Haifa via Venice, we had a four-day stop-over, the entire period being crowded with official business of various kinds, both national and international; the schedule was so heavy that even on Sunday I was engaged from morning until late in the night. The ox was in the well; hence the violation of Sunday.

On the 8th of July we left Zürich by special train for Calais where we were received with befitting ceremony aboard Her Majesty's ship, *Virago* by which we travelled across the English Channel to Dover. We were met there by the Duke of Kent and immediately set off on a special train for Victoria Station in London. Here a fascinating and unforgettable reception awaited us – Her Majesty the Queen, H.R.H. the Duke of Edinburgh, members of the Royal Family, and of the British nobility, and other dignitaries, Liberian representatives, students, officials and prominent citizens were lined up in the waiting-room at Victoria Station. The playing of the national anthems of Liberia and Great Britain, the Inspection of the Guard of Honour, the glittering horse-drawn carriage procession of the Household Cavalry with the traditional grandeur, pomp and pageantry so characteristic of the British, the resounding of the Liberian National Anthem played by about a dozen bands at different intervals all along the route of march from Victoria Station to Buckingham Palace as we drove past, and the enthusiastic cheering crowds will always remain a memorable event in our lives.

For three eventful days we were the happy guests of Her Majesty the Queen in Buckingham Palace where we received the most lavish courtesies, and the affectionate and ready attention and service of every member of the Queen's household. There was not a single incident to mar in any degree the pleasant atmosphere which permeated the section of the Palace in which we lived and it is our opinion that this historic building, while not ornate and florid, is elegant and possesses the comfort and attributes of a home.

After the official banquets, receptions and luncheons in Buckingham Palace, St. James's Palace, Guildhall and Westminster Abbey and the visit to Harwell, the Atomic Nuclear Research and Experimental Centre, we took leave of Her Majesty on Friday, July the 11th, thus terminating our State Visit. We then moved to the Dorchester Hotel for a seven-day Private Visit for the benefit of having contacts with industrialists and businessmen of various categories and offering inducement for investments and other businesses in Liberia, which we believe will be successful.

With the end of our private visit in London, we left for Liverpool on the evening of the 18th, and arrived in that great maritime city where the Lord Mayor and other officials of government welcomed us at the station. 'Mr. President, you and I have one thing in common; we are both Methodists,' were the opening words with which the Lord Mayor greeted us. The next day at a dinner given for us by the Lord Mayor of Liverpool, high tributes were paid to what the Mayor called Liberia's astonishing strides, and its era of progress and prosperity. Earlier that day we had paid a visit of inspection to the Evans Medical Plant, a firm which supplies pharmaceutical drugs and medicines to the Government, and were honoured by a luncheon given by the officials of the Company.

While in Liverpool I had the opportunity of conferring with the Chairman of the Board of Directors of Elder Dempster Lines and as a result of our discussion the M.V. *Aureol* will, beginning in November of this year, call here regularly on her southward and northward voyages. This is a gratifying accomplishment as it will be the beginning of the re-establishment of an old link with Great Britain which was severed years ago.

On Friday, July 20, at 3.30 p.m., after official leave-taking by the Lord Mayor of Liverpool, high officials and other government representatives, we embarked aboard the *Aureol* which weighed anchor at 4.45 p.m. for her ten-day voyage to Monrovia. But for the initial delay of almost a day, because of engine trouble immediately after leaving Liverpool harbour, the voyage was pleasant, and was punctuated with cocktail parties, the observance of our 115th Independence Anniversary, the ship's gala night and the Captain's traditional farewell dinner.

In England we saw the great loyalty which binds the English people to their sovereign; we witnessed the traditional pageantry of a great kingdom and we admired their ancient institutions and the contributions which they have made towards culture, science and civilization; we were delighted with the interest shown on all sides, enjoyed their friendliness and were very favourably impressed with what we saw. We shall long remember this visit to a nation whose people we have always respected and admired and who have long-standing relations with our national history. Commenting on the material benefits of the two State Visits, we hope that some barriers have been broken down between our countries and that a great degree of understanding and goodwill has been engendered; that our trade relations will improve; that new cultural, commercial and economic links will be established and that the ties of friendship between us will be strengthened to facilitate the utilization of knowledge and skills in our developing situation. We also hope that newer avenues will be opened in our future relations.

Furthermore, the results of these visits, as you realize, will undoubtedly improve our relations with the international world. Consequently, this will demand more and more efficiency, greater effectiveness and an all-round high calibre of men in all Government services. We shall need to do more and more work, keep longer office hours, develop a greater interest in our respective professions and assignments and show a greater willingness to work and remain at work rather than quit early. Moreover, people of all ranks will be required to show more evidence of their patriotic spirit to serve so that even when civil servants are required to remain in office beyond working hours on special occasions they will not expect overtime payment.

We on our part must never relax our concern for the continued progress of our nation, but hope that every man and woman, every boy and girl will continue to go on working harder, more effectively, efficiently and productively so that we may deepen our loyalty to our national ideals, extend the dimensions of our patriotism to the limits of our country and offer our friendship and goodwill to the nations of the world. Thus will we broaden still further the base of Liberian democracy and make it a leading social and political philosophy in the world.

Our hearty thanks and appreciation go to the Secretary of State and the members of the Cabinet who directed the affairs of Government during our absence from the country. Our gratitude goes also to the Vice-President, the Speaker of the House of Representatives, all officials of Government and the citizens in general for the part which each played in facilitating the operation of the Government. United, you have dispensed your several responsibilities well, and I salute and thank you.

The Captain, the officers and crew of the M.V. *Aureol* were exceptionally kind to us on the voyage and we extend our profound gratitude for all the courtesies they afforded us. We feel that everything was done to make the ten-day voyage as pleasant as possible for us. We wish them a very pleasant journey to their destination and a safe return home to their families.

Finally, I ask you, citizens, friends and representatives of foreign governments and all foreign residents to join us in giving thanks to God for His manifold mercies vouchsafed us on our several journeys, and to pray that He may continue to guard and guide this nation in the years ahead, so that the ideals of our country and the concept of democracy may become a great vitalizing force, in these times when a comprehensive vision of nationhood and dedicated work to its ideals constitute a categorical imperative.

Speech at a Dinner tendered in Honour of a British Parliamentary Delegation

Executive Mansion, Monrovia, 15 March 1963

We share and practise in common many aspects of the democratic way of life.

Introductory Note

The independence of Liberia was a consequence of Anglo-Liberian relationship and early contacts. Liberia learned much from Anglo-Saxon jurisprudence. On the occasion of the visit of a British Parliamentary Delegation to Liberia, President Tubman mentioned these salient points and their relevance to our history, and was pleased to review the many ties of friendship which exist between Liberia and the United Kingdom.

Monrovia, 15 March 1963

HERE THIS evening we have the distinguished pleasure, honour and privilege of welcoming, on behalf of the Government and people of Liberia, the first British Parliamentary Delegation to visit this country.

The fact that these Parliamentarians have come from Great Britain, the nation that first gave recognition to the birth of our nation, the nation whose august sovereign, Queen Victoria, was the first to extend an official welcome to the first President of Liberia, Joseph Jenkins Roberts, and the first state to extend the hand of friendship and assistance to this nation as a free, sovereign and independent state, makes this visit particularly impressive, historic and unique; especially so when the arrival of these honourable delegates in this country coincides with the birthday of President Joseph Jenkins Roberts, the father of this nation.

When we consider the friendly ties which have existed between our two countries for over a century now, when we realize that the present activation of business interests in the nation is already paying dividends, and when we take into account the increased opportunities for training and education which quite an appreciable number of our young people seek in the schools of Great Britain, we know that such a visit can go a long way to improving and strengthening these relationships and creating new ones.

In the name of the Government and people of Liberia, therefore, I am happy to extend to you delegates our very warm welcome and our wishes for a most pleasurable and rewarding stay in Liberia.

While it is true that our form of Government is not patterned exactly upon the British parliamentary system, nevertheless we share and practise in common many aspects of the democratic way of life. We know that the fundamental principles and freedoms have always been priceless possessions which your nation has treasured and that you have actively participated with other nations in bringing liberty and justice to millions of peoples around the world, particularly in Africa. It is because of the intrinsic principles of justice and equality embodied in your system of government that the parliamentarian government of England is the oldest in the world. As an outgrowth of the wholesale change in forms of government, even among the oldest nations of the world, the English-speaking countries can lay claim to having the most enduring forms of government on our planet.

Because of our association with the legal structure of your nation, we are proud to mention that that great instrument, the Magna Carta, which guaranteed the preservation of English liberties and which has befittingly been called the 'cornerstone of English liberty' is recognized by us as the sheet anchor of our democracy. While it is true that the Magna Carta did not grant democracy to the English people, it nevertheless still constitutes an outstanding landmark in the history of human liberty, in that it laid the foundation of our important writ of *habeas corpus* and started the principle of 'no taxation without representation', so basic to our democratic way of life. It has been our privilege to have incorporated into the laws of our country some of the fundamental precepts embodied in the British parliamentary system.

Upon the gracious invitation of Her Majesty Queen Elizabeth II, we made a State Visit last year to the United Kingdom. The very high consideration and courtesy which we received from the Queen, the Duke of Edinburgh, the Royal Household, the friendliness and enthusiasm of the people of Britain and the general interest evinced in our visit made a very deep impression on us, one that we shall never forget. We came away encouraged by the reality of the ties which bind us and hopeful for a future of greater understanding and co-operation between our two countries and our respective peoples. We shall always remember that visit as one which brought our two countries closer together in the strengthening of the long-standing relations which have been of great value to us.

We hope that for the brief duration of your stay among us, you will see some indications of the material and spiritual progress which we have endeavoured to make over the years; that in our political and social institutions you will find the flowering of some of the ideals and ideas for which free men in all ages have fought and which our own forefathers struggled to maintain and perpetuate in Liberia. But most of all, we hope that you will see in the Liberian people themselves a friendly and hospitable people, desirous of improving their relations with the British Government and people; and that you will discover in our boys and girls, and our men and women, the eagerness to absorb knowledge which, when combined with true understanding, will enable its possessors to become not only wage-earners but worthwhile contributors in the competitive race for social progress and human survival.

Finally, we hope that you will have an insight into some of our human problems, towards the solution of which we have directed our energies and which we are tackling with courage and a sense of realism, in the hope that here liberty shall always dwell, so that generations of Liberians will continue to cherish and hold before them the vision of a united and happy people.

To the Inaugural Session of the Seminar of the International Alliance of Women

Monrovia, 29 July 1963

I share the conviction that the total political emancipation of the women of the world will usher in a new day in the history of mankind.

Introductory Note

Ever since the end of the Second World War, the women of the world have become increasingly conscious of new rights and freedoms to which they are entitled, especially those rights and freedoms guaranteed to them under the Charter of the United Nations. President Tubman recognized what this new spirit of emancipation can mean for the peace and progress of the world.

Monrovia, 29 July 1963

IN AN age when the rôle of women has become increasingly more and more significant, I am very happy that our nation's capital should have been selected for the convening of this Seminar. On behalf of the Government, people of Liberia and myself, I extend to you, the Officers and Members of the International Alliance of Women and other delegates, a hearty welcome, and hope that your stay here will be both interesting and enjoyable. May I also hope that the results of your Seminar will be most fruitful, and will contribute to the strengthening and enriching of the great objectives with which you have associated yourselves.

Ever since the dawn of history, in all periods, women have appeared on the world stage whose bold thought and fearless actions have left their imprints on the minds and the hearts of their generations and in the recorded chronicles of their times. Deborah of Biblical times, Jeanne d'Arc of France, Florence Nightingale of England, Harriet Beecher Stowe and the Negro Harriet Tubman of the United States and Matilda Newport of Liberia are some of the great female personalities whose life work transcended national boundaries and whose names will live forever in the grateful memories of posterity. In their day they devoted their time and talent to some supreme need of society and by the generosity and nobility of their souls worked to increase the sum total of human life and happiness.

Many changes have taken place since the times in which the great personalities I have mentioned lived. The rôle of women has expanded nationally and internationally, their abilities have been recognized, their talents are being more and more utilized and their contributions continue to enhance human life and experience. In many areas of the world women, in addition to their divine rôle, have become the *sine qua non* of our modern day society. That the International Alliance of Women, to which the Federation of Liberian Business Women is affiliated, has branches in thirty-nine countries of the world, is proof of the growing influence of the rôle of women in our contemporary society.

Let me here pay tribute to these affiliated societies for the awakening spirit which pervades them and for the great objectives which motivate their members. In the years ahead I feel sure that membership in the International Alliance of Women will continue to grow significantly and with its growth and expansion there will come about a greater participation by women in the political, social, educational and religious affairs of mankind.

In the history of our own nation, women figured prominently even before suffrage was granted to them. Through their vision and initiative, several social welfare institutions exist in the nation today for whose maintenance they carry the principal responsibilities. Among the several institutions, I may mention the Catherine Mills Rehabilitation Centre in Paynesville, the Refuge Home for the Aged in Monrovia, the Antoinette Tubman Child and Welfare Centre in Virginia and the Wilson Refuge Home in Harper, Cape Palmas, as examples. In addition, women are to be found playing vital rôles in the church, in the Red Cross Society, in the professions and not least, in the political activity of the nation. In fact, women figure in almost every area of our national life.

I share the conviction that the total political emancipation of the women of the world will usher in a new day in the history of mankind. I predict for our own nation a greater future because the women are determined not only to play the domestic rôle, but to take a more creative part in the affairs of the state. Current history, newspaper, radio and broadcasting reports reveal that among the women of the world there is a greater awakening and a more active participation by them and that by actual performance they are playing leading rôles in every field and in every avenue of human endeavour. On our part we shall continue with greater intensity to do everything humanly possible to encourage and assist the organizations sponsored by women in our nation and throughout the world, deeply convinced that their interest and work emanate from the great human compassion which fills the hearts of women generally.

If the women of the world continue to assure dynamic leadership in areas where disintegration is taking place in our social and moral values, and if organizations such as this one can influence thought and stir the world to nobler action for peace and genuinely good human relations, then we shall be building a strong and mighty bulwark for universal peace and brotherhood, not only in our time but for all times. I am certain that by encouraging the interests and developing the initiative in yourselves and others, by accepting the opportunities for leadership in your varied activities and by dedicating yourselves to your tasks, you will be adding to the growth of all nations and to the encouragement of the best in the struggle for survival.

I know that the members of the International Alliance of Women, together with the women of the entire world, irrespective of race, colour, creed, religion, clime or coast, are very happy about the eventual outcome of the talks held in Moscow recently, and the signing of a partial Nuclear Test Ban Treaty. Perhaps the representatives at this Seminar might become signatories to the Treaty for a partial Test Ban. I have decided that the Liberian Government will associate itself with this great act by applying to become a signatory since a resolution at the Addis Conference suggested that Africa become a nuclear free zone. And if you want Africa to be a nuclear free zone, then Africa must not possess nuclear weapons. We think that if sufficient interest is generated by nations and peoples who will commit themselves to a total treaty for banning nuclear testing and disarmament, this treaty will become an accomplished fact and the universal peace about which we have talked so long may be established.

Since the last world war numerous conferences have been convened and many resolutions adopted concerning the ideal of peace and universal brotherhood. Now that the great nuclear powers have taken the initial step, the time is ripe, and I feel that other nations should follow in their wake and take the bold and positive action, so long awaited, toward achieving the true objectives of peace, not only in our time but in all times.

I salute and congratulate the International Alliance of Women for the success which the organization has achieved and for its programme for future dynamic, spiritual, political and social growth, development and expansion.

I commend the officers and members of this organization for their endeavours to raise the status of womanhood throughout the world and to organize them into associations for their mutual benefits, so that their contributions to mankind can be more constructive and beneficial. I pray that this association may contribute greatly to the glory of God and redound to the happiness of mankind in his search for peace on earth.

A Panegyric to the Memory of President John F. Kennedy of the United States

Monrovia, 25 November 1963

> *He was a patriot whose integrity baffled the scrutiny of inquiry. . . .*
> *He lived nobly as a man, as a hero, as a statesman and fell nobly*
> *in his advocacy and struggle for political and social justice.*

Introductory Note

The death of President John F. Kennedy grieved the nations of the world. In him nearly every nation found an advocator for its own national cause, whether that cause stood for freedom, peace, justice, progress, or the development of human equality. President Kennedy, therefore, became an international symbol. The sorrow of the Liberian people at the passing of so great a man, who had signified to the world a new era of hope and peace, was given expression by their President during a special and extraordinary ceremony held in Monrovia at the same time as his funeral service was being celebrated in Washington, D.C., United States of America.

Monrovia, 25 November 1963

BECAUSE OF the manner by which the illustrious President Kennedy of the United States met his death, I find myself impelled to exclaim, as did David upon the death of King Saul and his son Jonathan in battle on Gilboa:

'How are the mighty fallen!'

Overwhelmed with grief and anguish, I attempt to present to you a panegyric on the life of John F. Kennedy, thirty-fifth President of the United States. We have assembled here to express our sorrows, our heads bowed down in solemn sadness and our hearts bewailing his sudden and cruel departure.

In the history of men and nations events and incidents occur which puzzle and bewilder the thinking, understanding and reasoning of the human mind and necessitate the natural question: WHY? To what end has this happened, or in other words, what is the cause of this destructive calamity? In most cases we are left aghast, perplexed, stupefied, incapable of making an analysis of the situation. Such was the case when reports of the tragic and brutal assassination of President John F. Kennedy resounded around the world. Strong men gave way to expressions of grief; women and children wept.

I believe in Divine dispensation but often, when some men are smitten in the course of life, we wonder, we marvel, we shudder; yet our faith in Him Who is the Great Dispenser and Absolver of human events restores our hopes, calms our fears, strengthens our nerves, and we yield in submissive acquiescence to the course of Divine wisdom, for there seems to be some truth in the lines written by Robert Burns:

> God nothing does or suffers to be done, but
> That we would do the same if we could see
> The end of things as well as He.

What a striking parallel! Abraham Lincoln signed the Emancipation Proclamation one hundred years ago and two years thereafter, in 1865, was killed by an assassin's bullet. John F. Kennedy proposed and sent to Congress Civil Rights legislations, not only for the implementation and enforcement of the decision of the Supreme Court of the United States outlawing racial discrimination and segregation, but also to give all Americans equal political, economic and social rights, privileges and benefits under the law and he, too, has fallen victim to the ruthless and unholy bullet of an assassin.

President John F. Kennedy is dead, cut off in the midst of his usefulness, mowed down by the wicked hand of a vile and despicable assassin; dead before his work of extending his country's image to mankind was consummated; dead before the peoples of the world could benefit fully from the lofty humanitarian principles in which he believed and for which he unshakably stood and fought so conscientiously and heroically; dead at a time when his country needed his leadership most and when the world looked to that leadership to help steer the course between war and peace. In bitter anguish we lament this tragic and great loss of an outstanding world-renowned statesman, a literary creative genius, a fearless fighter and a world citizen.

John F. Kennedy was a man on whom nature seemed to have impressed the stamp of greatness; he was a patriot whose integrity baffled the scrutiny of inquiry; whose manly virtue never shaped itself to circumstances; who, always great, always himself, stood amidst the varying tides of party strife firm as a rock, which, far from land, lifts its projecting top over the waves and remains unshaken by the storms; the friend who knew no guile and deep in the bottom of whose heart was rooted a feeling of warmth and understanding, over whose remains nations of different and varying ideologies, creeds and ideals unite with equal sympathy and grief to heap encomiums. He lived nobly as a man, as a hero, as a statesman, as a patriot and fell nobly in his advocacy and struggle for political and social justice.

He was the descendant of a line of distinguished personalities who made recognized contributions to their country, and he, by the brilliance of his many achievements in politics, in the realm of scholarship and in war, added to the distinction of his family's tradition. His scholarly performance at Harvard University was rounded off by foreign travels with his father who was U.S. Ambassador to Great Britain and his contacts with literary, political, industrial and business entrepreneurs and top ranking professional men made an important impression on his imaginative, fertile and creative mind. These experiences invariably helped to strengthen his appreciation for the traditions of his country and to broaden the basis of his faith in the democratic way of life, which were later given fuller expression in the fundamental human principles that guided his political, social and religious philosophies of life.

President Kennedy was a man of destiny; in 1946 he was elected to the House of Representatives by a district in Massachusetts; in 1952 he was elected to the United States Senate where he won the respect and admiration of his colleagues and attracted the attention of world statesmen. He was noted for his outstanding ability, the forcefulness and clarity of his logic, the recognized acumen of his assessment, his analysis of important situations, and his judicious and correct decision-making. It was this last attribute which was in my opinion his great strength and which is an outstanding characteristic necessary for leadership, for according to the great Napoleon Bonaparte:

'The rarest attribute among generals is two o'clock in the morning courage; that courage which amidst the most unforeseen events leaves full freedom of judgment and promptness of decision – nothing, nothing is so difficult as to decide.'

I visualize him as Senator in the Senate of the United States championing measures before that august body with the precise logic and great conviction which he possessed. I have seen pictures and movies of him before great crowds during his political campaign, captivating men, women and children by his exceptional personal magnetism, his calm confidence, and his human warmth; I have heard him at the United Nations, through radio broadcasts, extol the rôle of that bastion of human rights and urge total moral and financial support for its great work; I have seen him in the White House and discussed with him matters affecting Africa, Liberia and the world; I have, through the medium of the movies, seen him at home and abroad, always with calm confidence and a grave concern for world peace, displaying the inner workings of his fertile mind, brimful of ideas for his country and for mankind; I have noted a great personality whose ready wit and comprehension of world affairs were all-embracing.

In the death of President Kennedy mankind has lost a staunch friend; the cause of peace has been deprived of one of its boldest and most courageous proponents and advocates; his own nation, the United States, dispossessed of one of her most lofty, valiant and gallant sons and leaders; the Kennedy family bereft of a devoted and ardent husband, father, son and brother; the developing nations of Africa and the world robbed of a champion of freedom, a great sympathizer, whose understanding of their problems and difficulties was above the ordinary.

I was first attracted to Senator John F. Kennedy after reading his book entitled Profiles in Courage, and I met him personally on an official visit to the United States in the fall of 1961. I was fascinated by his immense knowledge of world affairs, particularly Africa, of his mental and physical grasp of the international situation at the time, his patience, understanding and sympathetic attitude to the problems of others and his willingness to be of assistance when convinced of the necessity that justified it. These are some of the attributes which the late President Kennedy was possessed, and that definitely impressed me with his true greatness.

We in Liberia have felt the sympathetic and understanding quality of his generous and great heart, the tender fellowship of his soul, and this nation associates itself with the Government and people of the United States, his family, relatives and friends in their hour of distress, bereavement and grief.

There appears to be a unique similarity between the life work of John F. Kennedy, President of the United States and Pope John XXIII of the Holy See, both functioning in different spheres of human endeavour, for only three and four years respectively, and both being Catholics. His Holiness the late Pope John enunciated liberal policies for an Ecumenical Communion, an ideal that still lives and is still gathering momentum; the late President John F. Kennedy subscribed to and supported the principles of freedom, human brotherhood, peace and universal civil rights for all men, a stand which will ever remain fresh in the memory of the people he loved. We pray that the ideals for which these two great leaders fought will continue to remain vitalizing forces for man's ultimate survival in a world free of hate, fear and racial prejudice.

What must be the plenitude of the sorrow and sufferings of his disconsolate widow, robbed – so cruelly and suddenly robbed – of her husband who, as the penetrating shot that slew him entered his head, fell into her arms in the cold grip of death! We condole and sympathize with her, and her children, and with the father, mother and brothers, sisters and other relatives, and direct them to the mercies of Him Whose sympathy, peace, grace and strength abundantly and forever flow.

'How are the mighty fallen!' Despite our horror of violent death, shall the tragic falling of great men weaken our faith? A short time ago, and he who is the occasion of our sorrows was the ornament of his country's glory and the idol of nations around the world. He stood on the eminence and glory covered him. From that eminence he has fallen suddenly, he has fallen forever by the vicious and despicable hand of an assassin. His intercourse with the living world is now ended; and those who will hereafter find him must seek him in the grave. There, cold and lifeless, is the heart which just a while ago, less than a week, was the seat of friendship. There, dim and sightless, are the eyes whose radiant and enlivening orb beamed with intelligence; and there, closed forever, are those lips to whose accent many have so often and lately listened with deep respect and admiration.

I salute the new President of the United States, Lyndon Johnson, upon whose shoulders have fallen the arduous burden and responsibilities of President of the United States, and whose long, continued and proved experience and ability in statecraft will be invaluable at a time like this, when there seems to be a lull in international tension, and international relations appear to have almost reached a crossroads, a time when the primary question seems to be 'Which way?' May Divine guidance be extended to him in the great task to which he has been called.

And finally, in closing, may I return to John F. Kennedy, and leave with you the words of Tennyson, the poet:

> With silence only as their benediction
> God's Angels come;
> Where in the shadow of a great affliction
> The soul sits dumb.
>
> Yet would we say what every heart approveth,
> Our Father's will;
> Calling to Him the dear Ones that He loveth
> Is mercy still.

God calls our loved ones but we lose not wholly
What He hath given;
They live in word and deed as truly
As in His heaven.

Not upon us and ours the solemn Angel
Hath evil wrought;
The funeral anthem is a glad evangel
The good die not!

Speech in Honour of Dr. Eric Williams, Prime Minister and External Affairs Minister of Trinidad and Tobago

Monrovia, 23 February 1964

The people of Trinidad and Tobago, and of Liberia are no strangers to each other.

Introductory Note

African nationalism and independence have strengthened links of affinity between Africa and the West Indies, but these links are older than the African movement of nationalism and independence. West Indians can proudly point to their contributions to Africa in terms of migration and the awakening in Africa of the desire to become independent from colonial rule. The Prime Minister of Trinidad and Tobago, His Excellency Dr. Eric Williams, however, can claim his own unique moral, intellectual and spiritual contribution to all Africans and people of African descent. President Tubman spoke well of the Prime Minister's contribution and leadership, and the historic links between the people of Trinidad and Tobago and Liberia.

Monrovia, 23 February 1964

AS FAST as science breaks down geographical barriers between nations, so advantage is fast being taken of the interpersonal relationships which the removal of these barriers tends to engender. And as rapidly as interpersonal relationships are taking place, the more apparent the fact becomes that the integrating factors outnumber the disintegrating forces existing between men and nations. I am happy that in this approach there has been a marked recognition of probable solutions to some of the tantalizing problems of mankind.

It is therefore a very great pleasure indeed that we are tonight privileged to be hosts to such an outstanding personality as Dr. Eric Williams, Prime Minister and Minister of External Affairs of Trinidad and Tobago since 1962, a man who has a brilliant literary record and now enjoys an enviable political career. On behalf of the Government, people of Liberia, Mrs. Tubman and myself, I extend a very warm welcome to our honoured guest and wish him and his entourage a most pleasurable and rewarding stay in our country.

Under the stimulus of the 'wind of change' the freedom movement has gathered momentum, gained popularity and achieved great results. Because of it this huge continent has been transformed and its people catapulted into the limelight of political and social history. What attitudes its people will now adopt, what institutional programmes they will initiate, what steps they will take in the fields of knowledge, science and technology and their practical application, and what realistic approaches they will bring to these problems are some of the crucial issues which face the leaders and people of today.

Clearly, our rate of progress and development lies to a large extent in our practical solutions of some of these vital issues, and in our combined action for their implementation. But we labour under no illusion. Events on our continent in recent months have brought to us the stark realities of some of the complexities of our situation. Nevertheless we are encouraged by the direction in which we seem to be heading rather than by the barriers which spring up in our pathway. It is enough that we all share a common concern about the peril we face should our desire for African unity become only matter for a footnote of history.

The people of Trinidad and Tobago and of Liberia are no strangers to each other. Our racial identity, our yen for freedom and our desire to bring unity, progress and prosperity to our peoples and nations make our kinship with you close and real indeed. On our part, for over a century we have maintained our autonomy, built a strong and respectable nation and developed our institutions upon the principles of freedom, liberty and justice. Over the years we have come to value the priceless possession of a free people – the freedom to be free. Along with other freedom-loving peoples of the world we shall continue to cherish this freedom, fight for it, and if necessary, die for it.

The history of Trinidad and Tobago convinces me that you also value democratic institutions to the extent that your people and nation have been able to experience a steady growth in political independence over the years. Be assured, Mr. Prime Minister, that you have friends in Africa who by reason of their racial affinity with you share your aspirations, ambitions, hopes and fears and who are dedicated to support and fight for the freedom movement until all men are indeed and in truth free to direct their own affairs in keeping with their political and social philosophy. As in the past we welcomed all emerging states to nationhood, so now we extend the right hand of fellowship and brotherhood to your nation and people, in the hope that there will develop between our two nations and peoples the closest and most valued ties of friendship and amity.

It is a pleasure at this time to pay special compliments to the Liberians of West Indian origin who have made their homes in Liberia, have become positive assets and are contributing substantially to the peace, progress and prosperity of the nation. They have proved themselves to be law-abiding citizens, skilful artisans and craftsmen, reputable businessmen and women, and reliable and efficient professionals. We are proud of them and grateful for their contributions.

We are particularly proud and happy to honour tonight a great leader who, after a brilliant literary career, and after having worked with the Caribbean Committee and Research Council, became the founder and political leader of the people's national movement, its first Chief Minister and Minister of Finance in 1956, its first Premier in 1959, and its first Prime Minister in 1962; led the Trinidad and Tobago delegations to London for the U.S. bases talks in 1960, the West Indian Federation Conference in 1961 and the Trinidad and Tobago Independence Conference in

1962. As an outstanding literary figure, our guest has written several books —
The Negro in the Caribbean, Capitalism And Slavery, Education In The
British West Indies, History Of The People Of Trinidad and Tobago,
Documents of West Indian History, Volume I, and British Historians and
The West Indies — in addition to contributions to several learned journals.
I salute this great leader and literary genius.

Under your wise and dedicated leadership I foresee the birth of a greater
national consciousness, a genuine and concerted struggle to build up a sound
economy, the desire to bring unity, happiness and prosperity to your people,
and your state playing a significant rôle in the comity of nations.

Our ultimate hope of a happy existence for all mankind now rests
basically on the success of the United Nations Organization, that great
bastion of human liberties. But the organization can be strong only to the
extent that member states will believe in it and support it morally and
financially, as an effective instrument for saving mankind from the ravages
of war and destruction. May those of us who cherish dearly the guiding
tenets of this great body resolve to help spread its influence, so that not
only may it capture the imaginations of men of all nations, but that it will
also become an instrument to turn their wills into the ways of justice, peace
and truth. May the people of your nation benefit from the principles to
which you have always subscribed and which you now offer to the world
through your seasoned and enlightened statesmanship, your tested patriotism and your unselfish devotion.

In coming to these shores, you will in this brief visit, I trust, be given
an insight into some of the guiding principles which have led us in the past
and present, and a glimpse of some of our national ideals and aspirations.
We hope that this visit will bridge, to some extent, whatever gap might
have existed between us and thus bring our two nations and peoples into a
better framework of mutual understanding and co-operative endeavours.

To the United Nations Conference on Social Defence

Monrovia, 18 August 1964

We shall endeavour to uproot by every reasonable and legal method that may be practicable, the cause of juvenile delinquency and end the plague that besets the youth of this age.

Introductory Note

Like any growing industrial nation Liberia has not escaped the problem of juvenile delinquency, and numerous social welfare agencies are battling to keep the high crime wave under control. President Tubman was pleased with the honour which was accorded to Liberia, to play host to a conference on the universal plague of juvenile delinquency, and he pledged Liberia's support in the active interest which the United Nations undertook to provide more meaningful lives for the youth of the world.

Monrovia, 18 August 1964

YOUR PRESENCE in this part of Africa at this time is indicative of the United Nations' concern and interest in the welfare, safety and progress of nations and peoples everywhere, regardless of clime, coast, race or creed. It therefore gives me great pleasure to extend to you on behalf of the Government and people of Liberia a welcome that emanates from a genuine feeling of fraternity, happiness and cordiality. It is our hope that your deliberations and decisions will see fruition in the attainment of practical formulas that will retard and diminish, if not halt, the great danger implicit in juvenile delinquency.

Mankind today lives in grave concern and in some degree of uncertainty about the security of life, limb and property due to the mounting wave of crime throughout the world. Juvenile delinquency has become a tragic phenomenon, and there is decidedly an alarming deterioration in moral values. The allocation of a considerable percentage of the resources of nations for the prevention of crime, the vast sums expended to track down criminals and bring them to justice, the number of institutions built for reformatory purposes and the vast programmes for rehabilitation of wrong-doers, are facts known to everyone present here. These social evils are coeval with the history of civilization, but even after centuries of crime and the meting out of punishment, the deterrents provided by society have not succeeded in stopping or diminishing the commission of crime. In fact, it is alleged that progress in civilization seems to have worked as much for the criminal as it has for society as a whole, since modern methods of communication and transportation are valuable assets in the organization of crime. The part which newspapers, novels, detective stories, the movies, the radio and television play falls into the same category of mixed blessings. Obviously there is need today for a new social philosophy which will focus more on the latent good in the individual rather than emphasize his evil inclinations.

I have often wondered why Robin Hood, the famous outlaw, became the hero of pageant, myth, story and play. His courage and fairness in outlawry made him the incarnation of beloved banditry, and dating from the days of the crusades the ideal gangster has come down to the present as a hangover from the romantic life of that outlaw. What a strange contradiction of values at a time and in a society where we profess to set so much premium on the dignity of the individual!

What effective measures can society take to protect itself and ensure the happiness and security of its members? What kind of civic and religious instructions can we promulgate that these evils of society may be stamped out and the abilities and capabilities of man sublimated toward constructive ends? How can we psychologically condition the minds of youth to the fact that crime does not pay and that the way of honour is the only acceptable path that leads to recognized fame and fortune? Why is the crime wave rising in our society, especially among youth today, when so much more is being offered them than ever before in the history of mankind? Unless we can find satisfactory and practical answers to these questions, we may be labouring in vain.

Statistics are appalling, but it is startling to realize that in almost every corner of the world today a picture of the reckless and daring gangster is being engraved in the idealizing mind of the youngsters who, for the love of adventure and curiosity, begin to imitate these traits. Will the criminal or the police win in the end? Discouraging as this may sound we know that the organized police of today have greater opportunities to combat professional crime, although the success of this will depend largely on the attitude of the public.

We may wonder whether to paint the criminal in his real light in the newspapers, to destroy his glamour in motion pictures, or to revise the story of Robin Hood, would debunk the modern imaginary concept of the criminal. This may be a step forward, but more personal interest in and emphasis on family life and the rearing of children, insistence by parents and guardians upon moral and spiritual values rather than upon material ones; corrective measures by parents, institutions of learning and moulding of children during their formative and adolescent years, will be and should be major steps toward ridding society of the cankerous sore of crime.

In addition to these, since example is better than precept, parents, guardians, teachers, and Sunday School officers should by their conduct, so win the admiration and respect of the children and youth, that their tendency will be towards emulating the virtuous qualities in parents, teachers and guardians rather than being diverted to delinquency.

It is our hope that in Liberia, under the stimulus and guidance provided by the Nation Youth Organization, the programme at Boys' Town in Schiefflein, the Boy Scouts, the Girl Guides, the YMCA, the YWCA, the Sunday Schools, Bible Classes, Civic Programmes and other institutions and programmes contemplated to capture the imagination of the young and turn their energies and abilities into creativity and usefulness, will diminish and prevent this mounting crime wave.

I congratulate the United Nations' specialized agencies, under whose auspices this Conference is being held, and hope that the results achieved here will be fully implemented in time. The Liberian Government and people will do all within their power toward resolving the inquiries of this important social problem. Full co-operation will be given the specialized agencies of the United Nations in their endeavour to reform, revitalize and draw out the good that is in youth. We shall endeavour to uproot, by every reasonable and legal method that may be practicable, the cause of this evil and end the plague that besets the youth of this age – this dreadful plague which, growing out of the ruthless, irresponsible commercialization of means and media of communication, transportation, and entertainment and from unprincipled social practices, causes youth to be lost in the abyss of evil communication and contact so prevalent in the world today, and which tend to corrupt good morals.

May God prosper the work of your hands for the redemption of the youth of the world.

Speech delivered to the Second Conference of Non-aligned States

Cairo, United Arab Republic, 7 October 1964

> *It is befitting that the smaller states come together periodically in an effort to assist not only in the elimination of the historic injustice brought about by a cruel system but also seek to contribute to the strengthening of internal confidence and peace in the world.*

Introductory Note

In this speech President Tubman gave his views on the significance of a meeting of non-aligned nations in the quest for peace. The moral impact of such a meeting would not go unnoticed by those nations who engaged in acts which undermined the activities of agencies set up for peaceful purposes. Non-alignment, he further believed, should become a vital and spiritual force mediating between the contending forces of peace and war, hatred and friendship, broken international relationships and sacred treaties and obligations.

Cairo, United Arab Republic, 7 October 1964

IT IS exhilarating that within less than three months of my attendance at the Second OAU Summit in the ancient, historic and modernized city of Cairo, I again find myself happily on the soil of Egypt with its fascinating pyramids, sphinx, mummies and other relics and antiquities that bewitch the soul.

Having accepted the invitation to attend this second Conference of Non-Aligned States as a member, I consider it a pleasure and an obligation to register on behalf of myself and the Liberian delegation our pleasure in accepting the invitation and subscribing to the conditions and provisions of the Declaration of the Organization adopted and promulgated in Belgrade.

For the benefit of making studies and surveys of international conditions which constitute constant threats to world peace, establishing co-operation among nations and seeking formulae for analysing and dissolving world problems, it is our honour and pleasure to be associated with this array of distinguished national and international personalities, the largest number of Heads of States and Governments ever to have met together at one time and in one place in the history of mankind.

The city of Cairo has in recent years become one of the focal points of international diplomacy because of the number of conferences which have been convened here. We extend congratulations to His Excellency President Gamal Abdul Nasser and the people of the United Arab Republic for making available the necessary facilities for this conference, and for their precise organizational arrangements and hospitality, which have from the outset afforded working comfort and stimulated interest in the tasks that lie before us.

We live in an era of perhaps the greatest technological and industrial achievements of man. No other time offered him such opportunities of living fully, happily and securely. Correspondingly, no other time offers greater opportunities for destroying what his creative genius has taken centuries to develop. And yet it is one of the paradoxes of our times that each nation blames the other for the tensions, unrest and uncertainties extant in the world, while refusing resolutely to take up the challenge of the present. The result has been that, even though we have conceived the shape of the ideal peace, we have faltered in the pathway to its implementation, for which humanity waits so breathlessly. The test of our century will be whether man will give ascendancy to the fascination of industrial development and the great dynamism of power, whether he will move bodily in the direction of permanent world peace and human brotherhood; or whether, while extolling the inevitability of history, he will fail to make the concomitant sacrifices to achieve these truly desirable goals.

When in 1961 twenty-five Heads of States and Governments met in Belgrade, exchanged views on the international situation and took the position that no government or people should abandon their responsibility in regard to the safeguarding of world peace, they opened a new dimension in international diplomacy. The connotation of non-alignment laid down by that first conference appears to be sound and appropriate, and, since earlier experiments for achieving world peace have been tried, the time has come for a revolution in man's viewpoint and attitude, a new and practical approach, whereby thinking is done in terms of a world rather than a local community framework. In this era of apparent peace, there are nations which possess weapons for mass destruction of such annihilating power that it is not enough merely to postpone their use. What is needed and required is the unreserved will and determination of nations and peoples that war is a crime; that the ruthless murder of human beings is genocide and a crime against humanity; that there be created and developed a new man with an aversion and horror for war; and an intense and relentless resolve by nations to pursue this policy for the attainment of peace, not only in our time but for all times.

Non-alignment can never or should never be viewed as a refusal to choose between good and evil, moral or immoral, to take sides with blocs or to remain neutral in a dynamic world. On the contrary the political actions of states ought to make it possible for them to enter various agreements — commercial, economic, technical, and undertake other national and international activities with other nations without affecting their independence of thought and action.

The non-aligned nations are concerned with justice, freedom, independence and human well-being. Equally so, they are concerned about the ending of colonial rule and imperialism everywhere in the world, where these forms have received their death knell, and where the force and significance of nationalism have turned the conscience of the peoples of the world from unreality to reality, and directed attention to the crossroads of a new human endeavour.

Non-alignment should become a vital, moral and spiritual force, a helpful influence between the contending forces of peace and war, hate and love, broken human relationships and sacred treaties and obligations. Non-alignment should be made a great and formidable international causeway through which nations can find the path to conciliation, reconciliation and the adjustment of differences between nations, and can evolve an era of universal peace founded on justice, equality and equity.

Because the majority of the human family of which we are a part has not been involved in the disruptive interplay of power politics, we should be equipped with the tools for objective and unconstrained analysis of the major problems which beset our times. In this respect, we ought therefore to accept the challenge which history and fate offer us, as a rare opportunity to be of immense assistance in the pursuit of world peace, human brotherhood and international coexistence.

We do not need to think within the framework and rigidity of the old order; neither do we need to cloud our thinking with our own prejudices and obsessions with some of the unfortunate and inhumane sufferings that have been directed against us, lest we become biased and fall back into the old ways. We should instead initiate and maintain a new order based upon genuine co-operation and coexistence between all nations, large and small, founded in and dedicated to freedom, equality and social justice and as a corollary of the fundamental principles enshrined in the Charter of the United Nations, which is itself the product of this new order.

We should continue, in conformity with the Charter of the United Nations, to awaken the hopes and aspirations of the hitherto depressed three-quarters of the world's population to the realization that that world body and our efforts are mutually and naturally an inevitable development in humanity's desire to cope realistically with the multilateral problems of maintaining peace, human brotherhood and economic well-being, and to assure them of their freedom.

Since the Belgrade Conference in 1961 to which reference has already been made, many changes have occurred among the great powers whose vying ideological, political and economic outlooks engendered the cold war and sustained it through almost two decades. On some occasions these differing ideologies have assumed dangerous proportions and there were times when these incidents made mankind's quest for peace appear hopeless, but, with intensified and persistent efforts at the United Nations and at the Geneva Conference, where representatives of the non-aligned nations played an important and effective rôle, the efforts initiated at Belgrade and those of the Organization of African Unity, combined with a realistic understanding by the nuclear powers, have until now averted a nuclear holocaust. The great contending powers have thus evinced reason and sanity for the sake of their own security; and shown some sense of humanity's danger in the possession of nuclear and thermo-nuclear weapons and devices. They have further evinced this by voluntarily concluding, in Moscow in August, 1963, a Partial Test Ban Treaty, and other antecedent agreements that have inspired hope and faith and caused some easing of tension throughout the world.

I pay special tribute to the great nuclear powers for their restraint, in untiring and sustained efforts of the non-aligned states, which constituted a part of the membership of the Geneva Conference of eighteen.

I pay special tribute to the great nuclear powers for their restraint, in spite of muddled and capricious thinking, and for the rationality they have evinced in reaching this partial rapprochement. We urge that as this is only a beginning, they will not relent until by perseverance, mutual understanding and good conscience, total disarmament has been achieved.

This new attitude and development appear to be narrowing the gap between these nuclear powers and it is my impression and conviction that these powers are not irresponsible, but that their constructive ability to rate first things first is patently apparent. They are cognizant of the dangers and threats to humanity, that could destroy and annihilate all the achievements of men, nations and science throughout the centuries.

The pace, however, appears to be rather slow and lagging, and I therefore advocate that our decision at this conference should be to urge acceleration of efforts to resolve all differences and points of disagreement on disarmament.

At the Seventeenth Session of the General Assembly of the United Nations in 1962, the Secretary-General submitted a Report on the Economic and Social Consequences of Disarmament. The report noted that international economic relations would benefit from disarmament. It further noted that the position of the primary producing countries, which include almost all of us, would improve as a result of the accelerated economic growth which disarmament could make possible.

It should fall within the efforts of our discussions and decisions to strengthen the hands of the United Nations and its Secretary-General in order that tangible results may follow from this report.

There still remain pockets of disagreement between the major powers. These disagreements have also contributed to the slow pace by which confidence and good faith can be built up. It is our hope that this conference will put itself in a position to offer reasonable and fair suggestions to the contending factions which may prove to be of assistance and thus promote the acceleration of action.

There is also the backlog of resistance against wiping out the last vestiges of colonialism, apartheid and racial discrimination. We cannot accept these situations as permanent and the African States appeal to all nations and peoples to lend assistance to the destruction of these hydra-headed dragons on the African and other continents.

The United Nations Conference on Trade and Development has thrown some encouraging light upon our faltering economic paths. The decisions of that conference have made it plain that there is need for changes in the policies of international economic co-operation and the direction in which these changes should go. We should insist upon the establishment on a broad basis of an international machinery as an integral part of the United Nations, qualified to apply the new international economic policies to trade, and to its relations with development, so as to contribute to the acceleration of economic growth in all countries and, most especially, the developing countries, regardless of size, or economic and social system.

With this broader perspective initiated in Geneva last March, let our actions at the United Nations follow up this initiative.

Fellow colleagues, we have assembled in Cairo to reason together. Let us agree and proclaim that we seek a world in which the internal and external policies of our states and all states are to provide all peoples, indeed humanity, with economic well-being and political freedom and stability. It is befitting that the smaller states come together periodically in an active effort, not only to assist in the elimination of the historic injustice brought about by a cruel system, but also to seek to contribute to the strengthening of international confidence and peace in the world.

To the attainment of these ends, let us throw our combined weight behind a truly constructive plan designed to search for and reach a permanent workable solution to the vexing problems of our time. If we can achieve this honestly enough and quickly enough, believing in the strength of our conviction, we shall create a new revolutionary force to channel man's behaviour into purposeful and effective action. This is our challenge; it is the challenge to all men of goodwill.

Welcome Remarks during the Visit of Lord Mountbatten to Liberia

Monrovia, 8 October 1964

We shall continue to strive to bring our nation and people the blessings of peace, dignity and unity.

Introductory Note

President Tubman was pleased to have an outstanding British citizen visit Liberia. In these remarks are his recollections of his own visit to Britain, and expressions of admiration for the brilliant career of Lord Mountbatten. It was furthermore his desire that our visitor should have an appreciation of our concept and practice of democracy in Liberia.

Monrovia, 8 October 1964

I MOST heartily and warmly welcome you and the members of your party on behalf of Mrs. Tubman, the Government, the people of Liberia and myself, and express profound gratitude that you found it possible to accept the invitation extended to you by Mrs. Tubman and myself at the banquet given in our honour by Her Majesty Queen Elizabeth II at Buckingham Palace on July 15, 1962.

It is to be regretted that circumstances beyond my control necessitate my absence at a time when it would have given me the utmost pleasure to renew my pleasant association with you. I am happy, however, that Your Lordship has been kind enough not only to make the visit in response to our invitation, but also to live in our official residence as our guest.

Notwithstanding my absence from the country, I assure you that Mrs. Tubman and my eldest son will regard it a pleasure to see that you, your daughter, her husband and the other members of your party are received into our family circle in the best Liberian tradition; and I am sure that officials of the Government and the Liberian people will also accord you and the members of your party all courtesies as an indication of our esteem and friendship.

The warm and brilliant welcome at Victoria Station, the glittering pageantry that attended our arrival in London, the enthusiastic receptions accorded us everywhere we went, the dazzling ceremonial function given in our honour and the extraordinary considerations extended to us by the Royal Family when we visited the United Kingdom, will always remain a pleasant memory and an unforgettable experience. It is only natural therefore that we should have left England with nothing but respect, admiration and warm regards for Her Majesty the Queen, His Royal Highness Prince Philip her husband, the members of the Royal Family and the people of the United Kingdom. That visit strengthened, in more ways than one, the ties of friendship which have subsisted between your great country and ours since the early years of our nationhood.

Following this visit we were guests of Their Majesties the King and Queen of Sweden where we had lavish courtesies bestowed upon us by Their Majesties, members of the Royal Family, the Government and people of Sweden, and it is interesting to note that Her Majesty the Queen is Your Lordship's sister.

Even greater than these associations and honours is the fact that we have been attracted by the elegance, refinement, genuineness, warmth and human element of the Members of the Royal Family. I still remember the touching telegram of condolence sent to me, despite the war and its anxieties, by His Majesty King George VI on the death of my late wife, six months after I assumed the Presidency of Liberia, a telegram which the Queen Mother recalled when I met her in London. These and other reasons intensify our pleasure at having you visit us.

Your personal history of valour, understanding and statesmanship is well known, Lord Mountbatten. As the youngest Vice-Admiral in the history of the Royal Navy, you performed military services for your country in the last World War, during which your display of valour and outstanding services won for you the respect of the allied countries and led to your being awarded decorations by seven allied countries for these services, and we are pleased to note that you are the only person still in active service who served in both World Wars. So well did you represent your country as its last Viceroy in India, and you were held in such high esteem by the Indian people that you were requested by them to become the First Constitutional Governor-General, upon that nation's accession to independence.

As a further token of the high regard and affection in which you were held by the people of India, they bestowed on you the nickname 'Pandit' Mountbatten – a name which I am given to understand means not only 'a wise and learned man' but also, appropriately in your case, 'a man much loved by the people'.

I trust that your stay in Liberia will help to increase your understanding of the ideals of democracy we have tried to cultivate, of our struggles during the past century, and of the degree of progress we have endeavoured to achieve. We shall continue to strive to bring our nation and people the blessings of peace, dignity, unity, increased prosperity and happiness and to blend our efforts with all nations that believe in and fight for freedom and human equality.

Again, Lord Mountbatten, on behalf of the Government, the people of Liberia, Mrs. Tubman and myself, I extend to you a very warm and hearty welcome.

Speech at Dinner during Dedication and Opening of the Embassy of the Federal Republic of Germany

Monrovia, 1 March 1965

German-Liberian contacts have been long-standing in diplomatic, trade and cultural relations, and strong ties of friendship have been maintained between the two nations and peoples.

Introductory Note

We have in these remarks a contribution to Liberian diplomatic history which is still unwritten. President Tubman on this occasion gave an insight into Liberia's relationship with Germany which every Liberian should read about and appreciate.

Monrovia, 1 March 1965

THE PURPOSE for which we have been invited here by His Excellency Ambassador Norbert Hebich is memorable in that it is to witness and participate in the dedication and opening of the Embassy of the Federal Republic of Germany. Because of the close ties of friendship that subsist and have subsisted between the German Government and people and the Government and people of Liberia from the time of this country's early incipiency, we are especially happy and proud that this building, constructed as the extra-territorial possession of the Federal Republic of Germany, is also a substantial contribution to the civic improvement of the capital.

On behalf of the Government and people of Liberia I am happy to extend congratulations to the Ambassador and through him to His Excellency President Loebke for this achievement in our nation. It is certainly one which does great credit to the ingenuity, engineering skill and artistry of a people, the reconstruction of whose economy since World War II has made West Germany one of the world's great economic and industrial powers.

German-Liberian contacts have been long-standing in diplomacy, trade and cultural relations, and interest has long been sustained in Liberia and strong ties of friendship have been maintained between the two nations and peoples. This achievement is yet another manifestation of the continuation of the good relations policy which has existed between us and we opine that it will be a happy augury for a closer and more creative and co-operative partnership here and abroad. We are proud to associate ourselves with you in the joy which you must experience today and we hope that these buildings, situated on this beautiful compound with its superb landscaping, will add significantly to creating an atmosphere conducive to productive work. May it become the happy home of many worthy representatives of your great nation.

Liberia and Liberians can never forget the period when they were encountering the greatest persecution, libel and slander in our history, when international opprobium, scathing invectives, threats and attempts at destroying the autonomy and the very existence of this nation were afoot. At that time certain European powers suggested that Liberia be handed over to the German Government in lieu of the African colonies that were taken away and distributed among the colonial allies of the 1914 World War. However, the German Government turned down that offer. We cannot forget that during World War II, although Liberia was one of the states fighting against the German Government, and was without any coastal defences, German submarines attacking enemy ships came between the Liberian coast line and these ships and fired torpedoes and shells at them, away from the direction of the Liberian coast so as not to damage Liberian lives and properties. This was extraordinary.

It is to be especially noted that in the midst of our austerity, the Federal Republic of Germany is making substantial contributions in the nature of loans, grants and scholarships as well as laying the basis of new incentives for private investments. Ours has been, is, and I earnestly hope will ever be, a Republican democracy based upon the free enterprise system, not only peace-loving but also peace-living, peace-practising, and adverse to war, strife, subversion and any philosophy aimed at world domination and the imposition upon other nations and peoples of our own beliefs, systems of Government or peculiar ideologies by force, artifice, intrigue or chicanery.

Mr. Ambassador, your nation has today taken another important step in cementing the diplomatic ties between our two nations and peoples. These buildings are a source of pride to the Government and people of the Federal Republic of Germany and a tribute to our nation. They will testify to the goodwill and friendship of two friendly Governments. In areas where we have reaped mutual benefits from our past and present associations, may our future relationship bring us greater rewards in those joint efforts whereby peace and harmony will be truly established, so that in our efforts to work hand in hand toward our goals we will bring to our respective nations and the world peace, solidarity, prosperity and progress.

On the Occasion of the Sudden Death of Ambassador Adlai Stevenson, United States Permanent Representative to the United Nations

Monrovia, 15 July 1965

To one who served his country and bore the torch of freedom as a beacon of hope and aspiration in the United Nations.

Introductory Note

President Tubman was an admirer of Ambassador Adlai Stevenson, especially because he was engaged in the eternal quest for peace. Because of his own dedication and that of his nation to peace, a cornerstone of Liberia's foreign policy, he mourned the loss of this great man to a great cause.

Monrovia, 15 July 1965

HOW UTTERLY appalling and greatly lamented is the loss sustained by the human race in the death of Mr. Adlai Stevenson! The people of Liberia and myself fully share the deep sense of grief occasioned by the sudden death of this great man who served his country and bore the torch of freedom as a beacon of hope and aspiration in the United Nations as Permanent Representative of the United States; who served his country magnificently, and laboured with great understanding and zeal to propagate and extol the image of his country; who worked ceaselessly in the forefront for the rights and dignity of the human personality in an attempt to influence the hearts and minds of men and thereby pave the way for universal brotherhood and world peace.

We in Liberia deeply deplore and mourn his death as a tragedy at a time when the United Nations Organization is in need of his calm patience, wisdom and understanding in seeking solutions to some of the vexing problems which plague the human race.

MAY HE REST FROM HIS EARTHLY LABOURS IN PEACE.

To the Nation on his return from Zürich, Switzerland

Monrovia, 2 October 1965

Disarmament has meaning and attraction only to the extent that it represents a genuine lessening of world tension and the existence of an effective peaceful control over international disputes.

Introductory Note

In 1965, President Tubman returned to Monrovia from a health trip to Zürich preoccupied with thoughts of a growing tendency by the great powers of the world not to listen to repeated and insistent appeals by the United Nations to disarm. In the decade since 1957 which saw the birth of the space age, there seemed to be no desire to lessen the tensions of a growing arms race. Everyone now realized that it would never be possible to localize another world holocaust. There was a universal fear of the entire world becoming an inferno which the United Nations could never avert, no matter how hard it tried. For developing nations, especially, their growth would be stifled and every chance for their leaders to give their peoples an opportunity for progress and advancement would be hopeless, because the world now seemed to stand in a hopeless state, quite unable to save itself from its own machinations. The President voiced these fears, and the concern of the entire world, and feared most for the fate of the developing nations, and also for what seemed the apparent ineffectiveness of the United Nations.

Monrovia, 2 October 1965

OUR SAFE arrival today after more than six weeks' absence gives cause for praise and thanksgiving to God, first for being back home in reasonably good health and secondly for returning to a home where peace, order and the rule of law prevail.

Five years ago I had a vacation granted to me by the Legislature but after this period another vacation became a necessity, and we therefore took the liberty of going to Zürich, Switzerland, for this purpose. During my stay abroad I had a number of medical tests and examinations, and the specialists pronounced that there was nothing organically wrong, but that I was overworked and tired, and they recommended regularity and better apportionment of my work time, rest and other activities.

Mrs. Tubman, who also underwent several medical tests and examinations, was found to be in reasonably good health, except for minor ailments that required correctives, which were administered.

As this was neither a State nor Official Visit, the members of our party consisted of people from our own level – ordinary, honourable, honest, loyal

and patriotic. Each of them had medical tests and examinations and was
found to be in good health except Counsellor Joseph T. Cisco who had to
undergo surgery. Because our time had expired we unfortunately had to
leave him hospitalized in Switzerland. However, according to reports
received from Zürich, his operation, while serious, was successful and his
progress back to normal health satisfactory.

A vacation such as the one just completed provided opportunity for calm
and deliberate reflection, especially since the madness of war appears to
hover over much of the earth where 'judgment seems to have fled to brutish
beasts and men have lost their reason'. One is tempted to ask, 'Where are
the nations of the world heading?' Internal crises in the smallest country
soon become the concern of the whole world, for if these crises continue for
any length of time the probability of intervention and involvement by some
great powers without recourse to the United Nations, and the resultant
devastation which necessarily ensues, rightfully set people wondering if the
Armageddon spoken of by the Prophet in Holy Writ is near at hand. The
existence of nuclear weapons – an outgrowth of twentieth-century scientific
research, experiments and genius – and the growing danger of their proliferation make even the smallish skirmish or brush-fire war the gravest threat to
world peace and security.

The deadly cancer of war gnaws at the vitals of nations and peoples, yet
we turn our attention not to the causes and origins, but to the symptoms.
Today brother still kills brother, and the heavens resound to the echo of
man's seeming attempt to annihilate himself. Above the noise of the sound
of bombs, the burst of shells and shots, threats and counter-threats and the
shedding of blood of innocent men, women and children, not to mention the
destruction of precious treasures of art, we see preoccupation with economic
grandeur, political prestige and the development of even more powerful,
fearful and destructive arms, armaments, weapons and accoutrements of
war. The inevitable result, predicated upon this trend of modern science
and technology, may portend the end of the human race with all of its
scientific and cultural achievements, unless remedial action is found and
applied. However, it appears to me that some concrete action should be
taken and a new approach made in trying to formulate criteria for the
solution of some of these problems.

In curative medicine the aetiology of a disease is generally sought and
treated in preference to the symptoms which, if treated in isolation, will
reappear. Similarly, in world affairs reason suggests that the same order of
priority obtain, because so long as the main rudiments of international discord and turmoil remain, unrest and tensions will continue to exist and
delays in attacking the causes may lead to war and chaos. One of the
imminent hazards in the world today is the possession of nuclear weapons,
which are capable of devastations of unimaginable magnitude.

In the United Nations, there are several efforts and proposals considered
for disarmament: bans on underground nuclear tests, prevention of the
spread of nuclear weapons and so forth, in an effort to ameliorate this
dangerous situation. Liberia is anxious and eager that the spread of atomic
and nuclear weapons be halted and that a ban on underground tests and
disarmament be effectuated. Liberia will use its best efforts to pursue a
course designed to attain this.

The pronouncements from international conferences on disarmament give cause for some hope; but we should not mistake the shadow for the substance. Disarmament has meaning and attraction only to the extent that it represents a genuine lessening of world tension and the existence of an effective peaceful control over international disputes.

History is replete with failures of the efforts of men and nations to deal with the symptoms of war apart from the cause. Within memory are the efforts and achievements of a noble, intricate and hard-won disarmament treaty in an attempt to control naval power, the intent of which was similar to that aimed today at controlling atomic weapons. The proponents of these measures, and the signatories to that treaty were as peace-loving, as hard-working and as hopeful for mankind as are those working for similar goals today. But they and their efforts failed after they had concluded and ratified the treaty.

The causes of their failure were many, but it is worthy of note that those efforts were, for the most part, conducted outside the League of Nations. While men busily worked on treatment of the symptoms of war, the instrument devised to strike at the cause itself rusted from neglect and disuse.

The United Nations Charter is an obligation voluntarily concluded between nations pledging most sacredly and solemnly to observe and execute the provisions therein contained. The fundamental and organic law of the United Nations and its primary and principal aim and objective is to prevent and avert war so that men and nations may live together in peace, understanding and friendship. Nevertheless, because of human nature and its foibles, misunderstanding and disturbances will ever and anon arise, but in all such cases the United Nations will seek to bring us to a realization of the spiritual and nobler element of our nature as against the animal part of us in an effort to have all such differences peacefully resolved.

A greater number of nations have subscribed to the Charter of the United Nations since its incipiency than have ever been subscribed to any other single international instrument. We have seen that the United Nations has averted war in many instances, and where hostilities have actually commenced has been able to stop them and bring about peaceful adjudication. With these incidents as object lessons, if nations and member states disregard and continue to violate the provisions of the Charter of this Organization just as it suits their interest and purpose, how can they be expected to keep any other international treaty, obligations or protocol into which they may enter?

There can be no more comprehensive and all-embracing commitment than the United Nations Charter, which assures, among other things, the four freedoms guaranteed by the Atlantic Charter. If we do not keep and perform the obligations implicit in this Charter, how can we be expected to keep inviolate any treaty on disarmament, or to prevent the spread of nuclear weapons and devices by any other specific treaty?

I am prone to believe that the institution of a Special Commission might be helpful in reviewing the Charter of the United Nations and insisting that member states conform to the conditions to which they have already subscribed and in addition to seek further for the reasons and causes of the apparent irreconcilable breach between nations, especially between East and West.

It has been suggested that East and West could exist together peacefully under what has been called the principle of co-existence. We might try to act upon this principle, because East and West were placed on this planet by God, or if the materialists or atheists object to saying God, then by nature; and neither can exterminate or destroy the other without exterminating or destroying themselves and the earth. An International Protocol or Agreement defining the term 'co-existence' and outlining the principles of peaceful co-existence between differing and vying political ideologies and systems of government, without resort to force or subversion, might be presented to the United Nations by this Special Commission to be approved and subscribed to by member states.

The small and developing nations are as responsible as the great ones for the deterioration of the influence and effectiveness of this World Body. This is unfortunate because if the United Nations should fail, we would suffer most, for we would be the first and greatest losers should the world revert to international anarchy.

Recognizing the ever-present danger of anarchy and destruction, I call today for Liberia and Liberians, for Africa and Africans, and for all nations and peoples who fervently seek peace to join in demanding a rebirth of influence, confidence, authority and effectiveness for the United Nations because it remains the best, indeed the only instrument in our hands potentially capable of eradicating war and all its terrors.

As Woodrow Wilson said to those who opposed the League of Nations more than forty years ago: 'You will say, "Is the League an absolute guarantee against war?" No; I do not know any *absolute* guarantee against the errors of human judgment or the violence of human passion, but I tell you this: with a cooling space of nine months for human passion, not much of it will keep hot – I ask you this: If it is not an absolute insurance against war, do you want no insurance at all? Do you want nothing?'

To the nations for which the United Nations is the best protection, we must ask, 'Do we want the United Nations or do we want nothing?' Because if we do not support and insist upon the support of others for this sole instrument for peace, we will one day have nothing.

To those nations which ask our adherence to treaties and agreements for control or limitation of armaments we say: Of course we agree that dangerous instruments must be controlled, but first you must use your power to help us obtain a strong United Nations capable of dealing promptly and forcefully with threats to peace and security. We must ask you to join us in making the United Nations a force capable of protecting those in need of protection, and we will readily and gladly join you in limiting or, rather, destroying the hated arms of destruction.

We address and direct this appeal for a revitalized, enlarged, strengthened and effective United Nations to all member states. We say to them that the Charter of this Organization provides the path to peace but that the path is obviously uncertain. *Let us improve it.* Let us not shrink from the task of amendment and improvement if that is what is required. Let us raise this appeal in favour of a United Nations which is vigorous, which is purposeful in the pursuit of peace, and which is respected and honoured by members who are dedicated to it.

This call is for an organization endowed with the *power* to enforce peace, with the *will* to exercise that power, and with the *imagination* and *wisdom* to exert that will for the good of all mankind. We must recognize that the United Nations provides the best and only foundation upon which such an organization can be built. We must use every gift within our command to see that it becomes the force for good, for peace and for progress that it can and must be.

Our goal should be that propounded by Edmund Burke who said: 'The proposition is peace. Not peace through the medium of war; not peace to be hunted through the labyrinth of intricate and endless negotiation; not peace to arise out of universal discord; not peace to depend upon the juridical determination of perplexing questions, or the precise marking of the shadowy boundaries of a complex government. It is simple peace; sought in its natural course and in its ordinary haunts. It is peace *sought in the spirit* of peace and laid in principles purely *pacific*.'

My fellow countrymen, I have elected to speak to you along these lines because of what I consider the serious international gloom that hangs over all nations and peoples. There can be no security or safety when there are recurring instances and events that take us to the brink of war, from which we escape by manoeuvres or tactics.

The issues involved in the present world crisis are of such tremendous proportions that sacrifices and tolerance are required. Individual national honour and prestige, if necessary, should to some extent be waived in favour of international interests – the interest of peace among all nations and peoples of the earth.

We need to marshal all the human forces that we can to assist governments and the United Nations in averting what would appear to be an inevitable approaching global danger. I have learned with great pleasure that His Holiness the Pope will be visiting and addressing the United Nations General Assembly and feel that his presence and what he says will have universal acclaim and contribute greatly to the realization of the necessity for peace in this particular era of the world. It would also be most helpful if the leaders of Buddhism, Judaism, Islam, Hinduism, Confucianism, Shintoism and other sects were to consider it necessary and sufficiently important to visit and address the United Nations in an appeal for peace and understanding among men and nations. In addition to this, all religious leaders and denominations should marshal the full force of their influence, and the consistency of their prayers and fasting, for the reign of peace. Let us pray to that God who wrought the great reconciliation between God and man that He may come and His will be done on earth as it is in heaven.

May God grant that through the United Nations man may begin a conscientious march toward enlightenment and practise the doctrine of 'live and let live'. May we have peace in this century.

During our absence from the country the affairs of state have been ably administered by the Cabinet under the direction of the Secretary of State with the advice and assistance of the Vice-President, the Speaker of the House of Representatives and the co-operation of other officials of Government, citizens and residents. To all of you we extend grateful thanks and appreciation for this manifestation of your loyalty and patriotism.

And finally,

Lord, while for all mankind we pray,
Of every clime and coast,
Oh, hear us for our Nativeland,
The land we love the most.

Speech at Dinner Honouring the Israeli Prime Minister, Levi Eskhol

Monrovia, 2 June 1966

We fail to see any reason whatever that could justify any irreconcilable differences between the peoples of the Middle East. Their history is outstanding, too sacred and universally recognized not to admit of unity, friendship and brotherhood.

Introductory Note

President Tubman spoke about the ties of friendship between Israel and Liberia and of their common concern for world peace. He recalled Israel's historic contribution to world religions, its great humanitarian traditions, and further expressed gratitude to the Israeli Government for technological assistance to developing nations. He also spoke about his concern for peace in the Middle East, especially between Israel and her neighbours.

Monrovia, 2 June 1966

THE WARMTH that thrills our hearts as we welcome you and Mrs. Eshkol to Liberia is of the highest magnitude. The Government and people of Liberia are as happy as Mrs. Tubman and myself to have you as our honoured guests, and we hope that you and the members of your party will thoroughly enjoy your brief stay with us.

Your presence brings to mind pleasant recollections and treasured memories of the splendid relationship that has existed between our two nations and peoples since the birth of the State of Israel, which was heightened by our memorable State Visit to that great and progressive Promised Land of the Bible. The fraternal understanding, co-operation and cordial relations between our two countries were further strengthened by the visit to Liberia of our late and lamented friend, your revered President Izhak Ben-Zvi, in 1962 which opened a new chapter in Israeli-Liberian friendship.

Moreover, our contacts with Israel—a land of living Biblical culture, antiquity, hope, promise and progress, extends beyond the birth of the present State of Israel. We had known Israel long before the founding of Liberia; when like Israel our forefathers were bowed down and stricken with humiliation, oppression and slavery, they sang the song of 'Moses and the Lamb'.

It is noteworthy, Mr. Prime Minister, that like Liberia, Israel's adherence to the Charter of the United Nations confirms its beliefs that the people of every nation are endowed with the right of free choice and that our most sacred obligation is to guarantee to all that choice which, once attained should be nurtured, preserved and protected from wanton and unjustified assaults.

In our world today, when nations are rising up against nations, peoples against peoples, when there are wars here and rumours of wars there, and when the world and its inhabitants seem stultified with blind obsession for world domination, we note the sanity and soberness that seem regularly and consistently to characterize your policies and attitudes, both nationally and internationally.

We cannot over-emphasize, in the interest of ourselves and all mankind, the necessity for some agreement and arrangement to save us from the inevitable calamities that must follow any global conflict, whether it be nuclear or conventional. Man has created a new earth but he has not made or created a new spirit and a new heart within himself to be able to live in this new world of his creation in peace and security. With the instruments for mass destruction that man has in his possession, it seems imperative that if he is to continue to inhabit the earth in any degree of safety, he must dispassionately, selflessly and rationally analyse the dreadful import of the unlimited and illimitable power of these weapons in an effort to safeguard against destroying, not only the human race, but all that he possesses and the earth itself.

Your Prophets, Mr. Prime Minister, prophesied that there would be no more sea; there is virtually no more sea at the present time. The aeroplanes, the missiles, the space ships have diminished and almost done away with the necessity for the sea as a dividing line between continents, nations and peoples and have made us one world.

The great works of healing, even the raising of the dead, the works of miracles – dividing the sea, causing the sun to stand still – which have been performed and experienced in the Middle East, have not been known to occur anywhere else upon the face of the globe. These have been wrought by great religious leaders, prophets, sages and kings – Judaism, Mohammedanism, Christianity.

We fail to see any reason whatever that could justify any irreconcilable differences between the peoples of the Middle East. Their history is too pronounced and outstanding, too sacred and universally recognized not to admit of unity, friendship and brotherhood.

In the present circumstances, we should pray for the fulfilment of the prophecy of another of your great prophets, the prophet Isaiah, who prophesied: 'They shall beat their swords into plow-shares, and their spears into pruning-hooks: nation shall not lift up sword against nation, neither shall they learn war any more. The wolf also shall dwell with the lamb, and the leopard shall lie down with the kid; and the calf and the young lion and the fatling together; and a little child shall lead them.'

Although a relatively small and developing nation yourself, your contributions to other developing countries are doing much to assist them, and they are confident that there is no evil motive, intrigue or artifice attending this assistance. The Liberian nation and people are recipients and beneficiaries of your assistance programme and express their gratitude.

Again, Mrs. Tubman and I, on behalf of this evening's guests and the people of Liberia, extend to Mrs. Eshkol and you, Mr. Prime Minister, a very, very fond welcome and assure you of the freedom, not only of our territories and homes, but also of our hearts.

Speech at Dinner in Honour of the Prime Minister of Israel

Monrovia, 3 June 1966

We plead for universal peace. We plead for peace among nations and men. We plead for regional peace. We plead for peace in the Far East, in the Middle East, in Africa and everywhere upon the face of the earth.

Introductory Note

President Tubman's plea for universal peace was an indication of his own deep concern for peace in the Middle East, especially in the crisis between Israel and several neighbouring Arab states. This was a matter which had always claimed his attention and had brought him requests to negotiate for a peaceful settlement. We have here an expression of his desire for a solution of a problem between neighbours whom he described as having more in common for unity than disunity.

Monrovia, 3 June 1966

TO EVERY beginning there is an ending. I speak of things material and of things terrestial. There are things terrestial that are everlasting, having beginnings but no endings. The things that are without beginning and without ending are eternal. The difference between everlasting and eternal is that some beginnings and endings spread over a long period of time while others spread over short periods of time; they are very brief.

But it is not the duration or the length of time between beginning and ending that counts most, it is what is crowded into the period between beginning and ending that counts – what is accomplished.

And so I am happy to say that I believe that the three or four day visit of His Excellency the Prime Minister and Mrs. Eshkol and members of their party, counts as much as if the duration of their visit had been several months or years.

We in Liberia believe in the Fatherhood of God and the brotherhood of man. We of Africa, enslaved, oppressed and deprived, argue that God has made of one blood all nations of men that dwell upon the face of the earth. Now that the tide seems to be turning, now that we are coming into our own share of the benefits and privileges of the dignity of man and nations, that principle has not changed. If it was right then, it is right now.

And we insist and contend that we must adhere to the same principle that we laid down then and act upon it and live up to it now, in this new era of African redemption and liberation.

In our discussions touching matters of disarmament and a halt to the proliferation of nuclear weapons, I have learned that, as I said before, all

662

men are brothers. We believe in Psalm 133 which says, 'Behold, how good and how pleasant it is for brethren to dwell together in unity!'

We plead for universal peace. We plead for peace among nations and men. We plead for regional peace. We plead for peace in the Far East, in the Middle East, in Africa and everywhere upon the face of the earth.

APPENDICES

To the Parliament of Sierra Leone
Freetown, 20 June 1959

> *There are few countries in the world today which have been founded*
> *under the same historical circumstances as Sierra Leone and Liberia.*
> *We have been able despite our stormy past to surmount our diffi-*
> *culties and to make a remarkable degree of progress.*

Introductory Note

In response to an invitation from Her Britannic Majesty, Queen Elizabeth
II, President Tubman visited Sierra Leone on the eve of the preparations
of that country for independence. It was the beginning of the laying of the
foundation of renewed friendship with the countries of Africa. The President further took the occasion to define in this major address his view on
how African unity should be achieved and the form it should take. We
have here his celebrated formula for *The Associated States of Africa* for
unity in Africa.

Freetown, 20 June 1959

THERE ARE few countries in the world today which have been founded under
the same historical circumstances as Sierra Leone and Liberia. Sierra Leone,
like Liberia, owes its origin to philanthropic movements organized for the
specific purpose of solving a social problem. The early history of our two
countries contains some dark and dismal chapters. But the heartening factor
is that we have been able, despite our stormy past, to surmount our many
difficulties, to survive in the midst of hardships and to make a remarkable
degree of progress.

For this outstanding accomplishment, I have no doubt that the names of
Granville Sharpe, Henry Smeathman, Captain Thompson, Mr. Irwin, the
Rev. P. Frazer and Tribal Kings Tom and Naimbana are as dear to you as
are our own Captain R. F. Stockton, Eli Ayres, Elijah Johnson, Thomas
Buchanan, Joseph Jenkins Roberts, and tribal kings Peter, George, Zoda,
Long Peter, Governor, Jimmy and scores of others.

These were some of the men – dedicated, devoted and determined – who
suffered, bled and died that our respective countries might live and contribute towards the advancement of the continent of Africa and civilization
everywhere. And these are the men who, by demonstrations of courage, perseverance and sacrifices, strove to ignite the torch of freedom which we their
descendants have jointly borne aloft – you since May 9, 1787 and we since
January 7, 1822.

As we of this generation review the past – a past studded with classical
examples of close collaboration and reciprocal respect so well displayed by
our forebears, we can be proud of the fact that throughout the years of our

667

existence, relations between our two countries and peoples have been peaceful, harmonious and mutually beneficial.

Side by side, despite our long and difficult journey, we have worked together. We have never been discouraged but have remained solidly dedicated to the principles of democracy and freedom, justice and equality for all men of all races, creeds and colours. Ours is therefore a devotion which has been embedded in our systems of government, not to be shaken by the approach of any traducing ideologies. We stand firm for the practical application of the principles of democracy because of our deep regard for individual liberty and the dignity of man.

As the oldest independent state in West Africa and for many years the only republic in Africa, Liberia has never been unmindful of her great mission to the peoples of this continent. Nor has she ever tried to evade her solemn responsibility which destiny placed upon her shoulders. In every instance and at all international councils where her representatives were present, they have stood up boldly and manfully because Liberia desires freedom for all peoples wherever dispersed over the globe.

Because of her long years of experience in statecraft and international affairs, Liberia has learnt that the pathway to freedom is easier to traverse by the guiding light of reason, the strong arm of negotiation and the virtue of sobriety. Moreover, the difficult and tempestuous seas through which the Liberian people, by the help of an All-wise Providence, have been able to navigate their Ship of State, avoiding the hidden snares and fearful torrents, have taught them to place the highest premium upon their hard-won liberty, independence and sovereignty. It has simultaneously created in them the deepest feelings of appreciation, respect and reverence for the sovereign rights of other independent nations and peoples. It has taught us Liberians to bind up our national wounds and consolidate our forces at home and with other nations before launching out into the deep.

Even though Liberia is intensely desirous of achieving unity and solidarity with all nations and peoples of Africa, it is principally out of due deference for the inherent rights of other independent peoples of this continent that she has proceeded cautiously, and, after giving careful consideration to so delicate a subject, has proffered the creation of an all-African organization to be known and styled as *The Association States of Africa*.

Such an organization could be bound together by a single convention of friendship, navigation and commerce, while allowing sufficient flexibility for each signatory nation to maintain its national sovereignty and its peculiar identity. Member states of this organization could feel free to work more closely together in an atmosphere of equal confidence and equal respect.

Furthermore, as a permanent machinery providing for continuing consultation among African States on problems of common interest as well as for the peaceful solutions of any and all disputes, the Association States of Africa could speak in one accord at international forums for the peoples of Africa. It would therefore become the recognized voice of Africa speaking not only for one nation or only for Africans, but for all the African nations as well as for all dependent and suppressed peoples. This is the type of association which we think to be most feasible. However, we are open to the views of others, for no individual or nation should assume to have a monopoly on knowledge.

Mr. Speaker and members of the Sierra Leone House of Representatives,

I am deeply gratified by this opportunity to address you and I extend to you the sincere thanks of the Government and people of Liberia for the warm reception which we have been given by the Government and people of your friendly and progressive country. In this age when the continent of Africa is aglow with the achievement of freedom, and, as you have so well pointed out, when Nigeria and other territories including your own country are also heading for independence, it behoves us all to think soberly, act wisely and reassess our policies in the light of these new developments.

The entire universe with its divisions and subdivisions was made by the unseen hand of the Supreme Being known to Christians as God, to Mohammedans as Allah, and to the other great religions of the world by various other titles of reverence. While these divisions have existed for millions of years, they were not named by the Creator but by man, the created. It was man who differentiated the races of the earth into Caucasoid or white, Mongoloid or yellow, Negroid or black, and Australoid or brown. It was also man who designated the geographical divisions and sub-divisions of the earth as continents, islands, oceans, seas, rivers, lakes and named the planets of the solar system.

Even though man has made a few mistakes, such as that the earth was flat or that the sun revolves around the earth, so well and so perfectly has he succeeded that for centuries his appellations to these bodies and things have remained unchanged. But notwithstanding these numerous geographical divisions and sub-divisions, notwithstanding the classifications of the races of man, one fact remains indisputable – they are all component parts of the one planet called the earth and all peoples wherever dispersed are members of the human family.

It is in recognition of this fact that I accept the principles of Wendell Wilkie's 'One World' philosophy. We are all interdependent, and any race, nation or group of people which embarks upon a policy of complete independence is doomed to failure. Each needs the other in one manner or another, and so long as this planet exists, so long shall the races, nations and peoples of the earth remain interdependent.

This is a great day for Africa and its over 200 million inhabitants who are assuming a new rôle in national and international affairs. But with this new rôle comes the tremendous responsibility of pursuing a wise and correct course of conduct that would bring to the peoples of this continent approbation and success rather than disrepute and failure. The age in which we live today requires sober, dispassionate, unselfish and well considered actions.

Africa will for quite some time to come need the genuine friendship and co-operation of our friends and benefactors across the seas; they too will need us, our friendship and Africa. Consequently, there is no necessity for nursing our old prejudicies, or harbouring feelings of bitterness. The past is history; the present is ours to utilize to the best advantage of ourselves so as to brighten the future for our posterity.

We in Liberia were happy to welcome to our shores the Governor of Sierra Leone, His Excellency Sir Maurice Dorman and Lady Dorman; and it gives me pleasure to state that their visit has already added new strength and vigour to the bonds of friendship which have subsisted between our two countries for more than a century. It is with even greater anticipation that we look forward to the royal visit of Her Majesty the Queen and His Royal

Highness The Duke of Edinburgh later this year; for the people of Liberia cherish their long friendship with the people of Great Britain.

Again I thank you for the opportunity afforded me of visiting your august body and addressing you. I feel very much at home here, for I myself was a member of the Legislature of Liberia as a senator for twelve years and there I began to mould my ideas and views on international relations. I realize also that for all legislators there are times when debate becomes turbulent; there are times when members have a tendency to measure their forensic ability in the interest of what they perceive to be right and sometimes to air and demonstrate that ability. But all this is understandable and is not incompatible with legislative procedure, for the Legislature has been defined by one of the Speakers of the House of Representatives of Liberia on a festive occasion as follows: 'The Legislature has always been and must always be the theatre of contending opinions; the public forum where the opposing forces of political philosophy meet to measure their strength; a place where the public good must meet the assault of local or sectional prejudice. In a word, the appointed place where the nation seeks to utter its thoughts and to register its will.'

Finally, I express the hope and prayer that the years ahead will be laden with abundant success in the social, economic and political advancement of your country and your government and in the well-being and prosperity of the people of Sierra Leone.

Opening Speech at the First West African Summit Conference

Sanniquellie, Nimba County, 16 July 1959

Freedom, unity and co-operation should be the noble objective of all peoples. But these will never be assured if we fail to create the right conditions which all Africans, despite their varying customs, traditions and culture, can whole-heartedly support. Thus, in our determined search for African unity, let us endeavour to evolve that formula which will be sufficiently flexible for each nation to maintain its national sovereignty and its peculiar identity. We should show a willingness to co-operate with all African countries and peoples regardless of their choice of association.

Introductory Note

This was perhaps the first international occasion which was afforded the President to make clear his views on African unity and the approach to its realization. Together with his address to the Parliament of Sierra Leone in 1959 we have his manifesto on African unity in which he articulated succinctly the position of the Liberian Government during the famous Sanniquellie Summit.

Sanniquellie, Nimba County, 16 July 1959

I AM happy to be able once more to extend to you, our visiting friends, distinguished sons of Africa, and to the members of your delegation a very warm welcome to Liberia, and to express the hope that your stay among us will not only be pleasant and enjoyable, but will mark the beginning of a new chapter in the history of African brotherhood, mutual co-operation and solidarity.

Long before either of you ever came to our shores, the people of this country, who have always been proponents of the principles of liberty, justice and equality for all the people of this continent, had come to admire and respect you because they had heard and read of your valiant struggles for the liberation and independence of your respective peoples who are their brothers. They had followed with pride, sympathy, great admiration and even with fervent prayers your courageous battles so nobly pitched, fought and won for the attaining of freedom and independence for your countries. They have rejoiced in your successes and by these achievements you have reinforced their strength and their determination to fight until the last enemy of freedom, justice, equality and human dignity is defeated and the soul of the African is once more free and unfettered.

I must therefore pay tribute to you both for the magnificent, sagacious and forthright manner in which you have boldly led your nations and peoples to independence. Your achievements have met with the respect and admiration of the Liberian people and, I dare say, Africans and most of the nations and peoples of the earth. For you have proved your firm devotion and your unflinching dedication to a worthy cause — the sacred right of all peoples, regardless of race, colour or creed and regardless of geographical location, to govern themselves and to enjoy the blessings of self-determination which a Beneficent Creator has bestowed upon all men everywhere.

Today I am particularly happy that, for the first time in the long history of our continent, and because of our profound interest in the future of this continent, we have mutually agreed to lay aside our respective onerous duties and responsibilities of State and meet in the calm and serenity of Sanniquellie, a typical African community more than two hundred miles in the interior, to discuss in an atmosphere of frankness, calm, equal respect and confidence matters affecting our three countries and our brothers of Africa.

We must not be content to have this meeting chronicled merely as the first time the Chiefs of States of three independent African countries have met. That would be unworthy of our rich and noble African heritage. But let us resolve that from our actions, deliberations and decisions at this meeting will go forth a message of encouragement, hope and confidence to our brothers, and of peace and goodwill to all men.

We can be sure that this meeting will be keenly followed by our brothers in Africa, and particularly those who still live under foreign rule. What we achieve will in some measure strengthen their determination in their struggle and accelerate their march to freedom and independence.

Let me make it clear that we glory in the fact that this is not a meeting to plan and plot the subjugation and suppression of peoples or nations. It is not designed to consult upon and plan the strategy for waging a hostile political, social or economic campaign against any nation, groups of nations or race of peoples. Nor is it intended to be pre-occupied with the attainment of any selfish, national, political, social or economic predominance of any one nation or group of nations over any other nation or nations, nor any one of us over the other two.

On the contrary, its primary objective is the quest for a formula or formulae to hasten and effect the liberation and independence of the subjected people of our continent; to bring unity, harmony, coherence and mutual understanding among ourselves and our brothers; and finally, to consider ways and means for contributing towards world peace and better understanding between the peoples of our continent and all nations and peoples everywhere. What better, what nobler and more beneficial objective could be conceived and pursued?

It is my opinion that a practical approach to a mutually acceptable formula should take full account of all the essential elements which make for mutual confidence, oneness of purpose and willingness to participate in joint actions for our common good. Mutual confidence in international relations is absolutely necessary, but it can only be obtained in a climate of mutual trust, candour and honesty. There must be a willingness to meet and negotiate on a basis of reciprocal respect coupled with a conscientious willingness to make wise and judicious compromises in the larger interest of the millions of our continent who are yet being deprived of their liberties and of their sovereign rights.

Joint action against a common threat inevitably involves agreement on principles in any specific context wherein the peace, progress and prosperity of the African continent appear to be at stake. Common measures might therefore range all the way from moral condemnation backed by socio-economic and political sanctions, to negotiation of settlements through the United Nations and other International forums.

To generate that needed and essential incentive in us all towards our determined goal of African unity and solidarity, we need first of all to create a spirit of mutual confidence devoid of personal ambitions and aspirations either as individuals or as nations. We need to strive to be understanding and understandable in our ideals, policies and programme and make it clear that we aim at the triumph of principles.

In the interest of developing a greater appreciation for the more enduring value of mutual respect for the national ideals and national sovereignty of our respective nations within the framework of unity and solidarity we need to avoid any adherence to or emphasis upon the idea of any apparent material advancement which any one of our countries may happen to enjoy over the other. For this could determine the very structure we are endeavouring to erect and thus divide rather than unite us.

Teeming millions of our peoples have for centuries been the victims of oppression, suppression and intolerable hardships. Our entire continent has been subjected to all the miseries and degradation known to man. Not only have our lands been partitioned, but our homes have been pillaged and expropriated without commensurate compensation. Despite these facts we have never despaired. We have kept the faith with God and ourselves. Because of our faith, we have not only contributed immeasurably to the progress and advancement of the nations of the world, but today a new Africa is rapidly emerging.

It is therefore with joy and great expectation that we look forward in the near future to the independence of Nigeria, Togoland, Somaliland, the Cameroons and other states of Africa.

Africa, our beloved continent, has bestirred itself. It has come forth into the limelight and its peoples are taking their places in the international galaxy of nations. But be that as it may, let us not deceive ourselves. We have only begun to begin. The greatest portion of Africa and Africans have yet to attain the great blessings of freedom and independence, and despite the quickened pace of our development, we are still under-developed countries. We face great obstacles, but nothing can stand against the concerted will and determination of a united people.

It is indeed heartening to note that we have all resolved to assist, foster and speed up the time for the total liberation of Africa and Africans. This is indeed a challenge which offers a tremendous opportunity for all of the leaders of this continent to portray and prove their ability and to justify the confidence reposed in them. It seems to me that one of the finest means of meeting that challenge and displaying the qualities of true responsible leadership should be the prosecution of sound and correct policies enunciated within the framework of co-operation and consultation with other African states and peoples.

Freedom, unity and co-operation should be the noble objectives of all peoples. But these will never be assured if we fail to create the right conditions which all Africans, despite their varying customs, traditions and culture, can whole-heartedly support. Thus, in our determined search for African unity, let us endeavour to evolve that formula which will be sufficiently flexible for each nation to maintain its national sovereignty and its peculiar identity. We should show a willingness to co-operate with all African countries and peoples regardless of their choice of association.

It appears necessary, in view of this brief survey of some fundamental issues which I have attempted to explore, that we formulate a programme in the interest of the attainment of our basic objectives. I therefore propose for our consideration the following topics:

1 – African Unity
2 – Freedom and independence in Africa
3 – The Cameroons
4 – Racial Discrimination in South Africa
5 – Nuclear Tests in the Sahara
6 – Conference of the Independent African States.

While some of these points have heretofore claimed our attention at conferences dealing with Africa or have been the subject of study by our individual governments, we in Liberia have felt an urgency for an informal and frank exchange of views among us.

Finally, I should like to mention for the benefit of any who may question the propriety of this meeting being confined to the three of us, that it is because thus far only Ghana, Guinea and Liberia have put forward definite proposals on African unity; and we have felt it necessary to meet and review these proposals as well as any other matters which may affect Africa in general.

It is our feeling that all discussions on African unity at this time should be of an exploratory nature and no decision, conclusion or agreement on such a far-reaching, intricate and delicate matter should be taken until other African territories with fixed dates for independence have achieved their independence and other independent states have been consulted and can fully participate as foundation members in a meeting or conference which should finally be agreed upon so as to decide a specific form that unity should take which will be satisfactory to all and spontaneously supported by all. These are only our views and we shall welcome for consideration any suggestions which you, our great and good friends, may desire to offer.

I regard it as significant that as we meet here to discuss some problems of unity among ourselves and freedom and independence for our peoples, the Ministers of Foreign Affairs of the United States, the United Kingdom, the Soviet Union and France are in session in Geneva seeking to ease world tension and to narrow the gap, if not close it, between East and West. I also note that negotiations have been going on for quite some time among some of the representatives of these same countries for an agreement to ban nuclear tests. Although no agreement has been reached, hope is inspired by the fact that no such explosions have occured since the beginning of that conference.

I suggest that we extend to them our ardent wishes for their success in finding a satisfactory solution which would avert an imminent threat to world peace and save mankind from the terrible consequences of radioactive fallout.

Permit me, Gentlemen, once again to welcome you and assure you of our appreciation for your presence here with us in Sanniquellie. It is my hope that your stay among us will be most pleasant and enjoyable, and that the results of our meeting will redound to the lasting benefit of the peoples of our beloved and revered Mother Africa.

Address at the University College of Fourah Bay

Fourah Bay, Freetown, Sierra Leone, 16 June 1959

It is essential that we become more internationally minded; that we lay aside our prejudices, open our hearts and work together.... Our educational systems should be geared to this principle and our young men and women should be taught the art and science of international partnership.

Introductory Note

In the new Africa which was being fashioned education would be the key instrument for the fulfilment of the hopes and aspirations of the new nations in their search for unity and meaningful values. The President extended an invitation for joint co-operation between the University of Liberia and the University College of Fourah Bay for partnership in the building of a new Africa based on a common bond of friendship and respect, and for the achievement of new values.

Freetown, 16 June 1959

TO US in Liberia education is the cornerstone of our democratic institutions, the firm foundation of our social, economic and political advancement and the solid bulwark of our national unity. It is the guiding light by whose radiant beams our citizens are hurling back the frontiers of illiteracy, defeating the century-old enemy of their progress and marching confidently in the vanguard of a rapidly emerging Africa.

From the early beginnings of our Republic, even though our Pioneer Fathers were in the throes of poverty and disease, even though they were being constantly attacked by powerful forces which threatened their very existence at every stage of their long and difficult journey towards national independence, they were never deterred from their determination to lay the basis of a sound educational system which would withstand the test of time.

It is that system of education which has provided our nation with stalwart men and women who have single-handedly charted its course and courageously defended its autonomy during some of the most critical periods in its history. It is that system of education which has given stamina to our youth, and strength, vitality, endurance and sobriety to our nation. And it is that same system of education which we are today revitalizing, revamping and expanding to meet the challenge of an ever-changing world.

Based upon our past experiences, I am convinced that education, whether it be liberal or technical, general or specialized, is of paramount importance

675

in every country, but particularly in those countries where the successful prosecution of the policies and programmes of Government depends to a large
extent upon the judgment and opinions of the great majority of the population. Consequently, since we of Africa voluntarily desire to pursue the pathway of democracy, and since we earnestly intend to make the democratic
system of Government acceptable and attractive to our peoples, we should
first strive assiduously to democratize knowledge. The masses of our population should be afforded ample opportunity to get an education.

The young men and women of Africa should be taught to appreciate the
dignity of labour. They should be prepared to utilize their knowledge for the
manufacture of material products to benefit their respective nations. They
should be made to realize that the acquisition of education is not essentially
for self-aggrandizement or sentimental reasons, but for practical purposes.
Finally, they should be able to differentiate between oppression, whether it be
disguised or exposed, and the legitimate burdens that stem from the inevitable exigencies that arise during the course of normal democratic processes.

In this age of keen competition among men and nations for the conquest of
outer space, in this age when our world is witnessing one of the hottest con-
tests ever waged by men for the supremacy of their ideas, the problems of
this vast continent and its diversified population cannot be solved by
emotional imbalance or hasty action. On the contrary, they require the
seasoned, unprejudiced and sober consideration of the statesmen of Africa.
Therefore it is essential that African statesmanship be guided by reason and
a unanimity of purpose.

The peoples of Africa must cultivate the virtue of working together in a
climate of equality and brotherhood not only among themselves, but with all
men everywhere; for no nation, no people can fully develop themselves in
isolation. There must be a constant interchange of knowledge, skills and
economic resources to ensure progress on a world-wide basis.

Africa, with its wealth of untapped and yet undiscovered mineral resources, its diverse cultural patterns and traditions, its rare fauna and flora,
and its vast agricultural possibilities is one of the finest natural laboratories
in the world. Here on our own continent are excellent materials begging to be
investigated, evaluated and brought to the attention of the world. But to do
this requires the skill and experience of the trained mind.

Without this training, experience and specialized knowledge we cannot do
it ourselves. And it is because of this inadequacy of our own technology and
experience in any one area of our development that we shall, for a long time
to come, need help from abroad. Let us not forget: the foreign world needs
Africa.

This is the reason why it is essential that we become more internationally
minded; that we lay aside our prejudices, open our hearts and work together
under the umbrella of mutually satisfactory international co-operation. Our
educational systems should be geared to this principle; and our young men
and women should be taught the art and science of international partnership.

It is in this perspective that I am gratified by this opportunity to speak to
the student body of this institution which for a hundred and thirty-two years
has cast its influence upon the lives and thoughts not only of the people of
Sierra Leone, but of West Africa and perhaps this entire continent. Founded
in 1827 by the Church Missionary Society, Fourah Bay College, with its

beautiful campus on the slopes of Mount Aureol, is a living monument to the foresight and tenacity of purpose of those early Missionaries who sacrificed the flower of their lives, came to Africa and established the College here as a training centre for teachers and clergymen.

Over the years this College has sent forth scores of able men and women who have contributed towards the emancipation of the minds of their fellow citizens from the shackles of ignorance and moral turpitude; and I am happy to state that the people of my own native land have been morally and spiritually benefited by the training of some of your finest graduates. I note that this spirit of selflessness and of sharing with others the training and ex-perience gained within the portals of this institution is inculcated into the lives of your students; for engraved upon the crest of this institution is the motto: 'Not for self, but for others'. This is a great lesson which we should never forget.

I heartily congratulate the Principal, Faculty and student body for this institution, and I express the hope that in the years ahead Fourah Bay College and our own University of Liberia will be fully affiliated for the further advancement of the frontiers of higher learning to the mutual satis-faction of our respective Governments and peoples.

Address to the Graduates of Cape Palmas High School

Harper, Cape Palmas, 14 December 1964

You are to be the personal trustees of the new Liberia.

Introductory Note

In Maryland County, his home, the President addressed a joint convocation of three graduating classes of three secondary schools – one a Government institution and two parochial schools. He commended them for this type of co-operation and noted further with appreciation the increase in the number of graduates from secondary schools in the entire nation. He reminded the graduates of what their rôle should be in building a new Liberia, and challenged them to pursue higher goals in learning.

Harper, Cape Palmas, 14 December 1964

IT IS my pleasure to greet the Principals, Faculties, graduating classes and students of our Lady of Fatima High School, Catholic; the Bishop Ferguson High School, Protestant; and the Cape Palmas High School, public, on this happy and eventful occasion unique in the history of this county and country, when two of our institutions of learning of different religious sects and a public one have merged their commencement and closing exercises to celebrate them under a single umbrella. This arrangement is indeed appropriate and judicious.

Four hundred and thirty-three students are expected to graduate from the high schools of Liberia this year. Of this number, three hundred and sixty-six plan to enter college, while sixty-seven will go into the broad bivouac of life and begin life in the practical demonstration of the saleable skills they have acquired from their high school education and training. Of the fifty-seven graduates from the high schools in Cape Palmas, forty-seven contemplate going on to college.

As these graduates leave the sheltered walls of the various institutions having finished the prescribed courses of study, I wonder just what attitudes of mind, what character traits and what philosophies of life they have developed? Just how much of the social and educational experiences has helped in the moulding of their character? How well have they applied themselves so that every opportunity for growth and development has been utilized to the fullest?

In this address, I want to bring to the attention of these three graduating classes three important reminders which are of great significance to our national programme of development. They are reminders which are applicable to all who enter our institutions of learning and who must become aware that it is principally through education that any people can rise to and enjoy freedom. They must learn what the love, understanding of and com-

678

mitment to freedom implies; they must know that freedom is not held by the representative of any segment of society or class. For the love of freedom cuts through the whole fabric of mankind, and commitments are made to it under all kinds of circumstances. It is because we believe that social injustice, economic exploitation and poverty are bound to give way under the pressure of a people with a high level of education, that we, in our society, have come to value it.

Let us now examine each of these reminders.

The first is the growing importance of education in our society.

Through the ages man has been eternally seeking for the better values of life. He has yearned for better food, shelter and clothing; he has formed better human relationships and in the establishment of a home he has eventually evolved a homogeneous society. In this search he turned to religion which satisfied his spiritual longing and provided him standards by which to guide his conduct, and to a philosophy which gave him a sense of direction. But man also looked to education as the process and to the school as the institution which could help him to develop his innate capacities to enable him to function effectively and successfully in carrying out his personal responsibilities as well as his responsibilities as a citizen of a free nation that would undertake the fashioning of a new world society.

'If a nation expects to be ignorant and free in a state of civilization, it expects what never was and never will be.' These words, spoken by a great American statesman, perhaps sum up the importance which the Founding Fathers attached to education and so made it one of the chief cornerstones of their survival and happiness. Schools were immediately established where Christian education was provided which instilled in the minds of the youths the fear of God and gave them the rudiments of knowledge. For them education was the safeguard of true democracy, and since they had come to these shores in search of an asylum, they would make it a vital and living force in their nation building.

Experience has taught us that there is one force at the disposal of man more powerful than atomic or hydrogen bombs. It is the force of knowledge. And if we are to escape the millstone of ignorance and the ravages of hunger; if we are to escape the limitations and exploitations of advancing nationalism; if we are to escape disease and death; and if we are to escape family disintegration and the opiate of religious dogma, then we will have to continue to loose education among the masses as others have done in the past in the history of mankind. For education is the one universal experience needed by the world more than any other single thing. It is the yeast of a free society and the 'spearhead of social reform'.

During the last century our schools have advanced and progressed and new processes have been discovered to improve the conditions of learning. At its best education must be rooted in the hearts and minds of the people of this nation reaching upward to the enjoyment and maintenance of this hard-won freedom. There is therefore no rational ground for temerity or marking time but there is an urgent command to move forward and storm the citadels of ignorance, sickness, poverty and lethargy, for we stand on the threshold of a magnificent age.

Reminder two is of the increased educational opportunities provided by Government, Missions and other Agencies in the nation.

The growing educational needs of the young and old of this nation, the urgency for more qualified teachers to man the schools, the need for better and more up-to-date educational aids and facilities, the desire to close the illiteracy gap and the increase in Government and other appropriations for education have, during the past years, necessitated the building of numerous elementary and high schools. Correspondingly the enrolment for elementary and high schools has become larger than ever before and will continue to increase for years to come. In this group are boys and girls who formerly did not ascend to this level of instruction and for whom the opportunity to receive either an elementary or a high school education is a new experience. It will be dangerous to neglect their needs and interests. Above all, the high schools now operate in a new social context of which they must take account. The changed conditions in our society, the influence of cinema, television, the Church, shops, banks, fraternal and social organizations, everything in our communities which tend to capture one's imagination, have their impact on youth. It is clear that the high schools of this nation will have to adjust to meet the needs of all our young people. In the years to come they will be required to prepare or they will fail to prepare the students for college, careers and citizenship.

But let us understand that there is no simple formula for re-shaping the structure of our high schools which prepare our youth. The high school must be something more than a bridge between the elementary school and college. It must focus attention not only on the preparation of one segment or another of its students, but also on the development in all of them of a core of useful habits, ideas, aspirations and assumptions that will make them, to the best of their abilities, creative and contributing citizens.

To understand fully what such an institution as the high school can best teach, it is necessary to explore two pervasive theories about education. One is the assumption that all that is taught is to be grasped and absorbed by the student. The rate at which knowledge fades after the final quiz in history, mathematics, and languages is rapid. What is taught simply cannot be equated with what is learned and remembered. Nor is it true that what is not taught will not be learned. When we wish to do so, we learn without teachers, and, sometimes, despite them.

In our high schools today two main tasks should concern the teachers – (a) to develop the ability to communicate and to be communicated with; and (b) to introduce them to the quantitative techniques on which modern science and technology rest. If the schools succeed in these tasks they shall have given their graduates the necessary equipment for future development. What is important is that the high schools of the nation do well what they have to do. For they should serve a democratic society at a point in the lives of the young when their future is vague and undefined.

But the high schools must do more; they must raise the sights of their students and lead them to the richest and noblest in their culture to the limits of their abilities with the common attributes of our culture. If this is done our high schools will imbue the young people with a sense of community that will assist in making their future work worthwhile whether in college or in the busy school of life. At least these students can be endowed with enough awareness of the world in which they will live to give them a sense of the value of their labour and of its relation to others. I hope that that same awareness outside the job will help them lead useful lives as parents and students.

And so we come to reminder three: you are expected to become a responsible and participating citizen in your social milieu.

You live in an age where great advances have been made in all branches of human endeavours; where discoveries and inventions have brought unparalleled powers that man never possessed before; and where unlimited possibilities exist for human progress, survival and happiness. But unless he is guided by mellow wisdom, sober judgment and a clear, righteous and ordinate purpose, man, who in reason, understanding and concept resembles God, may descend to the level of man the brute, may be subjected to brutish propensities and become a carnivorous animal predatory in character. Education therefore for responsible participation is one of the duties which devolve upon you who are graduating from the high schools of the nation. Wherever you will be, your sense of responsibility, your awareness that you have a duty to perform upon whose faithful and efficient performance the nation, the church and the society in which you live may depend, must be your primary concern. The interest of decency should stimulate in you the determination to do what your hands find and do it with all your might, with all your power, with all your grace and with the application of your intellectual, spiritual and moral forces, of honour, integrity, honesty and of your fear of God as the great source of all knowledge and perfect power; because a responsible citizen is one who is aware of his duties to his country and fellowmen and accomplishes them in the best tradition of his race.

If out of the three hundred and sixty-six students who plan to go to college two hundred should emerge successfully fired with a revolutionary idea to face the challenge of this century, don't you see that the history of this nation will shift? What is more, you will make a significant mark on the history of mankind. If a school is judged by the results it produces in the lives of its students, then we would wish that excellence in scholarship should be combined with a sense of responsibility and participation as end results of our educational goals.

You may remember the story or myth of how all the inhabitants of the earth at one time agreed that at a signal they would give a mighty shout together to reach the ear of the inhabitants of Mars. At the given signal there was silence. Each man decided to listen to the shout of the others. If our nation's youths must reach the dizzy heights of fame, scholarship and achievement, the time to act together is now when your educational opportunities and advantages excel those of any previous generation of Liberians; when every avenue along political, social, cultural, trade and industry is being opened up. The issue depends upon you, for someone has wisely said that the fashion of winning democracy in peace or war must be for each individual to act as a personal trustee of the result. You are to be the personal trustees of the new Liberia.

Let me admonish you not to be content with what you have today achieved but rather let the hunger to hunt be still in you and carry you forward in the years ahead. Remember that:

No student is truly trained unless in addition to getting the mastery of the tools of life that come through the discipline of routine tasks, he adds his own personal curiosities to a lively and original interest in the work he has to do.

No student is trained unless in addition to learning to do a man-like job and cultivating a lively spirit of insistent inquiry, he also gets from his contacts with the master spirits of the race those qualities of mind and behaviour and standards of judgment which constitute a true gentleman.

No student is truly trained unless he realizes that he does not live alone to himself, but is a part of an organic community life that is the source of most of the privileges he enjoys.

I challenge you to set your gaze higher and higher until it is possible for education to be beyond mere academic facts, and thus help enlighten the people in terms of the social, economic, and political significance of the times so that they can make their choice in the light of wisdom.

To you who will be leaving these institutions today, to the students who are yet to finish their high school education and to all parents and guardians connected with the training and education of the young for intelligent, effective and dedicated participation in Church and State, remember:

1. The growing importance of education in our society.
2. The increased educational opportunities provided by Government, missions and other agencies in the nation.
3. That as a result of the opportunities, privileges and facilities which our system of education today bestows, the students who graduate from our schools are expected to become responsible, participating and contributing citizens in their social settings.

Again I commend the uniqueness of the arrangement to hold these three commencements simultaneously, and I hope that it will tend to strengthen the educational programme in Maryland County by bringing teachers and students into closer and more understandable working relationships.

To the Principals and Faculties of the Government, the Bishop Ferguson and Our Lady of Fatima High Schools I extend congratulations for the contribution you have made to the country, Church and society by the preparation of these young men and women for the certificates of proficiency which will be presented to them for their success in the future as they enter the realm of the veritable reality of life to stand or fall, succeed or retrogress from the sound foundation which you have given them within the walls of your high schools. Take courage, press forward with ever-increasing devotion, love and determination in the teaching profession of this nation, realizing that, to a large extent, you are responsible for the perpetuity, development and progress of our nation; that you are moulders of the future leaders of Liberia. I pray God's blessings upon you and the graduating classes of 1964 so that you may be strong, courageous, patriotic and religious and in all of your words and actions remember to think like men of action and act like men of thought.

To all Units – Armed Forces of Liberia
Monrovia, 8 February 1967

We are gratified that the Liberian army throughout the years has constantly discharged the duty assigned to it under our system of Government with brilliance, honour, fortitude and intrepidity, thereby reflecting credit to itself, the people and the country.

Introductory Note

The behaviour and performance of the Army of Liberia are constantly under review so as to determine any departure from its constitutional function as essentially a peace army opposed to active warfare unless circumstances necessitate such action. The people of Liberia and their leaders have come to expect that it will never deviate from this normal behaviour. The President commended them for their peaceful behaviour.

Monrovia, 8 February 1967

I SALUTE you brave and gallant men, the protectors and defenders of the pillars and foundation of our freedom, liberties and tested free enterprise system of Government, on this gala morning marking the 12th Anniversary of Armed Forces Day in Liberia.

The celebration of Armed Forces Day 1967 is evidence of the successful fulfilment of your traditional rôle under provisions of the constitution that the military or army shall be kept in direct subordination; which means obedience and unquestionable loyalty to civil authority.

Whatever the historical records of armies and armed services the world over, particularly in Africa today, we are gratified to note that the Liberian Army throughout the years including 1966, a year in which *coups d'état* and other subversive activities took a full course and became the order of the day on this continent, has consistently discharged the duty assigned to it under our system of Government with brilliance, honour, fortitude and intrepidity thereby reflecting credit to itself, the people and the country.

A soldier under our constitution has a unique and awesome responsibility and is obligated, constrained and unconditionally committed to the fulfilment of the provision of his oath of office on which he is admitted into the armed services of the nation. His sense of devotion to duty, honour, alertness, faithfulness, steadfastness and loyalty to the Republic and to the Commander-in-Chief must at all times remain unshakable, uncontrovertible, and unquestionably beyond any spectrum of suspicion.

I therefore call upon you as Commander-in-Chief of the Armed Forces of the nation and command you in the name of the Republic and in the interest of its people and your service to re-dedicate yourselves to the principles of constant and eternal vigilance, resolute courage, realizing that the safety, perpetuity and security of this country, its people and their God-given liberties rest and depend on your behaviour.

May God strengthen and make more loyal the Liberian Armed Forces in the years ahead and save the state.

Eulogium on the life and character of Mary Euphemia Barclay, B.A., widow of the former President of Liberia, Edwin J. Barclay

Monrovia, 18 January 1967

An example of moral rectitude and possessed of that fine common sense, courage and love of justice which characterized her forebears, she was a true conservative Democrat, and none of the many recognitions that came to her succeeded in swerving her from her ideals of human equality, respectability and service to others.

Introductory Note

We have here a moving tribute paid to a noble lady by the President. Perhaps no one else was better able to perform such a task than he; and he did it from his own depth of close association with one of the nation's finest families. It is above all a memorable tribute to Liberian womanhood.

Monrovia, 18 January, 1967

AFTER FOUR score and three years the beautiful soul of Euphemia Barclay that had expressed itself under conditions of time and space, on the morning of January fifteenth took its flight from the tenements of clay that retained it and entered the limitless sphere of Eternity.

Mrs. Barclay was a noble lady, a typical example of moral rectitude and containment, possessed of that fine common sense, courage and love of justice which characterized her forebears, the late Honourable Alfred Davis, a former Attorney-General, and her mother, Mrs. Mary Jane Seton, one of the stalwarts of the Grebo element.

Born in an atmosphere of freedom, she was a true conservative Democrat and none of the many recognitions that came to her in her natural life of eighty-three years succeeded in swerving her from her ideals of human equality, respectability and service to others less fortunate than herself. In the home Mrs. Barclay was at her best; her whole career and the dominating purpose of her life was identified with the interest of her husband and her household. She believed in God and in the Church which she joined in early childhood, and in the good old-fashioned way relied upon God. She possessed a quiet dignity and an untiring loyalty, a scholarly bearing and an unpretentious enthusiasm, a tested dependability, a gracious thoughtfulness and an illuminating mind, a purified conscience and an infused will.

Wedded in matrimony to one of Liberia's greatest sons, an intellectual of the intelligentsia and literati of the nation, a patriot, soldier, statesman and jurist, Mrs. Barclay kept the faith and honour that her position required.

I have happy recollections of her impressive mannerisms first as the

685

gentle consort of the Secretary of State and later as First Lady of the Land in the Executive Mansion, when I often visited her husband, who was a close friend of mine, in their private living apartment. I remember how sometimes the three of us played a game called 'Pick Up Sticks' which President Barclay told me was one of the few games that she loved most. If the question arose that a misplay had been made or she felt that the game was not going right she was not argumentative about it but would express in modest and well-chosen terms what she thought had been done contrary to the rules of the game.

One could not contend with or dislike her because she was not contentious and was likeable, offering no occasion for quarrel, not even with her husband, as he told me, and through her winsome personality this noble lady made a host of friends whom she grasped to her soul with hoops of steel.

I have said that she believed in God and the Church, and in the good old-fashioned way relied upon God. As evidence of this I refer to two acts of charity and benevolence shown by her; a few years ago the pastor and officials of the First Methodist Church of Monrovia decided that they desired to extend their church edifice. They approached Mrs. Barclay and requested her to sell them a plot of land adjoining the present church edifice on its southern side. It did not require any persuasion or entreaty, she immediately gave the plot of land to the church without cost and refused to accept compensation. For the present Trinity Cathedral now under construction she offered twenty thousand dollars for a pipe organ – another benevolent act of charity whereby she spread her bread upon the proverbial water. She was charitable and gave to charity.

For thirteen years in the Executive Mansion she was a brilliant example of hospitality, kindness, decency and prudence; but of all that I have said or that I could say I am convinced that no greater eulogy or panegyric could better portray her real sterling life work and character than the words of the wise men written in the thirty-first chapter of Proverbs from the tenth to the thirty-first verse, which I now quote:

'Who can find a virtuous woman? For her price is far above rubies.

'The heart of her husband doth safely trust in her, so that he shall have no need of spoil.

'She will do him good and not evil all the days of her life.

'She seeketh wool, and flax, and worketh willingly with her hands.

'She is like the merchants' ships; she bringeth meat to her household, and a portion to her maidens.

'She considereth a field, and buyeth it: with the fruit of her hands she planteth a vineyard.

'She girdeth her loins with strength, and strengtheneth her arms.

'She perceiveth that her merchandise is good: her candle goeth not out by night.

'She layeth her hands to the spindle, and her hands hold the distaff.

'She stretcheth out her hand to the poor; yea, she reacheth forth her hands to the needy.

'She is not afraid of the snow for her household: for all her household are clothed with scarlet.

'She maketh herself coverings of tapestry; her clothing is silk and purple.

'Her husband is known in the gates, when he sitteth among the elders of the land.

'She maketh fine linen, and selleth it; and delivereth girdles unto the merchant.

'Strength and honour are her clothing; and she shall rejoice in time to come.

'She openeth her mouth with wisdom; and in her tongue is the law of kindness.

'She looketh well to the ways of her household, and eateth not the bread of idleness.

'Her children arise up, and call her blessed; her husband also, and he praiseth her.

'Many daughters have done virtuously, but thou excellest them all.

'Favour is deceitful, and beauty is vain; but a woman that feareth the Lord, she shall be praised.

'Give her of the fruit of her hands; and let her own works praise her in the gates.'

In Maurice Maeterlinck's beautiful fantasy of childhood, 'The Blue Bird', there is a touching scene when a little boy and his younger sister find themselves at the close of the day, in a village cemetery. As they stand there facing the rows of tombstones in the twilight, the little girl is frightened. And so is her brother. And then he turns the magic cap, which he wears, in which is fastened the magic stone, and a miracle happens. Instead of the rows of tombstones, there stretch before them beautiful blooming tulips. The little girl, a bit bewildered but completely freed from fear, looks up into the face of her brother and asks, 'Where are the dead?'

To which he confidently replies, 'There are no dead.'

I know that today and now Mrs. Barclay and her beloved husband, who preceded her to the undiscovered country almost twelve years ago, have met somewhere in heaven's auroral day to talk of things of earth they never can forget.